The Wiley Handbook of Entrepreneurship

The Wiley Handbook of Entrepreneurship

Edited by
Gorkan Ahmetoglu
University College London
London, UK

Tomas Chamorro-Premuzic
University College London
London, UK

Bailey Klinger
EFL Global & Harvard University
Cambridge, USA

Tessa Karcisky
University of Cologne
Cologne, Germany

WILEY Blackwell

This edition first published 2017
© 2017 John Wiley & Sons Ltd

All rights reserved. No part of this publication may be reproduced, stored in a retrieval system, or transmitted, in any form or by any means, electronic, mechanical, photocopying, recording or otherwise, except as permitted by law. Advice on how to obtain permission to reuse material from this title is available at http://www.wiley.com/go/permissions.

The right of Gorkan Ahmetoglu, Tomas Chamorro-Premuzic, Bailey Klinger and Tessa Karcisky to be identified as the authors of this editorial material in this work has been asserted in accordance with law.

Registered Office(s)
John Wiley & Sons, Inc., 111 River Street, Hoboken, NJ 07030, USA
John Wiley & Sons Ltd, The Atrium, Southern Gate, Chichester, West Sussex, PO19 8SQ, UK

Editorial Office
The Atrium, Southern Gate, Chichester, West Sussex, PO19 8SQ, UK

For details of our global editorial offices, customer services, and more information about Wiley products visit us at www.wiley.com.

Wiley also publishes its books in a variety of electronic formats and by print-on-demand. Some content that appears in standard print versions of this book may not be available in other formats.

Limit of Liability/Disclaimer of Warranty
While the publisher and authors have used their best efforts in preparing this work, they make no representations or warranties with respect to the accuracy or completeness of the contents of this work and specifically disclaim all warranties, including without limitation any implied warranties of merchantability or fitness for a particular purpose. No warranty may be created or extended by sales representatives, written sales materials or promotional statements for this work. The fact that an organization, website, or product is referred to in this work as a citation and/or potential source of further information does not mean that the publisher and authors endorse the information or services the organization, website, or product may provide or recommendations it may make. This work is sold with the understanding that the publisher is not engaged in rendering professional services. The advice and strategies contained herein may not be suitable for your situation. You should consult with a specialist where appropriate. Further, readers should be aware that websites listed in this work may have changed or disappeared between when this work was written and when it is read. Neither the publisher nor authors shall be liable for any loss of profit or any other commercial damages, including but not limited to special, incidental, consequential, or other damages.

Library of Congress Cataloging-in-Publication Data

Names: Ahmetoglu, Gorkan, editor. | Chamorro-Premuzic, Tomas, editor. |
  Klinger, Bailey, editor. | Karcisky, Tessa, editor.
Title: The Wiley handbook of entrepreneurship / [edited by] Gorkan Ahmetoglu,
  Tomas Chamorro-Premuzic, Bailey Klinger, Tessa Karcisky.
Description: Hoboken, NJ : John Wiley & Sons, 2017. | Includes index. |
  Identifiers: LCCN 2017009408 (print) | LCCN 2017020117 (ebook) | ISBN
  9781118970799 (Adobe PDF) | ISBN 9781118970720 (ePub) | ISBN 9781118970836
  (cloth)
Subjects: LCSH: Entrepreneurship.
Classification: LCC HB615 (ebook) | LCC HB615 .W538 2017 (print) | DDC
  338/.04—dc23
LC record available at https://lccn.loc.gov/2017009408

Cover Design: Wiley
Cover Image: © phive2015/Gettyimages

Set in 10/12, WarnockPro by SPi Global, Chennai, India
Printed and bound in Malaysia by Vivar Printing Sdn Bhd

10 9 8 7 6 5 4 3 2 1

Contents

Preface *xv*
Acknowledgments *xxiii*

Section 1 Entrepreneurship: Theory and Research
   1a: Understanding Entrepreneurship *1*

1 A Future of Entrepreneurship Research: Domain, Data, Theory, and Impact *3*
Per Davidsson
Introduction *3*
Narrowing and Broadening the Field *3*
Richer, Better, and More Varied Data *6*
The Quest for Increased Theoretical Precision *7*
  Abstraction, Conceptual Clarity, and Operationalization *9*
  Sample Size, Data Quality, Statistical Significance, and Practical Relevance *12*
    Expanding the null hypothesis *13*
    Stating predictions as comparisons *13*
    Developing non-nil predictions *13*
    Specifying other than linear functional forms *13*
  Recognizing Context *13*
Increased Demands for Practical Relevance *14*
Conclusion *17*
References *17*

2 Entrepreneurship as a Process: Empirical Evidence for Entrepreneurial Engagement Levels *25*
Peter van der Zwan and Roy Thurik
Introduction *25*
Merits of Entrepreneurship as a Process *27*
Three Stylized Facts *28*
  Latent Entrepreneurship *29*
  Different Roles Throughout the Process *29*
  Country Differences *30*
Conclusion and Recommendations for Future Research *31*
References *33*

3   Types and Roles of Productive Entrepreneurship: A Conceptual Study   *37*
Sander Wennekers and André van Stel

Introduction   *37*
   Ensuing Research Questions   *39*
   Methodology   *39*
Typologies and Types   *39*
   From Typologies/Dimensions to Major Types   *41*
   Twelve major types of entrepreneurship   *43*
   Further Reduction to Four Main Types   *44*
Entrepreneurial Roles   *45*
   General Entrepreneurial Roles   *45*
   Specific Entrepreneurial Roles   *46*
Intermediary Effects and Final Contributions   *50*
   Intermediate Effects   *51*
   Final Contributions   *54*
Causal Chains per Main Type of Entrepreneurship: A Synthesis   *57*
   Ambitious Innovators   *57*
   Ambitious Replicators/Adapters   *58*
   Solo Self-Employed   *59*
   Managerial Employers (Rest Group)   *60*
Discussion and Conclusions   *61*
   Summarizing and Interpreting the Main Findings   *61*
   Implications for Research   *62*
   Implications for Policy   *63*
   Conclusion   *65*
   References   *65*

4   Toward a Theory of Entrepreneurial Behavior   *71*
Bruce T. Teague and William B. Gartner

Introduction   *71*
The Current State of Entrepreneurial Behavior Scholarship   *72*
(Re)defining Entrepreneurial Behavior   *73*
   Defining Behavior   *73*
   Defining Entrepreneurial Behavior   *74*
The Role of Behavior in Existing Theories and Frameworks   *76*
A Theory of Entrepreneurial Behavior   *78*
   Behavioral Repertoire   *80*
   Sources of Behavioral Variation   *81*
   Level of Mastery   *83*
Implications of a Theory of Entrepreneurial Behavior   *84*
Toward an Entrepreneurial Behavior Research Agenda   *85*
   Next Steps   *86*
Conclusions   *87*
References   *88*

Section 2   The Individual: Psychology of Entrepreneurship *95*

5   The Psychology of Entrepreneurship: A Selective Review and a Path Forward *97*
Kelly G. Shaver and Amy E. Davis
Introduction   *97*
Why Ask Why?   *97*
The Personality Approach   *98*
  Single Traits   *98*
    Achievement Motivation   *98*
    Risk Propensity   *99*
  Broad Sets of Dimensions   *100*
    Inventories of Traits   *100*
    Latent Dimensions   *101*
The Social Cognition Approach   *102*
  Career Reasons   *103*
  Attribution Processes   *104*
  Social Cognitive Theories   *104*
    Expectancy Theory   *105*
    Theory of Planned Behavior   *105*
Entrepreneurial Teams   *106*
  Approaches to Teams   *106*
  Team Structure   *107*
Toward a More Inclusive Future   *107*
  Culturally Inclusive and Specific   *108*
    Gender   *108*
    Race and Ethnicity   *108*
    Life Course and Personal Context   *108*
    Country of Origin   *109*
  Methodologically Inclusive and Specific   *109*
    Theoretically Precise   *109*
    Multiple Dimensions   *110*
    Replication   *110*
    Teams Over Time   *110*
Conclusion   *111*
References   *111*

6   Tools Entrepreneurs Need for Converting Dreams To Reality—And Achieving Success   *119*
Robert A. Baron
Introduction   *119*
Motivation: What Goals Do Entrepreneurs Seek   *120*
Cognitive Tools: Creativity, Opportunity Recognition, and Avoiding Cognitive Traps   *121*
  Opportunity Recognition of Creation: Recognizing or Creating Practical Uses of Ideas   *122*

The Personal Side of Entrepreneurial Success: Characteristics and Skills That Contribute to Success *125*
  Personal Characteristics: Self-Efficacy, the "Big Five," and Willingness to Improvise *126*
  From Desire to Achievement: The Role of Self-Regulation *127*
  Passion: Deep, Emotional Commitment to Entrepreneurship and the Roles it Involves *128*
The Social Side of Entrepreneurial Success II: Forming High Quality Social Networks and Getting Along With Others *129*
  How do Entrepreneurs Build their Social Networks? *130*
Dealing with Adversity—and Failure *131*
  Coping With Stress *132*
    Psychological Capital *132*
  Dealing with Business Failure: When One Dream Ends Another (Should) Begin *133*
Putting it All Together: The Successful Entrepreneur's Tool Kit *133*
Tools for Changing the World—or at Least Some Corner of it *134*
References *136*

7 Creativity and Entrepreneurship: A Process Perspective *139*
Maike Lex and Michael M. Gielnik
Introduction *139*
Creativity and Entrepreneurship: A Conceptual Differentiation *140*
The Effect of Creativity on Entrepreneurship *141*
Toward a Cumulative Process Model of Creativity in Entrepreneurship *143*
Key Assumptions of the Cumulative Process Model *145*
  Creativity and its Underlying Components *145*
  The Entrepreneurial Process and its Constituting Phases *145*
  An Ambidexterity Perspective on Creativity in the Entrepreneurial Process *147*
A Cumulative Process Model on Creativity in Entrepreneurship *149*
  Prelaunch *149*
  Launch *151*
  Postlaunch *154*
  The Cumulative Process Model: A Summary *157*
An Interactionist Perspective on Creativity in Entrepreneurship *157*
Practical Implications: Promoting Creativity to Promote Entrepreneurship *159*
Future Research *161*
Conclusion *162*
References *163*

8 The Dark Side of the Entrepreneurial Personality: Undesirable or Maladaptive Traits and Behaviors Associated with Entrepreneurs *173*
Angelo S. DeNisi and Benjamin N. Alexander
Introduction *173*
  Recent Interest and Older Views *174*
Entrepreneurial Personality and Entrepreneurship Outcomes *175*
  Personality and Entrepreneurial Intentions *175*

Personality and Entrepreneurial Success 177
    Broader Impact 179
  Future Research on the Dark Side of the Entrepreneurial Personality 180
    Untangling Outcomes and Trait Phenomena 180
    Basic Issues 182
  Conclusion 183
  References 184

9 **Female Entrepreneurship and IQ** 187
  Rik W. Hafer
  Introduction 187
  Measuring Female Entrepreneurship and IQ 188
    The Female Entrepreneurship Index 188
    National IQ 190
  The Model and Data 191
  Regression Results 194
    Robustness Tests 195
    Caveats 197
  Conclusions and Policy Implications 198
  References 198
  Appendix A 201
  Appendix B 204
  Acknowledgments 204

10 **The Person in Social Entrepreneurship: A Systematic Review of Research on the Social Entrepreneurial Personality** 205
  Ute Stephan and Andreana Drencheva
  Introduction 205
  Theoretical Background 206
    Social Entrepreneurship 206
    Personality 207
  Review Approach and Overview of the Reviewed Studies 207
  Review Findings 208
    Motivation 208
      General values, motives, interests 211
      Specific motives 213
    Traits 216
    Identity 217
    Leadership and Managerial Skills 218
  Discussion and Opportunities for Future Research 220
    Building on Strengths and Insights of the Current Research 222
  References 223
  Acknowledgment 229

11 **An Individual Differences Approach to Studying Entrepreneurial Tendencies** 231
  Gorkan Ahmetoglu and Tomas Chamorro-Premuzic
  Introduction 231
  The Pillars of Individual Differences Psychology 232

The Psychological Approach to Entrepreneurship 233
A Critical Evaluation of the Psychological Approach
to Entrepreneurship 234
   A Critical Evaluation of the Group Differences Approach 234
   A Critical Evaluation of Comparisons Between More
   and Less Successful Entrepreneurs 236
An Individual Differences Approach to Understanding Entrepreneurial
Tendencies 236
   (Re)defining Entrepreneurial Tendencies 237
   The Practical Importance of Theoretical Preciseness 238
   Recommendations for Researching Entrepreneurial Tendencies 239
   How Do We Assess Entrepreneurial Tendencies? 240
   How Do General Entrepreneurial Tendencies Manifest in Contextual
   Behavior? 242
      Classification of Entrepreneurial Behaviors 242
   How Do General Entrepreneurial Tendencies and Contextual
   Behavior Manifest in Entrepreneurial Output? 245
Discussion 247
   Implications for Entrepreneurship Research 248
   Implications Beyond Business Creation 249
   Other Considerations 249
   Existing and Future Research 250
Conclusion 251
References 251

Section 2a: Genetics of Entrepreneurship 257

12 Biology and Entrepreneurship 259
Ahmed Nofal, Nicos Nicolaou, and Noni Symeonidou
Introduction 259
Genetics and Entrepreneurship 260
   Quantitative Genetics in Entrepreneurship 260
      Tendency to Engage in Entrepreneurship 260
      Genetic Influences on Physiology 261
      Genetic Covariation with Individual Attributes 261
      Gene X Environment Interactions 262
      Gene X Environment Correlations 262
      Opportunity Recognition 262
      Entrepreneurial Intention 262
      Entrepreneurial Performance 263
   Molecular Genetics in Entrepreneurship 263
      Candidate-Gene Studies 263
      Genome-Wide Association Studies (GWAS) 264
Hormones in Entrepreneurship 265
Physiology in Entrepreneurship 266
Neuroscience in Entrepreneurship 266
   Quantitative Electroencephalogram 267

Functional Magnetic Resonance Imaging   *267*
Conclusion   *267*
References   *268*

13 "Born, Not Made" and Other Beliefs About Entrepreneurial Ability   *273*
Daniel P. Forbes
Introduction   *273*
"Born, Not Made": Beliefs and Evidence   *274*
Understanding How People Think About Entrepreneurs   *277*
   Essentialist Lay Beliefs   *277*
   Genetic Essentialist Lay Beliefs About Entrepreneurs   *278*
   Born-Not-Made and General Beliefs About Entrepreneurial Ability   *280*
Implications of Belief in Born-Not-Made   *280*
   Implications for the Judgments People Make About Their Own Entrepreneurial Abilities   *281*
   Implications for the Judgments People Make About Others' Entrepreneurial Abilities   *283*
Discussion   *284*
References   *286*
Acknowledgments   *291*

Section 3   The Organization: Corporate Entrepreneurship and Entrepreneurial Teams
3a: The Organization   *293*

14 Corporate Entrepreneurship & Innovation: Today's Leadership Challenge   *295*
Donald F. Kuratko
Introduction   *295*
What Constitutes the Domain of Corporate Entrepreneurship?   *296*
The Importance of a Climate Conducive for Innovative Activity   *298*
Managerial Levels and Contributions to Entrepreneurial Efforts   *300*
Ingredients for an Effective Corporate Entrepreneurial Strategy   *302*
Challenges with Implementation of Corporate Entrepreneurship   *304*
Future Expectations   *305*
References   *307*

Section 3b: Entrepreneurial Teams   *313*

15 Unraveling the Black Box of New Venture Team Processes   *315*
Ekaterina S. Bjornali, Mirjam Knockaert, Nicolai Foss, Daniel Leunbach and Truls Erikson
Introduction   *315*

The New Venture Team as a Focal Object of Inquiry *316*
   Internal Factors *316*
   External Factors *317*
Disentangling NVT "Processes" in the Input-Processes-Outcome Framework *318*
Toward a Framework for Studying NVT Processes *318*
   Prefounding Phase *319*
   Postfounding phase *319*
Selected Theories Within the Theoretical Foundations *321*
   Faultline Theory *321*
      Future Research Directions *324*
   Behavioral Integration and Shared Cognition *324*
      Future Research Directions *325*
   Shared Leadership *326*
      Future Research Directions *327*
   Creativity and Imagination *328*
      Future Research Directions *329*
   Organizational and Team Justice *330*
      Future Research Directions *331*
   Transactive Memory Systems *332*
      Future Research Directions *332*
Measuring New Venture Team Processes *333*
   Methodological Issues in NVT Studies *333*
      Collinearity *334*
      Dominant Survey Method *334*
      Cross-Sectional Designs *334*
   Meeting Methodological Challenges *335*
      Improving Survey Instruments *335*
      Simulation Exercises: Agent-Based Modeling *335*
      Neurostudies *336*
      Towards a Mixed Methods Approach *337*
Concluding Remarks *337*
References *338*

Section 4 National and International Entrepreneurship
     4a: National Entrepreneurship 349

16 The Knowledge Spillover Theory of Entrepreneurship and the Strategic Management of Places *351*
David B. Audretsch and Erik E. Lehmann
Introduction *351*
The Challenge of Inequality of Places *353*
   Globalization and Regionalization *353*
      The Mediating Role of Entrepreneurship in Transforming Places *353*
   Transforming Regions to Places *355*

The Knowledge Spillover Theory of Entrepreneurship   *356*
   Defining the Knowledge Spillover Theory of Entrepreneurship   *356*
   The Emergence of the Knowledge Spillover Theory of Entrepreneurship   *358*
   Knowledge Spillover Theory and Places   *360*
   The Knowledge Filter and the Strategic Management of Place   *363*
   Absorptive Capacity of Place   *366*
Emergence of a Strategic Management Approach of Place   *368*
Conclusions   *371*
References   *372*

17 The Effect of New Business Formation on Regional Development   *379*
Michael Fritsch
Introduction   *379*
The Basic Relationships   *380*
The Magnitude of Direct and Indirect Effects   *383*
Differences in the Contribution of New Business Formation to Economic Growth Across Industries and Regions   *385*
The Persistence of Regional Entrepreneurship   *389*
Policy Implications   *391*
Avenues for Further Research   *392*
Final Remarks   *396*
References   *396*

18 National Culture and Entrepreneurship   *401*
Gabriella Cacciotti and James C. Hayton
Introduction   *401*
Method   *401*
Conceptualization of National Culture in Entrepreneurship Research   *402*
   National Culture as Values   *403*
      Definition   *403*
      Measures   *403*
      Outcomes   *404*
   National Culture as Norms and Practices   *408*
      Definition   *408*
      Measures   *409*
      Outcomes   *410*
Summary   *412*
Directions for Future Research   *414*
Conclusion   *416*
References   *416*

19 Management of Entrepreneurial Ecosystems   *423*
Erkko Autio and Jonathan Levie
Introduction   *423*
Entrepreneurial Ecosystems: Definitions and Policy Challenges   *425*

Management of Complex Socioecological Ecosystems *428*
  Stakeholder Consultation *429*
  Stakeholder Participation *430*
Scottish Innovation-Based Entrepreneurial Ecosystem *431*
  Method *431*
  REAP Scotland *432*
  Field Trial in Scotland *435*
  Case Reflection *438*
Discussion *442*
Conclusion *445*
References *446*

Section 4b: International Entrepreneurship *451*

20 International Entrepreneurship and Networks *453*
Salman Ahmad and Pavlos Dimitratos
Introduction *453*
International Entrepreneurship: Definition *454*
Network Perspective *456*
Networks and International Entrepreneurship *457*
  Important Themes: Intersection of International Entrepreneurship and Networks Research *458*
    Network Creation and International Entrepreneurship *460*
    Network Types and International Entrepreneurship *460*
    Network Structures and International Entrepreneurship *463*
    Network Dynamics and International Entrepreneurship *464*
    Network's Benefits and International Entrepreneurship *465*
Theoretical Basis: Intersection of International Entrepreneurship Networks Research *468*
  Transaction Cost Economics (TCE) *469*
  Organizational Learning *469*
  Resource-Based View *470*
  Social Capital *470*
  Knowledge-Based View *471*
  Other Theories *471*
Practical Implications *472*
Future Research *472*
Conclusion *472*
References *473*

Index *485*

Preface

Although definitions of entrepreneurship vary, few dispute its importance in bringing positive change to the world. It is no wonder, therefore, that the academic field of entrepreneurship permeates a broad spectrum of disciplines. So much so, that the study of entrepreneurship has become an integral part of economics, management, and business studies. More recently, there has also been growing interest in entrepreneurship from the field of psychology. However, despite the large amount of interdisciplinary research and collaboration around this subject, a great deal of opportunities remain. Globalization and changes in technology are impacting every aspect of life, with entrepreneurship often driving such changes. Indeed, the impact of entrepreneurship is felt at many levels, including the individual, organizational, regional, national, and international.

Gaining a deeper understanding of the entrepreneurship phenomenon is no doubt of fundamental value to businesses, governments, and society at large. To that end, the aim of the current handbook is to provide an overview of the academic research in this field. This book contains chapters from leading researchers in the field to provide a thorough foundation for knowledge exchange around entrepreneurship. It is an attempt to provide the latest thinking around some of the most important areas of focus in the field: individuals, teams, and organizations who engage in entrepreneurship, and their regional, national, and international impact.

Thus this handbook intends to demonstrate the importance of entrepreneurship as a research discipline, highlighting what is known as well as what is still unknown, so as to inspire and guide future research in this area. This volume comprises four parts, each with a unique view on entrepreneurship on differing levels—Entrepreneurship: Theory and Research; The Individual: Psychology of Entrepreneurship; The Organization: Corporate Entrepreneurship and Entrepreneurial Teams; and National and International Entrepreneurship. With contributions from nearly 40 experts, this book was written for scholars and students with an interest in entrepreneurship. This volume may also be of interest to audiences of related fields such as psychology, business strategy, finance and venture capital, organizational behavior, and economics.

Chapter Summaries

Section I. Entrepreneurship: Theory and Research

Understanding Entrepreneurship

1 A Future of Entrepreneurship Research: Domain, Data, Theory, and Impact In this chapter Per Davidsson offers observations and speculations about current and possible future developments in the field of entrepreneurship research. The main topics focused on include the delineation of the "entrepreneurship research" field and community; data and data sources; the quest for increased theoretical precision, and demands for practical relevance and real-world impact. Davidsson goes on to conclude that the future of entrepreneurship research offers both challenges and opportunities, and he predicts that it will remain an exciting field for scholarly study.

2 Entrepreneurship as a Process: Empirical Evidence for Entrepreneurial Engagement Levels In this chapter Peter van der Zwan and Roy Thurik focus on several stages of the entrepreneurial process. These stages both incorporate the "cognitive" and "behavioral" type of stages. They highlight that at a certain moment in time an individual is engaged in any of these stages, and for this individual there is a likelihood of moving to the next stage. Implicit in this model are thresholds that indicate the transition from one stage to another. They argue that several strands of literature are integrated in this particular process, such as the literature on entrepreneurial intentions, nascent entrepreneurship and entrepreneurial survival. Van der Zwan and Thurik combine these streams of literature and show that the individual-level determinants of entrepreneurship deserve a separate treatment depending on the stage in the entrepreneurial process. They show evidence that the empirically validated determinants of self-employment or entrepreneurship differ across the several stages in the entrepreneurial process.

3 Types and Roles of Productive Entrepreneurship: A Conceptual Study Sander Wennekers and André van Stel recognize in this chapter that there are three recurring questions that appear in literature: What is entrepreneurship? What economic and social contributions does entrepreneurship make? How does entrepreneurship make these contributions? Many interesting answers have been given to these questions, but these answers do not result in a clear-cut, unambiguous picture. On the contrary, confusion prevails. Wennekers and van Stel aim to dispel this confusion by assessing which different dimensions and which major types of entrepreneurship can be identified. They then go on to decipher which entrepreneurial roles are being fulfilled by these major types. Wennekers and van Stel finally address how the causal chains from these entrepreneurial roles are linked to their final contributions.

4 Toward a Theory of Entrepreneurial Behavior Bruce T. Teague and William B. Gartner begin this chapter by reviewing several of the most prominent entrepreneurship frameworks in order to demonstrate that the entrepreneurship field lacks a theory of entrepreneurial behavior. However, they suggest that each of these existing frameworks would benefit from, and be complemented by, an entrepreneurial behavioral theory. Drawing from multiple streams of research, Teague and Gartner offer a preliminary theory of entrepreneurial behavior. Several propositions are offered which are then followed by recommendations for new research opportunities.

Section II. The Individual: Psychology of Entrepreneurship

5 The Psychology of Entrepreneurship: A Selective Review and a Path Forward   Kelly G. Shaver and Amy E. Davis highlight that the creation of a new business is not an event, but a process undertaken by one person or by a team of people. As many writers have acknowledged, the cognitive processes, personal motives, actions performed, and interpersonal processes involved are all fair topics for psychological inquiry. In this selective review Shaver and Davis show how the "psychology of entrepreneurship" has evolved from a relatively simplistic beginning to a recent view that is much more highly nuanced. They first describe several of the ideas borrowed from psychology (mostly, though not exclusively, from personality and social psychology) that have been adapted for use in entrepreneurship. They then address the issues that arise when "the founder" changes to a "founding team." Finally, Shaver and Davis conclude with an argument for greater complexity in future work on entrepreneurial psychology.

6 Tools Entrepreneurs Need for Converting Dreams to Reality—And Achieving Success   In this chapter Robert A. Baron seeks to uncover some key in entrepreneurial success on the basis of current knowledge. To accomplish this task, in each section of the chapter Baron considers one component of why entrepreneurs fail or succeed, describing extant evidence concerning its importance. From this an overall picture of the personal ingredients in entrepreneurial success emerges. Despite many factors that contribute to an entrepreneur's success or failures being beyond the control of entrepreneurs, Baron adds to existing evidence and theory by suggesting that entrepreneurs themselves do indeed play a central role in the entrepreneurial process.

7 Creativity and Entrepreneurship: A Process Perspective   Maike Lex and Michael M. Gielnik open this chapter with a reminder that creativity has often been described in literature as a key predictor of entrepreneurial success. Yet, there is surprisingly little empirical research on the effect of creativity on entrepreneurial success with some of the studies yielding nonsignificant results. In this chapter, they review the literature on creativity and entrepreneurship and argue that it has in general adopted a relatively basic approach to the main effects of creativity on entrepreneurship. Gielnik and Lex go beyond this basic approach by adopting a more differentiated perspective on the role of creativity in entrepreneurship. Specifically, they argue that both creativity and entrepreneurship comprise different components and phases which need to be taken into account in order to fully understand the effect of creativity in entrepreneurship. In addition, they posit that it is important to consider contextual factors which systematically promote or hinder the effect of creativity within the entrepreneurial process. Building on these assumptions, they develop a theoretical model on the role of creativity in the entrepreneurial process. Their model integrates past theoretical and empirical research into a comprehensive framework and illuminates both the positive and negative effects of creativity in the different phases of the entrepreneurial process.

8 The Dark Side of the Entrepreneurial Personality: Undesirable or Maladaptive Traits and Behaviors Associated with Entrepreneurs   In this chapter Angelo S. DeNisi and Benjamin N. Alexander endeavor to extend the arguments made in recent papers on the "dark side" of the entrepreneurial personality and to integrate additional perspectives germane to the issue. DeNisi and Alexander examine the distinct mechanisms proposed in recent commentaries and also discuss the different outcomes that might be associated with dark-side traits. Specifically, they address the potential dark-side effects on the decision to become an entrepreneur and on the success or failure of any entrepreneurial enterprises, and also, more broadly, the impact other stakeholders in society. In their view, the entire question of a potential dark side to the entrepreneurial personality becomes much more interesting, and much more important, when trying to predict who will be successful as an entrepreneur and how they will impact other stakeholders and the larger society. Not only is this important for scholarship but it clearly has practical implications as well. DeNisi and Alexander end the chapter by suggesting some tentative directions for future research on the role of personality in entrepreneurship and also offer some thoughts on the appropriate methodologies for pursuing this research.

9 Female Entrepreneurship and IQ   Rik W. Hafer begins this chapter by reviewing previous work which has found that human capital development is a key factor for a growing economy, as well as reviewing literature that has shown nation-level IQ to be a robust predictor of entrepreneurial activity. From this Hafer tests whether IQ helps predict female entrepreneurship. This is measured using the recently developed Female Entrepreneurship Index (FEI). Based on a sample of 77 countries, the statistical results indicate that IQ is a statistically and economically significant predictor of female entrepreneurship. Hafer concludes the chapter by asserting that the results suggest that to improve female entrepreneurial activity, policymakers, especially in developing countries, may find it productive to engage in policies that increase their cognitive skills, such as increasing basic education and improving health care.

10 The Person in Social Entrepreneurship: A Systematic Review of Research on the Social Entrepreneurial Personality   Ute Stephan and Andreana Drencheva present a systematic literature review of research on the social entrepreneurial personality in this chapter. The review synthesizes the findings of 50 empirical studies. It differentiates four aspects of the social entrepreneurial personality: motivations, traits, identities, and skills. The three research approaches are describing the personality of social entrepreneurs, comparing them to another group, and relating personality aspects to social entrepreneurship intentions, activities, and performance outcomes. Stephan and Drencheva offer a multidimensional and refined account of who social entrepreneurs are, their diversity, and differences and similarities with commercial entrepreneurs and other individuals. The review then concludes by proposing several fruitful avenues for future research, including paying attention to heterogeneity among social entrepreneurs, encouraging more theory-based research, research relating personality to personal and venture-level outcomes, and research that considers more dynamic and contextualized perspectives.

11 An Individual Differences Approach to Studying Entrepreneurial Tendencies   In this chapter Gorkan Ahmetolgu and Tomas Chamorro-Premuzic offer an individual differences framework for the study of entrepreneurial tendencies. They form a theoretical argument to suggest that there is a distinction between the study of entrepreneurial tendencies and the study of the tendencies of entrepreneurs. Thus, unlike most research on the psychology of entrepreneurship that tend to answer the questions, "Who becomes an entrepreneur?" and "Why are some entrepreneurs more successful than others?" this chapter deals with the questions: "Who is more entrepreneurial?", and "What do entrepreneurial l people do?" This distinction generates a different set of research questions, requiring different research designs to the ones currently employed in literature. The aim is to encourage more research on entrepreneurial individuals, identified based on their enduring psychological and behavioral tendencies. Ahmetoglu and Chamorro-Premuzic conclude this chapter by discussing the implications of an individual differences framework for studying entrepreneurial tendencies and offer potential avenues for future research.

Genetics of Entrepreneurship

12 Biology and Entrepreneurship In this chapter, Ahmed Nofal, Nicos Nicolaou and Noni Symeonidou discuss the role that biology plays in entrepreneurship. They argue that literature hitherto has provided an incomplete explanation about the drivers of entrepreneurship, despite there being a wealth of literature that examines various factors influencing the tendency of people to engage in entrepreneurship including individual attributes, contextual factors and industry characteristics. They postulate that this incompleteness may be due to the lack of research on the biological aspects of entrepreneurship and thus acknowledge that researchers have started examining the role of biological factors in influencing key entrepreneurial phenotypes. Nofal, Nicolaou and Symeonidou examine how genetics, hormones, physiology, and neuroscience may affect entrepreneurial phenotypes. These phenotypes include the tendency to engage in entrepreneurship, opportunity recognition, entrepreneurial intention, and entrepreneurial performance. Fueled by recent evidence, they also investigate how biological factors may interact and correlate with environmental factors to influence entrepreneurship. Finally, they discuss some future research avenues for entrepreneurship scholars interested in the biological perspective.

13 "Born, Not Made" and Other Beliefs About Entrepreneurial Ability Daniel P. Forbes, in this chapter, calls attention to an understudied ability-related belief that "entrepreneurs are born, not made"; a belief that is likely to have significant implications for entrepreneurial behavior. He begins by observing that although the belief that entrepreneurs are born is prevalent among many members of the general population and is sometimes promoted by scholars, it is inconsistent with the accumulated scientific evidence. He then goes on to review recent psychological research on the concept of "essentialism," the idea that members of large social groups possess an underlying set of immutable characteristics. Extending those ideas, Forbes applies them to the case of occupational groups and introduces a construct to capture the belief that entrepreneurs possess an underlying essence that is fixed and inborn. Finally, he goes on to propose ways in which this belief is likely to affect the choices people make about the creation and management of new ventures.

Section III. The Organization: Corporate Entrepreneurship and Entrepreneurial Teams

The Organization

14 Corporate Entrepreneurship & Innovation: Today's Leadership Challenge In this chapter Donald F. Kuratko introduces the new leadership challenge by addressing that idea that as organizations seek to continually develop innovation, firms are increasingly turning to corporate entrepreneurship/innovation as a strategy. Corporate entrepreneurship, which is viewed as a dynamic deviation from prior routines, strategies, business models, and operating environments to embrace new resource combinations that hold promise for new innovations, has more to do with entrepreneurial leadership than ever before. Kuratko recapitulates that the characteristics of seeking opportunities, taking risks beyond security, and having the tenacity to push an idea through to reality combine into a special perspective known as an entrepreneurial mindset which has become the standard by which true leadership is now measured. Kuratko goes on to review literature with the aim of understanding the entire domain of what constitutes corporate entrepreneurship/innovation. He then discusses the importance of a climate conducive to innovative activity, the levels of management and their contribution to entrepreneurial efforts, the ingredients for an effective corporate entrepreneurial strategy, as well as the challenges with actual implementation. Finally, he draws upon the future expectations of leaders in this field.

Entrepreneurial Teams

15 Unraveling the Black Box of New Venture Team Processes Ekaterina S. Bjornali, Mirjam Knockaert, Nicolai Foss, Daniel Leunbach, and Truls Erikson begin this chapter by elaborating on what is unique about their object of inquiry, and suggest a framework for studying new venture team (NVT) processes. They argue that NVT processes are relatively ill-understood in the entrepreneurship literature, and so describe various theoretical and empirical research avenues that may be pursued in order to improve the general understanding of these processes. They then describe the selected theories within the theoretical foundations of entrepreneurial theorizing and subjectivism, and suggest future research opportunities for each of the selected theoretical perspectives. Bjornali, Knockaert, Foss, Leunbach, and Erikson then outline the methodological challenges and suggest selected methods that can address these challenges, before lastly providing a conclusion.

Section IV. National and International Entrepreneurship

National Entrepreneurship

16 The Knowledge Spillover Theory of Entrepreneurship and the Strategic Management of Places David B. Audretsch and Erik E. Lehmann argue in this chapter that regional competitiveness and entrepreneurial activities are strongly linked together by knowledge spillovers. According to the knowledge spillover theory of entrepreneurship (KSTE), the regional context in which decision-making is derived influences one's determination to become an entrepreneur. In particular, a context that is rich in knowledge generates entrepreneurial opportunities from those ideas. Audretsch and Lehmann highlight that by commercializing ideas that evolved from an incumbent organization via the creation of a new firm, entrepreneurs not only serve as a conduit for the spillover of knowledge, but also for the ensuing innovative activity and enhanced economic performance through resource allocation. Audretsch and Lehmann's knowledge spillover theory of entrepreneurship brings together contemporary theories and thoughts of entrepreneurship with prevailing theories of economic growth, geography, and strategy and therefore explains not just why some people choose to become an entrepreneur, but also why this matters significantly for regional competitiveness and society.

17 The Effect of New Business Formation on Regional Development   Michael Fritsch begins this chapter by reviewing the current state of knowledge about the effects of new business formation on regional development. He argues that the effects are diverse and include the creation and destruction of employment, introduction of innovations, structural change, and increasing productivity, among others. He then goes on to provide an explanatory approach that highlights the competitive challenge that start-ups pose to incumbent firms and also discusses important implications. Fritsch's overview of empirical research particularly deals with the development of start-up cohorts, identification of different types of indirect effects and their magnitude, differences based on characteristics of entry, and regional variation. He develops a general conclusion that the diverse indirect effects of new business formation on development are much more important than the growth effects created by newcomers. Further he addresses the fact that the diverse indirect effects of entry on development are currently less than fully understood. Finally, he draws on conclusions for policy and puts forward a number of important questions for further research

18 National Culture and Entrepreneurship   In this chapter Gabriella Cacciotti and James C. Hayton offer a review of the current literature to shed light on the main challenges and issues associated with the research on the relationship between national culture and entrepreneurship. They note that scholars have used two different approaches to defining national culture: culture as values and culture as norms and practices. While this theoretical pluralism may suggest researchers' enthusiasm for the topic, it also creates a challenge, as scholars try to make sense of the diverse theoretical frameworks used to explain the role of national culture in entrepreneurship. In this review, Cacciotti and Hayton analyze the literature that is related to each approach. They also highlight their limitations and use them as a starting point to propose a more coherent approach to defining and measuring national culture in entrepreneurship research. Cacciotti and Hayton conclude this chapter by proposing fear of failure as one of the cognitive variables able to capture the mechanisms through which national culture influences entrepreneurial behavior.

19 Management of Entrepreneurial Ecosystems   Erkko Autio and Jonathan Levie open this chapter by calling attention to the increasing policy interest toward entrepreneurial ecosystems. Yet, little is actually known about how entrepreneurial ecosystems work and what the related policy challenges are. Drawing on research on ecological economics and community governance, they develop a theoretical framework for entrepreneurial ecosystem management. Using a Scottish entrepreneurial ecosystem initiative as an example, Autio and Levie conclude that policy approaches that emphasize deep stakeholder engagement are likely to give rise to better informed, targeted, and more effectively implemented policy initiatives in entrepreneurial ecosystems than will market failure and structural failure approaches.

International Entrepreneurship

20 *International Entrepreneurship and Networks* Salman Ahmad and Pavlos Dimitratos begin the chapter by highlighting that until the 1990s, international entrepreneurship was not a separate field of study. However, during the last two decades, international entrepreneurship has attracted the interest of many scholars and is now being recognized as a distinguished field of significant potential. In addition to this, network research has emerged as a popular subject among researchers of international entrepreneurship who endeavor to identify the influence and impact of relationships at both the individual and organizational levels, and to determine how resources are mobilized to support international business activities. Although networks are increasingly perceived as a key element of international entrepreneurial activities, Ahmad and Dimitratos argue that many questions are unanswered about the content of interactions and relationships between networks and international entrepreneurship. They conduct a systematic literature review to spot different themes of network studies in the context of international entrepreneurship. They highlight the theories used to comprehend the interaction between networks and international entrepreneurship. Ahmad and Dimitratos then identify different methodological approaches used to study networks in the domain of international entrepreneurship, and finally suggests future research avenues for network research in the international entrepreneurship field.

Acknowledgments

We are grateful to Wiley for encouraging us to work on this project.

To my immediate and extended family, which I'm very lucky and proud to be a part of.
Gorkan Ahmetoglu

For my students: in the hope that they will be entrepreneurial and use psychology to drive real-world innovation.
Tomas Chamorro-Premuzic

In thanks for the support and partnership of my wife, Ruby.
Bailey Klinger

To my future husband.
Tessa Karcisky

Section 1

Entrepreneurship: Theory and Research

1a: Understanding Entrepreneurship

1

A Future of Entrepreneurship Research: Domain, Data, Theory, and Impact

Per Davidsson[a,b]

[a] Queensland University of Technology, Australia
[b] Jönköping International Business School, Sweden

Introduction

Over the past couple of decades, entrepreneurship research has undergone tremendous growth as well as maturation and institutionalization (Aldrich, 2012; Davidsson, 2016b; Meyer et al., 2012). Overall, this has no doubt been for the better, and when we sometimes feel that we have not come far enough, fast enough, it is probably because so much knowledge about the phenomenon is now taken for granted. One may have to revisit some of the early literature or engage in an extended conversation with a complete newcomer to the field in order to realize how much we have actually learned.

In this chapter I will offer some observations and speculations about current developments as well as likely and desirable scenarios for the future. The particular topics I will discuss are (a) the delineation of the "entrepreneurship research" field and community; (b) data and data sources; (c) the quest for increased theoretical precision; and (d) demands for practical relevance and real-world impact. My observations come from the perspective of an experienced "business school" researcher (with escapes into applied psychology and applied economics) who was an early (i.e., 1980s) entrant into the emerging field of entrepreneurship research, who has predominantly worked with large-scale survey and archival data, and who views outlets like the *Journal of Business Venturing* and *Entrepreneurship Theory & Practice* as main communication channels.

Narrowing and Broadening the Field

Over time, the field of entrepreneurship research has drifted away from having a considerable overlap with issues of small business management to having—at least in "business school research"— an increased overlap with research on innovation and strategy (Baker

---

The Wiley Handbook of Entrepreneurship, First Edition.
Edited by Gorkan Ahmetoglu, Tomas Chamorro-Premuzic, Bailey Klinger, & Tessa Karcisky.
© 2017 John Wiley & Sons Ltd. Published 2017 by John Wiley & Sons Ltd.

& Pollock, 2007; Dino, 2015; Salter & McKelvey, 2016).[1] There seems to be increasing consensus around *creation of new economic activities* as the core of what entrepreneurship is and what entrepreneurship research should study (Carlsson et al., 2013; McMullen & Dimov, 2013; Wiklund, Davidsson, Audretsch, & Karlsson, 2011).[2] Yet, characterizations of the field as being a "hodgepodge" (Shane & Venkataraman, 2000) or a "potpourri" (Low, 2001) remain relevant to an extent. The journal *Small Business Economics* has added "An Entrepreneurship Journal" to its name, but has not dropped the stronger connotation to organizational size from its title. *Entrepreneurship Theory & Practice* (*ETP*) features special issues on family business on a regular basis, and *Family Business Review* (*FBR*) is commonly included in the set of "entrepreneurship journals" as are the *Journal of Small Business Management* and *International Small Business Journal* (e.g., Teixeira, 2011). The Entrepreneurship Division of the Academy of Management (ENT) has retained "the characteristics, actions, and challenges of owner-managers and their businesses" as one of two alternative understandings of its stated domain (Mitchell, 2011).

It is not difficult to understand why this is so. Why would *Small Business Economics'* publisher, Springer, take the risk of dropping a well-established brand name? Why would ENT choose to alienate a large proportion of its membership, or *ETP* willingly forgo the citation volumes generated by their special issues on family business? However, there is an undeniable problem. Critics justifiably argue that self-employment and small business activity do not equate to entrepreneurship (Henrekson & Sanandaji, 2014) and there is objective, quantitative evidence that *FBR* is an outlier compared to other journals associated with the field of entrepreneurship (Teixeira, 2011, p. 17). Self-employment, small business, and family business are organizational and governance contexts that are interesting and important objects of study. However, only occasionally does an interest in these phenomena coincide with a focus on creation of new economic activities. If the latter is our arrived-upon and agreed-upon understanding of "entrepreneurship" then a separation of entrepreneurship from the self-employment, small business, and family business contexts is the better long-term solution for all parties. I think it is time to complete the separation.

I would argue that criteria like innovativeness and growth-orientation should not be the basis for separation. That would not only be impractical but also an example of methodologically unsound sampling on the dependent variable. Instead, I think the divider should be *entry* versus *state*. The *state* of being self-employed or an established small organization has no definitional or otherwise obvious connection to "creation of new economic activities." *Entry* does. True, we know that representative empirical populations of entry attempts are dominated by a "modest majority" and that this is also problematic for some purposes (Crawford, Aguinis, Lichtenstein, Davidsson, & McKelvey, 2015; Davidsson & Gordon, 2012). Nonetheless, apart from utter failures, the members of the modest majority perform, at least to some small extent, what I have

---

[1] However, regarding entrepreneurship and innovation studies see also Landström, Åström, & Harirchi (2015).
[2] I regard creation/emergence of new organizations as minor variations on the same theme (see Davidsson, 2016c, Ch. 2, and Gartner, this volume).

argued elsewhere (Davidsson, 2016c) are the essential functions of entrepreneurship in driving the economy forward:

1) They provide customers with new choice alternatives, potentially giving some of those customers more value for their money.
2) They stimulate incumbent actors to improve their market offerings in their turn, which increases efficiency and/or effectiveness of those actors.
3) If perceived to be successful, they attract other new entrants to the market, thus further increasing competitive pressures toward improved efficiency and effectiveness.

To this list—which essentially reflects wealth creation—we should perhaps add wealth redistribution and note that the alignment of the two is of utmost societal importance (Baumol, 1990). We may to varying degrees have qualms about uber-rich and uber-powerful plutocratic dynasties, but spectacular cases of what Baumol calls "productive entrepreneurship" are in my book a far preferable means of creating and destroying these dynasties compared to the alternative mechanisms of radical wealth redistribution (i.e., war, revolution, robbery, and confiscation) that mankind has witnessed through history.

The above places entrepreneurship in the economic but not necessarily in the commercial domain. As long as there is a market-like situation with equivalents of customers and incumbents present, we can welcome the broadening of the field exemplified by the recent surge in research on "social" and "green" entrepreneurship (Shepherd & Patzelt, 2011; Zahra, Gedajlovic, Neubaum, & Shulman, 2009). In fact, this is a refreshing move away from a narrow focus on "'the art of enriching oneself by starting and growing one's own business" which at one point threatened to come to dominate entrepreneurship research, at least in business schools (Davidsson & Wiklund, 2001).

Refreshing also is the disciplinary broadening of the field. After some debate about "entrepreneurship is a distinctive domain" versus "entrepreneurship belongs in the disciplines" (Sorenson & Stuart, 2008; Venkataraman, 1997) most have probably come to agree with Low (2001) that these perspectives are not contradictory but complementary. We need strong disciplinary theory and methods insights applied to the phenomenon of "creation of new economic activity" (Wiklund et al., 2011).

There used to be only a few individuals with strong disciplinary identities in economics, psychology, or sociology (e.g., Acs, Aldrich, Audretsch, Baron, Frese, Parker, Shaver) who participated regularly in the interdisciplinary community or entrepreneurship researchers, plus a few, significant "transient" visitors to the field (Landström & Persson, 2010). We now see the development of subcommunities of researchers identifying firstly as, for example, psychologists, sociologists, economists, and so on, who devote most of their research interest and effort to studying entrepreneurial phenomena through their particular, disciplinary lens. This is accompanied by infrastructure development that facilitates intradisciplinary dissemination and debate. For example, *Applied Psychology: An International Review* recently published a Special Issue on entrepreneurship. This is definitely a positive development because coopetition within the discipline may be a prerequisite for *really good* disciplinary research on entrepreneurship to result. There are one or two catches, though. We would probably not like to see these disciplinary subcommunities become completely isolated from each other, and we would probably like them all to embrace the same basic notion of entrepreneurship as the "creation of new economic activity." If they do not, they are not working in the same distinct domain and may therefore be little helped by each other's efforts.

Richer, Better, and More Varied Data

One of the most exciting and unambiguously positive current developments in entrepreneurship research is the evolution of the data scene. Increasingly, studies use large-scale, longitudinal, and often multilevel data sets of a scope and quality early entrepreneurship researchers could only dream of (e.g., Amaral, Baptista, & Lima, 2011; Bakker & Shepherd, 2015; Campbell, 2005; Coad, Frankish, Roberts, & Storey, 2013; Sørensen, 2007). Moreover, entrepreneurship-specific data sets like the Global Entrepreneurship Monitor (GEM) and Panel Study of Entrepreneurial Dynamics (PSED) (including its successors and counterparts around the globe) are ever growing, public-domain resources that have provided the empirical basis for hundreds of published studies (Bergmann, Mueller, & Schrettle, 2014; Davidsson & Gordon, 2012; Davidsson, Gordon, & Bergmann, 2011). While these data sets are subject to the modest majority "problem" their sheer—and increasing—size makes it a gradually more feasible prospect to gain insights from them into the generative mechanisms behind the emergence of the select minority of "gazelles" or "unicorns" that populate the right tail of empirical distributions (Crawford et al., 2015). GEM provides only scant and cross-sectional information on the microlevel, but due to the increasing number of countries and years it lends itself to increasingly interesting aggregate-level analyses, especially when combined with country-level data from other sources (Acs, Autio, & Szerb, 2014; Levie, Autio, Acs, & Hart, 2014). PSED-type studies are being conducted in an increasing number of countries and recently a five-cohort data set with longitudinal, venture-level data was made publicly available (Reynolds, Hechavarria, Tian, Samuelsson, & Davidsson, 2016).

As regards the special case of data on "entrepreneurial culture"—prevailing mindset, attitudes, and beliefs—I can recall back in the 1990s having to collect primary data from representative samples of individuals in order to obtain any data of this kind (Davidsson, 1995; Davidsson & Wiklund, 1997). Today, researchers can combine country-level entrepreneurship data with culture data from the World Values Survey (Hechavarria & Reynolds, 2009) and even on the regional level amazingly rich "mentality" data are available in some countries (Obschonka et al., 2015; Stuetzer, Obschonka, Brixy, Sternberg, & Cantner, 2014).

Digitization, the Internet, and social media mean that all kinds of electronic traces are left which can serve as unobtrusive data sources for creative researchers (e.g., Aggarwal & Singh, 2013; Fischer & Reuber, 2011). Further, phenomena like incubators, accelerators, start-up weekends, and crowdfunding platforms provide new sources from which to sample and collect data on start-ups (Amezcua, Grimes, Bradley, & Wiklund, 2013; Mollick, 2014). Some of these contexts may provide excellent opportunities to apply the "catch early and follow-over-time" methodology pioneered by the PSED to more homogeneous and higher-potential start-up cohorts (Davidsson & Gordon, 2012). For creative investigators willing to put in some work there seem to be endless opportunities for finding new types of data that can help address novel questions and generate new insights.

More established approaches like experimentation and simulation are also being increasingly applied to entrepreneurial phenomena (e.g., Grégoire & Shepherd, 2012; Keyhani, Lévesque, & Madhok, 2015). This too contributes to getting a more complete illumination of entrepreneurial phenomena from a variety of angles on multiple levels of analysis.

The one exception from the positive data trend would be the collection of primary data from representative samples through surveys. When I conducted my above-mentioned studies on culture and entrepreneurship in the 1990s in Sweden, I attained a 70% response rate in mail surveys directed to the general population on a topic that would not necessarily interest them. Barring mandatory government surveys, this level of cooperation is impossible to achieve today from any sample, anywhere, on any topic, by any mode of survey data collection. Similarly, when we started data collection for the Comprehensive Australian Study of Entrepreneurial Emergence (CAUSEE) study in 2007 (see Gruenhagen et al., 2016) it was still possible to use landline phone numbers for sampling without severe bias. Not so today (Steffens, Tonelli, & Davidsson, 2011). Much more fragmented and diverse use of communication technologies increases the challenges of building a sampling frame in the first place, and the proliferation of telemarketing and spamming has made audiences much less cooperative. Being more concerned with the theoretical suitability of the sample than whether it exactly matches the empirical population in a particular place at a particular time (see Davidsson, 2016c, Chapter 5) I do not think it is a major problem[3] that we no longer have a single mode of contact that works "for all" as long as researchers invest enough effort into constructing a theoretically sound sampling frame. However, the sharply reduced rate of voluntary participation is worrying.

The "improvements" in survey methodology that have occurred—how easily and cheaply surveys can be created and distributed online, and the presence of panels of individuals who are willing to fill out surveys "professionally" for peanuts—only serve to increase those worries. What all my rather comprehensive experience in survey research tells me is that, in order to get business founders to (repeatedly) provide quality data, you need to talk to them and build rapport with them, which means that the interviewer must have some business knowledge. Further, you need to show respect for them and their business, which means being willing to call back when it suits them, and having an advanced, computer-aided questionnaire design which remembers previous answers through skip patterns and adapted question wording or response alternatives (Gruenhagen et al., 2016). It is a lot of work but that is also why serious survey data are—literally—worth infinitely more than some pay-per-click survey responses received from a largely self-selected sample of unknown composition invited via email or other nonprobabilistic, electronic means.

The Quest for Increased Theoretical Precision

Early entrepreneurship research was to a large extent characterized by relatively atheoretical "mapping of the territory," that is, finding out what the empirical realities of entrepreneurial phenomena look like. This is not synonymous with bad or primitive research but

---

[3] Other than for GEM, where correct statistical representation is essential for country comparisons (Steffens et al., 2011).

rather a necessary step in sound knowledge development. One cannot effectively build or test theory about a poorly understood phenomenon (Hambrick, 2007; Locke, 2007) and still today we may sometimes jump too quickly to large-scale theory testing without sufficient, close-up familiarity with the phenomena (Dimov, 2011). Hence, we should not dismiss contemporary efforts that aim primarily at empirical fact-finding, either.

This said, a field of research cannot forever remain in a state where empirical fact-finding is the main game. For example, one of the findings from the 1990s *Business Dynamics in Sweden* study which really hit the media was that "seven out of ten new jobs are created by small firms" (Davidsson, Lindmark, & Olofsson, 1994). An empirical fact like that is not particularly exciting for people outside that time–space context. At the end of the day it is the sense-making of theory that makes empirical facts travel through space and stand the test of time (and today we know it is "new firms" rather than established "small firms" that create the job surplus; see Haltiwanger, Jarmin, & Miranda, 2013). Further, even within the context, a sound theoretical understanding is needed in order to take some action on the revealed information.

There is widespread perception that emphasis on theory in published entrepreneurship research accelerated around the year 2000. To substantiate this point, I checked the main body text occurrences of "theory" and its derivatives in the first five, regular-issue manuscripts published in *Journal of Business Venturing* in 1995, 2000, 2005, 2010, and 2015. The results are displayed in Figure 1.1.

It is interesting to note that in the year 2000, it was still not unusual to have articles with no mention of theory. Further, it may be noted that the minimum number of mentions of theory in the first five articles of 2015 exceeds the maximum number in 1995 and even in 2000. In all, this admittedly small test clearly indicates that the increase in

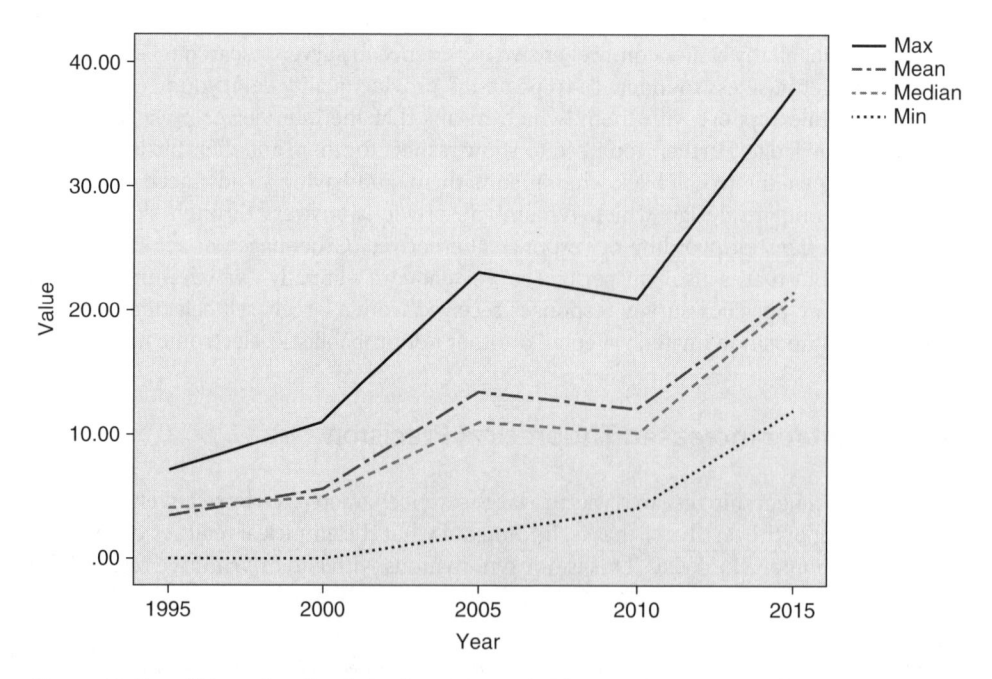

Figure 1.1 Use of "theory" and its derivatives in Journal of Business Venturing articles over time.

theory emphasis is substantial and still ongoing. For the reasons stated above, this is in many ways sound development. However, theorization does not automatically lead to true and correct understanding. Theoretical storytelling may seem to make sense, but so can pure fiction. To arrive at a really sound theoretical understanding of phenomena requires much more than rhetorical skill and statistically significant results. I would argue that a number of factors coalesce to create a strong need for increased theoretical precision in future research in entrepreneurship. For example:

- Increased theorization implies increased level of abstraction, which calls for greater attention to conceptual clarity (Bacharach, 1989; Suddaby, 2010).
- The same increase in abstraction also increases challenges of operationalization (Davidsson, 2016c).
- Increased sample sizes and data quality (Edwards & Berry, 2010) and growing understanding of the limitations of statistical inference (Bettis, 2012; Bettis, Ethiraj, Gambardella, Helfat, & Mitchell, 2016; Schwab, Abrahamson, Starbuck, & Fidler, 2011) make achieving mere "statistical significance" for a directional relationship trivial or relatively meaningless.
- Increased pressures for practical relevance (Frese, Rousseau, & Wiklund, 2014; Gulati, 2007; Khazragui & Hudson, 2015; McKenna, 2015) also make "statistically significant effects" rather meaningless without further information on the absolute and relative size of these effects.
- Increased realization of the importance of context calls for further exploration of how and why empirical relationships vary across countries, cultures, regions, industries, and time periods (Welter, 2011; Zahra, Wright, & Abdelgawad, 2014).

These issues are discussed below.

Abstraction, Conceptual Clarity, and Operationalization

A legitimate field of inquiry ought to achieve clarity about its most central concepts. I will here use the notion of *entrepreneurial opportunity* to illustrate the need for greater conceptual clarity. In the last couple of decades this concept has become one of the most central in our field; "opportunity" even has a central role in the ENT Division's domain statement (Mitchell, 2011).

The popularity of the notion of opportunity is understandable. If our main task is to study the creation of economic activities we need a starting point that precedes the up-and-running business, which makes the "opportunity" a candidate. Further, on an abstract, aggregate level the existence of opportunity can be said to follow directly from the theoretical assumption of disequilibrium. On this aggregate level it may even be possible to meaningfully measure the available (relative) "amount" of opportunity (Anokhin, Troutt, Wincent, & Brandyberry, 2009). To this we can add that the notion of "opportunity" is intuitively appealing and therefore hard to avoid in a lay conversation about entrepreneurship.

When we move to the micro-level and let time, change, and the possibility of failure enter the picture the notion of "entrepreneurial opportunity" becomes a conceptual mess, making it unfit for research purposes. Hansen, Shrader, and Monllor (2011) found no less than six distinct meanings of "opportunity" in the literature. My own deep dive into the topic revealed that only a minority of researchers define the term and that inconsistencies in meaning flourished not only across but also within works, even when a definition was offered (Davidsson, 2015b, 2016a, 2016c). An "opportunity" sometimes refers to the entire set of external circumstances that make (the success of) an entrepreneurial venture possible. At other times it means a single external circumstance—a new technology or a regulatory change, for example—upon which some profitable business might be built. Often it refers to a founder's subjective idea, which may be rudimentary and vague or fleshed out in great detail. The favorability which makes the entity earn the "opportunity" label may be theoretically assumed, empirically proven by a positive outcome, a (possibly delusional) belief on the part of the entrepreneurial agent, or not justified in any manner. When we look more closely, it becomes clear that whether an entity deserves the opportunity label or not depends on who is supposed to act on it, who is doing the evaluation, where in the entrepreneurial journey we find ourselves, and what other agents do.

No wonder, then, that there has been limited progress, due in part to failure to measure these elusive and hopelessly complex entities (Shane, 2012). A field cannot rely on central concepts of this nature because we cannot develop meaningful theory based on a concept that apparently cannot be clearly defined and consistently applied even within a given paper. I have outlined elsewhere how I believe the several important phenomena associated with "opportunity" can be more effectively approached through three separate and clearly defined concepts: *external enablers*, *new venture ideas*, and *opportunity confidence* (Davidsson, 2015b; 2016c). This triplet makes clear distinctions between the agent and the object acted upon, between the objective and the subjective, and between the contents and the favorability of that entity. Like Suddaby (2010), I believe we need to be much more careful in defining our central concepts, explicating their essential properties, and locating them in time and space. "Entrepreneurial opportunity" is but one example of this challenge.

On a more self-critical note, I have enjoyed an amazing number of citations for my coauthorship of the article "The Role of Social and Human Capital Among Nascent Entrepreneurs" (Davidsson & Honig, 2003). One reason for its popularity is probably that it was one of the first in entrepreneurship to use the theoretical concept *human capital* (HC) rather than just discussing effects ascribed to empirical variables like "experience" and "education." In some ways applying the more abstract notion of HC and using already gained theoretical insights surrounding it is no doubt an improvement. But it comes with some responsibility. When we discuss possible effects of "education" or "industry experience" and measure these variables as the number of years of involvement in these activities, there is a high degree of correspondence between what we discuss conceptually and what we measure empirically. How about "human capital?" In the early days it was an aggregate (population) level concept used by economists and sociologists (Becker, 1962; Coleman, 1988; Schultz, 1961). At that aggregate level, the population's average number of years of formal schooling can be a pretty accurate indicator of the country's level of human capital (although it is not the only indicator being used). At the individual level, however, even with a rather narrow HC definition like "skills and knowledge that individuals acquire through investments in schooling, on-the-job training, and other types of experience" (Unger, Rauch, Frese, & Rosenbusch, 2009) the correlation between the theoretical variable and the empirical measure "years of education" can be quite small, considering the variance in school quality, inherent talent, and effort.

What does that imply? A positive relationship between human capital—knowledge and skills—and entrepreneurial success is almost definitional. When Unger et al. (2009) find that HC explains about *one percent* (r=.098) of the variance in success, should we really believe that? Or should we rather conclude that the measurement of HC in most studies is rather weak? In the worst case scenario, Davidsson and Honig's (2003) failure to find support for the hypothesis that HC is positively associated with establishment of a viable firm only shows that the measures were too weak, or the sample too small, to confirm an effect that is bound to exist. Unger et al. (2009) probably provide a more important contribution by finding that the relationship is stronger for more direct measures of knowledge and skills than for indicators like years of education and experience. This suggests that if we want to test the theoretical effects of HC, we need to be more careful in our measurement of it.[4]

Issues of conceptualization and operationalization also pertain to the dependent variable (DV). If our main task is to study the creation of new economic activities, then our most important DVs concern entry into, progress, and success in that journey. For starters, this calls for clear conceptualizations of the start and end points of the process, which is no trivial task (Davidsson, 2016c; McMullen & Dimov, 2013; Schoonhoven, Burton, & Reynolds, 2009). I have come to the conclusion that the starting point should be defined by a combination of intentionality and action (Katz & Gartner, 1988; McMullen & Dimov, 2013). Mere intention without action is clearly unsatisfactory while including actions undertaken before there was an intention to start a business risks leading to something of an infinite regress. While the latter type of actions may create resources that benefit a start-up I would argue against viewing them as part of the venture creation process (Davidsson, 2015a). A venture creation process commences when an intention to create a new economic activity is backed by action towards realizing that intention.

As regards the end point of the process there are several alternatives. A main problem in the literature is the tendency to theorize drivers of *success* while using *continuation* of the start-up effort as operationalization (Davidsson & Gordon, 2012). This major misalignment of theory and operationalization leads to incorrect conclusions. Continuation of a doomed effort only represents waste of resources, which is about as far from success as one can get. However, rather than discarding continuation as a bad operationalization I would argue that continuation and success are two theoretically distinct concepts with, in part, different antecedents and consequences, which are both worthy topics of study. In Davidsson (2016c, Chapter 7) I elaborate on a string of conceptually distinct DVs from start to finish of the entrepreneurial journey. On the individual level there is *intention, engagement, persistence* and *success* whereas on the venture level there is *initiation, continuation, emergence success* and *business performance*.[5] Today I would probably wish

---

[4] In fairness, many of the studies included in Unger et al.'s (2009) meta-analysis probably did not have their theoretical focus on HC relationships but included HC indicators as control variables. However, this only reflects the widespread lack of appreciation of making reproducibility rather than single-study statistical significance the central truth criterion (Hubbard & Lindsay, 2013a; Open Science Collaboration, 2015). If we really wish to build solid knowledge about the role of human capital (or something else) in entrepreneurship we need multiple, serious replications of entire theoretical models based on strong operationalizations of the core concepts, not just meta-analyses of zero-order correlations built on simple indicators. The surge in meta-analyses is part of a promising start toward building more solid evidence, but not the optimal or ultimate solution (see also O'Boyle, Rutherford, & Banks, 2014).

[5] See also Davidsson (2012) and van der Zwan and Thurik (Chapter 2).

to add yet another distinction. One important transition is from the preoperational state to becoming a regular participant in the market, that is, achieving *operational status*. Nonetheless, many may trade for a long time before they achieve *emergence success*, which I define as generating a cumulative surplus exceeding all start-up and running costs; or they may never reach the latter status. This motivates distinguishing both theoretically and empirically between the achievement of operational status and emergence success, respectively.

Entrepreneurship researchers are not alone in struggling and sometimes being a bit careless with their dependent variables (see, e.g., Miller, Washburn, & Glick, 2013). However, this is clearly an area where increased precision is called for. What could be more important than the conceptualization and operationalization of the very phenomenon that we are trying to explain?

Sample Size, Data Quality, Statistical Significance, and Practical Relevance

So far I have discussed the need for clear concepts. The increased precision we now shift to concerns the relationships among concepts. I have noted above the delight we should take in the improved data now available to entrepreneurship researchers. Further below I will discuss the increased pressures to demonstrate impact on practice. Somewhat paradoxically, access to large-scale, high-quality data in combination with increased demands for practical relevance also drives increased demands for theoretical precision. The current mainstream culture accepts theoretical arguments leading to hypotheses of the kind "X has a positive (or negative) effect on Y," where the criterion for research success is statistical significance at a defined level, usually $p < .05$, which should mean "less than five percent risk of a false positive if no such effect exists in the underlying population." Little attention is paid to effect size, that is, the actual magnitude of the estimated effect.

In a world of small samples and/or large random measurement errors, this approach may make some sense (or represent the least bad we could reasonably hope for) because the estimate is known to be imprecise, yet it is also known that for a result to come out significant the real-world effect would have to be rather large.[6] If we have population data, significance as truth criterion does not make any sense. The "estimate" *is* the population parameter; it is not surrounded by any statistical uncertainty of the type statistical inference can help us assess (let alone resolve). If we have a very large probability sample, any tiny effect will come out as "statistically significant." Unless the effect concerns a small but real effect on saving lives—and it rarely does in entrepreneurship research—it is hardly of much interest that an effect of minuscule magnitude is unlikely to be completely absent in the underlying population when in fact it only explains a negligible fraction of the variance in the DV in the sample. If we have a very large sample that we can argue is theoretically relevant but which is not the product of probability sampling or random assignment, statistical significance testing again has no meaningful role. In all these cases, our first concern should instead be *effect size*, that is, the magnitude of the estimated effect. Thus our theoretical interest ought to be directed at the absolute and relative size of the effect, the statistical uncertainty of the effect sometimes being a secondary concern and in other cases a nonissue. This is also what practitioners

---

[6] A caveat being that the result might be entirely driven by *systematic* measurement error rather than real-world effect.

care about: How large is the effect compared to cost or compared to other ways of influencing the dependent variable?

Edwards and Berry (2010) note the increasing meaninglessness of merely confirming that "X has a positive effect on Y." As remedies they discuss the following (and other) ways of increasing theoretical precision, thereby making hypotheses more interesting and meaningful:

Expanding the null hypothesis
This entails demanding theoretical predictions that a parameter not merely differs from zero but that it deviates from zero by some minimum threshold amount. This should be standard practice when using population data and nonrandom (but theoretically relevant) samples. In fact, attention to the magnitude of the effect should always be the primary concern.

Stating predictions as comparisons
This entails theorizing not just that the effect of X on Y is greater than zero, but either that "the effect of X_1 on Y is greater than the effect of X_2 on Y" or "the effect of X on Y_1 is greater than the effect of X on Y_2." This type of prediction is occasionally seen in entrepreneurship (e.g., Naldi & Davidsson, 2013). Davidsson and Honig (2003) found reason to discuss relationships of this nature, for example that the importance of social capital relative to human capital seemed to increase the further you get into the entrepreneurial journey, and the same for specific relative to general forms of capital. Albeit not hypothesized, these exploratory observations may actually be more interesting and important contributions than some of the hypothesized (and conceptually near self-evident) results.

Developing non-nil predictions
This requires the theorist to specify a range within which an effect should fall in order to be consistent with the theory. This would oblige us to take note not just of "disappointingly weak" effects but also "suspiciously strong" ones. The latter may be driven by common-method bias in measurement (Podsakoff, MacKenzie, Lee, & Podsakoff, 2003), multicollinearity, or omitted variables in the model (Shugan, 2007) and hence not help increase our understanding of the phenomena under study.

Specifying other than linear functional forms
A linear relationship is sometimes a reasonable assumption within the range of variance represented in the data at hand, but conceptually it rarely makes sense to assume that each increment of an X-variable would have an equally strong effect on Y. For example, the first prior start-up experience or year of industry experience should be relatively more important than the fifth or the 19th. Nonlinear predictions occur with some regularity in the entrepreneurship literature (e.g., Kreiser, Marino, Kuratko, & Weaver, 2013; Senyard, Baker, Steffens, & Davidsson, 2014). However, it is probably more common that researchers induce nonlinearity through variable transformations undertaken for technical reasons without reflecting on the fact that this changes the variable relationship to a nonlinear one.

Recognizing Context

Several influential authors in entrepreneurship and management have recently pointed out the importance of context and the possible consequences of not paying sufficient attention to contextual variation (George, 2014; Johns, 2006; Welter, 2011;

Zahra & Wright, 2011; Zahra et al., 2014). Developing contingent predictions, which is another of Edwards and Berry's (2010) recipes for more theoretically precise hypotheses, is one way of dealing with context. For example, in Chandler, McKelvie, and Davidsson (2009) we hypothesize and find that rationalistic hypotheses derived from Transaction Cost Economics hold up in resource-scarce environments but not in munificent ones.

Theorizing contingent relationships, often with a context-based moderator, is now the norm in entrepreneurship research. As a case in point, at the time of writing the most recent issue of the *Journal of Business Venturing* features six articles, five of which offer hypotheses. All five include some kind of contingent relationship. This indicates that entrepreneurship research has become relatively advanced in terms of considering context. There are some caveats, though. First, moderation effects are often quite small (Aguinis, Beaty, Boik, & Pierce, 2005). As discussed above, small effects are not necessarily of much theoretical or practical interest even if they are "statistically significant." Second, contingent effects are less likely to replicate than are main effects (Open Science Collaboration, 2015). Third, whereas only a few moderating effects can be considered in any one analysis, it may be the case that the entire causal system differs by context.

The latter is at least implicitly considered in the other main approach to dealing with contextual variation that has become commonplace in entrepreneurship research, namely to restrict the empirical study to a single, narrow context. For example, Kapoor and Furr (2015) focus on the solar photovoltaic industry whereas Cliff, Jennings, and Greenwood (2006) center on law firms in the Greater Vancouver area. This has advantages in operationalization by allowing more precise, customized measures and in analysis by reducing problems of unmeasured heterogeneity (Davidsson, 2016c). The obvious downside is that our main interest is not in those particular industries and regions. Academic interest is usually directed at a broader, conceptual category of entrepreneurial phenomena whereas practitioner interest typically concerns some other particular place and time (Davidsson, 2002).

This means that both types of stakeholders should embrace replication. While theoretical concepts often remain relevant across time and space, their interrelationships are likely to show considerable contextual variation. If we want to become a more advanced field of research by developing more solid knowledge that has greater practical impact, then replicability rather than single-study statistical significance should be the main truth criterion (Davidsson, 2016c, Chapter 9; Hubbard & Lindsay, 2013a, 2013b). It is therefore encouraging to see the launch of new outlets like the *Journal of Business Venturing Insights* and *Academy of Management Discoveries* explicitly invite replication studies. For journal editors who are nervous about replication studies not getting cited it may be interesting to know that the few explicit replication studies in entrepreneurship that I know of tend to do *far better* than the average same-year, same-journal article in terms of citations (Dahlqvist, Davidsson, & Wiklund, 2000; Frank, Kessler, & Fink, 2010; Honig & Samuelsson, 2014; Obschonka, Andersson, Silbereisen, & Sverke, 2013; Weismeier-Sammer, 2011).

Increased Demands for Practical Relevance

Early entrepreneurship research was arguably driven mainly by an interest in important economic phenomena that were neglected by policymakers as well as by mainstream academic discourses (e.g., Birch, 1979). With this strong focus on the phenomena, and the need to engage in exploratory, empirical fact-finding about them, it was quite easy and natural to produce research that would appear relevant and accessible for practitioners, at least on the aggregate, policy-oriented level (e.g., Delmar & Davidsson, 2000; Reynolds, Carter, Gartner, & Greene, 2004).

Over time, a large portion of entrepreneurship got absorbed into the culture and incentive-system of North American, business school research. This arguably brought increased theoretical and methodological sophistication to the field but also a sometimes excessive, singular focus on theoretical contributions in top tier, peer-review publications. As a result, entrepreneurship research also became part of the ongoing and sometimes self-critical debates regarding "rigor versus relevance" (Frank & Landström, 2015; Frese et al., 2014; Gulati, 2007) and "the research-practice gap" (Bansal, Bertels, Ewart, MacConnachie, & O'Brien, 2012). Researchers—in particular those who study economic phenomena (see Harzing, 2005)—respond to incentives, and as long as these rather singularly focus on impressing one's peers the rigor–relevance debate is likely to have but marginal impact at the fringes. Just as increased access to research funding is likely to have played a significant part in the quantitative growth of the field to date, the threat of funding drying up will likely have stronger effects on redirection toward practical relevance than have any self-evaluative debates among academics.

This is what is happening; in the UK, the Research Excellence Framework now explicitly requests academic institutions to provide evidence of the impact of research on business or policy practice (Khazragui & Hudson, 2015; McKenna, 2015) and other countries are following suit by adapting their research evaluation systems (Morgan, 2014). The mechanisms may be different in the US, but there is no doubt in my mind that if business school research is being perceived as detached from practice the funding will dry up, be it donation based or somehow derived from taxpayers' pockets. As I see it, this would also be fair enough. Management and organization, including the entrepreneurship branch of these fields, are fundamentally applied areas of research. If they were to develop solely into domains for academics' exchange of ideas there would be little reason for governments (i.e., taxpayers) and donors to fund it. This said, I think there are some points that need to be considered in any discussion of these issues:

- **The illusion of relevance.** Simple, empirical fact-finding may appear accessible and relevant, but it may also be an example of overly simplistic research that does not help anyone draw the right conclusions. I found reason some years ago to seriously discuss the harmful impact that bad entrepreneurship research can have on practice (Davidsson, 2002) and this type of research is hardly what we would like to see increased. In this sense, there is no contradiction between rigor and relevance; practice can only be served well by good research, and doing good research requires some rigor.
- **The illusion of irrelevance.** As a field of research grows and matures, the topics of individual articles may seem increasingly narrow and esoteric from a practitioner's point of view. However, to some extent this may be a levels fallacy. At early stages it may be possible to address broad questions in single papers. At a more advanced stage, the contribution of the single paper may be restricted to the influence of some moderator variable or some methods detail. This does not mean that the field as a whole is becoming less relevant. Entrepreneurship research undoubtedly has more relevant insights to offer practice today than it had 10 or 20 years ago, and is also likely to produce

much more new, useful knowledge per annum than it did back then. It is rather the demands on the research *translation* function (Shapiro, Kirkman, & Courtney, 2007) that increases as the field becomes more theoretically and methodologically sophisticated, making individual papers' contributions more narrowly focused.

- **The illusion of separation and detachment.** Many entrepreneurship researchers do in fact engage in practice on a regular basis. They may be directly involved in business start-ups, invest in them, consult for them, sit on their boards, or provide advice in other capacities. They may, like myself, regularly interact with policymakers on a face-to-face basis and conduct contract research as an input to policy decisions. They may write practice-oriented reports, magazine articles, and blog posts. At the very least they influence practice indirectly in the classroom. The question here is whether this engagement sufficiently serves the purposes of implementing research-based insights into practice or of canvassing practice for problems to address in academic research. Sometimes one can get the impression that researchers themselves (subconsciously?) do not fully believe in the practical value of research, and then the two activities can become unduly separated.
- **It is a two-way street**. I am not under the impression that business practitioners show a high level of professionalism in terms of keeping up to date with research-based insights of potential value to their professional conduct. In this regard, business people behave differently from how we hope and believe that, for example, pilots and medical doctors behave (Romme, 2016). Then again, business schools share a lot of responsibility for this lack of professionalism by not providing students with the skills and mindset necessary for making the keeping up with developments in research a natural part of their professional identity. Notwithstanding this, as an individual academic I have reason to ask "If I provide a practitioner with good, research-based advice and they do not act upon it, why should the failure to have impact be attributed to me?"
- **Relevance for whom and impact on what?** Regardless of whether the funding comes from taxpayers or other sources, it is hardly the duty of academics and universities to unquestioningly assist particular people or organizations in their quest for profits (or other goals) or to provide proponents of particular ideologies with arguments to help their electoral success. Apart from defensible forms of contract research, the goal should rather be to benefit "society-as-a-whole," which requires consideration of all stakeholders affected by the creation of new economic activities. If researchers agree on that principle and (a) try to stay true to it and (b) interpret its implications somewhat differently, this is probably a good thing.

Despite all these reservations, there are sound reasons for increased pressures towards practical relevance and impact. Practitioners—and educators—have dramatically changed their business start-up toolbox in the last decade or so. Foremost among the newly adopted tools are the models, language, and recipes offered under the rubrics of Lean Start-Up and Business Model Canvas (Blank, 2013; Osterwalder & Pigneur, 2013a; Ries, 2011). These are nonacademic, semi-academic or—in the case of Osterwalder and Pigneur—products of a different research tradition than the dominant track in business schools. Many of the ideas they propose on frugality, incrementalism, and adaptation have parallels in leading themes in entrepreneurship research, such as effectuation (Sarasvathy, 2001), bricolage (Baker & Nelson, 2005) and a critical view on business planning (Honig & Karlsson, 2004). These strands of research have enjoyed an above-average impact on practice and teaching in their own right, and they may have facilitated the uptake of the even more popular ideas offered by Blank (2013), Ries (2011), and Osterwalder and Pigneur (2013a and 2013b). Yet, the latter arguably win the volumes game quite easily. This raises the question of whether future business school research on entrepreneurship ought to leave more room for "design school" research that—in an engineering-like manner—aims at developing practical "tools" and other *primary* types of outputs rather than journal papers (Davidsson & Klofsten, 2003; Osterwalder & Pigneur, 2013b; van Burg & Romme, 2014). If we were to reinvent business research from scratch today, we might actually find it odd not to have more of that perspective represented.

Conclusion

In this chapter I have discussed some likely and more or less desirable current and future developments in entrepreneurship research. My selections and conjectures are no doubt biased, and readers may therefore want to consult also some other gazes into the crystal ball (Carlsson et al., 2013; Choi & Majumdar, 2014; Clarke & Cornelissen, 2014; Shepherd, 2015; van Burg & Romme, 2014; Wiklund et al., 2011; Zahra & Wright, 2011). At any rate, it is safe to say that entrepreneurship remains an important societal phenomenon that is not yet fully understood, and that entrepreneurship research remains an exciting field in which to be active.

References

Acs, Z. J., Autio, E., & Szerb, L. (2014). National systems of entrepreneurship: Measurement issues and policy implications. *Research Policy, 43*(3), 476–494.

Aggarwal, R., & Singh, H. (2013). Differential influence of blogs across different stages of decision making: the case of venture capitalists. *MIS Quarterly, 37*(4), 1093–1112.

Aguinis, H., Beaty, J. C., Boik, R. J., & Pierce, C. A. (2005). Effect size and power in assessing moderating effects of categorical variables using multiple regression: A 30-year review. *Journal of Applied Psychology, 90*(1), 94–107.

Aldrich, H. E. (2012). The emergence of entrepreneurship as an academic field: A personal essay on institutional entrepreneurship. *Research Policy, 41*(7), 1240–1248.

Amaral, A. M., Baptista, R., & Lima, F. (2011). Serial entrepreneurship: Impact of human capital on time to re-entry. *Small Business Economics, 37*(1), 1–21.

Amezcua, A. S., Grimes, M. G., Bradley, S. W., & Wiklund, J. (2013). Organizational sponsorship and founding environments: A contingency view on the survival of business-incubated firms, 1994–2007. *Academy of Management Journal, 56*(6), 1628–1654.

Anokhin, S., Troutt, M. D., Wincent, J., & Brandyberry, A. A. (2009). Measuring arbitrage opportunities: A minimum performance inefficiency estimation technique. *Organizational Research Methods, 13*(55–66).

Bacharach, S. B. (1989). Organizational theories: Some criteria for evaluation. *Academy of Management Review*, 496–515.

Baker, T., & Nelson, R. E. (2005). Creating something from nothing: Resource construction through entrepreneurial bricolage. *Administrative Science Quarterly, 50*(3), 329–366.

Baker, T., & Pollock, T. G. (2007). Making the marriage work: The benefits of strategy's takeover of entrepreneurship for strategic organization. *Strategic Organization, 5*(3), 297–312.

Bakker, R. M., & Shepherd, D. (2015). Pull the plug or take the plunge: Multiple opportunities and the speed of venturing decisions in the Australian mining industry. *Academy of Management Journal.* doi: 10.5465/amj.2013.1165

Bansal, P., Bertels, S., Ewart, T., MacConnachie, P., & O'Brien, J. (2012). Bridging the research–practice gap. *The Academy of Management Perspectives, 26*(1), 73–92.

Baumol, W. J. (1990). Entrepreneurship: Productive, unproductive and destructive. *Journal of Political Economy, 98*(5), 893–921.

Becker, G. S. (1962). Investment in human capital: A theoretical analysis. *Journal of Political Economy, 70*(5), 9–49.

Bergmann, H., Mueller, S., & Schrettle, T. (2014). The use of Global Entrepreneurship Monitor data in academic research: A critical inventory and future potentials. *International Journal of Entrepreneurial Venturing, 6*(3), 242–276.

Bettis, R. A. (2012). The search for asterisks: Compromised statistical tests and flawed theories. *Strategic Management Journal, 33*(1), 108–113.

Bettis, R. A., Ethiraj, S., Gambardella, A., Helfat, C., & Mitchell, W. (2016). Creating repeatable cumulative knowledge in strategic management. *Strategic Management Journal, 37*(2), 257–261.

Birch, D. L. (1979). *The job generating process.* Cambridge, MA: MIT Program on Neighborhood and Regional Change.

Blank, S. (2013). Why the lean start-up changes everything. *Harvard Business Review, 91*(5), 63–72.

Campbell, B. A. (2005). Using linked employer–employee data to study entrepreneurship issues. In S. A. Alvarez, R. Agarwal, & O. Sorenson (Eds.), *Handbook of Entrepreneurship Research* (pp. 143–166). New York: Springer.

Carlsson, B., Braunerhjelm, P., McKelvey, M., Olofsson, C., Persson, L., & Ylinenpää, H. (2013). The evolving domain of entrepreneurship research. *Small Business Economics, 41*(4), 913–930.

Chandler, G. N., McKelvie, A., & Davidsson, P. (2009). Asset specificity and behavioral uncertainty as moderators of the sales growth–employment growth relationship in emerging ventures. *Journal of Business Venturing, 24*(4), 373–387.

Choi, N., & Majumdar, S. (2014). Social entrepreneurship as an essentially contested concept: Opening a new avenue for systematic future research. *Journal of Business Venturing, 29*(3), 363–376.

Clarke, J. S., & Cornelissen, J. P. (2014). How language shapes thought: New vistas for entrepreneurship research. In J. R. Mitchell, R. K. Mitchell, & B. Randolph-Seng (Eds.), *Handbook of Entrepreneurial Cognition* (pp. 383–397). Cheltenham, England: Elgar.

Cliff, J. E., Jennings, P. D., & Greenwood, R. (2006). New to the game and questioning the rules: The experiences and beliefs of founders who start imitative versus innovative firms. *Journal of Business Venturing, 21*, 633–663.

Coad, A., Frankish, J., Roberts, R. G., & Storey, D. J. (2013). Growth paths and survival chances: An application of Gambler's Ruin theory. *Journal of Business Venturing, 28*(5), 615–632.

Coleman, J. S. (1988). Social capital in the creation of human capital. *American Journal of Sociology, 94*, S95–S120.

Crawford, G. C., Aguinis, H., Lichtenstein, B., Davidsson, P., & McKelvey, B. (2015). Power law distributions in entrepreneurship: Implications for theory and research. *Journal of Business Venturing, 30*(5), 696–713.

Dahlqvist, J., Davidsson, P., & Wiklund, J. (2000). Initial conditions as predictors of new venture performance: A replication and extension of the Cooper et al. study. *Enterprise and Innovation Management Studies, 1*(1), 1–17.

Davidsson, P. (1995). Culture, structure and regional levels of entrepreneurship. *Entrepreneurship & Regional Development, 7*, 41–62.

Davidsson, P. (2002). What entrepreneurship research can do for business and policy practice. *International Journal of Entrepreneurship Education, 1*(1), 5–24.

Davidsson, P. (2012). Engagement, persistence, progress and success as theoretically distinct aspects of business creation processes. In A. Zacharakis et al. (Ed.), *Frontiers of Entrepreneurship Research 2011* (Vol. 31). Wellesley, MA: Babson College.

Davidsson, P. (2015a). Data replication and extension: A commentary. *Journal of Business Venturing Insights, 3*, 12–15.

Davidsson, P. (2015b). Entrepreneurial opportunities and the entrepreneurship nexus: A re-conceptualization. *Journal of Business Venturing, 30*(5), 674–695.

Davidsson, P. (2016a). Entrepreneurial opportunities as propensities: Do Ramoglou & Tsang move the field forward? *Journal of Business Venturing Insights.* doi:10.1016/j.jbvi.2016.02.002

Davidsson, P. (2016b). The field of entrepreneurship research: Some significant developments. In D. Bögenhold, J. Bonnet, M. Dejardin, & D. Garcia Pérez de Lema (Ed.), *Contemporary entrepreneurship* (pp. 17–28). New York, NY: Springer.

Davidsson, P. (2016c). *Researching entrepreneurship: Conceptualization and design* (2nd ed.). New York, NY: Springer.

Davidsson, P., & Gordon, S. R. (2012). Panel studies of new venture creation: A methods-focused review and suggestions for future research. *Small Business Economics, 39*(4), 853–876.

Davidsson, P., Gordon, S. R., & Bergmann, H. (Eds.). (2011). *Nascent entrepreneurship*. Cheltenham, England: Elgar.

Davidsson, P., & Honig, B. (2003). The role of social and human capital among nascent entrepreneurs. *Journal of Business Venturing, 18*(3), 301–331.

Davidsson, P., & Klofsten, M. (2003). The business platform: Developing an instrument to gauge and assist the development of young firms. *Journal of Small Business Management, 41*(1), 1–26.

Davidsson, P., Lindmark, L., & Olofsson, C. (1994). *Dynamiken i svenskt näringsliv (Business dynamics in Sweden)*. Lund, Sweden: Studentlitteratur.

Davidsson, P., & Wiklund, J. (1997). Values, beliefs and regional variations in new firm formation rates. *Journal of Economic Psychology, 18*, 179–199.

Davidsson, P., & Wiklund, J. (2001). Levels of analysis in entrepreneurship research: Current practice and suggestions for the future. *Entrepreneurship Theory & Practice, 25*(4, Summer), 81–99.

Delmar, F., & Davidsson, P. (2000). Where do they come from? Prevalence and characteristics of nascent entrepreneurs. *Entrepreneurship & Regional Development, 12*, 1–23.

Dimov, D. (2011). Grappling with the unbearable elusiveness of entrepreneurial opportunities. *Entrepreneurship Theory & Practice, 35*(1), 57–81.

Dino, R. N. (2015). Crossing boundaries: Toward integrating creativity, innovation, and entrepreneurship research through practice. *Psychology of Aesthetics, Creativity, and the Arts, 9*(2), 139–146.

Edwards, J. R., & Berry, J. W. (2010). The presence of something or the absence of nothing: Increasing theoretical precision in management research. *Organizational Research Methods, 13*(4), 668–689.

Fischer, E., & Reuber, A. R. (2011). Social interaction via new social media: (How) can interactions on Twitter affect effectual thinking and behavior? *Journal of Business Venturing, 26*(1), 1–18.

Frank, H., Kessler, A., & Fink, M. (2010). Entrepreneurial orientation and business performance—a replication study. *Schmalenbach Business Review, 62*, 175–198.

Frank, H., & Landström, H. (2015). What makes entrepreneurship research interesting? Reflections on strategies to overcome the rigour–relevance gap. *Entrepreneurship & Regional Development, 28*(1–2), 1–25.

Frese, M., Rousseau, D. M., & Wiklund, J. (2014). The emergence of evidence-based entrepreneurship. *Entrepreneurship Theory & Practice, 38*(2), 209–216.

George, G. (2014). Rethinking management scholarship. *Academy of Management Journal, 57*(1), 1–6.

Grégoire, D. A., & Shepherd, D. A. (2012). Technology-market combinations and the identification of entrepreneurial opportunities: An investigation of the opportunity-individual nexus. *Academy of Management Journal, 55*(4), 753–785.

Gruenhagen, J., Davidsson, P., Gordon, S. R., Salunke, S., Senyard, J., Steffens, P., & Stuetzer, M. (2016). *Comprehensive Australian Study of Entrepreneurial Emergence (CAUSEE). Handbook & user manual, version 7*. Brisbane, Australia: QUT Business School, Australian Centre for Entrepreneurship Research.

Gulati, R. (2007). Tent poles, tribalism, and boundary spanning: The rigor–relevance debate in management research. *Academy of Management Journal, 50*(4), 775–782.

Haltiwanger, J., Jarmin, R. S., & Miranda, J. (2013). Who creates jobs? Small versus large versus young. *Review of Economics and Statistics, 95*(2), 347–361.

Hambrick, D. C. (2007). The field of management's devotion to theory: Too much of a good thing? *Academy of Management Journal, 50*(6), 1346–1352.

Hansen, D. J., Shrader, R., & Monllor, J. (2011). Defragmenting definitions of entrepreneurial opportunity. *Journal of Small Business Management, 49*(2), 283–304.

Harzing, A.-W. (2005). Australian research output in economics and business: High volume, low impact? *Australian Journal of Management, 30*(2), 183–200.

Hechavarria, D. M., & Reynolds, P. D. (2009). Cultural norms & business start-ups: The impact of national values on opportunity and necessity entrepreneurs. *International Entrepreneurship and Management Journal, 5*(4), 417–437.

Henrekson, M., & Sanandaji, T. (2014). Small business activity does not measure entrepreneurship. *Proceedings of the National Academy of Sciences, 111*(5), 1760–1765.

Honig, B., & Karlsson, T. (2004). Institutional forces and the written business plan. *Journal of Management, 30*(1), 29–48.

Honig, B., & Samuelsson, M. (2014). Data replication and extension: A study of business planning and venture-level performance. *Journal of Business Venturing Insights, 1*(1–2), 18–25.

Hubbard, R., & Lindsay, R. M. (2013a). From significant difference to significant sameness: Proposing a paradigm shift in business research. *Journal of Business Research, 66*(9), 1377–1388.

Hubbard, R., & Lindsay, R. M. (2013b). The significant difference paradigm promotes bad science. *Journal of Business Research, 66*(9), 1393–1397.

Johns, G. (2006). The essential impact of context on organizational behavior. *Academy of Management Review, 31*(2), 386–408.

Kapoor, R., & Furr, N. R. (2015). Complementarities and competition: Unpacking the drivers of entrants' technology choices in the solar photovoltaic industry. *Strategic Management Journal, 36*(3), 416–436.

Katz, J., & Gartner, W. B. (1988). Properties of emerging organizations. *Academy of Management Review, 13*(3), 429–441.

Keyhani, M., Lévesque, M., & Madhok, A. (2015). Toward a theory of entrepreneurial rents: A simulation of the market process. *Strategic Management Journal, 36*(1), 76–96.

Khazragui, H., & Hudson, J. (2015). Measuring the benefits of university research: Impact and the REF in the UK. *Research Evaluation, 24*(1), 51–62.

Kreiser, P. M., Marino, L. D., Kuratko, D. F., & Weaver, K. M. (2013). Disaggregating entrepreneurial orientation: The non-linear impact of innovativeness, proactiveness and risk-taking on SME performance. *Small Business Economics, 40*(2), 273–291.

Landström, H., Åström, F., & Harirchi, G. (2015). Innovation and entrepreneurship studies: One or two fields of research? *International Entrepreneurship and Management Journal, 11*(3), 493–509.

Landström, H., & Persson, O. (2010). Entrepreneurship research: research communities and knowledge platforms. In H. Landström, & F. Lohrke (Ed.), *Historical foundations of entrepreneurship research* (pp. 46–76). Cheltenham, England: Elgar.

Levie, J., Autio, E., Acs, Z., & Hart, M. (2014). Global entrepreneurship and institutions: An introduction. *Small Business Economics, 42*(3), 437–444.

Locke, E. A. (2007). The case for inductive theory building. *Journal of Management, 33*(6), 867–890.

Low, M. (2001). The adolescence of entrepreneurship research: Specification of purpose. *Entrepreneurship Theory & Practice, 25*(4, Summer), 17–25.

McKenna, H. P. (2015). Research assessment: The impact of impact. *International Journal of Nursing Studies, 52*(1), 1–3.

McMullen, J. S., & Dimov, D. (2013). Time and the entrepreneurial journey: The problems and promise of studying entrepreneurship as a process. *Journal of Management Studies, 50*(8), 1481–1512.

Meyer, M., Libaers, D., Thijs, B., Grant, K., Glänzel, W., & Debackere, K. (2012). Origin and emergence of entrepreneurship as a research field. *Scientometrics*, 1–13.

Miller, C. C., Washburn, N. T., & Glick, W. H. (2013). The myth of firm performance. *Organization Science, 24*(3), 948–964.

Mitchell, R. K. (2011). Increasing returns and the domain of entrepreneurship research. *Entrepreneurship Theory & Practice, 35*(4), 615–629.

Mollick, E. (2014). The dynamics of crowdfunding: An exploratory study. *Journal of Business Venturing, 29*(1), 1–16.

Morgan, B. (2014). Research impact: Income for outcome. *Nature, 511*(7510), S72–S75.

Naldi, L., & Davidsson, P. (2013). Entrepreneurial growth: The role of international knowledge acquisition as moderated by firm age. *Journal of Business Venturing, 29*(5), 687–703.

O'Boyle, E. H., Rutherford, M. W., & Banks, G. C. (2014). Publication bias in entrepreneurship research: An examination of dominant relations to performance. *Journal of Business Venturing, 29*(6), 773–784.

Obschonka, M., Andersson, H., Silbereisen, R. K., & Sverke, M. (2013). Rule-breaking, crime, and entrepreneurship: A replication and extension study with 37-year longitudinal data. *Journal of Vocational Behavior, 83*(3), 386–396.

Obschonka, M., Stuetzer, M., Gosling, S. D., Rentfrow, P. J., Lamb, M. E., Potter, J., & Audretsch, D. B. (2015). Entrepreneurial regions: Do macro-psychological cultural characteristics of regions help solve the "knowledge paradox" of economics? *PloS One, 10*(6). doi: 10.1371/journal.pone.0129332

Open Science Collaboration. (2015). Estimating the reproducibility of psychological science. *Science, 349*(6251), 943–951.

Osterwalder, A., & Pigneur, Y. (2013a). *Business model generation: A handbook for visionaries, game changers, and challengers.* Hoboken, NJ: Wiley.

Osterwalder, A., & Pigneur, Y. (2013b). Designing business models and similar strategic objects: The contribution of IS. *Journal of the Association for Information Systems, 14*(5), 237.

Podsakoff, P. M., MacKenzie, S. B., Lee, J.-Y., & Podsakoff, N. P. (2003). Common method biases in behavioral research: A critical review of the literature and recommended remedies. *Journal of Applied Psychology, 88*(5), 879–903.

Reynolds, P. D., Carter, N. M., Gartner, W. B., & Greene, P. G. (2004). The prevalence of nascent entrepreneurs in the United States: Evidence from the Panel Study of Entrepreneurial Dynamics. *Small Business Economics, 23*(4), 263–284.

Reynolds, P. D., Hechavarria, D., Tian, L., Samuelsson, M., & Davidsson, P. (2016). *Panel Study of Entrepreneurial Dynamics: A five cohort outcomes harmonized data set* (Tech. Rep.). Retrieved from https://www.researchgate.net/publication/294292920_Panel_Study_of_Entrepreneurial_Dynamics_A_Five_Cohort_Outcomes_Harmonized_Data_Set

Ries, E. (2011). *The Lean Startup: How today's entrepreneurs use continuous innovation to create radically successful businesses.* New York, NY: Crown Books.

Romme, G. (2016). *The quest for professionalism: The case of management and entrepreneurship.* Oxford, England: Oxford University Press.

Salter, A. J., & McKelvey, M. (2016). Evolutionary analysis of innovation and entrepreneurship: Sidney G. Winter—recipient of the 2015 Global Award for Entrepreneurship Research. *Small Business Economics.* doi: 10.1007/s11187-016-9702-4

Sarasvathy, S. (2001). Causation and effectuation: Towards a theoretical shift from economic inevitability to entrepreneurial contingency. *Academy of Management Review, 26*(2), 243–288.

Schoonhoven, C. B., Burton, M. D., & Reynolds, P. D. (2009). Reconceiving the gestation window: The consequences of competing definitions of firm conception and birth. In P. D. Reynolds & R. T. Curtin (Eds.), *New firm creation in the United States* (pp. 219–237). New York, NY: Springer.

Schultz, T. W. (1961). Investment in human capital. *The American Economic Review, 51*(1), 1–17.

Schwab, A., Abrahamson, E., Starbuck, W. H., & Fidler, F. (2011). Researchers should make thoughtful assessments instead of null-hypothesis significance tests. *Organization Science, 22*(4), 1105–1120.

Senyard, J., Baker, T., Steffens, P., & Davidsson, P. (2014). Bricolage as a path to innovativeness for resource-constrained new firms. *Journal of Product Innovation Management, 31*(2), 211–230.

Shane, S. (2012). Reflections on the 2010 AMR Decade Award: Delivering on the promise of entrepreneurship as a field of research. *Academy of Management Review, 37*(1), 10–20.

Shane, S., & Venkataraman, S. (2000). The promise of entrepreneurship as a field of research. *Academy of Management Review, 25*(1), 217–226.

Shapiro, D. L., Kirkman, B. L., & Courtney, H. G. (2007). Perceived causes and solutions of the translation problem in management research. *Academy of Management Journal, 50*(2), 249–266.

Shepherd, D. A. (2015). Party on! A call for entrepreneurship research that is more interactive, activity based, cognitively hot, compassionate, and prosocial. *Journal of Business Venturing, 30*(4), 489–507.

Shepherd, D. A., & Patzelt, H. (2011). The new field of sustainable entrepreneurship: studying entrepreneurial action linking "what is to be sustained" with "what is to be developed." *Entrepreneurship Theory & Practice, 35*(1), 137–163.

Shugan, S. M. (2007). Errors in the variables, unobserved heterogeneity, and other ways of hiding statistical error. *Marketing Science, 25*(3), 203–216.

Sørensen, J. B. (2007). Closure vs. exposure: Mechanisms in the intergenerational transmission of self-employment. *Research in the Sociology of Organizations, 25*, 83–124.

Sorenson, O., & Stuart, T. E. (2008). Entrepreneurship: A field of dreams? *The Academy of Management Annals, 2*(1), 517–543.

Steffens, P. R., Tonelli, M., & Davidsson, P. (2011). How do we reach them? Comparing random samples from mobile and landline phones. In A. Maritz (Ed.), *Proceedings of AGSE Entrepreneurship Research Exchange 2011*. Melbourne, Australia: Swinburne University.

Stuetzer, M., Obschonka, M., Brixy, U., Sternberg, R., & Cantner, U. (2014). Regional characteristics, opportunity perception and entrepreneurial activities. *Small Business Economics, 42*(2), 221–244.

Suddaby, R. (2010). Editor's comments: Construct clarity in theories of management and organization. *Academy of Management Review, 35*(3), 346–357.

Teixeira, A. A. C. (2011). Mapping the (in)visible college(s) in the field of entrepreneurship. *Scientometrics, 89*(1), 1–36.

Unger, J. M., Rauch, A., Frese, M., & Rosenbusch, N. (2009). Human capital and entrepreneurial success: A meta-analytical review. *Journal of Business Venturing, 26*(3), 341–358.

van Burg, E., & Romme, A. G. L. (2014). Creating the future together: Toward a framework for research synthesis in entrepreneurship. *Entrepreneurship Theory & Practice, 38*, 369–397.

Venkataraman, S. (1997). The distinctive domain of entrepreneurship research: An editor's perspective. In J. Katz & J. Brockhaus (Eds.), *Advances in entrepreneurship, firm emergence, and growth* (Vol. 3, pp. 119–138). Greenwich, CT: JAI Press.

Weismeier-Sammer, D. (2011). Entrepreneurial behavior in family firms: A replication study. *Journal of Family Business Strategy, 2*(3), 128–138.

Welter, F. (2011). Contextualizing entrepreneurship—conceptual challenges and ways forward. *Entrepreneurship Theory & Practice, 35*(1), 165–184.

Wiklund, J., Davidsson, Audretsch, D. B., & Karlsson, C. (2011). The future of entrepreneurship research. *Entrepreneurship Theory & Practice, 35*(1), 1–9.

Zahra, S. A., Gedajlovic, E., Neubaum, D. O., & Shulman, J. M. (2009). A typology of social entrepreneurs: Motives, search processes and ethical challenges. *Journal of Business Venturing, 24*(5), 519–532.

Zahra, S. A., & Wright, M. (2011). Entrepreneurship's next act. *Academy of Management Perspectives, 25*(4), 67–83.

Zahra, S. A., Wright, M., & Abdelgawad, S. G. (2014). Contextualization and the advancement of entrepreneurship research. *International Small Business Journal, 32*(5), 479–500.

2

Entrepreneurship as a Process: Empirical Evidence for Entrepreneurial Engagement Levels

Peter van der Zwan[a] and Roy Thurik[a,b]

[a] Department of Business Studies, Leiden Law School, Leiden University
[b] Montpellier Business School, France

Introduction

Recently, some metastudies have examined the individual-level determinants of entrepreneurship or self-employment (Simoes, Crespo, & Moreira, 2016; Walter & Heinrichs, 2015), focusing on the question "Who is an entrepreneur?" These studies investigate the occupational choice decision at the individual level by comparing entrepreneurs with wage workers (or a different comparison group) based on their individual-level characteristics (see also Grilo & Thurik, 2008; Parker, 2009, Chapter 4). To mention a few of these individual-level determinants (Simoes et al., 2016), the probability of being self-employed—a commonly used proxy for entrepreneurship—is higher for men, older individuals, married individuals, individuals with children, individuals with self-employed parents, individuals with a self-employed spouse, and immigrants.

In these occupational choice models, entrepreneurship is viewed as a single state that an individual can adopt. More generally, studies on the topic of "determinants of entrepreneurship" tend to focus on one stage of the entrepreneurial process—being an entrepreneur or self-employed—and compare the individuals in this single stage with individuals in a comparison group, such as paid employment. Conclusions drawn from these single-state, static analyses do not necessarily maintain for the stages that are prior to (or beyond) the actual venture start-up and that go together with different levels of entrepreneurial engagement. This is why several scholars have advocated the view of entrepreneurship as a process (Baron, 2007; Gartner, 1988; Moroz & Hindle, 2012; Shane & Venkataraman, 2000; Van der Zwan, Thurik, & Grilo, 2013).

The present chapter adopts such a process approach because the integration of several stages that together shape the entrepreneurial decision may provide answers to relevant questions. For example, an analysis that includes various stages could reveal why some individuals are able to convert their start-up attempts into an actual business, whereas others experience difficulties. Moreover, some people are attracted to entrepreneurship or seriously consider starting a business but do not manage to actually found a business.

The Wiley Handbook of Entrepreneurship, First Edition.
Edited by Gorkan Ahmetoglu, Tomas Chamorro-Premuzic, Bailey Klinger, & Tessa Karcisky.
© 2017 John Wiley & Sons Ltd. Published 2017 by John Wiley & Sons Ltd.

In other words, the evidence on some determinants of entrepreneurship, as commonly found in the occupational choice literature, may be more nuanced when considering separate phases of the entrepreneurial process. Hence, research considering entrepreneurship as a single state may provide an incomplete picture of the entrepreneurial potential hidden within individuals. Research that considers the various stages, can subsequently reveal in detail how this entrepreneurial potential can be released or why it is hampered. This may have implications for policy interventions that do not necessarily work out similarly across different engagement levels.

This entrepreneurial potential has also been referred to as "latent entrepreneurship," defined as the preference of individuals for entrepreneurship rather than paid employment (Blanchflower, Oswald, & Stutzer, 2001; Grilo & Irigoyen, 2006). The literature on latent entrepreneurship suggests that many people in both higher-income and lower-income countries would rather be entrepreneurs than wage workers (Gohmann, 2012; Grilo & Irigoyen; 2006). Latent entrepreneurship can be considered a separate stage in the entrepreneurial process, one that precedes one's intentions to engage in entrepreneurship (i.e., "how hard people are willing to try," Ajzen, 1991, p. 181) and is a necessary condition for actual involvement in entrepreneurship (Verheul, Thurik, Grilo, & Van der Zwan 2012). Just as those who intend to become entrepreneurs do not always become so, those who are latent entrepreneurs may in the end decide not to set up a business.

This chapter has two aims. First, it emphasizes the benefits of addressing entrepreneurship as a process. Second, it provides an overview of established empirical findings in the area of the entrepreneurial process, an overview which has not been provided in earlier research. We zoom in on the relevance of several well-known individual-level determinants across the various phases of the entrepreneurial process, and present a concise overview of possible differences across countries. The chapter's empirical approach is important given that there is an underrepresentation of the empirical view of the entrepreneurial process (Brixy, Sternberg, & Stüber, 2012), and is in contrast to earlier studies about entrepreneurship as a process that are mainly theoretical (Moroz & Hindle, 2012).

An important reason for addressing entrepreneurship as a process from an empirical point of view is that there exist discrepancies between the various stages of the process. In other words, there is selection between phases (Brixy et al., 2012), a few examples of which follow. Although we know from previous research that entrepreneurial intentions tend to precede entrepreneurial behavior, it is also true, as mentioned above, that intentions do not necessarily lead to actual involvement in entrepreneurship. Kautonen, Gelderen, and Fink (2015) found that approximately 80% of respondents in their Austrian and Finnish sample who engaged in entrepreneurial behavior reported having previous intentions to do so. Their study, however, also revealed that 37% of individuals with intentions had taken action to start a business, but approximately 63% had not taken action one year later. In terms of the transition from nascent entrepreneurship—actively taking steps to start a business—to actual entrepreneurship, Parker and Belghitar (2006) found that one year later, one third of the nascent entrepreneurs who comprised their American sample had started a business, almost half were still taking steps to start a business, and one fifth had given up their start-up attempts. Also using an American sample, Hopp and Sonderegger (2015) found that one quarter of nascent entrepreneurs had started their venture and approximately half had disengaged from their nascent activities after five years. According to Figure 2 in Hechavarría, Matthews, & Reynolds (2016), approximately 60% of American start-ups were still trying to start a business approximately four years after conception (basically understood as the first attempts to start a business). Finally, Bergmann and Stephan (2013) show that the fraction of nascent entrepreneurs who have recently made the transition to new business ownership—"transition ratio"—is low in a considerable number of countries. In sum, although many individuals have intentions to start a business or are actively taking steps to start a business, significant fractions of these groups never end up doing so. A process perspective could shed more light on the underlying reasons behind this intentions–behavior gap and the difference between nascent and actual entrepreneurship.

In this chapter, we focus on several stages of the entrepreneurial process. These stages incorporate both the "cognitive" and "behavioral" stages (Davidsson, 2005). At a particular moment in time, an individual is engaged in any of these stages, and there is a certain likelihood that this individual will move to the next stage. Implicit in this model are thresholds that indicate the transition from one stage to another. In the majority of studies cited below, one may move (1) from "never considered starting a business" to "thinking about starting a business"; (2) from "thinking about starting a business" to "taking steps to start a business"; (3) from "taking steps to start a business" to "owning a young business"; and (4) from "owning a young business" to "owning an established business." Intriguingly, several strands of literature are integrated in this particular process, such as the literature on entrepreneurial intentions (Schlaegel & Koenig, 2014), nascent entrepreneurship (Davidsson, 2006), and entrepreneurial survival (van Praag, 2003). Entrepreneurial exit can be considered a critical component of the entrepreneurial process (DeTienne, 2010), and hence, exit can also be added as a stage (Stam, Thurik, & Van der Zwan, 2010). Below, we combine these streams of literature and show that the individual-level determinants of entrepreneurship (as indicated, for example, by Walter & Heinrichs, 2015, and Simoes et al., 2016) deserve separate treatment depending on the stage of the entrepreneurial process. That is, we show evidence that the empirically validated determinants of self-employment or entrepreneurship differ across the several stages of the entrepreneurial process.

The successive stages above have been referred to as the "entrepreneurial ladder" (Van der Zwan, Thurik, & Grilo, 2010), a concept that has also been adopted in other studies (e.g., Minola, Donina, & Meoli, 2016). By modeling the successive stages as a process, one can gain insight into the overall ease or difficulty of moving through the various stages (Van der Zwan et al., 2010, 2013). The transitions can also be analyzed separately, and the remainder of this chapter will present some examples of such an analysis.

Merits of Entrepreneurship as a Process

We acknowledge that entrepreneurship consists of a series of behaviors that have to be performed sequentially over time (Davidsson, 2005). Davidsson (2005) defines the entrepreneurial process as "all cognitive and behavioral steps from the initial conception of a rough business idea, or first behavior towards the realization of a new business activity, until the process is either terminated or has led to an up and running business venture regular sales" (p. 4). In addition to the distinction between cognition and behavior in this definition, a common distinction made in other studies is that between the "discovery" and "exploitation" of entrepreneurial opportunities (Shane & Venkataraman, 2000).

Entrepreneurship as a process is at the heart of the data collection effort of the Panel Study of Entrepreneurial Dynamics (PSED), which follows individuals over time as they start their businesses (Reynolds, 2010). Different cognitive and behavioral steps are taken throughout the process of starting a business (Reynolds, 2010), such as thinking about the new business, preparing a business plan, hiring employees for pay, and submitting a patent, trademark, or copyright application. Baron (2007) distinguishes among the prelaunch phase (activities prior to the new venture launch), the launch phase (activities related to the launch of the venture), and the postlaunch phase (activities related to the period after the launch). Work based on the PSED reveals how businesses are formed (Hechavarría et al., 2016; Parker & Belghitar, 2006) and emphasizes the important role of the individual in the start-up process.

In the first section of this chapter, we noted the justification of a process approach. In general, we argue that the process approach has the following three advantages over a traditional approach where entrepreneurship is viewed as a single state that can be adopted:

1) First, one can gain a summary measure of the ease or difficulty of moving through the various stages of the entrepreneurial process (Van der Zwan et al., 2010). The research question to be answered here is: What determines the probability of moving forward in the entrepreneurial process? This is particularly useful in drawing cross-national comparisons.

2) Second, one can retrieve information about the ease or difficulty of making a transition between two successive stages of the entrepreneurial process. This is related to the transition ratio in Bergmann and Stephan (2013) reflecting the "efficiency" of the start-up process, which is especially convenient from a cross-national perspective. Thus, one may also gain insight into the relative difficulty of making a specific transition in the entrepreneurial process. For example, it is shown by Van der Zwan et al. (2010) that the probability of transitioning from "thinking about starting a business" to "taking steps to start a business" is higher than that of making other transitions. Hence, a process perspective may reveal which regions or countries have better entrepreneurial conditions or which transition(s) in the process pose(s) fewer difficulties to individuals.

3) Third, a process approach may hint at a specific position in the process where certain groups of people experience more difficulties in making a transition than other groups of individuals. This is also relevant from a policy perspective. When conditions for certain groups are not beneficial at a certain transition, government may take action at a particular rung of the entrepreneurial ladder where a specific group is hampered in its progress. In other words, the determinants of entrepreneurial engagement can differ across the various phases of the entrepreneurial process (Baron & Markman, 2005). Variables that are not important for a specific stage in the entrepreneurial process may entail an important influence for another stage. This is also emphasized by Baron (2007), who states that "the impact of specific variables may change appreciably over different phases of the process" (p. 30).

Three Stylized Facts

This section elaborates on three stylized facts that have emerged from the existing literature on the entrepreneurial process and its determinants.

Latent Entrepreneurship

The first stylized fact based on empirical evidence refers to latent entrepreneurship, defined as an individual's preference for entrepreneurship versus wage work. Earlier studies on latent entrepreneurship have revealed the importance of the some individual-level determinants of latent entrepreneurship (Blanchflower et al., 2001; Bönte, & Piegeler, 2013; Gohmann, 2012; Grilo & Irigoyen, 2006; Grilo & Thurik, 2005, 2006). This evidence is based mainly on demographic variables. For example, men are more likely than women to prefer to be an entrepreneur rather than a wage worker. Furthermore, there exists a U-shaped relationship between an individual's age and his/her preference for entrepreneurship, such that the youngest and oldest individuals are most likely to prefer an entrepreneurial career. Interestingly, prior studies have not detected a significant relationship between educational attainment and the preference for entrepreneurship. Lastly, risk-taking propensity plays a decisive role here: risk tolerance increases the probability of being a latent entrepreneur. Hence, whereas the important role of an individual's risk-taking propensity for entrepreneurship has been emphasized in numerous earlier studies, the literature on latent entrepreneurship stresses the importance of this variable in a very early stage of the entrepreneurial process. Indeed, the process perspective may be particularly useful in the context of risk-taking propensity because the role of risk may change across the different stages of the entrepreneurial process (Baron, 2007), playing an especially important role in the earliest phases.

The concept of latent entrepreneurship can also be used to explain why certain groups of individuals have relatively low levels of entrepreneurial engagement. One prominent example refers to women, who are the focus in Verheul et al.'s (2012) study. It is generally known that women are less likely than men to engage in entrepreneurial activities and Verheul et al. (2012) find that the relatively low self-employment rate of women can be explained partly by a lower willingness to engage in entrepreneurship compared with men, that is, lower levels of latent entrepreneurship. In addition, the lower engagement among women is partly explained by the existence of gender-specific obstacles that are more prevalent in the latent entrepreneurship (preference) stage than in the actual entrepreneurship (action) stage. All in all, latent entrepreneurship plays an important role in explaining women's lower engagement in entrepreneurship than men's.

Different Roles Throughout the Process

Our second observation relates to the difference in importance of a particular variable throughout the entrepreneurial process. Gender is a prominent example and is a widely researched individual-level determinant of entrepreneurship. While gender determines entrepreneurial engagement, the importance of gender decreases as one's involvement in the process increases. In other words, the higher likelihood of men than women to engage in entrepreneurship depends on the stage in the entrepreneurial process, and the "advantage" of men over women diminishes at more mature stages of the entrepreneurial process (Van der Zwan et al., 2010, 2013). For example, based on the sample of Van der Zwan, Verheul, & Thurik (2011), it appears that men are twice as likely as women to think about engaging in entrepreneurship but that this advantageous position for men becomes less pronounced as the level of involvement increases. That is, the probability of owning an established business is approximately equal for women and men once they own a young business (Van der Zwan et al., 2013). Moreover,

Brixy et al. (2012) conclude that although women are "less likely than men to even think about becoming an entrepreneur . . . once in the process, women tend to proceed to start a firm more often than men" (p. 116). In a similar fashion, Parker and Belghitar (2006) do not find a gender effect for the transition from nascent entrepreneurship to actual entrepreneurship status.

Most studies find that the probability of being an entrepreneur increases with an individual's age but decreases beyond a certain threshold (Simoes et al., 2016). Van der Zwan et al. (2010) similarly conclude that the probability of moving forward in the entrepreneurial process decreases with age after a certain age. Not surprisingly, there are differences in terms of the importance of age across the various stages of the process. For example, the inverse U-shaped relationship between an individual's age and entrepreneurial engagement is in sharp contrast with the U-shaped relationship that has been found between age and latent entrepreneurship (Lévesque & Minniti, 2006). Latent entrepreneurs tend to be young individuals (Brixy et al., 2012; Grilo & Irigoyen, 2006; Verheul et al., 2012). Similarly, age negatively impacts the transition in the entrepreneurial process from "never considered starting a business" to "thinking about starting a business" (Van der Zwan et al., 2011, 2012), implying that it is the youngest individuals in particular who consider an entrepreneurial career.

Moreover, for educational attainment, we find a different role depending on the stage or transition in the process. While there exists a significant positive relationship in the earliest stage (from "never considered starting a business" to "thinking about starting a business"), the relationship between education and entrepreneurial involvement becomes nonsignificant or significantly negative at later stages (Van der Zwan et al., 2013). This suggests that higher educated individuals indeed have a higher likelihood of considering an entrepreneurial career but that the importance decreases as the level of entrepreneurial engagement increases. Brixy et al. (2012) interpret the decreasing prevalence of highly educated individuals in later stages of the process as a sign of selection because of the higher opportunity costs of entrepreneurship for these individuals.

Mickiewicz, Nyakudya, Theodorakopoulos, and Hart (2016) also find that some determinants are more important for specific phases in the entrepreneurial process. For the earliest stages, opportunity costs play a more important role such that it can be expected that individuals with more resources are discouraged from engaging in these earliest stages of entrepreneurship. For the more advanced stages in the entrepreneurial process, this resource effect dominates in the sense that individuals with more resources are more likely to reach these advanced stages. For example, Mickiewicz et al. (2016) find that household income and specific entrepreneurial knowledge and skills are of particular importance for the more advanced stages in the entrepreneurial process. Regarding income level, Brixy et al. (2012) find that individuals with lower incomes are more likely to have intentions to start a business or to actively take steps to set up their own business.

Country Differences

The third observation refers to country differences. Although the evidence presented here is based on cross-sectional data, the focus on multiple countries in combination with the entrepreneurial stages has an advantage over longitudinal designs, which usually focus on a single country. Differences between countries in terms of transitions between entrepreneurial stages—and, in particular, new business ownership—also receive attention in Bergmann and Stephan (2013).

When focusing on a particular example, Van der Zwan et al. (2013) find that American citizens on average have the highest odds of considering an entrepreneurial career. That is, among the country dummy variables in their empirical analysis, there are only two countries—Czech Republic and Greece—that have positive and nonsignificant coefficients and are thus on par with the United States. Regarding actually founding a new firm—that is, focusing on the transition from "taking steps to start a business" to "owning a young business"—we observe that citizens of almost every country have a higher likelihood than the United States to move beyond the "taking steps to start a business" stage. In other words, compared to individuals in other developed countries, individuals in the United States are more likely to think about starting an entrepreneurial career, but there appear to be difficulties for the subsequent transitions in the entrepreneurial process.

In addition to country-specific transition probabilities, country differences also exist regarding the influence of a particular variable on moving beyond a specific stage such as gender (Van der Zwan et al., 2012). Considerable cross-country variation is identified regarding gender differences in the transitions from "never considered starting a business" to "thinking about starting a business" and from "owning a young business" to "owning a mature business." Especially in some European former transition economies, females face difficulties taking steps to start a business ("thinking about starting a business" to "taking steps to start a business") and moving from "owning a young business" to "owning a mature business" (see Van der Zwan et al., 2012).

The setup of entrepreneurship as a process also provides ample opportunities to focus on the impacts of country-level variables on an individual's likelihood of moving beyond a certain stage of entrepreneurial engagement. For example, Kibler and Kautonen (2016) focus on the perceived degree of moral legitimacy and find that this is an important variable for various stages in the entrepreneurial process. Specifically, this variable is relevant not only for considering an entrepreneurial career but also for preparing to start a business and actually founding and running a business. In addition to demonstrating the importance of country-level variables for every transition, there could also be a relevant influence for a single stage. For example, Van der Zwan et al. (2013) conclude that there is a high inclination to think about a business when average risk tolerance in a country is high.

Conclusion and Recommendations for Future Research

This chapter has emphasized the benefits of a process view of entrepreneurship for the investigation of the determinants of entrepreneurship. While the majority of existing studies focus on the binary choice between entrepreneurship and paid employment, we have presented several reasons why it is helpful to integrate levels of entrepreneurial engagement. We have focused on the importance of variables over the course of the entrepreneurial process, also sometimes referred to as the entrepreneurial ladder. We have highlighted the differential influence of gender, age, and educational attainment on entrepreneurial decisions depending on the phase of the entrepreneurial process. In addition, we highlighted striking country differences at specific phases of the process.

There are various opportunities for further research. The present chapter has focused only on individual-level factors, whereas Baron (2007) notes two other groups of variables that also deserve attention in research on the entrepreneurial process: group or interpersonal factors, such as in terms of social networks (Afandi, Kermani, & Mammadov, 2016) and role models; and societal-level variables (Kibler & Kautonen, 2016). Another topic on which more knowledge is required relates to country differences. We have not yet obtained a complete understanding of how countries at different levels of economic development rank on the different rungs of the entrepreneurial ladder. Some evidence is assembled in Van der Zwan et al. (2011), which found that the transition from nascent entrepreneurship to a new business was especially difficult in China and the United States. Furthermore, we do not have a complete picture of different determinants over the course of the entrepreneurial process in various countries. Although the case of gender was investigated in Van der Zwan et al. (2012), other common individual-level determinants are also worth investigating.

New research is being developed on the biological determinants of entrepreneurship, such as genes and hormones (see Thurik, 2015; Van der Loos et al., 2013a, 2013b) for early attempts. Moreover, studies are taking the first steps to connect the world of psychiatric measures for nonclinical reasons and manifestations of entrepreneurial behavior. Attention deficit hyperactivity disorder (ADHD) is used as "a proof of concept" phenomenon (see Verheul et al., 2015, 2016; Thurik, Khedhaouria, Torrès, & Verheul, 2016). Linking these initiatives to the engagement-level approach is bound to lead to new insights.

Future research should follow an integrative approach by adopting a process perspective. In this way, a more comprehensive picture of the determinants of entrepreneurship depending on the stage in the entrepreneurial process is obtained. For example, "in entrepreneurship research, an urgent need exists to empirically and theoretically investigate the intention-behavior link" (Fayolle & Liñán, 2014, p. 665). Indeed, although the theory of planned behavior (Ajzen, 1991) is an established means to investigate entrepreneurial intentions (Kautonen et al., 2015), there are not many studies that investigate the effect of entrepreneurial intentions on entrepreneurial behavior (Schlaegel & Koenig, 2014). Moreover, the relation between nascent entrepreneurship and actual entrepreneurial behavior has not been the focus in much research, which calls for investigations on how individuals proceed in the process beyond nascent entrepreneurship (Parker & Belghitar, 2006). Such research would help identify the stages of the process at which people experience difficulty in making the transition to another stage.

Data availability is an important issue. The Panel Study of Entrepreneurial Dynamics (PSED) is a longitudinal survey conducted in the United States that follows nascent entrepreneurs over a four-year period in PSED I and a six-year period in PSED II. It focuses on the transition between nascent entrepreneurship to actual venture start-up. Cross-national analyses in a longitudinal context should become possible with the emergence surveys comparable to the PSED. So far, cross-national analyses have been performed with two cross-sectional surveys surveys that do not have a panel data design. One is the Flash Eurobarometer surveys on entrepreneurship conducted on behalf of the European Commission—with interviews mainly in European countries and the United States—which were performed in 2001, 2002, 2003, 2004, 2007, 2010, and 2013 and contain information on latent entrepreneurship and various phases in the entrepreneurial process. The other cross-national survey with information about levels of entrepreneurial engagement is the Global Entrepreneurship Monitor (GEM), with yearly surveys in dozens of countries from 1999 onwards. GEM contains measures of entrepreneurial intentions (expecting to start a business in the next three years), nascent entrepreneurship (actively taking steps to start a business), young business ownership (business in existence for less than 3.5 years), and established business ownership (businesses in existence for more than 3.5 years). The increased availability of available years and rounds of these cross-sectional surveys, together with the emergence of longitudinal designs in countries other than the United States, opens up possibilities for a more rigorous empirical investigation of the entrepreneurial process and how individuals climb the entrepreneurial ladder.

References

Afandi, E., Kermani, M., & Mammadov, F. (2016) Social capital and entrepreneurial process. *International Entrepreneurship and Management Journa*, 1–32.

Ajzen, I. (1991). The theory of planned behavior. *Organizational Behavior and Human Decision Processes*, 50(2), 179–211.

Baron, R. A. (2007). Entrepreneurship: A process perspective. In J. R. Baum, M. Frese, & R. A. Baron (Eds.), *The organizational frontiers series: The psychology of entrepreneurship* (pp. 41–65). Mahwah, NJ: Erlbaum.

Baron, R. A., & Markman, G. D. (2005). Toward a process view of entrepreneurship: The changing impact of individual level variables across phases of new venture development. In M. A. Rahim, R. T. Golembiewski, & K. D. Mackenzie (Eds.), *Current topics in management* (Vol. 9, pp. 45–64). New Brunswick, NJ: Transaction.

Bergmann, H., & Stephan, U. (2013). Moving on from nascent entrepreneurship: Measuring cross-national differences in the transition to new business ownership. *Small Business Economics*, 41(4), 945–959.

Blanchflower, D. G., Oswald, A., & Stutzer, A. (2001). Latent entrepreneurship across nations. *European Economic Review*, 45(4), 680–691.

Bönte, W., & Piegeler, M. (2013). Gender gap in latent and nascent entrepreneurship: Driven by competitiveness. *Small Business Economics*, 41(4), 961–987.

Brixy, U., Sternberg, R., & Stüber, H. (2012). The selectiveness of the entrepreneurial process. *Journal of Small Business Management*, 50(1), 105–131.

Davidsson, P. (2005). The types and contextual fit of entrepreneurial processes. *International Journal of Entrepreneurship Education*, 2(4), 407–430.

Davidsson, P. (2006). Nascent entrepreneurship: Empirical studies and developments. *Foundations and Trends in Entrepreneurship*, 2(1), 1–76.

DeTienne, D. R. (2010). Entrepreneurial exit as a critical component of the entrepreneurial process: Theoretical development. *Journal of Business Venturing*, 25(2), 203–215.

Fayolle, A., & Liñán, F. (2014). The future of research on entrepreneurial intentions. *Journal of Business Research*, 67(5), 663–666.

Gartner, W. B. (1988) Who is an entrepreneur? is the wrong question. *American Journal of Small Business*, 12(4), 1132.

Gohmann, S. F. (2012). Institutions, latent entrepreneurship, and self-employment: An international comparison. *Entrepreneurship Theory and Practice*, 36(2), 295–321.

Grilo, I., & Irigoyen, J. M. (2006). Entrepreneurship in the EU: To wish and not to be. *Small Business Economics, 26*(4), 305–318.

Grilo, I., & Thurik A. R. (2005) Latent and actual entrepreneurship in Europe and the US: Some recent developments. *International Entrepreneurship and Management Journal, 1*(4), 441–459.

Grilo, I., & Thurik, A. R. (2006). Entrepreneurship in the old and new Europe. In E. Santarelli (Ed.), *Entrepreneurship, growth, and innovation.* (pp. 75–103). New York, NY: Springer.

Grilo, I., & Thurik, R. (2008). Determinants of entrepreneurial engagement levels in Europe and the US. *Industrial and Corporate Change, 17*(6), 1113–1145.

Hechavarría, D. M., Matthews, C. H., & Reynolds, P. D. (2016). Does start-up financing influence start-up speed? Evidence from the Panel Study of Entrepreneurial Dynamics. *Small Business Economics, 46*(1), 137–167.

Hopp, C., & Sonderegger, R. (2015). Understanding the dynamics of nascent entrepreneurship—prestart-up experience, intentions, and entrepreneurial success. *Journal of Small Business Management, 53*(4), 1076–1096.

Kautonen, T., Gelderen, M., & Fink, M. (2015). Robustness of the theory of planned behavior in predicting entrepreneurial intentions and actions. *Entrepreneurship Theory and Practice, 39*(3), 655–674.

Kibler, E., & Kautonen, T. (2016). The moral legitimacy of entrepreneurs: An analysis of early-stage entrepreneurship across 26 countries. *International Small Business Journal, 34*(1), 34–50.

Lévesque, M., & Minniti, M. (2006). The effect of aging on entrepreneurial behavior. *Journal of Business Venturing, 21*(2), 177–194.

Mickiewicz, T., Nyakudya, F. W., Theodorakopoulos, N., & Hart, M. (2016). Resource endowment and opportunity cost effects along the stages of entrepreneurship. *Small Business Economics.* doi: 10.1007/s11187-016-9806-x

Minola, T., Donina, D., & Meoli, M. (2016). Students climbing the entrepreneurial ladder: Does university internationalization pay off? *Small Business Economics, 47*(3), 565–587.

Moroz, P. W., & Hindle, K. (2012). Entrepreneurship as a process: Toward harmonizing multiple perspectives. *Entrepreneurship Theory and Practice, 36*(4), 781–818.

Parker, S. C. (2009). *The economics of entrepreneurship.* Cambridge, England: Cambridge University Press.

Parker, S. C., & Belghitar, Y. (2006). What happens to nascent entrepreneurs? An econometric analysis of the PSED. *Small Business Economics, 27*(1), 81–101.

Reynolds, P. D. (2010). New firm creation in the United States: A PSED I overview. *Foundations and Trends in Entrepreneurship, 3*(1), 1–150.

Schlaegel, C., & Koenig, M. (2014). Determinants of entrepreneurial intent: A meta-analytic test and integration of competing models. *Entrepreneurship Theory and Practice, 38*(2), 291–332.

Shane, S., & Venkataraman, S. (2000). The promise of entrepreneurship as a field of research. *Academy of Management Review, 25*(1), 217–226.

Simoes, N., Crespo, N., & Moreira, S. B. (2016). Individual determinants of self-employment entry: What do we really know? *Journal of Economic Surveys, 30*(4), 783–806.

Stam, E., Thurik, R., & Van der Zwan, P. (2010). Entrepreneurial exit in real and imagined markets. *Industrial and Corporate Change, 19*(4), 1109–1139.

Thurik, A. R. (2015). Determinants of entrepreneurship: the quest for the entrepreneurial gene. In D. B. Audretsch, C .S. Hayter, & A. N. Link (Eds.), *Concise guide to entrepreneurship, technology and innovation* (pp. 28–38). Cheltenham, England: Elgar.

Thurik, A. R., Khedhaouria, A., Torrès, O., & Verheul, I. (2016). ADHD symptoms and entrepreneurial orientation of small firm owners. *Applied Psychology, 65*(3), 568–586.

Van der Loos M. J. H. M., Rietveld, C. A., Eklund, N., Koellinger, P. D., Rivadeneira, F., Abecasis, G., . . . Thurik, A. R. (2013a). The molecular genetic architecture of self-employment, *PLoS ONE, 8*(4), e60542.

Van der Loos, M. J. H. M., Haring, R., Rietveld, C. A., Baumeister, S. E., Groenen, P. J. F., Hofman, A., . . . Thurik, A.R. (2013b). Serum testosterone levels in males are not associated with entrepreneurial behavior in two independent observational studies. *Physiology and Behavior, 119*, 110–114.

Van der Zwan, P., Thurik, R., & Grilo, I. (2010). The entrepreneurial ladder and its determinants. *Applied Economics, 42*(17), 2183–2191.

Van der Zwan, P., Verheul, I., & Thurik, A. R. (2012). The entrepreneurial ladder, gender, and regional development. *Small Business Economics, 39*(3), 627–643.

Van der Zwan, P., Verheul, I., & Thurik, R. (2011). The entrepreneurial ladder in transition and non-transition economies. *Entrepreneurship Research Journal, 1*(2), Article 4.

Van der Zwan, P., Verheul, I., Thurik, R., & Grilo, I. (2013). Entrepreneurial progress: Climbing the entrepreneurial ladder in Europe and the United States. *Regional Studies, 47*(5), 803–825.

van Praag, C. M. (2003). Business survival and success of young small business owners. *Small Business Economics, 21*(1), 1–17.

Verheul, I., Block, J., Burmeister-Lamp K., Thurik, R., Tiemeier H., & Turturea, R. (2015). ADHD-like behavior and entrepreneurial intentions, *Small Business Economics, 45*(1), 85–101.

Verheul, I., Rietdijk, W. J. R., Block, J., Larsson, H., Franken I. H. A., & Thurik, A. R. (2016). The association between attention-deficit/hyperactivity (ADHD) symptoms and self-employment, *European Journal of Epidemiology, 31*(8), 793–801.

Verheul, I., Thurik, R., Grilo, I., & Van der Zwan, P. (2012). Explaining preferences and actual involvement in self-employment: Gender and the entrepreneurial personality. *Journal of Economic Psychology, 33*(2), 325–341.

Walter, S. G., & Heinrichs, S. (2015). Who becomes an entrepreneur? A 30-years-review of individual-level research. *Journal of Small Business and Enterprise Development, 22*(2), 225–248.

3

Types and Roles of Productive Entrepreneurship: A Conceptual Study

Sander Wennekers[a,b] and André van Stel[c,d]

[a] Retired; formerly Panteia/EIM, The Netherlands
[b] Rotterdam School of Management, The Netherlands
[c] Trinity College Dublin, Ireland
[d] Kozminski University, Poland

Introduction

Three questions that keep returning in the literature are: What is entrepreneurship? What economic and social contributions does entrepreneurship make? How does entrepreneurship make these contributions? Many interesting answers have been given to these questions, but these answers do not result in a clear-cut, unambiguous picture. On the contrary, confusion prevails.

Regarding the first question, it still holds that "entrepreneurship is an ill-defined concept" (Wennekers & Thurik, 1999, p. 29). Entrepreneurship is a multifaceted phenomenon and the heterogeneity of entrepreneurs in the economy is huge. In fact, Gartner (1985, p. 696) argued that the diversity among entrepreneurs and their ventures "may be larger than the differences between entrepreneurs and non-entrepreneurs and between entrepreneurial firms and non-entrepreneurial firms." Many different meanings of the terms entrepreneurship and corporate entrepreneurship have been proposed (Hébert & Link, 1989; Sharma & Chrisman, 1999). In itself this plethora of concepts and definitions only represents the heterogeneity and multiformity that exists in reality. It may, however, cause problems when a resulting conceptual unclarity leads to a mismatch between conceptualizations and data operationalizations in empirical research, when it confounds the analysis of the determinants and effects of entrepreneurship, and when it misguides entrepreneurship policies of governments. In order to streamline the discussion, Sternberg and Wennekers (2005) distinguish between an occupational and a behavioral notion. In the occupational perspective, entrepreneurship refers to owning and managing a business for one's own account and risk. Here individuals are the unit of measurement. The behavioral perspective regards entrepreneurial behavior "in the sense of seizing an economic opportunity" (Sternberg & Wennekers, 2005, p. 193). Shane and Venkataraman (2000) make a further distinction within this latter perspective, namely, independent versus corporate entrepreneurship. In the case of corporate

The Wiley Handbook of Entrepreneurship, First Edition.
Edited by Gorkan Ahmetoglu, Tomas Chamorro-Premuzic, Bailey Klinger, & Tessa Karcisky.
© 2017 John Wiley & Sons Ltd. Published 2017 by John Wiley & Sons Ltd.

entrepreneurship not only individuals (the "intrapreneurs") but also the business itself can be the unit of measurement. Consequently firms can also be called "entrepreneurial" (Miller, 1983, p. 771).

Within these different perspectives a great variety remains, such as freelancers, family business entrepreneurs, serial entrepreneurs, new technology-based firms, social entrepreneurs and intrapreneurs. Obviously there are many entrepreneurships, and many types of entrepreneurs. Regarding the first question (What is entrepreneurship?), this chapter aims to contribute to a structured overview of relevant dimensions and possible typologies, and to a selection of a smaller number of major entrepreneurship types that make specific economic and social contributions.

As for the second and third questions—what economic and social contributions does entrepreneurship make, and how?—we want to make three points:

First, entrepreneurship is often positively associated with macroeconomic performance (see, e.g., Carree & Thurik, 2010). Even so, different entrepreneurship types may make different contributions to society. However, because in most empirical studies the population of entrepreneurs is treated as a homogeneous group, our knowledge concerning how different types of entrepreneurs may contribute differently to value creation at the aggregate level is still rather limited (Stam & van Stel, 2011). For instance, regarding the groups of ambitious and high-growth entrepreneurs, Stam et al. (2012) state that these groups of entrepreneurs are crucial for macroeconomic growth and hence, that policymakers should target a limited number of "high-potential" entrepreneurs in order to realize macroeconomic growth. In contrast, Daunfeldt and Halvarsson (2015) find that for the small group of firms that actually realize high growth, this growth is seldom persistent and instead most high-growth firms can be labelled "one-hit wonders." Accordingly, Daunfeldt and Halvarsson (2015) doubt whether policymakers can improve economic outcomes by targeting them. van Stel, Wennekers, and Scholman (2014) take a position in between these two extremes by suggesting that macroeconomic growth can be realized through a small number of high-growth firms or, alternatively, a bigger number of low- to medium-growth firms.

A similar controversy exists around another type of entrepreneur, namely, the solo self-employed. While some authors suggest these workers are "relatively unproductive" (Stam, 2014, p. 23), other authors suggest that solo self-employed make an important contribution by enabling large firms to be more flexible, thereby contributing to macroeconomic performance in an indirect way (Burke, 2011).

Second, we want to add another distinction, that is, a differentiation between static and dynamic contributions. The former concept refers to the crucial role of entrepreneurs and businesses in the continuous production flow of goods and services in a capitalist economy and to their importance for the continuity of employment. The latter concept refers to the role of the so-called agents of change, in terms of the introduction of new products and production processes, the conquest of new markets, and the creation of new jobs. Many entrepreneurs primarily make static contributions. Together they form the "economic core" (Kirchhoff, 1994, cited in Wennekers & Thurik, 1999, p. 48). Agents of change are a rarer phenomenon.

Third, entrepreneurs do not always make *direct* social and economic contributions at the macro level. Instead it is useful to distinguish between first-order effects, including firm survival, firm growth, productivity and the emergence of new industries, and final contributions, such as economic growth and employment creation. First-order effects can often be seen as intermediary linkages toward the latter (Wennekers & Thurik, 1999).

Ensuing Research Questions

To summarize, our ensuing research questions for this chapter are as follows:

1) Which different dimensions and which major types of entrepreneurship can be identified?
2) Which entrepreneurial roles are being fulfilled by these major types?
3) What are the causal chains from these entrepreneurial roles to their final contributions, that is, what intermediate linkages are involved?

Questions 1, 2 and 3 are dealt with in the following three sections of this chapter, and a further section, "Causal Chains per Main Type of Entrepreneurship: A Synthesis," then brings the three questions together. Finally, the last section of the chapter provides discussion and conclusions.

Methodology

Consequently this is a conceptual chapter. It is based on our reading of several strands of literature, including entrepreneurial history, small business economics, and corporate entrepreneurship. In addition, we make use of our own direct and indirect observations of real-life entrepreneurs which we have been able to do over many years of research and teaching in this field. These observations include interviews with and (auto-)biographies of entrepreneurs. Finally, we use data from international data sets when they can help to illustrate an issue or to estimate the prevalence of certain types of entrepreneurship.

Typologies and Types

In colloquial speech the notion of entrepreneurship is ubiquitous. Outside the economic domain this notion even includes "political entrepreneurs" and "cultural entrepreneurs." Why are so many different people and phenomena being called "entrepreneurial?" An answer to this question can be found in the linguistic roots of the word entrepreneur. As is well-known, this term is derived from the French verb *entreprendre*, which was already in use in the 12th century with the connotation "to do something" (Hoselitz, 1951/1960, p. 235). The French noun *entrepreneur* in the sense of "a person who is active, who gets things done," came about in the 15th century (Wennekers, 2006, p. 21–25). Obviously, these linguistic roots provide a solid basis for the wide-ranging usage of the term "entrepreneur."

However, in this chapter we focus on the various meanings and manifestations of entrepreneurship inside the economic domain only. In addition, the chapter will be exclusively devoted to productive entrepreneurship as defined by Baumol (1990). Whereas "productive" entrepreneurship adds value to society, "unproductive" entrepreneurship does not, and "destructive" entrepreneurship may even be damaging to society. Productive entrepreneurship includes all activities that create value to society, ranging from producing bread in a bakery to highly innovative activity engaged in by high-tech firms. A typical example of unproductive entrepreneurship is rent-seeking entrepreneurship where entrepreneurs exploit the legal system of a country to their own benefit but where there is no value for society at large. Finally, for a typical example of destructive entrepreneurship one can think of organized crime (Baumol, 1990).

Within the realm of productive entrepreneurship, a first relevant distinction is the one between the occupational and the behavioral notion of entrepreneurship, as discussed in this chapter's introduction. And within the latter perspective, we also added a distinction between independent and corporate entrepreneurship. Finally, the entrepreneurship domain also includes those listed companies and subsidiary firms that innovate very little, are risk averse, and imitate the moves of competitors instead of leading the way (Miller, 1983, p. 771); these organizations can, thus, hardly be called "entrepreneurial" in a behavioral sense, but they nonetheless bear the risks and uncertainties of the market (Cantillon, 1755; Kirzner, 1997; Knight, 1921) and have to exercise judgment about business opportunities and the allocation of scarce resources (Casson, 1982; Knight, 1921; Say, 1971/1803) in order to survive. Figure 3.1 clarifies these notions.

Against the background of these general categorizations, heterogeneity and multiformity of real-life entrepreneurship are astonishing. Consequently many supplementary categorizations can be made, based, for instance, on the demographics of entrepreneurs but also on characteristics of the entrepreneurial activity or on the organizational form of the venture. Often these categorizations may be expressed as dichotomies. Examples of the first group are categorizations by gender, age, and education. Examples of the second group are ambitious versus less ambitious entrepreneurs, innovative versus imitative entrepreneurs, profit-oriented versus social entrepreneurs, and so forth. Examples of the third group are independent versus corporate entrepreneurs, start-ups versus incumbent entrepreneurs, solo self-employed versus employer entrepreneurs, and so on. Obviously, these categorizations are not mutually exclusive. Instead they can

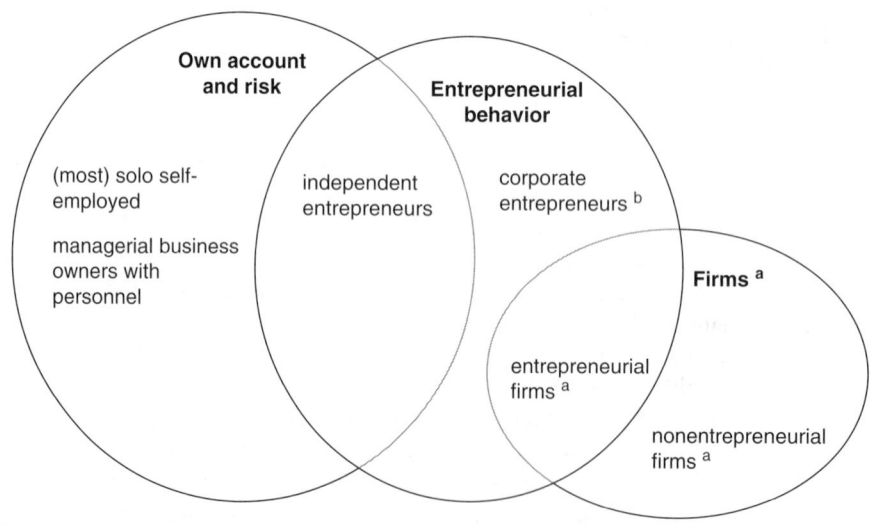

[a] Corporations and subsidiary firms managed by an appointed CEO.
[b] Corporate entrepreneurs are the entrepreneurial employees that constitute the entrepreneurial firms.

Figure 3.1 The entrepreneurship domain.

Table 3.1 Entrepreneurship dimensions (dichotomies).

Characteristics of the entrepreneurial activity	
Ambitious entrepreneurship	Other
Innovative entrepreneurship	Imitative (replicative) entrepreneurship
International entrepreneurship	Other
Social entrepreneurship	Profit-oriented entrepreneurship
Opportunity entrepreneurship	Necessity entrepreneurship
Green entrepreneurship	Other
Craftsman entrepreneurship	Opportunist entrepreneurship
Single firm entrepreneurship	Serial and Portfolio entrepreneurship
Organizational form of the venture	
Independent entrepreneurship	Corporate entrepreneurship
Solo self-employment	Employer entrepreneurship
Start-ups	Incumbent entrepreneurship
Family business entrepreneurship	Other
Academic entrepreneurship	Other
Team entrepreneurship	Other
Franchisee entrepreneurship	Other
Demographic characteristics	
Younger entrepreneurs	Older entrepreneurs
Higher educated entrepreneurs	Lower educated entrepreneurs
Female entrepreneurs	Male entrepreneurs
Immigrant entrepreneurs	Other
Disabled entrepreneurs	Other

best be viewed as dimensions. A real-life entrepreneur may be characterized on several of these dimensions, such as an "ambitious, innovative, international start-up entrepreneur" or an "academic, green, team, employer entrepreneur." In total we have identified around 20 different dimensions (dichotomies). We have listed the identified dimensions in Table 3.1, and will briefly discuss their relevance for studying the social and economic contributions of entrepreneurship. When the complement of a category is a rest-group rather than a distinct class, we have left the corresponding cell states "Other."

From Typologies/Dimensions to Major Types

By combining all these dimensions we might distinguish 2 to the power 20 = around 1 million different "types." Some of these types will be virtually "empty." A first reduction is possible by skipping the least likely combinations such as *innovative x nonambitious* entrepreneurship, and inconsistent combinations such as *start-ups x family business* entrepreneurship.

In addition, an important criterion can be found in the fact that we want to study the social and economic contributions of entrepreneurship. In that respect, the contributions of the dimensions belonging to the type-group "demographic characteristics" are usually *not directly* connected to these demographic characteristics themselves. Instead, they are often *indirect* in the sense that their members are overrepresented in certain entrepreneurial types from the type-group "characteristics of the entrepreneurial activity" or "organizational form." For instance, women are underrepresented in the entrepreneurial type *employer* entrepreneurship (Piacentini, 2013), but that does not mean women entrepreneurs are intrinsically less able to create jobs; they just choose solo self-employment relatively more often. Thus, in selecting a smaller number of major entrepreneurship types, we will leave age, education, gender, and country of origin out of consideration. This will also hold for some dimensions of the type-group "organizational form."

Given these preliminary considerations, we will now derive and discuss a number of mutually exclusive major types that in our view are most relevant for studying the social and economic contributions of entrepreneurship. Four dimensions are clearly relevant in this respect. These are ambitious versus nonambitious, innovative versus replicative, start-up/young (enterprise) versus incumbent, and solo self-employed versus employer. First, as for the role of ambitions, many types of ambitions have been identified, including making money, hiring employees, and making societal contributions (Stam et al., 2012, p. 24–25). Here we will focus on the ambitions of a relatively select group of entrepreneurs to grow their firms. Second, as for innovative versus replicative entrepreneurship, in our view innovative entrepreneurs are those who try something really and radically new. Conversely, replicative entrepreneurs may be characterized by routines, competencies, and products that vary only minimally, if at all, from those of existing organizations (Koellinger, 2008). In between these two extremes there are the adapters and incremental innovators. As their incremental innovations build on other, more original (breakthrough) innovations, and hence are not really new, we will take these together with the replicators.[1] Third, as for start-ups and young enterprises versus incumbents, we know from the literature that the former are more dynamic than older firms (Barron, West, & Hannan., 1994; Hannan & Freeman, 1984). On the other hand, incumbents are more often reluctant to innovate radically as they want to protect their vested interests and because established routines may prohibit new approaches (i.e., inertia). In addition, they have a relatively low share in new job creation compared to their share in total employment (Andrews, Criscuolo, Gal, Menon, & Pilat, 2014). Fourth, solo self-employed and employer entrepreneurs usually differ in both their objectives and their behavior, and consequently their roles in the economy also differ. This will be elaborated upon in the next section. A fifth dimension that may be relevant for subdividing (most of) the ensuing major types is "individuals versus firms." By individuals we mean independent entrepreneurs with a controlling stake in their enterprise, while firms represent the phenomenon of "corporate entrepreneurship."[2]

However, we do not consider all possible combinations of these five dimensions. Our initial distinction is that of employers versus solo self-employed. Next, we divide the

---

[1] Here we differ from Koellinger (2008, p. 29) who includes all entrepreneurs "who carry out any type of innovative behavior" with the innovative entrepreneurs.

[2] Alternatively corporate entrepreneurship may be conceptualized as the entrepreneurial employees that constitute an entrepreneurial firm (Bosma, Wennekers, & Amorós, 2012). Here we do not follow that course.

employers into ambitious versus nonambitious. The ambitious employers are further divided into four major types, based on the dimensions *innovative/replicative* and *young/incumbent*, while distinguishing between the two subcategories individuals versus firms for each of these four major types. The nonambitious employers are a rest group, which may also be subdivided into individuals versus firms. Finally, we divide the solo self-employed into two major types, based on whether they fulfil an enabling role for client firms ("enablers"), or whether their main goal is to create employment for themselves as they are often "outsiders" in the social arena that lack access to wage jobs.[3] Consequently we identify the following twelve major types.

Twelve major types of entrepreneurship

1) Employer x ambitious x innovative x young
   a) independent employer firm entrepreneurs (owner-managers with a controlling stake)
   b) corporate spin-offs and subsidiary firms (managed by an appointed CEO)[4]
2) Employer x ambitious x replicative x young
   a) independent employer firm entrepreneurs
   b) corporate spin-offs and subsidiary firms[5]
3) Employer x ambitious x innovative x incumbent
   a) independent employer firm entrepreneurs
   b) employer firms managed by an appointed CEO (i.e. corporations or subsidiary firms)
4) Employer x ambitious x replicative x incumbent
   a) independent employer firm entrepreneurs
   b) employer firms managed by an appointed CEO
5) Other employers (rest group)
   a) nonambitious independent employer firm entrepreneurs
   b) "nonentrepreneurial" employer firms managed by an appointed CEO
6) Solo self-employed
   a) enablers
   b) outsiders.

It is partly a matter of taste and opinion whether the category of "nonentrepreneurial" corporations and subsidiary firms (5b) belongs to the domain of entrepreneurship, or not. An argument in favor is that these businesses also run risks and also have to coordinate and allocate scarce resources. With that argument in mind, we include them for the sake of completeness.

Taken together these 12 mutually exclusive major types add up to the full spectrum of productive entrepreneurship. However, for a clear understanding of this categorization, we want to emphasize that these types are to some extent snapshots or temporary phases. A young firm may fail or it will ultimately become an incumbent firm. A solo

---

[3] One may also distinguish a third group of solo self-employed, namely, those who work business-to-consumer (B2C) instead of business-to-business (B2B) as the "enablers" do. Solo self-employed working B2C often deliberately prefer self-employment over wage-employment because of the higher job satisfaction and autonomy in work.

[4] If a spin-off is fully independent of its mother firm, its owner-manager(s) belong(s) to 1a.

[5] See note 4.

self-employed business may suddenly start growing and recruit personnel. An ambitious entrepreneur may change strategy and enter a new phase of consolidating market share. Nonetheless, at any moment in time our classification fully covers the domain of productive entrepreneurship.

As for the contributions of these major types, the large "rest group" (5) provides mostly *static* contributions to society (employment; income/production; well-being). The types 1–4 specialize in *dynamic* effects (job creation; economic growth; new industries). Some solo self-employed, particularly those in (6a), contribute to the dynamic effects of groups 1–4, while most solo self-employed in (6b) deliver mainly static effects.

Further Reduction to Four Main Types

Finally, for practical reasons types 1a, 1b, 3a, and 3b may be taken together as "ambitious innovators," while types 2a, 2b, 4a, and 4b may be grouped together as "ambitious adapters and replicators." Finally 6a and 6b will be taken together as the solo self-employed, and 5a and 5b will be combined as managerial employers. We then end up with only four main types (see Table 3.2).

However, in our text we will sometimes see reason to subdivide innovators and replicators into young versus incumbent or into individual entrepreneurs versus firms; to subdivide managerial employers into individual employer entrepreneurs versus (publicly listed or subsidiary) firms and companies; and to subdivide the solo self-employed into enablers versus outsiders.

With that in mind, we will now tentatively indicate the relative prevalence of these types.

First, as is well-known, the solo self-employed are the most numerous category. In the Organisation for Economic Cooperation and Development (OECD) area, more than 60% of all nonagricultural entrepreneurs are now, on average, solo self-employed, although this statistic varies between around 50% in France and almost 80% in the UK (figures for 2008; Van Stel, Wennekers, & Scholman, 2014). In terms of the distinction "enablers versus outsiders," the notion of enabling solo self-employed may be approximated by what Rapelli (2012) calls the independent professionals (I-pros), defined as "independent workers without employees engaging in a service activity and/or intellectual service not in the farming, craft or retail sectors" (Rapelli, 2012, p. 11). The main characteristic of this group is that they offer their own labor (knowledge and skills) rather than selling goods. Rapelli (2012) estimates the share of I-pros in total solo self-employment to have been 37% in the European Union (the number of member states at the time being 27) in 2011. The remainder group of solo self-employed (non-I-pros) are likely to include many individuals preferring self-employment over wage-employment because of the higher job satisfaction associated with higher autonomy in work (Benz & Frey, 2008). Therefore the group of outsiders is likely to be much smaller than the remaining 63%. Indeed, if we approximate outsider entrepreneurs by the concept of "necessity entrepreneurship" as utilized by the Global Entrepreneurship Monitor, their share varies from some 20% on average in innovation-driven economies to some 30% on average in factor- and efficiency-driven economies (Kelley, Singer, & Herrington, 2016).

As for the employers, we assess that in many countries the rest group of managerial employers easily makes up more than 50%, while within the category of ambitious employers the adapters and replicators are probably more abundant than the innovators. This leaves the crucial category of ambitious innovators as the most scarce entrepreneurial type. Policymakers' current great interest in precisely this group is therefore quite understandable.

Entrepreneurial Roles

As stated in the introduction to this chapter, entrepreneurship is a multifaceted and heterogeneous phenomenon. This heterogeneity has given rise to a plethora of definitions of entrepreneurship, two well-known ones being:

> Entrepreneurship is an activity that involves the discovery, evaluation and exploitation of new opportunities to introduce new goods and services, ways of organizing, markets, processes, and raw materials through organizing efforts that previously had not existed. (Shane, 2003, p. 4, based on Shane & Venkataraman, 2000)
>
> The essential act of entrepreneurship is new entry. New entry can be accomplished by entering new or established markets with new or existing goods or services. (Lumpkin & Dess, 1996, p. 136)

These two definitions share a behavioral perspective (Sternberg & Wennekers, 2005) and an emphasis on elements of "newness" (Wennekers & Thurik, 1999). Both also explicitly include two different modes of entrepreneurship, that is, the creation of new independent enterprises and corporate entrepreneurship within existing businesses (Shane & Venkataraman, 2000). However, they exclude a large part of the solo self-employed and the independent small business owners. Those entrepreneurs fit best in an occupational perspective, that is, they are called entrepreneurs because they own and manage their business for their own account and risk.

Related to this heterogeneity, entrepreneurs (however defined) have, throughout economic history, played many roles. An overview is given by Hébert and Link (1982, 1989), who list 12 distinct roles. Other distinctions are conceivable and other roles can be added to the list, particularly that of realizing the start-up of a new business or venture (Wennekers & Thurik, 1999). Some of these roles pertain to all or at least most entrepreneurs, while other roles are specific for certain types of entrepreneurs only. Below we will discuss some prominent examples of both categories of roles.

General Entrepreneurial Roles

The following two roles appear to be applicable for (almost) all entrepreneurs:

1) Bearing the risk associated with uncertainty (Hébert & Link, 1989, p. 41). The first to write about *entrepreneurial risk-taking* was Cantillon in the early 18th century, who viewed an entrepreneur as "someone who buys at a certain cost price and sells at an uncertain price" (Hoselitz, 1951/1960, p. 240). This view of bearing risk and uncertainty as a characteristic of entrepreneurship is shared by many of the (neo)classical authors, most notably Say and Marshall (van Praag, 1999), and later on Knight (1921) and the (neo-)Austrians such as Von Mises (Hébert & Link, 1982). An exception is Schumpeter (1911/1934) who argues that risk falls on the owner of the means of production, and "hence never on the entrepreneur *as such*."

2) Exercising *entrepreneurial judgment* about business opportunities and judgmental decision-making about the implementation of scarce resources (Westhead, Wright, & McElwee, 2011). Some 20th-century economists who can clearly be associated with this view are Knight (1921), Casson (1982), and Foss (1993). A classical author who has written about entrepreneurial judgment and the coordination of scarce resources is J. B. Say (van Praag, 1999).

Specific Entrepreneurial Roles

Based on a wide literature we have also identified six roles that apply to specific types of entrepreneurs only:

1) **Exploration and experimentation**
The role of exploration and experimentation is carried out by all entrepreneurs who try something really new and thus contribute to variety and learning (Wennekers, 2006, p. 90). In the footsteps of Cantillon and Knight, McGrath (1999, 13–14) takes uncertainty as a fundamental underlying characteristic of such entrepreneurial initiatives, in the sense of "introducing a new combination of resources," and takes failure as one of the possible outcomes. However, in a "real options approach," she does not view failure negatively, as shameful and something to be avoided. Instead, she also points out "failure's possible benefits." To give one example, McGrath (1999, p. 16) points to the positive association of simultaneous high rates of founding and exiting with "economic vibrancy." Another benefit is that "it is often easier to pinpoint why a failure has occurred than to explain a success" (McGrath, 1999, p. 28), making failure analysis very helpful for learning. McGrath (1999, p. 14) also states that "because of spill over and learning effects, it is often more useful to evaluate the collective contribution of entrepreneurial initiatives to wealth creation than to assess each initiative on its own. The initiative that fails may still improve knowledge or methods of production." She adds (p.15): "On a larger scale failed first movers are associated with the emergence of entirely new industries (Aldrich & Fiol, 1994)."

2) **Introduction of radical innovations**
According to Joseph Schumpeter's *The Theory of Economic Development* (first published in German in 1911) the key role of entrepreneurs is innovation, which in Schumpeter's vocabulary is indicated as "new combinations" (of productive means). This concept of new combinations may refer to the introduction of new products and new methods of production, the opening of new markets, the "conquest of a new source of supply" and a "new organization of any industry." Schumpeter, however, excludes new combinations that "may in time grow out of the old by continuous adjustment in small steps." Instead he explicitly means new combinations that "appear discontinuously." These radical innovations often imply the creation of a new industry, and "the competitive elimination of the old," a process also known as "creative destruction" (Schumpeter, 1942). In *The Theory of Economic Development* Schumpeter held the view that "new combinations are, as a rule, embodied . . . in new firms." In his later writings Schumpeter (1942) came to view innovative incumbent large businesses with R&D laboratories as the major agents of change. The former view is now known as the "Schumpeter Mark I regime," and the latter view as the "Schumpeter Mark II regime" (Carree, van Stel, Thurik, & Wennekers, 2002; Malerba & Orsenigo, 1995). Whatever the regime, creation of new information

(Shane, 2003, pp. 19–21) based on external changes and to be explored by innovative entrepreneurs, and creative action (De Jong & Marsili, 2015) are key elements of "Schumpeterian opportunities."

The role of "early ventures in the formative years of a new industry" includes challenges that are different from those faced by entrepreneurs "that simply carry on a tradition pioneered by thousands of predecessors in the same industry" (Aldrich & Fiol, 1994, pp. 645–646). In addition to "the normal pressures facing any new organizations, they also must carve out a new market, raise capital from skeptical sources" and "recruit untrained employees." Radical innovations must also gain "cognitive and socio-political legitimacy." Cognitive legitimation refers to the spread of knowledge about a new industry. Sociopolitical legitimacy refers to "public acceptance of an industry, government subsidies to the industry, or the public prestige of its leaders" (Aldrich & Fiol, 1994, p. 648).

3) **Introduction of incremental innovations**
The Austrian Economics school claims that "due to constant shifts in, and movements along, the demand and supply functions" (Westhead, Wright, & McElwee, 2011), markets are never in equilibrium. Consequently there are always opportunities to exploit "gaps in the market," by introducing new product variations and (incremental) process improvements in order to develop and serve potential markets, or by expanding and penetrating underdeveloped markets through focused marketing efforts and the opening up of new establishments. Subsequently, through this "dynamic competitive process of entrepreneurial discovery," markets tend towards equilibrium (Kirzner, 1997, p. 62). In the footsteps of Mises and Hayek, Kirzner is presently the most prominent representative of this approach that "defines the essence of entrepreneurship as alertness to profit opportunities" (Hébert & Link, 1989, p. 46).

In this view, competition in the sense of "dynamic rivalry" and not in the neoclassical sense of "perfect competition" plays a key role. Kirzner (1997, p. 73) says:

> The (market) process is made possible by the freedom of entrepreneurs to enter markets in which they see opportunities for profit. In being alert to such opportunities and in grasping them, entrepreneurs are competing with other entrepreneurs. . . . It is . . . the rivalrous process we encounter in the everyday business world, in which each entrepreneur seeks to outdo his rivals in offering goods to consumers (recognizing that, because those rivals have not been offering the best possible deals to consumers, profits can be made by offering consumers better deals).

The Kirznerian process of entrepreneurial discovery is often associated with the production and exploitation of *incremental* innovations (Cromer, Dibrell, & Craig, 2011; Stam & Nooteboom, 2011). However, also see De Jong and Marsili (2015) who suggest that many real-life business opportunities show a mix of Schumpeterian and Kirznerian characteristics.

4) **Replicative or imitative entrepreneurship**
The diffusion of innovations, also known as imitative or replicative entrepreneurship, is closely linked to the previously discussed role of the introduction of incremental innovations. As Schumpeter (1911/1934) points out, entrepreneurs often appear in "swarms" or "clusters," because the appearance of a few radical innovators

paves the way for imitation by many other new entrepreneurs who will replicate their innovation, and "later by existing firms serving the same market who must compete or go under" (Ziegler, 1985, p. 103). According to Ziegler the first imitators are often entrepreneurial firms founded by former employees of the "innovator-entrepreneur." Ziegler also points out that: "in this paradigm imitation is an important phenomenon in the diffusion of innovation."

Minniti and Lévesque (2010, pp. 305–306) highlight the "crucial role" of "a high number of imitative entrepreneurs" (in addition to "research-based entrepreneurs"), "who increase competition and product supply" for generating economic growth. In their approach they take a "Kirznerian" view of entrepreneurs, and conceptualize imitators as entrepreneurs who are "alert to opportunities," who "do not incur R&D costs" but who "are willing to incur upfront costs in the hope of realizing profit expectations," either by "imitating existing product or technology, or transforming a new invention into marketable technological change."

Finally, Aldrich and Fiol (1994, p. 647), based on Klepper and Graddy (1990), point out that "there is an enormous range of variation in the time required for industries to become established," as "some industries went from origin to stability (defined as the year when the number of firms reached a peak and remained more or less the same for a few years) in only two years, whereas others took more than 50 years."

Henceforth in this chapter, the roles 1) exploration and experimentation and 2) radical innovation will be taken together under the heading "exploration and creation." This role thus includes experimentation with new technologies, product development and testing, market research, experimenting with various business models and revenue models, and so on. The roles 3) incremental innovation and 4) replicative entrepreneurship are also closely related (De Jong & Marsili, 2015, section 3). They will be taken together under the heading "exploitation of opportunities."

Exploration (& creation) and exploitation (of opportunities) may be seen as two successive major phases in a "cycle of innovation" (Stam & Nooteboom, 2011). This is depicted in Figure 3.2, which also pays attention to the risks of each phase (i.e., chaos and inertia respectively). In addition, variety of content, a key characteristic of exploration and experimentation, gradually lessens in the movement towards exploitation, followed by "an opening up of variety of context" as indicated in the lower half of the figure, which includes generalization and differentiation of existing practice. See Stam

Figure 3.2 Exploration and exploitation as successive phases of the cycle of innovation. *Source: Stam (2014), based on Stam and Nooteboom (2011).*

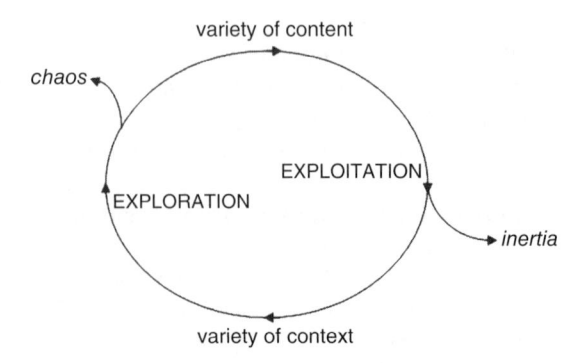

and Nooteboom (2011) for a further description of how this ongoing process may subsequently lead to new rounds of "Schumpeterian novel combinations."

Finally, and somewhat related to the distinction we made between dynamic and static contributions, we add a distinction between dynamic exploitation and static exploitation.[6] Dynamic exploitation implies expansion through capitalizing on proven new products, reaching out to additional customers and/or new markets, opening new shops or establishments, and so on. Static exploitation aims at survival and/or maintaining market share and profitability through efficient management of resources, due attention for customers, and defensive/late adoption of innovations and new shop formulas, and so on.

5) **Enabling role of entrepreneurs on behalf of client firms**

    A specific role of (mostly) enterprises without employees, that are active in the B2B market, is enabling the entrepreneurship of the client firms hiring them "by enabling de-risking strategies, reducing financial constraints, increasing entrepreneurial strategic agility as well as facilitating market entry by start-ups" (Burke, 2011, p. 25). These enterprises often do this by providing labor services on a project by project basis. Accordingly they help lower the risks of their clients who can employ flexible and/or temporary labor services "instead of having to commit to long term employment contracts" (Burke, 2011). These labor services may greatly lower the risks when entrepreneurs are testing out the viability of a new venture (Bhidé, 2000), and may enhance their agility to alter business strategy when necessary. According to Burke (2009) these lower risks also minimize the amount of finance required during the start-up or pilot phase. In addition, commercial labor services by micro enterprises also lower the costs of client firms that need temporary specialized services with high downtime or idleness hazards. This also reduces the minimum efficient scale, facilitating market entry by business start-ups. A final example of the enabling role of entrepreneurs working on behalf of client firms is that they offer the possibility of performance-related pay schemes, enhancing productivity and lowering costs. On the other hand, the enabling entrepreneurs are often not themselves involved in the key entrepreneurial function of "creating/finding and exploiting profit opportunities" (Burke, 2011). Thus they are the "enablers of entrepreneurship rather than the entrepreneurial agents themselves" (Burke, 2011).

6) **Self-employment as work opportunity for outsiders**

    Entrepreneurship in the sense of self-employment is often the only viable route to work and income for outsiders in the social arena who are "vulnerable to labor market exclusion" (OECD, 2013) and lack access to wage jobs. These outsiders include immigrants, ethnic minorities, high school drop-outs, disabled persons, and long-term unemployed.

    Shapero and Sokol (1982) refer to their conditions as "displacements." Such displacements may also pertain to women for whom self-employment is the only feasible way to combine paid work with care tasks and/or home tasks. Given that more than 25 million EU residents are unemployed and actively seeking work, while many others are discouraged workers or people outside the labor market for other

---

[6] Dynamic contributions stem from the entrepreneurial roles exploration (and creation) and dynamic exploitation.

reasons (OECD, 2013), so-called "inclusive entrepreneurship" can be an important source of new work opportunities including "improved employability from engaging in entrepreneurship."

A related phenomenon, "necessity entrepreneurship," refers to people who choose self-employment "because they have no better options for work" (Wennekers van Stel, Carree, & Thurik, 2010, p. 42). In lesser developed countries the number of necessity entrepreneurs may be quite substantial, in an order of magnitude of more than 40% of all self-employed in some developing countries (Kelley et al., 2016). In innovation-driven economies, on average some 20% of entrepreneurs have a necessity motive (Kelley et al., 2016).

Table 3.2 summarizes the discussion. In a highly schematic manner the table indicates to what extent each of the four main entrepreneurship types fulfills each of the five major entrepreneurial roles that were distilled out of the underlying six specific entrepreneurial roles discussed in the preceding paragraphs. XX points to a key role, X means a considerable role, (x) indicates a possible minor role. A blank cell means that no role is foreseen for the corresponding entrepreneurship type. The next section discusses how these various roles translate into intermediate effects and final contributions to the economy and society at large and then in the section "Causal Chains per Main Type of Entrepreneurship: A Synthesis" below, we will discuss in detail the specific roles and contributions for each of the four main types.

Intermediary Effects and Final Contributions

For a further conceptual development of these specific roles, it is useful to distinguish between final contributions (such as economic growth, job creation, and well-being/job satisfaction/happiness) and first-order effects acting as intermediate linkages toward these final effects. (For early attempts to identify intermediate linkages between entrepreneurship and economic growth, see Wennekers & Thurik, 1999; Thurik, Wennekers, & Uhlaner, 2002; and Wennekers, 2006.) Henceforth we will label these

Table 3.2 Main entrepreneurship types x major entrepreneurial roles.

Roles Types	Exploration and creation	Dynamic exploitation	Static exploitation	Enabling role	Work opportunity for outsiders
Ambitious innovator (radical and substantial)	XX	X			
Ambitious replicator/adapter (including incremental innovation)	X	XX			
Solo self-employed				XX	XX
Rest group (managerial employers)		(x)	XX		

linkages as "intermediate effects." In addition, we make a distinction between internal and external effects. The former are (intermediary) effects that concern the entrepreneur and/or the enterprise, while external effects have a bearing on other enterprises (meso effect) or on the economy as a whole (macro effect).

Intermediate Effects

Major external intermediate effects are higher meso-economic and macroeconomic productivity, enhanced international competitiveness, and the creation of new industries and new niches. Major internal intermediate effects are firm survival, and participation, autonomy, and (subsistence) income for relevant social groups. Finally, firm growth can be both an external and an internal effect. How these effects relate to the specific roles discussed above is visualized in Table 3.3. In this table, the symbol X indicates a major effect and (x) a minor effect.

The table includes the roles "exploration and creation" and "exploitation of opportunities," subdivided into dynamic and static exploitation, as stated before. However, while these aggregate roles are conceptually distinct, empirically it is difficult to disentangle their effects. It is often the joint forces of innovation (exploration) and imitation/adaptation (dynamic exploitation) that create the main contributions of entrepreneurship. With that in mind we will attempt to elaborate the specific effects of the identified entrepreneurial roles. For each of these roles, as indicated in the table, we will now discuss the intermediate effects acting as linkages toward the final contributions that will be discussed in the next section.

1) **Exploration and creation**

   The entrepreneurial role of exploration and creation by new entrants and other new ventures has wide-ranging first order effects in the economy. Major effects are the

Table 3.3 Entrepreneurial roles x intermediate effects.

Intermediate effects	External effects		Partly external and partly internal effects	(mostly) Internal effects	
Roles	Creation of new industries and niches	Productivity and competitiveness	Firm growth	Firm survival	Participation, autonomy and income
Exploration and creation	X	X	X		
Dynamic exploitation	(x)	X	X		
Static exploitation		(x)		X	(x)
Enabling role		X	X	(x)	
Self-employment as work opportunity for outsiders			(x)		X

introduction of breakthrough innovations and the subsequent creation of new industries and new niches (Baumol, 2004; Schumpeter, 1911/1934). An historical example that comes to mind is the creation of the motor vehicle industry by a large number of initially small manufacturers in the late 19th and early 20th century, and that of related industries such as automobile tires (Klepper, 2002). Another example is the creation of the personal computer market in the 1970s and early 1980s through joint effects of very different business start-ups such as Intel (microprocessors), Microsoft (BASIC; DOS) and Apple (personal computers). A third example is the emergence of online shopping in the late 1990s and early 2000s, following the invention of the World Wide Web. To a certain extent the creation of new industries and niches may also imply creative destruction of older industries. An example is the devastating effect of the increasing popularity of webshops on traditional physical bookstores. On the other hand there are also many examples of "non-destructive creation," such as "air conditioners and new drugs and vaccines," that "create and satisfy entirely *new* wants" (Bhidé, 2004).

Another major effect of exploration and creation by new entrants is increasing (meso-economic and macroeconomic) productivity and international competitiveness, related to the enhanced rivalry, learning, variety and selection that are triggered by new entry (Nooteboom, 1999; Thurik et al, 2002). Higher productivity means a higher per capita output, and it includes improved efficiency, higher quality, and the production of totally new goods and services (Bhidé, 2004). Although the (labor) productivity of young firms (0–6 years) is on average relatively low, their productivity rises quickly in subsequent years (Verhoeven, 2004), and the overall macro effect of entry and turbulence on productivity (growth) and competitiveness appears to be positive.

More generally, new business start-ups, new products, and new business ideas enhance the degree of competition in an economy, triggering "a restructuring of the economy through a wide array of reactions including . . . business exits, mergers, re-engineering (diffusion), and new innovations by incumbents" (Thurik et al., 2002, p. 164). Ultimately, selection of the most viable firms and "creative destruction" of inefficient and outdated businesses lead to a restructuring of the economy. At the aggregate level of industries, regions, and national economies these processes lead to higher levels of productivity, as well as to economic growth and employment growth (Baumol, 2004; Fritsch & Mueller, 2004). van Praag and Versloot (2007, p. 371), in their survey on the value of entrepreneurship, conclude: "Entrepreneurs may lag behind in the levels of productivity, but they are catching up to the production efficiency of the control group due to a higher growth rate."[7]

More specifically, exploration and creation are advantageous for firm growth in the sense that the emergence of new industries and the realization of higher productivity create growth opportunities for ambitious entrepreneurs. But here it holds, as stated before, that it is the joint forces of exploration and (dynamic) exploitation that create the main contributions of entrepreneurship. Rapidly growing firms may just as likely be the ambitious imitators as the initial innovators, but precise figures

---

[7] This refers to relatively high growth rates of both value added and productivity (van Praag & Versloot, 2007, p. 377).

on this distinction are not available. We do however know that a higher incidence of ambitious entrepreneurs has a positive effect on the percentage of high-growth firms (Teruel & de Wit, 2011).

2) **Dynamic and static exploitation of opportunities**

As stated earlier, dynamic exploitation entails business expansion through capitalizing on proven new products, reaching out to additional customers and/or new markets, and opening new shops or establishments, while static exploitation aims at business survival and/or maintaining market share and profitability through efficient management of resources, due attention for customers, and defensive/late adoption of innovations. However, both types of exploitation play a role in the dissemination of invention, leading to "widespread utilization of new or improved products and processes" (Baumol, 2004, p. 14). In particular, Baumol (2004, p. 17) emphasizes the "invaluable contribution of 'mere imitation.'" He continues: "History is replete with examples of substantial improvements that were contributed by the imitators. In part, these improvements are elicited by the need to adapt the technology to local conditions, including differences in size of the market, in the nature of consumer preferences, in climatic conditions and in the character of available complementary inputs." The crucial value of imitation for long-term technological development is corroborated by the research findings of evolutionary anthropology (McGowan, 2014). Exploitation thus plays a major role in the full development of new industries and in the accompanying growth of productivity and competitiveness. Obviously however, static exploitation plays a more modest role in these processes than dynamic exploitation.

An interesting example of the role of exploitation of opportunities, in which nontechnological innovation comes to the fore, is the growth of a highly diversified restaurant sector in many European countries during the past decades, in reaction to growing prosperity, an increasing number of immigrants, and changing lifestyles. A more recent example is the proliferation of niches around the development of apps for mobile devices (smartphones and mobile computers).

As for the effect of entrepreneurship on firm growth, again it must be pointed out that it is the joint forces of exploration and (dynamic) exploitation that matter. An interesting example is again the automobile industry in the US that began in 1895. Klepper (2002, p.43) says: "Paralleling entry, the number of firms rose through 1909, peaking at 271, and then fell sharply. By 1923 only 104 firms were left in the industry." Automobile sales during this latter period had risen quite strongly, illustrating the extremely high firm growth of the surviving producers.[8]

Finally, static exploitation is almost by definition aimed at firm survival through its continuous focus on efficient management of resources and on permanent efforts to keep regular customers satisfied. For solo self-employed and small business owners, another effect of these efforts is to maintain autonomy and (subsistence) income.

3) **Enabling role**

As explained in a previous section, the enabling role is tailor-made for enterprises without employees and other small enterprises that are active in the B2B market

---

[8] The production of only the Model T Ford increased from around 10,000 in 1909 to almost one million in 1920 (www.mtfca.com/encyclo/fdprod.htm).

and perform labor services on behalf of client firms. They help mitigate the risks, lower the costs, and enhance the agility of their clients who can employ flexible and/or temporary labor services "instead of having to commit to long term employment contracts" (Burke, 2011). In addition, many of these enterprises also play an enabling and accelerating role in the innovative processes of their clients. This contribution to innovation is often based on their specialized expertise acquired in previous assignments.

De-risking, agility, and gradual innovation are among the key ingredients of an entrepreneurial success strategy for the minority of client firms that not only survive after start-up but also become really successful (Burke, 2009). Through their contribution to these success factors enabling entrepreneurs thus also contribute to higher productivity, competitiveness, and firm growth of their clients. Indirectly enabling entrepreneurs may also contribute to the expansion of new industries and niches, as this process often takes the form of gradual reform and diffusion by entrepreneurial (client) firms that build on an innovation platform provided by earlier more revolutionary innovators (Burke, 2009, p.37).

4) **Self-employment as work opportunity for outsiders**

Social inclusion of all groups, including ethnic minorities, high school drop-outs, disabled persons, long-term unemployed, and women, is an explicit policy goal of the European Union (OECD, 2013, p. 23–24), the more so because more than 25 million EU residents are unemployed and actively seeking work, while many others are outside of the labor market for other reasons. In most EU-member states active labor market policy measures, as a way to fight social exclusion, so far have focused mainly on wage jobs while support for business start-ups represents less than 10% of these expenditures. However, there is a growing awareness that start-up activities may generate important benefits. Self-employment, in these cases also known as inclusive entrepreneurship, can be an important source of new work opportunities; it may thus generate increasing participation in the labor market and in society in general, and as a result may lead to decreasing dependency on social security, to an increasing sense of autonomy, and to opportunities for better balancing private life and work. In addition, it may offer a new source of income for those who set up a business successfully or who gain "improved employability from engaging in entrepreneurship" (OECD, 2013). Finally, although there is no specific empirical evidence for this effect, it seems likely that inclusive entrepreneurs may also fulfil an enabling role on behalf of client firms and may thus contribute to their firm growth.

Final Contributions

Table 3.4 visualizes how the intermediate effects may ultimately lead to final economic and societal contributions. The discussion will now be done "backwards," that is, we start with the final contributions and examine how they are linked to the various intermediate effects. For reasons of simplicity we discuss economic growth and job creation together.

1) **Economic growth and job creation**

The causal relationships between the growth of productivity, production, and employment are complex. In the long run and assuming that the supply of labor is fully employed, it is by definition productivity growth that determines the rate of

Table 3.4 Intermediate linkages x final (economic and societal) contributions.

Final contributions	Dynamic contributions		Static contributions	
Intermediate effects	Economic growth	Job creation	National product and employment	Well-being: Inclusive economy, job satisfaction and happiness
Creation of new industries and niches	X	X		
Productivity and competitiveness	X	(x)	(x)	
Firm growth	X	X		
Firm survival			X	
Participation, autonomy and income			(x)	X

economic growth. In that respect the positive first-order effect of entrepreneurship on productivity growth is of crucial importance. However, production growth may also be viewed as the outcome of processes on the supply and the demand side. First, in open economies, production growth is to a large extent determined by foreign demand. Thus increasing international competitiveness, another first-order effect of entrepreneurial exploration and exploitation, is also of great importance for economic growth. Second, at the supply side, economic growth by definition takes the form of firm growth, either in the sense of growing firms or in the sense of a growing number of businesses. Growing firms are particularly important because of their dynamic qualities. Finally, there is ample evidence that in the long run the introduction and expansion of new industries and niches, based on new products and processes, play a major role in these processes (Baumol, 2004).

At the macro level, employment growth follows production growth (Kaldor, 1966). At the underlying industry level, job creation is determined by the net effect of business dynamics (entry, firm growth and decline, and exits) in which entry and firm growth play the driving role. In their survey based on a large number of empirical studies, van Praag and Versloot (2007, p. 361) found that "in the long run, entrepreneurial firms create positive externalities leading to more employment, also in other, i.e., older, larger, and incumbent firms." However, the jobs created by entrepreneurial businesses are "less secure due to higher volatility and higher probabilities of firm dissolution." A (multi-regional) study by Fritsch and Mueller (2004) indicates both indirect effects of new business formation (such as crowding out of competitors and improved competitiveness) and direct effects, that is, the jobs created in the new entities. While the net employment effect of new businesses on regional employment is initially negative, "due to crowding out effects and to failing newcomers," in the longer run there is a positive net effect that peaks about eight years after entry. Recent research by the OECD (Andrews et al., 2014, based on Criscuolo, Gal, & Menon, 2014) shows that "young firms systematically create more jobs than they destroy." In particular, "young firms represent only around 20% of total employment, but they account for almost 50% of total job creation in the economy, while their share in job destruction is around 25%" (Andrews et al., 2014, p. 73).

2) **Annual national product and aggregate employment**
Each year, on the January 1, all national statistics start afresh from zero, and a new national product has to be brought about. This remarkable feat is basically the contribution of the many million incumbent entrepreneurs and businesses around the globe. While this is common sense knowledge, nowadays there is a tendency to overlook or forget these basic facts due to an understandable emphasis on innovation and dynamism. Nonetheless, the national product cannot be taken for granted, and the role of the nonglamorous rank and file of entrepreneurship in creating it is worthy of study and investigation. In order to survive and to continue making their contributions, the many solo self-employed and managerial employer entrepreneurs and firms have to assess changing business opportunities, they must coordinate and allocate scarce resources, they must satisfy the wants of their customers, they must compete with other entrepreneurs, and they run risks. They also play a major role in the continuity of aggregate employment.

3) **Inclusive economy, job satisfaction, and happiness**
Time and again it has been shown that self-employed people, on average, enjoy a higher (or at least not lower) rate of job satisfaction compared to employees, "in spite of longer working hours, poorer working conditions, heightened job stress and higher risk" (Noorderhaven, Thurik, Wennekers, & Stel, 2004, p. 451). Likewise, the survey study by van Praag and Versloot (2007, p . 376) concludes that entrepreneurs have lower median incomes than wage employees, but that nonetheless "they are more satisfied with both their jobs and their lives." In addition, a recent study using a large European data set shows self-employed persons to report significantly higher levels of job satisfaction with the work they do, but lower levels of satisfaction in terms of job security (Millán, Hessels, Thurik, & Aguado, 2013). It seems quite likely that the higher job satisfaction of self-employed individuals is to a large extent caused by their higher rate of autonomy and self-determination (Noorderhaven et al., 2004; Benz & Frey, 2008).

Entrepreneurship can make another contribution to happiness and well-being through its positive influence on job creation, both through job opportunities for outsiders who become self-employed and through jobs for employees created by growing firms. These mechanisms are highly relevant as unemployment is known to increase unhappiness in two ways. First, there are the effects for the unemployed themselves. Winkelmann and Winkelmann (1998) conclude that unemployment has a large detrimental effect on life satisfaction. In their study it was also shown that the "non-pecuniary effect is much larger than the effect that stems from the associated loss of income." Nonpecuniary effects have to do with damage to "social relationships, identity in society and individual self-esteem." These effects underscore the importance of self-employment as a road toward participation in society. They also resonate with the earlier findings of Clark and Oswald (1994, p. 658), who conclude that unemployed people (in Great Britain) "have much lower levels of mental well-being than those in work." Second, Di Tella, MacCulloch, and Oswald (2001) show that a higher average unemployment rate at the country level negatively influences overall life-satisfaction. In addition, they also find that "unemployment depresses reported well-being more than does inflation" (p. 340).

Clearly, self-employment as a road toward participation in the economy also contributes to the establishment of an "inclusive economy," which Acemoglu and Robinson (2013, p. 74) define as an economy with institutions "that allow and encourage participation by the great mass of people in economic activities that make best use of their talents and skills and that enable individuals to make the choices they wish."

Causal Chains per Main Type of Entrepreneurship: A Synthesis

As a brief wrap-up of the preceding sections, we will now discuss the entire causal chain per main type of entrepreneurship. For each of the four main types this synthesis thus covers the whole trajectory from entrepreneurial roles through intermediary effects toward their final contributions. The causal chains are visualized in Figure 3.3 to Figure 3.6.

Ambitious Innovators

The relatively small group of ambitious innovators includes all employer entrepreneurs/firms that are both ambitious and innovative, regardless whether they are young or incumbent entrepreneurs/firms. However, in our classification this category comprises only the really innovative, while the incremental innovators and the adapters are subsumed under the heading "replicators/adapters." As for their entrepreneurial roles, the ambitious innovators are specialists in exploration and creation. In particular, radical innovation is exclusively their domain. Some of them sell their business or venture after it has proven to be feasible, but others are also involved in the consecutive dynamic exploitation phase, in which they build and expand their venture, reach out to more customers and/or new markets, and open new shops or establishments. Apart from growing their own firms, ambitious innovators also create external effects for other businesses and for the economy as a whole. Some of these ambitious innovators, often new start-ups and young firms (Schumpeter, 1911/1934), are the creators of new industries and niches which, in due time, will be fully developed by large numbers of replicators/adapters. Another (intermediary) external effect of exploration and creation is enhanced rivalry, learning, and selection, which in turn lead to higher productivity and international competitiveness of the business sector. In some cases ambitious innovators trigger a process of creative destruction, in other cases their innovations merely add new and supplementary products to the existing stock. As a final consequence of their entrepreneurial roles and the ensuing external effects, ambitious innovators are a crucial condition for future economic growth and new job creation, and in the long run the net effect for national product and employment is positive. Figure 3.3 summarizes these causal chains, where the main roles, intermediate effects and final contributions of this type of entrepreneurship are indicated in bold, and where broad arrows

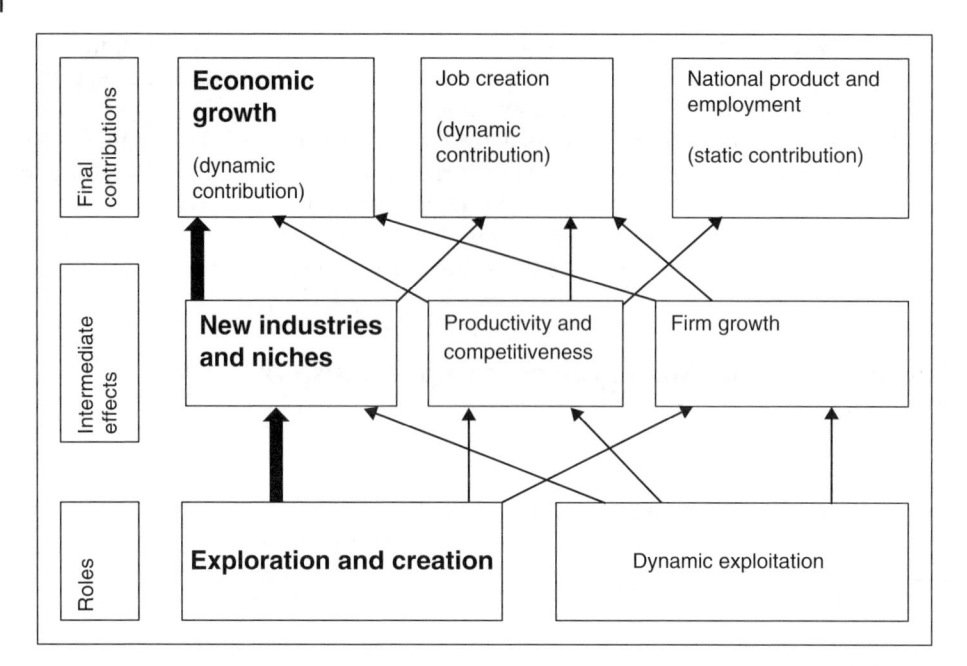

Figure 3.3 Roles, intermediate effects and final contributions of ambitious innovators.

represent stronger effects than thin arrows (as the broad arrows connect the main roles, intermediate effects, and final contributions). This denotes that the ambitious innovators excel in exploration and creation, are particularly important for the emergence of new industries, and consequently act as an engine for economic growth.

Ambitious Replicators/Adapters

The relatively large category of ambitious replicators and adapters includes all ambitious employer entrepreneurs and firms that are not radically innovative. So in addition to the purely replicative (ambitious) entrepreneurs, that apply established routines and offer well-known goods and services, this group also comprises entrepreneurs that contribute incremental innovations or who adapt innovations made by others and that are ambitious in the sense that they all want to grow their firms. In an economic sense the contributions of these entrepreneurs and firms can often be seen as a "follow-up" to the more radical innovations made by others. In that respect innovators and replicators/adapters are closely related and unknowingly work in tandem. As for their entrepreneurial roles, the emphasis is on dynamic exploitation, as they all attempt to expand their business. Some do this by simply grasping the market opportunities created by the innovations of other entrepreneurs, others grow their business by introducing new product variations and incremental process improvements. Obviously the activities of the latter ambitious replicators/adapters also entail a good deal of exploration and experimentation. Consequently, and apart from growing their own firms, this large group also creates large external effects for other firms and for the economy as a whole. These effects include enhanced rivalry, learning, and selection, which in turn lead to

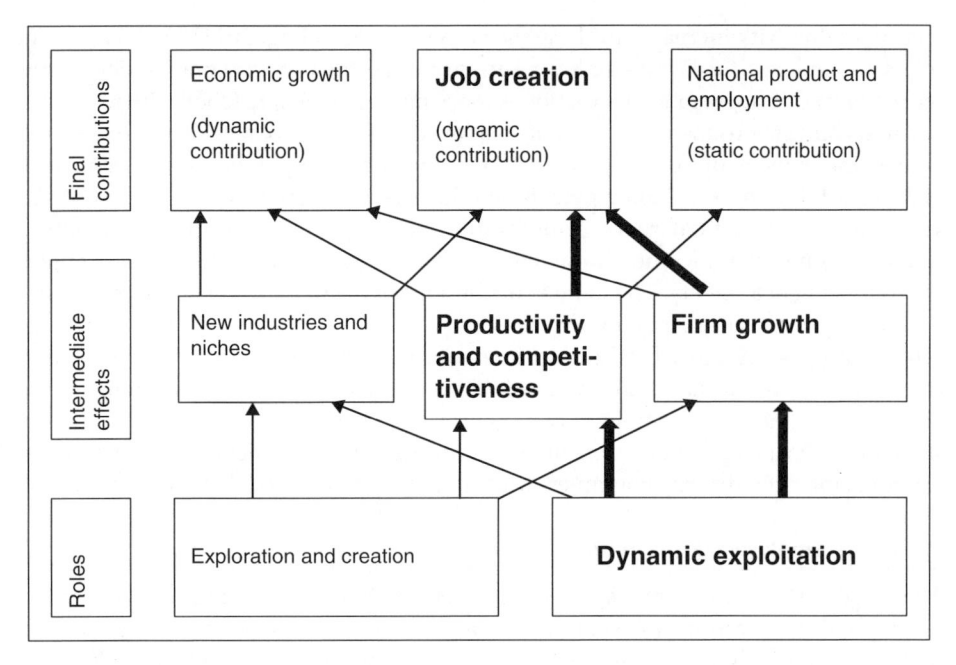

Figure 3.4 Roles, intermediate effects and final contributions of ambitious replicators/adapters.

higher productivity and international competitiveness of the business sector. In addition these entrepreneurs and firms also play a role in fully developing new industries. Thus, where the activities of ambitious innovators are an essential precondition for future economic growth and job creation, it is often the many ambitious replicators and adapters that actually realize the potential and deliver the promise. Figure 3.4 summarizes the causal chains for the ambitious replicators/adapters. Here the emphasis is on dynamic exploitation, productivity and competitiveness, firm growth and ultimately on job creation. Nonetheless, the differences with Figure 3.3 are subtle, indicating that ambitious innovators and ambitious replicators/adapters are closely related types of entrepreneurs.

Solo Self-Employed

The solo self-employed form the most numerous category of entrepreneurs with roughly some two third of entrepreneurs working on their own. This group consists of two main subgroups which are quite distinct in terms of their roles and contributions to economy and society. First, there are the "enabling" solo self-employed. As described earlier, they contribute to competitiveness at the industry level by enabling their client firms to be more flexible. In particular, solo self-employed improve the performance of their client firms "by enabling de-risking strategies, reducing financial constraints, increasing entrepreneurial strategic agility as well as facilitating market entry by start-ups" (Burke, 2011, p. 25). Hence, an important part of the economic contribution of the enabling solo self-employed is indirect, in the sense that their flexible activities, which may also be innovative in nature, enable the entrepreneurship of their client firms and secure productivity increases in these firms (Burke & Cowling, 2015). Although some solo self-employed turn into employer entrepreneurs, the (direct) contribution of solo self-employed to aggregate job creation is more limited (Kraaij & Elbers, 2016).

The second subgroup consists of self-employed workers who have only limited alternative employment options. These outsiders include immigrants, ethnic minorities, high school drop outs, disabled persons and long-term unemployed. This type of solo self-employment particularly contributes to participation in society and the ability of generating one's own income. These intermediate effects, in turn, greatly contribute to the well-being of a society. The main contributions of the (two main subgroups of) solo self-employed are summarized in Figure 3.5.

In an earlier section we discussed various approximations of the relative size of these two subgroups of the solo self-employed. While these estimates are wide-ranging, the bottom line is that neither of these two subgroups is marginal. Also, it appears that the share of the enablers is on average higher in innovation-driven economies than in factor- and efficiency-driven economies, while the reverse holds for the outsiders.

Managerial Employers (Rest Group)

The large rest group of managerial employers includes the young and incumbent employer firm entrepreneurs that are not ambitious with respect to firm growth, as well as the similarly nonambitious incumbent corporations and subsidiary firms. As for their roles in the economy, like all entrepreneurs they must bear the risk associated with uncertainty (Hébert & Link, 1989, p. 41) and they have to exercise entrepreneurial judgment about business opportunities and to engage in judgmental decision-making about the implementation of scarce resources (Westhead et al., 2011). In particular, they are often replicators and adapters, mainly aimed at firm survival, through a continuous focus on efficient management of resources and on permanent efforts to keep their customers satisfied. As a consequence they may also have a positive influence on productivity and international competitiveness, and on the labor market participation and income generation for large numbers of employees. Their mostly static contributions

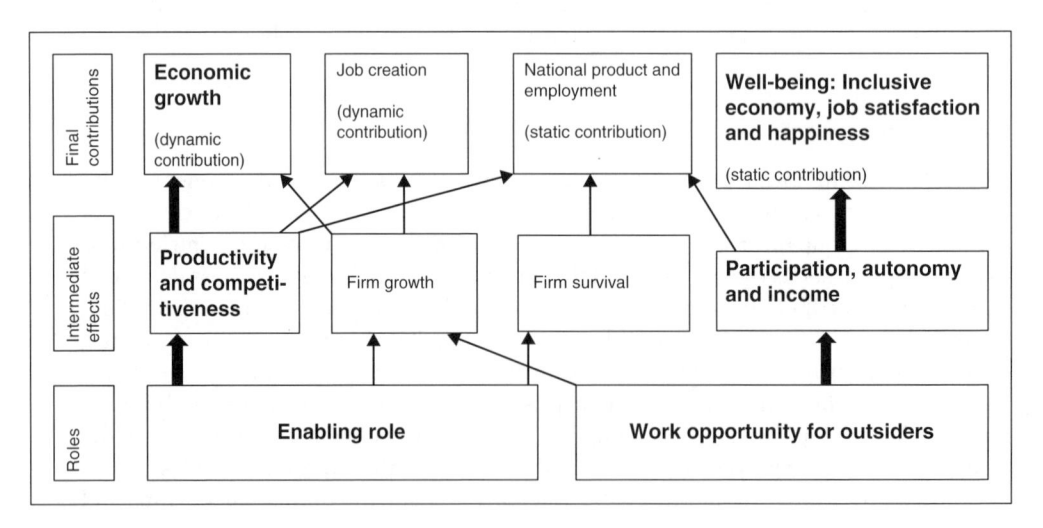

Figure 3.5 Roles, intermediate effects, and final contributions of solo self-employed.

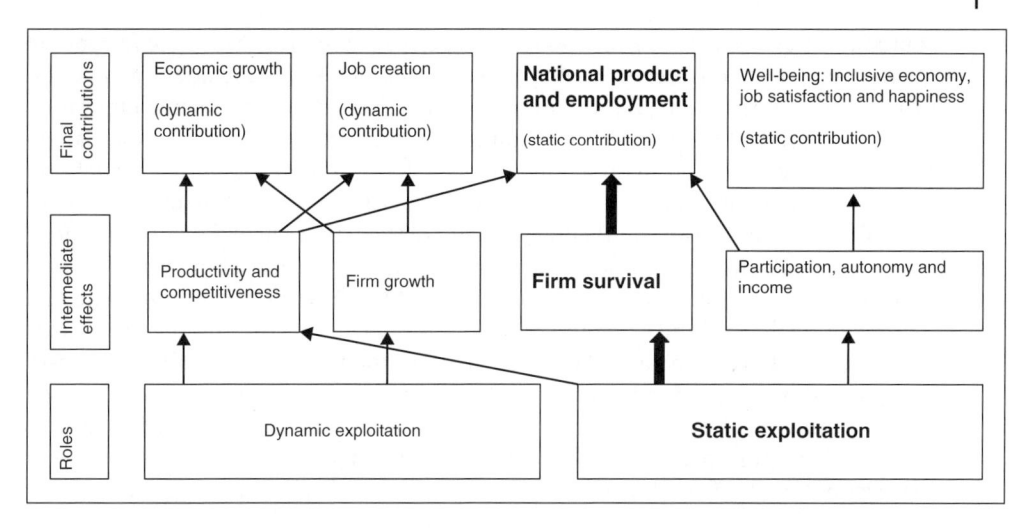

Figure 3.6 Roles, intermediate effects, and final contributions of managerial employers.

to the economy are definitely not without merit. As mentioned above, each year, on the January 1, all national statistics start afresh from zero, and a new national product has to be brought about. This remarkable feat is to a large extent due to the efforts of the many managerial employers. Likewise, they also play a major role in the continuity of aggregate employment.

Figure 3.6 summarizes the causal chains for managerial employers.

Discussion and Conclusions

Summarizing and Interpreting the Main Findings

In this chapter we have addressed three questions. First, we discussed the different dimensions and the major types of entrepreneurship that can be identified. We discerned about 20 different dichotomized dimensions, grouped in three categories, that is, characteristics of the entrepreneurial activity, organizational form of the venture, and demographic characteristics. Types of entrepreneurship were derived by combining several of these dimensions. Here we focused on dimensions that are particularly relevant for studying the social and economic contributions of entrepreneurship, including ambitious versus less ambitious, innovative versus replicative/adaptive, start-up/young firm entrepreneur versus incumbent, and solo self-employed versus employer. After a further reduction we ended up with the following four main types: ambitious innovators, ambitious replicators/adapters, managerial employers, and the solo self-employed. The latter are the most numerous entrepreneurial type, while the ambitious innovators are the most scarce. In addition, we sometimes found it logical to subdivide innovators and replicators into young versus incumbent, or into individual entrepreneurs versus firms, and to subdivide the solo self-employed into enablers versus outsiders.

Second, we examined the entrepreneurial roles that are being fulfilled by these main types. Apart from two general roles that are played by (almost) all entrepreneurs, that is, risk bearing, and judgmental decision-making about the allocation of scarce resources, we have discerned five roles that have a special relevance for specific types of entrepreneurship. These are: (1) Exploration and creation, which include experimentation and radical innovation; (2) Dynamic exploitation, based on incremental innovation and replication/adaptation, and focused on business expansion; (3) Static exploitation, aimed at survival and/or maintaining market share and profitability through for example efficient management of resources and defensive/late adoption of innovations; (4) Enabling role of (mostly solo) entrepreneurs on behalf of client firms hiring them; and (5) Self-employment as work opportunity for outsiders in the labor market.

Our third research question concerned the causal chains from these entrepreneurial roles to their final social and economic contributions, including the intermediate effects and linkages that are involved. Major external intermediate effects are higher mesoeconomic and macroeconomic productivity, enhanced international competitiveness, and the creation of new industries and new niches. Major internal intermediate effects are firm survival and participation, autonomy, and (subsistence) income for relevant social groups. Finally, firm growth can be both an external and an internal effect.

Implications for Research

Our survey of the field has raised several issues that warrant further research. First and foremost, our chapter is obviously a plea for the further development of statistical indicators for measuring the various main types of entrepreneurship. This is an essential prerequisite for more meaningful empirical research into the effects of entrepreneurship. The efforts of the Global Entrepreneurship Monitor to develop an index of ambitious entrepreneurship (see, for example, Autio, 2005) is a good example of what we mean. Also see van Stel et al. (2014) for an example of empirical research that explicitly distinguishes between solo self-employed and employer entrepreneurs. In addition, statistical agencies should also pick up this challenge.

Second, while the distinction between real/radical innovators and incremental innovators/adopters is intuitively clear, empirically it is sometimes difficult to disentangle their roles and effects. To some extent they fulfill similar roles in the economy, that is, exploration/creation and dynamic exploitation, although with a different emphasis on these two roles. And accordingly they have comparable intermediary effects on productivity and competitiveness, and on firm growth. A major distinction is the importance of radical innovators for the creation of new industries, while ambitious adopters and incremental innovators seem crucial for their further expansion and development. Thus, it is often the joint forces of innovation (exploration) and imitation/adaptation (dynamic exploitation) working in tandem that create the main final contributions of entrepreneurship to economic growth and job creation. For a better understanding of these processes we need more empirical research at the sector level, including studies of the history and evolution of industries (see Klepper, 2002, p. 58) and case studies of real markets (as proposed by Coase, 1992[9]). A related issue for further empirical research is the role of competition in the sense of rivalry, and its effect on both learning and selection, in the expansion of new industries.

Third, a major and encompassing research issue with great relevance for the future would be the development of a "green economy." While there is no single clear definition

---

[9] Also see *The Economist* December 16, 2010, on "Why do firms exist?"

of the green economy, this (future) economy is characterized by green products that are organically produced or use inexhaustible energy and resources, and by new production methods based on "cradle-to-cradle" or "circular economy" principles. This will among others include conservation, pollution control, reducing the material content of products, designing for durability, "replacing products, possession and waste with services, rental and maintenance and recycling, respectively" and redesigning transport systems (Mazzucato & Perez, 2014, p.12). While such an economy is expected to pervade and transform all sectors and domains of society, it also creates many new industries and niches. Green entrepreneurs may be start-up businesses that act as change agents, and in addition, both the expansion of new industries and the pervasion and transformation of the entire economy by green products and technologies will also be the work of ambitious imitative entrepreneurs who use these new technologies and act upon existing opportunities. An important research question is whether a full development of the green economy will require a willingness of national states to shape a "coherent and stable set of (green) government policies" and to act as "lead market-creating investors" in order to generate a "green direction" for steering R&D, business strategies and consumer preferences strongly towards sustainability (Mazzucato & Perez, 2014, pp. 13–15).

Some other likely future technological advances that deserve empirical study by entrepreneurship researchers are medical technology, artificial intelligence, and the Internet of things. Here again, the role of change agents in initiating new applications and that of adopters in further diffusing these applications must be taken into account. Another relevant distinction is that between the pace of innovation, which may be high, and the impact of innovation on total factor productivity, which may be more modest (Gordon, 2015). A related issue is the impact of these technologies on employment.

Finally, earlier indications for a U-shaped interpretation of entrepreneurial history in the years 1870–2000 (Gordon, 2015, p. 697; Wennekers et al., 2010) deserve further scrutiny. After a period, beginning around 1870, in which individual innovative entrepreneurs "deserve credit for most of the inventions of the Second Industrial Revolution" (Gordon, 2015, p. 698), by the 1920s innovation became dominated by the research labs of large corporations. This phase was the heyday of corporate entrepreneurship, while the importance of independent entrepreneurs diminished. Then, from the 1970s onwards the advent of personal computers, the Internet, and smartphones was again dominated by individual entrepreneurs. However, particularly in the US, "after 2000 the high-tech sector experienced a large decline in start-ups and fast-growing young firms," while the percentage of people younger than 30 who owned stakes in private companies had already declined from 1989 onwards (Gordon 2015, p. 718). Does this recent "decline in business dynamism" suggests an undulating pattern instead of a U-shape, and is corporate entrepreneurship becoming dominant again?

Implications for Policy

First, a brief road map for policymakers might be derived from our survey of the roles and types of entrepreneurship. As a first step it seems sensible for policymakers to clearly state their policy goal. Is it economic growth, job creation, or an inclusive economy? Next they might infer the most appropriate entrepreneurship type for attaining this goal, from the analysis in this chapter. Subsequently they should benchmark their country regarding the prevalence of this type of entrepreneurship, and finally they must reflect on the most conducive ecosystem for promoting it.

Second, in many highly developed economies, entrepreneurs with ambitions to grow their business are scarce (Bosma et al., 2012). This lack of ambition is a critical impediment for economic development, as "growth in the absence of aspiration is extremely rare" (Stam et al., 2012, p. 134). For these countries it will pay to stimulate entrepreneurial growth ambitions among both innovative and replicative entrepreneurs. Two transitions appear to be promising here – ambitious and experienced managers becoming independent entrepreneurs and going into business for themselves, and incumbent solo self-employed and small business owners becoming more eager to grow (Stam et al., 2012).

Policymakers have various measures at their disposal to stimulate ambitious entrepreneurship. Although it may be tempting to direct relatively large amounts of public money to a small group of targeted individuals with high potential to achieve high firm growth, this remains an uncertain undertaking, as persistent spells of high growth are the exception rather than the rule (Daunfeldt & Halvarsson, 2015). Rather than targeting high potentials, general measures to reduce growth barriers for ambitious ventures may be more promising. This may require a wider scope specifically for new high-performance ventures to use flexible labor (including solo self-employed workers, especially freelancers and I-pros; Burke, 2011; Rapelli, 2012) in order to reduce their costs and risks. Still, as flexible workers are more loosely connected to the firm and hence may be more likely to leave, entrepreneurs will also like to work with a fixed core of permanent employees. In this respect, governments may think of lowering employment protection for employees, in order to make it more attractive for entrepreneurs to offer permanent contracts to their employees. Besides alleviating the insider–outsider problem on the labor market (Lindbeck & Snower, 2001), such reduction in employment protection will likely lead to higher labor mobility (Millán, Millán, Román, & van Stel, 2013) which in turn will positively influence productivity growth (Stephan, 1996).

Another area where growth barriers may be reduced involves an improved availability of external risk capital for ambitious ventures. According to Stam (2014, p. 5), "Accessibility to finance, preferably provided by actors with knowledge of the entrepreneurial process, is of crucial importance for investments in uncertain entrepreneurial projects with a longer term pay-off." As banks are often reluctant to invest in uncertain projects, it is important that external risk capital is being made available through formal and informal venture finance. However, it may be argued that particularly informal venture finance, including business angel finance, is of importance as, in contrast to formal venture capital, this type of finance typically focuses on very early-stage (i.e., start-up) firms, where the uncertainty is largest and finance constraints most acute (Burke, van Stel, Hartog, & Ichou, 2014). A possible policy response may be to make investments in firms by private investors more attractive.

Finally, R&D, innovation, and innovative entrepreneurship also play a key role. According to some, "inclusive growth must be government-led and innovation-driven" and "growth policy must be innovation policy" (Mazzucato & Perez, 2014, pp. 22–24). This implies a willingness of national states to shape a "coherent and stable set of government policies" and to act as "lead market-creating investors."

Conclusion

There are semantic and conceptual reasons why all those who run a business, either tiny, medium-sized, or large, and either for their own account or as a manager, may rightfully be called "entrepreneurs." Nonetheless, as this chapter has once again reconfirmed, these entrepreneurs can be very different in their ambitions, in their innovativeness, in other behavioral characteristics, and consequently in their impact on the economy. And these differences cannot to any large extent be explained by the occupational status of these economic agents (self-employment/independent business ownership versus wage-employment/corporate entrepreneurship). Simply and only labeling all these agents as entrepreneurs may greatly confuse both empirical entrepreneurship research and economic policy. In empirical research it may cause a mismatch between conceptualizations and data operationalizations and may thus distort the analysis of the determinants and effects of entrepreneurship. Likewise it may confound the public debate on entrepreneurship and consequently it may misguide entrepreneurship policies of governments. Our chapter should be seen as a plea for a widespread and structural use of more precise terms to adequately distinguish between the various types of entrepreneurs, indicating whether they are necessity solo self-employed, independent professionals, or employer entrepreneurs, whether they are ambitious or not, radically innovative, adaptive or imitative, and so on. The application of a more precise terminology in the entrepreneurship domain will promote more meaningful empirical research, a more stuctured policy discourse, and more tailor-made entrepreneurship policy-making.

References

Acemoglu, D., & Robinson, J. A. (2013). *Why nations fail: The origins of power, prosperity and poverty*. London, England: Profile Books.

Aldrich, H. E., & Fiol, C. M. (1994). Fools rush in? The institutional context of industry creation. *Academy of Management Review, 19*(4), 645–670.

Andrews, D., Criscuolo, C., Gal, P., Menon, C., & Pilat, D. (2014), Entrepreneurship and business dynamics in the Netherlands—enabling experimentation. In H. van der Wiel, H. van der Kroon, & J. Snijders (Eds.), *Entrepreneurship in the Netherlands: The top sectors*, Zoetermeer, Netherlands: Panteia.

Autio, E. (2005). *Global Entrepreneurship Monitor: 2005 report on high-expectation entrepreneurship*. Retrieved from http://www.gemconsortium.org

Barron, D. N., West, E., & Hannan, M. T. (1994). A time to grow and a time to die: Growth and mortality of credit unions in New York, 1914–1990. *American Journal of Sociology, 100*(2), 381–421.

Baumol, W. J. (1990). Entrepreneurship: Productive, unproductive and destructive. *Journal of Political Economy, 98*(5), 893–921.

Baumol, W. J. (2004). Entrepreneurial enterprises, large established firms and other components of the free-market growth machine. *Small Business Economics, 23*, 9–21.

Benz, M., & Frey, B. S. (2008). Being independent is a great thing: Subjective evaluations of self-employment and hierarchy. *Economica, 75*, 362–383.

Bhidé, A. V. (2000). *The origin and evolution of new businesses.* New York, NY: Oxford University Press.

Bhidé, A. (2004, 17 November). *Entrepreneurs in the 21st century—Non-destructive creation: How entrepreneurship sustains prosperity.* Lecture, Royal Society of Arts, London, England.

Bosma, N., Wennekers, S., & Amorós, J. E. (2012). *Global Entrepreneurship Monitor 2011 extended report: Entrepreneurs and entrepreneurial employees across the globe.* Retrieved from http://gemconsortium.org/report

Burke, A. E. (2009). Strategies for entrepreneurial success. *Journal of Strategic Management Education, 5*(1), 33–44.

Burke, A. E. (2011). The entrepreneurship enabling role of freelancers: Theory with evidence from the construction industry. *International Review of Entrepreneurship, 9*(3), 1–28.

Burke, A. E., & Cowling, M. (2015). The use and value of freelancers: The perspective of managers in large firms and SMEs. *International Review of Entrepreneurship, 13*(1), 7–20.

Burke, A. E., van Stel, A. J., Hartog, C. M., & Ichou, A. (2014). What determines the level of informal venture finance investment? Market clearing forces and gender effects. *Small Business Economics, 42*(3), 467–484.

Cantillon, R. (1755). *Essai sur la Nature du Commerce en Général* (first published 21 years after the author's death in 1734).

Carree, M. A., & Thurik, A. R. (2010). The impact of entrepreneurship on economic growth. In D. B. Audretsch & Z. J. Acs (Eds.), *Handbook of entrepreneurship research.* Berlin, Germany: Springer: 557–594.

Carree, M. A., van Stel, A. J., Thurik, A. R., & Wennekers, A. R. M. (2002). Economic development and business ownership: An analysis using data of 23 OECD countries in the period 1976–1996. *Small Business Economics, 19*(3), 271–290.

Casson, M. C. (1982). *The entrepreneur: An economic theory.* Oxford, England: Martin Robertson.

Clark, A. E., & Oswald, A. J. (1994). Unhappiness and unemployment. *The Economic Journal, 104*, 648–659.

Coase, R. H. (1992). *The institutional structure of production* (Occasional Paper No.28), Chicago, IL, University of Chicago Law.

Criscuolo, C., Gal P., & Menon, C. (2014). The dynamics of employment growth: New evidence from 18 countries, OECD Science, Technology and Industry Policy Paper, Paris: OECD Publishing.

Cromer, C. T., Dibrell, C., & Craig, J. B. (2011). A study of Schumpeterian (radical) vs. Kirznerian (incremental) innovations in knowledge intensive industries. *Journal of Strategic Innovation and Sustainability, 7*(1), 28–42.

Daunfeldt, S-O., & Halvarsson, D. (2015). Are high-growth firms one-hit wonders? Evidence from Sweden. *Small Business Economics, 44*(2), 361–383.

De Jong, J. P. J., & Marsili, O. (2015). The distribution of Schumpeterian and Kirznerian opportunities. *Small Business Economics, 44*(1), 19–35.

Di Tella, R., MacCulloch, R. J., & Oswald, A. J. (2001). Preferences over inflation and unemployment: Evidence from surveys of happiness. *American Economic Review, 91*(1), 335–341.

Foss, N. J. (1993). Theories of the firm: Contractual and competence perspectives. *Journal of Evolutionary Economics, 3*, 127–144.

Fritsch, M., & Mueller, P. (2004). The effects of new business formation on regional development over time. *Regional Studies, 38*, 961–975.

Gartner, W. B. (1985). A conceptual framework for describing the phenomenon of new venture creation. *Academy of Management Review, 10*(4), 696–706.

Gordon R. J. (2015). *The rise and fall of American growth: The U.S. standard of living since the Civil War*, Princeton University Press.

Hannan, M. T., & Freeman, J. (1984). Structural inertia and organizational change. *American Sociological Review, 49*(2), 149–164.

Hébert, R. F., & Link, A. N. (1982). *The entrepreneur: Mainstream views and radical critiques*. New York, NT: Praeger.

Hébert, R. F., & Link, A. N. (1989). In search of the meaning of entrepreneurship. *Small Business Economics, 1*, 39–49.

Hoselitz, B. F. (1951/1960). The early history of entrepreneurial theory. In J. J. Spengler & W. R. Allen (Eds.), *Essays in economic thought: Aristotle to Marshall*. Chicago, IL: Rand McNally.

Kaldor, N. (1966). *The causes of the slow rate of economic growth of the United Kingdom: An inaugural lecture*. Cambridge, England: Cambridge University Press.

Kelley, D., Singer, S., & Herrington, M. (2016). *Global Entrepreneurship Monitor, 2015/16 Global Report*. Retrieved from http://www.gemconsortium.org

Kirchhoff, B. A. (1994). *Entrepreneurship and dynamic capitalism*. Westport, CT: Praeger.

Kirzner, I. M. (1997). Entrepreneurial discovery and the competitive market process: An Austrian approach. *Journal of Economic Literature, 35*, 60–85.

Klepper, S. (2002). Firm survival and the evolution of oligopoly. *RAND Journal of Economics, 33*(1), 37–61.

Klepper, S., & Graddy, E. (1990). The evolution of new industries and the determinants of market structure. *RAND Journal of Economics, 21*, 27–44.

Knight, F. H. (1921). *Risk, uncertainty and profit*. Boston, MA: Houghton Mifflin.

Koellinger, P. (2008). Why are some entrepreneurs more innovative than others? *Small Business Economics, 31*, 21–37.

Kraaij, A., & Elbers, E. (2016). Job creation by the solo self-employed during the first years of business. *International Review of Entrepreneurship, 14*(1), 103–122.

Lindbeck, A., & Snower, D. J. (2001). Insiders versus outsiders. *Journal of Economic Perspectives, 15*(1), 165–188.

Lumpkin, G. T., & Dess, G. G. (1996). Clarifying the entrepreneurial orientation construct and linking it to performance. *Academy of Management Review, 21*(1), 1–37.

Malerba, F., & Orsenigo, L. (1995). Schumpeterian patterns of innovation. *Cambridge Journal of Economics, 19*(1), 47–65.

Mazzucato, M., & Perez, C. (2014). *Innovation as growth policy: The challenge for Europe* (Working Paper SWPS 2014-13), Science Policy Research Unit, University of Sussex, England.

McGowan, K. (2014, November). Brilliant impersonators. *Aeon Magazine*.

McGrath, R. G. (1999). Real options reasoning and entrepreneurial failure. *Academy of Management Review, 24*(1), 13–30.

Millán, J. M., Hessels, J., Thurik A. R., & Aguado, R. (2013). Determinants of job satisfaction: A European comparison of self-employed and paid employees. *Small Business Economics, 40*, 651–670.

Millán, A., Millán, J. M., Román, C., & van Stel, A. (2013). How does employment protection legislation influence hiring and firing decisions by the smallest firms? *Economics Letters, 121*(3), 444–448.

Miller, D. (1983). The correlates of entrepreneurship in three types of firms. *Management Science, 29*(7), 770–791.

Minniti, M., & Lévesque, M. (2010). Entrepreneurial types and economic growth. *Journal of Business Venturing, 25*, 305–314.

Noorderhaven, N., Thurik, A. R., Wennekers, S., & van Stel, A.(2004). The role of dissatisfaction and per capita income in explaining self-employment across 15 European countries. *Entrepreneurship Theory and Practice, 28*, 447–466.

Nooteboom, B. (1999). Learning, innovation and industrial organization. *Cambridge Journal of Economics, 23*, 127–150.

OECD/EU (2013). *The missing entrepreneurs: Policies for inclusive entrepreneurship in Europe*. Paris, France: OECD Publishing. Retrieved from http://www.oecd.org/publications/the-missing-entrepreneurs-9789264188167-en.htm

Piacentini, M. (2013). *Women entrepreneurs in the OECD: Key evidence and policy challenges* (OECD Social, Employment and Migration Working Papers, No. 147). OECD Publishing, Paris.

Rapelli, S. (2012). *European I-Pros: A Study*. London, England: Professional Contractors Group.

Say, J. B. (1971). *A Treatise on Political Economy, or the Production, Distribution and Consumption of Wealth* (first ed., 1803). New York, NY: A.M. Kelley.

Schumpeter, J. A. (1911/1934). *The theory of economic development* (trans. of 2nd ed. 1926). Cambridge, MA: Harvard University Press

Schumpeter, J. A. (1942). *Capitalism, socialism and democracy*. New York, NY: Harper and Row.

Shane, S. (2003). *A general theory of entrepreneurship: The individual-opportunity nexus*, Cheltenham, England: Elgar.

Shane, S., & Venkataraman, S. (2000). The promise of entrepreneurship as a field of research. *Academy of Management Review, 25*(1), 217–226.

Shapero, A., & Sokol, L. (1982). The social dimensions of entrepreneurship. In C. A. Kent, D. L. Sexton, & K. H. Vesper (Eds.), *Encyclopedia of entrepreneurship*, 72–90. Englewood Cliffs, NJ: Prentice-Hall.

Sharma, P., & Chrisman, J. J. (1999). Toward a reconciliation of the definitional issues in the field of corporate entrepreneurship. *Entrepreneurship Theory and Practice, 23*(3), 11–27.

Stam, E. (2014). *The Dutch entrepreneurial ecosystem*. Utrecht, Netherlands: Birch Research. doi: 10.2139/ssrn.2473475

Stam, E., Bosma, N., Van Witteloostuijn, A., De Jong, J., Bogaert, S., Edwards, N., & Jaspers, F. (2012). *Ambitious entrepreneurship: A review of the academic literature and new directions for public policy. Report for the advisory council for science and technology policy (AWT) and the Flemish council for science and innovation (VRWI)*. The Hague, Netherlands: Advisory Council for Science and Technology Policy.

Stam, E., & Nooteboom, B. (2011). Entrepreneurship, innovation and institutions. In D. Audretsch, O. Falck, & S. Heblich (Eds.), *Handbook of research on innovation and entrepreneurship* (pp. 421–438), Cheltenham, England: Elgar.

Stam, E., & van Stel, A. J. (2011). Types of entrepreneurship and economic growth. In A. Szirmai, W. Naudé, & M. Goedhuys (Eds.), *Entrepreneurship, innovation, and economic development* (pp. 78–95). Oxford, England: Oxford University Press.

Stephan, P. E. (1996). The economics of science. *Journal of Economic Literature, 34*(3), 1199–1235.

Sternberg, R., & Wennekers, S. (2005). Determinants and effects of new business creation: Investigations using Global Entrepreneurship Monitor data. *Small Business Economics, 24*(3), 193–203.

Teruel, M., & de Wit, G. (2011). *Determinants of high-growth firms: Why do some countries have more high-growth firms than others?* (Research Report 201107). Zoetermeer, Netherlands: Panteia/EIM.

Thurik, A. R., Wennekers, S., & Uhlaner, L.M. (2002). Entrepreneurship and economic performance: A macro perspective. *International Journal of Entrepreneurship Education 1*(2), 157–179.

van Praag, C. M. (1999). Some classic views on entrepreneurship. *De Economist, 147*, 311–335.

van Praag, C. M., & Versloot, P. H. (2007). What is the value of entrepreneurship? A review of recent research. *Small Business Economics, 29*(4), 351–382.

van Stel, A., Wennekers, S., & Scholman, G. (2014). Solo self-employed versus employer entrepreneurs: Determinants and macro-economic effects in OECD countries. *Eurasian Business Review, 4*(1), 107–136.

Verhoeven, W. (2004). Firm dynamics and labour productivity. In G. Gelauff et al. (Eds.), *Fostering productivity: Patterns, determinants and policy implications* (pp. 211–241). Amsterdam, Netherlands: Elsevier.

Wennekers, S. (2006). *Entrepreneurship at country level: Economic and non-economic determinants (PhD thesis)*. Erasmus Research Institute of Management, Rotterdam, Netherlands.

Wennekers, S., & Thurik, A. R. (1999). Linking entrepreneurship and economic growth. *Small Business Economics, 13*(1), 27–55.

Wennekers, S., van Stel, A., Carree, M., & Thurik, A. R. (2010). The relationship between entrepreneurship and economic development: Is it U-shaped? *Foundations and Trends in Entrepreneurship, 6*(3), 167–237.

Westhead, P., Wright, M., & McElwee, G. (2011). *Entrepreneurship: Perspectives and cases*. Harlow, England: Pearson Education.

Winkelmann, L., & Winkelmann, R. (1998). Why are the unemployed so unhappy? Evidence from panel data. *Economica, 65*, 1–15.

Ziegler, C. A. (1985). Innovation and the imitative entrepreneur. *Journal of Economic Behavior and Organization, 6*, 103–121.

4

Toward a Theory of Entrepreneurial Behavior[1]

Bruce T. Teague[a] and William B. Gartner[b,c]

[a] *Eastern Washington University*
[b] *California Lutheran University*
[c] *Copenhagen Business School, Denmark*

> *Different people, or the same people in different situations, can employ different strategies for performing a given task. A theory of their performance would include ... describing the strategy they are using in a given instance together with a specification of the circumstance under which this particular strategy will be used.*
> Herbert Simon, discussing behavioral theory (1992, p. 155).

Introduction

Behavior is central to entrepreneurship and new venture creation (Bird, 1989; Bird, Schjoedt & Baum, 2012; de Jong, Parker, Wennekers, & Wu 2015; Dyer, Gregersen, & Christensen, 2008; Gartner, 1988; Karlsson & Honig, 2009). And there has been a steady stream of research on this topic. For instance, Bird et al. (2012, p. 895) identified 91 articles published on entrepreneurs' behavior between 2004 and 2010. We did a quick database search of the same journals used in Bird et. al. (2012) and we found more than 60 articles had been published which either (a) use measures of behavior as dependent or independent variables, or (b) make entrepreneurs' behavior the focus of inductive study, since their review. Yet, in spite of this long history of interest on behavior in entrepreneurship (e.g., Alvarez & Barney, 2007; Baron & Henry, 2010; Bird, 1989; Gartner, 1988; Schumpeter, 1934; Shane, Locke, & Collins, 2003), we still lack a theory

---

[1] The origin of this chapter took place while Bruce Teague was a Visiting Professor at the Copenhagen School of Business. Versions of this chapter were presented at the RENT Conference in Luxembourg, November 19–20, 2014 and at the USASBE Conference in Tampa, FL, USA, January 22–25, 2015. Subsequent drafts were sponsored by the Danish Strwategic
Research Council and have been carried out within the PACE project (http://www.badm.au.dk/pace) and while William B. Gartner was a Visiting Professor at Linneaus University, Vaxjo, Sweden.

The Wiley Handbook of Entrepreneurship, First Edition.
Edited by Gorkan Ahmetoglu, Tomas Chamorro-Premuzic, Bailey Klinger, & Tessa Karcisky.
© 2017 John Wiley & Sons Ltd. Published 2017 by John Wiley & Sons Ltd.

of entrepreneurial behavior per se. As a result, little progress has been made in critical research questions, such as: (1) determining what constitutes an entrepreneurial behavior, (2) developing a logic for why and how behaviors are influenced by specific contextual cues, and (3) how these behaviors influence the environmental context of the developing new venture (Bird et al., 2012; Bird, Schjoedt, & Hanke, 2014).

This chapter makes several theoretically important contributions (Whetten, 1989). First, we integrate a number of perspectives on the study of behavior drawn from multiple research streams. Second, we draw upon this broad literature to develop a theory of entrepreneurial behavior, formalized as a new model, to guide future research. From this model, we derive several testable propositions, which might be the focus of future study. Finally, we consider the implications of this theory of entrepreneurial behavior for future research.

This chapter now proceeds as follows. We begin with a brief review of the literature related to entrepreneurial behavior. Our review concurs with Bird et al. (2012): progress in this area is limited. Following this review, we consider several highly cited entrepreneurship theories and frameworks to (a) highlight the often hidden role of behavior, (b) demonstrate that a theory of entrepreneurial behavior is currently lacking, and (c) show how such a theory would complement and enhance knowledge gained from these existing perspectives. Next, we develop a theory of entrepreneurial behavior and derive a set of testable propositions. Finally, we discuss the implications of a theory of entrepreneurial behavior for future research.

The Current State of Entrepreneurial Behavior Scholarship

In an attempt to be inclusive, Bird et al. (2012) sought to find all articles in which the behavior of entrepreneurs was measured, whether it was the primary focus of the study, or not. While a large number of entrepreneurship articles exist that use indicators of behavior as either dependent or independent variables, a much smaller subset actually attempts to explain entrepreneurial behavior. A few studies stand out. For instance, using a mixed-methods design, Dyer et al. (2008) found that a group of unusually successful entrepreneurs tended to rely on a set of behaviors that included questioning, observing, and experimenting, along with two cognitive patterns (associational thinking and desire to change the status quo). They demonstrated that the propensity to engage in these behaviors was significantly related to the propensity for innovativeness in the new ventures started (Dyer et al., 2008). In another study, Karlsson and Honig (2009) shed light on how entrepreneurs use business plans across the life of their ventures. Their study indicates that early on, creating business plans may serve an external legitimacy role, but, as the business develops, it tends to diverge from the plan and over time entrepreneurs rarely use, refer back to, or update the original plan (Karlsson & Honig, 2009). Other studies have demonstrated influences of environmental factors on: sellers' behavior in entrepreneurial acquisitions (Graebner & Eisenhardt, 2004); the role of environmental dynamism in moderating the influence of transactional and transformational leadership behaviors (Ensley, Pearce, et al., 2006); and how prior human capital, prior management experience, and prior marketing experience influence the propensity to use network ties in approaching potential investors (Zhang, Souitaris, Soh, & Wong, 2008). Finally, though entrepreneurs' behavior was not the primary focus, work on user innovation (Shah, 2003; Shah & Tripsas, 2004, 2007), studies emerging from the effectuation research stream (Dew, Read, Sarasvathy, &, Wiltbank, 2011; Sarasvathy, 2008; Sarasvathy & Dew, 2005), and insights into the process of bricolage (Baker & Nelson, 2005) have also informed our knowledge of entrepreneurial behavior. This sample from the extant literature demonstrates that while progress may be limited, our knowledge of entrepreneurial behavior is advancing.

Unfortunately, these studies are exceptions. Much of the work that does measure the behavior of entrepreneurs falls into one of several categories that do little to advance our understanding of how entrepreneurs act. First, many studies rely on single-item or categorical survey measures of behavior, which demonstrate potential associations between selected behaviors and outcome measures, such as, venture launch and profitability but do not directly advance our knowledge or understanding of behavior (e.g., Chrisman, McMullan, & Hall, 2005: Haber & Reichel, 2007). Second, other studies attempt to capture associations between entrepreneurial perceptions and simple behavioral measures, often related to financing behaviors (Alsos, Isaksen, & Ljunggren, 2006; Orser, Riding, & Manley, 2006). Third, a subset of studies suffers from research designs that inhibit our ability to draw strong behavioral inferences. For example, a study of small firms relied on recollections up to 37 years in the past to categorize frequency and timing of bootstrapping behaviors using five-item Likert type measures (Ebben & Johnson, 2006). Another study asked employees to speculate about their likelihood of behaving entrepreneurially in response to reading the description of a CEO's behavioral display (Brundin, Patzelt, & Shepherd, 2008). Such studies may accomplish other laudable research objectives, but they do not advance our understanding of entrepreneurial behavior: the study of what individuals are actually doing when they behave entrepreneurially. Finally, in many studies in which entrepreneurial behavior is measured, behavior is assigned an indirect or relatively unimportant role in explaining some other outcome of interest. As a result, we conclude that the extant literature has significant room for development with respect to our understanding of entrepreneurial behavior as it is enacted in everyday working life.

(Re)defining Entrepreneurial Behavior

Entrepreneurial behavior is a subset of all human behavior, which is a subset of the still larger set (category) of all behavior. In order to carefully define the subset, we must first define the set. In other words, we must begin with a careful and scientifically driven definition of behavior. This section begins by discussing a rigorously developed definition of behavior. Once a definition of behavior is established, we use it as foundation from which to consider the definition of entrepreneurial behavior. We conclude that the definition developed by Ahmad and Seymour (2008) best meets the needs of the field. Their definition is consistent with the general definition of behavior developed; it meets the established criteria for a strong scientifically useful definition; and it resonates with existing usage in our literature.

Defining Behavior

Given that dozens of scientific societies exist with behavior as their explicit focus, it would be both arrogant and ignorant to define behavior based solely on intuitive and contextually situated criteria. Such a definition would also jeopardize the consilient development of our field within the broader scientific understanding of human behavior and behavior in general (Wilson & Ros, 1999). If we acknowledge the need to begin with a definition of behavior that has general applicability, then four primary criteria might be used to screen an effective definition: it should be operational, essential, widely applicable, and succinct (Joyce, 1916).

A definition is operational if it clearly identifies characteristics that define inclusion or exclusion from the defined subset (Tuckman, 2012). In other words, it allows scholars to determine whether or not a phenomenon qualifies to be a member of the set or not. A definition is essential if it circumscribes phenomena that we think qualify, while excluding those we think should not. (This is similar to the idea of face validity.) A definition is widely applicable if researchers in different areas can apply the same definition and phenomena are not excluded simply because of the context within which they occur. Finally, a definition is succinct if it is, "free of unnecessary descriptive or explanatory elements that do not aid in the operational interpretation of the definition, and does not have so many clauses, caveats, and modifiers as to encumber usage" (Levitis, Lidicker, & Freund, 2009).

Using these criteria, researchers recently employed an iterative survey design involving 181 respondents drawn from three different scholarly societies interested in the study of behavior (Levitis et al., 2009, p. 108). A perfect consensus was not achieved; however, strong general agreement coalesced around certain qualities that the authors used to offer the following general definition of behavior: "the internally coordinated responses (actions or inactions) of whole living organisms (individuals or groups) to internal and/or external stimuli, excluding responses more easily understood as developmental changes" (Levitis et al., 2009, p. 109).

This definition meets all four criteria, discussed earlier. It also allows for important but subtle points to be recognized within behavioral study, such as the fact that inaction can occasionally qualify as behavior. The authors cite an example in which a guard dog recognizes its owner and does not bark. The authors argue that this inaction results from the dog recognizing the owner and selecting the appropriate behavioral response, which is not barking, in this instance. Finally, this definition allows behavior to be measured as either an individual or group level phenomenon. We believe this definition provides a strong foundation upon which to elaborate and develop a framework that explores entrepreneurial behavior.

Defining Entrepreneurial Behavior

Entrepreneurial behavior represents a subset of all possible behaviors that would be included in the suggested definition. For instance, as Bird and colleagues (2014) have noted, entrepreneurial behavior is specifically a human behavior. However, at this point, we must make some choices about how best to circumscribe entrepreneurial behavior for purposes of future study. Similar to the general definition of behavior, a definition of entrepreneurial behavior should also meet the four criteria of a good scientific definition.

It is worth noting that some who study behavior have argued that intentional behavior should be distinguished from unintentional or reflexive behaviors (Davidson, 2001; Greve, 2001). While this may prove useful, it appears to be a distinction that offers little advantage to a general theoretical framework for the study of entrepreneurial behavior.

Though most behaviors of scholarly interest will be intentional, we are not yet ready to argue that unintentional action cannot be interesting. Regardless, this distinction should be obvious in the operational and methodological choices of the researcher. Thus, we have chosen to adopt the more generally used construct label: behavior.

As soon as we attempt to define a behavior as entrepreneurial, we run into conceptual issues with which we must reconcile ourselves. Intuitively, one might initially suggest that entrepreneurial behavior is the behavior of entrepreneurs. However, defining who is an entrepreneur (Gartner, 1988) based on whether they started an organization, or created a new market offering (Davidsson, 2003), or some other required outcome condition is inherently problematical.

It should readily become apparent that there are serious problems associated with defining entrepreneurial behavior as being tied to the behavior of entrepreneurs. To begin with, much of the behavior of interest occurs prior to the start-up process or before the new market offering. Shah and Tripsas (2007), for instance, demonstrate that user entrepreneurs are relatively prevalent in certain areas of the economy, and they frequently engage in behaviors of interest to entrepreneurial scholars prior to thinking about starting a new venture. Similarly, a definition of entrepreneurial behavior that is tied to an outcome (e.g., new venture start-up) would be problematic in terms of defining and motivating interest in research problems (it would be difficult to convince scholars to invest large quantities of time in research that might be later determined irrelevant based on an unknown and unknowable outcome). Selecting behaviors as relevant based upon an outcome variable would also result in bias due to data truncation. Observing a variety of behaviors under varying conditions with a full range of outcome possibilities is critical to developing an accurate understanding of entrepreneurial behavior—especially if the goal is that we might be able to enhance entrepreneurial success rates, or decrease costs associated with failed start-ups.

Finally, we need to be open to understanding ancillary and complementary behaviors engaged in by nascent entrepreneurs. To better understand this concept, let us consider a different behavioral context. Imagine that we want to understand swimming behavior. We might be tempted—as unfamiliar outsiders—to focus on behaviors that specifically involve swimming. We could study a variety of individuals ranging from absolute novice to international caliber competitor. We might examine their behaviors, practice habits, time spent in the pool, types of workouts, stroke technique training, and so on. No doubt, we would learn quite a lot from this study. However, we also might miss the importance of seemingly unrelated behaviors such as dry-land workouts (weight training, band training, etc.), nutrition and diet, rest, and cross-training (which often appears unrelated to the actual sport). In other words, if we define the behavior of interest around a specific activity, rather than around the behaviors engaged in by individuals with a particular intention (to improve as swimmers), then we would develop incomplete or even incorrect understandings of the behavior of interest. We suggest this is a concern for entrepreneurship researchers, as well.

Because definitions of entrepreneurship and entrepreneurial behavior, have, in the past proved problematical (e.g., Bruyat & Julien, 2000; Cunningham & Lischeron, 1991; Gartner, 1990; Hébert & Link, 1988; Ireland, Hitt, & Sirmon, 2003), we have settled on a modification of a definition of entrepreneurial behavior generated by Ahmad and

Seymour (2008) that melded both "top down," theory-driven definitions with "bottom up," operational definitions of entrepreneurship into this specification:

> Entrepreneurship is about identifying and acting upon (enterprising human activity) opportunities that create value (be that economic, cultural or social). Typically, entrepreneurial activities require the leveraging of resources and capabilities through innovation, but the opportunities themselves always relate to the identification of either new products, processes or markets." (Ahmad & Seymour, 2008, p. 14)

We use their definition of entrepreneurial activity as our definition of entrepreneurial behavior: "Enterprising human action in pursuit of the generation of value, through the creation or expansion of economic activity, by identifying and exploiting new products, processes or markets" (Ahmad & Seymour, 2008, p. 14). Notice that this definition is inclusive of the research Shah and her colleagues have done on user entrepreneurs, as well as the research from the effectuation perspective (Dew et al., 2009, 2011; Sarasvathy 2001, 2008) and bricolage (Baker & Nelson, 2005).

Though this definition is not perfect, it adheres to the four requirements earlier stated for a good definition: it is operational, essential, widely applicable, and succinct. It should also be reiterated that a definition that achieves perfect consensus is highly improbable, as demonstrated by the research of Levitis et al. (2009).

The Role of Behavior in Existing Theories and Frameworks

In this section, we consider some of the more visible models and theories in the entrepreneurship literature and compare them to this definition to demonstrate that although behavior can be found within them, they are not truly behavioral theories.[2] This is expected given that each was designed to serve a different research purpose. However, this review demonstrates that a new model is needed in order to facilitate growth in behaviorally oriented research.

As is common in the entrepreneurship literature, we will begin with the works of Schumpeter (1934) and Kirzner (1973/1978). In both cases, the entrepreneur was far more a catalyst in the study of microeconomic phenomena than a person of research interest. In the case of Schumpeter's work, his primary interest was in explaining economic growth given the assumptions of economic equilibrium prevalent in microeconomic theories of the period. Though he was interested in higher order dynamic processes, Schumpeter conceived behavioral action on the part of the entrepreneur as key to this process (Schumpeter, 1934). For instance, he writes, "Now, it is this 'doing the things,' without which possibilities are dead, of which the [entrepreneur's] function consists (1934, p. 88, quoted in McMullen and Shepherd (2006, footnote 8). While Schumpeter emphasizes that behavioral action on the part of the entrepreneur is critical, his theory is not intended for exploring entrepreneurial behavior.

Similarly, Kirzner has been clear in many of his writings (e.g., Kirzner, 1978, 1983, 1997, 2009) that for his purposes, the entrepreneur served a construct role,

---

[2] While we have selected a few of the most cited models, we do not offer these examples as an exhaustive review of the literature.

facilitating the return to equilibrium in the presence of nonuniform distribution of information (i.e., relaxing the perfect information assumption). Inspired by the work of his mentor, Ludwig von Mises, he focuses on entrepreneurial alertness which is *predicated* on successful action (for futher elaboration see McMullen & Shepherd, 2006).

Among more recent work, Shane and Venkataraman (2000) describe their framework as follows "(1) we focus on the existence, discovery, and exploitation of opportunities; (2) we examine the influence of individuals and opportunities, rather than environmental antecedents and consequences; and (3) we consider a framework broader than firm creation" (p. 219). As such, this framework works at a highly conceptual level, but explicitly does not address the study of what Shane and Venkataraman refer to as the firm creation process, itself. Yet they provide excellent arguments for the importance of understanding entrepreneurial behavior as a complement to the opportunity discovery process:

> "Entrepreneurial behavior is transitory (Carroll & Mosakowski, 1987). Moreover, estimates of the number of people who engage in entrepreneurial behavior range from 20 percent of the population (Reynolds & White, 1997) to over 50 percent (Aldrich & Zimmer, 1986). . . . Therefore, when we argue that some people and not others engage in *entrepreneurial behavior* [italics added for emphasis], we are describing the tendency of certain people to respond to the situational cues of opportunities—not a stable characteristic that differentiates some people from others across all situations." (pp. 218–219)

Although Shane and Venkataraman's framework does not focus on behavior, they acknowledge that behavior is critical to entrepreneurship and that a behavioral understanding of entrepreneurship is complementary to their own framework.

Alvarez and Barney (2007) offer creation theory as an alternative that explains opportunity within the context of individual agency. In offering their theory, they explicitly note that both discovery and creation theories of opportunity are built around explaining "the same dependent variable—*actions* [italics added for emphasis] that entrepreneurs take to form and exploit opportunities" (p. 12). In other words, both are built around the assumption that new venture opportunities are a result of entrepreneurial behavior. Whereas discovery theory is characterized by search behaviors, due to the assumption that opportunities exist independent of individual action, creation theory emphasizes that entrepreneurs "do not search, they act." They write: "creation theory assumes that entrepreneur's actions are the essential source of these opportunities . . ." (p. 15).

While creation theory expands our understanding of opportunity within entrepreneurship and broadened the conversation surrounding the opportunity construct, it is not a theory of entrepreneurial behavior. We believe that a strong understanding of entrepreneurial behavior represents a critical complement to creation theory.

More recently, McMullen and Shepherd (2006) offered a framework with a theoretical underpinning built on entrepreneurial action. Their two-stage conceptual model attempts to systematically develop connections from knowledge and motivation to opportunity. In stage 1 (attention stage), prior knowledge and personal strategy lead to recognition of a third-person opportunity. In stage 2 (evaluation stage), knowledge (i.e., feasibility assessment) and motivation (i.e., desirability assessment) lead to entrepreneurial action (i.e., perception of first-person opportunity). Though the authors present this as a theory of entrepreneurial action, behavior is implicit to the resulting model. This is primarily a cognitive model in which cognitive processes influence the perception and evaluation of opportunities. Implicitly, behavior plays a role in the personal strategy (motivation) element of the attention stage; explicitly it plays a role in entrepreneurial action, which is associated with what the authors call "first-person opportunity." In spite of the fact that behavior plays a role in leading to recognition of the third-person opportunity, and the outcome of interest is action (i.e., behavior), this model does not help researchers who are explicitly interested in understanding entrepreneurial behavior more generally.

In contrast to the models already reviewed, two recent theories offer more explicit insight into entrepreneurial behavior, Sarasvathy's (2001, 2008) effectuation logic, and the accidental entrepreneurs of Shah and Tripsas (2007). Sarasvathy's (2001, 2008) effectuation logic has implications for cognitive understanding of entrepreneurship (e.g., effectual versus causal logics of development) that leads to a particular behavior pattern (i.e., the development of effectual networks and effectual network commitments). Through effectual network development, Sarasvathy develops an explanation for how the means of the entrepreneur (i.e., who I am, what I know, and whom I know) lead to new means and goals, resulting in a feedback loop that eventually results in new markets and other effectual artifacts (Sarasvathy, 2008, p. 101). While we consider the work of Sarasvathy and her colleagues quite encouraging, we believe that like the other models reviewed, it would be complemented by a more general understanding of entrepreneurial behavior.

Finally, Shah and Tripsas (2007) offered an interesting extension to the entrepreneurship literature with their work on "user entrepreneurs." They develop a description of the "classic model of the entrepreneurial process" and then extend that model to include user innovation processes that lead to opportunity identification. Their model (2007, p. 129) is built around a feedback cycle in which users begin with an unmet (personal) need, which they respond to by creating a preliminary solution. The preliminary solution is improved through feedback obtained from community and public interaction. As such, their model is a process-oriented model with motivational and behavioral implications. Though behavior is not the focus of their model, behavior is important to it, especially in the user experimentation and solution creation stage. Similarly, forming or not forming a new venture is behavior. However, as with the other models, this is not a true behavioral model per the earlier definition offered.

While these frameworks demonstrate significant advances in our field's understanding of entrepreneurship, we believe they show gaps in the entrepreneurship literature as related to entrepreneurial behavior. That is, the field of entrepreneurship has made significant advances with respect to our understanding of opportunity and our understanding of cognitive processes that drive entrepreneurial action. But, they deemphasize the significant role of behavior in our current theories and frameworks. While there appears to be broad agreement that entrepreneurial behavior matters, little progress has been made in advancing this knowledge (Bird et al., 2012).

A Theory of Enterpreneurial Behavior

Our theory (see Figure 4.1) makes five key assumptions about behavior. First, people who pursue entrepreneurship, whether individually or in teams, will possess a set of behaviors, developed over time, that can be enacted individually or in combination,

A Theory of Enterpreneurial Behavior | 79

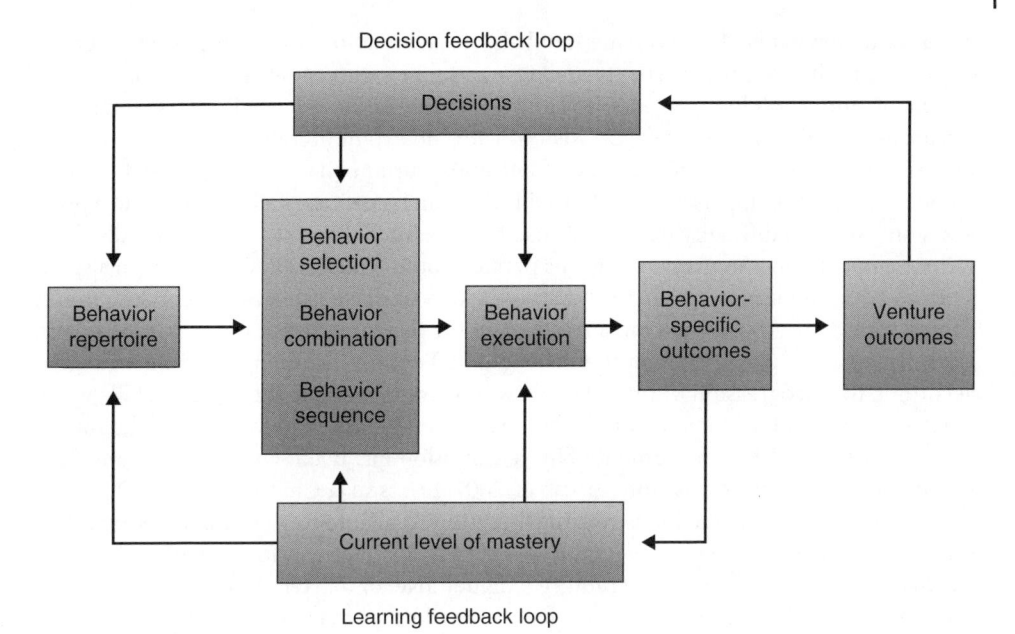

```
                      Decision feedback loop
         ┌─────────────────── Decisions ◄───────────────────────┐
         │                        │                              │
         │               ┌─────────────────┐                    │
         │               │    Behavior     │                    │
         │               │    selection    │                    │
         ▼               │                 │                    │
   ┌──────────┐          │    Behavior     │   ┌──────────┐   ┌──────────┐   ┌──────────┐
   │ Behavior │─────────►│   combination   │──►│ Behavior │──►│ Behavior-│──►│  Venture │
   │repertoire│          │                 │   │execution │   │ specific │   │ outcomes │
   └──────────┘          │    Behavior     │   └──────────┘   │ outcomes │   └──────────┘
        ▲                │    sequence     │         ▲        └──────────┘
        │                └─────────────────┘         │              │
        │                         ▲                  │              │
        │                         │                  │              │
        └────────────── Current level of mastery ◄───┘              │
                                  ▲                                  │
                                  └──────────────────────────────────┘
                       Learning feedback loop
```

Figure 4.1 Model of entrepreneurial behavior.

to solve problems. We call this set of behaviors a *behavioral repertoire*. Second, that behavioral repertoire can be expressed in many different ways, that is, differences (variation) in what individuals do occurs because: (a) individuals or teams select different behaviors to solve similar problems; (b) individuals or teams may use multiple behaviors in different combinations to solve similar problems; or, (c) individuals or teams sequence a set of behaviors in a different order to solve similar problems. For example, most entrepreneurs or entrepreneurial teams likely possess "selling" as a constituent of their behavioral repertoire. The activity of selling might be executed by an entrepreneur using any of a variety of behaviors, or the entrepreneur (or team) might use a combination of behaviors that are different, or the entrepreneur (or team) might use these behaviors in a sequence that is different from that of other entrepreneurs. Third, we expect each behavior enacted to result in a unique behavior-specific outcome. For example, attempting to make early sales via a crowdfunding site is expected to yield a specific crowdfunding result that would be qualitatively and measurably different from that of selling at a trade show. Each of these behaviors, then, results in different outcomes. (Note: This is not a contradiction of assumption 2. In certain circumstances, different behaviors may result in similar outcomes, while, in certain circumstances, different behaviors may result in different outcomes. In each case, there will be a specific outcome.) Fourth, individuals perform a behavior within the constraints of the expertise that they have developed in regard to that behavior. We call this their *level of mastery*. Therefore, we assume that any enacted behavior can be characterized by some level of proficiency or expertise in execution. This is consistent with the findings of Ericsson and his colleagues (e.g., Ericsson, 2006; Ericsson & Charness, 1994; Ericsson, Roring, & Nandagopal, 2007). In other words, we would assume, then, that a behavior could be qualitatively performed better or worse based on proficiency or learned expertise. In order to further explicate this element of behavioral variation, we distinguish the terms behavior and skill. We reserve the term behavior for complex observable actions such as selling, planning, pitching, forecasting, and so on. In our theory, "skill" refers to specific learnable subunits of behaviors. Consistent with the extant literature (see the works of Ericsson and colleagues), our theory of entrepreneurial behavior recognizes that any complex behavior comprises of a set of skills that can be conceptually arranged in a progression based on difficulty or level of mastery exhibited. For example, if an individual were learning to play an instrument, this person would typically practice and learn such skills as common scales, timings, and so on. None of these skills represents the more complex behavior of playing a musical score on the instrument, but these skills are necessary in order to play music on the instrument. These skills, then, could be arranged according to a progression of mastery. We would assume that if the specific skills were mastered, then, the musician would also be able to demonstrate mastery of the musical composition on the instrument. This assumption has been validated in numerous studies on expert skill acquisition (Ericsson, 2007; Ericsson & Charness, 1994). Our fifth assumption is that a behavior is not meaningfully available to the individual or team unless it has been minimally developed to a level of adequate performance (Ericsson et al., 2007). Often, however, it may require a higher level of mastery to provide meaningful benefit. This idea is developed under the heading of mastery, that occurs later in the chapter. We offer these five assumptions to suggest that, the accomplishment of a particular activity such as "selling" requires us to see this activity as more complicated than is often viewed. So, if one asks an entrepreneur: "Did you engage in selling?" we should appreciate that an answer of "yes" tells us very little of what behaviors specifically occurred or the quality or mastery of the behaviors engaged in.

What follows is an elaboration of the model in more detail.

Behavioral Repertoire

If we are to make behavioral variation a focus of serious inquiry in future research, we need a means of understanding why two individuals may select completely different behavioral responses when confronted with the same challenge. One of the fascinating things about human beings is our capacity to adapt both cognitively and behaviorally through acquired learning and systematic training (Bruel-Jungerman, Davis, & Laroche, 2007; Buonomano & Merzenich, 1998; Ericsson, 2007, Ericsson et al., 2007; Ericsson, Krampe, & Tesch-Romer, 1993; Merzenich, 2009). This capacity for neurological adaptation and refinement allows each individual to develop sets of behavioral options, each decidedly unique over time (Merzenich, 2008), and each developed to a different level of specific skill content and possible level of performance (Ericsson, 2006, Ericsson, et al., 2007). The presence of a differently developed set of behaviors available to each individual leads us to suggest that the behavioral repertoire of the individual should be a focal construct in the study of entrepreneurial behavior. The behavioral repertoire is the set of behaviors that an individual has developed to at least an adequate level of performance ability (for a more thorough overview of adequate versus other levels of performance, including a more nuanced understanding of the popularized "10,000 hour rule," see Ericsson 2006, 2007). The behavioral repertoire construct provides a theoretical basis for exploring questions such as why the same entrepreneur may invoke different behaviors when confronted with apparently similar problems. Additionally, it allows us to explore why different entrepreneurs with seemingly similar levels of behavioral mastery of a given behavior might invoke it differently in response to the same contextual cue. Finally, the behavioral repertoire can be scaled to units of analysis beyond the individual. For instance, it seems intuitive that a start-up team can also be characterized as possessing a behavioral repertoire that is composed of the behaviors present in each individual's behavioral repertoire, along with the emergent behavioral routines, which arise through the interaction of this particular set of individuals. Behaviors will be selected alone, or in combination, from the behavioral repertoire in response to perceived and interpreted contextual cues.

The behavioral repertoire is important to our behavioral theory of entrepreneurship for three reasons. First, it allows us to represent human actors as possessing different behavioral capacities, due both to the combination of available behaviors and due to the level of mastery developed in each. Second, it allows us to capture the fact that individuals possess behavioral capacities beyond those that are exhibited in particular sample situations. We call these behaviors, which are possessed but not utilized to solve a general problem, *latent behaviors*. This brings us to the third reason the behavioral repertoire is critical to a correct theoretical understanding of entrepreneurship behavior as a phenomenon of scholarly interest. It allows us to more precisely understand exaptation as it often occurs in new venture beginnings (Dew et al., 2011; Murmann, 2003). Exaptation refers to the application of a behavior (in this case) for a purpose other than that which it was originally developed. In essence, the behavioral repertoire functions as a constraint upon the primary sources of behavioral variation that we posit in the next section: behavioral selection, behavioral sequence, and behavioral combination.

Proposition 1 The behavioral repertoire of the entrepreneur or the start-up team will constrain the available behavioral solutions when faced with a new challenge.

Sources of Behavioral Variation

If individuals or teams have multiple behaviors at their disposal with which to solve complex problems, and if these behaviors can be used in combination to solve that problem, then there are deducible ways in which individuals will be expected to systematically vary though faced with a similar challenge. First, individuals or teams may differ in the behavior they select to solve a particular problem. For example, when Scott's fertilizer sued TerraCycle in 2006, Tom Szaky (an accomplished web designer prior to starting this company) chose to respond by creating a web page to promote his company's side of the argument, rather than fighting Scott's in court. An entrepreneur without this behavior in their repertoire would have likely selected a different behavioral response to this threat. Thus, behavioral selection is one source of variation. The second source of variation recognizes that complex problems typically require complex solutions—in other words, multiple behaviors. Thus, individuals or teams may vary in the combination of behaviors that they enact to solve the problem. Finally, most entrepreneurial ventures are created over long periods of time. Therefore, the combination of behaviors selected can vary due to temporal ordering, or what we refer to as *behavioral sequencing*. Each of these three sources of variation will influence behavior-specific outcomes, which will ultimately cause different venture level outcomes to emerge.

Proposition 2a Entrepreneurs will vary with respect to the behavior they choose in response to similar challenges as they progress through the start-up process.

Proposition 2b Entrepreneurs will utilize different combinations of behavior in responding to similar challenges as they progress through the start-up process.

Proposition 2c Entrepreneurs may use the same categories of behavior but vary in the temporal sequence in which behaviors are enacted.

Another way in which we expect individual behavior to vary is in execution. Many factors may influence execution of a behavior, but we expect that the level of behavioral mastery will be most predictive. For example, the quality of a piano recital can be influenced by many factors, including piano tuning, key response, room acoustics, and so on, but we would expect a concerto pianist to perform at a high level under most reasonably occurring variations of these conditions, whereas we expect an accomplished amateur to sound less polished than the expert in any combination of these conditions. Thus, we expect developed mastery to most influence the execution of any behavior.

Proposition 3 Entrepreneurs who perform the same behavior will still exhibit different performance of the behavior, referred to as execution, due primarily to their current level of acquired mastery.

In the preceding discussions, we have identified four sources of variation in individual or team behavior: behavior selection, behavior combination, behavior sequence, and behavior execution. The variation explained by these four sources will causally influence *behavior-specific outcomes*. Behavior-specific outcomes are a critical element of this theory, because these are the immediate and measureable results of the behavior. For example, when developing a business model for a new venture, the written business model is the behavior-specific outcome. This resulting business model can be assessed for detail, content, quality of data used, and so on. We suggest that behavioral variation be assessed by developing measures of performance that are specific to the behavior itself, rather than a more distally hoped for benefit of the behavior (e.g., venture growth). We expect that these behavior-specific outcome measures will improve the field's ability to explain variation in new venture outcomes. In other words, we suggest that the relationship between the performance of a specific behavior and the desired new venture benefit is mediated by the behavior-specific outcome. For example, a common behavior early in new venture creation is planning (which is often reflected in asking questions about whether an entrepreneur has written a business plan, e.g., Delmar & Shane, 2003; Honig, 2004; Honig & Karlsson, 2004; Karlsson & Honig, 2009; Liao & Gartner, 2006). Our theory suggests that individuals or teams will vary with respect to (a) whether they write a business plan; (b) the behaviors they couple with writing a business plan, such as product development and refinement, investment seeking, and so on; (c) when they write the business plan (i.e., prior to creating a product, after market testing a product, etc.); and/or (d) the quality of the business plan. Obviously, the intent is that a good business plan will improve the venture outcomes; however, variation in the behavior must be measured and evaluated based on the behavior-specific outcome (e.g., the correctness of the choice relative to other possible behaviors, the behavioral combination it is part of, its place in the temporal sequencing of start-up behaviors, and the quality of the resulting information achieved by writing the plan). It is for this reason that the study of behavior necessitates the use of behavior-specific outcomes.

Because our theory is a behavioral theory, it focuses on explaining variation in behavior across different individuals and circumstances. We believe that variation in behavioral selection, execution and performance will be the strongest predictors of venture level outcomes. As such, we believe that it is critical for researchers to capture behavior-specific outcome measures if we wish to better understand venture level outcomes.

Proposition 4 Differences in behavior-specific outcomes will explain variation in venture level performance outcomes.

Level of Mastery

Level of mastery refers to the acquired capacity to perform a given behavior. This label is used to represent the current level at which an entrepreneur is able to perform a specific behavior. This builds directly upon the expert skill development literature. Where the expert skill acquisition literature defines a process through which skills may be developed by most members of the population, level of mastery represents a snapshot measure of the current level attained, recognizing that this level is malleable through additional directed practice, or disuse. Within this literature, directed practice appears to be the most viable explanation for how a person's level of mastery in any given behavior is developed (Ericsson, 1998, 2006, 2007; Ericsson et al., 1993, Ericsson & Charness, 1994, Ericsson & Lehmann, 1996). Directed practice occurs when an individual works to acquire the next most challenging skill associated with that behavior. Thus, a novice diver will typically learn to successfully perform a simple forward dive, first. Once they become proficient at that, then learning to perform a backward facing dive might be the next skill associated with development of the behavior we call diving. As such, this type of skill, or discrete subcomponent of a complex behavior, can be individually learned and mastered. Each time a new skill is mastered, it increases the general mastery of the behavior; however, mastery of one or more skills may not necessarily constitute mastery of the more general behavior.

Proposition 5 Individuals may possess the capacity to execute the same behavioral response but will differ in their mastery of the behavior.

An example of this proposition might be reflected in studies of pitching (Chen, Yao & Kotha, 2009; Maxwell, Jeffrey, & Lévesque 2011; Maxwell & Lévesque, 2014; Parhankangas & Ehrlich 2014; Pollack, Rutherford, & Nagy, 2012; Williams, 2013) where the differences in the success of the pitches (as determined by the acquisition of resources from others or in winning a pitching competition) might be reflected in the mastery of the behaviors of pitching.

The behavioral repertoire is expected to change over time due to two feedback loops: the decision feedback loop and the learning feedback loop. These two feedback loops recognize the role of cognition in understanding variation in entrepreneurial behavior. The decision feedback loop begins when a behavior-specific outcome is perceived and evaluated by the entrepreneur and other relevant stakeholders affected by the behavior. Based upon the behavior-specific outcome, the entrepreneur receives feedback with respect to the efficacy of the behavior or behaviors selected, the sequence of behaviors, and the combination of behaviors, as well as the current sufficiency or insufficiency of the current behavior repertoire. The learning feedback loop also begins with feedback received based on the behavior-specific outcome, but this feedback loop allows for improvement in expertise over time, which results in increasing levels of mastery. Increasing levels of mastery then modifies the behavior repertoire available for future use. Each of these feedback loops is amenable to systematic study as part of elucidating the behavioral variation of entrepreneurs.

Proposition 6a Positive venture outcomes will increase the probability of the entrepreneur deciding to use a behavioral response when facing similar future challenges.

Proposition 6b Negative venture outcomes will decrease the probability of the entrepreneur deciding to use a behavioral response when facing similar future challenges.

Proposition 6c Behavior-specific outcomes provide feedback that can result in changed level of mastery with respect to that behavior.

Implications of a Theory of Entrepreneurial Behavior

Our chapter has implications for three distinct audiences: academic scholars, practitioners, and policymakers. Here, we provide just a few of the implications. First, our primary objective is to communicate with researchers who are interested in understanding and explaining variation in venture start-up processes and the resulting venture outcomes. Our current work suggests that the variation observed in the venture creation process is the direct result of our five key assumptions.
As such, future studies need to help us answer the following questions:

1) How do we capture and measure the behavioral repertoire of the entrepreneur or the start-up team?
2) How and why do people vary in their selection of behavioral response to a given challenge in the start-up process?
3) How and why do people vary in their temporal sequencing of behavioral responses to a given challenge in the start-up process?
4) How and why do people choose to combine particular behaviors in response to a given challenge in the start-up process?

Additionally, our work implies that we must account for the performance of the behavior, not just the existence of the behavior, if we want to understand venture level outcomes. For instance, our work suggests that not only do we need to know that an individual created a business plan, but also we need to evaluate the quality of content in the business plan if we are to accurately understand whether or not it influenced the venture outcome.

Similarly, would-be entrepreneurs may benefit from an evaluation of their behavioral repertoire as well as that of the start-up team—as it is created. Carefully crafting the behavioral repertoire with attention paid to both behavioral variety and behavioral mastery may prove essential to venture success. Additionally, consistent with the work on expert skill acquisition, our work suggests that the behavioral repertoire (of the individual entrepreneur or the team) is not simply a static endowment, but rather a dynamic variable which can be systematically enhanced to the advantage of the new venture.

Finally, from a pedagogical perspective, our work suggests that there is likely benefit to treating entrepreneurship as a collection of behaviors in which mastery is developed via directed practice as a function of time. This implies that if we, as a research community, can identify necessary (but perhaps not sufficient) behaviors and threshold levels of mastery required, then we can improve our efforts to systematically enhance entrepreneurial success.

Toward an Entrepreneurial Behavior Research Agenda

Previous reviews of the existing literature on entrepreneurial behavior have concluded that little progress has been made on key questions, such as (1) determining what constitutes an entrepreneurial behavior, (2) developing a logic for why and how behaviors are influenced by specific contextual clues, and (3) understanding how these behaviors influence the environment in which the new venture is developing (Bird et al., 2012, 2014). In this chapter, we contribute answers to the first two of these critical questions by drawing on multiple literatures in order to define entrepreneurial behavior, and then developing a theoretical model to explain why and how behaviors may be influenced by specific contextual clues. Though we do not offer a direct answer to the third question—our model focuses on understanding sources of behavioral variation and relates these to venture outcomes via behavior-specific outcomes—the theory presented establishes a solid foundation upon which environmental influence can be explored with minor adaptation to the model.

This chapter contributes a novel theory of entrepreneurial behavior and identifies key sources of variation that are expected to influence behavioral outcomes and thus explain variation in behavioral selection and execution across (a) different entrepreneurs facing similar situations, and (b) the same entrepreneur facing different situations. In elaborating sources of variation, the theory also introduces two new constructs that warrant significant investigation in future studies: the behavioral repertoire and behavior-specific outcomes. We believe studies modeled after the Dyer et al. (2008), Sarasvathy (2001), and Shah and Tripsas (2007) would make valuable contributions to this area. Additionally, exploratory qualitative analyses that seek the discovery and use of novel behaviors on the part of entrepreneurs would also yield important insights. This is also an area in which narrative methods, particularly those embracing the structural approach (Pentland, 1999; Riessman, 2008; Webster & Mertova, 2007) would be of tremendous value. If we can develop a sufficient inventory of entrepreneurial behaviors, then comparative methods common in other areas of behavioral research will become useful (de Waal, 1988, 1991; de Waal & Luttrell, 1989; Thierry et al., 2008). Studies such as those described here would establish a foundation upon which studies following the expert skill acquisition methodologies could be developed (Ericsson, 1985, 2006, 2007; Ericsson & Lehmann, 1996; Ericsson & Simon, 1980; Pentland, 1999, Riessman, 2008; Webster & Mertova, 2007).

Two other areas deserve consideration in future studies. First, the theory of entrepreneurial behavior suggests two primary avenues for acquisition of new behaviors to the behavioral repertoire: learning and strategic acquisition of team members. Future studies should explore the trade-offs between these two approaches and explore the conditions under which each proves most beneficial to the entrepreneurial start-up. Second, the field of entrepreneurship would also benefit from future studies that explore the possible interaction between an entrepreneur's behavioral repertoire and the developing entrepreneurial identity.

Finally, we should note that a limitation of the chapter is that it does not specifically link cognition to behavioral variation. Further development in this area would facilitate better understanding of how environmental cues are perceived, prioritized, and used in the selection of behavioral response by entrepreneurs. This would likely lay the foundation for systematic study of variation across different categories of entrepreneur, which would advance our understanding of entrepreneurial behavior and of entrepreneurship in general.

Next Steps

Besides the suggestions for research identified earlier, we offer the following specific recommendations for scholarship that focuses on the behavior of entrepreneurs.

We believe that a more systematic inventory of prior scholarship on entrepreneurial behavior needs to be undertaken. As we have noted before, scholarship on entrepreneurial behavior is not always labeled as such, and, finding those nuggets of research that offer insights into the behavior of entrepreneurs will require a rather dogged and laborious search through previous academic scholarship compared to what has been undertaken in past reviews. For example, from our own scholarship on this topic, an article such as "A longitudinal study of cognitive factors influencing start-up behaviors and success at venture creation" (Gatewood, Shaver, & Gartner, 1995) which is ostensibly about attribution theory, self-efficacy, and locus of control, also provides insights into the specific actions individuals undertook to successfully start new ventures. We would assume that there are numerous examples of similar kinds of articles, therefore, a more thorough exploration of the academic literature may reveal substantial information on this topic.

Second, a more comprehensive recognition of the behavior of entrepreneurs within their life course (e.g., Aldrich & Kim, 2007; Davis & Shaver, 2012; Jayawarna, Rouse, & Kitching, 2013; Reynolds, 1991) would broaden the context of acknowledging the importance of prior experiences, family background, and other circumstances in regards to the development of behavioral repertoires and expertise. As noted earlier, the process of entrepreneurship for any one individual is likely to have a genesis and foundation that is significantly earlier than the initial inception or recognition of an idea. What behaviors individuals pick up along the way, and, how these behaviors are honed and developed over time, needs a generous acknowledgment of the prior history of their experiences.

Third, while the examples of scholarship in this chapter have tended to focus on entrepreneurial behavior within the context of the creation of independent new ventures, we recognize a broader sense of entrepreneurial activity (as suggested in the definition of entrepreneurial behavior offered). We celebrate efforts to critically explore the nature of entrepreneurship as a phenomenon (Calas, Smircich, & Bourne, 2009; Rindova, Barry, & Ketchen, 2009; Tedmanson, Verduyn, Essers, & Gartner 2012) and welcome creative ways of both conceptualizing and observing various ways individuals engage in entrepreneurial behaviors (e.g., Hjorth, 2005; Hjorth & Holt, 2016).

Fourth, we reemphasize the usefulness of expanding the methods that might elucidate aspects of entrepreneurial behavior. While we have mentioned narrative methods earlier, we note additional connections to this perspective (Down & Warren, 2008; Downing, 2005; Martens, Jennings, & Jennings 2007). We also suggest such approaches as ethnography (Dana & Dana, 2005; Johnstone, 2007; Robinson & Blenker, 2014; Stewart & Aldrich, 2015); autoethnography (e.g., Engstrom, 2012; Fletcher, 2011; Poldner, 2013; Scherdin, 2007; Steyaert, 2011); and innovative ways of capturing behaviors in real time (e.g., Lackeus, Lundqvist, & Middleton 2015) as ways to get closer to observing and reporting on the entrepreneurial behavior of individuals.

Finally, we recognize that our focus on entrepreneurial behavior as the both the ontological and epistemological lens for peering into the phenomenon of entrepreneurship is parallel and concurrent with complimentary approaches that would come under such labels as "entrepreneurship as practice" (e.g., Anderson, Dodd, & Jack, 2010; Chalmers & Shaw, 2015; De Clercq & Voronov, 2009; Geiger, Keating, & McLoughlin, 2013; Johannisson, 2011; Nicolini, 2012; Terjesen & Elam, 2009); "entrepreneuring and process views" (e.g., Bhave, 1994; Birley, 1986; Chell, 2007; Gartner, 1985; Gherardi & Perrotta, 2014; Jack & Anderson, 2002; Rindova, Barry, & Ketchen, 2009; Steyaert, 2007); and "entrepreneurial action" (e.g., Corbett & Katz, 2012; Gordon, 2012; McMullen & Shepherd, 2006; Shaver, 2012). The good news in these many approaches is that they all focus on entrepreneurial behavior. We expect that clarity in the terminology of these labels and their application to the study of entrepreneurial behavior will emerge as more dialogue and insights from research engages the scholarly, practitioner, and policy communities.

Conclusions

We began this chapter by reviewing the current state of knowledge about entrepreneurial behavior. Though exemplars exist (e.g., Dyer et al., 2008; Karlsson & Honig, 2009; Graebner & Eisenhardt, 2004; Shah & Tripsas, 2007), they are few in number. In order to make progress on this problem, we needed to adequately define entrepreneurial behavior, which necessitated first identifying a strong scholarly definition of behavior.

Drawing upon multiple literatures, we adopt the Levitis et al. (2009) definition, in which behavior means, "the internally coordinated responses (actions or inactions) of whole living organisms (individuals or groups) to internal and/or external stimuli, excluding responses more easily understood as developmental changes" (p. 109). Starting with this definition of behavior, we then argued that a modification of the definition of entrepreneurial behavior developed by Ahmad and Seymour (2008) best serves the goals of consilient development of our field with other behavioral fields, while still facilitating constructive theory development for our current purposes. Thus, we define entrepreneurial behavior as follows: Entrepreneurial behavior is enterprising human action (or inaction—see general definition of behavior) in pursuit of the generation of value, through the creation or expansion of economic activity, by identifying and exploiting new products, processes, or markets."

Next, we used this definition, along with Herbert Simon's (1992) definition of behavioral theory, to review prominent existing frameworks and theories. We demonstrate that although behavior is often recognized as critical to entrepreneurship, and frequently implicit to these models, none currently meets the needs of a behavioral theory, though each would be complemented by the development of a theory of entrepreneurial behavior.

Having established the need for a theory of entrepreneurial behavior, we responded by proposing a new theory of entrepreneurial behavior. Our theory emphasizes two new constructs, the behavioral repertoire and behavior-specific outcomes. The behavioral repertoire represents the set of behaviors that an individual (or team) has developed to at least an adequate level of performance ability (see Ericsson, 2006, 2007 for detailed review), such that the behavior is available for enactment in response to perceived stimuli. Behavior-specific outcomes are performance outcomes specific to the behavior(s) enacted in response to the perceived situation. Thus, two entrepreneurs or start-up teams may write business plans, but these plans may differ substantially in their quality and content, which will then influence such venture outcomes as future planning, financial investment, and perceived venture legitimacy.

We argue that entrepreneurial behavior may vary across situations with the same individual, or across individuals in similar situations based on four qualities of behavior: (1) behavioral selection; (2) behavioral sequence; (3) behavioral combination (or temporal ordering); and (4) behavior execution. These sources of variation support propositions 1–3. Thus, business plans will vary with respect to existence, timing, combination with other behaviors (e.g., completion pitch, financing seeking, networking, etc.) and the quality and relevance of data and analyses contained. These sources of variation will influence behavior-specific outcomes (e.g., competition placement, financing decision, perceived legitimacy, etc.). In addition, entrepreneurs differ in the level of mastery to which they have developed any behavior that exists within their behavioral repertoire (proposition 5).

The theory of entrepreneurial behavior goes on to suggest that behavior-specific outcomes influence the venture level outcomes with which we are ultimately interested (proposition 4). Our theory also accounts for the dynamic nature of behavior and the development of expertise over time by specifying two feedback loops, the decision feedback loop and the learning feedback loop. The decision feedback loop is driven by venture outcome feedback (propositions 6a and 6b). The learning feedback loop is driven by feedback from behavior-specific outcomes (proposition 6c).

The question this chapter ultimately posits for entrepreneurship research is, "How do the entrepreneurs' behavioral choices influence their ultimate success or failure?" Simon (1992) emphasized the need for behavioral theory to understand and explain variation in behavioral selection across individuals faced with similar situations, and across different situations confronted by a given individual. Yet, in the extant entrepreneurship literature, the importance of behavioral variation is not adequately captured and systematically studied (Bird et al., 2012, 2014), leaving us with significant gaps as we attempt to understand the success or failure of new ventures.

The theory we offer in this chapter serves as a foundation for numerous new lines of research related to entrepreneurship. We invite and encourage new scholarship with an explicit focus on entrepreneurial behavior, the behavioral repertoire of the entrepreneur or start-up team, and the influence of behavior-specific outcomes as they influence venture level outcomes and provide feedback to behavioral choices and developing mastery. Entrepreneurship is driven by behavior (McMullen & Shepherd, 2006; Schumpeter, 1934) and governed by variation in behavioral choices, execution, and outcomes. Through the systematic study of entrepreneurial behavior, we are likely to gain greater appreciation of the subtlety and nuance of behavioral variation that ultimately results in entrepreneurial success or failure.

References

Ahmad, N., & Seymour, R. G. (2008). *Defining entrepreneurial activity: Definitions supporting frameworks for data collection* (OECD Statistics Working Papers, 2008/01). OECD Publishing. doi. 10.1787/243164686763

Aldrich, H. E., & Kim, P. H. (2007). A life course perspective on occupational inheritance: Self-employed parents and their children. *Research in the Sociology of Organizations, 25*, 33–82.

Aldrich, H., & Zimmer, C. (1986). "Entrepreneurship through social networks." University of Illinois at Urbana-Champaign's Academy for Entrepreneurial Leadership Historical Research Reference in Entrepreneurship.

Alsos, G. A., Isaksen, E. J., & Ljunggren, E. (2006). New venture financing and subsequent business growth in men-and women-led businesses. *Entrepreneurship Theory and Practice, 30*(5), 667–686.

Alvarez, S. A., &, J. B. Barney (2007). Discovery and creation: Alternative theories of entrepreneurial action. *Strategic Entrepreneurship Journal, 1*(1-2), 11–26.

Anderson, A. R., Dodd, S. D., & Jack, S. (2010). Network practices and entrepreneurial growth. *Scandinavian Journal of Management, 26* (2), 121–133.

Baker, T., & Nelson, R. E. (2005). Creating something from nothing: Resource construction through entrepreneurial bricolage. *Administrative Science Quarterly, 50*(3), 329–366.

Baron, R. A., & Henry, R. A. (2010). How entrepreneurs acquire the capacity to excel: Insights from research on expert performance. *Strategic Entrepreneurship Journal 4* (1), 49–65.

Bhave, M. P. (1994). A process model of entrepreneurial venture creation. *Journal of Business Venturing, 9*(3), 223–242.

Bird, B. J. (1989). *Entrepreneurial behavior*. Glenview, IL: Scott Foresman.

Bird, B., Schjoedt, L., & Baum, J. R. (2012). Editor's introduction. Entrepreneurs' behavior: Elucidation and measurement. *Entrepreneurship Theory and Practice, 36* (5), 889–913.

Bird, B., Schjoedt, L., & Hanke, R. (2014). Behavior of entrepreneurs: Existing research and future directions. In E. Chell & M. Karatas-Ozkan (Eds.), *Handbook of research in small business and entrepreneurship* (pp. 207–221). Cheltenham, England: Elgar.

Birley, S. (1986). The role of networks in the entrepreneurial process. *Journal of Business Venturing, 1*(1), 107–117.

Bruel-Jungerman, E., Davis, S., & Laroshce, S. (2007). Brain plasticity mechanisms and memory: A party of four. *The Neuroscientist, 13*(5), 492–505.

Brundin, E., Patzelt, H., & Shepherd, D. A. (2008). Managers' emotional displays and employees' willingness to act entrepreneurially. *Journal of Business Venturing, 23*(2), 221–243.

Bruyat, C., & Julien, P. A. (2000). Defining the field of research in entrepreneurship. *Journal of Business Venturing, 16,* 165–180.

Buonomano, D. V., & Merzenich, M. M. (1998). Cortical plasticity: From synapses to maps. *Annual Review of Neuroscience, 21*(1), 149–186.

Calas, M. B., Smircich, L., & Bourne, K. A. (2009). Extending the boundaries: Reframing "entrepreneurship as social change" through feminist perspectives. *Academy of Management Review, 34* (3), 552–569.

Carroll, G. R., & Mosakowski, E. (1987). The career dynamics of self-employment. *Administrative Science Quarterly, 32*(4) 570–589.

Chalmers, D. M., & Shaw, E. (2015). The endogenous construction of entrepreneurial contexts: A practice-based perspective. *International Small Business Journal, 35*(1)19–39.

Chell, E. (2007). Social enterprise and entrepreneurship towards a convergent theory of the entrepreneurial process. *International Small Business Journal, 25* (1), 5–26.

Chen, X. P., Yao, X., & Kotha, S. (2009). Entrepreneur passion and preparedness in business plan presentations: a persuasion analysis of venture capitalists' funding decisions. *Academy of Management Journal, 52* (1), 199–214.

Chrisman, J. J., McMullan, E., & Hall, J. (2005). The influence of guided preparation on the long-term performance of new ventures. *Journal of Business Venturing 20*(6), 769–791.

Corbett, A. C., & Katz, J. A. (2012). Introduction: The action of entrepreneurs. In A. C. Corbett & J. A. Katz (Eds.), *Entrepreneurial action: Advances in entrepreneurship, firm emergence and growth* (vol. 14, pp. ix–xix). Bingley, England: Emerald.

Cunningham, J. B., & Lischeron, J. (1991). Defining entrepreneurship. *Journal of Small Business Management, 29*(1), 45.

Dana, L. P., & Dana, T. E. (2005). Expanding the scope of methodologies used in entrepreneurship research. *International Journal of Entrepreneurship and Small Business, 2*(1), 79–88.

Davidson, D. (2001). Reasons, actions, and causes (1963). In D. Donaldson, *Essays on actions and events* (pp. 3–21). Oxford, England: Oxford University Press.

Davidsson, P. (2003). The domain of entrepreneurship research: Some suggestions. *Advances in Entrepreneurship, Firm Emergence and Growth, 6*(3), 315–372.

Davis, A. E., & Shaver, K. G. (2012). Understanding gendered variations in business growth intentions across the life course. Entrepreneurship Theory and Practice, 36 (3), 495–512.

De Clercq, D., & Voronov, M. (2009). Toward a practice perspective of entrepreneurship entrepreneurial legitimacy as habitus. *International Small Business Journal, 27*(4), 395–419.

de Jong, J. P., Parker, S. K., Wennekers, S., & Wu, C. H. (2015). Entrepreneurial behavior in organizations: Does job design matter? *Entrepreneurship Theory and Practice, 39*(4), 981–995.

de Waal, F. B. (1988). The communicative repertoire of captive bonobos (Pan paniscus), compared to that of chimpanzees. *Behaviour, 106*(3) 183–251.

de Waal, F. B. (1991). Complementary methods and convergent evidence in the study of primate social cognition. *Behaviour, 118*(3) 297–320.

de Waal, F., & Luttrell, L. M. (1989). Toward a comparative socioecology of the genus Macaca, different dominance styles in rhesus and stumptail monkeys. *American Journal of Primatology 19*(2): 83–109.

Delmar, F., & Shane, S. (2003). Does business planning facilitate the development of new ventures? *Strategic Management Journal, 24*(12), 1165–1185.

Dew, N., Read, S., Sarasvathy, S., & Wiltbank, R.,(2009). Effectual versus predictive logics in entrepreneurial decision-making: Differences between experts and novices. *Journal of Business Venturing 24*(4), 287–309.

Dew, N., Read, S., Sarasvathy, S., & Wiltbank, R. (2011). On the entrepreneurial genesis of new markets: Effectual transformations versus causal search and selection. *Journal of Evolutionary Economics 21*(2), 231–253.

Down, S., & Warren, L. (2008). Constructing narratives of enterprise: Clichés and entrepreneurial self-identity. *International Journal of Entrepreneurial Behavior & Research, 14*(1), 4–23.

Downing, S. (2005). The social construction of entrepreneurship: Narrative and dramatic processes in the coproduction of organizations and identities. *Entrepreneurship Theory and Practice, 29*(2),185–204.

Dyer, J. H., Gregersen, H. B., & Christensen, C. (2008). Entrepreneur behaviors, opportunity recognition, and the origins of innovative ventures. *Strategic Entrepreneurship Journal, 2*(4), 317–338.

Ebben, J., & Johnson, A. (2006). Bootstrapping in small firms: An empirical analysis of change over time. *Journal of Business Venturing 21*(6), 851–865.

Engstrom, C. (2012). An autoethnographic account of prosaic entrepreneurship. *Tamara Journal of Critical Organisation Inquiry, 10*(1), 41.

Ensley, M. D., Pearce, C. L., Hmieleski, K.M. (2006). The moderating effect of environmental dynamism on the relationship between entrepreneur leadership behavior and new venture performance. *Journal of Business Venturing 21*(2), 243–263.

Ericsson, K. A. (1985). Memory skill. *Canadian Journal of Psychology/Revue canadienne de psychologie, 39*(2), 188.

Ericsson, K. A. (1998). The Scientific study of expert levels of performance: General implications for optimal learning and creativity 1. *High Ability Studies, 9*(1), 75–100.

Ericsson, K. A. (2006). *The Cambridge handbook of expertise and expert performance.* Cambridge, England: Cambridge University Press.

Ericsson, K. A. (2007). Deliberate practice and the modifiability of body and mind: Toward a science of the structure and acquisition of expert and elite performance. *International Journal of Sport Psychology, 38*(1), 4.

Ericsson, K. A., & Charness, N. (1994). Expert performance: Its structure and acquisition. *American Psychologist, 49*(8), 725.

Ericsson, K. A., Krampe, R. T., & Tesch-Romer, C. (1993). The role of deliberate practice in the acquisition of expert performance. *Psychological Review, 100*(3), 363.

Ericsson, K. A., & Lehmann, A. C. (1996). Expert and exceptional performance: Evidence of maximal adaptation to task constraints. *Annual Review of Psychology, 47*(1), 273–305.

Ericsson, K. A., Roring, R. W., & Nandagopal, K. (2007). Giftedness and evidence for reproducibly superior performance: An account based on the expert performance framework. *High Ability Studies, 18*(1), 3–56.

Ericsson, K. A., & Simon, H. A. (1980). Verbal reports as data. *Psychological Review, 87*(3), 215.

Fletcher, D. E. (2011). A curiosity for contexts: Entrepreneurship, enactive research and autoethnography. *Entrepreneurship and Regional Development, 23*(1-2), 65–76.

Gartner, W. B. (1985) A framework for describing and classifying the phenomenon of new venture creation. *Academy of Management Review, 10*(4), 696–706.

Gartner, W. B. (1988). Who is an entrepreneur? is the wrong question. *American Journal of Small Business, 12*(4), 11–32.

Gartner, W. B. (1990). What are we talking about when we talk about entrepreneurship? *Journal of Business Venturing, 5*(1), 15–28.

Gatewood, E. J., Shaver, K.G., & Gartner, W. B. (1995). A longitudinal study of cognitive factors influencing start-up behaviors and success at venture creation. *Journal of Business Venturing, 10* (5): 371–391.

Geiger, S., Keating, A., & McLoughlin, D. (2013). Riding the practice waves: Social resourcing practices during new venture development. *Entrepreneurship Theory and Practice, 38*(5), 1207–1235.

Gherardi, S., & Perrotta, M. (2014). Gender, ethnicity and social entrepreneurship: Qualitative Approaches to the Study of Entrepreneuring. In E. Chell & M. Karatas-Ozkan (Eds.), *Handbook of research in small business and entrepreneurship* (pp. 130–147). Cheltenham, England: Elgar.

Gordon, S. R. (2012). Action's place the venture creation process. In A. C. Corbett & J. A. Katz (Eds.), *Entrepreneurial action: Advances in entrepreneurship, firm emergence and growth* (vol. 14, pp. 161–205). Bingley, England: Emerald.

Graebner, M. E., & Eisenhardt, K. M. (2004). The seller's side of the story: Acquisition as courtship and governance as syndicate in entrepreneurial firms. *Administrative Science Quarterly, 49*(3), 366–403.

Greve, W. (2001). Traps and gaps in action explanation: Theoretical problems of a psychology of human action. *Psychological Review, 108*(2), 435.

Haber, S., & Reichel, A. (2007). The cumulative nature of the entrepreneurial process: The contribution of human capital, planning and environment resources to small venture performance. *Journal of Business Venturing, 22*(1), 119–145.

Hébert, R. F., & Link, A. N. (1988). *The entrepreneur: Mainstream views & radical critiques*. Santa Barbara, CA: Praeger.

Hjorth, D. (2005). Organizational entrepreneurship with de Certeau on creating heterotopias (or spaces for play). *Journal of Management Inquiry, 14*(4), 386–398.

Hjorth, D., & Holt, R. (2016). It is entrepreneurship, not enterprise. Ai Weiwei as entrepreneur. *Journal of Business Venturing Insights, 5*(6), 50–54.

Honig, B. (2004). Entrepreneurship education: Toward a model of contingency-based business planning. *Academy of Management Learning & Education, 3*(3), 258–273.

Honig, B., & Karlsson, T. (2004). Institutional forces and the written business plan. *Journal of Management, 30*(1), 29–48.

Ireland, R. D., Hitt, M. A., & Sirmon, D. G. (2003). A model of strategic entrepreneurship: The construct and its dimensions. *Journal of Management, 29*(6), 963–989.

Jack, S. L., & Anderson, A. R. (2002). The effects of embeddedness on the entrepreneurial process. *Journal of Business Venturing, 17*(5), 467–487.

Jayawarna, D., Rouse, J., & Kitching, J. (2013). Entrepreneur motivations and life course. *International Small Business Journal, 31*(1), 34–56.

Johannisson, B. (2011). Towards a practice theory of entrepreneuring. *Small Business Economics, 36*(2), 135–150.

Johnstone, B. A. (2007). Ethnographic methods in entrepreneurship research. In H. Neergaard & J. P. Ulhoi (Eds.), *Handbook of qualitative research methods in entrepreneurship research* (pp. 97–121). Cheltenham, Engalnd: Elgar.

Joyce, G. H. (1916). *Principles of logic*. New York, NY:Longmans, Green and Co.

Karlsson, T., & Honig, B. (2009). Judging a business by its cover: An institutional perspective on new ventures and the business plan. *Journal of Business Venturing, 24*(1), 27–45.

Kirzner, I. M. (1973/1978). *Competition and entrepreneurship*, Chicago, IL: University of Chicago Press.

Kirzner, I. M. (1983). *Perception, opportunity, and profit: Studies in the theory of entrepreneurship*. Chicago, IL: University of Chicago Press.

Kirzner, I. M. (1997). Entrepreneurial discovery and the competitive market process: An Austrian approach. *Journal of Economic Literature, 35*(1), 60–85.

Kirzner, I. M. (2009). The alert and creative entrepreneur: A clarification. *Small Business Economics, 32*(2), 145–152.

Lackeus, M., Lundqvist, M., & Middleton, K. W. (2015). *Opening up the black box of entrepreneurial education*. Paper presented at the 3E Conference. April 23–24. Luneburg, Germany.

Levitis, D. A., Lidicker, W. Z. Jr., & Freund, G. (2009). Behavioural biologists do not agree on what constitutes behaviour. *Animal Behaviour, 78*(1), 103–110.

Liao, J., & Gartner, W. B. (2006). The effects of pre-venture plan timing and perceived environmental uncertainty on the persistence of emerging firms. *Small Business Economics, 27*(1), 23–40.

Martens, M. L., Jennings, J. E., & Jennings, P. D. (2007). Do the stories they tell get them the money they need? The role of entrepreneurial narratives in resource acquisition. *Academy of Management Journal, 50*(5), 1107–1132.

Maxwell, A. L., Jeffrey, S. A., & Lévesque, M. (2011). Business angel early stage decision making. *Journal of Business Venturing, 26*(2), 212–225.

Maxwell, A. L., & Lévesque, M. (2014). Trustworthiness: A critical ingredient for entrepreneurs seeking investors. *Entrepreneurship Theory and Practice, 38*(5), 1057–1080.

McMullen, J. S., & Shepherd, D. A. (2006). Entrepreneurial action and the role of uncertainty in the theory of the entrepreneur. *Academy of Management Review, 31*(1), 132–152.

Merzenich, M. (2008). *Think faster, focus better, and remember more—rewiring our brain to stay younger and smarter*. [Google TechTalks video]. Retrieved from https://www.youtube.com/watch?v=UyPrL0cmJRs.

Merzenich, M. (2009). *Growing evidence of brain plasticity*. [Ted video]. Retrieved from https://www.ted.com/talks/michael_merzenich_on_the_elastic_brain/transcript?language=en

Murmann, J. P. (2003, March). Evolutionary thought in management and organization theory at the beginning of the new millennium: A symposium on the state of the art and opportunities for future research. *Journal of Management Inquiry, 12,* 22–40.

Nicolini, D. (2012). *Practice theory, work and organization: An introduction.* Oxford, England: Oxford University Press.

Orser, B. J., Riding, A. L., & Manley, K. (2006). Women entrepreneurs and financial capital. *Entrepreneurship Theory and Practice, 30*(5), 643–665.

Parhankangas, A., & Ehrlich, M. (2014). How entrepreneurs seduce business angels: An impression management approach. *Journal of Business Venturing, 29*(4), 543–564.

Pentland, B. T. (1999). Building process theory with narrative: From description to explanation. *Academy of Management Review, 24*(4), 711–724.

Poldner, K. (2013).Un-dress: Stories of ethical fashion entrepreneuring (Doctoral dissertation). University of St.Gallen, School of Management, Economics, Law, Social Sciences and International Affairs, Netherlands.

Pollack, J. M., Rutherford, M. W., & Nagy, B. G. (2012). Preparedness and cognitive legitimacy as antecedents of new venture funding in televised business pitches. *Entrepreneurship Theory and Practice, 36*(5), 915–939.

Reynolds, P. D. (1991). Sociology and entrepreneurship: Concepts and contributions. *Entrepreneurship Theory and Practice, 16*(2), 47–70.

Reynolds, P. D., & White, S. B. (1997). *The entrepreneurial process: Economic growth, men, women, and minorities.* Westport, CT: Quorum Books.

Riessman, C. K. (2008). *Narrative methods for the human sciences.* Thousand Oaks, CA: Sage.

Rindova, V., Barry, D., & Ketchen, D. J. (2009). Entrepreneuring as emancipation. *Academy of Management Review, 34*(3), 477–491.

Robinson, S., & Blenker, P. (2014). Tensions between rhetoric and practice in entrepreneurship education: An ethnography from Danish higher education. *European Journal of Higher Education, 4*(1), 80–93.

Sarasvathy, S. D. (2001). Causation and effectuation: Toward a theoretical shift from economic inevitability to entrepreneurial contingency. *Academy of Management Review, 26*(2), 243–263.

Sarasvathy, S. D. (2008). *Effectuation: Elements of entrepreneurial expertise.* Cheltenham, England: Elgar.

Sarasvathy, S. D., & Dew, N. (2005). New market creation through transformation. *Journal of Evolutionary Economics, 15*(5), 533–565.

Scherdin, M. (2007). The invisible foot: Survival of new art ideas on the swedish art arena: An autoethnographic atudy of nonTV-TVstation (Doctoral dissertation). Uppsala University, Sweden.

Schumpeter, J. A. (1934). *The theory of economic development: An inquiry into profits, capital, credit, interest, and the business cycle* (vol. 55). New York, NY: Transaction.

Shah, S. K. (2003). Community-based innovation and product development: Findings from open source software and consumer sporting goods (Doctoral dissertation). Massachusetts Institute of Technology, MA.

Shah, S., & Tripsas, M. (2004). When do user-innovators start firms? Towards a theory of user entrepreneurship. Boston, MA: Harvard Business School Publishing.

Shah, S. K., & Tripsas, M. (2007). The accidental entrepreneur: The emergent and collective process of user entrepreneurship. *Strategic Entrepreneurship Journal, 1*(1-2), 123–140.

Shane, S., Locke, E. A., & Collins, C. J. (2003). Entrepreneurial motivation. *Human resource Management Review, 13*(2), 257–279.

Shane, S., & Venkataraman, S. (2000). The promise of entrepreneurship as a field of research. *Academy of Management Review, 25*(1), 217–226.

Shaver, K. G. (2012). Entrepreneurial action: Conceptual foundations and research challenges. In A. C. Corbett & J. A. Katz (Eds.), *Entrepreneurial action: advances in entrepreneurship, firm emergence and growth* (vol. 14, pp. 281–306). Bingley, England: Emerald.

Simon, H. A. (1992). What is an "explanation" of behavior? *Psychological Science 3*(3), 150–161.

Stewart, A., & Aldrich, H. (2015). Collaboration between management and anthropology researchers: Obstacles and opportunities. *The Academy of Management Perspectives, 29*(2), 173–192.

Steyaert, C. (2007). "Entrepreneuring" as a conceptual attractor? A review of process theories in 20 years of entrepreneurship studies. *Entrepreneurship and Regional Development, 19*(6), 453–477.

Steyaert, C. (2011). Entrepreneurship as in(ter)vention: Reconsidering the conceptual politics of method in entrepreneurship studies. *Entrepreneurship and Regional Development, 23*(1-2), 77–88.

Tedmanson, D., Verduyn, K., Essers, C., & Gartner, W. B. (2012). Critical perspectives in entrepreneurship research. *Organization, 19*(5), 531–541.

Terjesen, S., & Elam, A. (2009). Transnational entrepreneurs' venture internationalization strategies: A practice theory approach. *Entrepreneurship Theory and Practice, 33*, 1093–1120.

Thierry, B., Aureli, F., Nunn, C. L., Petit, O., Abegg, C., & de Waal, B. M. (2008). A comparative study of conflict resolution in macaques: Insights into the nature of trait covariation. *Animal Behaviour, 75*(3), 847–860.

Tuckman, B. W. (2012). *Conducting educational research*. Lanham, MD: Rowman & Littlefield.

Webster, L., & Mertova, P. (2007). *Using narrative inquiry as a research method: An introduction to using critical event narrative analysis in research on learning and teaching*. London, England: Routledge.

Whetten, D. A. (1989). What constitutes a theoretical contribution? *Academy of management review, 14*(4), 490–495.

Williams, A. (2013). A study on the art and science of pitching new businesses (Doctoral dissertation). Massachusetts Institute of Technology, MA.

Wilson, E. O., & Ros. J. (1999). *Consilience: The unity of knowledge*. New York, NY: Vintage Books.

Zhang, J., Souitaris, V., Soh, P.-H., & Wong, P-K. (2008). A contingent model of network utilization in early financing of technology ventures. *Entrepreneurship Theory and Practice, 32*(4), 593–613.

Section 2

The Individual: Psychology of Entrepreneurship

5

The Psychology of Entrepreneurship: A Selective Review and a Path Forward

Kelly G. Shaver[a] and Amy E. Davis[b]

[a] *College of Charleston*
[b] *MindCette, LLC*

Introduction

The creation of a new business is not an event, but a process undertaken by one person or by a team of people. As many writers have acknowledged, the cognitive processes, personal motives, actions performed, and interpersonal processes involved are all fair topics for psychological inquiry. In this selective review we will show how the "psychology of entrepreneurship" has evolved from a relatively simplistic beginning to a recent view that is much more highly nuanced. We will first describe several of the ideas borrowed from psychology (mostly, though not exclusively, from personality and social psychology) that have been adapted for use in entrepreneurship. We will address the issues that arise when "the founder" changes to a "founding team." We then conclude with an argument for greater complexity in future work on entrepreneurial psychology.

Why Ask Why?

Why do people start businesses? Why do some succeed at this endeavor when others do not? Why does a founding team have the "chemistry" so desirable to investors? More generally, why do people of any sort do what they do? One of the first things one notices about these questions is that they are more likely to arise when an action or an outcome is unexpected or counternormative. When a behavior is not only expected, but practically universal, questions about "why" tend not to be very interesting to psychology. For example, consider "why do people desire closeness with others, either in a romantic sense or a platonic sense?" Answers to this question likely involve biological, social, or cultural factors much more than they involve issues of individual psychological processes. The latter come into play primarily when attempting to explain why *some* people do things that others do not do. Or even within one person, why do *some* personal characteristics become most important when others fall into the background? The

The Wiley Handbook of Entrepreneurship, First Edition.
Edited by Gorkan Ahmetoglu, Tomas Chamorro-Premuzic, Bailey Klinger, & Tessa Karcisky.
© 2017 John Wiley & Sons Ltd. Published 2017 by John Wiley & Sons Ltd.

search for explanations follows behavior that is statistically rare. Nobody asks, "Why do most people not become entrepreneurs?" but rather "Why do some people do it?" Psychological answers to this question began with single traits, but in the future, the explanations will need to become more complex.

Given the fact that there are at least four books on psychological processes in entrepreneurship (Baum, Frese, & Baron, 2007; Brännback & Carsrud, 2016; Carsrud & Brännback, 2009; Mitchell, Mitchell, & Randolph-Seng, 2014) as well as collections that contain chapters on psychological processes (Acs & Audretsch, 2010; Fayolle, 2014), a comprehensive review of psychological processes and theories involved in explanations of entrepreneurial behavior is simply beyond the scope of a single chapter. Consequently, what follows is an admittedly selective illustration of the various forms that such explanations have taken in the past, followed by a discussion of what we believe would be a fruitful direction for future research to take.

The Personality Approach

Single Traits

Achievement Motivation

Beginning with McClelland's early work (1961) on the relationship between achievement strivings and entrepreneurial action a number of individual psychological traits have been advanced as possible explanations for entrepreneurial behavior. In addition to achievement motivation, frequently mentioned traits include such things as locus of control (Phares, 1971; Rotter, 1966), risk propensity (Jackson, Hourany, & Vidmar, 1972), and self-efficacy (Bandura, 1977, 1986, 2012). More recently, negative characteristics such as the "dark triad" of narcissism (Campbell & Miller, 2011; Smith, Sherry, Chen, Saklofske, Flett, & Hewitt, 2016), Machiavellianism (Castille, Kuyumcu, & Bennett, 2017; originally assessed by Christie & Geis, 1970), and psychopathy (Jonason & Jackson, 2016) have begun to be considered in entrepreneurship research, as has the psychological condition of attention deficit hyperactivity disorder (see, e.g., Wiklund, Wei, & Patzelt, 2016).

In his comprehensive theory of personality, Murray (1938) argued that a person's behavior could be explained by a combination of relatively enduring internal predispositions to action, called *needs*, and the situational factors, called environmental *press*, that might facilitate or inhibit the expression of a need. Murray developed a projective test, the Thematic Apperception Test (TAT) to measure a variety of needs (including achievement, which Murray called *n*Ach). A person's responses to the series of 20 pictures in the TAT reveal the individual's various needs. According to McClelland, Atkinson, Clark, and Lowell (1953) only four of the pictures are typically used to assess achievement needs.

In a later formulation of achievement motivation, Atkinson (1958) pointed out that the individual's responses to TAT pictures reveal only a motive for success (M_S). The tendency to approach success is also affected by the incentive value provided by success (I_S) and the (environmentally influenced) probability of success (P_S), with these two elements being inversely related. In addition to the motive to approach success, there is also a motive to avoid failure (M_{AF}), affected by both the probability of failure and the (negative) incentive value of failure. An individual's resultant achievement motivation is the difference between M_S and M_{AF}. Consequently, a person can have high resultant achievement motivation either by having an extreme desire for success paired with a moderate fear of failure, or a moderate desire for success coupled with essentially zero fear of failure. So from our perspective, an entrepreneur who is "driven" would have the same resultant achievement motivation as one who was "fearless." On the other hand, it is hard to imagine that two such entrepreneurs would have, say, identical propensities toward risk. There are other measures of achievement motivation (Carsrud, Brännback, Elfving, & Brandt, 2009) and not surprisingly, achievement has long been related to entrepreneurial performance (Johnson, 1990).

Risk Propensity

As Palich and Bagby (1995) note, the idea of risk was part of the first formal theory of entrepreneurship (Cantillon, 1755). Risk propensity is another personal characteristic popularly attributed to entrepreneurs, but current research suggests that there are limits. Within the psychological literature, an early discussion of risk by Jackson, Hourany, and Vidmar (1972) found different uses of the term. First, there was *monetary* risk, the willingness to trade security for a better payoff or more generally to take chances for possible financial gain. This sense of risk is most probably the one attached to entrepreneurial action. The second sense of risk identified by Jackson et al. (1972) is the *physical* risk that accompanies taking part in activities that could lead to personal injury. People may say that an entrepreneur who bets an entire personal fortune on a venture with a low probability of success is "working without a net," but that is not literally the case. A third category is *social* risk, the willingness to speak nothing but the truth regardless of the consequences. This particular risk might actually be smaller for an entrepreneur whose business success depends on the market than for a company employee whose success depends on the good graces of superiors. Finally, there is *ethical* risk, the willingness to contravene normative standards or to use deceit to gain one's objectives. We are reminded of Martin Shkreli's move in 2015 to raise the price of the antiparasitic drug widely used by HIV-positive individuals, Daraprim, by over 5,000 percent, an incident that suggests the possibility of an inverse relationship between monetary risk and ethical risk for the actions of an entrepreneur.

Risk propensity has been measured in a number of ways within the management and entrepreneurship literature. Some studies have used the Kogan and Wallach (1964) Choice Dilemmas Questionnaire (such as Brockhaus, 1980). This questionnaire invites respondents to indicate the odds of success they would need before undertaking a risky activity (sometimes the activity involves monetary risk, sometimes physical risk, sometimes social risk). MacCrimmon and Wehrung (1986, 1990) have reviewed 13 separate measures of risk, including those involving gambles (choice among multiple options, with variations in probabilities and sizes of payoffs), those based on investment decisions, and those derived from Zuckerman's sensation-seeking attitude scale (Zuckerman, Kolin, Price, & Zoob, 1964). Regardless of the psychological measures used to assess risk propensity, a number of meta-analyses (e.g., Jain, 2011; Niess & Biemann, 2014; Stewart & Roth, 2001, 2004) and narrative reviews (e.g., Chell, 2008; Shaver, Schjoedt, Passarelli, & Reeck, in press) suggest that although entrepreneurs may be slightly higher than others in risk propensity, that one dimension is surely insufficient as "the" explanation for entrepreneurial behavior.

Broad Sets of Dimensions

Inventories of Traits

When one's objective is to identify personal characteristics that contribute to entrepreneurial tendencies, performance, and even success, the path of least resistance is to choose scales that purport to measure specific traits thought to be important. Everyone expects that entrepreneurial behavior should be related to achievement motivation. After all, entrepreneurs routinely achieve goals that many of us consider nearly impossible. Similarly, the popular wisdom holds that entrepreneurs do what they do by taking risks that would make the rest of us uncomfortable. So achievement motivation and risk propensity are immediately plausible candidates for examination. As noted earlier, others in the same category are self-efficacy (Bandura, 1977, 2012), locus of control (Paulhus, 1983; Paulhus & Van Selst, 1993; Phares, 1971; Rotter, 1966), and desire for autonomy (van Gelderen, 2016; van Gelderen & Jansen, 2006). Note that all of these are dimensions on which the initial expectation is that entrepreneurs will be dramatically *different* from the rest of us.

But the search for expected differences is not the only way to examine the psychological attributes of entrepreneurs. The alternative is to begin with dimensions that presume to describe everyone, and only then ask where entrepreneurs fall on these dimensions. One of the major achievements of modern personality theory is the construction of a set of (a few) dimensions that together are expected to describe everyone. Some of the early broad-based personality assessment measures owe a debt to clinical practice, as they are patterned after the Minnesota Multiphasic Personality Inventory (MMPI, Hathaway & McKinley, 1942) originally constructed to identify various personality disorders. Rather than base the items on some form of psychodynamic theory, the creators of the MMPI used an *empirical* criterion. Specifically, they tested known groups (people already diagnosed with one or another personality or behavioral disorder) to identify items that were answered differently by the different groups. Only with a later version (MMPI-2) were normal adults included in the reference population. The current MMPI-2 has 567 true–false items and requires 90 to 120 minutes to complete, a time commitment completely impractical for testing entrepreneurs.

A different sort of atheoretical approach embodied in broad-dimension measures is the California Psychological Inventory (CPI; Gough, 1956, 1989). Like the MMPI-2, this test consists of (434) true–false questions. But here the attempt was to capture "folk concepts" that describe individuals, such as dominance, sociability, or independence. From the standpoint of entrepreneurship research, there are two fundamental problems with the CPI. The first problem is the fact that because the scales were constructed to reflect Gough's view of "folk psychology" (the explanations that would be provided by people without training in social science), many of the dimensions are correlated. These intercorrelations are not especially helpful when the research objective is to identify particular characteristics of entrepreneurs. Additionally, the scale takes from 45 to 60 minutes to complete. This may be tolerable in some populations that have been tested—for example, high school or college students—but would, like the MMPI-2, be unacceptable in research involving entrepreneurs who are constantly pressed for time.

A second approach is embodied in the Jackson Personality Inventory (JPI-R, Jackson, 1976, 1994). The JPI also consists of (320) true–false items. Unlike the "folk psychology" origins of the CPI, however, the JPI was originally designed to assess constructs specified in Murray's (1938) system of needs. It contains five scales with a total of 15 subscales. Though the JPI-R is theoretically derived, with much less in the way of scale overlap, it still requires some 45 minutes to complete.

Latent Dimensions

The third approach to defining human personality begins not with folk psychology or psychological theory, but rather with *words*—specifically, with a large number (3,320 as of November, 2016) of self-descriptions. This set is the International Personality Item Pool (IPIP) originally established by Goldberg and his collaborators (Goldberg et al., 2006). The complete description of the IPIP can be found at http://ipip.ori.org, a site originally created by staff of the Oregon Research Institute. Although the IPIP items are given in first-person form, this very open-source process also provides directions for constructing scales worded in the third person. Some of the items are worded in the positive direction, some are worded in the negative direction, and regardless of direction respondents are asked to say whether the descriptor is "very inaccurate," "moderately inaccurate," "neither inaccurate nor accurate," "moderately accurate," or "very accurate." Typically respondents are asked to describe some target person (self or other) using a large number of the descriptive statements (often a few hundred). Positively worded items are scored 1–5, negatively worded items are scored 5–1. When the items are scored, the results are subjected to some form of factor analysis to identify the several underlying dimensions onto which the items collectively load. The outcome, as Lewis and Bates (2014) note, is that "it is now uncontroversial to assert that a small number of latent factors—often five (Costa & McCrae, 1992) or, less frequently, three (Eysenck & Eysenck, 1975), or six (Lee and Ashton, 2004)—account for the bulk of reliable variance in a wide spectrum of traits and behaviors" (p. 9). It is important to note that the factors emerge from analyses of the descriptive words, not from examination of the behaviors of individuals selected for being at the extreme on some dimension.

The Big Five are Openness to experience, Conscientiousness, Extraversion, Agreeableness, and Neuroticism (here arranged in one of the common mnemonic orders, OCEAN). Each of these is a dimension that consists of separate elements. Openness to experience distinguishes people who are naturally curious and inventive from those who are cautious and consistent. Conscientiousness represents the poles of efficient/organized versus easygoing/careless. Conscientious people are dependable, organized, prefer planned to spontaneous behavior, and are interested in achievement. Extraversion differentiates people who are gregarious and outgoing from those who are solitary and reserved. Agreeableness represents the difference between friendliness/compassion and a detached, analytical nature. Finally, Neuroticism is the dimension that runs from sensitive/nervous to secure/confident.

Several studies have tested for differences in entrepreneurial performance based on the Big Five. In one such study, Ciavarella, Buchholtz, Riordan, Gatewood, and Stokes (2004) found that conscientiousness was positively related to venture survival. There was, however, an unanticipated negative relationship between openness to experience and long-term venture survival. Extraversion, emotional stability (the positive end of Neuroticism), and agreeableness were unrelated to venture success. Before concluding that an extraverted, emotionally stable, and agreeable person would make a terrible entrepreneur, it is worth noting that one study is rarely sufficient as a basis for such general conclusions. In a meta-analysis of 23 separate studies, Zhao and Seibert (2006) used the dimensions of the Big Five as an organizing principle to test for effects of various personality characteristics on entrepreneurial status. In other words, not all the research Zhao and Seibert reviewed actually employed the Big Five, but rather employed individual traits that could be characterized by Big Five dimensions. Their research showed that compared with managers, entrepreneurs were higher on conscientiousness and openness to experience and lower on neuroticism and agreeableness. Because these results differ somewhat from those of Ciavarella et al. (2004), it should be noted that the dependent variable was a difference between entrepreneurs and managers, not the survival of an entrepreneur's business.

The five-factor model has typically been found when the personality descriptors are used in the English language. Recently, however, analyses of the lexical structure of personality descriptors used in languages other than English have suggested that there should be a sixth latent personality trait in addition to the Big Five (Ashton & Lee, 2008; Ashton, Lee, & Goldberg, 2007). This is Honesty-Humility: the degree to which a person is sincere, honest, loyal, and modest versus sly, deceitful, greedy, and pretentious. When the sixth dimension is added, the group of traits is identified by the acronym HEXACO. This stands for Honesty/Humility, Emotionality, eXtraversion, Agreeableness, Conscientiousness, and Openness to experience. Extraversion, Conscientiousness, and Openness to experience are essentially the same in the two trait systems. By contrast, the three HEXACO dimensions of Humility, Agreeableness, and Emotionality together correspond to the elements of the Big Five's Agreeableness and Neuroticism. Given that so much of contemporary research in entrepreneurship takes place in countries where the native language is not English, it might serve the field well to use the HEXACO factors, rather than the big five factors, as dimensions on which to characterize entrepreneurs.

The Social Cognition Approach

A substantial amount of research in entrepreneurship has dealt not with inherent personality dispositions, but rather with how entrepreneurs might "think differently." This work is in the general area of social cognition (Fiske & Taylor, 1991), the subfield of social psychology that addresses the ways in which people obtain, remember, and use information about others. There have been two special issues of *Entrepreneurship Theory & Practice* devoted to the social cognition approach to entrepreneurship (Mitchell, Busenitz, Lant, et al., 2004; Mitchell, Busenitz, Bird, et al., 2007), a special issue of the *International Journal of Management Reviews* (Grégoire, Cornelissen, Dimov, & van Burg, 2015) as well as a number of separate summaries of the approach (Arend et al., 2016; Baron & Ward, 2004; Grégoire, Corbett, & McMullen, 2011). Indeed, there have been calls for "direct" measurement of cognitive processes in entrepreneurship through the methods of neuropsychology (de Holan, 2014; Shaver et al., in press). Again, our review here is selective, concentrating on only two aspects of research that have received significant attention.

Career Reasons

The major drawback of the broad-brush personality approach inherent in the Big Five or Big Six is that these personal dimensions are distal—general behavioral predispositions that guide behavior, other things equal. So although they might be of significant value in distinguishing a person who is likely to create *some* company from a person who will not do so, they are much less informative about why an entrepreneur would choose to create a particular kind of company, to attack a particular market, or to pursue a particular business strategy. For those operational details, some psychological characteristic more proximal to the events would be helpful.

New businesses are not created by accident; they are the product of considerable effort expended over time in the direction specified by the entrepreneur's intentions (Fayolle & Liñán, 2014; Krueger, 2009). Not surprisingly, where intentional behavior is concerned, many investigators have wondered about the reasons that might underlie this venture-formation behavior.

Initial examination of an entrepreneur's reasons began with an influential paper by Scheinberg and Macmillan (1988). With general guidance from such theories as need for independence, need for material incentives, need for social approval, or drive to fulfill personal values, these authors created a set of 38 reasons that an individual might pursue one career alternative (such as entrepreneurship) as opposed to another. After surveying over 1,400 independent business owners/founders in 11 countries, the authors conducted a factor analysis of the 38 items. Seventeen were dropped, and the remaining 21 produced six scales. In the years since, the set of "career reasons" has been reduced to a smaller number (Birley & Westhead, 1994), had items added (Shane, Kolvereid, & Westhead, 1991), and a parallel stream of research has also examined reasons for getting into business (Kolvereid, 1996).

In a thorough review of the reasons literature, Carter, Gartner, Shaver, & Gatewood (2003) grouped them into five broad categories and added items to reflect gender differences in the importance of self-realization. Using only these few new items and items that had achieved factor loadings of at least .5 in prior work, Carter et al. (2003) identified six dimensions: self-realization, financial success, roles (performing according to the expectations of others), innovation, recognition (desire for one's accomplishments to be known), and independence. The 18 items constituting these six factors were included in the US Panel Study of Entrepreneurial Dynamics (PSED I; Gartner, Shaver, Carter, & Reynolds, 2004). PSED I was a nationally representative longitudinal dataset that included nascent entrepreneurs (people in the process of starting businesses) and a comparison group (also nationally representative) of individuals who were not starting businesses. Interestingly, the results of this study showed *no* differences between nascent entrepreneurs and the comparison group on four of the six factors: self-realization, financial success, innovation, and independence. Only on roles (items such as to continue a family tradition and to follow the example of a person I admire) and recognition (items such as to achieve something and get recognition or gain a higher position for myself in society) were there nascent-comparison differences.

The career reasons items were also included in PSED II (but only 14 of the 18). In contrast to PSED I, PSED II contained no comparison group, but did gather extensive information about the structure of founding teams (Reynolds & Curtin, 2009). Factor analyses of the 14 career reasons in PSED II have shown three factors (Davis & Shaver, 2009) and when data from PSED I are combined with those from PSED II, factor analyses show two factors (Shaver, Blair, & Davis, 2014). Whether the number of factors is six, three, or two, it is clear that the career reasons are elements of social cognition that matter in the production of entrepreneurial behavior.

Attribution Processes

Not only are processes of social cognition involved in the production of entrepreneurial activity, they may also be involved in the continuation of such activity following early failures. The psychological literature is chock full of explanations for why people continue to engage in behavior that has brought them success. But not everyone succeeds. One of the psychologically most interesting features of entrepreneurs is that, following clear failures, they frequently redouble their efforts and move forward. By contrast, there is a long history of research in social psychology showing that responsibility for negative outcomes is to be avoided (e.g., Robbennolt, 2000) and entire theories on the attribution of blame (Malle, Guglielmo, & Monroe, 2014; Shaver, 1985).

Two explanations for the difference suggest themselves. First, most of the work on responsibility and blame has dealt with moral failures, but *business* failure may not carry the same societal stigma. Second, some of the same attribution processes implicated in responses to moral failure may operate—in a different way—in the case of entrepreneurial failure. Attribution principles distinguish causal explanations that are "stable" from those that are "variable"; they also distinguish those that are "internal" to the person from those that are "external" forces from outside the person. Using this four-fold classification, Gatewood, Shaver, and Gartner (1995) asked clients of a small business development center why they wanted to begin their proposed businesses. These explanations were coded (without knowledge of the respondent's sex) as internal/external and stable/variable. All respondents were contacted a year later, and roughly 60% of them responded. Females who had actually started their businesses had a year earlier expressed internal-stable reasons for entering business. By contrast, the males who had started companies had a year earlier expressed reasons that were external and stable. There are detailed instructions for accomplishing this sort of classification (Shaver, Gartner, Crosby, Bakalarova, & Gatewood, 2001). In addition, attribution approaches have been applied to strategic issues such as opportunity identification (Gartner, Shaver, & Liao, 2008), success among nascent entrepreneurs (Diochon, Menzies, & Gasse, 2007), or entrepreneurial failure (Mantere, Aula, Schildt, & Vaara, 2013).

Social Cognitive Theories

A number of social psychological theories have been adapted to the study of entrepreneurial behavior. In chronological order by date of the original theory (first citation listed), some of these are expectancy theory (Vroom, 1964; De Clercq, Menzies, Diochon, & Gasse, 2009; Renko, Kroeck, & Bullough, 2012), self-determination theory (Deci & Ryan, 1980, 2008, 2012; Iremadze, 2016; van Gelderen, 2010), the theory of planned behavior (Ajzen, 1985; Krueger, 2009), and regulatory focus theory (Higgins, 1998; Higgins & Cornwell, 2016; Hmieleski & Baron, 2008; McMullen & Kier, 2016). In part because of their relationships to entrepreneurial intentions, we shall confine the present discussion to expectancy and planned behavior.

Expectancy Theory

Although it was originally proposed as a theory of work motivation, expectancy theory (Vroom, 1964) is fundamentally psychological in character. The theory has three essential components: valence, instrumentality, and expectancy (hence, it is sometimes referred to as a "VIE" theory). Valence is the perceived attractiveness or worth of a particular outcome that might be obtained. The worth is "perceived" because different individuals can have different preference structures. There are first-level outcomes that can either be ends in themselves or be of value only because of the second-level outcomes to which they lead. Instrumentality is the perceived relationship between a first-level outcome and a corresponding second-level outcome. Finally, expectancy is the belief that a particular act will be followed by a particular outcome. In essence, expectancy is the subjective probability that outcome Y will follow the successful performance of behavior X. Originally the three elements of the theory were presumed to be multiplicative: if any one (valence, instrumentality, expectancy) is zero, there will be no motivation. Later research, however, more typically considers the three components separately (Renko, Kroeck, & Bullough, 2012; Van Eerde & Thierry, 1996).

The expectancy approach has been used in entrepreneurship research in both survey and experimental settings. Six items designed to test elements of the original VIE formulation were included in PSED I (Gatewood, 2004). Studies involving the PSED have shown clear differences in expectancy between nascent entrepreneurs and the members of the comparison group (Shaver, Gatewood, & Gartner, 2001) and that nascents with higher expectancies intend to put more effort into their ventures, though nascents motivated primarily by financial success expend effort regardless of their level of expectancy (Renko et al., 2012). In an experimental setting, Gatewood, Shaver, Powers, and Gartner (2002) tested the effort–performance linkage. With formal approval from the university's institutional review board, undergraduate students were given either positive or negative feedback about their likely entrepreneurial ability. Those who received positive feedback increased their expectancies concerning future business start-up, but interestingly did not alter their task quality or performance. As Renko et al. (2012) noted, future studies of entrepreneurial motivation would do well to include expectancy principles.

Theory of Planned Behavior

In the early years of attitude measurement and change within social psychology, it was taken for granted that an attitude included three components—cognitive, affective, and behavioral. The cognitive component was the individual's beliefs about the attitude object, the affective component was the person's positive or negative evaluation of the object (based on the beliefs), and the behavioral component was presumed to be a disposition to behave in a particular way toward the attitude object. The problem with this assumption, as Wicker (1969) persuasively pointed out, is that there was very little relationship between expressed attitudes and overt behavior. To try to improve this sort of prediction, Fishbein and Ajzen (1975) developed a revision to the previous attitude model. This model considered the various attributes of an attitude object separately (each one of these is a belief). Then there is a positive or negative evaluation of each attribute, and the sum of these belief X evaluation products is the affective response to the object. Perhaps their most important contribution was to argue for *behavioral* intentions: probable responses specific to time, location, and particular actions. In this sense, "I want to start a business" is different from "tomorrow morning at 10 am I will be visiting my attorney to have papers of organization drawn up for my business."

Over the years this formulation was expanded to include features representing the influence of other people and the likelihood of success. The fully revised model, called the theory of planned behavior (TPB; Ajzen, 1985) specifically included social norms (the opinions and expectations of others) and perceived behavioral control to reflect the fact that not all desired actions are in fact possible. In the TPB, there are reciprocal influences among social norms, perceived desirability, and perceived behavioral control, and together these affect entrepreneurial intentions. Indeed, Krueger (2009) has argued that the intentions themselves also exert reciprocal influence on the other elements. In the early attribution literature (Heider, 1958) intentions alone were never considered sufficient causes of action: some element of *effort* was also required. Heider recognized that the difference between personal causality and the causality inherent in physical systems was that only personal causality—involving both intention and exertion—was capable of redirecting action toward an "equifinal" goal if obstacles to goal attainment should get in the way.

In his discussion of entrepreneurial intentions, Krueger has suggested that principles from Bagozzi's theory of trying (Bagozzi, Dholakia, & Basuroy, 2003; Dholakia, Bagozzi, & Gopinath, 2007) should be incorporated into the study of entrepreneurial intentions. Finally, authors whose allegiance is to expectancy theory and those whose primary interest is TPB have been quick to point out the overlaps inherent in these two approaches to entrepreneurial motivation (Krueger, 2009; Renko et al., 2012) and to consider its relation to self-efficacy generally and to entrepreneurial self-efficacy specifically (McGee, Peterson, Mueller, & Sequeira, 2009; Zhao, Seibert, & Hills, 2005).

Entrepreneurial Teams

Approaches to Teams

Approximately half of all new entrepreneurs in the United States start their businesses with a team of at least one other person (Ruef, Aldrich, & Carter, 2003). But there is very little academic research on founding teams. In a 2012 review, Davidsson and Gordon found only two studies of teams out of 83 publications from panel-based data sets. Where research on founding teams does exist, it is devoted primarily to structural characteristics—past experience or educational background of team members, financial contributions, or network connections (Ruef et al., 2003)—rather than to the daily interactions among team members.

Teams are viewed as essential for many high-growth businesses that attract and require venture capital, so that members can specialize in complementary areas of the start-up, but teams are also common in the typical small start-up. Too often, researchers only collected data on one member of a team, often someone who was designated the primary owner/operator of the business. Thus, the bulk of research on entrepreneurs may leave out "hidden entrepreneurs" who were considered secondary owners and not in charge of the daily operations of the business. Data sets like the PSED II are unique, given that their sampling frame is households. In fact, a sizable fraction of business owners in the PSED II reported that they were not the primary owner/operator of the business. It is possible that the psychological predictors determining entry into entrepreneurship vary considerably depending on whether someone is the primary owner/operator or not.

There are both theories and research procedures showing the ways in which social and psychological processes can be examined in an entrepreneurial context. Early theoretical accounts of close interpersonal relationships are in an edited book by Kelley et al. (1983). Building on the concept of interdependence, Kelley et al. (1983) argue for the measurement of three central properties of an interaction between (typically only) two people. These properties are the frequency, diversity, and strength of the interaction. The essence of this approach has been captured by the Relationship Closeness Inventory (Berscheid, Snyder, & Omoto, 1989). Frequency of an interaction is the amount of time the partners (for our purposes these would be team members) spend in each other's company, both inside and outside of the work setting. Diversity is the number of specific, but different, activities that the partners (team members) engage in during a particular week. Strength is assessed by each partner's judgment of the extent to which the other partner influences one's thoughts, feelings, and behavior (in multiple domains).

Although originally the "close relationships" research was confined to the study of romantic partners, the general methods can easily be adapted to work on founding teams. For example, building on a meta-analysis by Bell (2007), O'Neill and Allen (2011) have used the Big Five personality inventory to create team-level measures of personality. This sort of aggregation can be done by combining the individual mean scores (when a trait is presumed to be additive), by indexing the variance (when a greater or lesser variation in the trait is presumed to be related to performance), or by using the maximum individual score (when the team's performance might be best related to the most capable individual). Other recent work has dealt with approach and avoidance motives (Gable & Impett, 2012) and the effects of differential power (Laurin, et al., 2016).

Team Structure

Research by Davis and Shaver (2012) demonstrated that, just as social networks change in composition over one's life course, the team composition of a business someone starts varies over that person's life course. For example, kin or spouse teams are most common when entrepreneurs are in their 30s, which is considered the launching stage of a career characterized by high rates of marriage, parenthood, and home ownership. One of the risks associated with self-organized teams is that team members may be too close in attitudes and perspective, thus reducing the team's ability to anticipate problems. This is the problem of homophily and it has a pervasive influence on social networks and results in the lack of diversity of entrepreneurial teams. Although demographic diversity has been studied (Steffens, Terjesen, & Davidsson, 2012), affective diversity, or diversity of psychological characteristics has been studied less so, particularly among entrepreneurial teams (Barsade, Ward, Turner, & Sonnenfeld, 2000; Kouamé, Oliver, & Poisson-de-Haro, 2015).

Toward a More Inclusive Future

Now is when we beg the reader's indulgence. The productive relationship between psychology and entrepreneurship can be expected both to continue and to expand in the future. But we believe, along with other voices, that this disciplinary interchange can be improved by beginning to consider it a research enterprise, rather than a large collection of individual studies. We all know the pressure, when submitting an article, to "tell a single story." Many factors contribute to this pressure. The scope of a project may be limited by the duration of access to a company or an incubator. The work may need to be done by the end of a summer or a term. Unlike our colleagues in the hard sciences, we may not have the internal or external funding needed to keep a "lab" going. By and large, our undergraduate and MBA students are seeking jobs, not doctoral placements, so there is little opportunity to train students who can later make independent contributions. When projects are completed, journals have suggested page limits for submissions. Promotion and tenure committees are often much better at counting than at reading. If we were somehow able to take an enterprise-level view, what might that look like?

Culturally Inclusive and Specific

Gender

It is still all too common to see articles describing "entrepreneurs" in which it is clear that all respondents are male. When seeking to predict, understand, or even promote entrepreneurial behavior, researchers and practitioners may be misguided in promoting a one-size-fits-all model of entrepreneurial behavior (see a special issue of *Entrepreneurship and Regional Development*, Brush & Cooper, 2012). At the same time, women entrepreneurs face a very different reality in becoming entrepreneurs than do men (Sullivan & Meek, 2012). Women are underrepresented in entrepreneurship and receive a very small amount of the venture capital funding (Brush, Carter, Gatewood, Greene, & Hart, 2006). Women are also underrepresented in key positions with which entrepreneurs must interact, so they may be excluded from important entrepreneurial networks or opportunities. Therefore, characteristics that might be highly associated with men becoming entrepreneurs may be very different from those associated with women becoming entrepreneurs. Indeed, Davis and Shaver (2012) found that the predictors of high-growth intentions differed greatly for men and women entrepreneurs. Thus, in studies that do not explicitly examine gender and have either no women or a smaller proportion of women in their sample, the relationships researchers find may not apply to all entrepreneurs.

Race and Ethnicity

Race and ethnicity can influence the types of opportunities nascent entrepreneurs recognize and then exploit. Race and ethnicity can also influence the networks entrepreneurs draw from when building their business ideas or launching their businesses, as well as influence the way in which they are received by customers, lenders, investors, and partners (e.g., see Bates & Robb, 2016). There are also race-based differences in the reasons that people select an entrepreneurial career (Edelman, Brush, Manolova, & Greene, 2010). The abilities of researchers to elucidate differences among entrepreneurs within and across different ethnic groups has been hampered by data sets with insufficient representation of entrepreneurs from minority groups. But this should not stop us from trying.

Life Course and Personal Context

Starting a business would be considered by life course scholars to be a significant life transition comparable to marriage, or becoming a parent. And just as marriage and parenthood have different causes and consequences on the lives of people depending on whether they are 19 or 45, for example, the predictors of starting a business at the beginning of a person's career can differ greatly from those of a person starting a business after decades in the labor market. For example, Davis and Shaver (2012) found that persons at the beginning of their careers (18–29 years old) had the greatest odds of intending to start high-growth businesses whereas individuals in their 30s were least likely to express intentions of starting a high-growth business. Further, whether individuals are living alone or are married with dependent children would likely influence the extent to which their psychological characteristics that may predispose them to entrepreneurial behavior are actually associated with starting a business.

Country of Origin

If the well-known Global Entrepreneurship Monitor (e.g., Kelley, Singer, & Herrington, 2016) studies have taught us anything, it is that there are wide differences in start-up rates across countries. This, despite there being three primary clusters of countries—factor-driven, efficiency-driven, and innovation-driven. There are substantial differences in ecosystems, participation by urban versus rural individuals, and political support for (in some cases even "tolerance of") entrepreneurial activity. It stands to reason that these country-level influences will have a bearing on what aspects of financial, social, and human capital are available to support entrepreneurial activity.

How can the various cultural and social supports/constraints be part of the research conversation? We propose two ways that this could happen. First, and simplest, would be for researchers to be clear and complete about who the participants were in their work. It is now becoming more common to include an operational definition of "entrepreneur" (such as "owner/manager," "founder," or even "founder with growth intentions"), but this should become the accepted standard, with manuscripts returned for correction prior to review. Moreover, manuscripts should be explicit about the country in which the research was performed, identify the distribution of race/ethnicity and gender (in at least a four-fold classification such as brown/white by female/male) of the participants, and provide information about the age of the participants. Second, just as some journals require specification of the appropriate JEL classification codes for content, the discipline should create an equivalent set of codes that represent the various demographic characteristics of the research participants.

Methodologically Inclusive and Specific

Theoretically Precise

As noted earlier, investigators approaching the study of entrepreneurship with a lens of expectancy theory and those using a lens of some version of the theory of planned behavior have already commented on the similarities between these two approaches. But the comparisons should not end there. How exactly is perceived behavioral control similar to, and different from, entrepreneurial self-efficacy? How is intrinsic versus extrinsic motivation similar to, and different from, the principles of self-determination theory? How is achievement motivation similar to, and different from, locus of control? How is an entrepreneur's internal attribution of success similar to, and different from, an overconfidence bias? This line of reasoning suggests that writers should be encouraged to do more than "draw on the principles of theory A." Rather, they should be asked also to identify the *other* theories that may overlap with theory A and present a conceptual comparison that allows the two or more theories either to make the same predictions, or better, to make differential predictions.

Multiple Dimensions

For many years, entrepreneurship was able to advance as a discipline, one single psychological characteristic at a time. That time has likely passed. Our attempts to understand the psychological characteristics of entrepreneurs should cease comparing entrepreneurs to "managers" (or any other comparison group) on one trait dimension at a time. Rather, we should be attempting—even within the context of a single research study—to locate both the entrepreneurs and the comparison individuals in an *N-dimensional space*. This is a reason to prefer either the Big Five or the HEXACO set of latent dimensions to, say, locus of control (by itself). Even if the investigator's choice is to use what we have called "single traits," more than one of them should be used at any given time.

Replication

The replication crisis in science has generated enough attention (e.g., Pashler & Wagenmakers, 2012) that it has its own Wikipedia page (https://en.wikipedia.org/wiki/Replication_crisis). Given the prevalence of psychological methods in entrepreneurship research, this is also a problem for our discipline. There are ways to minimize this problem. First and foremost, researchers need to provide detailed method sections—all the sophisticated analyses in the world will not help if readers have no idea what was actually done or said. If the study is an experiment, the exact instructions (that differ by conditions) should at minimum be included in an appendix that could be removed at the choice of an editor upon acceptance of the manuscript. If the study is a survey, the orienting instructions and stems of the questions should likewise be included. If the study is based on individual interviews, the questions and prompts should be stated, they should be delivered in the same order, and with the blessing of the research participants the interview sessions should be recorded so that the raw data can be shared (data sharing is mandated for any research supported by the US federal government) with anyone who desires to reanalyze the original material. In the entrepreneurship domain, the gold standard for sharing is probably the PSED (which has complete documentation, all data, all questionnaires, and all computer-aided-interview schedules available at http://www.psed.isr.umich.edu/psed/home). In addition to providing details of all methods, researchers should endeavor to perform either empirical replications (essentially identical procedures done either at different times or different institutional settings) or conceptual replications (tests of the same conceptual issues with different methods). Generating replicable data is more than just "better science," it is also critical if entrepreneurs and policymakers are to take our findings seriously.

Teams Over Time

If the research is being conducted on entrepreneurial teams—as we believe more should be in the future—longitudinal designs will be even more important than they are with individual entrepreneurs. Ideally, entrepreneurship researchers will come to value a multiplicity of methods, including experiments (Acs, Audretsch, Desai, & Welpe, 2010; Shaver, 2014), as well as the more usual interviews and surveys. When the target of investigation is entrepreneurial teams, however, longitudinal designs are practically a must. These might involve participant observation, personal diary records, or even "beeper" studies that ping participants at random times (for analysis methods see Nezlek, 2012, 2016). In any of these cases, what is critical is that the research be ongoing during the time that (a) team members might come or go, (b) the financing of the team's effort might change, or (c) a product might either launch or fail. It is relatively simple to determine causality if there is an environmental change followed by changes in the team's behavior (provided, of course, that accurate time records have been maintained). Much more difficult is the task of trying to assess the reciprocal causality that individual team members may have on one another. Perfect solutions to this problem are exceedingly difficult to find, but one that can be valuable is what we would call a "perturbation" approach in an analogy to some of the modern vehicle systems designed to keep a car in its own lane if the driver should fall asleep (or to brake even before a driver can do so). The system continually monitors the roadbed, "learning" the proper relationship of its sensors to the painted line. If the vehicle changes position relative to that line (and the human behind the wheel does nothing), then the vehicle corrects its own steering. To try to determine which team member is the one whose lead the other members follow, the researcher can (again, provided the records are sufficiently detailed) introduce an issue to some member of the team and track the communication patterns that ensue until the issue is resolved. But all of these operations require the time that is too often a luxury. On the other hand, precisely because longitudinal methods are so expensive, they are excellent candidates for funding either by national agencies or by companies who have a financial stake in knowing exactly what is happening within a start-up team. It is worth noting that a Scandinavian team led by Frédéric Delmar is as of this writing commencing just such a longitudinal study of entrepreneurial teams.

Conclusion

The relationship between psychology and entrepreneurship has been a productive one for a long time. As entrepreneurship researchers have become substantially more connected to the basic psychological literature, the research has become more interesting and more informative. We have provided examples of the use of single traits, broad personality dispositions, elements of social cognition, and theories imported from psychology. As valuable as all of this material has been to our understanding of the phenomenon that is entrepreneurial behavior, it is time to take a major leap forward to a more inclusive research future. We hope that our suggestions for better identification of the culture and personal context of entrepreneurs, the simultaneous use of multiple psychological dimensions, more detailed attention to methodological rigor and replication, and the longitudinal study of entrepreneurial teams will help the field reach its full potential.

References

Acs, Z., & Audretsch, D. (Eds.). (2010). *The handbook of entrepreneurship research: An interdisciplinary survey and introduction.* Dordrecht, Germany: Springer.

Acs, Z., Audretsch, D., Desai, S., & Welpe, I. (2010). On experiments in entrepreneurship research. *Journal of Economic Behavior & Organization, 76*(1), 1–2. doi: 10.1016/j.jebo.2010.06.007

Ajzen, I. (1985). From intentions to actions: A theory of planned behavior. In J. Kuhl & J. Beckmann (Eds.), *Action control: From cognition to behavior* (pp. 11–39). Berlin, Germany: Springer.

Arend, R. J., Cao, X., Grego-Nagel, A., Im, J., Yang, X., & Canavati, S. (2016). Looking upstream and downstream in entrepreneurial cognition: Replicating and extending the Busenitz and Barney (1997) study. *Journal of Small Business Management, 54*(4), 1147–1170. doi: 10.1111/jsbm.12233

Ashton, M. C., & Lee, K. (2008). The HEXACO model of personality structure. In G. J. Boyle, G. Matthews, & D. H. Saklofske (Eds.), *The SAGE handbook of personality theory and assessment. Vol 2: Personality measurement and testing.* (pp. 239–260). Thousand Oaks, CA,: Sage.

Ashton, M. C., Lee, K., & Goldberg, L. R. (2007). The IPIP-HEXACO scales: An alternative, public-domain measure of the personality constructs in the HEXACO model. *Personality and Individual Differences, 42*(8), 1515–1526.

Atkinson, J. W. (1958). *Motives in fantasy, action, and society: A method of assessment and study*. Oxford, England: Van Nostrand.

Bagozzi, R. P., Dholakia, U., & Basuroy, S. (2003). How effortful decisions get enacted: The motivating role of decision processes, desires & anticipated emotions. *Journal of Behavioral Decision Making, 16*(4), 273–295.

Bandura, A. (1977). Self-efficacy: Toward a unifying theory of behavioral change. *Psychological Review, 84*, 191–215.

Bandura, A. (1986). The explanatory and predictive scope of self-efficacy theory. *Journal of Social and Clinical Psychology, 4*(3), 359–373. doi: 10.1521/jscp.1986.4.3.359

Bandura, A. (2012). On the functional properties of perceived self-efficacy revisited. *Journal of Management, 38*(1), 9–44. doi: 10.1177/0149206311410606

Baron, R. A., & Ward, T. B. (2004). Expanding entrepreneurial cognition's toolbox: Potential contributions from the field of cognitive science. *Entrepreneurship: Theory & Practice, 28*(6), 553-573. doi: 10.1111/j.1540-6520.2004.00064.x

Barsade, S. G., Ward, A. J., Turner, J. D. F., & Sonnenfeld, J. A. (2000). To your heart's content: A model of affective diversity in top management teams. *Administrative Science Quarterly, 45*(4), 802–836. doi: 10.2307/2667020

Bates, T., & Robb, A. (2016). Impacts of owner race and geographic context on access to small-business financing. *Economic Development Quarterly, 30*(2), 159-170. doi:10.1177/0891242415620484

Baum, J. R., Frese, M., & Baron, R. A. (Eds.). (2007). *The psychology of entrepreneurship*. Mahwah, NJ: Erlbaum.

Bell, S. T. (2007). Deep-level composition variables as predictors of team performance: A meta-analysis. *Journal of Applied Psychology, 92*, 595–615.

Berscheid, E., Snyder, M., & Omoto, A. M. (1989). The Relationship Closeness Inventory: Assessing the closeness of interpersonal relationships. *Journal of Personality and Social Psychology, 57*, 792–807.

Birley, S., & Westhead, P. (1994). A taxonomy of business start-up reasons and their impact on firm growth and size. *Journal of Business Venturing, 9*(1), 7–31.

Brännback, M., & Carsrud, A. L. (Eds.). (2016). *Revisiting the entrepreneurial mind. Inside the black box: An expanded edition*. New York, NY: Springer.

Brockhaus, R. H. (1980). Risk taking propensity of entrepreneurs. *Academy of Management Journal, 23*, 509–520.

Brush, C. G., Carter, N. M., Gatewood, E. J., Greene, P. G., & Hart, M. M. (2006). The use of bootstrapping by women entrepreneurs in positioning for growth. *Venture Capital, 8*(1), 15–31. doi:10.1080/13691060500433975

Brush, C. G., & Cooper, S. Y. (2012). Female entrepreneurship and economic development: An international perspective (Special issue). *Entrepreneurship and Regional Development, 24*(1-2), 1–6. doi: 10.1080/08985626.2012.637340

Campbell, W. K., & Miller, J. D. (2011). *The handbook of narcissism and narcissistic personality disorder: Theoretical approaches, empirical findings, and treatments.* Hoboken, NJ: Wiley.

Cantillon, R. (1755). *Essai sur la nature du commerce en general* [Essay on the nature of trade in general]. London, England: Macmillan.

Carsrud, A. L., & Brännback, M. (2009). *Understanding the entrepreneurial mind: Opening the black box.* Dordrecht, Germany: Springer.

Carsrud, A. L., Brännback, M., Elfving, J., & Brandt, K. (2009). Motivations: The entrepreneurial mind and behavior. In A. L. Carsrud & M. Brännback (Eds.), *Understanding the entrepreneurial mind: Opening the black box* (pp. 141–165). Dordrecht, Germany: Springer.

Carter, N. M., Gartner, W. B., Shaver, K. G., & Gatewood, E. J. (2003). The career reasons of nascent entrepreneurs. *Journal of Business Venturing, 18*(1), 13–39.

Castille, C. M., Kuyumcu, D., & Bennett, R. J. (2017). Prevailing to the peers' detriment: Organizational constraints motivate Machiavellians to undermine their peers. *Personality and Individual Differences, 104,* 29-36. doi: 10.1016/j.paid.2016.07.026

Chell, E. (2008). *The entrepreneurial personality: A social construction* (2nd ed.). London, England: Routledge.

Christie, R., & Geis, F. L. (Eds.). (1970). *Studies in Machiavellianism.* New York, NY: Academic Press.

Ciavarella, M. A., Buchholtz, A. K., Riordan, C. M., Gatewood, R. D., & Stokes, G. S. (2004). The Big Five and venture survival: Is there a linkage? *Journal of Business Venturing, 19,* 465–483.

Costa, P. T., & McCrae, R. R. (1992). Normal personality assessment in clinical practice: The NEO Personality Inventory. *Psychological Assessment, 4*(1), 5–13. doi: 10.1037/1040-3590.4.1.5

Davidsson, P., & Gordon, S. (2012). Panel studies of new venture creation: a methods-focused review and suggestions for future research. *Small Business Economics, 39*(4), 853–876. doi: 10.1007/s11187-011-9325-8

Davis, A. E., & Shaver, K. G. (2009). Social motives in the PSED II. In P. D. Reynolds & R. T. Curtin (Eds.), *New firm creation in the United States: Initial explorations with the PSED II data set* (pp. 19–34). New York, NY: Springer.

Davis, A. E., & Shaver, K. G. (2012). Understanding gendered variations in business growth intentions across the life course. *Entrepreneurship: Theory & Practice, 36*(3), 495–512. doi:10.1111/j.1540-6520.2012.00508.x

De Clercq, D., Menzies, T. V., Diochon, M., & Gasse, Y. (2009). Explaining nascent entrepreneurs' goal commitment: An exploratory study. *Journal of Small Business & Entrepreneurship, 22*(2), 123–139.

de Holan, P. M. (2014). It's all in your head: Why we need neuroentrepreneurship. *Journal of Management Inquiry, 23*(1), 93–97. doi: 10.1177/1056492613485913

Deci, E. L., & Ryan, R. M. (1980). Self-determination theory: When mind mediates behavior. *Journal of Mind and Behavior, 1*(1), 33–43.

Deci, E. L., & Ryan, R. M. (2008). Self-determination theory: A macrotheory of human motivation, development, and health. *Canadian Psychology/Psychologie canadienne, 49*(3), 182–185. doi: 10.1037/a0012801

Deci, E. L., & Ryan, R. M. (2012). Self-determination theory. In P. A. M. Van Lange, A. W. Kruglanski, E. T. Higgins (Eds.), *Handbook of theories of social psychology* (Vol. 1., pp. 416–436). Thousand Oaks, CA: Sage.

Dholakia, U. M., Bagozzi, R. P., & Gopinath, M. (2007). How formulating implementation plans and remembering past actions facilitate the enactment of effortful decisions. *Journal of Behavioral Decision Making, 20*(4), 343–364. doi: 10.1002/bdm.562

Diochon, M., Menzies, T. V., & Gasse, Y. (2007). Attributions and success in new venture creation among Canadian nascent entrepreneurs. *Journal of Small Business & Entrepreneurship, 20*(4), 335–350.

Edelman, L. F., Brush, C. G., Manolova, T. S., & Greene, P. G. (2010). Start-up motivations and growth intentions of minority nascent entrepreneurs. *Journal of Small Business Management, 48*(2), 174–196. doi: 10.1111/j.1540-627X.2010.00291.x

Eysenck, H. J., & Eysenck, S. B. G. (1975). *Manual of the Eysenck personality questionnaire*. San Diego, CA: Educational and Industrial Testing Service.

Fayolle, A. (Ed.) (2014). *Handbook of research on entrepreneurship: What we know and what we need to know*. Cheltenham, England: Elgar.

Fayolle, A., & Liñán, F. (2014). The future of research on entrepreneurial intentions. *Journal of Business Research, 67*(5), 663–666. doi: 10.1016/j.jbusres.2013.11.024

Fishbein, M., & Ajzen, I. (1975). *Belief, attitude, intention, and behavior: An introduction to theory and research*. Reading, MA: Addison-Wesley.

Fiske, S. T., & Taylor, S. E. (1991). *Social cognition* (2nd ed.). New York, NY: McGraw-Hill.

Gable, S. L., & Impett, E. A. (2012). Approach and avoidance motives and close relationships. *Social and Personality Psychology Compass, 6*(1), 95–108. doi: 10.1111/j.1751-9004.2011.00405.x

Gartner, W. B., Shaver, K. G., Carter, N. M., & Reynolds, P. D. (2004). *Handbook of entrepreneurial dynamics: The process of business creation*. Thousand Oaks, CA: Sage.

Gartner, W. B., Shaver, K. G., & Liao, J. J. (2008). Opportunities as attributions: Categorizing strategic issues from an attributional perspective. *Strategic Entrepreneurship Journal, 2*(4), 301–315.

Gatewood, E. J. (2004). Entrepreneurial expectancies. In W. B. Gartner, K. G. Shaver, N. M. Carter, & P. D. Reynolds (Eds.), *Handbook of entrepreneurial dynamics: The process of business creation* (pp. 153–162). Thousand Oaks, CA: Sage.

Gatewood, E. J., Shaver, K. G., & Gartner, W. B. (1995). A longitudinal study of cognitive factors influencing start-up behaviors and success at venture creation. *Journal of Business Venturing, 10*(5), 371–391.

Gatewood, E. J., Shaver, K. G., Powers, J. B., & Gartner, W. B. (2002). Entrepreneurial expectancy, task effort, and performance. *Entrepreneurship: Theory & Practice, 27*(2), 187–206.

Goldberg, L. R., Johnson, J. A., Eber, H. W., Hogan, R., Ashton, M. C., Cloninger, C. R., & Gough, H. G. (2006). The international personality item pool and the future of public-domain personality measures. *Journal of Research in Personality, 40*(1), 84–96. doi: 10.1016/j.jrp.2005.08.007

Gough, H. G. (1956). *California Psychological Inventory*. Palo Alto, CA: Consulting Psychologists Press.

Gough, H. G. (1989). The California Psychological Inventory. In C. S. Newmark & C. S. Newmark (Eds.), *Major psychological assessment instruments* (Vol. 2. pp. 67–98). Needham Heights, MA: Allyn & Bacon.

Grégoire, D. A., Corbett, A. C., & McMullen, J. S. (2011). The cognitive perspective in entrepreneurship: An agenda for future research. *Journal of Management Studies, 48*(6), 1443–1477. doi: 10.1111/j.1467-6486.2010.00922.x

Grégoire, D. A., Cornelissen, J., Dimov, D., & van Burg, E. (2015). The mind in the middle: Taking stock of affect and cognition research in entrepreneurship. *International Journal of Management Reviews, 17*(2), 125–142. doi: 10.1111/ijmr.12060

Hathaway, S. R., & McKinley, J. C. (1942). *The Minnesota Multiphasic Personality Schedule*. Minneapolis, MN: University of Minnesota Press.

Heider, F. (1958). *The psychology of interpersonal relations*. New York, NY: Wiley.

Higgins, E. T. (1998). Promotion and prevention: Regulatory focus as a motivational principle. In M. P. Zanna (Ed.), *Advances in experimental social psychology* (Vol. 30, pp. 1–46). New York, NY: Academic Press.

Higgins, E. T., & Cornwell, J. F. M. (2016). Securing foundations and advancing frontiers: Prevention and promotion effects on judgment & decision making. *Organizational Behavior and Human Decision Processes, 136*, 56–67. doi: 10.1016/j.obhdp.2016.04.005

Hmieleski, K. M., & Baron, R. A. (2008). Regulatory focus and new venture performance: A study of entrepreneurial opportunity exploitation under conditions of risk versus uncertainty. *Strategic Entrepreneurship Journal, 2*, 285–299.

Iremadze, D. (2016). Towards entrepreneurial motivation: The self-determination theory approach. *Proceedings of the European Conference on Innovation & Entrepreneurship*, 960–970.

Jackson, D. N. (1976). *Jackson Personality Inventory manual*. Port Huron, MI: Research Psychologists Press.

Jackson, D. N. (1994). *Jackson Personality Inventory Research–Revised manual*. Port Huron, MI: Sigma Assessment Systems.

Jackson, D. N., Hourany, L., & Vidmar, N. J. (1972). A four-dimensional interpretation of risk-taking. *Journal of Personality, 40*(3), 483–501.

Jain, R. K. (2011). Entrepreneurial competencies: A meta-analysis and comprehensive conceptualization for future research. *Vision, 15*(2), 127–152. doi: 10.1177/097226291101500205

Johnson, B. R. (1990). Toward a multidimensional model of entrepreneurship: The case of achievement motivation and the entrepreneur. *Entrepreneurship: Theory & Practice, 14*(3), 39–54.

Jonason, P. K., & Jackson, C. J. (2016). The Dark Triad traits through the lens of Reinforcement Sensitivity Theory. *Personality and Individual Differences, 90*, 273–277. doi: 10.1016/j.paid.2015.11.023

Kelley, D., Singer, S., & Herrington, M. (2016). *GEM global report 2015/16*. Babson Park, MA: Babson College.

Kelley, H. H., Berscheid, E., Christensen, A., Harvey, J. H., Huston, T. L., Levinger, G., . . . Peterson, D. R. (1983). *Close relationships*. New York, NY: Freeman.

Kogan, N., & Wallach, M. A. (1964). *Risk taking: A study in cognition and personality*. New York, NY: Holt, Rinehart, & Winston.

Kolvereid, L. (1996). Organizational employment vs. self-employment: Reasons for career choice intentions. *Entrepreneurship Theory & Practice, 20*(3), 23–31.

Kouamé, S., Oliver, D., & Poisson-de-Haro, S. (2015). Can emotional differences be a strength? Affective diversity and managerial decision performance. *Management Decision, 53*(8), 1662–1676. doi: 10.1108/MD-08-2014-0540

Krueger Jr, N. F. (2009). Entrepreneurial intentions are dead: Long live entrepreneurial intentions. In A. L. Carsrud & M. Brännback (Eds.), *Understanding the entrepreneurial mind: Opening the black box* (pp. 51–72). Dordrecht, Netherlands: Springer.

Laurin, K., Fitzsimons, G. M., Finkel, E. J., Carswell, K. L., van Dellen, M. R., Hofmann, W., ... Brown, P. C. (2016). Power and the pursuit of a partner's goals. *Journal of Personality and Social Psychology, 110*(6), 840–868. doi: 10.1037/pspi0000048

Lee, K., & Ashton, M. C. (2004). Psychometric properties of the HEXACO personality inventory. *Multivariate Behavioral Research, 39*(2), 329–358.

Lewis, G. J., & Bates, T. C. (2014). How genes influence personality: Evidence from multi-facet twin analyses of the HEXACO dimensions. *Journal of Research in Personality, 51*, 9–17.

MacCrimmon, K. R., & Wehrung, D. A. (1986). *Taking risks: The management of uncertainty*. New York, NY: Free Press.

MacCrimmon, K. R., & Wehrung, D. A. (1990). Characteristics of risk taking executives. *Management Science, 36*(4), 422–435.

Malle, B. F., Guglielmo, S., & Monroe, A. E. (2014). A theory of blame. *Psychological Inquiry, 25*(2), 147–186. doi: 10.1080/1047840X.2014.877340

Mantere, S., Aula, P., Schildt, H., & Vaara, E. (2013). Narrative attributions of entrepreneurial failure. *Journal of Business Venturing, 28*(4), 459–473. doi: 10.1016/j.jbusvent.2012.12.001

McClelland, D. C. (1961). *The achieving society*. New York, NY: Van Nostrand.

McClelland, D. C., Atkinson, J. W., Clark, R. A., & Lowell, E. L. (1953). *The achievement motive*. East Norwalk, CT: Appleton-Century-Crofts.

McGee, J. E., Peterson, M., Mueller, S. L., & Sequeira, J. M. (2009). Entrepreneurial self-efficacy: Refining the measure. *Entrepreneurship: Theory & Practice, 33*(4), 965–988. doi: 10.1111/j.1540-6520.2009.00304.x

McMullen, J. S., & Kier, A. S. (2016). Trapped by the entrepreneurial mindset: Opportunity seeking and escalation of commitment in the Mount Everest disaster. *Journal of Business Venturing, 31*(6), 663–686. doi: 10.1016/j.jbusvent.2016.09.003

Mitchell, R. K., Busenitz, L., Lant, T., McDougall, P. P., Morse, E. A., & Smith, J. B. (2004). The distinctive and inclusive domain of entrepreneurial cognition research. *Entrepreneurship: Theory & Practice, 28*(6), 505–518. doi: 10.1111/j.1540-6520.2004.00061.x

Mitchell, R. K., Busenitz, L. W., Bird, B., Marie Gaglio, C., McMullen, J. S., Morse, E. A., & Smith, J. B. (2007). The central question in entrepreneurial cognition research 2007. *Entrepreneurship: Theory & Practice, 31*(1), 1–27. doi: 10.1111/j.1540-6520.2007.00161.x

Mitchell, J. R., Mitchell, R. K., & Randolph-Seng, B. (Eds.). (2014). *Handbook of entrepreneurial cognition*. Northhampton, MA: Elgar.

Murray, H. A. (1938). *Explorations in personality*. Oxford, England: Oxford University Press.

Nezlek, J. B. (2012). Multilevel modeling analyses of diary-style data. In M. R. Mehl, T. S. Conner, M. R. Mehl, & T. S. Conner (Eds.), *Handbook of research methods for studying daily life*. (pp. 357–383). New York, NY: Guilford Press.

Nezlek, J. B. (2016). A practical guide to understanding reliability in studies of within-person variability. *Journal of Research in Personality*. doi: 10.1016/j.jrp.2016.06.020

Niess, C., & Biemann, T. (2014). The role of risk propensity in predicting self-employment. *Journal of Applied Psychology, 99*(5), 1000–1009.

O'Neill, T. A., & Allen, N. J. (2011). Personality and the prediction of team performance. *European Journal of Personality, 25*(1), 31–42. doi: 10.1002/per.769

Palich, L. E., & Bagby, D. R. (1995). Using cognitive theory to explain entrepreneurial risk-taking: Challenging conventional wisdom. *Journal of Business Venturing, 10*(6), 425–438.

Pashler, H., & Wagenmakers, E.-J. (2012). Editors' introduction to the special section on replicability in psychological science: A crisis of confidence? *Perspectives on Psychological Science, 7*(6), 528–530.

Paulhus, D. (1983). Sphere-specific measures of perceived control. *Journal of Personality and Social Psychology, 44*(6), 1253–1265. doi: 10.1037/0022-3514.44.6.1253

Paulhus, D. L., & Van Selst, M. (1990). The spheres of control scale: 10 yr of research. *Personality and Individual Differences, 11*(10), 1029–1036. doi: 10.1016/0191-8869(90)90130-J

Phares, E. J. (1971). Internal-external control and the reduction of reinforcement value after failure. *Journal of Consulting and Clinical Psychology, 37*(3), 386–390. doi: 10.1037/h0031951

Renko, M., Kroeck, K., & Bullough, A. (2012). Expectancy theory and nascent entrepreneurship. *Small Business Economics, 39*(3), 667–684. doi: 10.1007/s11187-011-9354-3

Reynolds, P. D., & Curtin, R. T. (Eds.). (2009). *New firm creation in the United States: Initial explorations with the PSED II data set*. New York, NY: Springer.

Robbennolt, J. K. (2000). Outcome severity and judgments of "responsibility": A meta-analytic review. *Journal of Applied Social Psychology, 30*(12), 2575–2609. doi: 10.1111/j.1559-1816.2000.tb02451.x

Rotter, J. B. (1966). Generalized expectancies for internal versus external control of reinforcement. *Psychological Monographs: General and Applied, 80*(1), 1–28. doi: 10.1037/h0092976

Ruef, M., Aldrich, H. E., & Carter, N. M. (2003). The structure of founding teams: Homophily, strong ties and isolation among U.S. entrepreneurs. *American Sociological Review, 68*(2), 195–222.

Scheinberg, S., & Macmillan, I. C. (1988). An 11 country study of motivations to start a business. In B. A. Kirchhoff, W. A. Long, W. E. McMullan, K. H. Vesper, & W. E. W. Jr. (Eds.), *Frontiers of entrepreneurship research 1988* (pp. 669–687). Babson Park, MA: Babson College.

Shane, S., Kolvereid, L., & Westhead, P. (1991). An exploratory examination of the reasons leading to new firm formation across country and gender. *Journal of Business Venturing, 6*(6), 431.

Shaver, K. G. (1985). *The attribution of blame: Causality, responsibility, and blameworthiness*. New York, NY: Springer.

Shaver, K. G. (2014). Experimentation in entrepreneurship research. In A. L. Carsrud & M. Brännback (Eds.), *Handbook of research methods and applications in entrepreneurship and small business*. (pp. 88–111). Cheltenham, England: Elgar.

Shaver, K. G., Blair, C. A., & Davis, A. E. (2014, June). *The embedded entrepreneur: Gender, family stage, and psychological correlates of start-up success and failure*. Paper presented at the Diana International Research Conference, Stockholm, Sweden.

Shaver, K. G., Gartner, W. B., Crosby, E., Bakalarova, K., & Gatewood, E. J. (2001). Attributions about entrepreneurship: A framework and process for analyzing reasons for starting a business. *Entrepreneurship: Theory & Practice, 26*(2), 5–32.

Shaver, K. G., Gatewood, E. J., & Gartner, W. B. (2001, August). *Differing expectations: Comparing nascent entrepreneurs to non-entrepreneurs*. Paper presented at the Academy of Management, Washington, DC.

Shaver, K. G., Schjoedt, L., Passarelli, A., & Reeck, C. (in press). The cognitive neuroscience of entrepreneurial risk: Conceptual and methodological challenges. In M. J. Day, M. C. Boardman, & N. F. Krueger, Jr. (Eds.), *Handbook of research methodologies and design in neuro-entrepreneurship*. Cheltenham, England: Elgar.

Smith, M. M., Sherry, S. B., Chen, S., Saklofske, D. H., Flett, G. L., & Hewitt, P. L. (2016). Perfectionism and narcissism: A meta-analytic review. *Journal of Research in Personality, 64*, 90–101. doi: 10.1016/j.jrp.2016.07.012

Steffens, P., Terjesen, S., & Davidsson, P. (2012). Birds of a feather get lost together: New venture team composition and performance. *Small Business Economics, 39*, 727–743.

Stewart Jr, W. H., & Roth, P. L. (2001). Risk propensity differences between entrepreneurs and managers: A meta-analytic review. *Journal of Applied Psychology, 86*, 145–153.

Stewart Jr, W. H., & Roth, P. L. (2004). Data quality affects meta-analytic conclusions: A response to Miner and Raju (2004) concerning entrepreneurial risk propensity. *Journal of Applied Psychology, 89*(1), 14–21. doi: 10.1037/0021-9010.89.1.14

Sullivan, D. M., & Meek, W. R. (2012). Gender and entrepreneurship: A review and process model. *Journal of Managerial Psychology, 27*(5), 428–458. doi: 10.1108/02683941211235373

Van Eerde, W., & Thierry, H. (1996). Vroom's expectancy models and work-related criteria: A meta-analysis. *Journal of Applied Psychology, 81*(5), 575–586. doi: 10.1037/0021-9010.81.5.575

van Gelderen, M. (2010). Autonomy as the guiding aim of entrepreneurship education. *Education & Training, 52*(8–9), 710–721. doi:10.1108/00400911011089006

van Gelderen, M. (2016). Entrepreneurial autonomy and its dynamics. *Applied Psychology: An International Review, 65*(3), 541–567. doi: 10.1111/apps.12066

van Gelderen, M., & Jansen, P. (2006). Autonomy as a start-up motive. *Journal of Small Business and Enterprise Development, 13*, 23–32.

Vroom, V. H. (1964). *Work and motivation*. New York, NY: Wiley.

Wicker, A. W. (1969). Attitudes versus actions: The relationship of verbal and overt behavioral responses to attitude objects. *Journal of Social Issues, 25*(4), 41–78. doi: 10.1111/j.1540-4560.1969.tb00619.x

Wiklund, J., Wei, Y., & Patzelt, H. (2016). Impulsivity and entrepreneurial action. *Academy of Management Annual Meeting Proceedings*, 1–1. doi: 10.5465/AMBPP.2016.13945abstract

Zhao, H., & Seibert, S. E. (2006). The Big Five personality dimensions and entrepreneurial status: A meta-analytical review. *Journal of Applied Psychology, 91*, 259–271.

Zhao, H., Seibert, S. E., & Hills, G. E. (2005). The mediating role of self-efficacy in the development of entrepreneurial intentions. *Journal of Applied Psychology, 90*(6), 1265–1272. doi:10.1037/0021-9010.90.6.1265

Zuckerman, M., Kolin, E. A., Price, L., & Zoob, I. (1964). Development of a sensation-seeking scale. *Journal of Consulting Psychology, 28*(6), 477–482.

6

Tools Entrepreneurs Need for Converting Dreams To Reality—And Achieving Success

Robert A. Baron[a]

[a] *Oklahoma State University*

Introduction

I once worked at a university where the motto was "Why not change the world?" This could certainly be the basic credo for entrepreneurs. While only a tiny proportion set out to transform the world, all do seek some form of change, whether it is a better product, better service, a new raw material, or beneficial other change in what exists *now*. And some entrepreneurs *do* change the world—they use their creativity, energy, knowledge, and skills to create something new that truly has far-reaching effects. A few of my personal favorites: Bill Gates (cofounder of Microsoft), Chester Carlson (creator of the dry photocopying process), and Sam Walton (founder of Walmart); the list could continue, but the basic point is, I hope, clear.

In fact, of course, these entrepreneurs and companies—ones that really do change the world (or some part of it)—are only a tiny, elite group. As is well known, a large proportion of new ventures fail—or least disappear—during the first few years after their founding; Since all entrepreneurs start with dreams of success and are highly motivated to attain them, an important question arises: why do so many experience disappointment instead of realization of these dreams? The answer, must, of necessity, be complex, and involve a multitude of factors, many beyond the control of entrepreneurs—changes in technology, actions of competitors, shifts in potential customers' preferences, government regulations and so many others that they could not possibly be listed here. It is a basic theme of this chapter, however, that many of the causes of entrepreneurs' success or failure, involve the entrepreneurs themselves. The process of converting ideas into reality—and successful companies—is a long and complex one and to accomplish it, entrepreneurs need many skills, relevant knowledge and experience, personal characteristics, motives, and goals. Together, these aspects of human and psychological resources provide them with what might be viewed as the *tools* they need for success. To the degree entrepreneurs possess these tools, the likelihood of their success is increased; to the extent they do not—or fail to utilize them effectively—the likelihood of success is reduced.

The Wiley Handbook of Entrepreneurship, First Edition.
Edited by Gorkan Ahmetoglu, Tomas Chamorro-Premuzic, Bailey Klinger, & Tessa Karcisky.
© 2017 John Wiley & Sons Ltd. Published 2017 by John Wiley & Sons Ltd.

A key goal of the present discussion is, on the basis of current knowledge, identifying some key in entrepreneurial success. To accomplish this task, each section will consider one of these components, describing extant evidence concerning its importance. From this, it is hoped, an overall picture of the personal ingredients in entrepreneurial success will emerge. A related and important contribution that this chapter seeks is to add to existing evidence and theory that suggests entrepreneurs do indeed play a central role in the entrepreneurial process or, as Shane, Locke, and Collins (2003, p. 259) put it, without entrepreneurs "nothing happens, the entrepreneurial process simply does not occur."

Motivation: What Goals Do Entrepreneurs Seek

Why do people—including, of course, entrepreneurs do what they do in life—behave as they do in various situations? Clearly, for most persons most of the time, their behavior is far from random. Rather, it is directed toward attaining specific goals. Sometimes, these goals are obvious—for instance, an individual who is hungry stops at a restaurant for a meal or a snack. Similarly, an entrepreneur who needs external funding to launch her company writes a business plan and seeks interviews with venture capitalists or other potential sources of financing. In other instances, the goals are more complex or difficult to identify. Why do rock climbers risk life and limb climbing sheer rock walls? One possibility is that they enjoy the "high" that accompanies risk; another is that they want to do something no one else has done, as was true for the group of individuals who were the first to successfully reach the summit of Mt. Everest. These motives, however, are not directly visible, but must be inferred from their actions.

Whatever the specific goals individuals seek or whatever actions they view as helpful in reaching these goals, their purposeful, planned actions, reflects *motivation*. Although definitions of motivation differ, a basic one accepted widely by psychologists is: Motivation refers to internal states (often not open to direct observation) that *energize* and *guide* behavior, and underlie its *persistence* (e.g., Ryan & Deci, 2000). In addition, motivation is intimately linked with cognition—for instance one major theory of motivation, expectancy theory (Heneman & Schwab, 1972). This theory suggests that individuals' expectations that increased effort on performing various tasks well will help them to actually improve their performance on these tasks, and that this enhanced performance, in turn, will increase their likelihood of attaining desired outcomes (i.e., rewards). In describing the intimate links between cognition and motivation it has often been suggested (e.g., Baron, 2007) simply that motivation without cognition leads to undirected, random actions, while cognition without motivation lead to inaction—no overt actions occur. Only when the two function together does goal-directed, planned behavior occur.

A basic finding of research on goal setting is that difficult, challenging goals increase performance on many tasks and do so to a greater extent than less challenging goals (e.g., Locke & Latham, 2006). Yet, there are limits to this relationship; when goals are so challenging as to be realistically unattainable, performance and motivation may both decrease. In a sense, individuals "give up" on reaching extremely difficult goals, including ones they have set for themselves. Research findings indicate that under such conditions, the beneficial effects of goal difficulty may decrease and be replaced, instead, by feelings of discouragement and a resulting loss of motivation (e.g., Carver & Scheier, 1990; Wrosch et al., 2007).

These findings have important implications for entrepreneurs; they suggest that it is crucial to adopt challenging but *attainable* goals. Being very high in self-efficacy (Zhao, Seibert, & Hills, 2005), entrepreneurs are often tempted to choose unrealistically high goals. This puts them at particular risk of experiencing the discouragement and reduced motivation that may occur in such situations. Evidence for these effects has recently been reported by Baron, Mueller, and Wolfe (2016), who found that self-efficacy is positively related to the difficulty of the goals entrepreneurs set for themselves and their new ventures and, consistent with goal-setting research, the relationship between goal difficulty and performance is positive—but only up to a point, beyond which higher levels of goal difficulty are actually negatively related to performance. These findings suggest in concrete terms why entrepreneurs much be restrained in terms of establishing goals for themselves and their new ventures. Such restraint can be included among the basic tools needed by entrepreneurs to attain the success they seek.

Another way in which motivation is an important tool for entrepreneurs in their quest for success involves the specific motives that bring them to entrepreneurship. In the past, it was widely assumed that virtually all entrepreneurs are motivated primarily by the desire for financial gains. However, a growing body of theory and research (e.g., Baron, 2010; Rindova, Barry, & Ketchen, 2009) indicates that in fact, they have several different motives. A large number of studies have focused on the task of identifying these motives, and overall, have found that financial gains are one, but by no means the only or even most important, motive. In fact, a review of exiting evidence (Franklin & Baron, 2015) indicates that the desire for autonomy or independence is ranked as the most important by entrepreneurs. Financial gain is second, followed, in descending order, by the desire to grow and develop as a person, to escape from unpleasant work environments, to acquire status and recognition, to contribute to the well-being of their communities and societies, and to contribute to solving important social problems.

To the extent that entrepreneurs recognize their own motives, they can consciously choose goals relevant to them rather than pursue outcomes that are emphasized or expected by others (e.g., financial gains). If they pursue these "approved" motives, they will divert energy and attention from tasks that would contribute to their progress toward fulfilling their own actual motives. Thus, an important sense—that of recognizing and acting on their personal motives—is another factor that may be listed among the key ingredients in their ultimate success.

Cognitive Tools: Creativity, Opportunity Recognition, and Avoiding Cognitive Traps

In an important sense, entrepreneurship begins with ideas—ideas for something new, useful, and, hopefully, better than what exists at present. These ideas, in turn, emerge from the imaginations of individuals, although, of course, several persons may have the same or similar thoughts simultaneously. In other words, ideas emerge from, and reflect, individual creativity. However, the term "creativity" itself is, like many others, difficult to define as are the terms "love" or "justice." In general, however, creativity has been defined as something that is viewed as original and new by relevant persons—those working in the same or similar fields (e.g., Runco & Jaeger, 2012). Thus, a painting is viewed as creative to the extent that artists and art critics view it as new; similarly, an idea for a new product or service is creative to the extent that other persons—for instance, venture capitalists—have the knowledge and experience to evaluate it along this dimension.

But how does creativity itself emerge? One answer provided by cognitive scientists is that it originates, at least in part, in *concepts*—mental "containers" that include objects, events principles, and people. For instance, the concept of a vehicle includes cars, planes, boats, motorcycles, and—at the "edges"—elevators and escalators. Vehicles move people, have systems to start, stop, and steer. So while cars meet all of these criteria, elevators and escalators do not. Should they be included? This is uncertain, which is why, in a sense, all concepts become "fuzzy" at the edges.

Creativity is viewed in cognitive science as emerging, in part, from expansion, combinations, or adaptions of concepts to new applications. For example, Uber and Lyfft are examples of concept combination: The idea that people often need a vehicle to take people from one place to another—traditionally a task performed by taxis or limousines—was combined, by the entrepreneurs who founded these companies, with the fact that most people now have smartphones. Together, these facts suggested the idea of a company that could be contacted by smartphone and could then provide the transportation customers wanted. An example of concept expansion is provided by tablet computers (e.g., the iPad). The concept of a personal computer already existed, but it was then expanded to include a small, portable device that would perform a wide range of functions without the size and bulk of laptops or notebooks.

Although concepts are often a source of creative thought, it's important to note that they can also restrict such thought. For instance, consider the fact that the Inca, who had several means of transporting objects, never expanded these—or their concept of such means—to the wheel. Moreover, this was true despite the fact that wheels were used in children's toys. For some reason, they did not expand existing concepts of vehicles for carrying loads to using the wheel in carts.

Creativity also arises from other sources, but for the present purposes, this brief description provides a widely accepted view of the nature of creativity—and its role in ideas for something new. Since such ideas lie at the heart of entrepreneurship, some degree of creativity is another tool that can contribute to entrepreneurs' success. Such creativity does not have to be what is known as *exceptional creativity* of the kind shown by Einstein, Shakespeare, or Picasso, but some degree of creativity is often an essential component of entrepreneurship.

Opportunity Recognition of Creation: Recognizing or Creating Practical Uses of Ideas

Ideas can be viewed as the "raw materials" for entrepreneurship: they are a basic way in which the process starts. However, if they cannot be put to practical use—and in the context of business, this implies being used as the basis for products, services, or new production processes that can generate financial or social value—they have no further bearing on entrepreneurship. For instance, suppose an individual had the idea for a device that would instantly transport people from one place to another—even places far, far away. The creators of "Star Trek" had such an idea, presenting it in a television program and then in several successful films. Although this a highly attractive idea, as anyone who has spent endless hours in an airport waiting for a flight would agree, the technology for actually making it simply does not exist. Thus, having ideas is one potentially useful tool for entrepreneurs but such creativity does not necessarily lead to entrepreneurship. Rather, ideas are only useful in this respect if they relate to opportunities to use them as the basis for a new venture or other forms of entrepreneurship.

Identifying potential opportunities does not necessarily involve new ideas, but in many cases it does. In such instances, opportunity recognition refers to processes which lead to the discovery or creation of the means of generating value (financial or social) that are not currently being exploited (and that are perceived in a given society as permissible or acceptable). To be a bona fide opportunity, such a use of new ideas must include a potential market for their application and a means of actually converting these ideas into something real (i.e., tangible), such as a new product, service, raw material, or other beneficial outcomes. Further, doing so must be consistent with current laws and regulations, and be sufficiently new and useful so as to create competitive advantage—offering something that actual or potential competitors do not (e.g.,Webb, Tihanyi, Ireland, & Sirmon, 2009).

Much research has been conducted to identify the cognitive processes involved in opportunity recognition, and one that appears to play a role is *pattern recognition*— what is known in everyday speech as "connecting the dots." More formally, it refers to perceiving connections between various conditions, events, or markets that are not currently recognized by others (Baron, 2006; Grégoire, Barr, & Shepherd, 2010). For instance, Chester Carlson, developer of the original photocopier, recognized what he thought was an opportunity by perceiving a way in which several factors—available technology, the need for legible and rapidly produced copies of documents, and the superiority of his invention over what then existed—could be connected. The result was the "Xerox" machine—but only decades after his original idea; it took that long to convince the CEOs of existing companies that this was, in fact, an important opportunity.

In short, one view of opportunities suggests that they exist "out there" as patterns that have not yet been recognized by individuals—anyone!—but then, when a person with the right background experience and training appears, these patterns are identified and may form the basis for important entrepreneurial activity. Another view of opportunities is that they are created by entrepreneurs themselves—that they emerge not out of external conditions, but out of the cognitions of entrepreneurs (e.g., Alvarez & Barney, 2007). Recent findings suggests that these two views of opportunities are not competing, but complementary. Hmieleski, Carr, and Baron (2015) reported research indicating, in part, that opportunity creation is more likely than opportunity identification in contexts of high industry dynamism and high uncertainty, while opportunity recognition is more likely than opportunity creation in contexts of stable industries and high risk. These findings indicate that depending on the environments in which entrepreneurship occurs, opportunities are both discovered and created. Overall, the capacity to identify potential valuable opportunities should be included among the tools entrepreneurs need to succeed.

While creativity and effective opportunity recognition are important cognitive tools for entrepreneurs, another is the ability to resist what might be termed "cognitive traps." These are tendencies that are an intrinsic part of human cognition that can lead to errors in judgment, decisions, plans, and expectations. Many exist, either singly or in combination, but in the extent to which they operate, the results for entrepreneurs can be disastrous. A number of such errors or traps are described in Table 6.1 but here a few those most likely to interfere with entrepreneurs' success will be briefly reviewed.

Table 6.1 Cognitive errors with important consequences for entrepreneurs.

Cognitive error	Description	Relevance for entrepreneurship
Confirmation bias	Tendency to notice, process, and store only information consistent with current beliefs	Reduces capacity to be flexible in the face of changing conditions, and capacity to respond to negative information
Heuristics	Rules of thumb for making decisions and judgments quickly	Efficient in terms of reducing cognitive effort, but can lead to serious errors when more systematic and detailed analysis is required
Self-serving bias	Tendency to attribute positive outcomes to one's own talent, effort, etc., but negative ones to external factors beyond one's control	Reduces capacity to learn, since negative outcomes are perceived as generated by external agencies or factors
Optimistic bias	Tendency to expect more positive outcomes than is rationally justified	Leads to unrealistically high goals and aspirations and to underestimating the amount of time or effort needed to complete various tasks.
Fast-thinking effect	Faster speeds of thinking enhance risk-taking.	Entrepreneurs must often make decisions rapidly and this may increase their tendency to assume high risks.
Affect infusion	Influence on emotions and feelings on key aspects of cognition (e.g., decision-making, evaluation of various alternatives)	Can seriously distort judgments and decisions by entrepreneurs in a wide range of contexts
Sunk costs	Tendency to get trapped in bad decisions or failing course of action	Can prevent entrepreneurs from cutting their losses by walking away from poor decisions or strategies
The last is best effect	The last in a series of events is perceived most positively	Entrepreneurs who present last in business plan competitions or other contexts may gain an advantage

The confirmation bias. If we were totally rational beings, we would welcome information inconsistent with our current beliefs, since it would help make these more accurate. In fact, though, people tend to focus their attention on information that confirms their views and ignore or reject information that does not. Clearly, this can be a dangerous error for entrepreneurs who need to be aware of customer reactions to their products, the success or failure of their business strategies, and many other forms of information. To the extent that the confirmation bias prevents them from processing such information, it may interfere with their capacity to respond to valuable input in appropriate ways.

Self-serving bias and hubristic pride. A very basic cognitive bias is known as the self-serving bias (e.g., Forsyth, 2008). It refers to the strong tendency of individuals to attribute positive outcomes to internal causes—something about their actions or characteristics (e.g., talent), but to attribute negative outcomes to external causes—for instance, the actions of other persons or circumstances beyond their own control. The costs of this powerful bias are high, and may be especially high when this cognitive error results in what is known as hubristic pride. Hubristic pride develops as a result of initial success and refers to the extent to which such success "goes to their heads" (Tracy, Cheng, Robins, & Trzesniewski, 2009). That is, individuals experiencing it not only attribute success to themselves, but also assume that it derives from their "special" skills or talents, and that success will continue in the future and will occur in a wide range of contexts. As a result, they engage in actions such as failing to give credit to others who have also contributed to the success, resulting in such persons—often the best in a new venture—leave in search of better treatment. Overall, hubristic pride can generate many serious problems for entrepreneurs (e.g., overestimating the likelihood of success, ignoring negative information, and seeking to dominate, rather than influence, others). In short, hubristic pride is an extreme form of the self-serving bias, and avoiding it is another important tool that can contribute to entrepreneurs' success.

Sunk costs. Few people like to admit that they made an error, and as a result, people have a strong tendency to stick with initial decisions, even in the face of information indicating that they were incorrect. This is known as sunk costs, since it results in situations in which individuals resist changing course because they have too much invested to quit—financial resources, reputation, and loss of face (e.g., Garland, 1990; Staw & Ross, 1989). Given the uncertain and rapidly changing environments entrepreneurs face, they must be willing to respond to new conditions as they, emerge, so resisting the harmful effects of sunk costs can contribute measurably to their success.

Additional cognitive biases are described in Table 6.1. Overall, the basic takeaway for entrepreneurs is that these cognitive errors or traps can be very harmful to them and their companies, so by recognizing and resisting them, they may increase their own chances of success.

The Personal Side of Entrepreneurial Success: Characteristics and Skills That Contribute to Success

The field of entrepreneurship has often focused on two important and related questions: (1) are entrepreneurs different from other persons in measurable ways? (2) are successful entrepreneurs different from unsuccessful ones, again, in measurable ways? Both questions refer, in a sense, to what might be termed the "personal side" of entrepreneurship. That is, they both focus on entrepreneurs themselves and on what personal characteristics, skills, and knowledge they possess (or don't possess) that are relevant to their success. Research findings indicate that many of these aspects exist, but here we will focus on several that have been found to be especially important in this respect.

Before beginning, however, it is useful to briefly describe why it is reasonable to expect entrepreneurs to differ from other persons. An important answer is suggested by *attraction, selection, attrition* (ASA) theory (e.g., Schneider, Smith, Goldstein, 2000). This theory, which is widely accepted in several fields of management (e.g., human resource management, organizational behavior), suggests that initially, many persons may be attracted to a particular activity or a career. However, of these, only some find that they are actually suited for the activity or career and continue to pursue it. Finally, among the latter, only some succeed in reaching their goals while most others drop out along the way. The result is that only a very small proportion remain, and they are a highly selected group. This is true for all professions and this theory certainly applies to entrepreneurs. While many persons express interest in starting their own company, faced with the difficulties of doing so, only some actually do. And among these, only a few develop companies that survive and prosper. The result: entrepreneurs are different from other persons, just as surgeons are different from other persons and even other doctors, and star athletes are different from more ordinary ones. Thus, there is a strong theoretical basic for suggesting that entrepreneurs may indeed differ significantly from other persons because, simply, selective forces result in such differences. Some of these differences will now be reviewed.

Personal Characteristics: Self-Efficacy, the "Big Five," and Willingness to Improvise

Perhaps the variable found in research to distinguish entrepreneurs from others is self-efficacy—individuals' belief that they can successfully accomplish whatever they set out to accomplish (e.g., Zhao, Seibert, & Hills, 2005). This is one reason why, despite the odds being highly stacked against them, many start new ventures: they believe that they can effectively complete the tasks needed to make these companies a success. Thus, self-efficacy is one characteristic that helps entrepreneurs get started and also persist in their efforts to succeed. Self-efficacy, however, has a downside. It may lead individuals to undertake tasks for which, in reality, they lack the required resources, leading to what can be disastrous results. In a sense, they have chosen to play in a game they cannot win, with negative results virtually guaranteed. These negative effects can be magnified by a high level of optimism—a general, and often unjustified, belief, that ultimately all will turn out well. In combination, high levels of optimism and high levels of self-efficacy can prove deadly for entrepreneurs with limited resources.

Another way in which entrepreneurs differ from other persons involves the "Big Five" dimensions of personality—basic dimensions along which individuals differ with respect to dispositions or preferences that are stable over time and occur across different situations. Specifically, research findings indicate that entrepreneurs are high in *conscientious*—they are high in achievement, work motivation, and personal organization, and, in general, on-time with respect to completing various tasks and meeting responsibilities. They are also higher than others in *openness to experience*—high in curiosity, imagination, creativity, seeking new ideas, and *emotional stability* (termed *neuroticism* in the original framework) they are calm, stable, even-tempered, able to resist stress and other forms of adversity. They are not higher on two others dimensions—*agreeableness*—the tendency to be cooperative and altruistic, or *extraversion*—the tendency to be, friendly, and expressive. Although these latter characteristics do contribute to success in other contexts, they appear to be less relevant for entrepreneurs, given the highly competitive environments they face.

An additional characteristic that differentiates entrepreneurs from other is their tendency to experience high levels of positive affect, especially after success or even progress toward key goals (e.g., Foo, 2011). Overall, high levels of positive affect exert many beneficial effects—higher energy, greater openness to new ideas, greater capacity to innovate and improvise (make adjustment "on-the-fly"), and even personal health and psychological adjustment (Lyuobmirsky, King, & Diener, 2005). Positive affect, too, has a downside, especially at very high levels. When positive affect is extreme, it may lead individuals to think heuristically (using mental shortcuts) rather than systematically, which can be essential in making complex decisions. Further, it can reduce attention to negative information and also increase the propensity to take risks (Baron, Hmieleski, & Henry, 2012). Thus, a high level of positive affect is a kind of two-edged sword—within certain limits, it can facilitate many tendencies and actions positively related to entrepreneurs' success, but if extreme, it can produce opposite effects. Thus, positive affect is an important "plus" for entrepreneurs—but only if they learn to manage and restrain it effectively. If they can, its benefits offset its potential costs and it is one more valuable tool for entrepreneurs in their quest for success.

From Desire to Achievement: The Role of Self-Regulation

How do famous athletes, amazingly skilled surgeons, and acclaimed musicians or stars reach the pinnacles of success in their fields. A large body of research (e.g, Ericsson, 2014) suggests that the answer involves many hours or difficult, highly focused practice, termed deliberate practice in a large literature on expertise (e.g., Ericsson, 2014). As Michael Jordan, the star basketball player, put it "I'm not out there sweating for three hours every day just to find out what it feels like to sweat." And on a more humorous note, Mae West, film star of the 1930s, stated: "I never said it would be easy, I only said it would be worth it." Famous entrepreneurs agree with these sentiments and also indicate that their success was due largely to huge amounts of hard work. Thomas Edison, one of the most successful entrepreneurs in history, put it this way: "Genius is one percent inspiration and ninety-nine percent perspiration." In a basic sense, all these sentiments are related to the process of self-regulation.

In essence, the term self-regulation refers to a collection of skills and capabilities individuals use to select key goals, monitor progress toward them, and adjust their behavior (their thoughts, emotions, and actions) so as to enhance such progress. What are these skills and capabilities. Research findings indicate that among the most important are these:

1) Exerting *self-control*: performing actions that facilitate progress toward important goals (even if they are not enjoyable) while refraining from actions that are enjoyable but impede progress.
2) Demonstrating a combination of focus and persistence (staying focused on key goals and working persistently toward them).
3) Managing emotions and impulses—for instance, avoiding hasty or rash behavior and decisions, and having the ability to delay rewards until a time when they will be maximized.
4) Developing accurate *metacognition*—acquiring insightful self-knowledge, which involves monitoring and regulating one's own cognitive processes so that they facilitate progress toward key goals, and gaining greater understanding of what we know and don't know.

Clearly, these skills are important for everyone, but there are several reasons why they are especially valuable for entrepreneurs. First, in their efforts to create something new, entrepreneurs generally face situations in which the external rules or norms that guide behavior are lacking. Unless they actively seek guidance from an experienced mentor, they have no direct supervisors, teachers, or other persons who evaluate their performance, provide feedback, and advise them on how to improve. Further, since they are, by definition, attempting to create something new, they often face situations in which they must, basically, "make it up as they go along." Second, and especially for first-time entrepreneurs, they often find themselves performing tasks and filling roles they have not previously performed or occupied. As a result, it is crucial for entrepreneurs to accurately recognize what they know and do not know, so that they will seek help when it is truly needed.

In short, there are several reasons why skills with respect to self-regulation are especially important for entrepreneurs and should be included in any list of the tools they need for success.

Passion: Deep, Emotional Commitment to Entrepreneurship and the Roles it Involves

Passion is a word with many meanings—often it is applied to romance, but it is also used in the context of powerful commitments to a career, such as painting or music. For instance, Albert Einstein once remarked: "I have no special talents. I am only passionately curious." He was certainly being far too modest, but viewing passion as closely related to curiosity and the desire to know or do something different, is not far from the use of this term in the field of entrepreneurship, where it often refers to such things as entrepreneurs' powerful commitment to success, their strong desire to do something truly new, and even to be their own boss. A precise meaning of this term remained elusive until Cardon, Wincent, Singh, and Drnovsek (2009) proposed a model of passion based on existing theory and research primarily from psychology and other fields.

They defined passion as a strong, positive inclination toward entrepreneurial activities, coupled with a powerful identification with these activities. In other words, entrepreneurs high in passion love what they do and identify strongly with the role of being an entrepreneur. Further, Cardon et al. (2009) suggest that passion relates to three key aspects of entrepreneurship which form components of entrepreneurs' self-identity: the role of inventor—generating ideas for new products or services; the role of founder—performing the actions necessary to found and launch a new venture; and the role of developer—performing activities that help the new venture survive and grow. Research on passion (Murnieks, Mosakowski, & Cardon, 2014) has begun to investigate its role in the entrepreneurial process, and indicates that passion is positively related to entrepreneurs' self-efficacy, since passion generates positive affect and such affect has, in turn, been found to be positively related to entrepreneurs' self-efficacy. In addition, passion is positively related to their entrepreneurial behavior—for instance, the amount of time they spend working on their new ventures.

Overall, then, passion may be a valuable addition to the tools entrepreneurs need for success. Being passionate about the role they play (inventor, founder, developer) can help entrepreneurs to focus intently on these roles and behaviors related to them, and to generate or reflect positive feelings about these roles, and to combine them with self-regulation to provide both the energy and guidance needed for persistent efforts to attain important goals.

The Social Side of Entrepreneurial Success II: Forming High Quality Social Networks and Getting Along With Others

Entrepreneurs rarely, if ever, do it alone. To turn their ideas or dreams into reality—and to make this reality (e.g., new ventures) successful—they generally need help from others. This is one reason why a large majority of new ventures are started by founding teams, rather than single entrepreneurs. The help cofounders give each other, however, is often not enough. Rather, the new venture needs assistance from persons outside the company, since even with several members, no founding team has expertise in all the complex tasks the new venture must perform. How do they obtain this help? One very important way is through establishing social networks

Social networks are social structures composed of a set of members (which can be either individuals or organizations), and the ties between them—in essence, who knows whom, to what extent, and in what context. Social networks are important in many contexts, from sports to science, but they are especially crucial for entrepreneurs because, founding teams, in trying to create something new, have few concrete guidelines to follow and, consistent with their desire for increased autonomy, must make all the decisions, develop strategies, and deal with a myriad of unexpected problems. For instance, perhaps the founding members are knowledgeable about manufacturing new products and marketing them but know little or nothing about accounting, government rules concerning safety, the hiring of employees, or many other topics. An extensive social network can help provide such information

The combined benefits entrepreneurs derive from their social networks are often known as *social capital*. Social capital has been defined in several different ways, but in general, refers to: (1) the ability of individuals to obtain benefits from their social relationships with others, (2) the benefits themselves (Nahapiet & Ghoshal, 1998; Portes, 1998), and (3) the structure of individuals' social networks and their location in the larger social structure of the domain (e.g., industry) in which the new ventures are functioning. In brief, social capital refers to, and derives from, the social ties entrepreneurs have with others and the benefits they can obtain from these ties (Putnam, 2000). Not surprisingly, entrepreneurs with high levels of social capital (based on extensive and high-quality social networks) can readily obtain information and guidance when they need it; entrepreneurs lacking in social capital do not have such resources at their disposal.

In more general terms, social capital provides entrepreneurs with increased access to both tangible and intangible resources. Tangible benefits include financial resources and enhanced access to potentially valuable information. Intangible benefits include support, advice, and encouragement from others, as well as increased cooperation and trust from them. While the benefits provided by these latter (intangible) resources are somewhat difficult to measure in economic terms, they are often highly valuable to the persons who obtain them. The social ties on which social capital rests exist within social networks (Aldrich & Kim, 2007), and are often divided into two major types: (1) close or strong ties—for example, the strong, intimate bonds that exist between members of a nuclear family, very close friends, of member of an entrepreneurial team; and (2) loose or weak ties—social linkages between persons who are not close friends or on intimate social terms with each other (e.g., Adler & Kwon, 2002; Putnam, 2000).

Close (strong) ties are often viewed as leading to, or at least being associated with, what is known as *bonding social capital*—they generate relationships between individuals that are based on mutual trust. Establishing and maintaining such strong ties can be effortful, but once developed, they are a ready source of both tangible resources and information. Loose or weak ties, in contrast, lead to (or are associated with) bridging social capital—they are especially useful in providing individuals with information that might otherwise not be available to them, but since they do not involve high levels of mutual trust and confidence are less likely to provide tangible resources. On the other hand, they require little effort to establish or maintain. Over time, loose (weak) ties sometimes develop into strong ones, in which case they would lead to relationships based on mutual trust. Since social capital offers important benefits, and derives—to a large extent—from social networks, it is clear that one important ingredient in entrepreneurs' success is their capacity to build, and then reap benefits from, their social networks.

How do Entrepreneurs Build their Social Networks?

Although a large body of evidence offers support for the importance and benefits of social networks, until recently, relatively little attention has been directed to the question of how these networks develop and grow. In other words, how entrepreneurs build them. Often, they have a social network when they begin, but in order to obtain success, in most cases it is important to extend it in various ways. How can they accomplish this important goal? One answer is provided by research conducted by Fang, Chi, Chen, and Baron (2015). In this study, the authors sought to link the literature on social networks with that on what is known as political or social skills (Ferris, Perrewé, Anthony, & Gilmore, 2000). These refer to several skills that, together, assist individuals to get along well with others, to form relationships with them, and to influence them. Fang et al. (2015) predicted that such skills would be positively related to the breadth and quality of entrepreneurs' social networks. More specifically, entrepreneurs high in political skills develop networks with stronger ties and more rapidly adjust and expand these networks than entrepreneurs low in political skills Further, entrepreneurs are better at applying the social capital provided by their networks to enhance new venture performance. Fang et al. (2015) obtained the data on which these findings were based by using a mixed method of research employing a combination of questionnaire data (a measure of political skill) and detailed interviews with entrepreneurs, which followed Eisenhardt's (1989) approach to deriving theory from case studies, and using a number of different cases to replicate and validate theory derived from these qualitative methods (Eisenhardt & Graebner, 2007). In other words, the authors treated the cases they examined as experiments in which each case provided the basis for confirming or disconfirming conclusions and inferences based on the other cases (Yin, 1994).

The findings reported by Fang et al. (2015) indicate that entrepreneurs' political skills enhance their capacity to build effective social networks, and also to use resources provided by these networks to enhance the success of their companies. As they put it "Our field interviews with entrepreneurs suggest that political skill is an important individual characteristic that influences access to and mobilization of social capital" (2015, p. 205).

It should be noted that social or political skills have also been found, in other studies, to enhance new venture performance outside of social networks, in part, because such skills help entrepreneurs to gain access to potential customers, potential sources of financial support and also, crucially, to influence these persons or organizations to place orders for their products or offer financial support (Baron & Markman, 2003; Baron & Tang, 2009). As Baron and Markman (2003) note, social capital "opens the doors" to these persons, but social skills help determine whether these persons do actually provide what the entrepreneurs seek.

To summarize: the capacity to build high-quality, extensive social networks, and the ability to use the resources these networks provide, are additional tools that can help entrepreneurs achieve success.

Dealing with Adversity—and Failure

The road to success was anything but smooth for Colonel Harlan Sanders, founder of Kentucky Fried Chicken. In fact, it was extremely rocky. He had been fired from a dozen jobs, was 65 and living his car, and was essentially broke, when he developed the "secret" mix of herbs and spices for a very tasty fried chicken. The chain he founded was soon a success, making Colonel Sanders a wealthy man, and one whose face was familiar to tens of millions of persons around the globe.

Henry Ford—certainly one of the most successful entrepreneurs of all time—also had a large dose of failure early in his career. His first new venture, the Detroit Automobile Company, went bankrupt because it adopted a strategy almost guaranteed to produce failure: selling low-quality cars at high prices. He then reorganized this company into the Henry Ford Company, but it too collapsed over a dispute with a partner. His third company, almost a failure, was only saved when an angel investor rescued it from oblivion with needed financial assistance.

Walt Disney, too, experienced major failures before hitting on the formula that would make his company a huge success. Disney always wanted to be a cartoonist for newspapers, but was told, repeatedly, that he had no good ideas worth pursuing. He then decided to found a company of his own to produce cartoons, but it soon went bankrupt. He tried again, but his timing was bad: his new company started during World War II when most of his employees were called to military service. Once again, he was on the verge of failure, but for him, the third time was indeed charmed because the characters he invented for his cartoons—Mickey Mouse, Donald Duck, Goofy and others—soon gained great popularity. From this start, Disney built his company into one that started theme parks (Disneyland, Disneyworld), and continued to grow at a dizzying pace. So, Disney too, gained success only after several failures.

Although these are unique cases, they suggest three important principles: (1) resilience and faith in one's ideas or abilities is crucial for attaining entrepreneurial success, (2) these failures must be used as important lessons from which entrepreneurs can learn how to do it better the next time, and (3) failure does indeed often precede success in the highly challenging, stressful environment of entrepreneurship. These principles are confirmed by the fact that even today, a large proportion of successful entrepreneurs experienced major failures—sometimes several—before achieving success (e.g., Sarasvathy, Menon, & Kuechle, 2013).

Although some entrepreneurs recover from setbacks and even failure, many do not. This raises an important question: Why? What skills, characteristics, and personal strengths allow some entrepreneurs to try again, while others decide to give up and, perhaps, never to try again? Until recently, little research had been conducted to answer this question and so to identify additional tools entrepreneurs need for success. However, a growing body of research now offers important insights into this intriguing issue.

Coping With Stress

Stress, often defined as cognitive, emotional, and physiological reactions resulting from the perception by an individual that she or he cannot cope with current, seemingly overwhelming conditions—has been found to be a major source of psychological and health-related problems (e.g., Lupien, McEwen, Gunnar, & Heim, 2009). Given the unpredictable, dynamic and high-risk environments in which many entrepreneurs operate, it has often been assumed that as a group, they experience very high levels of stress—but is this actually true? At first glance, it appears to be a very reasonable suggestion and, in fact, many entrepreneurs report that they often experience high levels of stress while running their companies. However, recent research actually indicates that counterintuitively, entrepreneurs may actually experience lower levels of stress than persons in many other occupations. Baron, Franklin, and Hmieleski (2016) found that when compared to several other occupational groups on a standard measure of stress, entrepreneurs reported less stress on the same measure. Results indicated that this was due, in part, to the fact that, as ASA theory (attraction, selection, attrition, described earlier) suggests, only individuals who are relatively resistant to stress become entrepreneurs and then continue in this role. An additional factor involves what is known as *psychological capital*—a construct that expands that of social capital in important ways. Psychological capital has received a large amount of attention in several fields of management (e.g., organizational behavior) and has potentially important implications for the field of entrepreneurship.

Psychological Capital
Psychological capital refers to a combination of four variables: self-efficacy, optimism, hope, and resilience (Luthans, Avolio, Walumbwa, & Li, 2005). High self-efficacy provides the belief that current adversity and stress can be overcome; optimism is the belief that outcomes will be positive in almost any situation (Hmieleski & Baron, 2009); hope involves imagining multiple paths for coping with current stressful conditions (Snyder, Sympson, & Ybasco, 1996); and resilience provides confidence that current difficulties can be overcome, as they have been in the past—that it will be possible to "bounce back" from adversity (Tugade, Fredrickson, & Barrett, 2004).

Psychological capital has been shown to be related to several important work-related outcomes, such as superior performance on many tasks and positive work-related attitudes (e.g., job satisfaction, organizational commitment). Further, and most directly relevant, it has been found to be negatively related to perceived stress. For example, a meta-analysis of research on the impact of psychological capital (Avey, Reichard, Luthans, & Mhatre, 2011) indicates that it is negatively related to stress. This negative relationship, in turn, suggests that psychological capital provides individuals with personal resources that help protect them against the adverse of effects of stress (Baron, Franklin, & Hmieleski, 2016).

Consistent with previous research and theory concerning psychological capital, Baron et al. (2016) found that psychological capital was negatively related to perceived stress, but was positively related to entrepreneurs' feelings of subjective well-being—an indicant of individuals' overall satisfaction with their lives. In short, psychological capital not only contributes to resistance to stress, it also enhances the overall quality of life. In sum, psychological capital—and the variables that underlie it—represent ingredients in the achievement of entrepreneurial success.

Dealing with Business Failure: When One Dream Ends Another (Should) Begin

Winston Churchill, once remarked that "Success is not final, failure is not fatal: It is the courage to continue that counts." His words certainly seem to apply to Colonel Sanders, Henry Ford, and Walt Disney—all of whom failed but persevered. Clearly, however, the failure of a business is a highly disturbing experience for all entrepreneurs. Recent theory and research has helped to clarify what the effects of such an experience are. As noted by Ucbasaran, Westhead, Wright, and Flores (2010), these effects fall into three distinct categories.

Financial costs. These involve the loss of capital time and energy, and—if entrepreneurs have funded their own ventures—may leave them facing financial ruin. If the entrepreneurs have used their own resources, the effects on their personal lives and finances may be ones from which they cannot readily recover. Their credit is gone and they may be left with large debts. Further, they may be blamed, personally, for the failure of their companies and these financial losses.

Social costs. These are somewhat more subtle in nature than financial losses, but can be just as devastating. They include loss of reputation and this often makes if much more difficult for the entrepreneur to obtain support in the future. That, in turn, reduces the likelihood they will try again. Further, business failure may significantly weaken an entrepreneur's social network as the people in it attempt to distance themselves from the entrepreneur, and because the entrepreneur no longer has anything to trade—to offer members of her or his network in exchange for their help.

Psychological costs. These can include feelings of guilt, anger, or shame, reduction in motivation, and strong feelings of being overwhelmed, that is, a high level of stress, with all the physical and psychological costs it extracts. Such effects are weaker for entrepreneurs who have previously run successful businesses, but can nonetheless be intense.

Unfortunately, there is no single or simple means of dealing with these costs—they are real and unavoidable when a new venture fails. Entrepreneurs are deeply committed to and involved in their ventures, and so are especially vulnerable to these costs. Overall, then, it is important for them to develop the psychological and social capital that can help them cope with what, in many cases, is truly the shattering of their personal dreams—and these skills can contribute significantly to their success.

Putting it All Together: The Successful Entrepreneur's Tool Kit

Admittedly this review of the skills, knowledge, and characteristics entrepreneurs need to achieve success is incomplete. The ingredients are many—too many to include here—and, perhaps more importantly, we do not yet know what these are, or their relative importance. However, drawing on the information that is currently available,

Table 6.2 Key ingredients in entrepreneurial success—an incomplete list.

Tool	Description
Motivation	Understanding what you seek
Creativity	Breaking free of mental ruts
Identifying feasible opportunities	
Alertness	Actively searching for, finding, and evaluating opportunities
Self-regulation	Self-control, knowing what you know and do not, and knowing when to get out (avoid sunk costs)
Avoiding cognitive errors	Self-serving bias, confirmation bias, etc.
Building a strong founding team	
Developing effective social networks	
Social/political skills	Being able to get along well with others and form effective relationships with them
Manage emotions	Minimizing the effects of extreme positive affect
Passion	Strong commitment to entrepreneurial roles
Managing positive affect	
Planning and improvisation	
Managing stress	
Learning from mistakes	
Building subjective well-being	

Note: Although no complete list of the key factors contributing to entrepreneurial success is possible (there are too many and we don't yet know what all of these are), existing evidence points to these as being among the most important.

a tentative list of the variables that should be included on this list are presented in Table 6.2. Again, it should be emphasized that this is only a partial list and is intended merely as a beginning step in understanding the broad realm of factors that together may provide entrepreneurs with what they need to turn the possible—what their creative ideas suggest—into reality.

Tools for Changing the World—or at Least Some Corner of it

Years ago—when an independent field of entrepreneurship was just emerging—William Baumol—a famous economist who is perhaps best known in entrepreneurship for his views concerning the productive versus destructive form of this process, offered the following suggestion: trying to understand entrepreneurship without understanding entrepreneurs is like trying to understand Shakespeare without including Hamlet. To most persons outside academia, this seems to be only common sense: *of course* entrepreneurs are crucial. As Shane et al. (2003) noted, entrepreneurship only happens because specific individuals act to turn their ideas (and perhaps dreams) into reality—something tangible. Yet, the field of entrepreneurship has not always placed entrepreneurs center stage—rather, the effects of external environments and conditions quite apart from the entrepreneurs themselves, have been emphasized. Indeed, some have gone so far as to suggest that entrepreneurs are, to a large extent interchangeable: If one person does not recognize and act on an opportunity, someone else will, and there is little if anything special about the persons who are first on the scene.

In recent years, this view has softened considerably and, currently, it is widely recognized in all areas and foci of the field, that both sets of factors must be included in efforts to develop a comprehensive, informative model of the entrepreneurial process. And this model must, logically, include understanding of what tools entrepreneurs need to achieve their goals, whatever these goals may be.

But acquiring insight into the nature and interaction of these micro- and macro-level variables factors is important for another reason: it contributes in a major way to the primary goal the field of entrepreneurship seeks: *helping entrepreneurs*—assisting them on their journey to the success for which they strive. Indeed, at many universities the contributions of departments or programs of entrepreneurship are often judged, to an important extent, by such metrics as the number of new ventures started by its students, the number of business plan competitions students in the programs win, and ultimately, the extent to which, having obtained success, they seek to "give back" to the people and institutions that helped them in various ways, such as sharing their expertise with students, providing internships for them, and making financial gifts. Consistent with this view, state governments which are often generous in their support for entrepreneurship, expect concrete returns on their investment—successful new ventures that contribute to the economic well-being of their state. Of course, as members of the academic community, the field of entrepreneurship must also meet another central responsibility: contributing to knowledge in its domain. Often, however, this mission is seen as less central by many of its supporters (e.g., donors, state governments) than the practical economic benefits entrepreneurship can provide.

Given this duality of basic missions, how can the field best meet both? Adding to knowledge is in one sense, straightforward: conducting excellent research, publishing it in high-quality journals, winning recognition from colleagues in other fields. The mission of assisting entrepreneurs, however, is, somewhat more complex. Basically, it involves equipping future and current entrepreneurs with the kind of tools described in this chapter. The greater the extent to which they possess this equipment —skills, knowledge, understanding of their own motives, the self-discipline to act on them, several personal characteristics, and an effective balance between passion and reality (e.g., setting attainable goals)—the more likely they will be to succeed.

But we can't provide our students with this help unless we first identify and then obtain it. So, to put it succinctly, we can only fulfill one of our central missions—helping entrepreneurs to realize their dreams and so, perhaps, change the world—if we obtain accurate, comprehensive, and practical knowledge to share with them. This, in turn raises the key question: "How do we obtain such knowledge?" One answer—and an answer that has often been accepted without question—is: From highly successful entrepreneurs. While such input can certainly be informative, relying on it too heavily has a potential downside: human cognition is far from perfect and often people do not really know why they have done what they have done in the past, or what factors truly contributed to their success (or failure; e.g., Baron, 2013). Happily, augmenting the basically subjective information provided by successful entrepreneurs involves our second major mission: adding to knowledge in our field. In sum, understanding what entrepreneurs need in order to achieve success can contribute in important ways both to (1) helping our students reach their personal goals—their own definitions of success, and (2) expanding our knowledge of the entrepreneurial process generally. As Paloma Faith, a well-known songwriter and actress has put it: "There's nothing better than achieving your goals, whatever they might be," and that may be as true for entire fields as it is for individuals.

References

Adler, P., & Kwon, S. (2002). Social capital: Prospects for a new concept. *Academy of Management Review, 27*, 17–40.

Aldrich, H. E., & Kim, P. H. (2007). Small worlds, infinite possibilities? How social networks affect entrepreneurial team formation and search. *Strategic Entrepreneurship Journal, 1*(1–2), 147–165.

Alvarez, S. A., & Barney, J. B. (2007). Discovery and creation: Alternative theories of entrepreneurial action. *Strategic entrepreneurship journal, 1*(1-2), 11–26.

Avey, J. B., Reichard, R. J., Luthans, F., & Mhatre, K. H. (2011). Meta-analysis of the impact of positive psychological capital on employee attitudes, behaviors, and performance. *Human Resource Development Quarterly, 22*(2), 127–152.

Baron, R. A. (2006). Opportunity recognition as pattern recognition: How entrepreneurs "connect the dots" to identify new business opportunities. *Academy of Management Perspectives, 20*, 104–119.

Baron, R. A. (2007). Behavioral and cognitive factors in entrepreneurship: Entrepreneurs as the active element in new venture creation. *Strategic Entrepreneurship Journal, 1*, 167–182.

Baron, R. A. (2010). Job design and entrepreneurship: Why closer connections = mutual gains. *Journal of Organizational Behavior, 30*, 1–10.

Baron, R. A. (2013). *Enhancing entrepreneurial excellence: Tools for making the possible real*. Cheltenham, England: Elgar.

Baron, R. A., Franklin, R., & Hmieleski, K. M. (2016). Why entrepreneurs often experience low, not high, levels of stress: The joint effects of selection and psychological capital. *Journal of Management, 42*, 742–768.

Baron, R. A., Hmieleski, K. M., & Henry, R. A. (2012). Entrepreneurs' dispositional positive affect: The potential benefits—and potential costs—of being "up." *Journal of Business Venturing, 27*, 310–324.

Baron, R. A., & Tang, J. (2009). Entrepreneurs' social competence and new venture performance: Evidence on potential mediators and cross-industry generality. *Journal of Management, 35*, 282–306.

Baron, R. A., & Markman, G. D. (2003). Beyond social capital: The role of entrepreneurs social competence in their financial success. *Journal of Business Venturing, 18*, 41–60.

Baron, R. A., Mueller, B., & Wolfe, M. T. (2016). Self-efficacy and entrepreneurs' adoption of unattainable goals: The restraining effects of self-control. *Journal of Business Venturing, 31*, 55–71.

Cardon, M. S., Wincent, J., Singh, J., & Drnovsek, M. (2009). The nature and experience of entrepreneurial passion. *Academy of management Review*, *34*(3), 511–532.

Carver, C. S., & Scheier, M. (1990). Principles of self-regulation: Action and emotion. Guilford Press.

Eisenhardt, K. M. (1989). Building theories from case study research. *Academy of Management Review*, *14*(4), 532–550.

Eisenhardt, K. M., & Graebner, M. E. (2007). Theory building from cases: Opportunities and challenges. *Academy of Management Journal*, *50*(1), 25–32.

Ericsson, K. A. (2014). *The road to excellence: The acquisition of expert performance in the arts and sciences, sports, and games*. Hove, England: Psychology Press.

Fang, R., Chi, L., Chen, M., & Baron, R. A. (2015). Bringing political skill into social networks: Findings from a field study of entrepreneurs. *Journal of Management Studies*, *52*(2), 175–212.

Ferris, G. R., Perrewé, P. L., Anthony, W. P., & Gilmore, D. C. (2000). Political skill at work. *Organizational Dynamics*, *28*(4), 25–37.

Foo, M. D. (2011). Emotions and entrepreneurial opportunity evaluation. *Entrepreneurship Theory and Practice*, *35*(2), 375–393.

Forsyth, D. R. (2008). *Self-serving bias*. In W. A. Darity (Ed.), International encyclopedia of the social sciences (Vol. 7, 2nd ed.). Detroit, MI: Macmillan.

Franklin, R. & Baron, R. A. (2015). Entrepeneurs' motivation: A review (Unpublished manuscript). Oklahoma State University.

Garland, H. (1990). Throwing good money after bad: The effect of sunk costs on the decision to escalate commitment to an ongoing project. *Journal of Applied Psychology*, *75*(6), 728.

Grégoire, D. A., Barr, P. S., & Shepherd, D. A. (2010). Cognitive processes of opportunity recognition: The role of structural alignment. *Organization Science*, *21*(2), 413–431.

Heneman, H. G., & Schwab, D. P. (1972). Evaluation of research on expectancy theory predictions of employee performance. *Psychological Bulletin*, *78*(1), 1.

Hmieleski, K., & Baron, R. A. (2009). Entrepreneurs' optimism and new venture performance: A social cognitive perspective. *Academy of Management Journal*, *52*, 473–488.

Hmieleski, K. M., Carr, J. C., & Baron, R. A. (2015). Integrating discovery and creation perspectives of entrepreneurial action: the relative roles of founding CEO human capital, social capital, and psychological capital in contexts of risk versus uncertainty. *Strategic Entrepreneurship Journal*, *9*(4), 289–312.

Locke, E. A., & Latham, G. P. (2006). New directions in goal-setting theory. *Current directions in Psychological Science*, *15*(5), 265–268.

Lupien, S. J., McEwen, B. S., Gunnar, M. R., & Heim, C. (2009). Effects of stress throughout the lifespan on the brain, behaviour and cognition. *Nature Reviews Neuroscience*, *10*(6), 434–445.

Luthans, F., Avolio, B. J., Walumbwa, F. O., & Li, W. (2005). The psychological capital of Chinese workers: Exploring the relationship with performance. *Management and Organization Review*, *1*, 249–271.

Lyubomirsky, S., King, L., & Diener, E. (2005). The benefits of frequent positive affect: Does happiness lead to success? *Psychological Bulletin*, *131*(6), 803–855.

Murnieks, C. Y., Mosakowski, E., & Cardon, M. S. (2014). Pathways of passion identity centrality, passion, and behavior among entrepreneurs. *Journal of Management, 40*(6), 1583–1606.

Nahapiet, J., & Ghoshal, S. (1998). Social capital, intellectual capital, and the organizational advantage. *Academy of Management Review, 23*(2), 242–266.

Portes, A. (1998). Social capital: Its origins and applications in modern sociology. *Annual Review of Sociology, 24*(1), 1–24.

Putnam, F. (2000). *Bowling alone: The collapse and revival of American community.* New York, NY: Simon & Schuster.

Rindova, V., Barry, D., &. Ketchen, D. J. Jr. (2009). Entrepreneuring as emancipation. *Academy of Management Review, 34,* 477–491.

Runco, M. A., & Jaeger, G. J. (2012). The standard definition of creativity. *Creativity Research Journal, 24*(1), 92–96.

Ryan, R. M., & Deci, E. L. (2000). Intrinsic and extrinsic motivations: Classic definitions and new directions. *Contemporary educational psychology, 25*(1), 54–67.

Sarasvathy, S. D., Menon, A. R., & Kuechle, G. (2013). Failing firms and successful entrepreneurs: Serial entrepreneurship as a temporal portfolio. Small business economics, *40*(2), 417–434.

Schneider, B., Smith, D. B., & Goldstein, H. W. (2000). *Attraction–selection–attrition: Toward a person–environment psychology of organizations.* Mahwah, NJ: Erlbaum.

Shane, S., Locke, E. A., & Collins, C. J. (2003). Entrepreneurial motivation. *Human Resource Management Review, 13*(2), 257–279.

Snyder, C. R., Sympson, S. C., & Ybasco, F. C. (1996). Development and validation of the State Hope Scale. *Journal of Personality and Social Psychology, 70,* 321–335.

Staw, B. M., & Ross, J. (1989). Understanding behavior in escalation situations. *Science, 246*(4927), 216–220.

Tracy, J. L., Cheng, J. T., Robins, R. W., & Trzesniewski, K. H. (2009). Authentic and hubristic pride: The affective core of self-esteem and narcissism. *Self and identity, 8*(2–3), 196–213.

Tugade, M. M., Fredrickson, B. L., & Feldman Barrett, L. (2004). Psychological resilience and positive emotional granularity: Examining the benefits of positive emotions on coping and health. *Journal of personality, 72*(6), 1161–1190.

Ucbasaran, D., Westhead, P., Wright, M., & Flores, M. (2010). The nature of entrepreneurial experience, business failure and comparative optimism. *Journal of Business Venturing, 25*(6), 541–555.

Webb, J. W., Tihanyi, L., Ireland, R. D., & Sirmon, D. G. (2009). You say illegal, I say legitimate: Entrepreneurship in the informal economy. *Academy of Management Review, 34*(3), 492–510.

Wrosch, C., Miller, G. E., Scheier, M. F., & De Pontet, S. B. (2007). Giving up on unattainable goals: Benefits for health? *Personality and Social Psychology Bulletin, 33*(2), 251–265.

Yin, R. K. (1994). *Case study research: Design and methods.* London, England: Sage.

Zhao, H., Seibert, S. E., & Hills, G. E. (2005). The mediating role of self-efficacy in the development of entrepreneurial intentions. *Journal of Applied Psychology, 90*(6), 1265–1272.

7

Creativity and Entrepreneurship: A Process Perspective

Maike Lex and Michael M. Gielnik[a]

[a] *Leuphana University of Lüneburg, Germany*

Introduction

Creativity is widely acknowledged as a key predictor of entrepreneurship (e.g., Manimala, 2009; Shalley & Perry-Smith, 2008; Tsai, 2014; Ward, 2004; Zhou, 2008). Indeed, there are numerous theoretical reasons to expect a positive effect of creativity on entrepreneurs' success, such as creativity promoting entrepreneurs' ability to identify business opportunities and to overcome problems in the process of setting-up and managing a new venture (e.g., Hansen, Lumpkin, & Hills, 2011; Mcmullan & Kenworthy, 2015; Schumpeter, 1934; Ward, 2004; Zhou, 2008). However, there is surprisingly little empirical research on the effect of creativity on entrepreneurship with some of the studies yielding nonsignificant results (e.g., Heinonen, Hytti, & Stenholm, 2011; Heunks, 1998). In this chapter, we review the literature on creativity and entrepreneurship, which has generally employed a relatively basic approach to the main effects of creativity on entrepreneurship. We go beyond this relatively basic approach by adopting a more differentiated perspective on the role of creativity in entrepreneurship. Specifically, we argue that both creativity and entrepreneurship comprise different components and phases and that these need to be taken into account in order to fully understand the effect of creativity in entrepreneurship (Dimov, 2007; Gielnik, Frese, Graf, & Kampschulte, 2012; Zhou, 2008). Creativity consists of two disparate cognitive abilities, that is, divergent and convergent thinking, which are both required to generate new and useful ideas (Basadur, Graen, & Green, 1982; Brophy, 1998; Cropley, 2006; Guilford, 1950; Ward, Smith, & Finke, 1999). Divergent thinking represents people's ability to recognize links between seemingly unrelated pieces of information and to come up with unexpected combinations of such information, leading to the generation of multiple new and original ideas (Cropley, 2006; Mumford, Mobley, Reiter-Palmon, Uhlman, & Doares, 1991). Convergent thinking, in contrast, refers to a more analytical mode of thinking that focuses on a narrow range of familiar information in order to detect one single conventional solution (Cropley, 2006; Hennessey & Amabile, 2010; Mumford et al., 1991). Similarly, entrepreneurship represents a

The Wiley Handbook of Entrepreneurship, First Edition.
Edited by Gorkan Ahmetoglu, Tomas Chamorro-Premuzic, Bailey Klinger, & Tessa Karcisky.
© 2017 John Wiley & Sons Ltd. Published 2017 by John Wiley & Sons Ltd.

continuous process of exploring and exploiting business opportunities (Shane & Venkataraman, 2000). This entrepreneurial process can be broken down into three phases: the prelaunch phase in which entrepreneurs identify opportunities; the launch phase in which entrepreneurs set up a new venture; and the postlaunch phase in which entrepreneurs manage continuous innovation, growth, and survival of the new venture (Baron, 2007; Frese & Gielnik, 2014). Building on the assumptions that creativity and entrepreneurship encompass different components and phases, we develop a comprehensive theoretical model on the role of creativity in the entrepreneurial process. We build our cumulative process model on ambidexterity theory (Bledow, Frese, Anderson, Erez, & Farr, 2009) which provides a differentiated perspective on the generation and implementation of novel and useful ideas. Our cumulative process model integrates past theoretical and empirical research into a holistic framework and illuminates both the positive and negative effects of creativity in different phases of the entrepreneurial process.

Creativity and Entrepreneurship: A Conceptual Differentiation

Creativity and entrepreneurship are frequently viewed as inherently linked (Fillis & Rentschler, 2010; Manimala, 2009; Matthews, 2010; Sternberg & Lubart, 1999; Whiting, 1988) and have sometimes even been treated synonymously in past research (Hamidi, Wennberg, & Berglund, 2008). Indeed, there are certain parallels between creativity and entrepreneurship (Fillis & Rentschler, 2010; Shalley, Hitt, & Zhou, 2015; Ward, 2004).

Creativity is defined as the generation of new and useful ideas concerning products, services, processes, or procedures (Amabile, 1988; Anderson, Potocnik, & Zhou, 2014; Zhou & George, 2001). Similarly, entrepreneurship refers to the exploration and exploitation of business opportunities (Shane & Venkataraman, 2000), that is, situations in which novel products and services can be introduced to the market and are considered useful by potential customers (Eckhardt & Shane, 2003). These definitions reveal that the concepts of creativity and entrepreneurship are substantially related since both address the novelty and usefulness of an idea or product (Gielnik, 2013; Matthews, 2007; Ward, 2004). However, there are also important conceptual differences between the two constructs that need to be taken into account when investigating the effect of creativity in entrepreneurship (Dino, 2015). Entrepreneurship goes beyond creativity because it does not only comprise the generation of novel and useful ideas but also the refinement and implementation of these ideas into a viable business opportunity (Dimov, 2007; Gielnik, 2013; Wood & McKinley, 2010). More specifically, entrepreneurship represents a continuous process that starts with the generation of an idea which then needs to be elaborated, refined, and implemented with the help of entrepreneurial actions (Dimov, 2007). Important entrepreneurial actions include, for example, collecting information and feedback regarding the feasibility of the idea and advancing the initial idea based on the acquired information (Lumpkin & Lichtenstein, 2005; Ravasi & Turati, 2005). Also, entrepreneurs have to invest considerable effort to acquire financial resources and to attract high-quality employees that enable the implementation of the business opportunity (Baron, 2007; Ward, 2004). All these entrepreneurial activities require creativity (Mcmullan & Kenworthy, 2015; Shalley & Perry-Smith, 2008; Zhou, 2008). As such, creativity is not a synonym for entrepreneurship but rather a key factor that is essential in the entire entrepreneurial process to successfully explore and exploit business opportunities (Zhou, 2008).

The Effect of Creativity on Entrepreneurship

Scholars agree that creativity plays a key role in entrepreneurship (e.g., Dayan, Zacca, & Di Benedetto, 2013; Shalley & Perry-Smith, 2008; Tsai, 2014; Ward, 2004; Zhou, 2008). For instance, scholars have described creativity as the "spirit of entrepreneurship" (Tsai, 2014, p. 106) or as "the most critical trait of an entrepreneur" (Manimala, 2009, p. 121). While there is theoretical agreement that creativity positively affects an entrepreneur's success, empirical research on the role of creativity in entrepreneurship has provided inconsistent results (Gielnik, 2013). In the following, we review empirical research examining the link between creativity and entrepreneurship. An overview of empirical research on the link between creativity and entrepreneurship is provided in Table 7.1.

Table 7.1 Empirical results on the role of creativity in entrepreneurial success in the three phases of the entrepreneurial process.

Phase	Prelaunch	Launch	Postlaunch
Positive effects	DeTienne & Chandler (2004): Creativity training → Business opportunity identification	Audretsch & Belitski (2013); Lee, Florida, & Acs (2004): Regional creativity → Business creation	Baron & Tang (2011): Creativity → Radicalness of implemented innovations
	Hansen, Lumpkin, & Hills (2011): Creativity → Business opportunity identification (in part)	Knörr, Alvarez, & Urbano (2013): Creativity → Probability of becoming an entrepreneur	Morris & Fargher (1974) Creativity → Venture growth
	Shane & Nicolaou (2015): Creative personality → Business opportunity identification	Shane & Nicolaou (2015): Creative personality → Business creation	
No effects	Antonio, Lanawati, Wiriana, & Christina (2014): Creativity ✗→ Achievements in entrepreneurship education	Hull, Bosley, & Udell (1980): Creativity ✗→ Business creation	Heunks (1998): Creativity ✗→ Venture profit and growth
	Hansen, Lumpkin, & Hills (2011): Creativity ✗→ Business opportunity identification (in part)		
	Heinonen, Hytti, & Stenholm (2011): Creativity ✗→ Viability of generated business ideas		

On the one hand, there is indeed some empirical research indicating a positive effect of creativity in all phases of the entrepreneurial process (see Table 7.1). For example, focusing on the prelaunch phase, DeTienne and Chandler (2004) have provided empirical evidence for a positive effect of creativity on business opportunity identification. Using an experimental pretest–posttest control group design, the authors showed that participating in creativity training increases the number and innovativeness of identified business opportunities. Recently, Shane and Nicolaou (2015) have substantiated these results by showing that people with creative personalities are more likely than others to identify business opportunities. Moreover, research investigating the role of creativity in the launch phase has provided evidence that creativity also promotes actual business creation (e.g., Audretsch & Belitski, 2013; Lee, Florida, & Acs, 2004; Shane & Nicolaou, 2015). For example, the study by Shane and Nicolaou (2015) revealed that having a creative personality does not only increase people's opportunity identification but also their tendency to start a business. Moreover, using a county-level study covering the entire United States, Lee and colleagues (2004) found a positive and significant impact of a county's creativity level on its rate of business creation. Similarly, Audretsch and Belitski (2013) showed a positive effect of regional creativity on the number of businesses being started across 143 European cities. Supporting these regional-level results, Knörr, Alvarez, and Urbano (2013) showed in a study on the individual level that an individual's creativity raises the likelihood of them becoming an entrepreneur. Furthermore, studies examining creativity in the postlaunch phase have provided evidence that creativity also fosters entrepreneurs' success after having started a business (Baron & Tang, 2011; Morris & Fargher, 1974). For instance, based on a sample of 99 entrepreneurs in the United States, Baron and Tang (2011) theorized and showed a positive effect of entrepreneurs' creativity on the radicalness of innovations implemented in their new ventures. Radicalness of innovations is an important predictor of new venture performance (Rosenbusch, Brinckmann, & Bausch, 2011; Tushman & Anderson, 1986; Zahra & Bogner, 2000). In line with these results, Morris and Fargher (1974) demonstrated that entrepreneurs' creativity is positively related to the growth of their new ventures. These studies highlight the important role of entrepreneurs' creativity for their venture performance.

In contrast to the studies showing a positive impact of creativity in entrepreneurship, other studies have failed to demonstrate such an effect for the respective phases of the entrepreneurial process (see Table 7.1). Focusing on the prelaunch phase, Antonio and colleagues (2014) conducted a cross-sectional study with 283 university graduates and reported that individuals' creativity did not predict their achievements in entrepreneurship education. Furthermore, Hansen, Lumpkin, and Hills (2011) found only partial support for a link between entrepreneurs' creativity and their ability to recognize opportunities. While creativity was positively and significantly related to two activities underlying opportunity recognition, creativity did not affect three further important activities required for opportunity recognition (Hansen et al., 2011). Heinonen and colleagues (2011) also yielded nonsignificant results indicating that students' creativity did not have a direct effect on the viability of business ideas generated during an entrepreneurship course. Similarly, with regard to the launch phase, Hull, Bosley, and Udell (1980) failed to establish a link between creativity and business creation. Using a survey study with 307 university graduates, the authors showed that individuals' creativity did not distinguish between entrepreneurs and nonentrepreneurs. Regarding the postlaunch phase, a study with 200 entrepreneurs across six countries revealed that entrepreneurs' creativity did not influence the profit and growth of their ventures (Heunks, 1998). Taken together, these studies cast some doubt that creativity directly affects success in entrepreneurship.

In sum, empirical research on the role of creativity in entrepreneurship has yielded inconsistent results which, at least in part, directly contradict each other. For instance, whereas some studies (DeTienne & Chandler, 2004; Shane & Nicolaou, 2015) have demonstrated a positive effect of creativity on individuals' ability to identify business opportunities, other studies (Hansen et al., 2011; Heinonen et al., 2011) could not fully replicate such an effect. The contradictory results may result from the relatively basic approach adopted by past research (Dimov, 2007). Past research has mainly examined the link between creativity and entrepreneurship using relatively broad measures of creativity and entrepreneurship. Both creativity and entrepreneurship, however, are complex processes comprising multiple components and phases over time (Dimov, 2007; Gielnik et al., 2012; Nyström, 1993; Zhou, 2008). Accordingly, to fully understand the role of creativity in entrepreneurship, research needs to adopt a more differentiated perspective by distinguishing between different components of creativity and entrepreneurship (Baron, 2007; Gielnik et al., 2012; Gielnik, 2013; Zhou, 2008). Numerous scholars have called for such a differentiated perspective on creativity in entrepreneurship (e.g., Baron, 2007; Zhou, 2008). We follow these calls and propose an integrated theoretical model on the role of creativity in the entrepreneurial process. Our model provides a more fine-grained investigation of the specific effects of the two components of creativity, that is, divergent and convergent thinking, on different outcomes throughout the entrepreneurial process. Such a detailed examination helps to resolve apparent contradictions in past research and thus contributes to our understanding of the diverse effects of creativity in the different phases of the entrepreneurial process (Baron, 2007; Gielnik et al., 2012; Zhou, 2008).

Toward a Cumulative Process Model of Creativity in Entrepreneurship

We build our theoretical model on past research in the areas of creativity and entrepreneurship. Past research has provided fine-grained conceptualizations describing both creativity and entrepreneurship as complex processes that encompass multiple components (Baron, 2007; Gielnik et al., 2012; Gielnik, 2013; Zhou, 2008). We draw upon these fine-grained conceptualizations and incorporate them into our theoretical model. Accordingly, we build our theoretical model on the following three assumptions. First, entrepreneurship is a continuous and dynamic process comprising three different phases: the prelaunch, the launch, and the postlaunch phases (Baron, 2007). Each phase requires specific ways of entrepreneurial thinking and acting (Baron, 2007). Accordingly, an entrepreneur's success in each phase encompasses different dimensions that are differentially affected by creativity (Baron, 2007; Dimov, 2007). Second, creativity consists of two components—divergent and convergent thinking (Basadur et al., 1982; Brophy, 1998; Guilford, 1950; Ward et al., 1999), which have differential effects on success in entrepreneurship. Third, creativity is of continuing importance for an entrepreneur's success throughout the entire entrepreneurial process (Lin & Nabergoj, 2014;

Ogbari & Isiavwe, 2015; Shalley et al., 2015; Shalley & Perry-Smith, 2008; Zhou, 2008). More specifically, both divergent and convergent thinking are fundamental to an entrepreneur's success in each phase of the entrepreneurial process (Manimala, 2009). The relative importance and specific effects of entrepreneurs' divergent and convergent thinking, however, considerably change in the course of the entrepreneurial process (Baron, 2002, 2007; Baron & Markman, 2005; Baron & Shane, 2004; Shane, 2003). It follows from these assumptions that a differentiated perspective on creativity in entrepreneurship requires examining the specific effects of divergent and convergent thinking on different dimensions of entrepreneurial success in the three phases of entrepreneurship (e.g., Gielnik, 2013; Gielnik et al., 2012).

Recently, scholars have started to adopt such a differentiated perspective and investigated the effects of different components of creativity on success in different phases of the entrepreneurial process. For example, several studies have examined the effect of divergent thinking on business opportunity identification. Using both a correlational field study and an experimental design, Gielnik and colleagues (2012) provided evidence that divergent thinking has a significant positive effect on the originality of identified business opportunities which in turn positively predicts business growth. A recent field study substantiated these results by showing a positive effect of entrepreneurs' divergent thinking on the number of identified business opportunities and the innovativeness of newly introduced products or services (Gielnik, Krämer, Kappel, & Frese, 2014). Further support for a positive effect of divergent thinking on business opportunity identification stems from Karimi and colleagues (2014) who showed that training in divergent thinking promotes participants' ability to generate multiple and innovative business ideas. Taking a step further, Ames and Runco (2005) investigated the impact of entrepreneurs' divergent thinking on actual business creation. Based on a field survey study with actual entrepreneurs, the authors demonstrated that divergent thinking has a positive effect on the number of businesses started by an entrepreneur (Ames & Runco, 2005). Beyond these studies directly examining the effect of divergent thinking on entrepreneurship, empirical evidence from other academic fields indicates further links between divergent thinking and entrepreneurial success. For instance, past research suggests that divergent thinking helps an entrepreneur to develop and communicate an effective vision (Matthews, 2009; Strange & Mumford, 2005) which in turn positively affects business growth (Baum, Locke, & Kirkpatrick, 1998). Also, divergent thinking enables entrepreneurs to generate ideas on how to overcome barriers in the entrepreneurial process, which in turn helps to persistently pursue entrepreneurial goals (Frese & Fay, 2001; Markman, Baron, & Balkin, 2005; Zaccaro, Mumford, Connelly, Marks, & Gilbert, 2000). Apart from these studies focusing on divergent thinking, there is also some empirical research suggesting a positive effect of convergent thinking on entrepreneurial success. For instance, Chen, Chang, and Lo (2015) recently provided evidence that entrepreneurs with high levels of convergent thinking display more rational and effective conflict management styles, which in turn substantially promotes new venture performance (Liu, Fu, & Liu, 2009).

While these findings provide interesting insights into the role of creativity and its two components divergent and convergent thinking in entrepreneurship, the findings remain fairly fragmented and disconnected. We therefore aim to integrate the fragmented findings into a more inclusive model on creativity in entrepreneurship. Our theoretical model illuminates how and why divergent and convergent thinking promote or hinder different indicators of entrepreneurial success in the three phases of entrepreneurship. As such, our model contributes to our theoretical understanding of the differential effects of creativity in entrepreneurship. In the following, we first present the key assumptions underlying our process model in more detail. We then propose a comprehensive process model on the role of creativity in entrepreneurship. We conclude by summarizing the central contributions of our theoretical model.

Key Assumptions of the Cumulative Process Model

Creativity and its Underlying Components

To systematically examine the effect of creativity on entrepreneurship, we first need to precisely conceptualize creativity. Creativity can be conceptualized as a complex cognitive process that requires the two specific cognitive abilities of divergent and convergent thinking (Basadur et al., 1982; Brophy, 1998; Cropley, 2006; Guilford, 1950; Mumford et al., 1991; Runco, 2003; Runco & Acar, 2012; Ward et al., 1999).[1] Divergent and convergent thinking represent two disparate cognitive processes leading to different outcomes. As mentioned earlier, divergent thinking refers to people's capacity to think across different dimensions of information, to make associations among apparently unrelated information, and to create novel combinations of those seemingly unrelated concepts, resulting in the generation of a broad range of new and original ideas (Cropley, 2006; Hennessey & Amabile, 2010; Mumford et al., 1991). As such, divergent thinking is generally directed at increasing variability in generated ideas (Cropley, 2006). Convergent thinking, in contrast, represents a more disciplined and analytical way of thinking that focuses on a small amount of familiar and obviously relevant information with the goal of detecting one single best answer (Cropley, 2006; Hennessey & Amabile, 2010; Mumford et al., 1991). Accordingly, convergent thinking is mainly focused on narrowing variability to one single idea or solution (Cropley, 2006; Hennessey & Amabile, 2010). Scholars have widely acknowledged that both ways of thinking are required to come up with creative, that is, novel and useful, ideas (Brophy, 1998; Cropley, 2006; Runco, 2003). While divergent thinking allows the generation of a high number of original ideas, convergent thinking is important for evaluating and refining these ideas into novel and useful ideas (Bledow et al., 2009; Cropley, 2006; Runco, 2003). As such, the effects of both divergent and convergent thinking need to be taken into account in order to fully understand the role of creativity in the entrepreneurial process.

The Entrepreneurial Process and its Constituting Phases

To fully understand the role of creativity in entrepreneurship, we further need to clearly conceptualize entrepreneurship. Entrepreneurship represents not a one-time event, but rather a continuous and dynamic process that unfolds over time (e.g., Baron, 2007; Baron

---

[1] Past entrepreneurship research has conceptualized creativity in a number of different ways, e.g., as a stable personality characteristic (e.g., Heinonen et al., 2011; Heunks, 1998; Shane & Nicolaou, 2014) or as cognitive capability (e.g., Ames & Runco, 2005; Baron, 2006; Gielnik et al., 2012, 2014). Given that recent creativity research primarily describes creativity as a cognitive process rather than a stable trait (e.g., Anderson et al., 2014; Brophy, 1998; Cropley, 2006), we follow this common cognitive approach and conceptualize creativity as a cognitive process rather than a stable trait.

& Shane, 2004; Bygrave, 1989; Shane, 2003). The entrepreneurial process is dynamic in nature, meaning that it confronts entrepreneurs with a wide range of tasks in an ever-changing and unpredictable manner (e.g., Aldrich, 1999; Baron, 2007; Baron & Shane, 2004; Gartner, 1988; Harvey & Evans, 1995; Low & Abrahamson, 1997; Phan, Zhou, & Abrahamson, 2010; Shane & Venkataraman, 2000). While entrepreneurs' tasks rapidly change throughout the entire entrepreneurial process, there are some key entrepreneurial activities that are characteristic of different stages within the entrepreneurial process (e.g., Baron, 2007; Baron & Shane, 2004; Bygrave, 1989; Shane, 2003). Accordingly, entrepreneurship can be described as a dynamic process that moves through several distinct but closely intertwined phases (e.g., Baron, 2007; Baron & Shane, 2004; Bygrave, 1989; Shane, 2003). Scholars have suggested various process models that define different phases of the entrepreneurial process (e.g., Baron, 2007; Bhave, 1994; Bygrave, 1989, 2006; Hornsby, Naffziger, Kuratko, & Montagno, 1993; Shane, 2003). One prominent process model has been proposed by Baron (2007). Baron's (2007) process model is based on prior conceptualizations of the entrepreneurial process (e.g., Shane, 2003; Venkataraman, 1997) and provides a useful framework to systematically analyze the differential effects of potential influencing factors on an entrepreneur's success (Baron, 2007; Baron & Shane, 2004). We therefore build our theoretical model on the process model suggested by Baron (2007).

As seen earlier in this chapter, according to Baron (2007), the entrepreneurial process can be divided into three main phases: the prelaunch, the launch, and the postlaunch phases. The prelaunch phase refers to the time period prior to the actual launch of a new venture. In this phase, entrepreneurs primarily need to identify original and potentially useful business opportunities. Accordingly, entrepreneurs' success in this phase is captured by the number, originality, and usefulness of generated business opportunities (Baron, 2007; Baron & Shane, 2004). The second phase, the launch phase, comprises all entrepreneurial activities that are required for the actual launch of the new venture (Baron, 2007). Important entrepreneurial activities include, for example, acquiring a broad array of resources such as financial capital, potential partners, and high-quality employees,[2] choosing and establishing a legal form for the new venture, as well as developing strong marketing plans and strategies for exploiting the business opportunity. As such, meaningful measures of entrepreneurial success in this phase are the amount of resources acquired and the time that was needed to raise these resources as well as the actual business creation (Baron, 2007). The third phase, the postlaunch phase, encompasses all activities that are required after the start-up period. In this phase, entrepreneurs need to build the newly established venture into a viable, continuously innovating, and growing business (Baron, 2007; Baron & Shane, 2004). Specifically, entrepreneurs need to ensure continuous innovation and growth of the new venture, for example by introducing new products, services, or processes, attracting, leading, and retaining high-quality employees, and developing strong strategies for promoting and managing growth (Baron, 2007; Baron & Shane, 2004). Accordingly, meaningful

---

[2] According to Baron (2007), the assembly of resources is mainly required in the prelaunch phase. We argue that assembling resources is an ongoing task that is primarily required when preparing the launch of the new venture. We therefore depart from Baron (2007) and allocate the task to acquire resources into the launch phase (see also Frese & Gielnik, 2014).

success measures are financial measures capturing survival, continuous innovation, and growth of the new venture.

Baron's (2007) process model offers important insights into major tasks that are to be accomplished at different stages of the entrepreneurial process (Baron, 2007; Baron & Shane, 2004). However, the process model simplifies the dynamic nature of the entrepreneurial process which is not a linear sequence of phases but cumulative in nature (Baron, 2007; Baron & Shane, 2004). We therefore expand Baron's (2007) linear process model and emphasize that entrepreneurship is not a linear process moving through consecutive and sharply delineated phases (Baron, 2007; Baron & Shane, 2004), but rather a cumulative process in which every activity of a prior phase is also required in subsequent phases of the entrepreneurial process. Specifically, while the entrepreneurial process may indeed be composed of different phases that are characterized by specific key activities, these phases do not occur consecutively but rather simultaneously or cumulatively (Baron, 2007; Baron & Shane, 2004; Matthews, 2007). This means that all tasks that are considered to be important in earlier phases of the entrepreneurial process remain important at later stages as well. For instance, an entrepreneur's task to generate and evaluate business opportunities is not completed at the end of the prelaunch phase, but remains important in the launch and postlaunch phases. Indeed, to bring an initially generated and evaluated business opportunity to fruition, entrepreneurs need to continuously develop and extend the business opportunity in the launch phase (Ward, 2004). Moreover, entrepreneurs need to continually come up with new business opportunities in the postlaunch phase to ensure survival and growth of the new venture. In addition, while entrepreneurs start acquiring resources and implementing the business opportunity in the launch phase, these tasks remain crucial in the postlaunch phase as well (e.g., Baker & Nelson, 2005; Lin & Nabergoj, 2014; Tyebjee & Bruno, 1984). Consequently, the specific effects of divergent and convergent thinking are not only important in one phase—for example, the specific effects on assembling resources and actually launching the new venture in the launch phase—but also in all subsequent phases. We therefore propose a cumulative process model including three closely intertwined phases. Our cumulative process model highlights the repetitive and cumulative nature of the entrepreneurial process, meaning that all tasks of prior stages are required in later stages of the entrepreneurial process as well. As such, our model holds that all activities and tasks of one phase are proper subsets of each subsequent phase (see Figure 7.1). Our cumulative process model provides important insights into the major activities that dominate the entrepreneur at different stages of the entrepreneurial process while taking the cumulative nature of the entrepreneurial process into account.

An Ambidexterity Perspective on Creativity in the Entrepreneurial Process

Scholars have often acknowledged that creativity plays a crucial role throughout the entire entrepreneurial process (e.g., Lin & Nabergoj, 2014; Ogbari & Isiavwe, 2015; Shalley et al., 2015; Shalley & Perry-Smith, 2008; Zhou, 2008). The underlying assumption is that creativity is important for various entrepreneurial activities at different stages of the entrepreneurial process such as recognizing promising business opportunities before launching a new venture, assembling resources while actually launching the new venture, as well as promoting continuous innovation and growth after having launched a new venture (Mcmullan & Kenworthy, 2015; Perry-Smith & Mannucci, 2015;

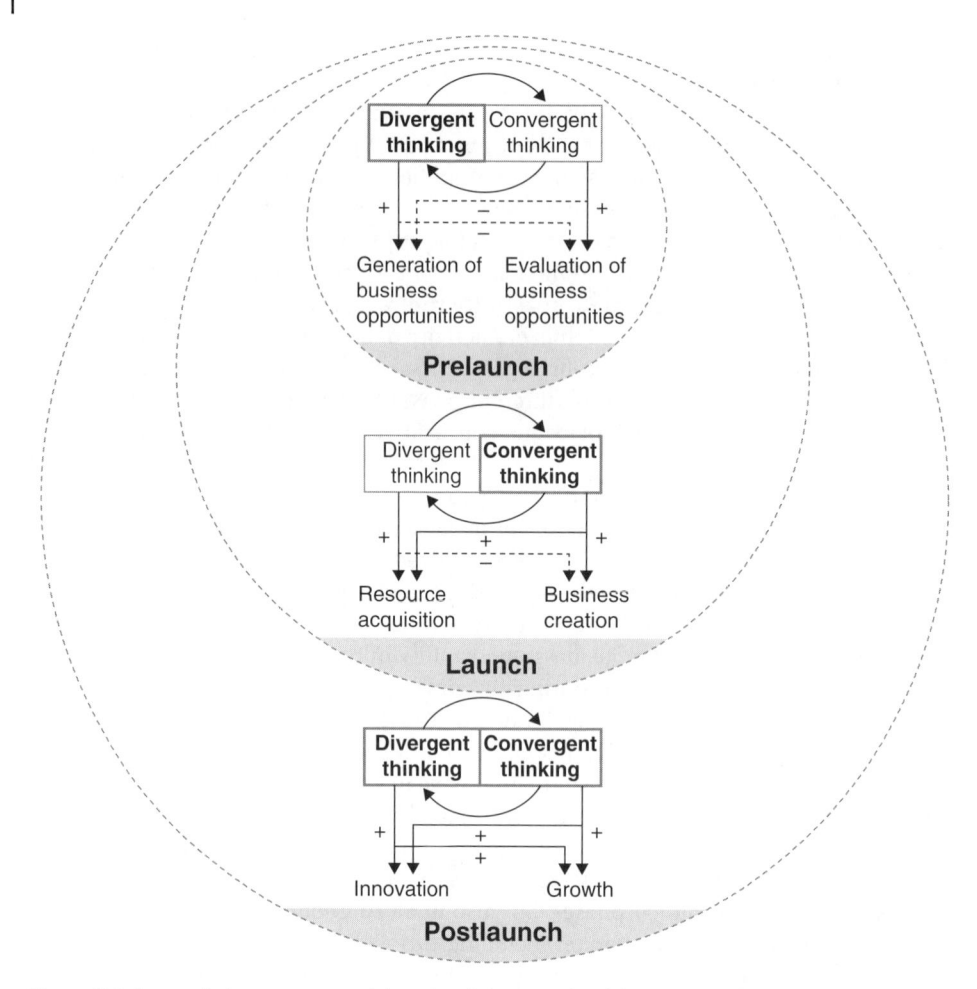

Figure 7.1 A cumulative process model on the changing role of divergent and convergent thinking throughout the entrepreneurial process.

Shalley & Perry-Smith, 2008). We concur with this assumption and take it a step further to develop a more nuanced model of creativity in entrepreneurship. Building on our more fine-grained conceptualizations of creativity and entrepreneurship, we argue that both divergent and convergent thinking are fundamental to an entrepreneur's success in each phase of the entrepreneurial process (Manimala, 2009). Each phase of the entrepreneurial process entails tasks that require the generation of multiple novel and original ideas—that is, divergent thinking—and tasks that call for the detection of one accurate answer—that is, convergent thinking (see Bledow et al., 2009; Brophy, 1998; Manimala, 2009). Moreover, given the dynamic nature of the entrepreneurial process, tasks requiring divergent thinking and tasks calling for convergent thinking continuously alternate and even occur simultaneously throughout the entrepreneurial process (see Cropley, 2006; Manimala, 2009; Wolf & Mieg, 2010). However, divergent and convergent thinking represent fundamentally different and even contradictory cognitive processes that compete for entrepreneurs' scarce resources (Bledow et al., 2009; Cropley, 2006; Getzels & Jackson, 1962). Accordingly, the need of both divergent and convergent thinking confronts entrepreneurs with inconsistent and seemingly incompatible psychological demands (Bledow et al., 2009).

Bledow and colleagues (2009) proposed a theoretical framework that helps to explain how entrepreneurs can successfully manage these inherently conflicting demands. In their ambidexterity theory, they describe how individuals and teams can manage innately conflicting demands of innovation within organizations. We borrow from this theoretical framework and apply it to the domain of entrepreneurship.

According to Bledow and colleagues (2009), apparently conflicting activities, such as divergent and convergent thinking, are not necessarily incompatible but complementary. In fact, divergent and convergent thinking are tightly intertwined and mutually dependent processes that need to be combined and integrated to generate synergistic outcomes (Bledow et al., 2009; Brophy, 1998). Accordingly, entrepreneurs need to actively capitalize on the mutual dependence and use the synergies that reside in prosecuting both divergent and convergent thinking (see Bledow et al., 2009). Moreover, given that the entrepreneurial process is chaotic in nature, entrepreneurs need to flexibly alternate from one kind of thinking to the other according to situational demands (Manimala, 2009; Wolf & Mieg, 2010). Indeed, empirical research supports this assumption by showing that entrepreneurs' ability to switch between divergent and convergent thinking promotes their success in terms of the number of granted and marketed patents (Wolf & Mieg, 2010).

In sum, we propose that entrepreneurs generally need to be able to perform both divergent and convergent thinking as well as to flexibly switch between these two types of thinking according to situational demands (see Bledow et al., 2009). Moreover, given that entrepreneurs' major tasks and activities shift in the course of the entrepreneurial process, the relative importance of an entrepreneur's divergent and convergent thinking may considerably vary across the different phases of the entrepreneurial process (Baron, 2002, 2007; Baron & Markman, 2005; Baron & Shane, 2004; Shane, 2003). We therefore propose a comprehensive process model that systematically analyzes the role of divergent and convergent thinking in each phase of the entrepreneurial process separately. The process model provides valuable insights into the specific effects of divergent and convergent thinking on an entrepreneur's success throughout the entire entrepreneurial process. Moreover, given that the tasks and activities of an entrepreneur build up cumulatively along the different phases of the entrepreneurial process, our cumulative process model elucidates how the effects of divergent and convergent thinking spill over and reappear in subsequent phases of the entrepreneurial process.

A Cumulative Process Model on Creativity in Entrepreneurship

Prelaunch

The prelaunch phase comprises an entrepreneur's activities prior to the actual launch of a new venture (Baron, 2007). In this phase, an entrepreneur's most important task is to identify an original and potentially useful business opportunity (Baron, 2007; Baron & Shane, 2004). The identification of a promising business opportunity can be seen as a two-step process requiring entrepreneurs, first, to generate new business ideas and, second, to evaluate and develop these ideas into an original and feasible business opportunity (Dimov, 2007). Past research has argued that both the generation of novel business ideas and the further development of these ideas into a business opportunity largely depend on entrepreneurs' creativity (Ardichvili, Cardozo, & Ray, 2003; Baron, 2006; Dimov, 2007; Phan et al., 2010; Shane, 2003; Ward, 2004; Zhou, 2008). We concur with this assumption and take it a step further by disentangling the concept of creativity into divergent and convergent thinking. Specifically, we argue that both divergent and convergent thinking strongly, but differently, affect entrepreneurs' success throughout the opportunity identification process as outlined in the following.

First, entrepreneurs need to generate a high number of original business ideas. This is important because generating a large amount of ideas enhances the probability of identifying original ideas (Simonton, 1989). Identifying original business ideas is crucial because original ideas are likely to result in more innovative products and services that provide a stronger competitive advantage and thus positively affect new venture performance (Baron & Tang, 2011; Drucker, 1998; Gielnik, Frese, et al., 2012; Gielnik, Krämer, et al., 2014; Porter, 1980; Shepherd & DeTienne, 2005; Zahra & Bogner, 2000). Building on past theoretical and empirical research, we argue that generating a high number of original business ideas is positively affected by entrepreneurs' divergent thinking and negatively influenced by entrepreneurs' convergent thinking (see Figure 7.1). Original business ideas usually represent novel combinations of familiar ideas, routines, or information (Baron, 2007). As described above, an individual's cognitive capacity to create novel and unexpected combinations of existing concepts corresponds to divergent thinking (Cropley, 2006; Hennessey & Amabile, 2010; Mumford et al., 1991). Accordingly, divergent thinking should have a positive impact on entrepreneurs' ability to generate multiple and original business ideas (see Figure 7.1). Indeed, empirical research has provided evidence that divergent thinking positively affects the number and originality of generated business ideas (Gielnik, Frese, et al., 2012; Gielnik, Krämer, et al., 2014; Karimi et al., 2014). Convergent thinking, in contrast, should have a negative effect on the number and originality of generated business ideas (see Figure 7.1). As outlined above, convergent thinking represents a more analytical and systematic way of thinking that results in the detection of one correct and conventional answer rather than multiple novel ideas (Cropley, 2006; Guilford, 1967; Hennessey & Amabile, 2010; Mumford et al., 1991; Ward et al., 1999). Accordingly, convergent thinking should limit entrepreneurs' capability to come up with a high number of original business ideas and thus have a negative effect at the beginning of the opportunity identification process.

After generating multiple original business ideas, entrepreneurs need to evaluate and refine these ideas into a viable and feasible business opportunity (Dimov, 2007). To do so, they have to thoroughly analyze the generated business ideas, select the most promising idea, and develop the selected idea into a viable business opportunity that is commercially feasible, compliant with legal and moral guidelines, and acceptable to potential customers (Baron, 2007; Chang, Hung, & Lin, 2014; Ward, 2004). As displayed in Figure 7.1, this process of evaluating, selecting, and refining initially generated ideas should be promoted by entrepreneurs' convergent thinking and hindered by divergent thinking (Brophy, 1998; Cropley, 2006; Erez & Nouri, 2010; Gielnik et al., 2012). Convergent thinking helps entrepreneurs to systematically analyze significant strengths and weaknesses of ideas and thus to evaluate the feasibility of initially generated business ideas (Cropley, 2006; Runco, 2003). Furthermore, convergent thinking facilitates focusing on a limited range of ideas and thus supports entrepreneurs in reducing the large amount of generated business ideas to one single best idea (Cropley, 2006; Nyström, 1993). Convergent thinking also enables entrepreneurs to acquire and systematically analyze information on potential competitors, industries, and markets (Cropley, 2006) which is important in order to evaluate and refine the selected idea into a viable business opportunity (Heinonen et al., 2011). As such, convergent thinking should positively affect the evaluation, selection, and refinement of business ideas (e.g., Erez & Nouri, 2010; Gielnik et al., 2012). Divergent thinking, in contrast, should negatively affect entrepreneurs' ability to evaluate, select, and refine business ideas (e.g., Gielnik et al., 2012). The unconventional way of thinking and the tendency to increase variability that are associated with divergent thinking should counteract the evaluation and selection of a limited number of business ideas (see Cropley, 2006).

In sum, we argue that the prelaunch phase calls for both divergent and convergent thinking (see Figure 7.1), and that identifying an original and feasible business opportunity requires entrepreneurs to generate multiple original business ideas using divergent thinking and then to evaluate and refine these ideas into one feasible business opportunity based on convergent thinking. It is important to note, however, that the tasks of generating and evaluating business ideas do not follow each other in neat sequence. Instead, opportunity identification is a dynamic and iterative process which requires entrepreneurs to generate and evaluate business ideas in continuing alternation (Dimov, 2007; Hills, Shrader, & Lumpkin, 1999; Lumpkin, Hills, & Shrader, 2004; Lumpkin & Lichtenstein, 2005). Accordingly, to identify an original and useful business opportunity, entrepreneurs need to to flexibly switch between divergent and convergent thinking according to situational demands.

While both divergent and convergent thinking are considered important for opportunity identification, divergent thinking should play a major role at this stage (Gielnik et al., 2014). The process of identifying an original and useful business opportunity is mainly characterized by creating novel combinations of ideas rather than detecting one single best answer (Eckhardt & Shane, 2003; Gielnik et al., 2014), thereby putting a stronger focus on divergent thinking than on convergent thinking (Gielnik et al., 2014). However, as outlined above, solely relying on divergent thinking would result in wild business ideas which may be completely novel and original but infeasible and thus useless (Cropley, 2006; Runco & Acar, 2012). Accordingly, identifying an original and useful business opportunity requires a combination of divergent and convergent thinking with a stronger emphasis on divergent thinking. The degree of emphasis placed on divergent thinking compared to convergent thinking should then determine the originality of the identified business opportunity (see Campos, Parellada, Quintero, Alfonso, & Valenzuela, 2015; Heunks, 1998). The underlying assumption is that highly original business opportunities represent completely novel and unexpected combinations of unrelated concepts which require an especially high degree of divergent thinking to be created (Campos et al., 2015). Therefore, a strong focus on divergent thinking should lead to more original business opportunities, whereas a low focus on divergent thinking should result in more incremental business opportunities (Campos et al., 2015).

Launch

The successful identification of an original and useful business opportunity is only the first step in the entrepreneurial process (Baron, 2007). Having identified an opportunity, entrepreneurs need to devote considerable effort to the actual launch of the new venture. Launching a new venture requires entrepreneurs to mobilize a wide range of resources (Baron, 2007; Shane & Venkataraman, 2000). For instance, they have to assemble financial resources such as venture capital, social resources such as social support by relatives and friends, human resources such as potential partners and employees, and informational resources such as information about the market and potential competitors (Baron, 2007; Perry-Smith & Mannucci, 2015). Acquiring all these resources has been described as one of the most critical steps in the entrepreneurial process (Baron, 2007; Shalley et al., 2015) that largely depends on an entrepreneur's creativity (Kirzner, 2009; Lin & Nabergoj, 2014; Matthews, 2007; Shalley et al., 2015; Shane, 2012). We concur with this assumption and take it a step further, suggesting that entrepreneurs' ability to assemble resources requires both divergent and convergent thinking (see Figure 7.1).

To obtain access to resources, entrepreneurs need to engage in several activities that demand both divergent and convergent thinking. For instance, entrepreneurs have to persuade potential investors, partners, and employees of the value and potential of their business opportunity which is, at that point of time, still unknown and full of risk (Chen, Yao, & Kotha, 2009; Phan et al., 2010; Ward, 2004). As such, entrepreneurs need to generate original ideas about how to convince other people to invest in their risky business opportunity and how to react to concerns raised by potential investors (Adner & Levinthal, 2008; Chen et al., 2009; Ward, 2004; Zhou, 2008). As outlined above, coming up with such original ideas calls for entrepreneurs' divergent thinking (Cropley, 2006; Hennessey & Amabile, 2010; Mumford et al., 1991). In addition, to really convince resource providers to actually invest money in the new venture, entrepreneurs also need to write and present a fully developed and highly elaborate business plan (Becherer & Helms, 2009). A business plan entails detailed information about how to set up, develop, and grow the new venture (Baron & Shane, 2004). Writing such a business plan requires entrepreneurs to seek, thoroughly evaluate, and carefully consider information about the prospective market, potential competitors, legal and financial conditions, as well as potential challenges and feasible solutions in starting and running the new venture (Chen et al., 2009). Based on the acquired information, entrepreneurs need to carefully plan the entire set-up and growth of the new venture (Chen et al., 2009). As described above, accumulating, evaluating, and using such information to carefully plan a new venture is facilitated by entrepreneurs' convergent thinking (Cropley, 2006). Therefore, acquiring resources should require entrepreneurs to perform both divergent and convergent thinking (see Figure 7.1).

Once entrepreneurs have acquired sufficient resources, they can actually launch the new venture (Baron, 2007; Baron & Shane, 2004). The launch of the new venture calls for various further important entrepreneurial activities and decisions such as determining the legal form of the venture, developing strong marketing plans and strategies for exploiting the business opportunity, protecting the product or service by ensuring intellectual property rights, and organizing the production and timely introduction to market (Baron, 2007; Baron & Shane, 2004). To successfully accomplish all these tasks, entrepreneurs need to systematically search for a wide array of information, thoroughly analyze the acquired information, and decide which is the one best option based on the information. For instance, to establish a specific legal form of the new venture, entrepreneurs need to seek information about various potential legal forms, evaluate the different possibilities with regard to the venture, decide on the one single legal form that matches the requirements of the venture, and execute the legal establishment of the venture in an efficient way (Baron & Shane, 2004; Leach & Leach, 1984). Furthermore, to come up with strong marketing plans and strategies, entrepreneurs need to thoroughly analyze the new venture's external environment and define marketing concepts that are perfectly aligned to its specific needs (Zahra & Bogner, 2000). As such, launching a new venture mainly requires entrepreneurial activities that focus on searching for information on different options, thoroughly evaluating the available options, and deciding on the best option using convergent thinking. Having decided on the one single solution, it is important that entrepreneurs stick to this solution and refrain from performing divergent activities that are targeted toward other ideas or activities than the efficient execution of the chosen solution (see Bledow et al., 2009; Brophy, 1998; Delmar & Shane, 2003; Shane & Delmar, 2004). Accordingly, launching a new venture is mainly focused on decreasing variability, which is facilitated by entrepreneurs' convergent thinking while being inhibited by divergent thinking (Cropley, 2006). It follows that entrepreneurs' success in launching a new venture may primarily depend on convergent thinking. Some levels of divergent thinking, however, are considered also to be important in order to succeed in the launch of a new venture. When launching a new venture, entrepreneurs usually encounter various obstacles and barriers such as skeptical investors, legal restrictions, or bureaucratic procedures that hinder the legalization of the venture (Kuuluvainen, 2009; Nieman, Hough, & Nieuwenhuizen, 2003). Facing such barriers, entrepreneurs need to come up with original ideas on how to overcome these barriers using divergent thinking (Cropley, 2006). Moreover, given that these sudden barriers rapidly occur while launching a new venture, entrepreneurs need to be able to alternate from convergent thinking to divergent thinking in a dynamic and flexible manner (see Figure 7.1).

Besides assembling resources and actually launching the new venture, entrepreneurs need to invest further effort to continuously develop and improve the business opportunity which was generated in the prelaunch phase (see Figure 7.1). In the launch phase, entrepreneurs receive valuable information and feedback regarding their business opportunity from important stakeholders and people they trust (Dimov, 2007; Wood & McKinley, 2010). Successfully processing and integrating such feedback calls for similar processes of divergent and convergent thinking as demanded in the prelaunch phase. First, receiving and processing feedback requires entrepreneurs to perform convergent thinking in order to carefully analyze the feedback and to select the most useful comments from the full set of feedback received (see Cropley, 2006). Having selected the most valuable feedback, they then need to apply divergent thinking to come up with original ideas on how to actively use that feedback and to advance the business opportunity based on the acquired feedback (see Cropley, 2006). Subsequently, entrepreneurs have to switch back to convergent thinking in order to analyze the generated ideas, select the most suitable ideas that enhance the business opportunity, and synthesize all ideas into the business opportunity (see Cropley, 2006). As such, the same processes described in the prelaunch phase continue in the launch phase. Entrepreneurs need to continuously engage in the same repetitive cycle of divergent and convergent thinking as in the prelaunch phase in order to actively integrate acquired feedback and to further refine and develop their business opportunity (see Figure 7.1).

In sum, successfully launching a new venture requires entrepreneurs to engage in both divergent and convergent thinking as well as to flexibly switch between these two thinking styles (see Figure 7.1). While the launch phase thus demands both divergent and convergent thinking, entrepreneurs' convergent thinking should play a major role in this phase. In the launch phase, entrepreneurs need to become more focused on one single business opportunity and take specific actions and decisions to implement the opportunity. To do so, they have to systematically gather and analyze information and integrate all acquired information into one thorough business concept (see Bledow et al., 2009; Heinonen et al., 2011; Nyström, 1993). Accordingly, entrepreneurs' main task at this stage is to reduce variability via convergent thinking. While divergent thinking is also considered important to actually launch a venture, the successful, timely, and efficient launch of the business should primarily depend on entrepreneurs' convergent thinking.

Postlaunch

After launching a new venture, entrepreneurs need to invest considerable effort to ensure and actively manage continuous growth of the newly established venture (Baum et al., 1998). Venture growth depends on a wide array of activities that require both divergent and convergent thinking (Gielnik, 2013; Gielnik et al., 2012). We therefore expect promoting venture growth in the postlaunch phase to call for similar levels of divergent and convergent thinking (see Figure 7.1). We further posit that both thinking styles foster venture growth through various mechanisms (Gielnik, 2013; Gielnik et al., 2012; Heunks, 1998).

One important mechanism that transmits the effects of both divergent and convergent thinking on venture growth is leadership (see Antonakis & Autio, 2007; Baron, 2007; Ensley, Hmieleski, & Pearce, 2006). Given that growing ventures demand an increasing number of skilled employees (Baum, Locke, & Smith, 2001; Gilbert, McDougall, & Audretsch, 2006), entrepreneurs need to devote substantial effort to attaining, motivating, and retaining qualified employees (Baron, 2007). Motivating and retaining employees requires entrepreneurs to perform both divergent and convergent thinking. First, entrepreneurs have to engage in divergent thinking to come up with original ideas for concepts that motivate employees such as inspiring visions and incentive systems (Fillis & Rentschler, 2010; Matthew, 2009). In addition, entrepreneurs need to perform convergent thinking to motivate employees by establishing concrete goals, processes, and structures within the new venture. Given that new ventures often lack well-defined standard operating procedures and structures compared to more established firms (Ensley et al., 2006), motivating and retaining employees in new ventures requires entrepreneurs to provide guidance, stability, and control in terms of consistent goals, processes, and structures (Ensley et al., 2006; Jansen, Vera, & Crossan, 2009; Williamson, 2000). Defining and sticking to specific goals, processes, and structures requires convergent thinking (see Cropley, 2006). As such, both divergent and convergent thinking are considered important to motivate and retain employees which in turn is crucial for a new venture's growth.

Furthermore, to enable the growth of their new venture, entrepreneurs need to handle unpredictable and suddenly occurring barriers that have the potential to adversely impact the new venture's survival and long-term growth (Lin & Nabergoj, 2014; Mcmullan & Kenworthy, 2015; Sarasvathy, 2001; Shalley et al., 2015; Shalley & Perry-Smith, 2008). Overcoming such barriers requires entrepreneurs to improvise and to adapt to the new situation which is mainly based on divergent thinking (Baker, Miner, & Eesley, 2003; Huang, Ding, & Chen, 2014; Sarasvathy, 2001). As such, entrepreneurs need to continuously perform divergent thinking to generate original ideas on how to handle sudden barriers such as rapid market shifts and resource shortages (Bledow et al., 2009; Fillis & Rentschler, 2010; Frese & Fay, 2001; Kirzner, 2009; Lin & Nabergoj, 2014; Mumford, Scott, Gaddis, & Strange, 2002;

Wiklund & Shepherd, 2009). However, entrepreneurs also have to engage in some levels of convergent thinking to thoroughly analyze the different ideas and select the most effective solution to overcome a particular barrier. In addition, overcoming unpredictable and uncontrollable barriers often requires entrepreneurs to rely on their intuition, which is based on knowledge and thus convergent thinking (Cropley, 2006).

To assure continuous survival and growth of the new venture, entrepreneurs further have to constantly engage in innovation (Porter, 1980; Roper, 1997; Rosenbusch et al., 2011; Thornhill, 2006). Continuous innovation is an important predictor of a new venture's success, growth, and long-term survival (e.g., Baron & Tang, 2011; Heunks, 1998; Ireland & Webb, 2007; Schumpeter, 1934). Innovation refers to the generation and implementation of novel and potentially useful ideas (Amabile, 1996; West & Farr, 1990). The literature has discussed different types of innovation, such as radical and incremental innovation or exploratory and exploitative innovation, that contribute to the performance and growth of a new venture (Groen, Wakkeee, & De Weerd-Nederhof, 2008; Harms, Walsh, & Groen, 2012; Huang et al., 2014; Kollmann & Stöckmann, 2014; Levinthal & March, 1993; Li, Vanhaverbeke, & Schoenmakers, 2008). Radical innovation represents the introduction of completely new products, services, or processes that incorporate fundamental changes and provide substantially higher benefits compared to existing products, services, or processes (Chandy & Tellis, 1998, 2000; Raisch & Birkinshaw, 2008; Tushman & Anderson, 1986). Incremental innovation, in contrast, refers to minor adaptations and improvements of existing products, services, or processes such as simple line extensions (Benner & Tushman, 2003; Raisch & Birkinshaw, 2008). Radical innovation departs from existing knowledge and is therefore classified into exploratory innovation which refers to the creation of knowledge that is novel to the respective firm (Benner & Tushman, 2003; Jansen, van den Bosch, & Volberda, 2006; Jansen et al., 2009; Levinthal & March, 1993; March, 1991; Phelps, 2010; Raisch & Birkinshaw, 2008; Tushman & Smith, 2002). Incremental innovation, in contrast, builds upon existing knowledge and is thus considered to be exploitative innovation which is defined as the application and development of existing knowledge (Benner & Tushman, 2003; Jansen, van den Bosch, et al., 2006; Jansen, Vera, et al., 2009; Levinthal & March, 1993; March, 1991; Raisch & Birkinshaw, 2008; Tushman & Smith, 2002). Although the different forms of innovation might call for somewhat different capabilities and activities (e.g., Gibson & Birkinshaw, 2004; He & Wong, 2004; March, 1991; Smith & Tushman, 2005), exploratory and exploitative innovation mainly demand similar processes that generally underlie innovation.

In general, innovation requires the generation, evaluation, selection, and implementation of novel and potentially useful ideas within existing ventures (Farr, Sin, & Tesluk, 2003). These steps of the innovation process strongly resemble entrepreneurs' tasks of exploring and exploiting business opportunities in the prelaunch and launch phases of the entrepreneurial process (see Amabile, 1997). Accordingly, ensuring innovation in the postlaunch phase calls for the same iterative cycle of divergent and convergent thinking as the identification of a business opportunity in the prelaunch phase and the implementation of the business opportunity in the launch phase (seee Heunks, 1998; Nyström, 1979). Specifically, similar to the identification of a business opportunity in the prelaunch phase, innovation first requires entrepreneurs' divergent thinking to generate original ideas and entrepreneurs' convergent thinking to evaluate, refine, and integrate these ideas (Bledow et al., 2009). For instance, to introduce an original and useful new product to market, an entrepreneur first needs to come up with multiple original ideas for a new product via divergent thinking (Bledow et al., 2009). To ensure that the final product is not only original but also useful, an entrepreneur then has to evaluate, elaborate, and integrate the generated ideas using convergent thinking (Bledow et al., 2009; Cropley, 2006; Runco, 2003). This includes, for instance, collecting, systematically analyzing, and interpreting information about the venture's external environment and strongly aligning the final product to the specific market needs (see Zahra & Bogner, 2000). Given that all these tasks are similar to the tasks required for identifying a business opportunity in the prelaunch phase, the early stages of the innovation process in the postlaunch phase call for the same repetitive processes of divergent and convergent thinking as required in the prelaunch phase.

Then, akin to the implementation of the business opportunity in the launch phase, later stages of the innovation process demand entrepreneurs' divergent and convergent thinking to carefully plan and implement the generated ideas (Bledow et al., 2009; Cropley, 2006; Runco, 2003). For example, introducing a new product to market requires entrepreneurs to create strict plans and assemble a wide range of resources that are required for the production, delivery, and promotion of the product (Baron, 2007; Lin & Nabergoj, 2014). Also, a high rate of innovation requires entrepreneurs to implement the generated ideas using the least time, effort, and financial resources possible (Frese & Fay, 2001; Hamidi et al., 2008). As outlined above, such an efficient planning and implementation process requires entrepreneurs to focus on one selected idea without wasting resources on other activities or ideas. Therefore, similar to the efficient planning and implementation of the business opportunity in the launch phase, planning and implementing the introduction of a new product to market requires entrepreneurs to concentrate on fully exploiting one elaborated idea instead of generating many diverse ideas, a requirement which is facilitated by an entrepreneur's convergent thinking and inhibited by divergent thinking (Ames & Runco, 2005; Bledow et al., 2009; Gielnik et al., 2012; Kuratko & Welsch, 2001; Phan et al., 2010; Ward, 2004). As such, comparable with the exploitation of the business opportunity in the launch phase, the planning and implementation stages of the innovation process mainly call for entrepreneurs' convergent thinking. However, as in the launch phase, suddenly occurring barriers also require some level of divergent thinking in order for entrepreneurs to successfully plan and implement the ideas. For instance, while trying to implement the idea for a new product, an entrepreneur may encounter unexpected challenges which make it necessary to develop new and original ideas to overcome such implementation barriers (Baer & Frese, 2003; Rosing, Frese, & Bausch, 2011; Van de Ven, 1986). As such, to successfully plan and implement the introduction of new products to market, entrepreneurs need to flexibly alternate from convergent thinking to divergent thinking (see Figure 7.1).

In sum, similar to exploring and exploiting a business opportunity in the prelaunch and launch phases, exploratory and exploitative innovation in the postlaunch phase requires both divergent and convergent thinking as well as flexible switching between these two thinking styles (see Figure 7.1). The different nature of exploratory and exploitative innovation, however, indicates that the two types of innovation call for different proportions of divergent and convergent thinking. Exploratory innovation departs from existing knowledge and focuses on developing completely new products or services that break new ground (Benner & Tushman, 2003; Huang et al., 2014; Jansen et al., 2006), thereby putting a stronger focus on creating novel combinations of existing concepts via divergent thinking (see Bledow et al., 2009). Exploitative innovation, in contrast, builds on existing knowledge and extends established products, services, or processes (Benner & Tushman, 2003; Huang et al., 2014; Jansen et al., 2006), which mainly requires entrepreneurs to rely on available information from a limited number of domains that are directly related to existing products, services, or processes based on convergent thinking (see Bledow et al., 2009). As such, entrepreneurs should place an emphasis on divergent thinking when engaging in exploratory innovation while stressing convergent thinking when working on exploitative innovation (see Bledow et al., 2009). Given that short performance periods of exploratory and exploitative innovation alternating with each other are considered most effective for a new venture's performance (Bledow et al., 2009; Huang et al., 2014), entrepreneurs should further continuously shift their focus between divergent and convergent thinking.

The Cumulative Process Model: A Summary

To conclude this section, our comprehensive process model reveals that an entrepreneur's success is a joint function of divergent and convergent thinking. While both divergent and convergent thinking play an important role throughout the entire entrepreneurial process, the specific role of these two thinking styles shifts in the course of the entrepreneurial process (Manimala, 2009; Matthews, 2009, 2010; Nyström, 1993). Divergent thinking is most critical for an entrepreneur's success in earlier phases of the entrepreneurial process when recognizing promising business opportunities and assembling required resources call for the generation of many novel and original ideas (Gielnik et al., 2014; Matthews, 2009, 2010; Nyström, 1993). Convergent thinking, in contrast, becomes increasingly important in later phases of the entrepreneurial process requiring the precise evaluation and more focused implementation of these ideas to actually launch the new venture (Manimala, 2009; Nyström, 1993). However, even tasks that demand precise evaluation and efficient implementation also call for entrepreneurs' divergent thinking, for instance when facing sudden and unforeseen challenges (see Bledow et al., 2009). Accordingly, although the relative importance of divergent and convergent thinking considerably changes in the course of the entrepreneurial process, both thinking styles are required throughout the entrepreneurial process. Moreover, given the dynamic and chaotic nature of the entrepreneurial process, the necessities of divergent and convergent thinking alternate throughout the entrepreneurial process in an ever-changing manner. As such, entrepreneurs need to engage in both divergent and convergent thinking as well as to flexibly switch between these two thinking styles to successfully start and run a new venture.

An Interactionist Perspective on Creativity in Entrepreneurship

Our basic model provides valuable insights into the potential positive and negative effects of creativity on an entrepreneur's success throughout the entrepreneurial process. Previous theoretical and empirical research suggests, however, that the effect of creativity on entrepreneurial success depends on boundary conditions (Woodman & Schoenfeldt, 1990; Zhou, 2008). We therefore extend our basic model by considering multiple conditions that may promote or hinder the effect of both divergent and convergent thinking on entrepreneurial success. Taking the boundary conditions into account further contributes to our understanding of the complex relationship between creativity and entrepreneurship (Dimov, 2007; Zhou, 2008).

One important boundary condition moderating the effect of divergent and convergent thinking on entrepreneurial success is the diversity of information that is available to the entrepreneur (Gielnik et al., 2012). Building on creativity research (e.g., Mumford, Baughman, Supinski, & Maher, 1996; Mumford et al., 1991; Perttula & Sipilä, 2007), Gielnik and colleagues (2012) have argued that the diversity of information provided by the environment determines the potential positive effects of divergent and convergent thinking on an entrepreneur's success. First, the positive effects of divergent thinking are enhanced when diverse information is provided, while being weakened when homogeneous and constrained information from only one specific domain is available (Gielnik et al., 2012). The underlying assumption is that divergent thinking requires entrepreneurs to combine various pieces of information from apparently unrelated domains (Cropley, 2006). Diverse information stemming from many domains should facilitate this process because it provides access to different domains that the entrepreneur can combine into novel and original ideas (Mumford et al., 1996). Constrained information from a limited number of domains, in contrast, directs an entrepreneur's thinking to a small number of domains and thus limits the number of domains an entrepreneur can draw upon to make linkages between different pieces of information (Runco & Chand, 1995). Constrained information thus may diminish the potential positive effects of divergent thinking on business idea generation (Gielnik et al., 2012). Indeed, using an experimental design with direct manipulations of the diversity of received information, Gielnik and colleagues (2012) provide empirical evidence that entrepreneurs' divergent thinking has a positive impact on the originality of generated business opportunities when obtaining diverse information but not when receiving constrained information. In contrast, the positive effects of convergent thinking should be increased by restricting the available information to a limited number of domains and diminished by providing diverse information (Gielnik et al., 2012). Convergent thinking requires entrepreneurs to focus on a low amount of information and to make associations within only one domain or a small number of directly related domains of information (Cropley, 2006). Such focused attention to a limited range of information should be facilitated by constraining information to these domains and diminished by overloading entrepreneurs with information from various domains (Brown, Tumeo, Larey, & Paulus, 1998; Coskun, Paulus, Brown, & Sherwood, 2000; Cropley, 2006).

The moderating effect of information diversity points toward further important factors that may affect the diversity of available information and thus the potential impact of divergent and convergent thinking. For instance, one factor influencing the diversity of available information is the degree of active information acquisition (Gielnik et al., 2014). A high degree of active information acquisition means that entrepreneurs invest considerable time and effort into information search and actively seek more information from various sources (Frese, 2009). Accordingly, a more active search for information provides a broader information basis from several domains and thus fosters the positive effect of divergent thinking while diminishing the potential effects of convergent thinking (Baron & Tang, 2009; Gielnik et al., 2014; Keh, Nguyen, & Ng, 2007; Lybaert, 1998; Song, Wang, & Parry, 2010). Indeed, Gielnik and colleagues (2014) provide empirical evidence that the degree of active information search moderates the effects of divergent thinking on business opportunity identification and innovativeness of products and services such that divergent thinking only has a positive and significant effect if active information search is high. Accordingly, entrepreneurs can leverage the full potential of their divergent thinking capacities only if they actively search for information (Gielnik et al., 2014).

Another important factor affecting the diversity of available information may be the heterogeneity of an entrepreneur's social network. An entrepreneur's social network potentially provides the entrepreneur with valuable information, knowledge, advice, and inspiring perspectives (Baron, 2007; Dimov, 2007; Shalley & Perry-Smith, 2008). Therefore, more heterogeneous social networks may equip an entrepreneur with more diverse information (Aldrich & Martinez, 2015; Baron, 2007; Dimov, 2007) and thus may affect the cognitive processes underlying creativity (Dimov, 2007; Hills, Lumpkin, & Singh, 1997; Lubart, 2010; Shalley & Perry-Smith, 2008). Specifically, heterogeneous social networks may increase the diversity of available information and thus stimulate the potential of divergent thinking while diminishing the potential impact of convergent thinking. Homogeneous social networks, in contrast, should restrict the available information to a narrow domain of information, thereby limiting the potential effects of divergent thinking and increasing the positive effects of convergent thinking.

In sum, past research indicates that there are numerous boundary conditions that promote or hinder the effect of creativity on entrepreneurship, making the relationship between creativity and entrepreneurship even more complex. While a detailed discussion of these ancillary conditions is beyond the scope of this chapter, future research on the role of creativity in entrepreneurship should take these conditions into account to provide a more comprehensive understanding of the complex relationship between creativity and entrepreneurship.

Practical Implications: Promoting Creativity to Promote Entrepreneurship

Our theoretical model offers important practical implications. First and most generally, our model supports the assumption that creativity generally has a positive effect on entrepreneurial success (see Shalley & Perry-Smith, 2008; Tsai, 2014; Ward, 2004; Zhou, 2008). Moreover, building on cognition-based approaches rather than trait-based perspectives on creativity, our model posits that creativity is not an innate and stable predisposition but rather an ability that can be systematically fostered by training specific cognitive processes such as divergent and convergent thinking (see Brophy, 1998; Karimi et al., 2014; Ma, 2006; Scott, Leritz, & Mumford, 2004; Shalley & Perry-Smith, 2008; Ward et al., 1999). As such, our model indicates that it may be beneficial to systematically train entrepreneurs' creativity by incorporating creativity techniques into entrepreneurship training (e.g., DeTienne & Chandler, 2004; Gibb, 2011; Hamidi et al., 2008; Ko & Butler, 2007; Lin & Nabergoj, 2014; Lourenço & Jayawarna, 2011; Ward, 2004). Indeed, there is empirical evidence that including creativity techniques into entrepreneurship trainings positively affects participants' entrepreneurial abilities (DeTienne & Chandler, 2004; Karimi et al., 2014). However, despite this empirical evidence and scholars' repeated calls for creativity training in entrepreneurship, very little has been done to systematically stimulate creativity among entrepreneurs (Karimi et al., 2014; Karimi, Biemans, Lans, Chizari, & Mulder, 2016; Lin & Nabergoj, 2014; Nielsen & Stovang, 2015; Sarri, Bakouros, & Petridou, 2010). Against this background, our theoretical model reemphasizes the importance of future entrepreneurship education to direct more attention to systematically promoting entrepreneurs' creativity by means of creativity techniques.

Moreover, and more specifically, our comprehensive theoretical model suggests that the creativity techniques to be included in entrepreneurship training should be directed at training both divergent and convergent thinking. Our theoretical investigation points out that entrepreneurs and people aiming to becoming entrepreneurs need to engage in both types of thinking. However, past research has highlighted that most people favor either divergent or convergent thinking (Basadur, 1995; Brophy, 1998, 2001, 2006).

Entrepreneurship trainers should therefore assess participants' tendencies to divergent and convergent thinking and teach them how to engage in the other way of thinking as well, for example by demonstrating to divergent thinkers the importance and potential advantages of engaging in convergent thinking in order to increase the usefulness and viability of identified business opportunities (see Basadur, 1995; Basadur et al., 1982; Brophy, 1998; Isaksen, 1983; Treffinger, 1983). Indeed, past research has provided evidence that people's cognitive capacities underlying creativity can be systematically nurtured by means of creativity techniques (Karimi et al., 2014; Runco & Okuda, 1991; Scott et al., 2004). As such, creativity techniques aimed at performing both divergent and convergent thinking should be an integrated part of entrepreneurship training.

Similarly, it may be beneficial to train entrepreneurs in their ability to flexibly switch between divergent and convergent thinking (see Bledow et al., 2009; Wolf & Mieg, 2010). Our theoretical investigation indicates that entrepreneurs need to continuously alternate between the two thinking styles according to situational demands. However, alternating between divergent and convergent thinking represents a challenging task that exceeds most people's capabilities (Brophy, 1998, 2006). Therefore, entrepreneurs and persons on their way to becoming entrepreneurs should be encouraged and systematically trained in flexibly switching between divergent and convergent thinking, for example by fostering their awareness of the dynamic nature of entrepreneurial task demands, their ability to carefully evaluate the task demands, and their reflexivity (see Bledow et al., 2009)

Beyond these general suggestions applying to the entire entrepreneurial process, our comprehensive model also allows more specific recommendations on how to increase an entrepreneur's success at specific stages within the entrepreneurial process. For instance, our model indicates that entrepreneurs and people aiming at becoming entrepreneurs should place emphasis on divergent thinking in earlier phases of the entrepreneurial process while increasing the focus on convergent thinking in later phases of the entrepreneurial process (see Gielnik et al., 2014). As such, entrepreneurship trainers should create awareness that the necessity of divergent and convergent thinking changes in the course of the entrepreneurial process which requires entrepreneurs to monitor and flexibly adapt to these changing demands. In general, it is important that entrepreneurship trainers highlight the dynamic nature of entrepreneurship (see Bledow, 2013; Bledow et al., 2009). Given that entrepreneurial success requires divergent and convergent thinking in an ever-changing manner with both thinking styles partly having negative effects, simplistic recommendations regarding general increases of these thinkings styles may have no or even detrimental effects (see Bledow, 2013; Bledow et al., 2009). Instead, to systematically foster entrepreneurial success, entrepreneurship trainers need to establish an understanding of the complex interplay between divergent and convergent thinking that dynamically determines an entrepreneur's success.

In addition, our interactionist perspective on creativity in entrepreneurship suggests that entrepreneurship training and interventions need to account for different boundary conditions in order to strengthen the potential positive effects and diminish the potential negative effects of creativity on entrepreneurial success. For instance, interventions could increase the positive effects of divergent thinking by training entrepreneurs in actively searching for appropriate information (Gielnik, Frese, et al., 2012; Gielnik, Krämer, et al., 2014). Specifically, entrepreneurs should be trained in searching for diverse information from different disciplines for tasks requiring divergent thinking while concentrating on constrained information from selected disciplines when working on tasks demanding convergent thinking (Gielnik, Frese, et al., 2012; Gielnik, Krämer, et al., 2014).

Finally, our theoretical model also provides important implications for the composition of entrepreneurial teams. As outlined above, most people are initially inclined toward divergent or convergent thinking (Basadur, 1995; Brophy, 1998, 2001, 2006). While people could and should be systematically trained in engaging in their less preferred way of thinking as well, engaging in the unfavored thinking style may demand considerable cognitive efforts (see Bledow et al., 2009). Therefore, entrepreneurial teams may be more efficient when being composed of both members proficient in divergent thinking and members preferring convergent thinking (see Bledow et al., 2009; Erez & Nouri, 2010). Such entrepreneurial teams can benefit from the complementary effects of members' divergent thinking and members' more constrained convergent thinking. Given that most ventures are started and run by entrepreneurial teams (Chowdhury, 2005; Kamm, Shuman, Seeger, & Nurick, 1990; Lechler, 2001), such a composition may contribute to the entrepreneurial success of many new ventures in the future.

Future Research

Our theoretical model provides important avenues for future research. First, future research should empirically test the main theoretical assumptions of our model. While our model is built on past theoretical and empirical research, empirical studies that systematically test our comprehensive model are lacking. For example, while there is some empirical research testing the effects of divergent thinking on opportunity identification at the beginning of the entrepreneurial process (e.g., Gielnik, Frese, et al., 2012; Gielnik, Krämer, et al., 2014; Karimi et al., 2014), empirical studies testing the theorized effects of convergent thinking throughout the entrepreneurial process are scarce. Therefore, empirical studies that systematically test the key assumptions of our comprehensive model would enhance our understanding of the role of creativity in the entrepreneurial process.

To adequately and fully test the main assumptions of our comprehensive process model, longitudinal studies examining the changing role of divergent and convergent thinking throughout the entrepreneurial process are required (Gielnik, 2013). Most entrepreneurship research to date, however, has relied on cross-sectional approaches, leaving the understanding of how the role of cognitive processes changes over time incomplete (Baron, 2007). Our theoretical model thus echoes the call for moving toward more longitudinal studies empirically examining an entrepreneur's success and the factors influencing it over time (Baron, 2007).

In addition, an important task of future research is to extend our theoretical model to a more comprehensive model. We build our model on Baron's (2007) process model disentangling the entrepreneurial process into the prelaunch, launch, and postlaunch phase. Drawing upon Baron's (2007) conceptualization of these three phases, we selectively analyzed the effects of divergent and convergent thinking on specific tasks that are typical for these phases. As such, our theoretical model offers a simplistic view of the entrepreneurial process which is in fact much more complex including several further entrepreneurial tasks and interactions (Baron, 2007). For instance, our model illuminates the role of creativity for opportunity identification by disentangling the effects of divergent and convergent thinking on both the generation and evaluation of business ideas. Opportunity identification, however, has been described as a complex and multidimensional process requiring a wider array of specific activities that may differentially depend on divergent and convergent thinking (e.g., Shane & Venkataraman, 2000).

Future research should thus employ a more fine-grained analysis of each stage of the entrepreneurial process in order to provide a more complete representation of the differential effects of divergent and convergent thinking in entrepreneurship (Baron, 2007).

To further refine our theoretical model on creativity in entrepreneurship, it would be interesting to examine potential interactions and reciprocal relations between cognitive processes and entrepreneurial outcomes (see Mcmullan & Kenworthy, 2015). While our model focuses on investigating the effects of divergent and convergent thinking on entrepreneurial outcomes, entrepreneurial outcomes in turn may have recursive effects on the amount of divergent and convergent thinking needed throughout the entrepreneurial process. For instance, entrepreneurs that display high levels of divergent thinking at the beginning of the entrepreneurial process may identify a more original business opportunity (Campos et al., 2015). The originality of the business opportunity in turn may affect the amount of divergent thinking required to implement this business opportunity and thus the positive and negative effects of divergent and convergent thinking at later stages of the entrepreneurial process. More detailed studies of such reciprocal effects may contribute to our understanding of the complex interplay between creativity and success in entrepreneurship.

Finally, an interesting avenue for future research would be to extend our theoretical model to the team level. Past research has highlighted that a team's cognitive processes differ from individuals' cognitive processes in various ways (Shalley & Perry-Smith, 2008). Therefore, future research should investigate the role of entrepreneurial team members' divergent and convergent thinking for entrepreneurial success in the team context. As it is entrepreneurial teams that start most ventures (Chowdhury, 2005; Kamm et al., 1990; Lechler, 2001), such an investigation would further contribute to our understanding of the role of creativity in entrepreneurship.

Conclusion

In this chapter, we have provided a comprehensive theoretical investigation of the role of creativity in entrepreneurship. While we concur with past research that creativity has a positive effect on an entrepreneur's success, we argue that the relationship between creativity and entrepreneurial success is more complex than expected. Building on past research on creativity and entrepreneurship, we posit that both creativity and entrepreneurship represent complex processes that need to be disentangled into smaller components to fully understand the role of creativity in entrepreneurship (Fillis & Rentschler, 2010). Drawing upon more fine-grained conceptualizations of both creativity and entrepreneurship, we propose a comprehensive theoretical model on the changing role of divergent and convergent thinking throughout the entrepreneurial process. Our theoretical model provides a detailed examination of the complex processes through which divergent and convergent thinking promote an entrepreneur's success at different stages of the entrepreneurial process in a cumulative manner. Such a detailed examination is important to fully understand and systematically foster the effect of creativity in entrepreneurship (Baron & Tang, 2011; Baum & Locke, 2004; Fillis & Rentschler, 2010). As such, our theoretical model provides an important step toward a more unified and inclusive framework that enhances our understanding of creativity in entrepreneurship. We hope that our model will spur further fine-grained investigations of the effects of divergent and convergent thinking on entrepreneurial success in order to fully understand the role of creativity in entrepreneurship.

References

Adner, R., & Levinthal, D. (2008). Doing versus seeing: Acts of exploitation and perceptions of exploration. *Strategic Entrepreneurship Journal, 2*, 43–52. doi: 10.1002/sej.19

Aldrich, H. E. (1999). *Organizational evolving*. London, England: Sage.

Aldrich, H. E., & Martinez, M. A. (2015). Why aren't entrepreneurs more creative? Conditions affecting creativity and innovation in entrepreneurial activity. In C. E. Shalley, M. A. Hitt, & J. Zhou (Eds.), *The Oxford handbook of creativity, innovation, and entrepreneurship* (pp. 445–456). Oxford, England: Oxford University Press.

Amabile, T. M. (1988). A model of creativity and innovation in organizations. *Research in Organizational Behavior, 10*, 123–167.

Amabile, T. M. (1996). *Creativity in context*. Boulder, CO: Westview.

Amabile, T. M. (1997). Entrepreneurial creativity through motivational synergy. *The Journal of Creative Behavior, 31*(1), 18–26. doi: 10.1002/j.2162-6057.1997.tb00778.x

Ames, M., & Runco, M. A. (2005). Predicting entrepreneurship from ideation and divergent thinking. *Creativity and Innovation Management, 14*(3), 311–316. doi: 10.1111/j.1467-8691.2004.00349.x

Anderson, N., Potocnik, K., & Zhou, J. (2014). Innovation and creativity in organizations: A state-of-the-science review, prospective commentary, and guiding framework. *Journal of Management, 40*(5), 1297–1333. doi: 10.1177/0149206314527128

Antonakis, J., & Autio, E. (2007). Entrepeneurship and leadership. In J. R. Baum, M. Frese, & R. A. Baron (Eds.), *The psychology of entrepreneurship* (pp. 189–207). Mahwah, NJ: Erlbaum.

Antonio, T., Lanawati, S., Wiriana, T. A., & Christina, L. (2014). Correlations creativity, intelligence, personality, and entrepreneurship achievement. *Procedia – Social and Behavioral Sciences, 115*, 251–257. doi: 10.1016/j.sbspro.2014.02.433

Ardichvili, A., Cardozo, R., & Ray, S. (2003). A theory of entrepreneurial opportunity identification and development. *Journal of Business Venturing, 18*, 105–123.

Audretsch, D. B., & Belitski, M. (2013). The missing pillar: The creativity theory of knowledge spillover entrepreneurship. *Small Business Economics, 41*(4), 819–836. doi: 10.1007/s11187-013-9508-6

Baer, M., & Frese, M. (2003). Climate for initiative and psychological safety, process innovation, and firm performance. *Journal of Organizational Behavior, 24*(1), 45–68.

Baker, T., Miner, A. S., & Eesley, D. T. (2003). Improvising firms: Bricolage, account giving and improvisational competencies in the founding process. *Research Policy, 32*, 255–276. http://doi.org/10.1016/S0048-7333(02)00099-9

Baker, T., & Nelson, R. E. (2005). Creating something from nothing: Resource construction through entrepreneurial bricolage. *Administrative Science Quarterly, 50*, 329–366. doi: 10.2189/asqu.2005.50.3.329

Baron, R. A. (2002). OB and entrepreneurship: The reciprocal benefits of closer conceptual links. In B. M. Staw & R. Kramer (Eds.), *Research in organizational behavior* (pp. 225–269). Greenwich, CT: JAI Press.

Baron, R. A. (2006). Opportunity recognition as pattern recognition. *Academy of Management Perspectives, 20*, 104–120. doi: 10.5465/AMP.2006.19873412

Baron, R. A. (2007). Entrepreneurship: A process perspective. In J. R. Baum, M. Frese, & R. A. Baron (Eds.), *The psychology of entrepreneurship* (pp. 19–39). Mahwah: Erlbaum.

Baron, R. A., & Markman, G. D. (2005). Toward a process view of entrepreneurship: The changing impact of individual level variables across phases of new venture development. In M. A. Rahim, R. T. Golembiewski, & K. D. Mackenzie (Eds.), *Current topics in management* (pp. 45–64). New Brunswick, NJ: Transaction.

Baron, R. A., & Shane, S. A. (2004). *Entrepreneurship: A process perspective*. Mason, OH: South-Western.

Baron, R. A., & Tang, J. (2009). Entrepreneurs' social skills and new venture performance: Mediating mechanisms and cultural generality. *Journal of Management, 35*(2), 282–306. doi: 10.1177/0149206307312513

Baron, R. A., & Tang, J. (2011). The role of entrepreneurs in firm-level innovation: Joint effects of positive affect, creativity, and environmental dynamism. *Journal of Business Venturing, 26*(1), 49–60. doi: 10.1016/j.jbusvent.2009.06.002

Basadur, M. (1995). Optimal ideation–evaluation ratios. *Creativity Research Journal*. doi: 10.1207/s15326934crj0801_5

Basadur, M., Graen, G. B., & Green, S. G. (1982). Training in creative problem solving: Effects on ideation and problem finding and solving in an industrial research organization. *Organizational Behavior and Human Performance, 30*(1), 41–70. doi: 10.1016/0030-5073(82)90233-1

Baum, J. R., & Locke, E. A. (2004). The relationship of entrepreneurial traits, skill, and motivation to subsequent venture growth. *Journal of Applied Psychology, 89*(4), 587–598. doi: 10.1037/0021-9010.89.4.587

Baum, J. R., Locke, E. A., & Kirkpatrick, S. A. (1998). A longitudinal study of the relation of vision and vision communication to venture growth in entrepreneurial firms. *Journal of Applied Psychology, 83*(1), 43–54. doi: 10.1037/0021-9010.83.1.43

Baum, J. R., Locke, E. A., & Smith, K. G. (2001). A multidimensional model of venture growth. *Academy of Management Journal, 44*(2), 292–303. doi: 10.2307/3069456

Becherer, R. C., & Helms, M. M. (2009). The value of business plans for new ventures: Company and entrepreneur outcomes. *Journal of Small Business Strategy, 20*(2), 81–97.

Benner, M. J., & Tushman, M. L. (2003). Exploitation, exploration, and process management: The productivity dilemma revisited. *Academy of Management Review, 28*(2), 238–256.

Bhave, M. P. (1994). A process model of entrepreneurial venture creation. *Journal of Business Venturing, 9*(3), 223–242.

Bledow, R. (2013). Kreative Leistung als selbstgesteuerte Integration psychischer Funktionen [Creative performance as a self-controlled integration of mental functions] In D. E. Krause (Ed.), *Kreativität, Innovation und Entrepreneurship* [Creativity, innovation and entrepreneurship] (pp. 43–58). Wiesbaden, Germany: Springer Fachmedien. doi: 10.1007/978-3-658-02551-9

Bledow, R., Frese, M., Anderson, N., Erez, M., & Farr, J. (2009). A dialectic perspective on innovation: conflicting demands, multiple pathways, and ambidexterity. *Industrial and Organizational Psychology, 2*(3), 305–337. doi: 10.1111/j.1754-9434.2009.01154.x

Brophy, D. R. (1998). Understanding, measuring, enhancing collective creative problem-solving efforts. *Creativity Research Journal, 11*(2), 123–150. doi: 10.1207/s15326934crj1103_2

Brophy, D. R. (2001). Comparing the attributes, activities, and performance of divergent, convergent, and combination thinkers. *Creativity Research Journal, 13*(3-4), 439–455. doi: 10.1207/S15326934CRJ1334_20

Brophy, D. R. (2006). A comparison of individual and group efforts to creatively solve contrasting types of problems. *Creativity Research Journal, 18*(3), 293–315. doi: 10.1207/s15326934crj1803_6

Brown, V., Tumeo, M., Larey, T. S., & Paulus, P. B. (1998). Modeling cognitive interactions during group brainstorming. *Small Group Research, 29*(4), 495–526. doi: 10.1177/1046496498294005

Bygrave, W. D. (1989). The entrepreneurship paradigm (I): A philosophical look at its research methodologies. *Entrepreneurship Theory and Practice, 14*(1), 7–26.

Bygrave, W. D. (2006). The entrepreneurship paradigm (I) revisited. In H. Neergar & J. Parm Ulhoi (Eds.), *Handbook of qualitative research methods in entrepreneurship* (pp. 17–48). Cheltenham, England: Elgar.

Campos, H. M., Parellada, F. S., Quintero, M. R., Alfonso, F., & Valenzuela, A. (2015). Creative thinking style and the discovery of entrepreneurial opportunities in startups. *Revista de Negócios, 20*(1), 3–12. doi: 10.7867/1980-4431.2015v20n1p3-12

Chandy, R. K., & Tellis, G. J. (1998). Organizing for radical product innovation: The overlooked role of willingness to cannibalize. *Journal of Marketing Research, 35*(4), 474. doi: 10.2307/3152166

Chandy, R. K., & Tellis, G. J. (2000). The incumbent's curse? Incumbency, size, and radical product innovation. *Journal of Marketing, 64*(3), 1–17. doi: 10.1509/jmkg.64.3.1.18033

Chang, J.-J., Hung, K.-P., & Lin, M.-J. J. (2014). Knowledge creation and new product performance: The role of creativity. *R&D Management, 44*(2), 107–123. doi: 10.1111/radm.12043

Chen, M. H., Chang, Y. Y., & Lo, Y. H. (2015). Creativity cognitive style, conflict, and career success for creative entrepreneurs. *Journal of Business Research, 68*(4), 906–910. doi: 10.1016/j.jbusres.2014.11.050

Chen, X.-P., Yao, X., & Kotha, S. (2009). Entrepreneur passion and preparedness in business plan presentations: A persuasion analysis of venture capitalists' funding decisions. *Academy of Management Journal, 52*(1), 199–214. doi: 10.5465/AMJ.2009.36462018

Chowdhury, S. (2005). Demographic diversity for building an effective entrepreneurial team: Is it important? *Journal of Business Venturing, 20*(6), 727–746.

Coskun, H., Paulus, P. B., Brown, V., & Sherwood, J. J. (2000). Cognitive stimulation and problem presentation in idea-generating groups. *Group Dynamics: Theory, Research, and Practice, 4*(4), 307–329. doi: 10.1037/1089-2699.4.4.307

Cropley, A. (2006). In praise of convergent thinking. *Creativity Research Journal, 18*(3), 391–404. doi: 10.1207/s15326934crj1803_13

Dayan, M., Zacca, R., & Di Benedetto, A. (2013). An exploratory study of entrepreneurial creativity: Its antecedents and mediators in the context of UAE firms. *Creativity and Innovation Management, 22*(3), 223–240. doi: 10.1111/caim.12036

Delmar, F., & Shane, S. (2003). Does business planning facilitate the development of new ventures? *Strategic Management Journal, 24*(12), 1165–1185. doi: 10.1002/smj.349

DeTienne, D. R., & Chandler, G. N. (2004). Opportunity identification and its role in the entrepreneurial classroom: A pedagogical approach and empirical test. *Academy of Management Learning & Education, 3*(3), 242–257. doi: 10.5465/AMLE.2004.14242103

Dimov, D. (2007). Beyond the single-person, single-insight attribution in understanding entrepreneurial opportunities. *Entrepreneurship: Theory and Practice, 31*(5), 713–731.

Dino, R. N. (2015). Crossing boundaries: Toward integrating creativity, innovation, and entrepreneurship research through practice. *Psychology of Aesthetics, Creativity, and the Arts, 9*(2), 139–146. doi: 10.1037/aca0000015

Drucker, P. F. (1998). The discipline of innovation. *Harvard Business Review, 76*(6), 149–157.

Eckhardt, J. T., & Shane, S. A. (2003). Opportunities and entrepreneurship. *Journal of Management, 29*(3), 333–349. doi: 10.1177/014920630302900304

Ensley, M. D., Hmieleski, K. M., & Pearce, C. L. (2006). The importance of vertical and shared leadership within new venture top management teams: Implications for the performance of startups. *Leadership Quarterly, 17*(3), 217–231. doi: 10.1016/j.leaqua.2006.02.002

Erez, M., & Nouri, R. (2010). Creativity: the influence of cultural, social, and work contexts. *Management and Organization Review, 6*(3), 351–370. doi: 10.1111/j.1740-8784.2010.00191.x

Farr, J. L., Sin, H.-P., & Tesluk, P. E. (2003). Knowledge management processes and work group innovation. In L. V. Shavinina (Ed.), *International handbook on innovation* (pp. 574–586). New York, NY: Elsevier Science.

Fillis, I., & Rentschler, R. (2010). The role of creativity in entrepreneurship. *Journal of Enterprising Culture, 18*(1), 49–81. doi: 10.1142/S0218495810000501

Frese, M. (2009). Towards a Psychology of Entrepreneurship: An Action Theory Perspective. *Foundations and Trends® in Entrepreneurship, 5*(6), 437–496. doi: 10.1561/0300000028

Frese, M., & Fay, D. (2001). Personal initiative: An active performance concept for work in the 21st century. *Research in Organizational Behavior, 23*, 133–187. doi: 10.1016/S0191-3085(01)23005-6

Frese, M., & Gielnik, M. M. (2014). The psychology of entrepreneurship. *Annual Review of Organizational Psychology and Organizational Behavior, 1*(1), 413–438. doi: 10.1146/annurev-orgpsych-031413-091326

Gartner, W. B. (1988). "Who is an entrepreneur?" is the wrong question. *American Journal of Small Business, 12*, 11–32.

Getzels, J. A., & Jackson, P. W. (1962). *Creativity and intelligence.* New York, NY: Wiley.

Gibb, A. (2011). Concepts into practice: Meeting the challenge of development of entrepreneurship educators around an innovative paradigm. *International Journal of Entrepreneurial Behaviour & Research, 17*(2), 146–165. doi: 10.1108/13552551111114914

Gibson, C. B., & Birkinshaw, J. (2004). The antecedents, consequences, and mediating role of organizational ambidexterity. *Academy of Management Journal, 47*(2), 209–226. doi: 10.2307/20159573

Gielnik, M. M. (2013). Kreativität und Entrepreneurship [Creativity and entrepreneurship]. In D. E. Krause (Ed.), *Kreativität, Innovation und Entrepreneurship* [Creativity, innovation and entrepreneurship] (pp. 77–92). Wiesbaden, Germany: Springer Fachmedien. doi: 10.1007/978-3-658-02551-9_4

Gielnik, M. M., Frese, M., Graf, J. M., & Kampschulte, A. (2012). Creativity in the opportunity identification process and the moderating effect of diversity of information. *Journal of Business Venturing, 27*(5), 559–576. doi: 10.1016/j.jbusvent.2011.10.003

Gielnik, M. M., Krämer, A.-C., Kappel, B., & Frese, M. (2014). Antecedents of business opportunity identification and innovation: investigating the interplay of information processing and information acquisition. *Applied Psychology: An International Review, 63*(2), 344–381. doi: 10.1111/j.1464-0597.2012.00528.x

Gilbert, B. A., McDougall, P. P., & Audretsch, D. B. (2006). New venture growth: A review and extension. *Journal of Management, 32*(6), 926–950. doi: 10.1177/0149206306293860

Groen, A. J., Wakkeee, I. A. M., & De Weerd-Nederhof, P. C. (2008). Managing tensions in a high-tech start-up: An innovation journey in social system perspective. *International Small Business Journal, 26*(1), 57–81. doi: 10.1177/0266242607084659

Guilford, J. P. (1950). Creativity. *American Psychologist, 5*, 444–454.

Guilford, J. P. (1967). *The nature of human intelligence.* New York, NY: McGraw-Hill.

Hamidi, D. Y., Wennberg, K., & Berglund, H. (2008). Creativity in entrepreneurship education. *Journal of Small Business and Enterprise Development, 15*(2), 304–320. doi: 10.1108/14626000810871691

Hansen, D. J., Lumpkin, G. T., & Hills, G. E. (2011). A multidimensional examination of a creativity-based opportunity recognition model. *International Journal of Entrepreneurial Behaviour & Research, 17*(5), 515–533. doi: 10.1108/13552551111158835

Harms, R., Walsh, S. T., & Groen, A. J. (2012). The strategic entrepreneurship process – New avenues for research. *International Journal of Entrepreneurial Behaviour & Research, 18*(2), 132–136.

Harvey, M., & Evans, R. (1995). Strategic windows in the entrepreneurial process. *Journal of Business Venturing, 10*, 331–347.

He, Z.-L., & Wong, P.-K. (2004). Exploration vs. exploitation: An empirical test of the ambidexterity hypothesis. *Organization Science, 15*(4), 481–494. doi: 10.1287/orsc.1040.0078

Heinonen, J., Hytti, U., & Stenholm, P. (2011). The role of creativity in opportunity search and business idea creation. *Education + Training, 53*(8/9), 659–672. doi: 10.1108/00400911111185008

Hennessey, B. A., & Amabile, T. M. (2010). Creativity. *Annual Review of Psychology, 61*(1), 569–598. doi: 10.1146/annurev.psych.093008.100416

Heunks, F. J. (1998). Innovation, creativity and success. *Small Business Economics, 10*(3), 263–272.

Hills, G. E., Lumpkin, G. T., & Singh, R. P. (1997). Opportunity recognition: Perceptions and behaviors of entrepreneurs. *Frontiers of Entrepreneurship Research, 17*, 168–182.

Hills, G. E., Shrader, R. C., & Lumpkin, G. T. (1999). Opportunity recognition as a creative process. In P. D. Reynolds, W. D. Bygrave, S. Manigart, C. M. Mason, G. D. Meyer, H. J. Sapienza, & K. G. Shaver (Eds.), *Frontiers of entrepreneurship research* (pp. 216–227). Wellesley, MA: Babson College.

Hornsby, J. S., Naffziger, D. W., Kuratko, D. F., & Montagno, R. V. (1993). An interactive model of the corporate entrepreneurship process. *Entrepreneurship Theory and Practice, 17*(2), 29–37.

Huang, S., Ding, D., & Chen, Z. (2014). Entrepreneurial leadership and performance in chinese new ventures: A moderated mediation model of exploratory innovation, exploitative innovation and environmental dynamism. *Creativity and Innovation Management, 23*(4), 453–471. doi: 10.1111/caim.12085

Hull, D. L., Bosley, J. J., & Udell, G. G. (1980). Renewing the hunt for the heffalump: Identifying potential entrepreneurs by personality characteristics. *Journal of Small Business Management, 18*(1), 11–18.

Ireland, R. D., & Webb, J. W. (2007). Strategic entrepreneurship: Creating competitive advantage through streams of innovation. *Business Horizons, 50*(1), 49–59. doi: 10.1016/j.bushor.2006.06.002

Isaksen, S. G. (1983). Toward a model for the facilitation of creative problem solving. *Journal of Creative Behavior, 17*(1), 18–31.

Jansen, J. J. P., van den Bosch, F. A. J., & Volberda, H. W. (2006). Exploratory innovation, exploitative innovation, and performance: Effects of organizational and environmental moderators. *Management Science, 52*(11), 1661–1674. doi: 10.1287/mnsc.1060.0576

Jansen, J. J. P., Vera, D., & Crossan, M. (2009). Strategic leadership for exploration and exploitation: The moderating role of environmental dynamism. *Leadership Quarterly, 20*(1), 5–18. doi: 10.1016/j.leaqua.2008.11.008

Kamm, J. B., Shuman, J. C., Seeger, J. A., & Nurick, A. J. (1990). Entrepreneurial teams in new venture creation: A research agenda. *Entrepreneurship: Theory and Practice, 14*(4), 7–17.

Karimi, S., Biemans, H. J. A., Lans, T., Aazami, M., & Mulder, M. (2014). Fostering students' competence in identifying business opportunities in entrepreneurship education. *Innovations in Education and Teaching International*, 1–15. doi: 10.1080/14703297.2014.993419

Karimi, S., Biemans, H. J. A., Lans, T., Chizari, M., & Mulder, M. (2016). The impact of entrepreneurship education: A study of Iranian students' Eentrepreneurial intentions and opportunity identification. *Journal of Small Business Management, 54*(1), 187–209. doi: 10.1111/jsbm.12137

Keh, H. T., Nguyen, T. T. M., & Ng, H. P. (2007). The effects of entrepreneurial orientation and marketing information on the performance of SMEs. *Journal of Business Venturing, 22*(4), 592–611. doi: 10.1016/j.jbusvent.2006.05.003

Kirzner, I. M. (2009). The alert and creative entrepreneur: A clarification. *Small Business Economics, 32*(2), 145–152.

Knörr, H., Alvarez, C., & Urbano, D. (2013). Entrepreneurs or employees: A cross-cultural cognitive analysis. *International Entrepreneurship and Management Journal, 9*(2), 273–294. doi: 10.1007/s11365-012-0235-2

Ko, S., & Butler, J. E. (2007). Creativity: A key link to entrepreneurial behavior. *Business Horizons, 50*(5), 365–372. doi: 10.1016/j.bushor.2007.03.002

Kollmann, T., & Stöckmann, C. (2014). Filling the entrepreneurial orientation–performance gap: The mediating effects of exploratory and exploitative innovations. *Entrepreneurship Theory and Practice, 38*(5), 1001–1027. doi: 10.1111/j.1540-6520.2012.00530.x

Kuratko, D. F., & Welsch, H. P. (2001). *Strategic entrepreneurial growth*. Fort Worth, TX: Harcourt College.

Kuuluvainen, A. (2009). Serial entrepreneur and entrepreneurial learning – A case study from Finland. *International Journal of Business and Globalisation, 4*(1), 55–70.

Leach, J. A., & Leach, L. N. (1984). Establishing a business: Fundamental aspects for information practitioners. *Library Trends, 32*(3), 327–336.

Lechler, T. (2001). Social interaction: A determinant of entrepreneurial team venture success. *Small Business Economics, 16*(4), 263–278. doi: 10.1023/A:1011167519304

Lee, S. Y., Florida, R., & Acs, Z. (2004). Creativity and entrepreneurship: A regional analysis of new firm formation. *Group Entrepreneurship, Growth and Public Policy, 23*, 1–24. doi: 10.1080/0034340042000280910

Levinthal, D. A., & March, J. G. (1993). The myopia of learning. *Strategic Management Journal, 14*, 95–112.

Li, Y., Vanhaverbeke, W., & Schoenmakers, W. (2008). Exploration and exploitation in innovation: Reframing the interpretation. *Creativity and Innovation Management, 17*(2), 107–126. doi: 10.1111/j.1467-8691.2008.00477.x

Lin, J., & Nabergoj, A. S. (2014). A resource-based view of entrepreneurial creativity and its implications to entrepreneurship education. *Economic and Business Review, 16*(2), 163–183.

Liu, J., Fu, P., & Liu, S. (2009). Conflicts in top management teams and team/firm outcomes: The moderating effects of conflict-handling approaches. *International Journal of Conflict Management, 20*(3), 228–250. doi: 10.1108/10444060910974867

Lourenço, F., & Jayawarna, D. (2011). Enterprise education: The effect of creativity on training outcomes. *International Journal of Entrepreneurial Behaviour & Research, 17*(3), 224–244. doi: 10.1108/13552551111130691

Low, M., & Abrahamson, E. (1997). Movements, bandwagons, and clones: Industry evolution and the entrepreneurial process. *Journal of Business Venturing, 12*(6), 435–458.

Lubart, T. I. (2010). Cross-cultural perspectives on creativity. In J. C. Kaufman & R. J. Sternberg (Eds.), *The Cambridge handbook of creativity* (pp. 265–278). New York, NY: Cambridge University Press.

Lumpkin, G. T., Hills, G. E., & Shrader, R. C. (2004). Opportunity recognition. In H. P. Welsch (Ed.), *Entrepreneurship: The way ahead* (pp. 73–90). London, England: Routledge.

Lumpkin, G. T., & Lichtenstein, B. B. (2005). The role of organizational learning in the opportunity-recognition process. *Entrepreneurship Theory and Practice, 29*(4), 451–472.

Lybaert, N. (1998). The information use in a SME : Its importance and some elements of influence. *Small Business Economics, 10*(2), 171–191. doi: 10.1023/A:1007967721235

Ma, H.-H. (2006). A synthetic analysis of the effectiveness of single components and packages in creativity training programs. *Creativity Research Journal, 18*(4), 435–446. doi: 10.1207/s15326934crj1804_3

Manimala, M. (2009). Creativity and entrepreneurship. In T. Rickards, M. A. Runco, & S. Moger (Eds.), *The* Routledge *companion to creativity* (pp. 119–131). London, England: Routledge.

March, J. G. (1991). Exploration and exploitation in organizational learning. *Organization Science, 2*(1), 71–87. doi: 10.1287/orsc.2.1.71

Markman, G. D., Baron, R. A., & Balkin, D. B. (2005). Are perseverance and self-efficacy costless? Assessing entrepreneurs' regretful thinking. *Journal of Organizational Behavior, 26*(1), 1–19. doi: 10.1002/job.305

Matthew, C. T. (2009). Leader creativity as a predictor of leading change in organizations. *Journal of Applied Social Psychology, 39*(1), 1–41. doi: 10.1111/j.1559-1816.2008.00427.x

Matthews, J. H. (2007). Creativity and entrepreneurship: Potential partners or distant cousins? In R. Chapman (Ed.), *Proceedings Managing Our Intellectual and Social Capital: 21st ANZAM 2007 Conference* (pp. 1–17). Sydney, Australia.

Matthews, J. H. (2009). What are the lessons for entrepreneurship from creativity and design? In G. Solomon (Ed.), *Proceedings of the Academy of Management Annual Meeting: Green Management Matters*. Chicago, IL: Academy of Management.

Matthews, J. H. (2010). Investigating design, creativity and entrepreneurial processes. In *Annual Meeting of the Academy of Management – Dare to Care: Passion and Compassion in Management Practice & Research* (pp. 6–10). Montreal, Canada.

Mcmullan, W. E., & Kenworthy, T. P. (2015). *Creativity and entrepreneurial performance a general scientific theory*. New York, NY: Springer. doi: 10.1007/978-3-319-04726-3

Morris, J. L., & Fargher, K. (1974). Achievement drive and creativity as correlates of success in small businesses. *Australian Journal of Psychology, 26*(3), 217–222.

Mumford, M. D., Baughman, W. A., Supinski, E. P., & Maher, M. A. (1996). Process-based measures of creative problem-solving skills: II. Information encoding. *Creativity Research Journal, 9*(1), 77–88. doi: 10.1207/s15326934crj0901_7

Mumford, M. D., Mobley, M. I., Reiter-Palmon, R., Uhlman, C. E., & Doares, L. M. (1991). Process analytic models of creative capacities. *Creativity Research Journal, 4*(2), 91–122.

Mumford, M. D., Scott, G. M., Gaddis, B., & Strange, J. M. (2002). Leading creative people: Orchestrating expertise and relationships. *Leadership Quarterly, 13*, 705–750. doi: 10.1016/S1048-9843(02)00158-3

Nielsen, S. L., & Stovang, P. (2015). DesUni: University entrepreneurship education through design thinking. *Education + Training, 57*(8/9), 977–991. doi: 10.1108/ET-09-2014-0121

Nieman, G., Hough, J., & Nieuwenhuizen, C. (2003). *Entrepreneurship: A South African perspective*. Pretoria, South Africa: Van Schaik.

Nyström, H. (1979). *Creativity and innovation*. Chicester, England: Wiley.

Nyström, H. (1993). Creativity and entrepreneurship. *Creativity and Innovation Management, 2*(4), 237–242. doi: 10.1111/j.1467-8691.1993.tb00102.x

Ogbari, M. E., & Isiavwe, D. T. (2015). Forecasting effect of creativity on entrepreneurial sustainability. *International Journal of Academic Research in Business and Social Sciences, 5*(7), 123–139. doi: 10.6007/IJARBSS/v5-i7/1715

Perry-Smith, J., & Mannucci, P. V. (2015). Social networks, creativity, and entrepreneurship. In C. E. Shalley, M. A. Hitt, & J. Zhou (Eds.), *The Oxford handbook of creativity, Innovation, and Entrepreneurship* (pp. 205–224). Oxford, England: Oxford University Press.

Perttula, M., & Sipilä, P. (2007). The idea exposure paradigm in design idea generation. *Journal of Engineering Design, 18*(1), 93–102. doi: 10.1080/09544820600679679

Phan, P., Zhou, J., & Abrahamson, E. (2010). Creativity, innovation, and entrepreneurship in China. *Management and Organization Review, 6*(2), 175–194. doi: 10.1111/j.1740-8784.2010.00181.x

Phelps, C. C. (2010). A longitudinal study of the influence of alliance network structure and composition on firm exploratory innovation. *Academy of Management Journal, 53*(4), 890–913. doi: 10.5465/AMJ.2010.52814627

Porter, M. E. (1980). *Competitive strategy*. New York, NY: Free Press.

Raisch, S., & Birkinshaw, J. (2008). Organizational ambidexterity: Antecedents, outcomes, and moderators. *Journal of Management, 34*(3), 375–409. doi: 10.1177/0149206308316058

Ravasi, D., & Turati, C. (2005). Exploring entrepreneurial learning: A comparative study of technology development projects. *Journal of Business Venturing, 20*(1), 137–164. doi: 10.1016/j.jbusvent.2003.11.002

Roper, S. (1997). Product innovation and small business growth: A comparison of the strategies of German, UK and Irish companies. *Small Business Economics, 9*(6), 523–537. doi: 10.1023/A:1007963604397

Rosenbusch, N., Brinckmann, J., & Bausch, A. (2011). Is innovation always beneficial? A meta-analysis of the relationship between innovation and performance in SMEs. *Journal of Business Venturing, 26*(4), 441–457. doi: 10.1016/j.jbusvent.2009.12.002

Rosing, K., Frese, M., & Bausch, A. (2011). Explaining the heterogeneity of the leadership-innovation relationship: Ambidextrous leadership. *Leadership Quarterly, 22*(5), 956–974. doi: 10.1016/j.leaqua.2011.07.014

Runco, M. A. (2003). *Critical creative processes*. Cresskill, NJ: Hampton.

Runco, M. A., & Acar, S. (2012). Divergent thinking as an indicator of creative potential. *Creativity Research Journal, 24*(1), 66–75. doi: 10.1080/10400419.2012.652929

Runco, M. A., & Chand, I. (1995). Cognition and creativity. *Educational Psychology Review, 7*(3), 243–267.

Runco, M. A., & Okuda, S. M. (1991). The instructional enhancement of the flexibility and originality scores of divergent thinking tests. *Applied Cognitive Psychology*. doi: 10.1002/acp.2350050505

Sarasvathy, S. D. (2001). Causation and effectuation: Toward a theoretical shift from economic inevitability to entrepreneurial contingency. *Academy of Management Review, 26*(2), 243–263.

Sarri, K. K., Bakouros, I. L., & Petridou, E. (2010). Entrepreneur training for creativity and innovation. *Journal of European Industrial Training, 34*(3), 270–288. doi: 10.1108/03090591011031755

Schumpeter, J. (1934). *The theory of economic development*. Cambridge, MA: Harvard University Press.

Scott, G., Leritz, L. E., & Mumford, M. D. (2004). The effectiveness of creativity training: A quantitative review. *Creativity Research Journal, 16*(4), 361–388. doi: 10.1207/s15326934crj1604_1

Shalley, C. E., Hitt, M. A., & Zhou, J. (2015). Introduction: Integrating creativity, innovation, and entrepreneurship to enhance the organization's capability to navigate in the new competitive landscape. In C. E. Shalley, M. A. Hitt, & J. Zhou (Eds.), *The Oxford handbook of creativity, innovation, and entrepreneurship* (pp. 1–14). Oxford, England: Oxford University Press.

Shalley, C. E., & Perry-Smith, J. (2008). The emergence of team creative cognition: The role of diverse outside ties, sociocognitive network centrality, and team evolution. *Strategic Entrepreneurship Journal, 2*, 23–41. doi: 10.1002/sej.40

Shane, S. (2003). *A general theory of entrepreneurship: The individual-opportunity nexus approach to entrepreneurship*. Aldershot, England: Elgar.

Shane, S. (2012). Reflections on the 2010 AMR decade award: Delivering on the promise of entrepreneurship as a field of research. *Academy of Management Review, 37*(1), 10–20. doi: 10.5465/amr.2011.0078

Shane, S., & Delmar, F. (2004). Planning for the market: Business planning before marketing and the continuation of organizing efforts. *Journal of Business Venturing, 19*(6), 767–785. doi: 10.1016/j.jbusvent.2003.11.001

Shane, S., & Nicolaou, N. (2014). Creative personality, opportunity recognition and the tendency to start businesses: A study of their genetic predispositions. *Journal of Business Venturing, 30*(3), 407–419. doi: 10.1016/j.jbusvent.2014.04.001

Shane, S., & Nicolaou, N. (2015). Creative personality, opportunity recognition and the tendency to start businesses: A study of their genetic predispositions. *Journal of Business Venturing, 30*(3), 407–419. doi: 10.1016/j.jbusvent.2014.04.001

Shane, S., & Venkataraman, S. (2000). The promise of entrepreneurship as a field of research. *Academy of Management Review, 25*(1), 217–226. doi: 10.2307/259271

Shepherd, D. A., & DeTienne, D. R. (2005). Prior knowledge, potential financial reward, and opportunity identification. *Entrepreneurship Theory and Practice, 29*(1), 91–112.

Simonton, D. K. (1989). Chance-configuration theory of scientific creativity. In B. Gholson, W. R. Shadish Jr., R. A. Neimeyer, & A. C. Houts (Eds.), *Psychology of science: Contributions to metascience*. Cambridge, England: Cambridge University Press.

Smith, W. K., & Tushman, M. L. (2005). Managing strategic contradictions: A top management model for managing innovation streams. *Organization Science, 16*(5), 522–536. doi: 10.1287/orsc.1050.0134

Song, M., Wang, T., & Parry, M. E. (2010). Do market information processes improve new venture performance? *Journal of Business Venturing, 25*(6), 556–568.

Sternberg, R. J., & Lubart, T. I. (1999). The concept of creativity: Prospects and paradigms. In R. J. Sternberg (Ed.), *Handbook of creativity* (pp. 3–15). New York, NY: Cambridge University Press.

Strange, J. M., & Mumford, M. D. (2005). The origins of vision: Effects of reflection, models, and analysis. *Leadership Quarterly, 16*(1), 121–148. doi: 10.1016/j.leaqua.2004.07.006

Thornhill, S. (2006). Knowledge, innovation and firm performance in high-and low-technology regimes. *Journal of Business Venturing, 21*(5), 687–703.

Treffinger, D. J. (1983). George's group: A creative problem-solving facilitation case study. *Journal of Creative Behavior, 17*, 39–48.

Tsai, K. C. (2014). Creativity is the spirit of entrepreneurship. *Business and Social Sciences, 2*(1), 106–115.

Tushman, M. L., & Anderson, P. (1986). Technological discontinuities and organizational environments. *Administrative Science Quarterly, 31*(3), 439–465.

Tushman, M. L., & Smith, W. K. (2002). Organizational technology. In J. R. Baum (Ed.), *Companion to organization* (pp. 386–414). Malden, MA: Blackwell.

Tyebjee, T. T., & Bruno, A. V. (1984). A model of venture capitalist investment activity. *Management Science, 30*(9), 1051–1066.

Van de Ven, A. H. (1986). Central problems in the management of innovation. *Management Science, 32*(5), 590–607.

Venkataraman, S. (1997). The distinctive domain of entrepreneurship research. In J. Katz & R. Brockhaus (Eds.), *Advances in entrepreneurship, firm emergence, and growth* (pp. 119–138). Greenwich, CT: JAI Press.

Ward, T. B. (2004). Cognition, creativity, and entrepreneurship. *Journal of Business Venturing, 19*(2), 173–188. doi: 10.1016/S0883-9026(03)00005-3

Ward, T. B., Smith, S. M., & Finke, R. A. (1999). Creative cognition. In R. J. Sternberg (Ed.), *Handbook of creativity* (pp. 189–212). Cambridge, England: Cambridge University Press.

West, M. A., & Farr, J. L. (1990). Innovation at work. In M. A. West & J. L. Farr (Eds.), *Innovation and creativity at work: Psychological and organizational strategies* (pp. 3–13). Chichester, England: Wiley.

Whiting, B. G. (1988). Creativity and entrepreneurship: How do they relate? *Journal of Creative Behavior, 22*, 178–183.

Wiklund, J., & Shepherd, D. A. (2009). The effectivenes of alliances and acquisitions: The role of resource combination activities. *Entrepreneurship Theory and Practice, 33*(1), 193–212.

Williamson, I. O. (2000). Employer legitimacy and recruitment success in small businesses. *Entrepreneurship Theory and Practice, 25*(1), 27–43.

Wolf, K. M., & Mieg, H. A. (2010). Cognitive determinants of the success of inventors: Complex problem solving and deliberate use of divergent and convergent thinking. *European Journal of Cognitive Psychology, 22*(3), 443–462.

Wood, M. S., & McKinley, W. (2010). The production of entrepreneurial opportunity: a constructivist perspective. *Strategic Entrepreneurship Journal, 4*(1), 66–84. doi: 10.1002/sej.83

Woodman, R. W., & Schoenfeldt, L. F. (1990). An interactionist model of creative behavior. *Journal of Creative Behavior, 24*(4), 279–290.

Zaccaro, S. J., Mumford, M. D., Connelly, M. S., Marks, M. A., & Gilbert, J. A. (2000). Assessment of leader problem-solving capabilities. *Leadership Quarterly, 11*(1), 37–64.

Zahra, S. A., & Bogner, W. C. (2000). Technology strategy and software new ventures' performance: Exploring the moderating effect of the competitive environment. *Journal of Business Venturing, 15*(2), 135–173. doi: 10.1016/S0883-9026(98)00009-3

Zhou, J. (2008). New look at creativity in the entrepreneurial process. *Strategic Entrepreneurship Journal, 2*(1), 1–5.

Zhou, J., & George, J. M. (2001). When job dissatisfaction leads to creativity: Encouraging the expression of voice. *Academy of Management Journal, 44*(4), 682–696. doi: 10.2307/3069410

8

The Dark Side of the Entrepreneurial Personality: Undesirable or Maladaptive Traits and Behaviors Associated with Entrepreneurs

Angelo S. DeNisi[a] and Benjamin N. Alexander[b]

[a] *Tulane University*
[b] *California Polytechnic State University*

Introduction

Recently, several authors have begun examining the role of the entrepreneurial personality more closely (i.e., DeNisi, 2015; Klotz & Neubaum, 2016; Miller, 2014). These authors have made several interesting points about both the upside and downside of various personality characteristics in entrepreneurs, which we view here as individuals starting a business venture (DeNisi, 2015). These works share a common origin in finding that, while there is a robust literature examining the positive role of certain personality traits in driving entrepreneurship outcomes, the negative implications of personality traits require more attention.

The present chapter endeavors to extend the arguments made in those recent papers on the "dark side" of the entrepreneurial personality and to integrate additional perspectives germane to the issue (see Kets de Vries, 1985). We examine the distinct mechanisms proposed in recent commentaries (dark traits, curvilinearity, etc.) and delineate between different outcomes. Specifically, we discuss the dark side of the entrepreneurial personality with regard to the decision to become an entrepreneur, entrepreneurial success, and broader social well-being. In our view, the entire question of a potential dark side to the entrepreneurial personality becomes much more interesting, and much more important, when we turn to trying to predict who will be successful as an entrepreneur and their impact on other stakeholders. Not only is this important for scholarship, but it clearly has practical implications as well. Individuals, groups, or firms interested in starting and funding new ventures would clearly like to know something about the probability of success. Depending upon what predicts or inhibits success, it may be possible to train new entrepreneurs in ways that will increase their chances of success.

There are more questions than answers about any dark side to the entrepreneurial personality. We strive to close these gaps and to suggest some tentative directions for

The Wiley Handbook of Entrepreneurship, First Edition.
Edited by Gorkan Ahmetoglu, Tomas Chamorro-Premuzic, Bailey Klinger, & Tessa Karcisky.
© 2017 John Wiley & Sons Ltd. Published 2017 by John Wiley & Sons Ltd.

future research on the role of personality in entrepreneurship. We also offer some thoughts on the appropriate methodologies for pursuing this research.

Recent Interest and Older Views

Much of the more recent interest in the issue of a dark side to the entrepreneurial personality was triggered by Danny Miller's (2014) paper in which he suggested that some of the personality variables that might help entrepreneurs could at the same time, in extreme cases, be problematic. Miller's (2014) analysis focuses primarily on personality traits that are associated with individuals who pursue entrepreneurial goals or careers— that is, what has been termed the *entrepreneurial personality*. Specifically, Miller discusses how traits that are often studied as part of the entrepreneurial personality, including need for achievement, power, and autonomy (see McClelland, 1965, 1987), are, in the extreme, aggressiveness, ruthlessness, social deviance, and indifference to other people. Similarly, other positive traits such as self-efficacy and self-assurance can become narcissism and lead to hubris, while the need for control can lead to obsessive behavior and mistrust. In each case, Miller (2014) argues that personality traits typically viewed as positive can become undesirable when they are represented at very high or low levels. He further suggests that such extreme personalities have negative implications for broader societal well-being.

However, it is important to clarify that Miller (2014) did not directly suggest that there are personality traits which, at extreme levels, might inhibit success or the propensity to become an entrepreneur. His focus, rather, was on how these traits might relate to societal implications. In highlighting these consequences, Miller (2014) discusses examples of famous and successful entrepreneurs whose impact on society was not entirely positive (e.g., John D. Rockefeller and Cornelius Vanderbilt). That is, entrepreneurs who possessed extreme levels of certain personality traits might well be successful using traditional measures of entrepreneurial success, but that success may come at a high cost for society and other stakeholders. Miller (2014) also noted that other, more recent and famous entrepreneurs, such as Steve Jobs, have likewise been described as ruthless in their dealings with others.

Subsequent commentaries on the Miller (2014) paper (DeNisi, 2015; Klotz & Neubaum, 2016, Miller, 2016) took issue with some of the earlier characterizations but agreed that further research on a potential dark side to the entrepreneurial personality was important. For example, Klotz and Neubaum (2016, p. 8) noted that "conceptualizing narcissism as one extreme of self-efficacy or self-assurance . . . is not completely accurate." That is, several of the traits which Miller argued are the extreme state of a trait typically construed positively, are actually distinct traits which can occur at different levels (e.g., Costa & McCrae, 1992; Watson & Clark, 1997). Watson, Clark, & Tellegen (1988) also point out that personality traits exist as a profile, not in isolation within an individual. That is, we all possess many personality traits, and the presence of some can offset or complement the presence of others. Accordingly, Klotz and Neubaum (2016) suggest that research on the dark side of the entrepreneurial personality would benefit from the application of multidimensional personality conceptions such as core self-evaluations (e.g., Judge & Bono, 2001; Judge, Locke, & Durham, 1997).

DeNisi (2015) took a different tack, noting that Miller's (2014) discussion of a dark side might only be another manifestation of the curvilinear, inverted U-shaped relationship we find with many predictor variables, a phenomenon widely known as the

Yerkes–Dodson Law (Yerkes & Dodson, 1908). DeNisi further noted that several entrepreneurship scholars had already proposed such an effect in traits such as positive affect (Baron, Hmieleski, & Henry, 2012) and optimism (Hmieleski & Baron, 2009). In addition, the various commentaries on Miller (2014) argued that there were also other personality traits that could and should be examined in the context of entrepreneurship.

Miller (2014) does not really suggest the kind of curvilinear relationship discussed by DeNisi (2015) but harked back to earlier work by Kets de Vries (1985), which approached the entrepreneurial personality through a psychoanalytic lens. De Vries' work was based on several interviews with entrepreneurs whose firms were experiencing problems, including failure. His analysis of those interviews suggested that traits such as a need for control, a sense of distrust, and a desire for applause or affirmation were likely important in stimulating individuals to choose entrepreneurship, but that these same traits could also lead to problems in its conduct. Kets de Vries (1985) did not suggest that positive traits, in the extreme, could lead to problems, but instead argued that the very things that helped make someone an entrepreneur could also hurt that person later, both professionally and personally. Miller (2014) took these arguments a step further in suggesting that it is the *level* of a personality trait that determines if the trait leads to different outcomes such as entrepreneurial success and societal problems.

Thus, while all of these recent papers raise issues about the role of personality in entrepreneurship, and especially the role of a potential dark side, they focus on different mechanisms and problems in calling for further research on the topic. We, too, will suggest directions for future research, but we begin by making clear the distinction between research on entrepreneurial intentions, entrepreneurial success, and societal impact, and the role personality traits—whether light or dark—may play in affecting each. DeNisi (2015) began by raising a question about what we were trying to predict with personality. He pointed out that Miller (2014) often focused on the entrepreneurial personality in characterizing the type of person most likely to become an entrepreneur (e.g., need for achievement and autonomy), but in other instances discussed the literature on traits that are related to success in entrepreneurship (e.g., self-efficacy and self-esteem). Deciding to become an entrepreneur is clearly not the same as being a successful entrepreneur (Zhao, Seibert, & Lumpkin, 2010), and neither DeNisi nor Zhao et al. inherently addresses Miller's (2014) valid concern with broader societal impact and implications for different stakeholders. All these issues are worthy of study in understanding the entrepreneurial personality and, to further this literature, researchers must be clear about which is their outcome of interest. In delineating between different outcomes, we do not aim to restate the aforementioned commentaries, but rather to clarify those discussions in terms of clearly identified outcomes. In a few cases, we also focus on personality dimensions that have been underutilized in this discourse.

Entrepreneurial Personality and Entrepreneurship Outcomes

Personality and Entrepreneurial Intentions

The traits that have been applied to predict entrepreneurial intentions or the decision to become an entrepreneur are varied and include need for achievement (McClelland, 1965), the Big Five (conscientiousness, openness to experience, emotional stability/neuroticism, agreeableness and extraversion), narcissism, and many more (see Zhao, Seibert, & Lumpkin, 2010). These traits are not associated with any dark-side personality, but they have been found to be related to entrepreneurial intentions. In addition, the literature on vocational behavior offers some additional insight into the choice to become an entrepreneur, unrelated to any negative effects. John Holland's (1985) research has been especially influential in this area. His theory of fit and career choice focuses on six vocational personality types— Realistic, Investigative, Artistic, Social, Entrepreneurial (or Enterprising), and Conventional—each having different abilities, interests and occupational preferences. Although all six types are useful in vocational research, we will focus briefly upon the entrepreneurial type (E-type). The E-type is typified by individuals who display entrepreneurial competence as well as a preference for entrepreneurial activities. These individuals do best in settings where the ability to convince and direct others is rewarded, where there is competition, where dominance and self-confidence are important, and where an understanding of business-related issues is valued. Holland (1985) notes that, although not all E-types become successful entrepreneurs, most entrepreneurs display these interests and abilities.

A substantial body of research links vocational behavior to the broader literatures on personality and competencies. Several studies have demonstrated that Holland's E-type is related to higher levels of conscientiousness and extraversion, as well as to lower levels of agreeableness and neuroticism (e.g., Costa, McCrae, & Holland, 1984; Gottfredson, Jones, & Holland, 1993). Other work has found that entrepreneurs are more creative and innovative than are other professionals (e.g., Engle, Mah, & Sadri, 1997). Separately, studies examining the role of adolescent entrepreneurial competence, which is part of early childhood experiences (e.g., Obschonka, Silbereisen, & Schmitt-Rodermund, 2010; Schmitt-Rodermund, 2004, 2007) reported that both personality and adolescent entrepreneurial competence predicted subsequent entrepreneurial intentions. These authors also reported, however, that these effects were moderated by entrepreneurial control beliefs: the belief that one can influence success; and the belief that one can obtain the resources needed to influence success.

Overall, research growing out of the vocational behavior literature is consistent with extant research on the entrepreneurial personality in finding that there are several personality variables that are consistently related to either the intention to start a business or the actual launch of a new business. The vocational behavior literature does not seem to contradict the literature on management and entrepreneurship, but instead seems to supplement and support it. A meta-analysis by Zhao and Seibert (2006) concluded that entrepreneurs differed from managers in conscientiousness, openness to experience, neuroticism, and agreeableness. These results appear consistent with the conclusions reached by Miller (2014) that individuals who decide to become entrepreneurs tend to have high needs for achievement, autonomy, and power. More generally, the personality literature also points to the importance of studying clusters of personality traits, such as core self-evaluations or psychological capital (Judge & Bono, 2001; Judge, Locke, & Durham, 1997; Luthans, Youssef, & Avolio, 2007), rather than individual traits. Both of the aforementioned commentaries by Zhao and Seibert (2006) and Miller (2014) highlight the importance of viewing personality more broadly.

There has been research, however, that has suggested a "dark triad" of personality traits encompassing Machiavellianism, psychopathy, and narcissism (Paulhus & Williams, 2002) which predict entrepreneurial intentions (Akhtar, Ahmetoglu & Chamorro-Premiuzic, 2013; Kramer, Cesinger, Schwarzinger & Gelléri, 2011). This work draws on a robust literature addressing psychopathy in organizational settings, though not overwhelmingly in an entrepreneurship context, wherein psychopaths appear to be professionally successful (Babiak & Hare, 2006).

However, research on these more negative traits, similar to the research in management and entrepreneurship, does not provide direct evidence of a dark side involved with the decision to become an entrepreneur. As DeNisi (2015) points out and we have summarized above, the various traits which positively predict the decision to become an entrepreneur may have contrary effects at their extremes, undermining entrepreneurial motivations rather than encouraging them. Though there is some evidence that "dark" personality traits are associated with entrepreneurial intentions, in fact, as noted by DeNisi (2015), there doesn't seem to be much potential for a "dark side" when predicting career choices. Thus, as there is another side to personality in those who decide to become an entrepreneur that is not a dark side, it is worth knowing more about who decides to become an entrepreneur. Holland's work on E-types should be brought into the fold in research that further explores the entrepreneurial personality and addresses interactions with particular traits, multidimensional personality profiles, and contextual moderators. As we will expand upon in the next section, the vocational behavior literature does point to some dark side for entrepreneurial success (e.g., Simon, Houghton, & Aquino, 2000).

Personality and Entrepreneurial Success

A true dark side to the entrepreneurial personality becomes more meaningful when predicting entrepreneurial success. Success can be understood as relating to the financial performance of the new venture and the entrepreneur's well-being. There are two motivating issues which are not mutually exclusive. First, the same traits which positively influence the decision to become an entrepreneur can become a liability in growing a new venture. Second, personality traits may exhibit a curvilinear relationship with success, fostering success at moderate levels and inhibiting it at extreme levels. There have been several studies focusing on personality predictors of entrepreneurial success. In particular, two meta-analyses—by Rauch and Frese (2007) and Zhao et al. (2010)—deserve special attention in this regard because both examined the effects of personality traits not just on entrepreneurial success but also on the decision to become an entrepreneur or to have entrepreneurial intentions.

Rauch and Frese (2007) meta-analyzed more than 100 articles examining both the relationship between personality traits and the decision to become an entrepreneur (62 studies), and between personality traits and entrepreneurial success (54 studies). Their study went beyond a simple calculation of effects and compared relationships between traits consistent with the tasks of entrepreneurs versus those which were not relevant to those tasks. The authors found that traits rated as more relevant to entrepreneurial tasks related to both the likelihood of starting a business and business success. These traits included need for achievement, innovativeness, proactive personality, generalized self-efficacy, stress tolerance, need for autonomy, locus of control and risk-taking. The authors also reported that, in every case, effects for business creation were not significantly different from effects for entrepreneurial success. This consistency fails to support the notion of a dark side to the entrepreneurial personality in entrepreneurial success.

Rauch and Frese's (2007) results differed only slightly from those reported in the meta-analysis by Zhao et al. (2010) who reported that conscientiousness, openness to experience, emotional stability (neuroticism), and extraversion were related to both entrepreneurial intentions and entrepreneurial success. However, an additional personality trait they assessed—risk propensity—was positively related to entrepreneurial intentions but not to success. Finally, Zhao they found few real differences when predicting different measures of success (relative growth, operational effectiveness, and profitability). Thus, both meta-analyses generally found that there were clearly definable personality traits that seemed to be related to both entrepreneurial intentions and entrepreneurial success. The one exception, risk propensity, was unrelated, not negatively related, to entrepreneurial success (Zhao et al., 2010).

Other studies provide indirect evidence regarding the reversal of traits' effects from the decision to become an entrepreneur or having entrepreneurial intentions to entrepreneurial success. As noted by Miller (2014), several scholars have suggested that optimism is an important trait for entrepreneurs (e.g., Kets de Vries & Miller, 1985). However, Hmieleski and Baron (2009) reported a negative relationship between an entrepreneur's optimism and the success of new ventures measured by revenue growth. These results suggest the possibility that optimism is positively related to the choice to become an entrepreneur, but negatively related to entrepreneurial success. Likewise, Hayward, Shepherd, and Griffin (2006) argued that hubris is what leads individuals to start new businesses in the face of high failure rates, but this same hubris also increases the likelihood that they will ultimately fail. Of course, Miller (2014) characterized hubris as the negative extreme of self-efficacy and self-assurance, both of which have been associated with entrepreneurship. Similarly, McCarthy, Schoorman, and Cooper (1993) noted that self-assured entrepreneurs night be more likely to engage in an escalation of commitment and so continue (or increase) commitment to a failing course of action. Psychopathy, while associated with entrepreneurial intentions, is negatively associated with management skills and overall accomplishments in corporate settings (Babiak, Neumann & Hare, 2010). Accordingly, it is possible that psychopaths will not succeed in leading organizations even if they are more likely to found them. Finally, Simon et al. (2000) discussed a dark side to control beliefs and ultimate success. Specifically, they posited an "illusion of control," a type of cognitive bias where an entrepreneur overestimates his or her entrepreneurial skills and therefore embarks on a new venture for which he or she is not prepared. These authors therefore stressed the importance of believing in one's ability to obtain resources as well as in one's ability to succeed in order to make realistic decisions.

In addition, the Yerkes–Dodson Law about curvilinearity may explain the influence of different personality traits. However, neither meta-analysis reported any indication of curvilinear relationships between the examined traits and entrepreneurial success. Further, neither study reported any hypotheses regarding curvilinearity. As noted above, Miller (2014) did not explicitly suggest that there should be such a relationship between personality and entrepreneurial success, but it is still interesting that no such effects have been examined. At the same time, several studies have provided evidence which suggests, but does not provide direct evidence of, curvilinearity. Hmieleski and Baron (2009) explained their finding on optimism by arguing that they identified a negative relationship between optimism and revenue because the entrepreneurs in their sample were already at the high end of optimism for the population. Therefore, the entrepreneurs who were higher in optimism might actually have been too optimistic, so divorced from reality that their ventures were less likely to succeed. Likewise, McCarthy, et al.'s (1993) arguments regarding self-assurance suggest negative implications for entrepreneurial success beyond a certain point.

Some extant research also points to a dark side of the entrepreneurial personality for entrepreneurs' well-being. Kets de Vries (1985), in recounting his interactions with entrepreneurs and their motivating desire for applause, described one entrepreneur's repeated experience of waking up screaming with a feeling of suffocation. Ambition at excessive levels may also compromise entrepreneurs' well-being by driving them toward isolation. At the same time, the role of personality in resource conservation, could, in considering personality as a multidimensional profile, provide clearer support for a positive relationship between entrepreneurial personality and well-being (Klotz & Neubaum, 2016; Miller, 2016).

In sum, there is little (if any) direct evidence of a dark side of the positive personality traits discussed by Miller (2014) for entrepreneurial success. That is, there is no clear empirical evidence that traits which increase the likelihood of entrepreneurship also reduce the likelihood of success (or increase the likelihood of venture failure). There is also no direct evidence of curvilinearity wherein particular traits positively influence entrepreneurial success up to a point and constrain it afterward. Nonetheless, there are some logical bases provided in the extant literature, upon which we have sought to expand, that suggest one or both of these dark-side personality effects might impact entrepreneurial success in a manner that researchers have yet to capture empirically. Finally, while there is some anecdotal evidence that certain traits may, beyond some point, negatively impact entrepreneurs' well-being, personality more comprehensively may serve to sustain entrepreneurs through the trials of launching and growing new ventures.

Broader Impact

The dark side of the entrepreneurial personality is also pertinent in understanding how entrepreneurs affect broader societal well-being and the well-being of particular stakeholders. Like entrepreneurial success, the same traits which predict the decision to engage in entrepreneurship or entrepreneurial success could have negative implications for those entrepreneurs' broader impact. In an early discussion of the entrepreneurial personality, Kets de Vries (1985) described the results of a number of interviews with entrepreneurs which indicated that certain personality traits could lead to problems for the entrepreneurs themselves, their companies, and those who might work with them. For example, the need for control which motivated the decision to become an entrepreneur also inspired invasive monitoring of employees.

Other less studied traits or disorders, such as Machiavellianism, psychopathy, and social dominance orientation may, alongside more studied narcissism, play a role in understanding the broader impact of the entrepreneurial personality's dark side. DeNisi (2015) and Klotz and Neubaum (2016) suggested that the "dark" traits described by Miller (2014) were not necessarily extreme manifestations of positive traits, but were actually different traits altogether. Negative characteristics, such as ruthlessness, which Miller (2014) journalistically ascribes to renowned entrepreneurs, appear to, at one and the same time, drive business success and cause more diffuse damage to business partners, unions, and society more generally. In one study, researchers found that one type of subclinical psychopathy was related to both entrepreneurial intentions and entrepreneurial outcomes (Akhtar et al., 2013). However, though the authors found that psychopathy was negatively related to social entrepreneurship, they did not examine its effects on community or societal well-being. While Miller (2014) does not suggest this, it is also possible in some cases that the entire basis for entrepreneurship may be predicated on antisocial motives.

In addition to impacting broader societal well-being, employees, and business partners, entrepreneurs' families may also suffer as a result of entrepreneurs' personality traits. Miller (2014) addresses the implications of entrepreneurs' success for their relations, especially with regard to family enterprises. The effects of the dark side of the entrepreneurial personality for family members in Miller's account ranged from neglect to psychological violence (Belanger, 2011; Kets de Vries, 1996).

Future Research on the Dark Side of the Entrepreneurial Personality

The remainder of this chapter builds on the preceding discussion of personality traits and outcomes. In the next section, we discuss some persistent questions revealed in our effort to parse the different outcomes from the personality traits that may or may not affect them. Second, we examine some basic issues, the resolution of which will support additional clarifying research on the dark side of the entrepreneurial personality.

Untangling Outcomes and Trait Phenomena

Our discussion thus far has suggested that there is very little (if any) empirical evidence that personality traits which researchers generally construe as positive for entrepreneurs, can yield negative outcomes either when extended to different outcomes or when manifested in the extreme. Nonetheless, we concur with earlier commentaries on the basis of ample anecdotal and suppositional support that there is much more to investigate concerning a dark side to personality in entrepreneurship. For example, as noted in several places, Miller (2014) did not suggest that extreme personality types would lead to failure, but rather to societal problems. We could find no empirical research examining this possibility, and so it remains an open question requiring further research. The examples used by Miller (2014) all represent extremely successful entrepreneurs who were ruthless or behaved unethically. Do all successful entrepreneurs behave in this manner and we only learn about it when they become famous enough for someone to study their lives? Alternatively, the individuals Miller (2014) discussed could be examples of persons who have extreme levels of certain traits and these extreme levels led them to be both extremely successful and extremely ruthless or unethical. Finally, it could be the extreme success they achieved that allowed them to behave as ruthlessly as they did. Whatever the case, mainstream management and entrepreneurship research has not typically considered impact on society as a dependent variable (Margolis & Walsh, 2003). Yet that is exactly what Miller (2014) was suggesting we should do, and such research would clearly yield important information about success or impact on a different level of analysis.

Turning to the more traditional outcome variables, future efforts should combine research on determinants of who becomes an entrepreneur with determinants of who becomes a successful entrepreneur. Setting aside for a moment the nontrivial issue of how we define success, there does seem to be, as discussed above, some reason to expect that certain traits which can lead a person to pursue an entrepreneurial career can also lead to failure. Perhaps this occurs only at the highest levels of a given trait (e.g., Hmieleski & Baron, 2009, relative to optimism; Hayward et al., 2006 relative to hubris), but it is also possible that the same traits that lead to entrepreneurship also contain the seeds for failure (e.g., McCarthy, Schoorman, & Cooper, 1993, relative to self-assurance and escalation of commitment).

Such a set of findings would be important because they would suggest that, once someone embarked upon an entrepreneurial career, they would need additional training or some type of intervention to keep them from failing. While this training would not alter underlying traits, it could provide entrepreneurs with personal and managerial tactics to mitigate those traits' negative effects. Furthermore, it could be that a combination of traits allows one to overcome the potentially negative effects of an isolated trait. A case in point would be Baron, Franklin and Hmieleski's (2013) findings that entrepreneurs' levels of self-efficacy, optimism, hope, and resilience (also referred to as psychological capital; Luthans et al., 2007) diminished the effects of stress on well-being. Baron and his associates have also examined several other potential moderating factors such as affect, various cognitive mechanisms, and social competence (Baron, 1998, 2008; Baron & Markham, 2003). These moderators could allow an entrepreneur to enjoy the benefits of a trait such as optimism, without suffering the potential ill-effects of being overly optimistic. Finally, clarifying the influence of trait clusters such as core self-evaluations (Judge & Bono, 2001; Judge, Locke, & Durham, 1997) and psychological capital (Luthans et al., 2007) would be fruitful for research on the entrepreneurial personality. In general, the interaction between personality traits and states including attitudes, moods, and emotions, also warrant more attention (e.g., Klotz & Neuman, 2016).

It is also important to conduct research to help us better understand when personality traits will and will not be related to different outcome. For example, as discussed above, Hmieleski and Baron (2009) attributed their results to the notion that entrepreneurs (at least those in their sample) were already quite high on optimism so that individuals who were at the highest levels in their sample were extremely high on optimism relative to the general population. If in fact, most entrepreneurs tend to possess certain traits, it is unlikely that researchers will detect relationships between these traits and performance, since the range will be restricted. Alternatively, this situation might produce counterintuitive results such as those reported by Hmieleski and Baron (2009) where researchers may unknowingly study only extreme levels of a given trait.

It would also be useful to directly study "dark" personality traits such as psychopathy, Machiavellianism, narcissism, hubris, dominance orientation, and obsessive behavior, and their role in determining negative effects for and of entrepreneurs. Whether these are simply the manifestation of extreme levels of more benign traits (as discussed by Miller, 2014), or are actually separate but important traits (such as discussed by DeNisi, 2015; Kets de Vries, 1985; Klotz & Neubaum, 2016), it is important to know if the individuals most likely to become entrepreneurs are more likely to possess these characteristics, what the implications of these traits are for entrepreneurial success and other broader outcomes, and what might be done about any negative effects.

Up to this point, our discussion has construed the entrepreneur and process of entrepreneurship atomistically. Some entrepreneurs, such as Elon Musk, are serial entrepreneurs who found multiple new ventures. The influence of personality and its possible dark side may be somewhat different when examined over multiple instances. More to the point, any of the outcomes related to entrepreneurship within and across instances of entrepreneurship is the product of a great many factors. The personality composition of a founding team or an eventual more traditional top management team, merits further examination in examining any dark side and may moderate otherwise negative influences (Klotz & Neubaum, 2016). Likewise, proximal situational forces in some contexts may be so strong that not even the darkest personality traits have a strong impact on any type of entrepreneurial outcome. Research along these lines also needs to consider contextual factors that might constitute a "strong situation" which can overwhelm the effects of any personality traits (Meyer, Dalal, Hermida, 2010; Mischel, 1968). More distal societal institutions may also operate to constrain the negative implications of any entrepreneur's personality as a facilitator for destructive tendencies.

Basic Issues

Beyond untangling outcomes and mechanisms, and proposing research questions for the future, several more basic issues remain that must be addressed to promote a better understanding of any dark side to the entrepreneurial personality. The first of these was noted earlier, but the fact remains that we do not have substantial empirical evidence to state that there is or is not a dark side—perhaps there is no "darkside" to the entrepreneurial personality. The extant research is speculative or based on a small number of interviews, and it really does not say much beyond the fact that any trait, when carried to the extreme can be a problem. The negative implications of extreme personality traits manifested at their extremes are likely present for entrepreneurs, managers, front-line employees, and for human beings generally in just about any social context. The assertion (or suggestion) that possession of extreme levels of certain traits could be problematic is simply not an important contribution to the literature on entrepreneurship or personality. Furthermore, as discussed above, it is not clear from the literature if a dark side of personality is important for whether or not individuals becomes an entrepreneur, whether or not they are successful, or how they impact other stakeholders. However, in the distinctions between these different outcomes lie more valuable contributions for the entrepreneurship literature.

Therefore, it is important that we move to a sensitive definition of these outcomes. While typical organizational outcome measures can be applied to assess one aspect of entrepreneurial success, an entrepreneur's well-being can be examined using outcomes such as life satisfaction or personal fulfillment as well as assessments of psychological and physical health. However, financial performance is not likely to be the sole reason for serial entrepreneurs' movements between ventures. As such, assessment of business success may be subject to different measures. Separately, Miller (2014) discussed the broader impact of negative traits on society as a whole, as well as on business partners, families, and other stakeholders. While there are metrics for addressing social and environmental impact including the Kullback-Leibler Divergence (KLD) measure, reputational indices, and private certifications, these measures are far less agreed upon by scholars and practitioners, and subject to limitations for making comparisons across businesses. The most validated measures tend to address particular types of output or impact (e.g., CO_2 emissions, poverty reduction), which complicate broad comparisons across firms engaged in multiple and different activities that affect different stakeholders.

Methodologically, research on the dark side of the entrepreneurial personality can take several forms. While no approach is perfect, and certain data is difficult to obtain, this work is most likely to be advanced through a combination of surveys, laboratory studies, and historiometric analysis. Survey research targeting groups of nascent entrepreneurs is promising. Faculty members at universities with entrepreneurship programs are in a strong position to develop longitudinal data collection efforts. Laboratory studies, perhaps presenting different entrepreneurship scenarios or using business strategy simulations, would also be revealing. Finally, historiometric analysis, which entails drawing on biographical accounts from archival sources like media reports can be used to assess, more systemically than has be done in this domain, the personalities of (in)famous entrepreneurs. Scholars have applied historiometric analysis in the past to study prominent business leaders and politicians (e.g., House, Spangler, & Woycke, 1991; Peterson, Smith, Martorana, & Owans, 2003; Resick, Whitman, Weingarden, & Hiller, 2009). Such analysis holds significant potential to provide insight into negative traits that might otherwise be obscured in surveys by social desirability bias.

Conclusion

Is the study of a potential dark side to the entrepreneurial personality important? To date, there is little direct empirical evidence that supports the existence of a dark side. Hmieleski and Baron (2009) *suggested* such a curvilinear relationship between optimism and performance to explain their negative relationship, while Hayward et al. (2006) *proposed* hubris (the extreme level of confidence and efficacy) as an explanation for why entrepreneurs engage in new ventures in light of high failure rates. However, neither study presented empirical data to support these suggestions and propositions. McCarthy et al. (1993) did present data indicating that entrepreneurs who were high in self-confidence were also more likely to expand their business when market conditions were negative (as predicted by the literature on escalation of commitment). However, these authors noted that this was not always a bad thing. Of course, there is evidence of problems associated with both escalation of commitment (see Staw, 1981) and hubris (e.g., Hayward & Hambrick, 1997), but this only suggests that these traits play a role in constraining entrepreneurial success without actually capturing those effects. As we noted, there is no empirical study (of which we are aware) that has actually tested traits' possible curvilinear effects, and future research in this area will need to better specify when traits are manifested at extreme levels or are actually different traits. However, if there are certain personality traits that negatively influence entrepreneurial outcomes, whether by reversed effects across outcomes, extreme levels of positively construed traits, or that are simply destructive in their nature (e.g., the dark triad), further investigation would be both practically and theoretically important.

Beyond a dark side to the entrepreneurial personality, our review has also revealed that there is only limited empirical evidence to suggest that any personality trait is negatively associated with entrepreneurial success, as success is typically defined. This absence suggests that such relationships may be atypical, but it also points to the need to examine other indicators of success as well as the broader impact of an entrepreneur's actions on different stakeholders. It is important, therefore, that future research look specifically for the kind of effects we have been discussing before we can conclude that personality does or does not negatively influence entrepreneurial outcomes.

Thus we must conclude that we don't know how much about the dark side of the entrepreneurial personality. It is clear from our review that researchers must distinguish between different entrepreneurship outcomes, even though it will often make sense to study multiple outcomes together. If there is a dark side, it is much more likely to be relevant in predicting entrepreneurial success or broader impact than entrepreneurial intentions. Though entrepreneurship is an essential economic vehicle, it is incontrovertible that some entrepreneurs have caused significant harm that is not captured in traditional measures of entrepreneurial success. Whether these effects are a function of certain personality traits, the dark side to the entrepreneurial personality, or just come with the territory of being a successful entrepreneur, is an important matter that merits future research.

It is also clear from our review that there may be other personality traits and personality profiles that deserve attention in studying entrepreneurial intentions, success, and broader impact. As noted, the literature on vocational interests may provide some additional insights into what kind of individual is most likely to become an entrepreneur, and this may also be related to entrepreneurial success and broader impact. Furthermore, as suggested, it may be more insightful to examine the impact of personality profiles and groups of traits on different entrepreneurial outcomes. It may be that the presence of a "positive" traits can ameliorate the effects of a "negative" trait, and it is also possible that certain personality profiles are associated with disastrous outcomes.

While the evidence for a dark side to the entrepreneurial personality is limited, the suggestions and implications in extant research and the practical value of clarification warrant additional scholarship. In this chapter, we have laid out several promising directions for future efforts by distinguishing among outcomes, isolating different trait phenomena and personality profiles, and broadening the scope to consider other factors such as how personality interacts with the broader context in which entrepreneurship occurs.

References

Akhtar, R., Ahmetoglu, G., & Chamorro-Premuzic, T. (2013). Greed is good? Assessing the relationship between entrepreneurship and subclinical psychopathy. *Personality and Individual Differences, 54*(3), 420–425.

Babiak, P., & Hare, R. D. (2006). *Snakes in suits: When psychopaths go to work.* New York, NY: Regan Books.

Babiak, P., Neumann, C. S., & Hare, R. D. (2010). Corporate psychopathy: Talking the walk. *Behavioral Sciences & the Law, 28*(2), 174–193.

Baron, R. A. (1998). Cognitive mechanisms in entrepreneurship: Why and when entrepreneurs think differently than other people. *Journal of Business Venturing, 13*(4), 275–294.

Baron, R. A. (2008). The role of affect in the entrepreneurial process. *Academy of Management Review, 33,* 328–340.

Baron, R. A., Franklin, R. J., & Hmieleski, K. M. (2013). Why entrepreneurs often experience low, not high, levels of stress: The joint effects of selection and psychological capital. *Journal of Management, 42*(3), 742–768.

Baron, R. A., Hmieleski, K. M., & Henry, R. A. (2012). Entrepreneurs' dispositional positive affect: The potential benefits—and potential costs—of being "up." *Journal of Business Venturing, 27,* 310–324.

Baron, R. A., & Markman, G. D. (2003). Beyond social capital: The role of entrepreneurs' social competence in their financial success. *Journal of Business Venturing, 18*(1), 41–60.

Belanger, C. (2011). L'echec des successions des fondateurs d'entreprise. *La Revue Gestion, 36*(1), 41–46.

Costa, P. T., Jr., & McCrae, R. R. (1992). The five-factor model of personality and its relevance to personality disorders. *Journal of Personality Disorders, 6*(4), 343–359.

Costa, P. T., McCrae, R. R., & Holland, J. L. (1984). Personality and vocational interests in an adult sample. *Journal of Applied Psychology, 69,* 390–400.

DeNisi, A. S. (2015). Some further thoughts on the entrepreneurial personality. *Entrepreneurship Theory and Practice, 39,* 997–1003.

Engle, D. E., Mah, J. J., & Sadri, G. (1997). An empirical comparison of entrepreneurs and employees: Implications for motivation. *Creativity Research Journal, 10,* 45–49.

Gottfredson, G. D., Jones, E. M., & Holland, J. L. (1993). Personality and vocational interests: The relation of Holland's six interest dimensions to five robust dimensions of personality. *Journal of Counseling Psychology, 40,* 518–524.

Hayward, M. L., & Hambrick, D. C. (1997). Explaining the premiums paid in large acquisitions: Evidence of CEO hubris. *Administrative Science Quarterly, 42,* 103–127.

Hayward, M. L., Shepherd, D. A., & Griffin, D. (2006). A hubris theory of entrepreneurship. *Management Science, 52*(2), 160–172.

Hmieleski, K. M., & Baron, R. A. (2009). Entrepreneurs' optimism and new venture performance: a social cognitive perspective. *Academy of Management Journal, 52,* 473–488.

Holland, J. L. (1985). *Making vocational choices: A theory of vocational personalities and work environments.* Englewood Cliffs, NJ: Prentice-Hall.

House, R. J., Spangler, W. D., & Woycke, J. (1991). Personality and charisma in the U.S. presidency: A psychological theory of leadership effectiveness. *Administrative Science Quarterly, 36,* 364–396.

Judge, T. A., & Bono, J. E. (2001). Relationship of core self-evaluations traits—self-esteem, generalized self-efficacy, locus of control, and emotional stability—with job satisfaction and job performance: A meta-analysis. *Journal of Applied Psychology, 86*(1), 80.

Judge, T. A., Locke, E. A., & Durham, C. C. (1997). The dispositional causes of job satisfaction. *Research in Organizational Behavior, 19,* 151–188.

Kets de Vries, M. (1985). The dark side of entrepreneurship. *Harvard Business Review, 63*(6), 29–39.

Kets de Vries, M. (1996). The anatomy of the entrepreneur: Clinical observations. *Human Relations, 49*(7), 853–883.

Kets de Vries, M. F. K., & Miller, D. (1985). Narcissism and leadership: An object relations perspective. *Human Relations, 38*(6), 583–601.

Klotz, A. C., & Neubaum, D. O. (2016). Research on the dark side of personality traits in entrepreneurship: Observations from an Organizational Behavior perspective. *Entrepreneurship Theory and Practice, 40*(1), 7–17.

Kramer, M., Cesinger, B., Schwarzinger, D., & Gelléri, P. (2011, December). Investigating entrepreneurs' dark personality: How narcissism, Machiavellianism, and psychopathy relate to entrepreneurial intention. In *Proceedings of the 25th ANZAM conference,* Wellington, New Zealand: Australia and New Zealand Academy of Management.

Luthans, F., Youssef, C. M., & Avolio, B. J. (2007). *Psychological capital: Developing the human competitive edge.* New York, NY: Oxford University Press.

Margolis, J. D., & Walsh, J. P. (2003). Misery loves companies: Rethinking social initiatives by business. *Administrative Science Quarterly, 48*(2), 268–305.

McCarthy, A. M., Schoorman, F. D., & Cooper, A. C. (1993). Reinvestment decisions by entrepreneurs: Rational decision-making or escalation of commitment. *Journal of Business Venturing, 8*(1), 9–24.

McClelland, D. C. (1965). N achievement and entrepreneurship: A longitudinal study. *Journal of Personality and Social Psychology, 1,* 389–392.

McClelland, D. C. (1987) Characteristic of successful entrepreneurs. *The Journal of Creative behavior, 21,* 219–233.

Meyer, R. D., Dalal, R. S., & Hermida, R. (2010). A review and synthesis of situational strength in the organizational sciences. *Journal of Management, 36*(1), 121–140.

Miller, D. (2014). A downside to the entrepreneurial personality? *Entrepreneurship theory and practice, 39,* 1–8.

Miller, D. (2016). Response to "Research on the dark side of personality traits in entrepreneurship: Observations from an Organizational behavior perspective." *Entrepreneurship Theory and Practice, 40,* 19–24.

Mischel, W. (1968). *Personality and assessment.* New York, NY: Wiley.

Obschonka, M., Silbereisen, R. K., & Schmitt-Rodermund, E. (2010). Entrepreneurial intention as developmental outcome. *Journal of Vocational Behavior, 77,* 63–72.

Paulhus, D. L., & Williams, K. M. (2002). The dark triad of personality: Narcissism, Machiavellianism, and psychopathy. *Journal of Research in Personality, 36,* 556–563.

Peterson, R., Smith, D. B., Martorana, P., & Owens, P. (2003). The impact of chief executive officer personality on top management team dynamics: One mechanism by which leadership affects organizational performance. *Journal of Applied Psychology, 88,* 795– 808.

Rauch, A., & Frese, M. (2007). Let's put the person back into entrepreneurship research: A meta-analysis on the relationship between business owners' personality traits, business creation, and success. *European Journal of Work and Organizational Psychology, 16*(4), 353–385.

Resick, C. J., Whitman, D. S., Weingarden, S. M., & Hiller, N. J. (2009). The bright-side and the dark-side of CEO personality: Examining core self-evaluations, narcissism, transformational leadership, and strategic influence. *Journal of Applied Psychology, 94*(6), 1365.

Schmitt-Rodermund, E. (2004). Pathways to successful entrepreneurship: Personality, parenting, entrepreneurial competence, and interests. *Journal of Vocational Behavior, 65,* 498–518.

Schmitt-Rodermund, E. (2007). The long way to entrepreneurship: Personality, parenting, early interests, and competencies as precursors of entrepreneurial activity among the "termites." In R. K. Silbereisen & R. M. Lerner (Eds.), *Approaches to positive youth development* (pp. 205–224). London, England: Sage.

Simon, M., Houghton, S. M., & Aquino, K. (2000). Cognitive biases, risk perception, and venture formation: How individuals decide to start companies. *Journal of Business Venturing, 15*(2), 113–134.

Staw, B. M. (1981). The escalation of commitment to a course of action. *Academy of Management Review, 6*(4), 577–587.

Watson, D., & Clark, L. A. (1997). Extraversion and its positive emotional core. In R. Hogan, J. J. Johnson, & S. R. Briggs (Eds.), *Handbook of personality psychology* (pp. 767–793). San Diego, CA: Academic Press.

Watson, D., Clark, L. A., & Tellegen, A. (1988). Development and validation of brief measures of positive and negative affect: The PANAS scales. *Journal of Personality and Social Psychology, 54*(6), 1063–1070.

Yerkes, R. M., & Dodson, J. D. (1908). The relation of strength of stimulus to rapidity of habit-formation. *Journal of Comparative Neurology and Psychology, 18,* 459–482.

Zhao, H., & Seibert, S. E. (2006). The Big Five personality dimensions and entrepreneurial status: A meta-analytic review. *Journal of Applied Psychology, 91*(2), 586–597.

Zhao, H., Seibert, S. E., & Lumpkin, G. T. (2010). The relationship of personality to entrepreneurial intentions and performance: A meta-analytic review. *Journal of Management, 36*(2), 381–404.

9

Female Entrepreneurship and IQ

Rik W. Hafer[a]

[a] *Lindenwood University*

Introduction

It has been a long-held view that entrepreneurs play a crucial role in a dynamic, growing economy. From the early writings of Smith (1776) through Knight (1921) and more recently Kirzner (1973, 1997) the entrepreneur has long been recognized as an integral cog in the economic machinery. Even though standard growth models show how factors of production are combined to produce output, entrepreneurship "fills in the institutional details to help make the [economic] growth process more understandable" (Holcombe, 1998, p. 60). This is a recurring theme in Acs and Armington (2006), and several of the papers in Audretsch, Keilbach, and Lehmann (2006). Unfortunately, as noted by Teece (2016) standard economic models are woefully lacking in properly addressing the role played by entrepreneurs.

Previous research has improved our understanding of why some individuals become entrepreneurs and why some countries are characterized as having more entrepreneurial activity.[1] An oversimplification is that much of this analysis often either treats entrepreneurship as male-dominated or is mute on possible gender differences. An example of this indifference is a recent paper (Hafer & Jones, 2015) in which the authors make no reference to any potential differences between female and male entrepreneurs.

The emergence of and role played by female entrepreneurs has not been ignored totally, however. The excellent reviews by Ahl (2006), Brush (2006), and Hughes, Jennings, Brush, Carter, and Welter (2012) highlight the extant issues, such as the role that gender plays in explaining entrepreneurial success (e.g., Coleman & Robb, 2012; Rietz & Henrekson, 2000; Wagner, 2007), or whether gender helps explain one's propensity to become (or not) an entrepreneur (Cowling & Taylor, 2001; Garcia, 2012; Koellinger, Minniti, & Schades, 2013; van der Zwan, Verheul, & Thurik, 2012). From these (and other) studies we find that gender gaps exist and are related to, among others, cultural effects—for example, women oftentimes postpone entrepreneurial activity until children are older—and

---

[1] From here on I mean productive entrepreneurship, where the entrepreneur is creating jobs and expanding incomes, not necessarily working in self-employment.

The Wiley Handbook of Entrepreneurship, First Edition.
Edited by Gorkan Ahmetoglu, Tomas Chamorro-Premuzic, Bailey Klinger, & Tessa Karcisky.
© 2017 John Wiley & Sons Ltd. Published 2017 by John Wiley & Sons Ltd.

bias—women find it more difficult to get financial backing for entrepreneurial activity relative to men (see Sauer & Wilson, 2016, and the articles cited therein.)

Another ongoing issue is whether differences in educational attainment explain differences in entrepreneurial activity. Gennaioli, La Porta, Lopez-de-Silanes, and Shleifer (2013) and van Pragg, van Witteloostuijn, and van der Sluis (2013) have found that differences in entrepreneurs' educational background has a proportionately greater effect on their productivity than differences in the educational attainment of workers has on their productivity. Similarly, Hartog, van Praag, and van der Sluis (2010) report that the measured return to education is greater for entrepreneurs relative to others. Given the evidence that the average woman, especially in developing countries (or often in low-income areas of developed countries) are often at an educational disadvantage relative to their male counterparts, differences in cognitive ability could provide an explanation for differences in female and male entrepreneurial activity.

Recent evidence indicates that differences in cognitive ability help explain differences in entrepreneurial activity. Instead of educational measures such as years of schooling, a number of investigations have used IQ as a proxy for cognitive skill. And the evidence suggests that, on average, those with higher IQs tend to be more successful entrepreneurs on the basis of several outcomes.[2] Hartog et al. (2010) reported that differences in IQ are better able to explain differences in entrepreneurs' incomes than they are in explaining differences in workers' wages. van Praag and Cramer (2011) found that childhood IQ is a significant (positive) predictor of the future size of the entrepreneurs' firms. And the evidence in Vinogradov and Kolvereid (2010) suggests that, among immigrants to Norway, the higher their home-country IQ the higher their rate of self-employment. The results from these (and other) studies suggest that high-IQ individuals on average are more likely to create new businesses and innovate in ways that expand products and markets. Hafer and Jones's (2015) work shows that after controlling for several economic and institutional factors, countries with higher levels of IQ tend to have higher levels of entrepreneurial activity. If national IQ and *overall* entrepreneurial activity are related, does a similar relationship hold between IQ and a more specific measure of female entrepreneurial activity? Answering that question is the objective of this chapter's study.

The following section gives an overview of the female entrepreneurship and IQ measures used in this study. Then I lay out the empirical model to be estimated along with a discussion of the control variables. My statistical results are the presented, followed by conclusions and policy implications.

Measuring Female Entrepreneurship and IQ

The Female Entrepreneurship Index

Some studies rely on outcome-based measures such as firm development or self-employment to test competing theories of entrepreneurship. Many also have used the survey-based Global Entrepreneurship Monitor (hereafter, GEM), of which Reynolds, Bosma, and Autio (2005) provide a useful overview and critique. Acs, Autio, and Szerb

---

[2] Some have argued that IQ is not a reliable measure, preferring instead scores on standardized exams, such as the Third International Mathematics and Science Study (TIMSS) and the Program for International Student Assessment (PISA) tests. On the reliability (or social acceptance issue) of IQ scores, Deary (2001) provides a pertinent discussion. On the choice between IQ and the standardized test scores, see the discussion below on the IQ data.

(2014) assert that while surveys like the GEM "provide an insight into the opinion climate that prevails in a given country, [they] tend to suffer from the obvious disassociation from actual activity . . . and tell us little about how opinions and attitudes translate into action within a given country" (p. 480).

Yet another alternative is the Global Entrepreneurship and Development Index (hereafter, GEDI), originally developed by Acs and Szerb (2010) and now maintained and published by the Global Entrepreneurship and Development Institute in Washington, DC. The GEDI combines individual-level measures of entrepreneurial activity along with broader institutional factors that capture the economic and legal environment within which such entrepreneurship occurs. The GEDI thus incorporates not only individual-level measures, taken from the GEM, but also the broader socioeconomic institutions that may help (open capital markets) or hinder (high levels of corruption) entrepreneurial activity. Acs and Szerb (2010) argue that any useful index of entrepreneurship must be "complex," reflecting the intricacy of the process and the institutional environment within which economic agents engage in entrepreneurial activity.

Terjesen and Lloyd's (2015) Female Entrepreneurship Index (FEI) is constructed in the same spirit as the GEDI. The FEI also combines individual-level aspects of entrepreneurial activity with a broader institutional-level assessment of the economic and social climate to derive an index of female entrepreneurship. As they put it, "The FEI's systematic approach enables cross-country comparison and benchmarking of the gender differentiated conditions that often affect high potential female entrepreneurship development" (p. 4).

The basic concepts underlying the construction of the FEI are outlined here.[3] The FEI uses both individual and institutional variables (factors) in its construction. There are 15 individual and 15 institutional variables, all of which come from recently available sources. The FEI is made up of three subindexes: Entrepreneurial Environment; Entrepreneurial Eco-System; and Entrepreneurial Aspirations. Each individual-level variable is matched with an institutional level measure at the so-called pillar level. Within each subindex there are five "pillars" that capture more specific aspects. To use one example, in the Entrepreneurial Environment subindex is the pillar "Opportunity Perception." While research shows that opportunity perception is important for start-ups, if women are socialized differently than men, they (women) may perceive the same opportunities in a different light (De Tienne & Chandler, 2007). This is recognized in constructing the FEI by incorporating a measure of legal rights to assess the parity of laws as they apply to women and men. For example, if in country X women do not share the same legal rights as men this would hinder potential female entrepreneurship. For this specific area individual level opportunity recognition is measured using pooled 2010–2012 data from the GEM and the institutional-level data from the World Bank's Women Business and the Law Database. These two sets of information are combined to create one subindex in the FEI. A similar process is used to create the other categories.

An obvious criticism of the FEI is that it is not measuring a tangible outcome: It is not calculating how many businesses women actually started in a country.[4] That is true, but

---

[3] This is based on Appendix 2 of Terjesen and Lloyd (2015).

[4] Some argue that the GEM fills this void. The problem is that the GEM is based on responses to an annual questionnaire survey of individuals asking them if they *plan* to start a new business within the coming year. While this provides a useful glimpse into an individuals' entrepreneurial aspirations, it does not tell us whether those who answered "yes" to the question actually carry through and open a new business (Nystrom, 2008). It also does not differentiate between the type of entrepreneurial activity: washing car windows in busy urban intersections or creating a firm that employs a dozen workers.

such a view is very limiting. One reason is that using specific data like new start-ups misses the socioeconomic environment within which such actions take place. A more complete and more complex process must surely influence an individual's decision to undertake some entrepreneurial activity. A construct like the FEI gives the researcher and policymaker the ability to determine the effects from different factors, such as differences in IQ, and to determine which policy levers may yield relatively better outcomes. And as Hafer and Jones (2105) report, their key findings using the GEDI were corroborated using a more standard measure of entrepreneurship, namely, new incorporations.

Is the FEI just the GEDI *redux*? The two series share a common framework and are, therefore, related. But Terjesen and Lloyd (2015) are clear that the FEI, in contrast to the genderless GEDI, targets *female* entrepreneurial activity by specifically utilizing two dozen gender-specific variables. To see how comparable the two indices are, Terjesen and Lloyd (2015) simulated the GEDI using their sample of countries and compared the rankings with the FEI. What they found was that differences in construction make the values of the two indices quite dissimilar in many areas of the world. Countries like Japan, Korea, Taiwan, Turkey, and Saudi Arabia, for example, have FEI rankings that are much lower than those based on the GEDI methodology. In contrast, some countries, such as Jamaica, Peru, and Mexico score much higher on the FEI scale compared to their GEDI rankings. Overall, while there are similarities, there are enough differences in the outcomes to warrant a separate examination.

National IQ

The national-level IQ data are taken from Lynn and Vanhanen (2012), which represents an updated and expanded version of their earlier data (Lynn & Vanhanen, 2002, 2006). There is a significant body of evidence supporting the use of the Lynn–Vanhanen (hereafter, LV) IQ data as a broad measure of human capital or cognitive skill. Lynn and Meisenberg (2010) test the relationship between IQ and results from widely used measures of educational attainment, the Third International Mathematics and Science Study (TIMSS) and the Program for International Student Assessment (PISA). They find that the correlation between IQ and educational attainment exceeds 0.90 based on a sample of 86 countries. The Spearman rank correlation between IQ and these education measures is similarly large. Lynn and Meisenberg (2010) use several additional assessment tools in their analysis, each corroborating the conclusion that IQ is highly correlated to these other measures of cognitive skill. Such findings have been supported by other researchers, such as Rindermann (2007) and Jones and Potrafke (2014).

Even though the IQ data are highly correlated with other measures of human capital development, they tend to dominate (statistically) other related measures when included in regression analyses. In an early use of the national-IQ data in economic growth analysis Jones and Schneider (2006) report that IQ is one of the most robust variables to survive their rigorous testing procedure.[5] In addition, Lynn and Vanhanen's (2012) comprehensive survey shows that scores of studies in psychology and economics have found that IQ and a wide variety of positive socioeconomic outcomes (e.g., better

---

[5] In contrast to Jones and Schneider's (and others) results, Moreale and Levendis (2014) argue that IQ is not a robust predictor of economic development. They find that it fails to explain economic growth when compared to end-of-period education; that is, educational attainment in the latter stages of the period over which economic growth is being measured. This, as Bils and Klenow (2000) argue, misplaces causal effects: *Current* education is likely the outcome of *past* prosperity, not the latter's predictor.

health, less crime, higher levels of income, faster economic growth, and better political institutions) are positively and significantly correlated.

This is not to say that the use of IQ is without controversy. "Cognitive skills" is a widely used phrase in the academic literature, usually viewed as a set of outcomes predicted in part by IQ scores (e.g., Burks, Carpenter, Goette, & Rustichini, 2009; Heckman, 2008). I consider the LV measure a metric of what psychologists refer to as *intelligence*, which encompasses a wide range of mental skills. As Deary (2001) points out, it is not the specific IQ number that is important but its distribution; that is, there are skills (e.g., spatial recognition) that those with lower IQs, on average, have more difficulty with compared to those with higher IQs. Indeed, this is the gist of the evidence provided in Jones (2016): It is not that having a high IQ guarantees each individual a certain outcome, but the empirical regularity is that countries with higher levels of national average IQ have predictably better macro socioeconomic outcomes.

For this study I matched the FEI and LV data sets and found 77 countries for which both variables overlap. Appendix A lists those countries along with the FEI and IQ values used here.

The Model and Data

To try and explain observed differences in the FEI across countries I use a regression model that takes the general form:

$$FEI_i = \alpha + \beta 1(IQ_i) + \beta_i(\text{Controls}) + \varepsilon_i \tag{1}$$

where FEI is the ith country's value of the Terjesen and Lloyd (2015) index, IQ is the ith country's LV datum, "Controls" is a set of economic and institutional variables that may explain a country's level of female entrepreneurship, α and the βs are coefficients to be estimated, and ε is the error term.

The initial set of control variables was chosen based on previous work. The set of controls includes measures of income, manufacturing employment, and two institutional measures, one measuring human development and the other economic freedom. I briefly describe each. Because the value of the FEI is measured using data circa 2015, I have attempted to use comparatively recent values for each of the control measures as well. Sources are listed in Appendix B.

The level of real GDP per capita (RGDPCAP) provides a benchmark of a country's relative standard of economic development and its overall economic size. It is measured in US dollars for the year 2011. The percent of labor employed in manufacturing (PercentMan) is included to account for any effects that a country's distribution of labor has on the degree of female entrepreneurial activity. An economy in which employment in manufacturing is predominant may offer fewer entrepreneurial opportunities relative to one that is more heavily weighted toward services. Bjornskov and Foss (2008) found this variable to be significant when the GEM is the dependent variable. Hafer and Jones (2015) also found that PercentMan had a negative and significant relationship with the GEDI. It seems reasonable to include PercentMan to test for labor market effects on the FEI. The values for PercentMan are matched to the FEI dates and come from the CIA *Factbook*.

Two institutional variables are included as controls for a broad range of socioeconomic influences. One is the United Nation's Human Development Index (HDI). The idea behind the HDI is that it captures those social characteristics that are representative of *successful* human development. The HDI is not, therefore, a simple alternative to an economic measure, such as real GDP, although RGDPCAP does enter into the calculation of the HDI. The HDI comprises three dimensions: health, education, and standard of living. The HDI is a geometric mean of the indexes for each dimension.[6] I use the values reported in the 2015 *Human Development Report.*

The other institutional variable is economic freedom. To assess the role of economic freedom I use the Economic Freedom of the World Index (EFWI), taken from Gwartney, Lawson, and Hall (2014). The freedom values are for 2012 and range in value from zero—no economic freedom—to a high of 10. Economic freedom is relevant in any study of entrepreneurship, because the level of government activity and entrepreneurial activity is likely to be related, as Boettke and Coyne's (2009) theoretical arguments suggest. On the empirical side Bjornskov and Foss (2008) and Nystrom (2008) have found that greater government intervention and regulation are negatively and significantly related to the GEM or the rate of self-employment in a country. These findings indicate that a smaller government, a business environment within which property rights are secured, and an economy characterized by less regulation of the credit, labor and business sectors are factors that increase the likelihood of greater entrepreneurial activity.

It has also been found that the government entitlement programs and how such programs are funded may adversely affect entrepreneurial activity (see Bjornskov & Foss, 2008; Henrekson, 2005). Because entrepreneurial income often is taxed as personal income, a punitive tax system does not reward or inspire entrepreneurship. Lastly, government's that do not establish and protect property rights are not likely to witness significant levels of entrepreneurial activity in their countries.

The set of control variables also includes two "noneconomic" variables. One is a (0, 1) variable that takes on a value of one if the country recently converted from Communist rule. Bjornskov and Foss (2008) and Hafer and Jones (2015) found that the estimated coefficient on this "PostCom" variable was significant, though each found that it took on a different sign: Bjornskov and Foss (2008) found it to be positively related to the GEM while Hafer and Jones (2015) found that it has a negative relation with the GEDI. This difference is likely explained by the fact that the two studies use different measures of entrepreneurship and that their country samples do not match. I also include a set of regional dummies based on Sala-i-Martin's (1997) demarcation of the world to account for any regional variation that is not captured by the other right-hand-side variables.

Summary statistics for the variables used are presented in Table 9.1. The average level of the FEI is about 45, ranging from Pakistan's low of 15 to a high of 83 for the United States. The countries used in this sample reveal a similarly wide dispersion in the other variables. Real GDP per capita ranges from Ethiopia's low of $945 to almost $63,000 for the UAE. The percent of labor employed in manufacturing (PercentMan) shows a wide variation, though it is interesting to note that the countries at the extremes are

---

[6] More detail on the construction of the HDI is available at the United Nations Development Programme website: http://hdr.undp.org/en/content/human-development-index-hdi

Table 9.1 Summary statistics.

Variable	Mean	Standard Deviation	Min	Max
FEI	44.94	15.98	15.20	82.90
RGDPCAP	$18,988.66	14,182.27	945.75	62,900
PercentMan	21.67	7.50	5.00	38.00
HDI	0.77	0.12	0.41	0.94
EFWI	7.00	0.79	3.89	8.54
IQ	89.67	10.29	60.10	107.1

Note: Sample size is 77.

Uganda (5%) and Algeria (38%). The institutional variables exhibit relatively high averages, though the ranges are wide. Malawi has the lowest HDI in the sample, and at 60 it has the lowest IQ. Norway has the highest HDI. Singapore has not only the highest value for the economic freedom index, but also for IQ. The country with the lowest economic freedom value is Venezuela.

Prior to the regression analysis, it is useful to consider the bivariate correlations between the variables. The correlation matrix is presented in Table 9.2. Of major interest is the result that IQ and the FEI are positively (and significantly) correlated. This is also true of the correlations between FEI and real GDP per capita, HDI and EFWI. Of course such simple correlations may not be robust once the effects of other variables are accounted for.

Table 9.2 Correlations.

Variable	FEI	RGDPCAP	Percent Man	Post Comm	HDI	EFWI	IQ
FEI	1.0						
RGDPCAP	0.789	1.0					
	(0.00)						
PercentMan	0.130	0.329	1.0				
	(0.26)	(0.00)					
PostComm	0.067	−0.015	0.298	1.0			
	(0.56)	(0.90)	(0.01)				
HDI	0.784	0.855	0.334	−0.016	1.0		
	(0.00)	(0.00)	(0.00)	(0.89)			
EFWI	0.662	0.462	−0.047	−0.013	0.535	1.0	
	(0.00)	(0.00)	(0.68)	(0.91)	(0.00)		
IQ	0.711	0.795	0.438	0.136	0.798	0.479	1.0
	(0.00)	(0.00)	(0.00)	(0.24)	(0.00)	(0.00)	

Note: p-values appear in parentheses.

Regression Results

Equation (1) is estimated using OLS, the results of which are reported in Table 9.3. The first column reports the outcome of estimating equation (1) without the IQ variable. This "baseline" regression reveals that most of the control variables achieve statistical significance. As expected, countries with higher levels of real income per capita tend to be characterized by higher levels of female entrepreneurial activity. A change

Table 9.3 Regression results. Dependent variable: Female Entrepreneur Index.

Variable	Specification 1	Specification 2
RGDPCAP	8.253***	6.915***
	(3.33)	(3.18)
	[0.53]	[0.44]
PercentMan	−0.152	−0.178
	(1.10)	(1.37)
	[0.07]	[0.08]
PostComm	4.249**	2.569
	(2.39)	(1.24)
	[0.11]	[0.06]
HDI	37.291*	23.126
	(1.80)	(1.22)
	[0.29]	[0.12]
EFWI	6.002***	5.034***
	(5.16)	(4.72)
	[0.30]	[0.25]
IQ		0.574***
		(2.78)
		[0.37]
R^2	0.76	0.79
F(pr)	31.80	32.48
	(0.00)	(0.00)

Notes: Absolute values of t-statistics appear in parentheses. Standardized regression coefficients appear in brackets. Significance at 1% level indicated by ***; at 5% by **; and at 10% by *. All equations include a constant term and regional dummies. All regressions are estimated using White's (1980) heteroskedasticity-consistent standard errors.

in RGDPCAP has the largest economic influence on FEI: its standardized regression coefficient (reported in brackets) is larger than for any other variable.

The results in column one of Table 9.3 also show that countries with higher levels of human development and economic freedom are more likely to have greater degrees of female entrepreneurship. Both the HDI and EFWI coefficients are positive and highly significant. Gauged by the standardized coefficients, their economic effects are about equal and second only to RGDPCAP. It appears that countries that have recently changed from Communism tend to have higher levels of female entrepreneurship compared with other countries in the sample. Finally, the labor market variable (PercentMan), negatively signed as expected, does not achieve statistical significance. The statistical significance of this variable may not be as robust as the others: Hafer and Jones (2015) found PercentMan to be negative and significant, but only when the economic freedom variable was absent. Even so, given its use in previous work I will include it in my regressions.

Holding constant the influence of the control variables, does adding IQ improve the overall explanation of female entrepreneurial activity? The answer, found in the second column of results in Table 9.3, is a resounding yes. Not only is the estimated coefficient on IQ highly significant, but its standardized coefficient indicates that its *economic* impact is large as well: The standardized coefficient on IQ (0.37) is only slightly less than that found for RGDPCAP. Adding IQ has differing effects on other estimated coefficients. The economic freedom variable is robust to adding IQ: The coefficient on EFWI is positive and significant at the 1% level, and its standardized coefficient is only slightly smaller compared to the baseline estimate. Including IQ adversely impacts other variables, however. In the expanded regression neither the PercentMan nor Post-Com variables, though they maintain their signs, are significant.

The results in Table 9.3 indicate that country-level IQ is a statistically significant and economically important variable in explaining cross-country differences in female entrepreneurship.

Robustness Tests

While it appears that national IQ helps predict FEI, is this finding robust to alternative specifications? To address this question I conducted several robustness tests. To conserve space I will report only the estimation results for IQ. (Complete results for this and the other tests are available upon request.)

It has been argued (Wicherts, Dolan, Carlson, & van der Maas, 2010a, 2010b) that the LV estimates of IQ for countries in sub-Saharan Africa are too low. Based on this criticism some previous work (e.g., Hunt & Wittmann, 2008; Jones & Schneider, 2010) simply raises these low-level scores to a minimum of 80. I use the same imperfect remedy and raise the IQ estimates for nine countries: Angola, Botswana, Ethiopia, Ghana, Malawi, Nigeria, South Africa, Uganda, and Zambia. Reestimating equation (1) with the raised IQ scores has little effect on IQ's effect: The estimated IQ coefficient is 0.674 with a t-statistic of 3.26. The role of IQ in explaining cross-country differences in the FEI is unaffected by this change.

I also experimented with estimating a series of regressions where an additional control variable is added to the model. The additional variables chosen were based on previous work, taking special care that the new controls should account for gender-related factors that might impact female entrepreneurship. Again to conserve space I report only the estimated IQ coefficient that occurs when the variable listed in the first column is added to equation (1). As before, I strive to use values for the new variables that closely match the dating of the FEI. Table 9.4 reports the outcome of those experiments.

The estimated IQ coefficient maintains its significance and economic effect in the presence of each additional measure, which includes income inequality (GINI), life expectancy, educational attainment, degree of urbanization, and the sex ratio (number of males for each female) at birth and for the population in the age range 15–64. The upshot of the additional empirical evidence is that, even in the presence of a wider

Table 9.4 Robustness results.

Variable added	Coefficient on IQ
GINI	0.557***
	(2.54)
	[0.36]
Life expectancy	0.472***
	(2.64)
	[0.30]
Education	0.482***
	(2.45)
	[0.31]
Urbanization	0.461***
	(2.46)
	[0.30]
Sex ratio (birth)	0.450***
	(2.59)
	[0.29]
Sex ratio (15–64)	0.479***
	(2.61)
	[0.31]

Notes: Absolute values of t-statistics appear in parentheses. Standardized regression coefficients appear in brackets. Significance at 1% level indicated by ***; at 5% by **; and at 10% by *. All equations include a constant term and regional dummies. All regressions are estimated using White's (1980) heteroskedasticity-consistent standard errors. Data sources are listed in Appendix B.

variety of control variables, national-level IQ is a significant and economically important predictor of differences in female entrepreneurial activity.

Caveats

The evidence linking IQ and the FEI is impressive. But let's be clear what we have, and what we don't have. The empirical results presented here corroborate the view that higher country-level IQ "contributes to higher-quality institutions, which in turn promote successful, productive entrepreneurship" (Hafer & Jones, 2015, p. 295). That conclusion was based on using the broader GEDI. As one reader has noted, the outcomes for the GEDI and the FEI may simply indicate that higher country-level IQ is associated with the "good" social and economic aspects that promote entrepreneurship: improving the "entrepreneurial environment ecosystem" as Terjesen and Lloyd's (2015) have called it. To that I answer "Yes."

If one accepts the premise that "identifying a country's strengths and weaknesses in terms of providing favorable conditions that could lead to high potential female entrepreneurship development" (Terjesen & Lloyd, 2015, p. 4) is important to explaining observed cross-country differences in female entrepreneurial activity, then identifying IQ as one of those important factors is significant. As the exhaustive review by Lynn and Vanhanen (2012) details, countries with higher levels of IQ do have better political systems, more established rule of law, better general health conditions, longer life expectancies, and so on. So, if one accepts that the FEI is a good proxy for female entrepreneurship—more women start businesses that employ workers, and so on—then finding IQ to be a significant and robust predictor of FEI across countries suggests that it will also help explain cross-country differences in female entrepreneurial activity at the more granular level. Note, however, that I explicitly have used a qualified "if" to recognize the simple fact that the FEI does not directly account for the number of start-ups by women. This is a fruitful area for future research.

But to address that issue within the context of this study, two points: First, recent research about gender-based factors has begun to focus on the "environmental institutions" that are likely to affect actual female entrepreneurial activity; for example, the existence of child-care services, family leave, family matters that influence female entrepreneurial activity, gender differences in access to educational training, legal rights, and gender-based cultural norms and expectations (see Terjesen & Lloyd, 2015, p. 5 for relevant citations.) Even though the FEI incorporates the role of individual decision-making in its subindex Entrepreneurial Aspirations, my results do not directly answer the narrow question of how many businesses are begun by women in high- versus low-IQ countries.

The second point is that while there is evidence that higher IQ individuals (gender unspecified) tend to have larger firms (van Praag & Cramer, 2011), are more adept at starting and running businesses (van Praag et al., 2013) and at expanding markets (Meisenberg, 2012), I am unaware of any study that addresses male versus female entrepreneurial activity using gender-based IQ. This in part suggests a lack of reliable data. In addition, the debate within psychology swirling around gender-based comparisons of IQ suggests that this may not be a fruitful path to take, as Flynn's (2012) summary of this contentious area of research suggests.

Given these caveats, are my results of any use? I believe that the answer is "Yes." Suppose that observed differences in IQ across countries represent (in part) underlying factors that are amenable to policy changes, such as improving educational attainment and health conditions. An important lesson from my results, then, is not that low-IQ countries are blocked from achieving higher levels of female entrepreneurship, but that enacting domestic policies to improve these environments would, if undertaken, not only improve cognitive skills but also female entrepreneurial activity.

Conclusions and Policy Implications

My results indicate that countries with higher relative levels of IQ, all else the same, are more likely to have those conditions that are recognized as promoting "high-potential" female entrepreneurial activity. This finding has important implications. If one considers IQ to be a broad measure of human capital, undertaking policies to improve female human capital should promote additional entrepreneurial activity by women. As shown by a large literature (e.g., Acs & Armington, 2006) such increases in entrepreneurial activity also are likely to improve the economic well-being of a county's citizens as increased entrepreneurial activity begets more economic growth.

The results also reinforce the need for additional research into the issue of gender-based differences in entrepreneurial activity. The evidence in this study suggests that one area in which additional research is needed concerns differences in educational attainment and cognitive ability by males and females, especially in less-than-developed economies. Previous work (Boserup, 1970; Klasen, 2002; Psacharopoulus, 1994, among others) suggests that one factor to explain less-than-stellar economic growth in some countries is the relative lack of education among its female population. Increased educational opportunities for women, which could be revealed in higher country-level IQs and a narrowing of any gender gap (Duckworth & Seligman, 2006; Flynn, 2012; Golsteyn & Schils, 2014) may help close any gaps in female and male entrepreneurship and improve overall economic development. Indeed, for many developing countries such policy actions would be fruitful additions to the list of actions already laid out by Acs, Astebro, Audretsch, and Robinson (2016).

References

Acs, Z. J., & Armington, C. (2006). *Entrepreneurship, geography, and American economic growth.* New York, NY: Cambridge University Press.

Acs, Z., Astebro, T., Audretsch, D., & Robinson, D. T. (2016). Public policy to promote entrepreneurship: A call to arms. *Small Business Economics, 47,* 35–51.

Acs, Z. J., Autio, E., & Szerb, L. (2014). National systems of entrepreneurship: Measurement issues and policy implications. *Research Policy, 43,* 476–494.

Acs, Z. J., & Szerb, L. (2010). *The Global Entrepreneurship and Development Index (GEDI).* Paper presented at the Opening up Innovation: Strategy, Organization and Technology conference, Imperial College, London, England.

Ahl, H. (2006). Why research on women entrepreneurs needs new directions. *Entrepreneurship Theory and Practice, 30,* 595–621.

Audretsch, D. B., Keilbach, D. B., & Lehmann, E. E. (2006). *Entrepreneurship and economic growth.* Oxford, England: Oxford University Press.

Bils, M., & Klenow, P. J. (2000). Does schooling cause growth? *American Economic Review, 90,* 1160–1183.

Bjornskov, C., & Foss, N. J. (2008). Economic freedom and entrepreneurial activity: Some cross-country evidence. *Public Choice, 134,* 307–328.

Boettke, P., & Coyne, C. J. (2009). *Context matters: Institutions and entrepreneurship.* Hanover, MA: Now Publishers.

Boserup, E. (1970). *Woman's role in economic development.* London, England: Earthscan.

Brush, C. G. (2006). Women entrepreneurs: A research overview. In M. Casson, B. Yeung, A. Basu, & N. Wadeson (Eds.), *The Oxford handbook of entrepreneurship.* Oxford, England: Oxford University Press.

Burks, S., Carpenter, J., Goette, L., & Rustichini, A. (2009). Cognitive skills affect economic preferences, strategic behavior, and job attachment. *Proceedings of the National Academy of Sciences, 106,* 7745–7750.

Coleman, S., & Robb, A. (2012). Gender-based firm performance differences in the United States: Examining the roles of financial capital and motivations. In K. D. Hughes & J. E. Jennings (Eds.), *Global women's entrepreneurship research: Diverse settings, questions and approaches.* Northampton, England: Elgar.

Cowling, M., & Taylor, M. (2001). Entrepreneurial women and men: Two different species? *Small Business Economics, 16,* 167–175.

Deary, I. (2001). *Intelligence: A very short introduction.* New York, NY: Oxford University Press.

De Tienne, D. R., & Chandler, G. N. (2007). The role of gender in opportunity identification. *Entrepreneurship Theory and Practice, 31,* 365–386.

Duckworth, A. L., & Seligman, M. E. P. (2006). Self-discipline gives girls the edge: Gender in self-discipline, grades and achievement test scores. *Journal of Psychology, 98,* 198–208.

Feenstra, R. C., Inklaar, R., & Timmer, M. P. (2015). The next generation of the Penn World Table. *American Economic Review, 105,* 3150–3182.

Flynn, J. R. (2012). *Are we getting smarter? Rising IQ in the twenty-first century.* Cambridge, England: Cambridge University Press.

Garcia, C. D. (2012). Gender and the multidimensional nature of entrepreneurial self-efficacy: Factor-analytic findings. In K. D. Hughes & J. E. Jennings (Eds.), *Global women's entrepreneurship research: Diverse settings, questions and approaches.* Northampton, England: Elgar.

Gennaioli, N., La Porta, R., Lopez-de-Silanes, F., & Shleifer, A. (2013). Human capital and regional development. *Quarterly Journal of Economics, 128,* 105–164.

Golsteyn, B. H. H., & Schils, T. (2014). Gender gaps in primary school achievement: A decomposition into endowments and returns to IQ and non-cognitive factors. *Economics of Education Review, 41,* 176–187.

Gwartney, J., Lawson, R., & Hall, J. (2014). *Economic freedom of the world annual report.* Vancouver, Canada: The Fraser Institute.

Hafer, R. W., & Jones, G. (2015). Are entrepreneurship and cognitive skills related? Some international evidence. *Small Business Economics, 44,* 283–298.

Hartog, J., van Praag, M., & van der Sluis, J. (2010). If you are so smart, why aren't you an entrepreneur? Returns to cognitive and social ability: Entrepreneurs versus employees. *Journal of Economics & Management Strategy, 19,* 947–989.

Heckman, J. J. (2008). Schools, skills, and synapses. *Economic Inquiry, 46,* 289–324.

Henrekson, M. (2005). Entrepreneurship: A weak link in the welfare state? *Industrial and Corporate Change, 14,* 437–467.

Holcombe, R. G. (1998). Entrepreneurship and economic growth. *The Quarterly Journal of Austrian Economics, 1,* 45–62.

Hughes, K. H., Jennings, J. E., Brush, C., Carter, S., & Welter, F. (2012). Extending women's entrepreneurship research in new directions. *Entrepreneurship Theory and Practice, 36,* 429–442.

Hunt, E., & Wittmann, W. (2008). National intelligence and national prosperity. *Intelligence, 36,* 1–9.

Jones, G. (2016). *Hive mind: How your nation's IQ matters so much more than your own.* Stanford, CA: Stanford University Press.

Jones, G., & Potrafke, N. (2014). Human capital and national institutional quality: Are TIMSS, PISA and national average IQ robust predictors? *Intelligence, 46,* 148–55.

Jones, G., & Schneider, W. J. (2006). Intelligence, human capital, and economic growth: A Bayesian averaging of classical estimates (BACE) approach. *Journal of Economic Growth, 11,* 71–93.

Jones, G., & Schneider, W. J. (2010). IQ in the production function: Evidence from immigrant earnings. *Economic Inquiry, 48,* 743–755.

Kirzner, I. (1973). *Competition and entrepreneurship.* Chicago, IL: University of Chicago Press.

Kirzner, I. (1997). Entrepreneurial discovery and the competitive market process: An Austrian approach. *Journal of Economic Literature, 35,* 60–85.

Klasen, S. (2002). Low schooling for girls, slower growth for all? Cross-country evidence on the effect of gender inequality in education on economic development. *World Bank Economic Review, 16,* 345–373.

Knight, F. (1921) *Risk, uncertainty, and profit.* Boston, MA: Hart, Schaffner & Marx; Houghton Mifflin Co.

Koellinger, P., Minniti, M., & Schades, C. (2013). Gender differences in entrepreneurial propensity. *Oxford Bulletin of Economics and Statistics, 75,* 213–234.

Lynn, R., & Meisenberg, G. (2010). National IQs calculated and validated for 108 nations. *Intelligence, 38,* 353–360.

Lynn, R., & Vanhanen, T. (2002). *IQ and the wealth of nations.* Westport, CT: Praeger.

Lynn, R., & Vanhanen, T. (2006). *IQ and global inequality.* Augusta, GA: Washington Summit.

Lynn, R., & Vanhanen, T. (2012). *Intelligence: A unifying construct for the social sciences.* London, England: Ulster Institute for Social Sciences.

Meisenberg, G. (2012). National IQ and economic outcomes. *Personality and Individual Differences, 53,* 103–107.

Moreale, J., & Levendis, J. (2014). IQ and economic development: A critique of Lynn and Vanhanen. *Forum for Social Economics, 43,* 40–56.

Nystrom, K. (2008). The institutions of economic freedom and entrepreneurship: Evidence from panel data. *Public Choice, 136,* 262–282.

Psacharopoulos, G. (1994). Returns to investment in education: A global update. *World Development, 22,* 1325–43.

Rietz, A. D., & Henrekson, M. (2000). Testing the female underperformance hypothesis. *Small Business Economics, 14,* 1–10.

Reynolds, P. D., Bosma, N., & Autio, E. (2005). Global entrepreneurship monitor: data, collection design and implementation 1998–2003. *Small Business Economics, 24,* 205–231.

Rindermann, H. (2007). The g-factor of international cognitive ability comparisons: The homogeneity of results with PISA, TIMSS, PIRLS and IQ-tests across nations. *European Journal of Personality, 21,* 667–706.

Sala-i-Martin, X. (1997). I just ran two million regressions. *American Economic Review, 87,* 178–183.

Sauer, R. M., & Wilson, T. (2016). The rise of female entrepreneurship: New evidence on gender differences in liquidity constraints. *European Economic Review, 86*, 73–86.

Smith, A. (1776/1937). *An inquiry into the nature and causes of the wealth of nations*. New York, NY: The Modern Library.

Teece, D. J. (2016). Dynamic capabilities and entrepreneurial management in large organizations: Toward a theory of the (entrepreneurial) firm. *European Economic Review, 86*, 202–216.

Terjesen, S., & Lloyd, A. (2015). *The 2015 Female Entrepreneurship Index*. Washington, DC: The Global Entrepreneurship and Development Institute.

van der Zwan, P., Verheul, I., & Thurik, A. R. (2012). The entrepreneurial ladder, gender, and regional development. *Small Business Economics, 39*, 627–643.

van Praag, C. M., & Cramer, J. S. (2011). The roots of entrepreneurship and labour demand: Individual ability and low risk aversion. *Economica, 68*, 45–62.

van Praag, M., van Witteloostuijn, A., & van der Sluis, J. (2013). The higher returns to formal education for entrepreneurs versus employees. *Small Business Economics, 40*, 375–396.

Vinogradov, E., & Kolvereid, L. (2010). Home country national intelligence and self-employment rates among immigrants in Norway. *Intelligence, 38*, 151–159.

Wagner, J. (2007). What a difference a Y makes: Female and male nascent entrepreneurs in Germany. *Small Business Economics, 28*, 1–21.

White, H. (1980). A heteroskedasticity-consistent covariance matrix estimator and a direct test for heteroskedasticity. *Econometrica, 48*, 817–838.

Wicherts, J. M., Dolan, C. V., Carlson, J. S., & van der Maas, H. L. J. (2010a). Another failure to replicate Lynn's estimate of the average IQ of sub-Saharan Africans. *Personality and Individual Differences, 20*, 155–157.

Wicherts, J. M., Dolan, C. V., Carlson, J. S., & van der Maas, H. L. J. (2010b). A systematic literature review of the average IQ of sub-Saharan Africans. *Intelligence, 38*, 1–20.

Appendix A

Countries Included in Sample, along with their FEI and IQ Scores.

Country	FEI2015	IQ
Algeria	27.4	84.2
Angola	26	71
Argentina	35.7	92.8
Australia	74.8	99.2
Austria	54.9	99
Bangladesh	17.9	81
Barbados	43.4	80
Belgium	63.6	99.3
Bolivia	29.7	87
Bosnia	31.6	93.2

Country	FEI2015	IQ
Botswana	36.4	76.9
Brazil	31.1	85.6
Chile	63.5	89.8
China	38.3	105.8
Colombia	52	83.1
Costa Rica	36.1	86
Croatia	49.9	97.8
Czech Republic	59.1	98.9
Denmark	69.7	97.2
Ecuador	32.3	88
Egypt	27.7	82.7
El Salvador	29.9	78
Estonia	55.4	99.7
Ethiopia	20.9	68.5
Finland	66.4	100.9
France	68.8	98.1
Germany	63.6	98.8
Ghana	25.8	69.7
Greece	43	93.2
Guatemala	23.2	79
Hungary	53.7	98.4
Iceland	68	98.6
India	25.3	82.2
Iran	20.6	85.6
Ireland	64.3	94.9
Israel	47.6	94.6
Italy	51.4	96.1
Jamaica	38.6	71
Japan	40	104.2
Korea	40.1	104.6
Latvia	56.6	95.9
Lithuania	58.5	94.3
Macedonia	41.2	90.5
Malawi	15.5	60.1

Country	FEI2015	IQ
Malaysia	39.2	91.7
Mexico	42.8	87.8
Montenegro	43.7	85.9
Netherlands	69.3	100.4
Nigeria	32.8	71.2
Norway	66.3	97.2
Pakistan	15.2	84
Panama	36.9	80
Peru	43.6	84.2
Poland	57.7	96.1
Portugal	49.8	94.4
Romania	49.4	91
Russia	35.6	96.6
Saudi Arabia	37	79.6
Singapore	59.8	107.1
Slovakia	54.8	98
Slovenia	55.9	97.6
South Africa	44.2	71.6
Spain	52.5	96.6
Sweden	66.7	98.6
Switzerland	63.7	100.2
Taiwan	53.4	104.6
Thailand	36.6	89.9
Trinidad	36.9	86.4
Tunisia	30.7	85.4
Turkey	39.3	89.4
UAE	52.6	87.1
Uganda	18.4	71.7
UK	70.6	99.1
Uruguay	44.5	90.6
USA	82.9	97.5
Venezuela	29	83.5
Zambia	29.1	74

Appendix B

Data Sources.

Variable	Source
FEI	Terjesen and Lloyd (2015)
RGDPCAP	Penn World Tables 8.1 (Feenstra, Inklaar, & Timmer, 2015)
PercentMan	*World Factbook* (CIA), various issues.
HDI	United Nations (http://hdr.undp.org/en/content/human-development-index-hdi)
EFWI	Gwartney, et al. (2012)
IQ	Lynn and Vanhanen (2102)
GINI	*World Factbook* (CIA), various issues.
Life-Expectancy	*World Factbook* (CIA), various issues.
Education	United Nations (http://hdr.undp.org/en/content/human-development-index-hdi)
Urbanization	*World Urban Prospects* (2011)
Sex Ratio	*World Factbook* (CIA), various issues.

Acknowledgments

I would like to thank Gorkan Ahmetoglu, Gail Heyne Hafer, Garett Jones, Heiner Rindermann, Siri Terjesen, and two anonymous readers for helpful comments and suggestions that have improved an earlier version of this paper. All errors are mine.

10

The Person in Social Entrepreneurship: A Systematic Review of Research on the Social Entrepreneurial Personality

Ute Stephan[a] and Andreana Drencheva[b]

[a] Aston University, UK
[b] University of Sheffield, UK

Introduction

Social entrepreneurs are individuals who start, lead, and manage organizations that seek to create social value by addressing societal challenges such as environmental degradation, ill-health or social exclusion (Mair & Martí, 2006). Policymakers increasingly hail social entrepreneurship as a tool to address societal challenges in novel ways and to alleviate strains on government welfare budgets.[1] Academics' interest in social entrepreneurship has grown dramatically over the past two decades as evident in a rising number of publications, including empirical studies (Gras, Moss, & Lumpkin, 2014; Short, Moss, & Lumpkin, 2009). Consequently, reviews of the social entrepreneurship literature no longer focus on mapping the entire field and definitional concerns (Dacin, Dacin, & Matear, 2010), but concentrate on specific areas of inquiry such as the tensions inherent in hybrid organizing (Battilana & Lee, 2014). No review has yet systematized what we know and do not know about the personality of social entrepreneurs, including their values, motives, traits, identities, and skills. As research into social entrepreneurship matures, it is important to take stock of what we know about the individuals involved in it.

Research on the "social entrepreneurial personality" to date is dispersed and it is seen by some as a niche area. This may be a reaction to early practitioner accounts of "heroic" social entrepreneurs who ingeniously overcome a multitude of obstacles (Bornstein, 2004; Leadbeater, 1997). Or it may be a reflection of the wider debate about the relevance of personality for entrepreneurship (Gartner, 1989; Rauch & Frese, 2007). After decades of debate, several meta-analyses now provide robust evidence that personality matters for business creation and the success of commercial entrepreneurs

---

[1] Examples are the European Commission's "Social Business Initiative" (European Commission, 2014), and the availability of financial support to this sector, for example, through the creation of Big Society Capital by the UK government and the White House' Social Innovation Fund in the US.

The Wiley Handbook of Entrepreneurship, First Edition.
Edited by Gorkan Ahmetoglu, Tomas Chamorro-Premuzic, Bailey Klinger, & Tessa Karcisky.
© 2017 John Wiley & Sons Ltd. Published 2017 by John Wiley & Sons Ltd.

(for an overview, see Frese & Gielnik, 2014). As any behavior, entrepreneurial action can be understood as a result of individual and situational factors—of both structure and agency (Davidsson, 2015). Thus, a personality lens draws attention to stable character differences between individuals and can help to understand one of the key individual factors at play in social entrepreneurial activity.

We suggest that a personality lens can provide an important perspective on why certain individuals but not others create social ventures and persist in their choice. While we do not propose that such interindividual differences alone explain entrepreneurial behavior, nor that they are the most important determinants of entrepreneurial behavior, applying *attraction-selection-attrition* (ASA) theory (Baron, Franklin, & Hmieleski, 2016; Schneider, 1987) to social entrepreneurship can help us understand the role of interindividual differences. ASA theory outlines that individuals are *attracted* to specific occupational choices (such as starting a social enterprise) because they perceive their personality characteristics, motivations, and skills to align with the requirements of that occupational choice. They then self-select into this career if they find they have indeed the required motivations, traits, and skills. Others may reinforce this *selection* because they similarly perceive such a fit (e.g., social investors or social enterprise support organizations providing finance and support to an individual whom they see as having the potential to be a social entrepreneur). Yet being a social entrepreneur may involve different requirements than the individual originally thought, and hence they may withdraw form their choice (the *attrition* phase).

In this systematic review, we take stock of research on the personality of social entrepreneurs to encourage an evidence-based discussion of what might constitute a social entrepreneurial personality and to stimulate future research. By outlining what we know and what we do not know about the person in social entrepreneurship, we seek to map particularly fruitful areas for future research. The review findings offer a refined account of who social entrepreneurs are—moving beyond simply equating social entrepreneurship with prosocial motivation. They shed light on the multitude of motivations at play in social entrepreneurship, and on differences and similarities with commercial entrepreneurs, and suggest important heterogeneity within the population of social entrepreneurs that is typically overlooked in research to date.

Before presenting the findings of our review, we define social entrepreneurship and personality. We then characterize the review method and present the findings of the review. We conclude by outlining avenues for future research.

Theoretical Background

Social Entrepreneurship

For the purpose of this review, we defined social entrepreneurs as individuals who lead and manage organizations that seek to create social value by addressing societal challenges such as environmental degradation, ill-health or social exclusion. We thus opt for a broad definition of a social entrepreneur emphasizing the goal to create social value (Mair & Martí, 2006). This is in line with occupational definitions of entrepreneurship, which include as entrepreneurs those who lead and manage an organization, or are self-employed (see Gorgievski & Stephan 2016). Our definition recognizes that social entrepreneurship can be realized either through commercial or nonprofit ventures

(Mair & Martí, 2006). We feel such a broad definition is useful as empirical research on social entrepreneurship is still in a relatively nascent stage. We hope future reviews may be able to define social entrepreneurs more narrowly, emphasizing social value creation through market-based activities (Stephan, Patterson, Kelly, & Mair, 2016) and "new entry," for example the creation of a new organization or market (Davidsson, 2016).

Personality

The term "personality" is often used inconsistently in the literature and has been associated with motives, values, traits, and skills, and even sociodemographic indicators. Based on extant theory in personality and social psychology, we differentiate four aspects of personality. Characteristic of all aspects of personality is that they describe the tendency or disposition of an individual to behave in a relatively consistent manner across a range of different situations and over time (Mischel, 2004).

First, individuals exhibit differences in their *motivation*, that is, what they find important and what energizes their behavior. Broad differences in motivations are captured by human values, which refer to abstract and enduring life goals (Schwartz, 2012). They influence especially deliberate and thoughtful actions; whereas traits (see below) are more closely related to typical everyday and spontaneous behavior (Roccas, Sagiv, Schwartz, & Knafo, 2002). Specific motivations are described by constructs such as motives for entrepreneurship.

Second, in the *trait* perspective, personality describes differences between individuals in patterns of feeling, thinking, and behavior. General and specific traits may be differentiated. An example for the former are the Big Five personality traits (Goldberg, 1990). Specific traits typically associated with entrepreneurial behavior are proactivity, self-efficacy, and creativity/innovativeness (Frese & Gielnik, 2014).

Third, the *identity* perspective highlights that individuals differ in their sense of self and how they see themselves. Identity is related to the roles that individuals fulfill or take on (e.g., as a leader at work, a social change activist, or a mother at home) and the social groups they feel they belong to (Hogg & Terry, 2000; Stets & Burke, 2000; Tajfel & Turner, 1986).

Fourth, individuals show stable differences in their *skills*, which are related to typical patterns of performing. Specific skills such as leadership and managerial skills have been highlighted as particularly relevant for social entrepreneurs (Thompson, Alvy, & Lees, 2000).

Our review retrieved studies speaking to each one of these four perspectives on personality. We present them clustered by these perspectives.

Review Approach and Overview of the Reviewed Studies

We conducted literature searches using Web of Science[2] covering sources published between 1970 and February 2016. We searched for the following keywords in titles, abstracts and keywords of papers: one set of keywords specified social entrepreneur (social entrepreneur, sustainab* entrepreneur, social venture, social enterprise,

---

[2] Web of Science is a leading multidisciplinary database of bibliographic information.

nonprofit, or not-for-profit) and was combined with a second set of keywords specifying personality (personality or trait or motiv*). This yielded 606 search results, which we coded for inclusion in the review based on reading the title and abstract of each paper. We complemented these results with (1) Google Scholar searches for which we scanned and coded the first 100 results, (2) searching the references of papers included in the review, and (3) scanning the table of contents of leading entrepreneurship journals (*Journal of Business Venturing, Entrepreneurship Theory and Practice*). We also set up search alerts in Web of Science, which allowed us to include new studies published between February and September 2016.

Our coding identified a set of 50 papers that studied aspects of the social entrepreneurial personality. We included only empirical studies as our aim is to provide an overview of the existing evidence-base on the social entrepreneurial personality. With regard to the specific aspect of personality under investigation, our data set included 37 papers presenting findings on motivation, 14 on traits, four on identity, and six on skills, especially leadership skills. Nine papers included findings relevant to more than one aspect of personality. We classified studies based on the actual measures of personality that they employed and their conceptual fit with the four personality aspects presented above. At times this diverged from how the authors had framed a study.

With regard to the research approach, most studies utilized a cross-sectional (38 papers) or a retrospective design (eight papers), with three longitudinal studies and two (quasi-) experimental studies.[3] Most findings were based on quantitative approaches (64%), while the 16 qualitative studies included case study designs, grounded theory, thematic, and narrative approaches. There were also two studies with mixed-method designs. We see three approaches: (1) research focusing on describing or mapping personality aspects of a sample of social entrepreneurs (21 studies), (2) comparing the personality of a sample of social entrepreneurs with another group (e.g., commercial entrepreneurs or the general population) (18 studies), and (3) relating personality aspects to social entrepreneurship intentions or activity in a nonsocial entrepreneur sample (e.g., general population, students, commercial entrepreneurs) (12 studies). Our review suggests that the investigation of social entrepreneurs' personality is gaining momentum as evidenced by the fact that the majority of the studies are published after 2010. Recent studies pay increasing attention to motivations and skills and consider multiple personality aspects in combination.

Review Findings

The review findings are summarized in Table 10.1.

Motivation

Motivation is the aspect of social entrepreneur personality that received most research attention (37 sources). Fourteen sources explored general motivational tendencies through values, motives, and vocational interests. These studies were predominantly

---

[3] Total number is higher than 50 as one paper reported findings from a cross-sectional and a quasi-experimental study.

Table 10.1 Overview of review findings.

Construct	Characteristic profile of social entrepreneurs	Social entrepreneurs compared to commercial entrepreneurs	Social entrepreneurs compared to other groups (general population, employees)
Motivation			
Values	Self-transcendence values	Higher self-transcendence values	Higher self-transcendence values[+]
	Openness to change values	Lower self-enhancement values	Lower self-enhancement values[+]
		Similar openness to change values	Higher openness to change values[+]
		Stronger radical environmental philosophies	Stronger liberal political views[⊥]
		Similar implicit spiritual orientation[t]	
Work motivation	Intrinsic motivation	Lower extrinsic motivation	Higher intrinsic motivation[*]
	Extrinsic motivation	Similar intrinsic motivation	Lower extrinsic motivation[*]
			Lower amotivation[*]
Interests	Social vocational interests		
Entrepreneurial motives	Independence	Lower need for achievement motive[±]	Higher independence motive[+]
		Higher need for autonomy motive	Higher income motive[+]
		Similar power motive	
		Similar implicit need for achievement, affiliation, and power[t]	
Social Entrepreneurial motives	Prosocial, other-oriented motives	Stronger affiliation motive	Stronger motivation to help clients with psychological problems[+]
		Higher responsibility motive	Lower general prosocial motivation to help the poor[+]
		Higher prosocial motives	Lower public service motivation[*]
Traits			
Big Five traits		No significant differences in openness to change, conscientiousness, extraversion, agreeableness and emotional stability	Higher extraversion[⊥]

(Continued)

Table 10.1 (Continued)

Construct	Characteristic profile of social entrepreneurs	Social entrepreneurs compared to commercial entrepreneurs	Social entrepreneurs compared to other groups (general population, employees)
Entrepreneurial traits	Entrepreneurial self-efficacy	Similar general self-efficacy	Higher entrepreneurial self-efficacy[&,#]
	Risk taking	Similar entrepreneurial self-efficacy[±]	Higher risk taking[&,⊥,+]
	Persistence	Similar risk taking[±]	Higher persistence[+]
	Optimism	Similar internal locus of control[±]	Higher optimism[⊥]
		Similar fear of failure	Internal locus of control[±]
		Similar personal initiative	
		Similar willingness to take responsibility	
		Higher creativity	
		Similar implicit self-confidence, perseverance, and patience[t]	
		Higher implicit emotional maturity[t]	
Social entrepreneurial traits	Empathy		Higher empathy[±]
	Moral obligation		Stronger belief that the world can be changed[⊥]
			Higher trust[⊥]
			Higher propensity to cooperate[⊥]

Identity

Identity	Career identity of service	Stronger service identity	Stronger autonomy identity[#]
	Career identity of entrepreneurship		No significant differences in career identity[&]
	Communitarian identity		
	Missionary identity		

Skills

Managerial skills		Implicit view that interpersonal and technical skills are less relevant[t]	
		Implicit view that political, time management and conceptual skills are similarly relevant[t]	

Construct	Characteristic profile of social entrepreneurs	Social entrepreneurs compared to commercial entrepreneurs	Social entrepreneurs compared to other groups (general population, employees)
Leadership skills		Similar employees' perceptions of charismatic leadership	
		Similar self-reports of transformational leadership and leadership vision	
		Visions more purposeful, long-term, and action-oriented	
		Lower self-reports of transactional leadership	

*Compared to managers in the public sector.
#Compared to philanthropists.
&Compared to volunteers.
+Compared to employees.
⊥Compared to the general population.
‡Conflicting evidence.
t"implicit" refers to *perceptions* of what traits/motives people *believe* to be associated with being a successful social entrepreneur.

conducted as theory-based quantitative survey research. The majority of publications (23 sources) examined specific motives for engaging in social entrepreneurship. Research on specific motives contained roughly equal shares of qualitative, explorative, and quantitative research.

General values, motives, interests
At their most general level, stable motivational tendencies are based on individuals' values. Four publications used the Schwartz theory of human values, which has been widely validated across 80 cultures and different research paradigms (Schwartz, 2012). One publication used the precursor to Schwartz's theory, the Rokeach value theory (Rokeach, 1973). The findings of these studies suggest that social entrepreneurs attribute great importance to other-oriented, prosocial values (self-transcendence values) and openness to change values (self-direction and stimulation, Bargsted, Picon, Salazar, & Rojas, 2013; Diaz & Rodriguez 2003; Egri & Herman 2000; Stephan, Huysentruyt, & Van Looy, 2010). Social entrepreneurs tended to endorse prosocial values more strongly than commercial entrepreneurs and employees, whilst at the same time de-emphasizing self-interested values (self-enhancement). However, openness to change values appear to be similarly important to social and commercial entrepreneurs, and were more important to both types of entrepreneurs compared to employees (e.g., in population-representative samples, Stephan et al., 2010). A similar pattern was observed for a study that investigated general entrepreneurial and social entrepreneurial intentions in a Spanish population sample. Although unexpectedly prosocial values were also

positively related to general entrepreneurial intentions, while conservation values (the opposite of openness to change values) were positively related to social entrepreneurial intentions (Sastre-Castillo, Peris-Ortiz, & Danvila-Del Valle, 2015).

Three studies investigated different types of values. One study found social entrepreneurs to be more likely to hold liberal political values compared to nonsocial entrepreneurs in a general population panel (Van Ryzin, Grossman, DiPadova-Stocks, & Bergrud, 2009). Two studies investigated proenvironmental values. One study found proenvironmental values associated "with radical environmentalist philosophies" to be more strongly endorsed by leaders of environmental nonprofit compared to environmental for-profit organizations (Egri & Herman 2000, p. 593). The other study provided intriguing evidence from a conjoint experiment on the conditions (low self-efficacy, hostile market environments) under which entrepreneurs may exploit environmentally harmful business opportunities and thus act on opportunities that are diametrically opposed to their proenvironmental values (Shepherd, Patzelt, & Baron, 2013).

Two further studies related values to outcomes apart from business opportunity exploitation. Stevens, Moray, Bruneel and Clarysse (2015b) found that social entrepreneurs' prosocial values correlate with a stronger emphasis on social goals for the organizations they lead. Stephan et al. (2010) related social entrepreneurs' prosocial and openness to change values to the type and quality of ideas they generate in an innovation challenge.

Three studies investigated general motivational drives as conceptualized in McClelland and Murray's work on motives[4] (McClelland, 1987). Two studies found that social compared to commercial entrepreneurs are characterized by lower need for achievement (De Hoogh et al., 2005; Diaz & Rodriguez, 2003), while one study found no difference between the two groups (Smith, Bell, & Watts, 2014). Social compared to commercial entrepreneurs were also characterized by a higher need for autonomy (Smith et al., 2014). In the most robust study in this set (De Hoogh et al., 2005), social entrepreneurs (nonprofit leaders) further exhibited similar power motivation compared to commercial entrepreneurs, but stronger affiliation (the need to relate to others in a positive way) and responsibility (a prosocial, moral motive) motives.

One study examined interests as set out in Holland's theory of vocational interest, a key theory in career psychology (Almeida, Ahmetoglu, & Chamorro-Premuzic, 2014). In a convenience sample of the general population, social entrepreneurial activity correlated with social vocational interest (e.g., characterized by an interest to help others, provide care, and nurture). While no particular dimension of interests corresponded to general entrepreneurial activity, artistic interests correlated with invention-oriented entrepreneurial activity.

Taken together the studies on general motivation support the intuitive assumption that social entrepreneurs are characterized by strong prosocial values or responsibility motives and share with commercial entrepreneurs the desire to seek out new situations and independence (e.g., as captured by openness to change values or need for autonomy). Evidence on whether social entrepreneurs also share the entrepreneurial drive for achievement and power (e.g., self-enhancement values, power and achievement

---

[4] We note that the motives, especially need for achievement, have also been treated as specific traits in the literature. We felt it most appropriate to present them as motivational concepts as they represent general goals (e.g., high performance) that give direction to behavior—consistent with the definition of motivation.

motives) was more mixed, but generally suggested that social entrepreneurs score lower in this domain compared to commercial entrepreneurs. This in turn may hamper the growth and scaling of the ventures that they lead. Interestingly studies that measured both prosocial and self-interested values found that these correlate at zero at the individual level (Stephan et al., 2010; Stevens, Moray, & Bruneel, 2015a). This suggests that there is no immediate trade-off between the values that underpin prosocial and growth-oriented behavior, although the same may not hold at the organizational level for the venture (Brown, McDonald, & Smith, 2013; Diochon & Anderson, 2011; Stevens et al., 2015a).[5]

Studies investigating general motivation built on established theory more so than studies in other streams. They also more often employed robust research designs including validated measures and statistical analyses that control for confounds and correlation among measures, as well as larger samples. Like studies that contextualize the effect of values, studies that move beyond documenting mean differences and relate motivations to venture performance and personal outcomes for the social entrepreneur remain scarce. Yet such research can help to build a fuller understanding of why, how, and when motivations may matter in social entrepreneurship.

Specific motives

Studies on specific motives typically focus on mapping these motives in a sample of social entrepreneurs, and less frequently compare them with commercial entrepreneurs or other samples. They employ both qualitative and quantitative approaches, which means that insight on social entrepreneurial motives stems from thematic analyses of open-ended interview answers by researchers, as well as from social entrepreneur self-reports in response to specific motivation questions.

Either type of study reveals that there is substantial heterogeneity in social entrepreneurs' motives, that is, a range of different and coexisting motives drive social entrepreneurs' actions (Allen & Malin, 2008; Braga, Proença, & Ferreira, 2014; Cohen & Peachey, 2015; Lukes & Stephan, 2012; Ross, Mitchell, & May, 2012; Seiz & Schwab, 1992b; Tigu, Iorgulescu, Ravar, & Lile, 2015; Yitshaki & Kropp, 2016). All but five studies[6] corroborated the importance of prosocial motives (helping others, creating a better life for future generations, a passion to give and change lives, etc.) for social entrepreneurs to start their ventures. Typically, prosocial motives were combined with intrinsic motives such as interest and passion for the work, profession or craft that a social entrepreneur engages in. Dissatisfaction with prior work and the opportunity to be independent also played a role.

Extrinsic motives, especially financial motives and reputation, were considered almost equally as often as prosocial motives. Many studies suggested the extrinsic motives were less important to social entrepreneurs than prosocial motives, yet they still played a role in motivating their actions both to start a business and to continue leading it (e.g., Greco, Morales Alonso, Vargas Perez, Pablo Lerchundi, & Petruzzelli, 2014; Koe, Omar, &

---

[5] The way values or organizational goals are measured appears to play an important role too. Existing measures of organizational goals, for instance, often force trade-offs, e.g., by assigning 100 points across different social or economic values (Lepoutre, Justo, Terjesen, & Bosma, 2013; Stevens et al., 2015a).
[6] These are (Chen, 2012, 2014; Chen & Bozeman, 2013; Wong & Tang, 2006; Yiu, Wan, Ng, Chen, & Jun Su, 2014).

Majid, 2014; Lukes & Stephan 2012; Seiz & Schwab 1992b). One study exploring the day-to-day work motivations found that intrinsic and extrinsic motivations coexisted (Chen, 2014).

Some studies suggested that within a sample of social entrepreneurs, the consideration of the relative balance of extrinsic/financial and prosocial motives can help to distinguish different types of social entrepreneurs (Campin, Barraket, & Luke, 2013; Migliore, Schifani, Romeo, Hashem, & Cembalo, 2015; Ruskin, Seymour, & Webster, 2016). Indeed, several in-depth studies mentioned at least one social entrepreneur who was primarily extrinsically motivated by financial gain (Ross et al., 2012; Tigu et al., 2015; Wong & Tang, 2006). Two of these studies suggested that being a social entrepreneur and seeing the positive impact of their work led to changes in motivation towards greater emphasis of prosocial aspects and the social mission (Parris & McInnis-Bowers, 2014; Tigu et al., 2015).

A number of studies pointed to the importance of context and personal experience for the motivation to start a social venture. This ranged from personal experience with a social need, for example experience of a traumatic event, lack of care for own elderly parent, visit to impoverished areas in childhood (Cohen & Peachey, 2015; Shumate, Atouba, Cooper, & Pilny, 2014; Wong & Tang, 2006; Yitshaki & Kropp, 2016), to relevant work experience in a specific industry sector, and supportive contexts in terms of role models, family traditions of volunteering, and fiscal incentives (Braga et al., 2014; Greco et al., 2014; Shumate et al., 2014; Wong & Tang, 2006). A study of commercial entrepreneurs in China suggested that reputational concerns and personal experience of disadvantage enhanced the likelihood that these entrepreneurs engaged in social entrepreneurial activities (Yiu et al., 2014). One study explored what may be a possible mechanism through which context and personal experiences influence prosocial and self-interested, extrinsic motivations to set up a social enterprise. Specifically Ruskin et al.'s (2016) qualitative research suggested that the repeated experience of self- or other-oriented emotions (e.g., passion and frustration or empathy and sympathy) acts as a precursor to developing self- and other-regarding entrepreneurial motives. This aligns with conceptual arguments made by Miller, Grimes, Mcmullen, and Vogus (2012).

Studies that compared motives of social and commercial entrepreneurs found the expected differences but also similarities. Social compared to commercial entrepreneurs were more likely to report to be driven by prosocial motives, while the opposite was true for extrinsic (especially financial) motives (Campin et al., 2013; Lukes & Stephan, 2012; Migliore et al., 2015). Yet there were also similarities in the emphasis put on intrinsic motivations such as work enjoyment, and desire to be creative and to perform well (Lukes & Stephan, 2012).

Three studies compared motives of social entrepreneurs and employees in the same industry sector. One study suggested that social entrepreneurs hold to a higher degree "entrepreneurial" motives (independence and income) than employees. They also exhibited stronger motivations to help their clients with psychological problems, but held lower general prosocial motivations to help the poor than their employed counterparts (Seiz & Schwab, 1992b). Two papers, seemingly based on the same study, investigated the day-to-day work motivations of social entrepreneurs (nonprofit leaders) compared to managers in the public sector (Chen, 2012; Chen & Bozeman, 2013). Drawing on self-determination theory (Ryan & Deci, 2000), they found that social entrepreneurs experienced relatively higher levels of intrinsic and lower levels of extrinsic motivation and amotivation. Social entrepreneurs also reported lower public service motivation and experienced generally higher levels of work satisfaction than employed managers in government organizations (Chen, 2012).

With regard to the consequences of motives, studies investigated the success in creating a venture, venture survival, choice of legal structure for the venture, and the personal work satisfaction of the entrepreneur. A longitudinal study based on the US Panel Study of Entrepreneurial Dynamics found that entrepreneurs who reported prosocial motives at the beginning of the start-up process were less likely to have succeeded in creating an organization four years later compared to those reporting financial motives (Renko, 2013). The odds for the social entrepreneurs' succeeding in creating their organization were further lowered when they also engaged in innovation. In a Spanish study, social compared to commercial entrepreneurs did not differ in the likelihood with which their ventures survived three and six years after they were started (Simón-Moya, Revuelto-Taboada, & Ribeiro-Soriano, 2012). Necessity- as opposed to opportunity-motivated commercial entrepreneurs had lower survival rates, but there were no differences between necessity- and opportunity-motivated social entrepreneurs. The relative strength of prosocial and extrinsic motives was linked to the choice of legal form (for-profit versus nonprofit) for fair trade social entrepreneurs (Child, Witesman, & Braudt, 2015). However, personal work histories and experience of previous work in the nonprofit versus for-profit sector appeared to be further influences on the choice of legal form. With regard to the satisfaction that social entrepreneurs derive from their work, intrinsic work motivations showed generally positive relationships, and extrinsic motivations showed generally negative relationships (Chen, 2014).

Overall, existing research has mapped both quantitatively and qualitatively the motives driving social entrepreneurs. Whilst prosocial motives are a key impetus for social entrepreneurs to start and lead their ventures, it is also clear that motivational explanations centering solely on these motives will fall short of providing a realistic account of why individuals pursue social entrepreneurial activity. Existing research shows that multiple motives are at work. Owing to the explorative nature of much of the research on motives, a conceptual framework to make sense of the multiple motives is still lacking. However, research on general motivations reviewed above suggests that content theories of motivation such as Schwartz's theory of human values may offer useful guidance in terms of the type of motives to investigate and to conceptualize potential tensions between different motives. In addition, process theories of motivation such as self-determination theory (Ryan & Deci, 2000) may be useful guides for understanding how and why motivations may change over time or be sustained by ongoing work at the social venture.

Some of the more surprising insights of existing research on social entrepreneurial motivation are arguably (1) findings of change of motivation over time, implying the need to differentiate start-up from continuance or ongoing work motivation; (2) the finding that prosocial start-up motivations may be associated with a lower likelihood of creating an operational venture; and (3) findings highlighting the importance of context—external, place-based, and social context, as well as personal biographical context. This calls for future research to adopt more process-based and contextualized research approaches and to explore situational triggers (see Shumate et al., 2014) that lead individuals to act on longstanding motivations and values. This echoes developments on research on entrepreneurial motivation more generally (Carsrud & Brännback, 2011; Stephan, Hart, Mickiewicz, & Drews, 2015).

Traits

Of the 14 studies that explored personality traits, all did so in a cross-sectional research design. Except for one study, all research was quantitative and survey-based. Two studies explored general traits (the Big Five). Most studies (80%) focused on specific "entrepreneurial" traits. However, the traits that were included under this label varied considerably across studies. In addition, five studies included what could be seen as traits specific to *social* entrepreneurship (see Table 10.1 for an overview).

Over half of the studies explored mean differences in the level of traits between social entrepreneurs and other samples from commercial entrepreneurs to volunteers or social activists to the general population. The pattern of results indicates that the comparison group matters. Trait differences between social and commercial entrepreneurs appear to be much less pronounced compared to differences between social entrepreneurs and other groups. More specifically, of the two studies investigating the general Big Five personality traits, one suggested that social entrepreneurs show higher levels of extraversion compared to a general population sample (US Civic Panel, Van Ryzin et al., 2009), while the other study found that social and commercial entrepreneurs did not differ significantly on these traits (openness, conscientiousness, extraversion, agreeableness, and neuroticism, Lukes & Stephan, 2012).

With regard to differences in specific entrepreneurial traits, the findings are more complex. Three studies compared social entrepreneurs to the general public, those in wage employment in the same sectors, or other groups of volunteers and philanthropists (Bargsted et al., 2013; Praszkier, Nowak, & Zablocka-Bursa, 2009; Seiz & Schwab, 1992a). These studies suggest that social entrepreneurs are characterized by higher levels of entrepreneurial traits such as entrepreneurial self-efficacy, risk-taking, persistence, and optimism. Findings for internal locus of control were mixed and varied depending on the specific comparison group.

Studies comparing commercial and social entrepreneurs tend to find few differences and suggest that both types of entrepreneurs share entrepreneurial traits. The two types of entrepreneurs seem to exhibit similar levels of general and entrepreneurial self-efficacy, risk-taking, internal locus of control, fear of failure, personal initiative, and willingness to take responsibility (Bacq, Hartog, & Hoogendoorn, 2016; Bargsted et al., 2013; Diaz & Rodriguez, 2003; Lukes & Stephan, 2012; Smith et al., 2014). However, one study also reported that social entrepreneurs showed lower entrepreneurial self-efficacy (Bacq et al., 2016) and another showed lower internal locus of control (Diaz & Rodriguez, 2003) compared to commercial entrepreneurs. Yet another study reported that social entrepreneurs exhibited higher levels of creativity and risk-taking compared to commercial entrepreneurs (Smith et al., 2014).

Another set of studies investigated the propensity to engage in social entrepreneurial activity; the investigations either used reports of intentions to become a social entrepreneur in the future (Hockerts, 2015; Koe et al., 2014) or used reports of social entrepreneurship related activities (Almeida et al., 2014). These studies provide further evidence that entrepreneurial traits, including entrepreneurial self-efficacy (Hockerts, 2015; Koe et al., 2014), are important for the engagement in social entrepreneurial activity.

A few studies pointed to traits that were suggested to help social entrepreneurs to deal with the specific requirements of their work. These may be considered *specific social entrepreneurial traits*. Amongst these were empathy and moral obligation (Bargsted et al., 2013; Hockerts, 2015).[7] Other traits were the belief that people and the world can be changed, and traits that may support the building of social capital (trust, propensity to cooperate). Social entrepreneurs scored higher in all of these compared to a general population sample (Praszkier et al., 2009). Finally, a scale development study suggested that specific entrepreneurial traits (proactivity, risk-taking, innovativeness) relate positively to traits associated with social entrepreneurship, specifically empathy and social responsibility (Rahman & Pihie, 2014).

Two studies explored what appear to be *implicit theories*. In one study, leaders of commercial and nonprofit environmental organizations were asked about their beliefs regarding the personality characteristics needed to successfully lead their organization. Both types of leaders pointed to largely similar traits and, indeed, motives (need for achievement, need for affiliation, self-confidence, need for power, perseverance, spiritual orientation, and patience) with the exception of emotional maturity, which was seen only in one type (Egri & Herman, 2000). Another study reported that students' implicit theories of social entrepreneurship (i.e., what they regard to be typical behaviors for social entrepreneurs) correlated with their own personality traits (Nga & Shamuganathan, 2010).

In summary, we observed many studies that use small samples and that do not appropriately control for confounds when exploring differences between social entrepreneurs and other groups. Hence the conclusions in this section are very tentative. The pattern of findings to date suggests that by and large commercial and social entrepreneurs are similar in the way they typically think, feel, and behave—that is, the overall picture is one of similarities in both general and specific entrepreneurial traits. Recent studies have started to explore specific social entrepreneurial traits related to empathy and moral obligation. These appear fruitful avenues if they can be anchored in robust theory. What is striking is the absence of studies in our review that link traits to social entrepreneurial outcomes—do traits influence strategic decisions, access to capital, and perhaps even performance? Future research could also employ a person-centric compared to the current variable-centric approach (Cervone, 2004; Zyphur, 2009) and ask whether it is perhaps the specific combination or profile of social and entrepreneurial traits, rather than each trait individually, that allows individuals to succeed as social entrepreneurs.

Identity

The third perspective on the social entrepreneurial personality focused on examining how individuals see themselves, either in relation to their roles or in relation to others. As an emerging stream of research, this perspective was used in only four studies. Two of these studies were qualitative in nature (Fauchart & Gruber, 2011; Jones, Latham, & Betta, 2008) and two were quantitative with cross-sectional designs (Bargsted et al., 2013; Sieger, Gruber, Fauchart, & Zellweger, 2016).

---

[7] In the Bargsted et al. (2013) study, social entrepreneurs scored lower on the specific trait of empathic distress than a range of comparision groups including commercial entrepreneurs—all of which were small samples. By comparison Hockerts (2015) found in large samples evidence for the expected relationship of empathy with social entrepreneurial intentions.

Studies explored the content of social entrepreneurial identity by identifying and differentiating individuals' career or social identities. Social entrepreneurs seem to be characterized by career identities of service and entrepreneurship. Social entrepreneurs reportedly have stronger autonomy identity compared to philanthropists and stronger service identity compared to commercial entrepreneurs, yet there seemed to be no significant career identity differences between social entrepreneurs and volunteers (Bargsted et al., 2013). Another approach differentiated and developed a scale to measure the social identities of firm founders based on their social motivations and relationships (Fauchart & Gruber, 2011; Sieger et al., 2016). These studies differentiated between Darwinian founders, who resemble our view of the self-interested and competitive commercial entrepreneur, and two types of socially oriented entrepreneurs. The socially oriented founders express a communitarian social identity as they support and are supported by their communities, or a missionary social identity as they aim to advance a particular cause and view society as their reference group. While differentiating between self-interested and socially oriented founders, the study also showed that some founders exhibit hybrid social identities by combining aspects of the pure types (Fauchart & Gruber, 2011).

Studies also examined how identity is shaped and crafted. One study examined how a social activist entrepreneur constructed his identity through dividing (e.g., rejecting mainstream or institutional principles, practices, and philosophies), undividing (e.g., endorsing local, participative, grass-roots and community initiatives), and suppressing discourse practices (nondiscourses to sideline or underplay issues and practices) (Jones et al., 2008). Focusing on social identities, Fauchart and Gruber (2011) suggested two routes that shape hybrid identities. First, founders' backgrounds may combine business and community experiences, which shapes their social motivations and relationships. Second, external pressures, such as demands from investors, can influence founders to combine social and self-interests.

Finally, the identity perspective also explored the relationship between identity and strategic decisions. Founders' social identities were argued to shape strategic decisions in relation to market segments, customer needs addressed, and capabilities and resources deployed. Socially oriented founders (i.e., those with communitarian or missionary social identities) were suggested to address novel customer needs and focus on activities that have the highest potential for social change, using artisanal production methods and promoting best practices to share with others or inspire change in the industry. Self-interested founders, on the other hand, were seen to focus on increasing profitability through cost efficiency (Fauchart & Gruber, 2011).

In summary, an identity perspective is emerging in research on the social entrepreneurial personality, in a similar way as to the trend in the broader entrepreneurship literature. While there is only a small number of studies currently, through diverse approaches these studies have investigated the content of identities, the process of developing identities, and initial links to firm outcomes, such as strategic decisions.

Leadership and Managerial Skills

All six studies that explored skills investigated either the concept of transformational leadership, the closely related concept of charismatic leadership or vision (one of the facets of transformational/charismatic leadership). The studies investigated differences in leader behavior for social compared to commercial entrepreneurs and also explored relationships with outcomes, such as performance and organizational cultures (see Table 10.1 for an overview). All studies were cross-sectional quantitative, and survey-based. One study also incorporated a qualitative analysis of social and commercial entrepreneurs' implicit theories about the managerial skills necessary to succeed in their work (Egri & Herman, 2000). The study reported that commercial compared to social entrepreneurs in the same sector viewed interpersonal and technical skills as more relevant for success in their jobs. There were no differences in political, time management, or conceptual skills.

Interestingly, employees' perception of charismatic leadership displayed by social and commercial entrepreneurs leading voluntary and for-profit small- and medium-sized organizations respectively, did not differ (De Hoogh et al. 2005). However, there was an interaction with leader motives: Social entrepreneurs who combined high power motivation with responsibility motivation were perceived to be more charismatic by their employees, while the same did not hold for commercial entrepreneurs. One study of nonprofit leaders and their middle-management subordinates suggested that their perceptions of visionary transformational leadership may largely converge (Taylor, Cornelius, Casey, & Colvin, 2014)—although this finding is at odds with extant evidence in leadership research that shows only modest overlap between self- and other-ratings of leaders (Fleenor, Smither, Atwater, Braddy, & Sturm, 2010).

Three studies investigated differences between social and commercial entrepreneurs' self-reports of their leadership styles. Egri and Herman (2000) found that North American social and commercial entrepreneurs (nonprofit and for-profit environmental leaders respectively) reported similar levels of transformational leadership, although commercial entrepreneurs reported making more use of transactional leadership (especially using contingent rewards and instrumental behavior). Similarly, Sarros, Cooper, and Santora (2011) found no differences in the use of leadership vision comparing samples of Australian for-profit and nonprofit leaders. Ruvio, Rosenblatt, and Hertz-Lazarowitz (2010) examined the content of entrepreneurial visions and found very few differences across 26 specific vision characteristics. The visions of the nonprofit entrepreneurs tended to be somewhat more purposeful, long-term, and action oriented.

Four studies related social entrepreneurs' transformational leadership behaviors to outcomes, including perceptions of organizational culture, effectiveness, and performance, as well as social value creation. They found mostly positive relationships. Sarros et al. (2011) reported a positive relationship between visionary leadership and more innovation-supportive organizational cultures. While neither the level of visionary leadership nor the extent of innovation-supportive culture differed between for-profit and nonprofit firms, the relationship between the two appeared to be mediated by different mechanisms. The findings suggested that visionary leadership may lead to innovation-supportive cultures via stimulating socially responsible cultures in social enterprises (nonprofits) but via stimulating competitive cultures in for-profit businesses. Ruvio et al. (2010) found vision associated with venture performance and growth among their sample of social enterprises (nonprofits) but not in their sample of for-profit businesses. Studying only nonprofit organizations, Taylor et al. (2014) reported a similarly positive link between visionary leadership behavior and several dimensions of perceived organizational effectiveness. However, a study by Felício, Martins Gonçalves, & da Conceição Gonçalves (2013) suggested a more nuanced picture. Social entrepreneurs' transformational leadership was more important for organizational performance and value creation in unfavorable contexts. This aligns with broader leadership research suggesting that transformational leaders may be particularly effective in times of uncertainty and crisis (Davis & Gardner, 2012).

Taken together, the reviewed studies suggest that even if transformational leadership is not necessarily more pronounced among social entrepreneurs, it appears to be linked to desirable organizational outcomes in social ventures. However, a few caveats are in order. All studies are based on self-report and conducted cross-sectionally. Thus the reverse relationships may also hold true, that leaders learn to be more transformational over time and/or that past performance strengthens transformational behaviors. More sophisticated designs using multisource data and conducting longitudinal or experimental research would allow the disentangling of causality. Such designs are already common in leadership research and social entrepreneurship researchers may draw inspiration from that field. Furthermore, it is striking that existing research solely focuses on transformational aspects of leadership, which may be another reflection of the "hero" bias in social entrepreneurship, and a more general bias to attribute heroic, charismatic, and visionary characteristics to leaders (Meindl, Ehrlich, & Dukerich, 1985). By contrast, emerging research suggests that leadership for social change might require collaborative, power-sharing, that is, "connective leadership" skills (Stephan et al., 2016). Social network approaches to leadership and connective leadership skills may thus be fruitful areas for future research in social entrepreneurship. Nevertheless, social entrepreneurship researchers keen to explore transformational leadership should be aware of critiques of the concept (Knippenberg & Sitkin, 2013).

Discussion and Opportunities for Future Research

Our review of empirical research on the personality of social entrepreneurs shows an increasing interest in this topic judging by the rapidly increasing number of publications. Our systematic search identified 12 empirical papers up to and including 2010, and 38 up to early 2016. The reviewed studies shed light on "who social entrepreneurs are." They suggest that social entrepreneurs are simultaneously driven by a range of motivations and values. They typically, but not always, are primarily motivated by prosocial concerns. Yet the enjoyment of their work, creativity, and even financial aspects among other motivations also play a role. Social entrepreneurs appear to share many personality traits with commercial entrepreneurs (self-efficacy, risk-taking, internal locus of control, proactivity) as well as benefit from similar transformational leadership skills. Yet they are also characterized by distinct social traits, such as empathy and moral obligation, and develop distinct identities.

It is encouraging that a substantial body of empirical work on the social entrepreneurial personality is developing, because social entrepreneurship research is often seen to lack empirical and quantitative work based on larger samples (Gras et al., 2014; Short et al., 2009). At the same time, however, there is much scope for future research. We summarize our recommendation in Table 10.2 and start by outlining three recommendations directly relating to the methodological quality of existing research on the social entrepreneurial personality.

Table 10.2 Summary of recommendations for future research.

Recommendation	Research criteria and questions
Pay attention to the operationalization of social entrepreneurship.	How are the "social" and "entrepreneurial" characteristics defined and measured?
Generate more generalizable findings.	How and when are there opportunities to conduct large-scale quantitative studies embedded in robust theory, using validated scales and appropriate statistical tests?
Conduct more theory-driven research to build a deeper understanding.	How is personality connected to venture-level and personal outcomes? How and when does personality matter?
Consider the substantial heterogeneity among social entrepreneurs possibly using personality profile approaches.	What types of social entrepreneurs are under investigation? How and why are they different from each other?
Develop dynamic and process approaches.	How may being a social entrepreneur change some aspects of personality? Over what time scales?
Investigate more contextualized perspectives.	How does the environment interact with personality to shape social entrepreneurial actions? What trigger points may exist?
Toward a holistic perspective.	Is there a dark side to the social entrepreneurial personality?

First, we encourage future research to pay more careful attention to the operationalization of social entrepreneurship. Future research will benefit from paying more attention to the hybrid nature of social entrepreneurship. For instance, if nonprofit organizations are the sampling frame, then their engagement with entrepreneurial activities should be ascertained. This can be in the form of requiring trading in the market through selling products/services (Stephan et al., 2016) and "new entry" through being the founder of an organization or creating new markets (Davidsson, 2016). Similarly, measures to capture the quality and extent of the social engagement and social change ambitions of social entrepreneurs may help to build more nuanced theories of social entrepreneurship.

Second, the quality of empirical studies in the review was extremely heterogeneous ranging from large sample quantitative studies or quasi-experimental studies to small sample quantitative studies conducting multiple simple group comparisons without controlling for confounding factors or single-case studies of an individual entrepreneur. Important insights can be gained from both qualitative and quantitative approaches, and indeed the qualitative studies provide in-depth insights into motivations and identities. To generate generalizable findings, more large-scale quantitative studies embedded in robust theory, using validated scales, and conducting appropriate statistical tests (e.g., in the simplest case multivariate analyses of covariance to ascertain mean differences between groups instead of multiple t-tests) are needed. Especially comparative studies need to control—at a minimum—for sociodemographic confounds. This is because, relative to commercial entrepreneurship, for example, a higher share of women and the highly educated engage in social entrepreneurship (Estrin, Mickiewicz, & Stephan, 2016). Similar systematic differences exist relative to employees.

Third, one trend in the reviewed studies is the increasing attention to connect social entrepreneur personality to outcomes, with encouraging results. For instance, motivations showed links to start-up success, strategic choices, and innovation, as well as personal satisfaction. More theory-driven research that connects personality to venture-level outcomes (financial and social performance) but also to personal outcomes for the entrepreneur can help to build a deeper understanding of how and when personality matters. Useful theoretical lenses range from person-environmental fit to strategic decision-making research, upper echelons, and strategic leadership lenses, to social influence, leadership research, and process theories of work motivation, among others.

Building on Strengths and Insights of the Current Research

The reviewed studies pointed to substantial heterogeneity among social entrepreneurs in terms of their personality. For instance, findings indicated diversity in motivations and identities consistent with different types of social entrepreneurs who are likely to take different strategic decisions about organizational goals, legal forms, accessing resources, growth strategies, markets, clients and beneficiaries (e.g., Fauchart & Gruber, 2011). This is consistent with past research in entrepreneurship more generally that connects personality characteristics to different types of strategic decisions (Gorgievski, Ascalon, & Stephan, 2011; Simsek, Heavey, & Veiga, 2010), as well as with emerging research drawing attention to the different types and organizational forms of social enterprises (Mair, Battilana, & Cardenas, 2012; Mair, Mayer, & Lutz, 2015). So called person-centric or profile approaches to personality (Cervone, 2004; Zyphur, 2009) would be particularly useful to define "social entrepreneur types" through constellations of high/low scores on particular values, motives, and traits.

How does becoming a social entrepreneur change identity, skills, motivations, possibly even traits? How does personality change over the life course of the venture? Existing research on the social entrepreneurial personality is largely static and assumes that motivations and traits, and to a lesser extent identities and skill, are entirely stable. Yet a few findings in the review suggest a more dynamic view as specific motivations and identities can change through the social entrepreneurial activity itself (Braga et al., 2014; Fauchart & Gruber, 2011). Such a view is consistent with the notion of "occupational socialization," that is, the very nature of the work we do, over time, shapes our motivations, even traits, and identities. Indeed, specific as opposed to general motives and traits are known to be malleable (Rauch & Frese, 2007). Emerging research suggests that even general traits may change, albeit slowly, depending on the work situation individuals find themselves in (Li, Fay, Frese, Harms, & Gao, 2014; Wu, 2016). These findings invite longitudinal and process research to explore how and when aspects of social entrepreneurs' personality change through being a social entrepreneur. They also invite more research on the day-to-day activities that social entrepreneurs' engage in from a work design perspective (Parker, 2014) to understand the very nature of social entrepreneurs' work.

Future research would also benefit from developing more contextualized perspectives on the social entrepreneurial personality. Most studies were squarely focused on aspects of social entrepreneurs' personality without consideration of context. A few studies on specific motives, however, highlighted important drivers in the personal or wider social and spatial context of the entrepreneur: from traumatic experiences, exposure to a family tradition of volunteering, to lack of social service provision for close others in a region. They further pointed to the interplay of personality with skills and human capital (education, experience in an industry sector, experience of working in a nonprofit). Future research could explore such associations more systematically to discern how the environment interacts with personality to shape social entrepreneurial actions. What trigger points may exist that "activate" existing personality traits and motivation such that individuals start working on a social venture? Process research approaches would allow the development of a more contextualized view that also pays attention to how events unfold dynamically. In addition, a more contextualized perspective and life history research may allow more light to be shed on the very antecedents of social entrepreneurs' personality, how they develop specific motivations, identities, and skills.

Finally, the existing research focuses on the many positive aspects of social entrepreneur personality—but might there also be a "dark side" to it? For instance, the study by Renko (2013) suggests that prosocially motivated entrepreneurs face greater difficulties in the start-up process. Such a finding aligns with recent research suggesting that very high levels of traits that typically have beneficial consequences for the individual and organization can also have detrimental effects for both (Kaiser, LeBreton, & Hogan, 2015). Research could explore not only positive but also potential negative outcomes of the strong prosocial stance and high levels of empathy that seem to characterize social entrepreneurs. For instance, over time these may incur costs to the social entrepreneurs' well-being or family life if his/her efforts to create positive social change are thwarted, or simply due to the sheer scale of the social need that their work addresses and which is unlikely to be resolved by one or even multiple social entrepreneurs (Stephan et al., 2016).

References

* Indicates a source included in the systematic review.

*Allen, J. C., & Malin, S. (2008). Green entrepreneurship: A method for managing natural resources? *Society & Natural Resources*, *21*(9), 828–844. doi: 10.1080/08941920701612917

*Almeida, P. I. L., Ahmetoglu, G., & Chamorro-Premuzic, T. (2014). Who wants to be an entrepreneur? The relationship between vocational interests and individual differences in entrepreneurship. *Journal of Career Assessment*, *22*(1), 102–112. doi: 10.1177/1069072713492923

*Bacq, S., Hartog, C., & Hoogendoorn, B. (2016). Beyond the moral portrayal of social entrepreneurs: An empirical approach to who they are and what drives them. *Journal of Business Ethics*, *133*(4), 703–718. doi: 10.1007/s10551-014-2446-7

*Bargsted, M., Picon, M., Salazar, A., & Rojas, Y. (2013). Psychosocial characterization of social entrepreneurs: A comparative study. *Journal of Social Entrepreneurship*, *4*(3), 331–346. doi: 10.1080/19420676.2013.820780

Baron, R. A., Franklin, R. J., & Hmieleski, K. M. (2016). Why entrepreneurs often experience low, not high, levels of stress: The joint effects of selection and psychological capital. *Journal of Management*, *42*(3), 742–768. doi: 10.1177/0149206313495411

Battilana, J., & Lee, M. (2014). Advancing research on hybrid organizing – Insights from the study of social enterprises. *The Academy of Management Annals*, *8*(1), 397–441. doi: 10.1080/19416520.2014.893615

Bornstein, D. (2004). *How to change the world: Social entrepreneurship and the power of new ideas*. New York, NY: Oxford University Press.

*Braga, J. C., Proença, T., & Ferreira, M. R. (2014). Motivations for social entrepreneurship – Evidences from portugal. *Tékhne, 12*(2014), 11–21. doi: 10.1016/j.tekhne.2015.01.002

*Brown, M. L., McDonald, S., & Smith, F. (2013). Jungian archetypes and dreams of social enterprise. *Journal of Organizational Change Management, 26*(4), 670–688. doi: 10.1108/JOCM-Sep-2012-0146

*Campin, S., Barraket, J., & Luke, B. (2013). Micro-business community responsibility in Australia: Approaches, motivations and barriers. *Journal of Business Ethics, 115*(3), 489–513. doi: 10.1007/s10551-012-1396-1

Carsrud, A., & Brännback, M. (2011). Entrepreneurial motivations: What do we still need to know? *Journal of Small Business Management, 49*(1), 9–26. doi: 10.1111/j.1540-627X.2010.00312.x

Cervone, D. (2004). Personality architecture: Within-person structures and processes. *Annual Review of Psychology, 56*(1), 423–452. doi: 10.1146/annurev.psych.56.091103.070133

*Chen, C.-A. (2012). Explaining the difference of work attitudes between public and nonprofit managers: The views of rule constraints and motivation styles. *The American Review of Public Administration, 42*(4), 437–460. doi: 10.1177/0275074011402192

*Chen, C.-A. (2014). Nonprofit managers' motivational styles: A view beyond the intrinsic-extrinsic dichotomy. *Nonprofit and Voluntary Sector Quarterly, 43*(4), 737–758. doi: 10.1177/0899764013480565

*Chen, C.-A., & Bozeman, B. (2013). Understanding public and nonprofit managers' motivation through the lens of self-determination theory. *Public Management Review, 15*(4), 584–607. doi: 10.1080/14719037.2012.698853

*Child, C., Witesman, E. M., & Braudt, D. B. (2015). Sector choice: How fair trade entrepreneurs choose between nonprofit and for-profit forms. *Nonprofit and Voluntary Sector Quarterly, 44*(4), 832–851. doi: 10.1177/0899764014542688

*Cohen, A., & Peachey, J. W. (2015). The making of a social entrepreneur: From participant to cause champion within a sport-for-development context. *Sport Management Review, 18*, 111–125. doi: 10.1016/j.smr.2014.04.002

Dacin, P. A., Dacin, M. T., & Matear, M. (2010). Social entrepreneurship: Why we don't need a new theory and how we move forward from here. *The Academy of Management Perspectives, 24*(3), 37–57.

Davidsson, P. (2015). Entrepreneurial opportunities and the entrepreneurship nexus: A re-conceptualization. *Journal of Business Venturing, 30*(5), 674–695. doi: 10.1016/j.jbusvent.2015.01.002

Davidsson, P. (2016). A "business researcher" view on opportunities for psychology in entrepreneurship research. *Applied Psychology, 65*(3), 628–636. doi: 10.1111/apps.12071

Davis, K. M., & Gardner, W. L. (2012). Charisma under crisis revisited: Presidential leadership, perceived leader effectiveness, and contextual influences. *The Leadership Quarterly, 23*(5), 918–933. doi: 10.1016/j.leaqua.2012.06.001

*De Hoogh, A. H. B., Den Hartog, D. N., Koopman, P. L., Thierry, H., Van Den Berg, P. T., Van Der Weide, J. G., & Wilderom, C. P. M. (2005). Leader motives, charismatic leadership, and subordinates' work attitude in the profit and voluntary sector. *The Leadership Quarterly, 16*(1), 17–38. doi: 10.1016/j.leaqua.2004.10.001

*Diaz, F., & Rodriguez, A. (2003). Locus of control, nAch and values of community entrepreneurs. *Social Behavior and Personality: An International Journal, 31*(8), 739–747. doi: 10.2224/sbp.2003.31.8.739

*Diochon, M., & Anderson, A. R. (2011). Ambivalence and ambiguity in social enterprise; narratives about values in reconciling purpose and practices. *International Entrepreneurship and Management Journal, 7*(1), 93–109. doi: 10.1007/s11365-010-0161-0

*Egri, C. P., & Herman, S. (2000). Leadership in the North American environmental sector: Values, leadership styles, and contexts of environmental leaders and their organizations. *Academy of Management Journal, 43*(4), 571–604. doi: 10.2307/1556356

Estrin, S., Mickiewicz, T., & Stephan, U. (2016). Human capital in social and commercial entrepreneurship. *Journal of Business Venturing 31*(4), 449–467.

European Commission. (2014). *The Social Business Initiative of the European Commission.*

*Fauchart, E., & Gruber, M. (2011). Darwinians, communitarians, and missionaries: The role of founder identity in entrepreneurship. *Academy of Management Journal, 54*(5), 935–957. doi: 10.5465/amj.2009.0211

*Felício, J. A., Martins Gonçalves, H., & da Conceição Gonçalves, V. (2013). Social value and organizational performance in non-profit social organizations: Social entrepreneurship, leadership, and socioeconomic context effects. *Journal of Business Research, 66*(10), 2139–2146. doi: 10.1016/j.jbusres.2013.02.040

Fleenor, J. W., Smither, J. W., Atwater, L. E., Braddy, P. W., & Sturm, R. E. (2010). Self–other rating agreement in leadership: A review. *The Leadership Quarterly, 21*(6), 1005–1034. doi: 10.1016/j.leaqua.2010.10.006

Frese, M., & Gielnik, M. M. (2014). The psychology of entrepreneurship. *Annual Review of Organizational Psychology and Organizational Behavior, 1,* 413–438.

Gartner, W. B. (1989). "Who is an entrepreneur?" is the wrong question. *Entrepreneurship: Theory & Practice, 13*(4), 47–68.

Goldberg, L. R. (1990). An alternative "description of personality": The Big-Five factor structure. *Journal of Personality and Social Psychology, 59*(6), 1216–1229. doi: 10.1037/0022-3514.59.6.1216

Gorgievski, M., Ascalon, M. E., & Stephan, U. (2011). Small business owners' success criteria, a values approach to personal differences. *Journal of Small Business Management, 49*(2), 207–232. doi: 10.1111/j.1540-627X.2011.00322.x

Gorgievski, M. J., & Stephan, U. (2016). Advancing the psychology of entrepreneurship: a review of the psychological literature and an introduction. *Applied Psychology, 65*(3), 437–468. doi: 10.1111/apps.12073

Gras, D., Moss, T. W., & Lumpkin, G. (2014). The use of secondary data in social entrepreneurship research: assessing the field and identifying future opportunities. In J. Short (Ed.), *Social entrepreneurship and research methods* (pp. 49–75). Bingley: Emerald. doi: 10.1108/S1479-838720140000009011

*Greco, A., Morales Alonso, G., Vargas Perez, A. M., Pablo Lerchundi, I., & Petruzzelli, A. M. (2014). Social companies as an innovative and sustainable way of solving social problems. A case study from Spain. *IFKAD 2014: 9th international forum on knowledge asset dynamics: Knowledge and management models for sustainable growth* (pp. 2516–2539). Matera, Italy: Institute of Knowledge Asset Management.

*Hockerts, K. (2015). Determinants of social entrepreneurial intentions. *Entrepreneurship: Theory and Practice*, 1–26. doi: 10.1111/etap.12171

Hogg, M. A., & Terry, D. J. (2000). Social identity and self-categorization processes in organizational contexts. *Academy of Management Review, 25*(1), 121–140. doi: 10.2307/259266

*Jones, R., Latham, J., & Betta, M. (2008). Narrative construction of the social entrepreneurial identity. *International Journal of Entrepreneurial Behavior & Research, 14*(5), 330–345. doi: 10.1108/13552550810897687

Kaiser, R. B., LeBreton, J. M., & Hogan, J. (2015). The dark side of personality and extreme leader behavior. *Applied Psychology, 64*(1), 55–92. doi: 10.1111/apps.12024

Knippenberg, D. van, & Sitkin, S. B. (2013). A critical assessment of charismatic-transformational leadership research: Back to the drawing board? *The Academy of Management Annals, 7*(1), 37–41.

*Koe, W.-L., Omar, R., & Majid, I. A. (2014). Factors associated with propensity for sustainable entrepreneurship. In C. T. B. Chui & W. E. W. Rashid (Eds.), *Proceedings of 4th International Conference on Marketing and Retailing (INCOMAR 2013)* (Vol. 130, pp. 65–74). Amsterdam, Netherlands: Elsevier Science. doi: 10.1016/j.sbspro.2014.04.009

Leadbeater, C. (1997). *The rise of the social entrepreneur*. London, England: Demos.

Lepoutre, J., Justo, R., Terjesen, S., & Bosma, N. (2013). Designing a global standardized methodology for measuring social entrepreneurship activity: The Global Entrepreneurship Monitor social entrepreneurship study. *Small Business Economics, 40*, 693–714. doi: 10.1007/s11187-011-9398-4

Li, W.-D., Fay, D., Frese, M., Harms, P. D., & Gao, X. Y. (2014). Reciprocal relationship between proactive personality and work characteristics: A latent change score approach. *Journal of Applied Psychology, 99*(5), 948–965. doi: 10.1037/a0036169

*Lukes, M., & Stephan, U. (2012). Nonprofit leaders and for-profit entrepreneurs: Similar people with different motivation. *Ceskoslovenska Psychologie, 56*(1), 41–55.

Mair, J., Battilana, J., & Cardenas, J. (2012). Organizing for society: A typology of social entrepreneuring models. *Journal of Business Ethics, 111*(3), 353–373. doi: 10.1007/s10551-012-1414-3

Mair, J., & Martí, I. (2006). Social entrepreneurship research: A source of explanation, prediction, and delight. *Journal of World Business, 41*(1), 36–44. doi: 10.1016/j.jwb.2005.09.002

Mair, J., Mayer, J., & Lutz, E. (2015). Navigating institutional plurality: Organizational governance in hybrid organizations. *Organization Studies, 36*(6), 713–739. doi: 10.1177/0170840615580007

McClelland, D. C. (1987). *Human motivation*. Cambridge, England: Cambridge University Press.

Meindl, J. R., Ehrlich, S. B., & Dukerich, J. M. (1985). The romance of leadership. *Administrative Science Quarterly, 30*(1), 78–102.

*Migliore, G., Schifani, G., Romeo, P., Hashem, S., & Cembalo, L. (2015). Are farmers in alternative food networks social entrepreneurs? Evidence from a behavioral approach. *Journal of Agricultural & Environmental Ethics, 28*(5), 885–902. doi: 10.1007/s10806-015-9562-y

Miller, T. L., Grimes, M. G., Mcmullen, J. S., & Vogus, T. J. (2012). Venturing for others with heart and head: How compassion encourages social entrepreneurship. *Academy of Management Review, 37*(4), 616–640. doi: 10.5465/amr.2010.0456

Mischel, W. (2004). Toward an integrative science of the person. *Annual Review of Psychology, 55,* 1–22. doi: 10.1146/annurev.psych.55.042902.130709

*Nga, J. K., & Shamuganathan, G. (2010). The influence of personality traits and demographic factors on social entrepreneurship start up intentions. *Journal of Business Ethics, 95*(2), 259–282. doi: 10.1007/s10551-009-0358-8

Parker, S. K. (2014). Beyond motivation: Job and work design for development, health, ambidexterity, and more. *Annual Review of Psychology, 65,* 661–691.

*Parris, D. L., & McInnis-Bowers, C. V. (2014). Social entrepreneurship questioning the status quo: Waste as a resource. *Journal of Economic Issues, 48*(2), 359–365. doi: 10.2753/JEI0021-3624480209

*Praszkier, R., Nowak, A., & Zablocka-Bursa, A. (2009). Social capital built by social entrepreneurs and the specific personality traits that facilitate the process. *Psychologia Spoleczna, 4*(10–12), 42–54.

*Rahman, R. S. A. R., & Pihie, Z. A. L. (2014). Validity and reliability of the social entrepreneurial personality. In V. Grozdanic (Ed.), *Processings of the 10th European Conference on Management, Leadership and Governance (ECMLG 2014)* (pp. 506–513). Reading, England: Academic Conferences.

Rauch, A., & Frese, M. (2007). Let's put the person back into entrepreneurship research: A meta-analysis on the relationship between business owners' personality traits, business creation, and success. *European Journal of Work and Organizational Psychology, 16*(4), 353–385. doi: 10.1080/13594320701595438

*Renko, M. (2013). Early challenges of nascent social entrepreneurs. *Entrepreneurship: Theory and Practice, 37*(5), 1045–1069. doi: 10.1111/j.1540-6520.2012.00522.x

Roccas, S., Sagiv, L., Schwartz, S. H., & Knafo, A. (2002). The Big Five personality factors and personal values. *Personality and Social Psychology Bulletin, 28*(6), 789–801. doi: 10.1177/0146167202289008

Rokeach, M. (1973). Rokeach Values Survey. *The nature of human values.* New York, NY: The Free Press.

*Ross, T., Mitchell, V. A., & May, A. J. (2012). Bottom-up grassroots innovation in transport: Motivations, barriers and enablers. *Transportation Planning and Technology, 35*(4), 469–489. doi: 10.1080/03081060.2012.680820

*Ruskin, J., Seymour, R. G., & Webster, C. M. (2016). Why create value for others? An exploration of social entrepreneurial motives. *Journal of Small Business Management, 54,* 1–23. doi: 10.1111/jsbm.12229

*Ruvio, A., Rosenblatt, Z., & Hertz-Lazarowitz, R. (2010). Entrepreneurial leadership vision in nonprofit vs. for-profit organizations. *Leadership Quarterly, 21*(1), 144–158. doi: 10.1016/j.leaqua.2009.10.011

Ryan, R. M., & Deci, E. L. (2000). Self-determination theory and the facilitation of intrinsic motivation, social development, and well-being. *The American Psychologist, 55*(1), 68–78.

*Sarros, J. C., Cooper, B. K., & Santora, J. C. (2011). Leadership vision, organizational culture, and support for innovation in not-for-profit and for-profit organizations. *Leadership & Organization Development Journal, 32*(3), 291–309. doi: 10.1108/01437731111123933

*Sastre-Castillo, M. A., Peris-Ortiz, M., & Danvila-Del Valle, I. (2015). What is different about the profile of the social entrepreneur? *Nonprofit Management and Leadership, 25*(4), 349–369. doi: 10.1002/nml.21138

Schneider, B. (1987). The people make the place. *Personnel Psychology, 40*(3), 437–453. doi: 10.1111/j.1744-6570.1987.tb00609.x

Schwartz, S. H. (2012). An overview of the Schwartz theory of basic values. *Online Readings in Psychology and Culture, 2*, 1–20. doi: 10.9707/2307-0919.1116

*Seiz, R. C., & Schwab, A. J. (1992a). Entrepreneurial personality traits and clinical social work practitioners. *Families in Society, 73*(8), 495–502.

*Seiz, R. C., & Schwab, A. J. (1992b). Value orientations of clinical social work practitioners. *Clinical Social Work Journal, 20*(3), 323–335. doi: 10.1007/BF00754643

*Shepherd, D. A., Patzelt, H., & Baron, R. A. (2013). "I care about nature, but...": Disengaging values in assessing opportunities that cause harm. *Academy of Management Journal, 56*(5), 1251–1273. doi: 10.5465/amj.2011.0776

Short, J. C., Moss, T. W., & Lumpkin, G. T. (2009). Research in social entrepreneurship: Past contributions and future opportunities. *Strategic Entrepreneurship Journal, 3*(2), 161–194. doi: 10.1002/sej.69

*Shumate, M., Atouba, Y., Cooper, K. R., & Pilny, A. (2014). Two paths diverged: Examining the antecedents to social entrepreneurship. *Management Communication Quarterly, 28*(3), 404–421. doi: 10.1177/0893318914538561

*Sieger, P., Gruber, M., Fauchart, E., & Zellweger, T. (2016). Measuring the social identity of entrepreneurs: Scale development and international validation. *Journal of Business Venturing, 31*(5), 542–572. doi: 10.1016/j.jbusvent.2016.07.001

*Simón-Moya, V., Revuelto-Taboada, L., & Ribeiro-Soriano, D. (2012). Are success and survival factors the same for social and business ventures? *Service Business, 6*(2), 219–242. doi: 10.1007/s11628-012-0133-2

Simsek, Z., Heavey, C., & Veiga, J. (2010). The impact of CEO core self-evaluation on the firm's entrepreneurial orientation. *Strategic Management Journal, 31*, 110–119. doi: 10.1002/smj.800

*Smith, R., Bell, R., & Watts, H. (2014). Personality trait differences between traditional and social entrepreneurs. *Social Enterprise Journal, 10*(3), 200–221. doi: 10.1108/SEJ-08-2013-0033

Stephan, U., Hart, M., Mickiewicz, T., & Drews, C.-C. (2015). *Understanding motivations for entrepreneurship.* London, England: Department for Business, Innovation and Skills.

*Stephan, U., Huysentruyt, M., & Van Looy, B. (2010, November 3–5). Corporate social opportunity recognition and the value(s) of social entrepreneurs. Paper presented at *NYU Stern Annual Social Entrepreneurship Conference*, New York, NY.

Stephan, U., Patterson, M., Kelly, C., & Mair, J. (2016). Organizations driving positive social change: A review and an integrative framework of change processes. *Journal of Management, 42*(5), 1250–1281. doi: 10.1177/0149206316633268

Stets, J. E., & Burke, P. J. (2000). Identity theory and social identity theory. *Social Psychology Quarterly, 63*(3), 224–237. doi: 10.2307/2695870

*Stevens, R., Moray, N., & Bruneel, J. (2015a). The social and economic mission of social enterprises: Dimensions, measurement, validation, and relation. *Entrepreneurship Theory and Practice, 39*(5), 1051–1082. doi: 10.1111/etap.12091

*Stevens, R., Moray, N., Bruneel, J., & Clarysse, B. (2015b). Attention allocation to multiple goals: The case of for-profit social enterprises. *Strategic Management Journal, 36*(7), 1006–1016. doi: 10.1002/smj.2265

Tajfel, H., & Turner, J. C. (1986). The social identity theory of intergroup behavior. *Psychology of Intergroup Relations.* doi: 10.1111/j.1751-9004.2007.00066.x

*Taylor, C. M., Cornelius, Casey, J., & Colvin, K. (2014). Visionary leadership and its relationship to organizational effectiveness. *Leadership & Organization Development Journal*, 35(6), 566–583. doi: 10.1108/LODJ-10-2012-0130

Thompson, J., Alvy, G., & Lees, A. (2000). Social entrepreneurship – A new look at the people and the potential. *Management Decision*, 38(5), 328–338. doi: 10.1108/00251740010340517

*Tigu, G., Iorgulescu, M.-C., Ravar, A. S., & Lile, R. (2015). A pilot profile of the social entrepreneur in the constantly changing Romanian economy. *Amfiteatru Economic*, 17(38), 25–43.

*Van Ryzin, G. G., Grossman, S., DiPadova-Stocks, L., & Bergrud, E. (2009). Portrait of the social entrepreneur: Statistical evidence from a US Panel. *Voluntas*, 20, 129–140. doi: 10.1007/s11266-009-9081-4

*Wong, L., & Tang, J. (2006). Dilemmas confronting social entrepreneurs: Care homes for elderly people in Chinese cities. *Pacific Affairs*, 79(4), 623–640.

Wu, C.-H. (2016). Personality change via work: A job demand–control model of Big-Five personality changes. *Journal of Vocational Behavior*, 92, 157–166. doi: 10.1016/j.jvb.2015.12.001

*Yitshaki, R., & Kropp, F. (2016). Motivations and opportunity recognition of social entrepreneurs. *Journal of Small Business Management*, 54(2), 546–565. doi: 10.1111/jsbm.12157

*Yiu, D. W., Wan, W. P., Ng, F. W., Chen, X., & Jun Su. (2014). Sentimental drivers of social entrepreneurship: A study of China's Guangcai (Glorious) Program. *Management and Organization Review*, 10(1), 55–80. doi: 10.1111/more.12043

Zyphur, M. J. (2009). When mindsets collide: Switching analytical mindsets to advance organization science. *Academy of Management Review*, 34(4), 677–688.

Acknowledgment

The first author acknowledges financial support provided by the European Union through its Seventh Framework Programme for research, technological development, and demonstration under the grant agreement 217622 (SELUSI project), which supported initial work on this chapter.

11

An Individual Differences Approach to Studying Entrepreneurial Tendencies

Gorkan Ahmetoglu[a] and Tomas Chamorro-Premuzic[a]

[a] *University College London, UK*

Introduction

The psychology of entrepreneurship generally starts with three basic assumptions: (a) entrepreneurship—the discovery and exploitation of profitable opportunities (Shane & Venkataraman, 2000)—is an important mechanism for innovation, job creation, and economic growth (Reynolds, Bygrave, & Autio, 2004); (b) people are the main agents in the process of finding and exploiting opportunities (i.e., this process cannot happen without the intervention of human agents; Hisrich, Langan-Fox, & Grant, 2007); and (c) there are individual differences between people in their tendency and ability to act as agents in this process (i.e., some people are more likely than others to engage in it and to do it more potently; Baum, Frese, Baron, & Katz, 2007). This logic has been the foundation for a large amount of research over the past 40 years, investigating the psychological factors involved in the entrepreneurial process. Key research questions have centered around the differences in cognitions, affect, and behavior of these agents as compared to others (Baron & Henry, 2010). The practical implications of this research are clear: if we understand the profile of people who recognize and exploit valuable opportunities, then we will be better able to identify, encourage, and support these individuals, thereby facilitating innovation, job creation, and economic growth.

This chapter proposes an individual differences framework for studying entrepreneurial tendencies. In particular, we offer a theoretical distinction between the study of entrepreneurial tendencies and the study of the tendencies of entrepreneurs. Thus, in contrast to most research on the psychology of entrepreneurship which concerns the questions: "Who becomes an entrepreneur?" and "Why are some entrepreneurs more successful than others?" (Baum et al., 2007), this chapter deals with the questions: "Who is more entrepreneurial?" and "What do entrepreneurial people do?" This distinction generates a different set of research questions, requiring different research designs to the ones currently employed. The aim is to encourage more research on entrepreneurial individuals, identified on the basis of their enduring psychological and behavioral tendencies.

The Wiley Handbook of Entrepreneurship, First Edition.
Edited by Gorkan Ahmetoglu, Tomas Chamorro-Premuzic, Bailey Klinger, & Tessa Karcisky.
© 2017 John Wiley & Sons Ltd. Published 2017 by John Wiley & Sons Ltd.

Following this introduction, this chapter comprises five more sections. To demonstrate how entrepreneurial tendencies can be studied within an individual differences framework, we first review the basic tenets of differential (i.e., individual differences) psychology. To theoretically differentiate the study of entrepreneurial tendencies to that of the tendencies of entrepreneurs, we summarize and critically evaluate the current literature on the psychology of entrepreneurship, in two further sections. We then follow this critical evaluation by proposing an individual differences framework for investigating entrepreneurial tendencies. Finally, before concluding, we summarize the implications of this approach and discuss future research avenues.

The Pillars of Individual Differences Psychology

Differential psychology is the study of individual differences in affect, behavior, and cognition (Revelle, Wilt, & Condon, 2011). In other words, it is the study of differences between people in what they think, feel, and do. The field is based on a number of tenets. First, individual differences may be transient or enduring (Chamorro-Premuzic, 2014). For instance, feeling anxious before a presentation is a transient state. This could be manifested in *cognitive* (e.g., rumination) *affective* (e.g., nervousness) or *behavioral* (e.g., "freezing") reactions. On the other hand, a person may have an enduring tendency to experience these reactions (or have a lower threshold for experiencing them), for instance by generally worrying, ruminating, and avoiding action, across most situations and over longer periods (Roberts & DelVecchio, 2000). These enduring states, or consistent patterns, of thought, feeling, and behaviors, are often referred to (by psychologists) as traits.[1] Measurement of traits, therefore, involves the assessment of habitual cognitive, affective, and behavioral tendencies.

A second assumption is that human psychology and behavior can be organized into a hierarchy (Eysenck, 1990). At its simplest level, behavior can be considered in terms of specific responses. However, some of these responses tend to co-occur, or correlate, and form general habits. Groups of habits that tend to co-occur form traits. For example, people who prefer meeting people to reading at home also tend to enjoy themselves at a party, suggesting that these two habits can be grouped together under the trait of sociability, or extraversion. In other words, this assumption suggests that people display broad predispositions to respond in certain ways across different situations and that these dispositions are organized in a hierarchical way. Accordingly, traits are the sum of states. Entrepreneurship research tends to deal with traits rather than states (e.g., Brandstätter, 2011).

A third assumption is that psychological traits are normally distributed across the population (Matthews, Deary, & Whiteman, 2009). That is, although people will display all levels of all traits (e.g., both introverted and extraverted behavior at different times), there are consistent differences in individuals' typical, or average, behaviors—their habits (Fleeson & Gallagher, 2009). For instance, although everyone will sometimes be sociable and at other times introverted, on average some people will behave more sociably than others. The normal distribution simply dictates that, statistically (or on a population level), some people will be extremely sociable, whereas others will be

---

[1] We use "traits" and "enduring tendencies" interchangeably throughout the chapter to aid the discussion.

extremely reserved, and most people will congregate around the average in terms of their sociability.

The reason enduring differences between people are of particular interest, is the notion of predictability. That is, if we assume that a person has individual tendencies that are stable across contexts and time, then we should be able predict how they will feel, think, and behave most of the time (Fleeson & Gallagher, 2009). This ability to predict people's actions lends itself to a number of practical contexts, including predicting performance. Performance is usually the *result* (or consequence) of behaviors (Hogan & Holland, 2003). Accordingly, sustained performance (i.e., rather than an episode of performance) is the result of stable patterns of behavior (i.e., traits).

A fourth assumption is that a person's general and enduring tendencies, will be expressed in work-related settings as trait-congruent behavior (Tett & Burnett, 2003). For instance, a sociable manager is more likely than a reserved manager to network with colleagues and communicate with their staff —a consequence of which may be variations in performance and output (i.e., what they produce). Accordingly, how people behave and perform across settings and time is a function of, and congruent with, their enduring psychological and behavioral tendencies.

These assumptions are relevant to entrepreneurship. First, if we assume that some people are more entrepreneurial (just as they are more sociable) than others, then it is reasonable to assume that entrepreneurial tendencies may not be episodic, but enduring in nature. Second, it follows that differences in enduring entrepreneurial tendencies will result in predictable behavior and performance output, that is congruent with these tendencies. Thus, an individual differences framework should provide valuable information in the understanding and prediction of the process of recognition and exploitation of profitable opportunities (i.e., entrepreneurship).

The Psychological Approach to Entrepreneurship

Based on these assumptions, the last four decades have seen an upsurge of literature devoted to individual differences in entrepreneurship (Baum et al., 2007). The investigation has most commonly focused on the psychological traits of entrepreneurs (Zhao & Seibert, 2006). The basic assumption in the field is that entrepreneurs are the agents behind entrepreneurial activity and therefore, by deduction, behind economic growth and innovation. For instance, Kirzner (1997) argues that entrepreneurs—through creativity, hard work, and a willingness to accept financial risk—innovate, pursue new opportunities, and create value for others. In the literature, entrepreneurs have been described as a "unique population" (Baron & Henry, 2010, p. 268), special breed (Stanworth & Kaufman, 1996), and "the single most important player in a modern economy" (Lazear, 2002, p. 1).

Research on this so called "trait approach" stretches back several decades (e.g., McClelland, 1961). Numerous psychological traits have been investigated, often focusing on personality (Chell, 2008). Methods of investigation have most commonly comprised examining differences between entrepreneurs and nonentrepreneurs, as well as between more and less successful entrepreneurs (e.g., Baum et al., 2007). Two broad research questions have, thus, been the focus: Why do some people but not others become entrepreneurs? Why are some entrepreneurs more successful than others?

Whilst initial narrative reviews in the 1980s and 1990s cast doubt on the usefulness of personal traits in entrepreneurship (see Aldrich, 1999), several recent meta-analyses have shown significant relations between personality traits and entrepreneurial behavior (Rauch & Frese, 2007; Stewart & Roth, 2001, 2007; Zhao & Seibert, 2006, Zhao, Seibert, & Lumpkin, 2010). Thus, Brandstätter (2011, p. 229) summarizing five meta-analyses on the personality aspects of entrepreneurship concludes: "There can be little doubt any more that personality traits contribute substantially to the way entrepreneurs think, what they aim for, what they do, and what they actually achieve . . . This topic is a fine example of the value of integrating personality psychology and economic-related behaviour."

A Critical Evaluation of the Psychological Approach to Entrepreneurship

A Critical Evaluation of the Group Differences Approach

The notion that personality is important for entrepreneurship today is widely taken for granted (Rauch & Frese, 2007). Indeed, this supposition in itself, in some ways, appears to have reached an empirical dead end. Yet, where empirical answers have been derived, in our view, a number of important questions remain. One important question regards the conceptual and methodological approach to assessing enduring entrepreneurial tendencies. In particular, we argue that whilst a group differences design (i.e., studying differences between entrepreneurs and nonentrepreneurs) is decidedly valuable for particular purposes, it is theoretically distinct from the investigation of enduring entrepreneurial tendencies. More specifically, we argue that the question "What are the tendencies (or traits) of entrepreneurs?" is different to the question "What are entrepreneurial tendencies?"

To clarify, let's refer back to the tenets presented in the previous section. As noted in that section, within an individual differences framework, judgments about enduring tendencies are made by observations of a persons habitual psychological and behavioral responses. Thus, to evaluate how extraverted a person is, assessments would be made of the extent to which this person habitually manifests *extraverted* behaviors, thoughts, or feelings. In other words, we would investigate stable patterns in manifestations that we consider extraverted (Fleeson, 2001), such as socializing, assertiveness, gregariousness, and forcefulness (Chamorro-Premuzic, 2014).

Now let's apply this logic to the assessment of entrepreneurial tendencies. Thus, to assess how entrepreneurial a person is, assessment would need to be made of the extent to which this person habitually manifests *entrepreneurial* behaviors, thoughts, or feelings; that is, we would investigate stable patterns in manifestations that we consider entrepreneurial (Fleeson, 2001). The issue arises here: a group differences approach *by design* operationalizes entrepreneurial tendencies as creating a business (or the act of becoming self-employed). This is problematic for a simple reason: business creation is an episodic event, not an enduring tendency. To be considered an enduring tendency, a person would have to start hundreds, or thousands, of businesses during a lifetime, which (unless one has a pathological reason to start companies) is highly unlikely.

Of course, people may engage in numerous behaviors both prior and subsequent to the act of creating an organization. Indeed, conceptually most researchers consider business creation to be a process (Baum et al., 2007), constituting a variety of behaviors before and after the actual act of application. However, whilst this is a common conceptual standpoint, it is not the operational one. The categorical distinction between groups as entrepreneurs and nonentrepreneurs is a function of one group having created a company and the other not. Thus, the mere act of a creating a company, by design, is the only metric that differentiates the groups (i.e., irrespective of the behavior prior or subsequent to the act).

Note that there needn't be an inherent issue with the group differences design. Indeed, a commonly recognized line of psychological research involves the comparison of the differences in personal traits of clinical populations to others. For instance, in clinical settings, researchers may be interested in examining the validity of a personality measure (e.g., the Big Five) in the prediction of a personality disorder diagnosis, by examining its correlations with diagnostic status (Butcher, Dahlstrom, Graham, Tellegen, & Kaemmer, 1989). In fact, personality trait scores have been found to be substantially related to diagnostic categories, thereby allowing practitioners to predict the onset of a disorder and/or assisting in the development of treatment plans (Quirk, Christiansen, Wagner, & McNulty, 2003). Clearly, group differences research can be useful.

The group differences research in entrepreneurship is arguably based on the same inherent assumption: that entrepreneurs are a unique population, who create things others cannot (Stanworth & Kaufman, 1996). This assumption would then substantiate research focused on predicting the diagnostic status of entrepreneurs. However, whilst there are similarities in assumptions, there are significant discrepancies in the theoretical and empirical foundations between the two approaches. In particular, psychiatric diagnoses rely on a set of diagnostic criteria related to enduring patterns of psychological and/or behavioral abnormalities (Kring, Johnson, Davison, & Neale, 2010). Diagnosis is often made by observation of manifestations of these abnormalities, by trained clinicians and psychiatrists. In basic terms, a person is categorized into a group, when there is a thorough and reliable assessment of the enduring manifestation of predetermined behavioral or psychological patterns. The group is then a function of a great amount of homogeneity between participants within the category group, in terms of the specified behavioral criteria (Kring et al., 2010).

In contrast, entrepreneurs are self-selected, and do not have to display any observable patterns of behavior, thoughts, or feelings in order to belong to the category. That is, mainstream research does not decide whether a person is an entrepreneur based on how they feel, think, and act. Rather, one automatically belongs to the category if one has created a company. This results in a far greater amount of heterogeneity between participants within the category group, in terms of their behavioral and psychological patterns, and therefore, in output (Gartner, 1989). Fundamentally, this means that the selection process does not incorporate opportunistic and innovative behaviors and output into the selection criteria. In fact, existing data indicates that, on average, these criteria are not met: most entrepreneurs do not produce much (or any) innovation, nor do they intend to (Reynolds, 2005, 2007); most never manage to produce significant growth (Aldrich, 1999; Uusitalo, 2001); and the majority simply fail within the first few years of conception (Baron & Henry, 2010; Taylor, 1999; van Praag, 2003).

Thus, unlike clinical diagnoses, a group differences approach in entrepreneurship, is unlikely to reveal useful information in relation to, or be measuring, the desired (or assumed) behavioral criteria, such as recognition and exploitation of opportunities, innovation and value creation. Consequently, we argue that it is not appropriately targeted to investigating entrepreneurial tendencies.

A Critical Evaluation of Comparisons Between More and Less Successful Entrepreneurs

What about research looking at more versus less successful entrepreneurs? Whilst there is no doubt about the practical value of this research stream, we think it is important to make a theoretical distinction between it and research dealing with the measurement of enduring tendencies. Measuring relationships between traits and performance, or inferring traits from these relationships, are distinct research endeavors to measuring traits per se.

To illustrate, say we conjecture that emotional intelligence is intricately linked to the performance of sales people. That is, we infer that emotional intelligence is key to success in this occupation. Say we then looked at the literature and found that there is a positive relationship between extraversion, conscientiousness, and performance in sales occupations (e.g., Barrick & Mount, 1991). Can we infer from this research that a person scoring high on extraversion and conscientiousness is more emotionally intelligent? Whether there is a correlation between these three measures is irrelevant, as approaching measurement of psychological tendencies this way wouldn't make much sense. Clearly, to infer how emotionally intelligent a person is, we would need to assess their emotional intelligence, not their standing on personality traits that correlate with sales performance.

For similar reasons, there should be a distinction between assessing a person's entrepreneurial tendencies and inferring them from the person's standing on the personality traits that correlate with new-venture success. Establishing a relationship between the Big Five traits of openness, conscientiousness, extraversion, neuroticism and business success (Zhao et al., 2010) is no doubt useful. However, can we infer from this research that openness, conscientiousness, extraversion, neuroticism are measures (or indicators) of *entrepreneurial* tendencies? Again, whether these Big Five traits may correlate with entrepreneurial tendencies is less relevant, because this isn't a suitable approach to measurement. To infer how entrepreneurial a person is, clearly we would need to assess this directly, by looking at their tendency to think, feel, and act entrepreneurially. Hence our argument that there is a significant theoretical distinction between the study of entrepreneurial tendencies and the study of tendencies of entrepreneurs (or successful ones). Whilst much research exists on the latter approach, we believe there is a gap in the literature in terms of the former.

An Individual Differences Approach to Understanding Entrepreneurial Tendencies

How should we assess entrepreneurial tendencies? As noted earlier, differential psychology is interested in looking for enduring patterns in affect, cognition, and behavior, with the assumption that most psychological tendencies are normally distributed. So, if we believe that people can be more or less entrepreneurial (i.e., that being entrepreneurial is a psychological and behavioral tendency), to assess how entrepreneurial a person is, we would need to investigate stable patterns in thoughts, feelings, and behaviors that we consider entrepreneurial (Fleeson, 2001). This leaves us with an important question: What thoughts, feelings, and behaviors do we consider entrepreneurial?

(Re)defining Entrepreneurial Tendencies

The defining and measurement of psychological constructs commonly start with a theoretical backdrop and the specifications of the conceptual dimensions to be measured, followed by assessments of these dimensions (Pervin & Cervone, 2010). For instance, McClelland's early work (1961) on the achievement motive conceptualized the theoretical foundations of a motivational construct that comprised three core dimensions: need for achievement, need for power, and need for affiliation. Subsequent empirical assessment of these dimensions has included projective measures (i.e., the Thematic Apperception Test; Murray, 1943) and various psychometric inventories, designed to assess these dimensions (Collins, Hanges, & Locke, 2004). Rotter (1954) developed the concept of *locus of control*, proposing a two-dimensional attributional construct, regarding people's beliefs about the amount of control they have over the outcomes of events in their lives. Consequent work has primarily used questionnaire-based assessment of the two dimensions (Furnham & Steele, 1993). It would appear reasonable, therefore, to apply a similar approach to conceptualizing the dimensionality and measurement of entrepreneurial tendencies.

The vast amount of literature on entrepreneurship would indicate this to be a substantive approach. Nevertheless, given the widespread focus on the predictors of business creation and success, this task is not without its hurdles. Most theorizing has focused on "what is needed to be an entrepreneur" (or achieve success as entrepreneur), and not "what is entrepreneurial," meaning little focus has been dedicated to defining a psychological construct (i.e., stable entrepreneurial behavioral or psychological patterns). Accordingly, the dimensions of entrepreneurial tendencies are not easily, or directly, accessible in the literature. The issue is further complicated in that clear distinction is often not made between personal tendencies (e.g., pursuing an opportunity) and outputs (e.g., introduction of a new product), or between episodic events (e.g., the recognition of an opportunity) versus enduring tendencies (e.g., tendency to recognize opportunities).

Nevertheless, the task is not beyond scope. First, although business creation has had a central role in entrepreneurial discussions, the literature is abundant with conceptual definitions that move beyond business creation and success—including some of the most widely accepted ones. Furthermore, whilst behavior and output are used interchangeably, it is possible to disentangle these components. Finally, distinctions between episodic behavior and enduring tendencies can be coordinated within an individual differences framework (see above).

In fact, looking at two of the most widely accepted definitions of entrepreneurship illustrates these points. For instance, Schumpeter's (1934) concept of innovation (i.e., anything that was carried out through new combinations) has been and still is fundamental to most definitions of entrepreneurship. The more recent definition of Shane and Venkataraman (2000) has included the dimensions of recognition and exploitation of profitable opportunities, which have since been widely adopted in the literature, as core dimensions of entrepreneurship (Baron & Henry, 2010). Indeed, our examination of several content analyses focusing on the dimensionality of entrepreneurship found these dimensions to be the most recurring (see Ahmetoglu, 2015).

These conceptual definitions are noteworthy for two reasons. First, the core dimensions in neither of these definitions relate to business creation (even if business creation could result from them). Second, although these dimensions can be studied as episodic events and outputs (Eckhart & Shane, 2003), theoretically, they can be investigated also as enduring personal tendencies. Take the example of opportunity recognition: a person in an organization may believe that they have spotted an opportunity to open up a trendy café in a rural area (cognitive), feel excited about the prospect (affective), and discuss the option with friends and family (behavioral). This is an episodic experience and reaction. On the other hand, the same person may have an enduring tendency to experience these reactions (or have a lower threshold for experiencing them), for instance by generally thinking about (or "seeing") different business opportunities also within their organization, feeling excited about these opportunities, and discussing them with people, across most situations (e.g., with colleagues, friends, and clients), and over longer periods (e.g., in their 20s and in their 30s). The person may never actually create a business, but may have recognized a number of innovative and valuable opportunities for their company while employed.

In this example, the person would not have been considered entrepreneurial in traditional group differences research (given that they have not created an organization). However, from an individual differences perspective, the person's recurring states of recognizing opportunities, if observed as a consistent pattern of thought, feeling, and behaviors across situations and time, would be referred to (by psychologists) as enduring tendencies (or traits). Furthermore, if one considers the concept of opportunity recognition as a core dimension of entrepreneurship, then from an individual differences perspective, this person would be said to have "elevated" (or high) entrepreneurial tendencies (at least on that dimension). The proposition here is that if one accepts that the recognition and exploitation of opportunities, and innovation are core dimensions of entrepreneurship, logically one should be able to investigate these dimensions within an individual differences framework.

The Practical Importance of Theoretical Preciseness

Viewing entrepreneurial tendencies through this theoretical lens generates a number of observations. First, given that most enduring psychological and behavioral tendencies (or constructs) are normally distributed (Matthews et al., 2009), it would be reasonable to expect there to be a normal distribution also in entrepreneurial tendencies. That is, statistically (or on a population level), some people should be far more entrepreneurial than others (and most people will fall around the mean level in terms of such tendencies).

Second, if we accept this view, then we also have to accept that these tendencies cannot be exclusive to business founders. That is, just as anyone can be sociable or emotionally intelligent, theoretically, anyone, regardless of his or her occupation, should be able to recognize and exploit an opportunity, and innovate (i.e., be entrepreneurial)—not only business founders (McKenzie, Ugbah, & Smothers, 2007). Certainly, managers in established organizations are likely to (in their job) engage in these activities, as are students, politicians, and academics. Within psychology, few, if any, psychological or behavioral tendencies can be exclusively reserved to a particular individual or group of individuals (Costa & Widiger, 2002; Fleeson & Gallagher, 2009).

Note that this does not make entrepreneurial tendencies any less relevant for the process of business creation and success. Indeed, the point is less about distancing the studies of entrepreneurial tendencies and tendencies of entrepreneurs *empirically*, as it is to distinguishing them *theoretically*. Yet, we do believe it will serve the field well to make this distinction for several reasons.

First, given that a person's stable psychological and behavioral tendencies predict specific behavioral activities and output (Ones & Viswesvaran, 2011), it would be reasonable to expect more-entrepreneurial business founders to behave differently and produce different output to less-entrepreneurial business founders. Furthermore, according to trait activation theory (Tett & Guterman, 2000), behavior and performance in specific situations should be congruent with a person's more general and stable patterns of thought, feelings, and behavior. It follows then, that more-entrepreneurial business founders will behave more entrepreneurially and produce more innovative output (e.g., Lumpkin & Dess, 1996).

Second, the principle of trait activation also holds that enduring tendencies are expressed as responses to relevant situational cues (Tett & Burnett, 2003). That is, both behavioral manifestations of general tendencies, as well as output resulting from behavioral manifestations, will be context-dependent. A person may be entrepreneurial, but different contexts will differentially allow and encourage these general tendencies to be expressed in contextual behavior and, therefore, result in output. Consequently, an entrepreneurial business founder may be expected to prefer, and react differently to, different environments, support mechanisms (e.g., investments or resources), team members and staff, industries, and national cultures, relative to a less entrepreneurial one. A more comprehensive understanding of these conditions would require different research endeavors to those more commonly employed in entrepreneurship research.

Ultimately, however, an entrepreneurial person, based on the same principle, may choose to work for an incumbent organization. The theoretical rationale behind the group differences research in entrepreneurship is the *attraction-selection-attrition* (ASA; Schneider, 1987) model, which states that people select occupations or organizations they perceive are in line with their psychological profile. Accordingly, the hypothesis is that some individuals but not others will choose to become entrepreneurs (Rauch & Frese, 2007). Whilst this logic is sound, it is not directly obvious from an ASA perspective that an entrepreneurial person, by default, will be attracted to the entrepreneurs' lifestyle. As noted, the probabilities of success and innovative activity in start-ups are minimal (Reynolds, 1997) and the probabilities of failure and task-related pressures are high (Taylor, 1999). In fact, the typical entrepreneur works longer hours and earns less than they would working for someone else (see Shane, 2008). Conversely, many incumbent organizations may promote innovation and possess cultures which allow the expression of entrepreneurial tendencies. It is not immediately clear, therefore, that an entrepreneurial person who weighs these options would choose self-employment over working for an incumbent organization (or a combination of both). These are practical considerations that, in our view, warrant the theoretical distinction between the study of entrepreneurial tendencies and tendencies of entrepreneurs.

Recommendations for Researching Entrepreneurial Tendencies

Based on the arguments presented above, we believe it is important to establish a framework for characterizing and researching individual differences in entrepreneurial tendencies. In our view, obtaining a comprehensive understanding of such tendencies requires measurement at the *psychological* (i.e., cognitive/affective), the *behavioral* (both general and contextual), and the *output* (i.e., performance) level, as well as consideration of relevant contextual factors.

Above, we have theoretically placed entrepreneurial tendencies along other psychological constructs. As such, a different set of research questions is generated, requiring different research designs to those more commonly found in current entrepreneurship research (e.g., Baum et al., 2007). Below we offer some recommendations as to the approaches that may be suitable for further investigation. We do not promote a particular assessment strategy, nor advocate a particular theory. Rather, our recommendations roughly follow a standard research approach to psychological constructs within the individual differences framework, which comprises three critical questions:

1) How do we assess entrepreneurial tendencies?
2) How do entrepreneurial tendencies manifest in contextual behavior?
3) How do entrepreneurial tendencies (and contextual behavior) manifest in entrepreneurial output?

How Do We Assess Entrepreneurial Tendencies?

The first task of measurement is defining what is to be measured. To assess a psychological construct, such as how entrepreneurial a person is, we first need to establish the dimensions of this construct. As noted above, although there is a wealth of theorizing on the questions "What is entrepreneurship?" and "Who is an entrepreneur?" we do believe that within an individual differences framework more work is needed to answer the question "What is entrepreneurial?" In particular, we urge that future work on the dimensionality of entrepreneurial tendencies starts with the theoretical bases of stable personal tendencies that are independent, rather than the metric, of particular episodic output (e.g., business entry or revenues), or the personal tendencies that predict (or are correlated with) episodic output.

Of course, agreeing the dimensions of a psychological construct is unlikely to have an objective answer. As Petrides and Furnham (2001, p. 428) note: "Asking what precisely should be part of a construct is like asking what sports should be in the Olympics; neither question can be answered objectively." The best one can hope for is a majority consensus.

For demonstration purposes, here we will use the dimensions of opportunity recognition, evaluation, exploitation, and innovation as core entrepreneurial dimensions, which are based on the rationale presented above. Although, we do not expect or intend there to be an agreement on these dimensions, we include them on the basis that they are some of the most recurrent themes in the literature, including in several content analyses focusing on the dimensionality of entrepreneurship (see Ahmetoglu, 2015), and can be studied at the individual level as enduring tendencies. Specification of theoretical dimensions of psychological constructs (in this case entrepreneurial tendencies) is important as it generates an operational definition that is accessible for assessment. From a measurement perspective then, the question is: How do we assess a person's tendency to think, feel, and behave entrepreneurially?

The measurement of personal tendencies takes several forms, and a number of methods are available, including life record data (actual behavioral records), self-report data (self-ratings), observer data (third-person ratings or observations of behavior), and test data (experimental research) (Ozer, 1999). A multi-method approach is therefore recommended (Pervin & Cervone, 2010). In psychology research, the assessment of psychological tendencies often starts by self-report data, or psychometric testing, which are generally accepted to be reliable and valid methods to obtain psychometric data (Roberts, Kuncel, Shiner, Caspi, & Goldberg, 2007). Given the hierarchical nature of tendencies, this is followed by measurement of factor structure, relationships to other individual differences constructs, as well as substructure of the dimensions. This method is not only used to reveal dimensionality (i.e., the correlation between dimensions), but also to locate tendencies in the more general "factor space" of individual differences (Chamorro-Premuzic, 2014). In plain terms, it indicates how much different habits tend to co-occur, and whether it is worth measuring any additional habits. It is also valuable for understanding which tendencies are more stable versus malleable/context-dependent, which in turn has important practical implications, for instance, in selection, investment, and development decisions.

Several psychometric measures conceptually aligned with our proposed operational definition exist, including the Entrepreneurial Alertness measure (Kaish & Gilad, 1991), various Innovativeness measures (e.g., Kirton, 1976), the individual level Entrepreneurial Orientation Scale (Langkamp Bolton & Lane, 2012) and more. Although many have primarily been developed and used to predict business creation and success, they are likely to be assessing tendencies that are enduring and general, and could potentially be combined in research to assess entrepreneurial tendencies. Based on the theoretical arguments presented above, our own research has been dedicated to the development and validation of a psychometric inventory specifically designed to assess entrepreneurial tendencies (META; Ahmetoglu, Leutner, & Chamorro-Premuzic, 2011), comprising individual differences in the core dimensions of opportunity recognition, opportunity exploitation, and innovation. This research reveals two relevant findings. First, analysis of the factor structure of the hypothesized (core) dimensions demonstrates that these are statistically independent. Second, entrepreneurial tendencies have been found to display discriminant validity in relation to the Big Five personality traits (Leutner, Ahmetoglu, & Chamorro-Premuzic, 2014), as well as a number of other established psychological constructs (see Ahmetoglu, 2015). Thus, this research denotes the existence of an empirically distinct psychological construct, meaning that entrepreneurial tendencies include different habits to the ones captured in traditional measures. This is an important foundation for further investigation.

Of course, self-reports can be compared to, and complemented by "other reports" of entrepreneurial tendencies. This involves getting a third-person perspective of an individual's enduring tendencies, and would be useful to counterbalance impression management or social desirability biases faced by self-reports (Morgensen et al., 2007). Nevertheless, given that others cannot observe the thoughts and feelings of an individual, such as how often a person recognizes, or thinks about, opportunities, or how often they have creative ideas, having self as well as other reports would be necessary for a comprehensive understanding. Establishing the dimensionality and measurement of a psychological construct is an important first step for understanding it within an individual differences framework. A second critical step, is to investigate how it manifests in contextual behavior.

How Do General Entrepreneurial Tendencies Manifest in Contextual Behavior?

Examining how entrepreneurial tendencies are expressed in specific situations is a key endeavor (Hogan & Holland, 2003). First, this research answers the question "What do entrepreneurial people do differently to others?" more specifically and across situations and time. Accordingly, it examines the contexts that release (or trigger) entrepreneurial tendencies and the contexts that suppress them. Second, context-specific tendencies are more proximal predictors of output (Hogan & Holland, 2003). Thus, their measurement is important for improving prediction of output. Third, establishing a relationship between general tendencies and context-specific behavior should improve prediction of individual output through the assessment of general tendencies, in the absence of contextual behavior data. Accordingly, we believe that it would be important for research to obtain observational and life record data, through records of actual behaviors, thoughts, and feelings across time and space. Because of space limitations, here we only focus on behavioral manifestations (although we do think it is worth researching all context-specific manifestations, including thoughts and feelings).

Detailed approaches to assessing entrepreneurial behaviors have been offered by Bird, Schjoedt, and Baum (2012) and Teague and Gartner (this volume). These provide great insights into the measurement of behavior. Nevertheless, there are some notable differences between work on the "behavior of entrepreneurs" and that presented here, examining "behavior of entrepreneurial people." For instance, Bird et al. (2012, p. 890) define entrepreneurs' behavior as "the concrete enactment by individuals (or teams) of tasks or activities . . . which are required in some combination to start and grow most new organizations." This definition gives a specific focus to entrepreneurs, does not differentiate between more and less entrepreneurial ones, and comprises any (relevant) behaviors, including those that may not be entrepreneurial in the current use of the term (i.e., innovative or opportunistic). Assessing the behaviors of entrepreneurial people requires a different classification methodology. Below, we offer a few approaches, inspired by Bird et al.'s (2012) framework for studying behaviors.

Classification of Entrepreneurial Behaviors

Given that it would be impractical to measure all the behaviors of entrepreneurial people (like how long they take to make breakfast, or their muscular movements when jogging), some categorization system of behavior is necessary. Here, we use Bird et al.'s (2012) recommendations about (a) granularity of behavior, and (b) taxonomy of behavior. Granularity of behavior involves decisions about the appropriate unit, or "chunk size" for study: that is, how abstract, versus specific, recorded behaviors should be. Chunks are usually more useful than specific components (Baum, 2002). For instance, behavior as "number of new service ideas presented to management" or "number of networking events attended," is more useful than the specifics about the word count of proposals, references used, body language, or tone of voice in communication. In principle, however, behavior can have a hierarchical structure, meaning granularity (or chunk size) of entrepreneurial behavior can be determined by the purpose of the research.

Beyond the granularity of behavior, ways of classifying behaviors as entrepreneurial, as opposed to anything else, are also necessary. That is, one needs a taxonomy of entrepreneurial behavior (Bird et al., 2012). As noted, this is different to monitoring the behaviors of entrepreneurs, and involves an additional question of "Should this behavior be considered entrepreneurial?"[2] Making such classifications has several caveats, including actor versus observer perceptions, intentionality, goal-orientation, and context specificity (Ahadi & Diener, 1989; Monson, Hesley, & Chernick, 1982). For instance, a person watching sci-fi movies to get ideas about future products, may subjectively consider this behavior to be entrepreneurial. However, an observer, without knowledge of the intention of the actor, may not choose to classify this behavior as such (on the basis of face validity). Thus, observers' perceptions may be insufficient to capture behaviors, and require subjective reports. What's more, if a person watching sci-fi movies generates ideas based on information contained in the movie, but doesn't intentionally watch these to obtain ideas (nor is conscious of the fact that the information helped them to), then the entrepreneurial behavior may not be accessible to classification, either by the actor or by an observer.

Conceptual challenges such as the above undoubtedly impede objectivity in classification of entrepreneurial behavior (or any behavior for that matter). Nevertheless, they needn't inhibit the generation of a taxonomy that has practical utility for prediction. In this regard, several approaches to classification are available. An obvious place to start is existing behavioral indices in relevant literature, that can be hypothesized to distinguish between more versus less entrepreneurial individuals. Examples of this include the Entrepreneurial Orientation literature (e.g., Lumpkin & Dess, 1996), the literature on innovative work behaviors within organizations (e.g., De Jong & Den Hartog, 2010; Scott & Bruce, 1994), or selections from current work on behavior of entrepreneurs noted in Bird et al. (2012) and Teague and Gartner (this volume). Consideration here should include making clear distinctions between behaviors, attitudes, traits (or general tendencies), and output, which have often been mixed in the literature (e.g., Bird et al., 2012). Making distinctions between these constructs is necessary for obtaining accurate understanding of how entrepreneurial tendencies are manifested in behavior in specific contexts. In principle, these existing indices may be expanded or extended, based on observational records or hypothesized entrepreneurial behaviors.

Having established relevant target behaviors to be analyzed, the next reasonable step would be to examine their (statistical) relationships to self or other rated general entrepreneurial tendencies (e.g., obtained by psychometric testing). Logically, for observed behaviors to be considered manifestations of general entrepreneurial tendencies, they should be significantly more prominent among people who report to be (or are rated by others as being) more entrepreneurial. The stronger the correlations between self (or other) rated tendencies and observed behavior, the more confident one would be in categorizing a behavior as a manifestation of the general tendency. Conversely, behavior that does not distinguish between more- or less-entrepreneurial people may be excluded from the taxonomy.

Of course, there may be other reasons for why a relationship between general tendencies and observed behavior may not be found. First, the association may not be there

---

[2] This is because, even with appropriate granularity, a researcher could in theory monitor differences in everything from the way entrepreneurial people organize their wardrobe, to the way they cycle. That is, without a prior theory about what behavior to monitor, research could involve analysis of the full spectrum of behavior across all contexts, which is clearly not a practical research approach.

because the dimensionality of the self, or other, reported tendencies is not comprehensive enough to capture the full spectrum of entrepreneurial tendencies,[3] in which case the behavioral research would add to theoretical latitude. Second, as the trait activation principle dictates, behaviors can only be observed if relevant situational cues are present, and forces that prohibit the behavior are absent (Tett & Guterman, 2000). Simply put, some situations will trigger entrepreneurial behavior whilst others will suppress it. To assess how an enduring entrepreneurial tendency manifests in context-specific behavior, therefore, one must observe people in situations where behaving entrepreneurially is possible, practical, and/or desirable. In other words, classification of behavior also requires systematic considerations of contexts.

It is beyond the scope of this chapter to review any situational taxonomies in detail. Nevertheless, for illustration purposes, it is easy to apply Tett and Burnett's (2003) principles of relevance (or expectations) and rewards, and the three sources of *task cues* (what are the tasks you need to do?), *social cues* (e.g., what do others expect from you?), or broader *organizational cues* (e.g., does the broader external environment encourage the behavior?) that inform the principles. For instance, an entrepreneurial employee is more likely to act entrepreneurially if the task of the job demands creativity and innovation, group norms favor tolerance, the organization provides enough opportunities to network (i.e., relevant expectations), and there are no obvious punishments for acting entrepreneurially (i.e., reward). Conversely, the employee is less likely to act entrepreneurially if their work includes repetitive and simple tasks, they work with conservative colleagues or managers, and the organizational culture is bureaucratic (O'Reilly, Chatman, & Caldwell, 1991).

The same logic can be applied to entrepreneurs. For instance, entrepreneurs in different industries (e.g., a start-up in a heavily regulated industry versus a tech start-up) may be faced with varying levels of relevance and reward for expressing entrepreneurial behavior (Shane, 2008). Likewise, different stages of the entrepreneurial process may provide differential relevance and rewards for behavior. For instance, early stages of the venture may necessitate the entrepreneur engaging in routine tasks (e.g., finding office space, implementing processes, recruitment etc.), cope with everyday demands of clients and staff, and face pressure from external investors or regulation (Shane, 2008).

These examples simply illustrate that systematic accounts of contexts in research would provide a more comprehensive understanding of the relationship between general tendencies and contextual behavior, and stresses the importance of measuring people across a multitude of situations (Bird et al., 2012). Needless to say, pinpointing the situations that trigger or release entrepreneurial behaviors and those that suppress them, would have significant practical implications, including guiding entrepreneurial people to specific environments, or making changes to existing environments to facilitate entrepreneurial behavior.

Still, arguably the key reason to why assessment of context-specific entrepreneurial behaviors (and indeed general entrepreneurial tendencies) are of interest, is prediction of sustained entrepreneurial output. That is, behaviors are of interest because they

---

[3] Or validity issues related to self-report inventories, including impression management and social desirability bias (Morgenson et al., 2007). This is unlikely to be a comprehensive explanation, however, given the wealth of literature on the validity of self-reports (Ones & Viswesvaran, 2011), especially in contextually based studies (e.g., Fleeson & Gallagher, 2009; Hogan & Holland, 2003; Tett & Guterman, 2000).

lead to tangible performance. A final method for corroborating the classification of entrepreneurial behavior, therefore, involves examining their statistical relationships to entrepreneurial output. Naturally, the stronger the relationship between observed behavior and entrepreneurial output, the more confidently one can categorize the former in an entrepreneurial behavior taxonomy. For instance, if the observed behavior of "number of networking events attended" is related to general entrepreneurial tendencies, *and* predicts whether a person innovates more often (produces higher rates of new products etc.), then including this behavior in an entrepreneurial taxonomy would be warranted.[4] In a way this is reversing the question and asking, "What are the behaviors of people who produce higher entrepreneurial output?" The same limitations of context specificity no doubt apply here too. That is, behavior, however entrepreneurial it may be, may not lead to output if the conditions that allow the output are not there. These limitations, however, can be (partially) mitigated in research, by systematic accounts of context, and the use of appropriate measures of output. Below we give a brief outline of both, starting with entrepreneurial output.

How Do General Entrepreneurial Tendencies and Contextual Behavior Manifest in Entrepreneurial Output?

How should we *operationalize* entrepreneurial output? There are several considerations of note. First, tangible output is different to behavior (and, of course, thoughts and cognitions). Output is the consequence of behavior but is not the behavior itself (Bird et al., 2012). For instance, behaviors may include doing research, deliberating, and drafting. These behaviors may result in the drafted prototype for a product, or a filed patent, which are tangible outputs.[5]

Second, as demonstrated throughout the chapter, we conceptualize entrepreneurial tendencies and behavior to be distributed across the population, and not be confined to business founders. It follows, therefore, that entrepreneurial output must also be distributed across the population. Within an individual differences framework, this output should vary between individuals, such that some individuals will produce higher entrepreneurial output than others (i.e., independent of whether they are entrepreneurs or not). Based on this conceptualization, therefore, several domain-specific output measures beyond business creation and success, are likely to be relevant, not only from

---

[4] Of course, there will again be caveats with this classification, and multiple explanations need to be kept in mind. For instance, what if the behavior correlates with entrepreneurial output but not with general (self or other rated) entrepreneurial tendencies? Here several explanations are available. First, it could again be that the self-report does not capture a particular dimension of entrepreneurial tendencies. Conversely, it could be a perceptual oversight; that is, people are not accounting for this behavior when rating entrepreneurial tendencies, even when they should. Third, it could mean that the researcher is using output which most people do not consider entrepreneurial. Finally, it could also simply mean that a behavior is related to output, but the behaviour itself is not a function of entrepreneurial tendencies. For instance, better nutrition may enable people to produce more prototypes for new products, but having better nutrition itself may not be a function of being entrepreneurial.

[5] Of course, the distinction may not always be so clear cut. For instance, behaviors may be intricately linked to smaller units of output: building an app involves several steps in the process, all of which involve smaller units of output (Baum, 2002). Therefore, a granularity approach similar to the one discussed with regards to behavior, may also be appropriate for output.

entrepreneurship studies, but also from the field of innovation studies (see Crossan & Apaydin, 2010), and the creativity literature (see Silvia, Wigert, Reiter-Palmon, & Kaufman, 2012). The choice of measure should, accordingly, vary depending on the line of research.

Third, to get substantive validity coefficients, the output measure of choice will need to be aligned with the level of analysis, whether that is the individual, group, or organizational level. Clearly, measuring the relationship between entrepreneurial tendencies and output in student, employee, or nascent entrepreneur samples, would need to employ measures that assess individual level output (e.g., Creative Achievement Questionnaire; Carson, Peterson, & Higgins, 2005; Entrepreneurial output inventory; Ahmetoglu et al., 2011), whereas research on the relationship between founders' entrepreneurial tendencies and output in medium-sized firms, or senior managers in incumbent firms, may be more interested in firm level output (e.g., the Entrepreneurial Intensity measure; Morris & Sexton, 1996). Needless to say, common moderators, such as industry, occupation, organization, seniority, and others, would also need to be taken into account when choosing a particular output measure. Establishing suitable metrics to assess entrepreneurial output, therefore, is an important element in making valid predictions.

As noted above, a final key step would be to examine the conditions under which entrepreneurial behavior leads to entrepreneurial output, and the conditions under which they do not. For instance, an entrepreneurial employee may obtain knowledge from unusual sources, and thereby generate and present a number of entrepreneurial ideas to management. However, if management is uninterested, or lacks resources or decision-making power, then these entrepreneurial behaviors may never materialize into output. Similarly, a young individual may have highly innovative business ideas and regularly spot opportunities to create value. However, if they are in a poor socioeconomic region deprived of funding or career prospects, no matter how entrepreneurially they behave, they may never get any of these ventures off the ground. Clearly, from this perspective, understanding the conditions under which general tendencies and contextual behaviors do versus do not lead to entrepreneurial output, may be consequential for socioeconomic activity of individuals, organizations, and perhaps regions. Situational taxonomies (e.g., relevance and reward) should be a relevant starting point for understanding these conditions.

It is worth clarifying that our aim is not to suggest what metrics researchers *should* be using to assess entrepreneurial tendencies and output. We do recognize that there may be more interest in studying revenues and profits of start-ups or incumbent organizations, than in studying a student exploiting an opportunity to provide snacks to others at university. Nevertheless, in an individual differences framework, entrepreneurial tendencies should be distributed among the population in a way that is relatively independent of the distribution of such organizational outputs. Statistically, many entrepreneurial people will not be directly contributing to, or have a major impact on, the revenues and profits of start-ups or incumbent organizations. Yet these individuals may nevertheless recognize many profitable opportunities, have innovative ideas, behave entrepreneurially, and produce more entrepreneurial output relative to others, even if these are smaller in scale. Focusing solely on revenues and outputs of organizations may result in failure to identify and recognize these individuals, which in turn may lead to missed opportunities to create value, suboptimal deployment of entrepreneurial talent, and discouragement of entrepreneurial activity. Thus, if the interest is the study of enduring entrepreneurial tendencies, then an individual differences framework of the complex interplay between general tendencies, specific behaviors, relevant output, and contextual moderators, described in this chapter, should be of interest.

Discussion

This chapter has proposed an individual differences framework for studying entrepreneurial tendencies. Most research on the psychology of entrepreneurship concerns two fundamental questions: "Who becomes an entrepreneur?" and "Why are some entrepreneurs more successful than others?" (Baum et al., 2007). In this chapter we have dealt with the questions: "Who is more entrepreneurial?" and "What do entrepreneurial people do and produce?"

In that sense, we looked at entrepreneurial tendencies from an individual differences lens and suggest that people differ in enduring tendencies to think, feel, and act entrepreneurially. From this lens, entrepreneurial tendencies cannot be "owned" by a particular subgroup of individuals (i.e., entrepreneurs). Rather, as with any other psychological and behavioral tendencies, they are distributed across the population. Individual differences are then a function of variations in the degree to which these tendencies are manifested across the population. In this framework, therefore, all people will display entrepreneurial tendencies to varying degrees, with some people having a higher average tendency to manifest them than others (Fleeson & Gallagher, 2009).

In plain terms, this means that people differ in the degree to which they are entrepreneurial, whether they are entrepreneurs, students, politicians, or employees. It also follows that entrepreneurial people—who think, feel, and do things differently—should also produce different output. This output, by the principle of trait activation, should be congruent with their psychological and behavioral tendencies (Motowidlo, Borman, & Schmit, 1997). If one is interested in the understanding and measurement of entrepreneurial behavior and output, therefore, pursuing the framework described in this chapter should be a constructive endeavor.

A number of theoretical and practical implications are engendered by the current framework. First, whilst studying group differences between entrepreneurs and nonentrepreneurs (or more or less successful ones) is useful for a variety of purposes, it is theoretically distinct from the study of enduring tendencies. From a measurement perspective, assessing how entrepreneurial a person is, should involve investigating how they generally think, feel, and behave across situations and over time (Fleeson, 2001). This naturally needs to start with a definition of what entrepreneurial tendencies are, which involves specifying the dimensions to be assessed. In the absence of a taxonomy, here we have suggested a classification based on core conceptual dimensions of entrepreneurship that are widely accepted in the literature and fit within an individual differences framework—namely opportunity recognition, exploitation, and innovation. In principle, however, both theoretical and empirical work is needed to come to a satisfactory taxonomy of entrepreneurial tendencies (even if we cannot expect universal agreement). Importantly, this work needs to investigate the dimensions from a "habitual behavior, thought, and feeling" perspective— not from a "what predicts business creation and success" perspective.

Implications for Entrepreneurship Research

Second, the proposed framework generates a different set of questions and hypotheses for entrepreneurship research. One question, which is of particular interest, is how more-entrepreneurial versus less-entrepreneurial business founders go about the process of business creation and development. In other words, what do entrepreneurial business founders do differently to their less entrepreneurial counterparts, in the pre-launch, launch, and postlaunch phases? What differences do we see in, for instance, ideation, gathering of resources, business planning, strategy, and output? How do different contexts (e.g., industry, region, business policy, national culture etc.) impact behavior and output of people with differing entrepreneurial tendencies? Is being entrepreneurial always a good thing? Can one be too entrepreneurial?

Several research hypotheses can be proposed. For instance, all else being equal, one should expect entrepreneurial business founders to be more focused on innovation and exploring new opportunities (e.g., new products, markets, channels of distribution, financing etc.; e.g., Kickul & Gundry, 2002; Morris & Sexton, 1996), than less-entrepreneurial founders. Accordingly, it would be reasonable to expect there to be differences also in how more- versus less-entrepreneurial business founders react to, or utilize, financial and nonfinancial investments, or the type of support they react to most favorably. For instance, providing larger funding to entrepreneurial founders (all else being equal) may yield a higher risk, but higher potential return strategy, because founders with such tendencies may be more likely to focus on innovation and new opportunities on a continuous and long-term basis. Similarly, one may conjecture that entrepreneurial founders should react more favorably to investors and stakeholders who afford more flexibility with regards to deviations in business trajectories. Finally, they may benefit more from working alongside people who are tolerant of explorative inclinations and more attentive to the executing of their ideas. The above hypotheses roughly correspond to the situational cues and pressures (i.e., task, social, and external/organizational) outlined in the trait activation theory, that may trigger differential responses (i.e., contextual behaviors) from people with differing dispositional tendencies. Finding empirical answers to the above (and related) questions and hypotheses, would appear to be a valuable avenue for future entrepreneurship research.

A second question concerns the extent to which enduring entrepreneurial tendencies can be recognized by alternative means, such as business ideas/plans. For instance, a highly entrepreneurial graduate may have a business idea that is less desirable to potential investors than a less-entrepreneurial graduate's idea. Based on the business plan, investors may opt to support the latter. However, a business idea/plan is an episodic event. As such, it may give limited information as to a founder's propensity to consistently recognize and exploit opportunities, and innovate in the long-term, which is information funding bodies are likely to be interested in.

This further raises the question of how well entrepreneurial tendencies may be captured by other traits that have been shown to predict entrepreneurial success, such as the Big Five. Given that we are conceptually comparing entrepreneurial tendencies to other enduring tendencies (or traits), a relationship is likely. However, as noted earlier, there are likely to be important distinctions. For instance, the Big Five traits that have been related to entrepreneurial success, such as conscientiousness, emotional stability, and extraversion, seem conceptually less related to recognition and exploitation of opportunities. Conscientiousness indicates diligence, reliability, and rule abidance, which would appear almost inversely related to innovative and opportunistic behavior

(Chamorro-Premuzic, 2014). Furthermore, these same traits have been related to general work-related performance (e.g., Barrick & Mount, 1991) which is arguably less to do with recognizing and exploiting opportunities or innovation. Thus, whilst the Big Five traits may be important for performance more generally, there are theoretical, empirical, and practical reasons to make a distinction between entrepreneurial tendencies and the traits that have been found to predict business creation and success. For researchers and practitioners interested in the measurement of entrepreneurial tendencies, therefore, examining these directly (i.e., rather than inferring them by other means), may be necessary. The current framework should hopefully provide guidance for such research efforts.

Implications Beyond Business Creation

Ultimately, however, we believe that research on entrepreneurial tendencies extends beyond entrepreneurs. Accordingly, a set of questions not traditionally tackled within entrepreneurship research may show relevance. For instance, under what conditions (if any) may entrepreneurial people choose to work for incumbent organizations? Which organizational ecosystems do entrepreneurial employees thrive in (and in which do they languish)? What do entrepreneurial employees do and produce differently to non-entrepreneurial employees?

Being an entrepreneur and being entrepreneurial are linguistically so intertwined that the separation has often escaped researchers. Yet, even on a statistical basis, it is improbable that all entrepreneurial people (or even most) will have become entrepreneurs. Indeed, there are convincing theoretical reasons for why they may not. The high likelihood of failure and the low likelihood of innovation raise significant questions as to how entrepreneurial the act of creating a business actually is. Sure, one can confidently assume that the founders of highly innovative and successful start-ups are also highly entrepreneurial. However, highly innovative and successful start-ups are rare (Shane, 2009). On a pure statistical level, therefore, the likelihood of being involved in innovation activity by founding a new venture may plausibly be lower than by strategically joining incumbent organizations or high-growth start-ups founded by others (Teece, 2016).

An interesting avenue for future research, therefore, would be to assess how, when and why, entrepreneurial people may opt for different career choices. This research could be aimed at identifying "enablers" versus "suppressors" of entrepreneurial tendencies, comparing occupations, industries, and organizations on various contextual dimensions. Such academic endeavor would no doubt be useful to institutions that fund and support entrepreneurial start-ups, but also to incumbent organizations that aim to retain and maximize the performance of entrepreneurial employees. It should likewise be advantageous more generally, for making informed career recommendations to individuals with regards to wage employment versus entrepreneurship paths, and the more specific roles and organizations to which they may be most suitable. Based on the arguments presented above, it may not always be appropriate to recommend that an entrepreneurial individual becomes an entrepreneur.

Other Considerations

Due to space limitations, we have had to omit both discussions on a number of other potential variables important for understanding entrepreneurial tendencies and elaboration of suggestions for research design and methodology. Of particular interest is the omission of *ability*. Clearly, discussing and measuring entrepreneurial tendencies must include not only the tendency to recognize and exploit opportunities, and to innovate, but also the ability to do so. Ability is likely to moderate the relationship between general tendencies and specific behavior and, in turn, output. There is an obvious distinction between the tendency to recognize opportunities and the ability to recognize good ones. Furthermore, ability may influence tendency and vice versa (Von Stumm, Hell, Chamorro-Premuzic, 2011). That is, the more able you are, the more likely you are to do it, and the more you do it, the more able you become. Ability, thus, may influence tendency, may moderate the general tendency-specific behavior relationship, and may moderate the specific behavior–output relationship. Although we have not had space to discuss these relationships and influences in detail, research clearly needs to account for them (along with other personal and external variables).

Existing and Future Research

We hope that the theoretical premises presented in this chapter inspire research on entrepreneurial tendencies considered within an individual differences framework. This may include applications of research designs beyond group differences, measurement of behavior and output beyond business creation and success, looking at new measurement methods of entrepreneurial tendencies (or applying existing ones in new ways), and testing additional hypotheses. Some of our own research has begun to investigate some of the propositions presented above. For instance, confirming the views discussed, our research suggests that entrepreneurial tendencies are distinct to the Big Five personality traits (Leutner, Ahmetoglu, & Chamorro-Premuzic, 2014), as well as a number of other established psychological constructs (see Ahmetoglu, 2015). Importantly, these entrepreneurial tendencies have been found to incrementally predict both specific entrepreneurial behavior (e.g., implementing new methods or changing organizational procedures to accomplish tasks, organizing events to generate alternative revenue, etc.), as well as output (e.g., patents registered, inventions sold, number of new products and services introduced, etc.) across contexts—whether the sample is entrepreneurs, employees, or students (Ahmetoglu et al., 2011; Ahmetoglu, Harding, Akhtar, & Chamorro-Premuzic, 2015; Akhtar, Ahmetoglu, & Chamorro-Premuzic, 2013; Almeida, Ahmetoglu, & Chamorro-Premuzic, 2014; Leutner et al., 2014). Confirming the importance of context, a recent study also showed that entrepreneurial employees are far more likely to feel engaged, and in turn generate entrepreneurial output, when they are in organizations characterized by innovative, as opposed to bureaucratic, cultures, where culture differences had little impact on the output of less-entrepreneurial employees (Akhtar, Ahmetoglu, Tsivrikos, & Chamorro-Premuzic, in press).

This preliminary research appears to support the hypotheses presented in this chapter. Needless to say, a lot more work is needed to get a thorough understanding of the interplay between enduring entrepreneurial tendencies, context-specific behaviors, output, and contextual moderators. In our view, research methodologies that move beyond self-reports to include other reports, records of actual behavior, records of actual output, experience sampling methods, and experimental as well as longitudinal research seem the most obvious avenues for such endeavors.

Conclusion

Fundamentally, we hope that the propositions presented in this chapter demonstrate that the distinction between entrepreneurial tendencies and the tendencies of entrepreneurs is a useful one to make. From an academic standpoint, this framework should hopefully encourage more research on entrepreneurial individuals, identified based on their general and enduring psychological and behavioral tendencies, rather than on their intentions to become, or already to be, entrepreneurs. From a practical perspective, the ability to identify and correctly manage entrepreneurial individuals who recognize and exploit new opportunities, and who innovate, may be a highly fruitful endeavor, not only on an individual, but also on an organizational and perhaps regional level. In our view, a more comprehensive and theoretically coherent framework for understanding and identifying such individuals is a necessary starting point.

References

Ahadi, S., & Diener, E. (1989). Multiple determinants and effect size. *Journal of Personality and Social Psychology, 56*(3), 398.

Ahmetoglu, G. (2015). *The entrepreneurial personality: A new framework and construct for entrepreneurship research and practice* (Doctoral dissertation, Goldsmiths, University of London). Retrieved from http://research.gold.ac.uk/11249/1/IMS_thesis_AhmetogluG_2015.pdf

Ahmetoglu, G., Harding, X., Akhtar, R., & Chamorro-Premuzic, T. (2015). Predictors of creative achievement: Assessing the impact of entrepreneurial potential, perfectionism, and employee engagement. *Creativity Research Journal, 27*(2), 198–205.

Ahmetoglu, G., Leutner, F., & Chamorro-Premuzic, T. (2011). EQ-nomics: Understanding the relationship between individual differences in trait emotional intelligence and entrepreneurship. *Personality and Individual Differences, 51*(8), 1028–1033.

Akhtar, R., Ahmetoglu, G., & Chamorro-Premuzic, T. (2013). Greed is good? Assessing the relationship between entrepreneurship and subclinical psychopathy. *Personality and Individual Differences, 54*(3), 420–425.

Akhtar, R., Ahmetoglu, G., & Chamorro-Premuzic, T. (in press). How to create an entrepreneurial organization. *Consulting Psychology Journal.*

Aldrich, H. (1999). *Organizations evolving.* London, England: Sage.

Almeida, P. I., Ahmetoglu, G., & Chamorro-Premuzic, T. (2014). Who wants to be an entrepreneur? The relationship between vocational interests and individual differences in entrepreneurship. *Journal of Career Assessment, 22*(1), 102–112.

Baron, R. A., & Henry, R. A. (2010). How entrepreneurs acquire the capacity to excel: Insights from research on expert performance. *Strategic Entrepreneurship Journal, 4*(1), 49–65.

Barrick, M. R., & Mount, M. K. (1991). The Big Five personality dimensions and job performance: A meta-analysis. *Personnel Psychology, 44*(1), 1–26.

Baum, J. R., Frese, M., Baron, R. A., & Katz, J. A. (2007). Entrepreneurship as an area of psychology study: An introduction. In J. R. Baum, M. Frese, & R. Baron (Eds), *The psychology of entrepreneurship* (pp. 1–18). Mahwah, NJ: Erlbaum.

Baum, W. M. (2002). From molecular to molar: A paradigm shift in behavior analysis. *Journal of the Experimental Analysis of Behavior, 78*(1), 95–116.

Bird, B., Schjoedt, L., & Baum, J. R. (2012). Editor's introduction. Entrepreneurs' behavior: Elucidation and measurement. *Entrepreneurship Theory and Practice, 36*(5), 889–913.

Brandstätter, H. (2011). Personality aspects of entrepreneurship: A look at five meta-analyses. *Personality and Individual differences, 51*(3), 222–230.

Butcher, J. N., Dahlstrom, W. G., Graham, J. R., Tellegen, A., & Kaemmer, B. (1989). *MMPI-2: Manual for administration and scoring.* Minneapolis: University of Minnesota Press.

Carson, S. H., Peterson, J. B., & Higgins, D. M. (2005). Reliability, validity, and factor structure of the creative achievement questionnaire. *Creativity Research Journal, 17*(1), 37–50.

Chamorro-Premuzic, T. (2014). *Personality and individual differences* (3rd ed.). West Sussex, England: Wiley-Blackwell.

Chell, E. (2008). *The entrepreneurial personality: A social construction* (2nd ed.). New York, NY: Routledge.

Collins, C. J., Hanges, P. J., & Locke, E. A. (2004). The relationship of achievement motivation to entrepreneurial behavior: A meta-analysis. *Human Performance, 17*(1), 95–117.

Costa, P. T., & Widiger, T. A. (2002). *Personality disorders and the five-factor model of personality* (2nd ed.). Washington, DC: American Psychological Association.

Crossan, M. M., & Apaydin, M. (2010). A multi-dimensional framework of organizational innovation: A systematic review of the literature. *Journal of Management Studies, 47*(6), 1154–1191.

De Jong, J., & Den Hartog, D. (2010). Measuring innovative work behaviour. *Creativity and Innovation Management, 19*(1), 23–36.

Eckhardt, J. T., & Shane, S. A. (2003). Opportunities and entrepreneurship. *Journal of Management, 29*(3), 333–349.

Eysenck, H. J. (1990). Biological dimensions of personality. In L. A. Pervin (Ed.), *Handbook of personality: Theory and research* (pp. 244–276). New York, NY: Guilford.

Fleeson, W. (2001). Toward a structure-and process-integrated view of personality: Traits as density distributions of states. *Journal of Personality and Social Psychology, 80*(6), 1011–1027.

Fleeson, W., & Gallagher, P. (2009). The implications of Big Five standing for the distribution of trait manifestation in behavior: Fifteen experience-sampling studies and a meta-analysis. *Journal of Personality and Social Psychology, 97*(6), 1097–1114.

Furnham, A., & Steele, H. (1993). Measuring locus of control: A critique of general, children's, health- and work-related locus of control questionnaires. *British Journal of Psychology, 84*(4), 443–479.

Gartner, W. B. (1989). Some suggestions for research on entrepreneurial traits and characteristics. *Entrepreneurship Theory and Practice, 14*(1), 27–38.

Hisrich, R., Langan-Fox, J., & Grant, S. (2007). Entrepreneurship research and practice: A call to action for psychology. *American Psychologist, 62*(6), 575–589.

Hogan, J., & Holland, B. (2003). Using theory to evaluate personality and job–performance relations: A socioanalytic perspective. *Journal of Applied Psychology, 88*(1), 100–112.

Kaish, S., & Gilad, B. (1991). Characteristics of opportunities search of entrepreneurs versus executives: Sources, interests, general alertness. *Journal of Business Venturing*, 6(1), 45–61.

Kickul, J., & Gundry, L. (2002). Prospecting for strategic advantage: The proactive entrepreneurial personality and small firm innovation. *Journal of Small Business Management*, 40(2), 85–97.

Kirton, M. (1976). Adaptors and innovators: A description and measure. *Journal of Applied Psychology*, 61(5), 622–629.

Kirzner, I. M. (1997). Entrepreneurial discovery and the competitive market process: An Austrian approach. *Journal of Economic Literature*, 35(1), 60–85.

Kring, A., Johnson, S., Davison, G. C., & Neale, J. M. (2010). *Abnormal psychology*. Hoboken, NJ: Wiley.

Langkamp Bolton, D., & Lane, M. D. (2012). Individual entrepreneurial orientation: Development of a measurement instrument. *Education+ Training*, 54(2/3), 219–233.

Lazear, E. P. (2002). *Entrepreneurship* (NBER Working Paper No. 9109), Cambridge, MA: National Bureau of Economic Research.

Leutner, F., Ahmetoglu, G., Akhtar, R., & Chamorro-Premuzic, T. (2014). The relationship between the entrepreneurial personality and the Big Five personality traits. *Personality and Individual Differences*, 63, 58–63.

Lumpkin, G. T., & Dess, G. G. (1996). Clarifying the entrepreneurial orientation construct and linking it to performance. *Academy of Management Review*, 21(1), 135–172.

Matthews, G., Deary, I. J., & Whiteman, M. C. (2009). *Personality traits* (3rd ed.). Cambridge, England: Cambridge University Press.

McClelland, D. C. (1961). *The achievement society*. Princeton, NJ: Van Nostrand.

McKenzie, B., Ugbah, S. D., & Smothers, N. (2007). "Who is an entrepreneur?" Is it still the wrong question? *Academy of Entrepreneurship Journal*, 13(1), 23–43.

Monson, T. C., Hesley, J. W., & Chernick, L. (1982). Specifying when personality traits can and cannot predict behavior: An alternative to abandoning the attempt to predict single-act criteria. *Journal of Personality and Social Psychology*, 43(2), 385.

Morgenson, F. P., Campion, M. A., Dipboye, R. L., Hollenbeck, J. R., Murphy, K., & Schmitt, N. (2007) Reconsidering the use of personality tests in personnel selection contexts. *Personnel Psychology*, 60(3), 683–729.

Morris, M. H., & Sexton, D. L. (1996). The concept of entrepreneurial intensity: Implications for company performance. *Journal of Business Research*, 36(1), 5–13.

Motowidlo, S. J., Borman, W. C., & Schmit, M. J. (1997). A theory of individual differences in task and contextual performance. *Human Performance*, 10, 71–83.

Murray, H. A. (1943). *Thematic Apperception Test*. Cambridge, MA: Harvard University Press.

O'Reilly, C. A., Chatman, J., & Caldwell, D. F. (1991). People and organizational culture: A profile comparison approach to assessing person-organization fit. *Academy of Management Journal*, 34(3), 487–516.

Ones, D. S., & Viswesvaran, C. (2011). Individual differences at work. In T. Chamorro-Premuzic, S. von Stumm, & A. Furnham (Eds), *The Wiley-Blackwell handbook of individual differences* (pp. 379–407). West Sussex, England: Wiley-Blackwell.

Ozer, D. J. (1999). Four principles for personality assessment. In L. A. Pervin & O. P. John (Eds.), *Handbook of personality: Theory and research* (2nd ed., pp. 671–686). New York, NY: Guilford

Pervin, L. A., & Cervone, D. (2010). *Personality: Theory and research* (11th ed.). Hoboken, NJ: Wiley.

Petrides, K. V., & Furnham, A. (2001). Trait emotional intelligence: Psychometric investigation with reference to established trait taxonomies. *European Journal of Personality, 15*(6), 425–448.

Quirk, S. W., Christiansen, N. D., Wagner, S. H., & McNulty, J. L. (2003). On the usefulness of measures of normal personality for clinical assessment: Evidence of the incremental validity of the Revised NEO Personality Inventory. *Psychological Assessment, 15*(3), 311–325.

Rauch, A., & Frese, M. (2007). Let's put the person back into entrepreneurship research: A meta-analysis on the relationship between business owners' personality traits, business creation, and success. *European Journal of Work and Organizational Psychology, 16*(4), 353–385.

Revelle, W., Wilt, J., & Condon, D. (2011). Individual differences and differential psychology: A brief history and prospect. In T. Chamorro-Premuzic, A. Furnham, & S. von Stumm (Eds.), *Handbook of individual differences* (pp. 3–38). Oxford, England: Wiley-Blackwell.

Reynolds, P. D. (1997). Who starts new firms? –Preliminary explorations of firms-in-gestation. *Small Business Economics, 9*(5), 449–462.

Reynolds, P. D. (2005). *Entrepreneurship in the United States: 2004 assessment*. Miami, FL: Florida International University, Pino Global Entrepreneurship Center.

Reynolds, P. D. (2007). New firm creation in the US: A PSED overview. *Foundations and trends in entrepreneurship, 3*(1), 1–151.

Reynolds, P. D., Bygrave, W. D., & Autio, E. (2004). *Global Entrepreneurship Monitor 2003 executive report*. Babson Park, MA: Babson College.

Roberts, B. W., & DelVecchio, W. F. (2000). The rank-order consistency of personality traits from childhood to old age: A quantitative review of longitudinal studies. *Psychological bulletin, 126*(1), 3–25.

Roberts, B. W., Kuncel, N. R., Shiner, R., Caspi, A., & Goldberg, L. R. (2007). The power of personality: The comparative validity of personality traits, socioeconomic status, and cognitive ability for predicting important life outcomes. *Perspectives on Psychological Science, 2*(4), 313–345.

Rotter, J. B. (1954). *Social learning and clinical psychology*. Englewood Cliffs, NJ: Prentice-Hall.

Schneider, B. (1987). The people make the place. *Personnel Psychology, 40*(3), 437–453.

Schumpeter, J. A. (1934). *The theory of economic development: An inquiry into profits, capital, credit, interest, and the business cycle*. New Brunswick, NJ: Transaction.

Scott, S. G., & Bruce, R. A. (1994). Determinants of innovative behavior: A path model of individual innovation in the workplace. *Academy of Management Journal, 37*(3), 580–607.

Shane, S. A. (2008). *The illusions of entrepreneurship: The costly myths that entrepreneurs, investors, and policy makers live by*. New Haven, CT: Yale University Press.

Shane, S. (2009). Why encouraging more people to become entrepreneurs is bad public policy. *Small Business Economics, 33*(2), 141–149.

Shane, S., & Venkataraman, S. (2000). The promise of entrepreneurship as a field of research. *Academy of Management Review, 25*(1), 217–226.

Silvia, P. J., Wigert, B., Reiter-Palmon, R., & Kaufman, J. C. (2012). Assessing creativity with self-report scales: A review and empirical evaluation. *Psychology of Aesthetics, Creativity, and the Arts, 6*(1), 19–34.

Stanworth, J., & Kaufmann, P. (1996). Similarities and differences in UK and US franchise research data: Towards a dynamic model of franchisee motivation. *International Small Business Journal, 14*(3), 57–70.

Stewart Jr, W. H., & Roth, P. L. (2001). Risk propensity differences between entrepreneurs and managers: A meta-analytic review. *Journal of Applied Psychology, 86*(1), 145–153.

Stewart Jr, W. H., & Roth, P. L. (2007). A meta-analysis of achievement motivation differences between entrepreneurs and managers. *Journal of Small Business Management, 45*(4), 401–421.

Taylor, M. P. (1999). Survival of the fittest? An analysis of self-employment duration in Britain. *The Economic Journal, 109*(454), 140–155.

Teece, D. J. (2016). Dynamic capabilities and entrepreneurial management in large organizations: Toward a theory of the (entrepreneurial) firm. *European Economic Review, 86*, 202–216.

Tett, R. P., & Burnett, D. D. (2003). A personality trait-based interactionist model of job performance. *Journal of Applied Psychology, 88*(3), 500–517.

Tett, R. P., & Guterman, H. A. (2000). Situation trait relevance, trait expression, and cross-situational consistency: Testing a principle of trait activation. *Journal of Research in Personality, 34*(4), 397–423.

Uusitalo, R. (2001). Homo entreprenaurus? *Applied Economics, 33*(13), 1631–1638.

van Praag, C. M. (2003). Business survival and success of young small business owners. *Small Business Economics, 21*(1), 1–17.

Von Stumm, S., Hell, B., & Chamorro-Premuzic, T. (2011). The hungry mind: Intellectual curiosity is the third pillar of academic performance. *Perspectives on Psychological Science, 6*(6), 574–588

Zhao, H., & Seibert, S. E. (2006). The Big Five personality dimensions and entrepreneurial status: A meta-analytical review. *Journal of Applied Psychology, 91*(2), 259–271.

Zhao, H., Seibert, S. E., & Lumpkin, G. T. (2010). The relationship of personality to entrepreneurial intentions and performance: A meta-analytic review. *Journal of Management, 36*(2), 381–404.

Section 2

The Individual: Psychology of Entrepreneurship

2a: Genetics of Entrepreneurship

12

Biology and Entrepreneurship

Ahmed Nofal, Nicos Nicolaou, and Noni Symeonidou[a]

[a] *University of Warwick, UK*

Introduction

Does biology matter for entrepreneurship? Over the past six decades, researchers have examined various factors that influence the tendency of people to engage in entrepreneurship including individual attributes (Baron, 2008; Cardon & Kirk, 2015; Simon, Houghton, & Aquino, 2000), contextual factors (Parker & van Praag, 2012; Zahra, Sapienza, & Davidsson, 2006), and industry characteristics (Shane, 2003). However, this rich literature has provided incomplete explanations about the drivers of entrepreneurship.

As biology influences many organizational phenotypes (Arvey, Li, & Wang, 2016; Song, Li, & Wang, 2015), researchers have suggested that this incompleteness may be due to the lack of research on the biological aspects of entrepreneurship (Nicolaou, Shane, Cherkas, Hunkin, & Spector, 2008; White, Thornhill, & Hampson, 2006). Recent research has therefore started examining the role of biological factors in influencing key entrepreneurial phenotypes such as the tendency to engage in entrepreneurship (Nicolaou, Shane, Cherkas, Hunkin, et al., 2008), opportunity recognition (Shane & Nicolaou, 2015b; Shane, Nicolaou, Cherkas, & Spector, 2010a), entrepreneurial intention (Nicolaou & Shane, 2010) and entrepreneurial performance (Shane & Nicolaou, 2013). This research emphasizes that although biology may *influence* entrepreneurship it does not *determine* who becomes an entrepreneur (Nicolaou, Shane, Cherkas, Hunkin, et al., 2008; Shane & Nicolaou, 2015a).

In this chapter, we discuss the role that biology plays in entrepreneurship. Specifically, we examine how genetics, hormones, physiology, and neuroscience may affect entrepreneurial phenotypes. Fueled by recent evidence, we also investigate how biological factors may interact and correlate with environmental factors to influence entrepreneurship. Finally, we discuss some future research avenues for entrepreneurship scholars interested in the biological perspective.

The Wiley Handbook of Entrepreneurship, First Edition.
Edited by Gorkan Ahmetoglu, Tomas Chamorro-Premuzic, Bailey Klinger, & Tessa Karcisky.
© 2017 John Wiley & Sons Ltd. Published 2017 by John Wiley & Sons Ltd.

Genetics and Entrepreneurship

Entrepreneurship researchers have investigated the influence of genetic factors in entrepreneurship (Nicolaou & Shane, 2009). This strand of research has dominated studies on biological factors in entrepreneurship. There are two main approaches that examine the influence of genetics on entrepreneurship: (1) quantitative genetics and (2) molecular genetics (Plomin, DeFries, Knopik, & Neiderhiser, 2012). We examine these approaches in turn.

Quantitative Genetics in Entrepreneurship

The quantitative genetics approach enables scholars to examine the broad heritability of entrepreneurial phenotypes. It uses the natural experiment of twins and adoptees to examine whether the variable of interest has a genetic component (Plomin et al., 2012). Twin studies compare the resemblance within monozygotic twins to the resemblance within dizygotic twins to investigate whether a phenotype is heritable.[1] Because monozygotic twins share 100% of their genes, unlike dizygotic twins who share on average 50% of their genes, a larger correlation between monozygotic than dizygotic twins in entrepreneurship would suggest that entrepreneurship is heritable (Nicolaou, Shane, Cherkas, Hunkin, et al., 2008). Indeed, twin studies have suggested that several entrepreneurial phenotypes are heritable such as self-employment (Shane, Nicolaou, Cherkas, & Spector, 2010b), opportunity recognition (Nicolaou, Shane, Cherkas, & Spector, 2009), and entrepreneurial performance (Shane & Nicolaou, 2013).

Adoption studies can also inform scholars about the heritability of entrepreneurial phenotypes by observing the resemblance between adopted children and both their biological and adoptive parents (Plomin et al., 2012). A similarity between an adopted child and adoptive parents would indicate that common environmental factors influence this entrepreneurial phenotype. Meanwhile, a similarity between an adopted child and biological parents would suggest that shared genes play a role in influencing this entrepreneurial phenotype. Empirical evidence on adoptees has also indicated that the tendency to engage in entrepreneurship is heritable (Lindquist, Sol, & Praag, 2015).

Tendency to Engage in Entrepreneurship

The tendency to engage in entrepreneurship is the most studied phenotype in the biological perspective in entrepreneurship. Empirical research has repeatedly shown that genetic factors influence individuals' propensities to engage in entrepreneurship. Nicolaou, Shane, Cherkas, Hunkin et al. (2008) used a sample of 870 monozygotic and 857 dizygotic twins and found that the tendency to engage in entrepreneurship is partly genetic. Schermer, Johnson, Jang, and Vernon (2015) provided recent evidence of the heritability of the tendency to engage in entrepreneurship. Lindquist et al. (2015), using a sample of adoptees, found that the tendency to engage in entrepreneurship has a genetic component.

Although researchers have shown that genes influence the tendency of people to engage in entrepreneurship, a direct effect of genes on any entrepreneurial phenotype

---

[1] Monozygotic twins are formed when one sperm fertilizes one egg, while dizygotic twins are formed when two sperms fertilize two different eggs.

remains highly unlikely (Shane & Nicolaou, 2015a). Nicolaou and Shane (2009) have presented four main mechanisms through which genes may influence entrepreneurship. First, genes may influence the tendency of people to engage in entrepreneurship through stimulating physiological effects. Second, genes may influence the tendency to engage in entrepreneurship through contributing to the covariance between individual attributes and entrepreneurship. Third, genes may influence the tendency to engage in entrepreneurship through gene x environment interactions. Fourth, genes may influence the tendency to engage in entrepreneurship through gene x environment correlations. We examine these in turn.

Genetic Influences on Physiology

The influence of genetic factors on the tendency of people to engage in entrepreneurship may be through physiological effects. These physiological effects may include factors such as physical appearance, hormones, and brain function (Arvey et al., 2016; Shane & Nicolaou, 2015a). For example, people tend to rate attractive looking entrepreneurs more favorably than less attractive entrepreneurs (Baron, Markman, & Bollinger, 2006). Because genetic factors affect people's physical appearance, researchers have suggested that genes may influence the tendency of people to engage in entrepreneurship through physical appearance (Shane & Nicolaou, 2015b).

Individual differences in hormones have also been linked to the tendency to engage in entrepreneurship. For instance, testosterone—an inherited androgen hormone formed in the testes of males, ovaries of females, and the adrenal glands of both males and females—has been associated with the tendency of people to engage in entrepreneurship (White et al., 2006). Thus, it is likely that genes may influence the tendency of people to engage in entrepreneurship through excretion of hormones such as testosterone. In a similar way, genes may trigger neurodevelopmental changes that influence the tendency of people toward entrepreneurship (Shane & Nicolaou, 2015b). In this regard, research has shown that Attention Deficit Hyperactivity Disorder (ADHD)[2] is associated with entrepreneurial orientation (Thurik, Khedhaouria, Torrès, & Verheul, 2016), actions and outcomes (Wiklund, Patzelt, & Dimov, 2016). Because genetic factors influence the tendency of people to have ADHD, researchers have suggested that genes may influence the tendency of people to engage in entrepreneurship through ADHD (Shane & Nicolaou, 2015a).

Genetic Covariation with Individual Attributes

Genetic factors may also predispose people to develop individual attributes that affect their tendency to engage in entrepreneurship (Nicolaou & Shane, 2009; Shane & Nicolaou, 2015b). Although it is plausible that genetic factors may influence entrepreneurial phenotypes through cognitive factors, attitudes, skills, and abilities, genetic studies have only examined the covariation between psychological traits and entrepreneurial phenotypes. For example, research into the heritability of the tendency to engage in entrepreneurship has shown that sensation seeking (Nicolaou, Shane, Cherkas, & Spector, 2008), extraversion (Shane et al., 2010b; Zhang et al., 2009), neuroticism (Zhang et al., 2009), openness to experience (Shane et al., 2010b) and creativity

---

[2] ADHD is a neurodevelopmental psychological disorder characterized by lack of focus, impulsivity, and hyperactivity (Wiklund, Patzelt, & Dimov, 2016).

(Shane & Nicolaou, 2015b) mediate the relationship between genes and the tendency of people to engage in entrepreneurship.

Gene X Environment Interactions

There is also evidence that genetic and environmental factors may interact to influence the tendency of people to engage in entrepreneurship. Researchers have labeled this mechanism gene X environment interaction (Nicolaou & Shane, 2009; Shane & Nicolaou, 2015b). Plomin, DeFries, and Loehlin (1977) explained that genetic factors may be sensitive to some environments, where an individual with a certain gene may react differently to a environmental stimulus than a person without that gene. For instance, Zhang and Ilies (2010) found that unfavorable family environments during childhood decreased the genetic influence on the tendency of people to engage in entrepreneurship during adulthood. In a similar way, Quaye, Nicolaou, Shane, and Harris (2012) indicated that education may moderate the relationship between genetic factors and the tendency to engage in entrepreneurship. Specifically, the authors suggested that dyslexia genes interact with education to influence the tendency of people to engage in entrepreneurship.

Gene X Environment Correlations

Together with gene X environment interactions, gene X environment correlations reveal the interplaying nature of genetic and environmental factors (Plomin et al., 2012; Plomin et al., 1977). Researchers have presented three types of gene X environment correlation: (1) passive, (2) evocative, and (3) active gene-environment correlation (Plomin et al., 2012; Plomin et al., 1977). Passive gene X environment correlations occur when individuals passively inherit environments that are correlated with their genetic predispositions in the sense that individuals tend to provide their genetically related offspring particular environments that are compatible with their genetic makeup (Nicolaou & Shane, 2009). Evocative gene-environment correlations occur when the surrounding environment tends to select individuals based on their genetic makeup (Nicolaou & Shane, 2009). Active gene-environment correlations suggest that individuals may select or establish environments that match their genetic composition so that their genetic and environmental makeup become compatible (Nicolaou & Shane, 2009).

Opportunity Recognition

Opportunity recognition is the hallmark of entrepreneurship (Shane & Venkataraman, 2000; Short, Ketchen, Shook, & Ireland, 2010). Accordingly, research has investigated whether opportunity recognition is heritable. Empirical evidence has shown that genetic factors may influence the tendency of people to recognize opportunities. Using a sample of 851 and 855 pairs of monozygotic and dizygotic twins respectively, Nicolaou, Shane, Cherkas, et al. (2009) found that genetic factors influence the tendency of people to recognize opportunities. They also found that genetic factors account for part of the covariance between opportunity recognition and the tendency to engage in entrepreneurship, such that genes may affect the tendency of people to engage in entrepreneurship through influencing the tendency to recognize opportunities.

Entrepreneurial Intention

Research has also shown that entrepreneurial intention is partly genetic. Nicolaou and Shane (2010) found that entrepreneurial intention has a genetic component and that common genes influenced entrepreneurial intention and the tendency to engage in entrepreneurship.

Entrepreneurial Performance

Research has also found evidence of the heritability of entrepreneurial performance. In a study of genetic covariation with individual differences, Shane and Nicolaou (2013) found that genetic factors influence entrepreneurial performance through three of the Big Five personality traits: (1) agreeableness, (2) openness to experience, and (3) extraversion.

Although a quantitative genetics approach allowed researchers to understand a significant part of the variance of many of entrepreneurial phenotypes, it does not identify any specific genetic polymorphisms associated with these phenotypes. We next discuss how to identify particular genes that may influence entrepreneurship.

Molecular Genetics in Entrepreneurship

What are the genetic polymorphisms that influence entrepreneurial phenotypes? The molecular genetics approach has delivered new insights into the genetic architecture of complex phenotypes. To identify which genes influence complex phenotypes, molecular genetics studies have followed two main pathways: (1) linkage and (2) association studies (Plomin et al., 2012). The former compares the polymorphic genetic markers among family members who share common phenotypes. If common genetic markers are detected, researchers may postulate that these genes influence the common phenotypes. Association studies compare a sample that possesses a particular phenotype to another control sample to identify whether there are differences between the two samples in terms of DNA markers. If researchers were to find that there is a difference between genetic markers across the two samples, they would be able to suggest plausible associations between genes and the phenotypes in question.

Although linkage studies can systematically detect single-gene disorders, they are less powerful than association studies in locating small effect size genes expected for most complex behavioral patterns (Plomin et al., 2012). As entrepreneurship is a complex phenomenon (Aldrich & Martinez, 2001) a focus on association studies is more relevant for examining the polygenic nature of entrepreneurial phenotypes (Nicolaou & Shane, 2009). Associations studies use two main methods: (1) candidate-gene and (2) genome-wide association studies (GWAS) (Plomin et al., 2012).

Candidate-Gene Studies

The candidate-gene method proposes that a particular gene may influence a phenotype based on its function (Plomin et al., 2012). By having insights into candidate genes that play a role in the etiology of certain disorders, the excretion of hormones, and the stimulation of physiological and neural factors, researchers may generate hypotheses about plausible relationships between these candidate genes and entrepreneurial phenotypes (Song et al., 2015). The guiding logic is based on the potential relationships between the functions of these genes and the phenotypes being examined. For example, based on their role in activating dopamine and serotonin hormones which have been associated with various organizational behaviors, Song, Li, and Arvey (2011) examined the influence of the dopamine receptor gene "DRD4 VNTR 7R" and the serotonin transporter gene "5-HTTLPR" on job satisfaction. They found a significant association between the two candidate genes and job satisfaction. In entrepreneurship, Nicolaou, Shane, Adi, Mangino, and Harris (2011) examined the influence of five dopamine receptor genes and four ADHD-related genes on the tendency to engage in entrepreneurship; they reported a significant association between the rs1486011 marker of the DRD3 gene and the tendency of people to engage in entrepreneurship. In another study, Wernerfelt, Rand, Dreber, Montgomery, and Malhotra (2012) examined the association between the tendency of people to engage in serial entrepreneurship and (1) the long-repeat genotype of the RS3 microsatellite in the arginine vasopressin 1a receptor promoter region (AVPR1a), (2) the 7- repeat genotype of the dopamine D4 receptor (DRD4), and (3) the low-activity Monoamine Oxidase A (MAOA) genotypes. Results showed that the long-repeat polymorphism of the RS3 microsatellite in the AVPR1a gene is associated with the tendency to engage in serial entrepreneurship. In a gene X environment interaction study, Quaye, Nicolaou, Shane, and Harris (2012) examined whether education and dyslexia genes, specifically ROBO1, KIAA0319, DCDC2 and DYX1C1, interact to influence the tendency to engage in entrepreneurship. Despite the presence of significant interactions between three dyslexia genes (ROBO1, KIAA0319, and DCDC2) and education on entrepreneurship, the authors indicated that all associations became insignificant after conducting Bonferroni corrections.

Candidate-gene methodology, in general, has achieved remarkable success in linkage studies (Plomin et al., 2012). But this method has been subject to the criticism that many candidate-gene studies have not been replicated (Johnson, 2009; van der Loos et al., 2011). Furthermore, behavioral geneticists believe that current knowledge is insufficient to predict functional candidate genes (Tabor, Risch, & Myers, 2002). Recently, researchers have developed an alternative method—genome-wide association study (GWAS) design—to identify which genes influence phenotypes, that overcomes many of the problems of the candidate-gene approach.

Genome-Wide Association Studies (GWAS)
GWAS methodology uses microarrays to genotype millions of single nucleotide polymorphisms (SNPs) on a small chip, thus locating genes with very small effect sizes (Plomin et al., 2012). The key advantage of GWAS methodology over candidate-gene methods is that GWAS methodology checks the entire genome in a hypothesis-free gene-agnostic approach (Yeo, 2011). Because GWAS have improved our understanding of the genetic architecture of numerous complex phenotypes (McCarthy et al., 2008), entrepreneurship researchers have urged scholars to adopt GWAS methodology rather than candidate-gene method to examine the genetic basis of entrepreneurial phenotypes (Koellinger et al., 2010).

GWAS of entrepreneurship have provided evidence of an association between the rs10791283 polymorphism of the OPCML gene on chromosome 11q25 with the tendency to engage in entrepreneurship at a 6×10^{-7} significance level (Quaye, Nicolaou, Shane, & Massimo, 2012). This was short of the 10^{-8} level that is usually considered adequate for genome-wide significance. van der Loos et al. (2013b) also failed to find any significant associations at the genome-wide level, but suggested that their findings are consistent with the polygenic nature of genes, such that a strong influence of a single gene on any entrepreneurial phenotype is highly unlikely.

Hormones in Entrepreneurship

The second strand of research on the biological perspective has examined the influence of hormones, with testosterone, dopamine, oxytocin, serotonin, cortisol, and progesterone receiving greater attention than other hormones in research on management (see Narayanan & Prasad, 2015). Hormones "shape behaviours by altering neural circuitry and we can simply monitor hormone levels and then associate these levels with various different behaviours" (Neave, 2007, p.51). Entrepreneurship research has only investigated the influence of testosterone on entrepreneurial phenotypes.

As previously mentioned, testosterone is an androgen hormone formed in the testes of males, ovaries of females, and the adrenal glands of both males and females (Shane & Nicolaou, 2015b; White et al., 2006). It varies from childhood to adulthood, from males to females, and from one season to another. Research has indicated that salivary testosterone influences the tendency of people to engage in entrepreneurship (Shane & Nicolaou, 2015b; White et al., 2006). White et al. (2006) suggested that individuals with higher testosterone level are more likely to take greater risks and are thus more likely to engage in entrepreneurship. van der Loos et al. (2013a) have also examined the association between serum testosterone and the tendency to engage in entrepreneurship. However, their results failed to report any significant associations. In a larger scale study, Greene, Han, Martin, Zhang, and Wittert (2014) suggested that potential omitted variable bias and reverse causality may distort results in studies that examine the association between testosterone levels and entrepreneurial tendencies. Accordingly, they used insulin as an instrumental variable to examine the influence of serum testosterone levels on the tendency toward entrepreneurship. They showed that there is an association between serum testosterone levels and the tendency to engage in entrepreneurship. In a forthcoming paper, using samples from the National Health and Nutrition Examination Surveys (NHANES), Understanding Society's Innovation Panel 6 (IP6), and the National Survey of Midlife Development (MIDUS I), Nicolaou, Patel, and Wolfe (2017) found that there is a positive influence of testosterone on the tendency of people to engage in entrepreneurship.

Bönte, Procher, and Urbig (2015) also examined the association between prenatal testosterone exposure and entrepreneurial intention. To measure prenatal testosterone exposure, the authors used the ratio of the length of the index finger to the length of the ring finger—a method called 2D:4D proxy. Lower ratios would indicate higher testosterone levels and vice versa. In addition to the direct influence of prenatal testosterone exposure on entrepreneurial intention, findings suggested that two stage factors, (1) general risk-taking and (2) domain-specific risk-taking, mediate part of the relationship between prenatal testosterone exposure and entrepreneurial intention respectively.

In addition to the tendency to engage in entrepreneurship and entrepreneurial intention, researchers found that commitment to strategic goals and entrepreneurial performance may be enhanced by hormonal changes. Research has shown that there is an association between entrepreneurial performance and commitment to strategic goals on one hand and 2D:4D prenatal testosterone levels on the other hand (Trahms, Coombs, & Barrick, 2010). In another recent study, Unger, Rauch, Weis, and Frese (2015) indicated that hormones may interact with other factors to influence entrepreneurial phenotypes. The authors found evidence of the interactive effect of prenatal testosterone and need for achievement on entrepreneurial success.

Physiology in Entrepreneurship

The third stream of research on the biological perspective in entrepreneurship examines the associations between physiology and entrepreneurial phenotypes. As indicated earlier, recent findings indicated that ADHD may be related to the tendency of individuals to engage in entrepreneurially oriented behaviors (Thurik et al., 2016). Further research also suggested that ADHD influences the tendency of people to engage and succeed in entrepreneurial actions (Wiklund et al., 2016). The authors indicated that impulsivity influences the tendency of people to engage in entrepreneurship, while, hyperactivity influences the consequence of these entrepreneurial actions. Other research has also, as discussed above, indicated that people perceive attractive looking entrepreneurs more favorably than non-attractive ones (Baron et al., 2006).

Furthermore, researchers have also suggested that dyslexics have a higher tendency to engage in entrepreneurship than their counterparts (Shane & Nicolaou, 2015b). Using a sample drawn from the US and the UK, Logan (2009) found that there is a positive association between dyslexia and the tendency of people to engage in entrepreneurship. The author also indicated that dyslexic entrepreneurs tend to be more comfortable in start-up and serial entrepreneurship activities.

While entrepreneurship research on physiology has been limited, other management areas have provided further studies on the role of physiology in organizational contexts (Chase, 1967; Shane & Nicolaou, 2015a). For example, Ilies, Dimotakis, and De Pater (2010) indicated that high blood pressure is associated with high workloads for employees who possess low job control and nonsupportive organizational environments. This finding may have some implications for entrepreneurship. Since job control moderates the relationship between blood pressure and workloads, entrepreneurship may show a positive association with lower blood pressure because entrepreneurs possess higher job control levels than employees.

Neuroscience in Entrepreneurship

The fourth stream of research on the biological perspective in entrepreneurship focuses on neuroscience. Driven by the advances in the neuroscience field and studies on neuroscience in the broader management field (Becker, Cropanzano, & Sanfey, 2011; Becker, Volk, & Ward, 2015; Hannah & Waldman, 2015; Laureiro-Martínez, Brusoni, Canessa, & Zollo, 2015a), researchers have called for the use of neuroscience techniques in examining entrepreneurial phenotypes (de Holan, 2014; Nicolaou & Shane, 2014; Nicolaou, Ucbasaran, Lockett, & Rees, 2017). However, entrepreneurship researchers have not yet reported any empirical evidence for the relationship between neuroscience and entrepreneurial phenotypes. Quantitative electroencephalogram (qEEG) and functional magnetic resonance imaging (fMRI) are the most adopted neuroscience techniques in organizational studies (Shane & Nicolaou, 2015a).

Quantitative Electroencephalogram

qEEG monitors brain activity of the scalp and recognizes brain responses to environmental stimuli (Becker & Menges, 2013). In the broader management field, research using qEEG has indicated that coherence values of the left front cortex, left hemisphere, and medial regions are negatively associated with transformational leadership, while coherence values of the right frontal, right temporal, and right occipital lobe are positively correlated with transformational leadership (Balthazard, Waldman, Thatcher, & Hannah, 2012). In another study, Hannah, Balthazard, Waldman, Jennings, and Thatcher (2013) found that leaders with less connectivity in the frontal lobes in the alpha range of the brain have higher degrees of adaptive decision-making.

Functional Magnetic Resonance Imaging

fMRI is a brain imaging technique that detects changes of oxygen levels in the brain's blood and localizes them (Niven & Boorman, 2016). The identified locations reflect activated brain regions. The advantage of fMRI over other neuroscience techniques is that it offers a high spatial resolution (Becker & Menges, 2013). Recent work from the decision-making literature has found that the activations of the ventral tegmental area, substantia nigra, ventral striatum, nucleus accumbens, and ventromedial prefrontal cortex are associated with exploration. Meanwhile, the activations of the dorsolateral prefrontal cortex, frontopolar cortex, locus coeruleus-norepinephrine circuit, frontopolar cortex, and inferior parietal lobule are associated with exploitation (Laureiro-Martínez, Brusoni, Canessa, & Zollo, 2015b).

Other research has shown that the activations in the bilateral insula, the right inferior parietal lobe, and the left superior temporal gyrus, are associated with recalling experiences with resonant leaders (Boyatzis et al., 2012). Recalling experiences with dissonant leaders were associated with (1) the right anterior cingulate cortex, (2) the right inferior frontal gyrus, (3) the bilateral posterior region of the inferior frontal gyrus, and (4) the bilateral inferior frontal gyrus.

Conclusion

Complementing previous work on individual differences in entrepreneurship, recent research indicates that some individuals are biologically predisposed to engage in entrepreneurial activities. While evidence shows that biological factors affect various entrepreneurial phenotypes, understanding the pathways through which biology influences entrepreneurship is complex. However, as more research appears, novel explanations are changing the way we approach entrepreneurship. For instance, research on the biological perspective has shown that ADHD is an asset that can stimulate entrepreneurial work environments. As a result, managers may coach employees with genetic predispositions toward ADHD to engage in entrepreneurial work activities, and turn what others may have perceived as a disadvantage into a great asset for the firm.

It is important to emphasize that biology has a probabilistic and *not* a deterministic association with entrepreneurship. Accordingly, organizations are cautioned against misinterpreting the findings of this biological perspective in entrepreneurship. In fact, researchers argue that environmental factors may matter more than biological factors in influencing entrepreneurship (Nicolaou & Shane, 2011).

There are a number of future research directions in this field. First, we still know extremely little about the interplay between biological and environmental factors in entrepreneurship. Additional research on the influence of gene x environment interactions and gene x environment correlations is needed. Second, there is a dearth of longitudinal studies in this area. Longitudinal studies may outline possible mechanisms through which biology influences entrepreneurship by recognizing how biological influences change over time. Third, additional molecular genetics studies are needed to gain insights into the genetic architecture of entrepreneurial phenotypes, preferably genome-wide association studies. Despite research showing that between 40% and 60% of the variance of entrepreneurship can be explained by genetic factors (Arvey et al., 2016), we know very little about which genes might be involved. Fourth, additional research on how physiological factors affect entrepreneurship is greatly encouraged. Given the negative effects that entrepreneurship may have on individuals' physiological patterns (Rietveld, van Kippersluis, & Thurik, 2014), further research would also advance our understanding of how physiology and entrepreneurship relate. Fifth, more research is needed to incorporate neuroscience techniques into the study of entrepreneurship. We know very little about the mechanisms through which neuroscience can help advance entrepreneurship theory and research.

Overall, additional work on the biological perspective is required to improve our understanding of entrepreneurial activities and unravel important implications for both research and practice.

References

Aldrich, H. E., & Martinez, M. A. (2001). Many are called, but few are chosen: An evolutionary perspective for the study of entrepreneurship. *Entrepreneurship Theory and Practice, 25*, 41–56.

Arvey, R. D., Li, W.-D., & Wang, N. (2016). Genetics and organizational behavior. *Annual Review of Organizational Psychology and Organizational Behavior, 3*(1), 167–190. doi: 10.1146/annurev-orgpsych-032414-111251

Balthazard, P. A., Waldman, D. A., Thatcher, R. W., & Hannah, S. T. (2012). Differentiating transformational and non-transformational leaders on the basis of neurological imaging. *The Leadership Quarterly, 23*(2), 244–258. doi: 10.1016/j.leaqua.2011.08.002

Baron, R. A. (2008). The role of affect in the entrepreneurial process. *Academy of Management Review, 33*(2), 328–340.

Baron, R. A., Markman, G. D., & Bollinger, M. (2006). Exporting social psychology: Effects of attractiveness on perceptions of entrepreneurs, their ideas for new products, and their financial success. *Journal of Applied Social Psychology, 36*(2), 467–492. doi: 10.1111/j.0021-9029.2006.00015.x

Becker, W. J., Cropanzano, R., & Sanfey, A. G. (2011). Organizational neuroscience: Taking organizational theory beyond the neural black box. *Journal of Management, 37*, 933–961.

Becker, W. J., & Menges, J. I. (2013). Biological implicit measures in HRM and OB: A question of how not if. *Human Resource Management Review, 23*(3), 219–228. doi: 10.1016/j.hrmr.2012.12.003

Becker, W. J., Volk, S., & Ward, M. K. (2015). Leveraging neuroscience for smarter approaches to workplace intelligence. *Human Resource Management Review, 25*(1), 56–67.

Bönte, W., Procher, V. D., & Urbig, D. (2015). Biology and selection into entrepreneurship—The relevance of prenatal testosterone exposure. *Entrepreneurship Theory and Practice.* doi: 10.1111/etap.12165

Boyatzis, R. E., Passarelli, A. M., Koenig, K., Lowe, M., Mathew, B., Stoller, J. K., & Phillips, M. (2012). Examination of the neural substrates activated in memories of experiences with resonant and dissonant leaders. *The Leadership Quarterly, 23*(2), 259–272. doi: 10.1016/j.leaqua.2011.08.003

Cardon, M. S., & Kirk, C. P. (2015). Entrepreneurial passion as mediator of the self-efficacy to persistence relationship. *Entrepreneurship Theory and Practice, 39*(5), 1027–1050. doi: 10.1111/etap.12089

Chase, R. B. (1967). Management uses of work physiology. *California Management Review, 10*(2), 91–94. doi: 10.2307/41164108

de Holan, P. M. (2014). It's all in your head: Why we need neuroentrepreneurship. *Journal of Management Inquiry.* doi: 10.1177/1056492613485913

Greene, F. J., Han, L., Martin, S., Zhang, S., & Wittert, G. (2014). Testosterone is associated with self-employment among Australian men. *Economics & Human Biology, 13*, 76–84. doi: 10.1016/j.ehb.2013.02.003

Hannah, S. T., Balthazard, P. A., Waldman, D. A., Jennings, P. L., & Thatcher, R. W. (2013). The psychological and neurological bases of leader self-complexity and effects on adaptive decision-making. *Journal of Applied Psychology, 98*(3), 393–411. doi: 10.1037/a0032257

Hannah, S. T., & Waldman, D. A. (2015). Neuroscience of moral cognition and conation in organizations. *Organizational Neuroscience,* 233–255.

Ilies, R., Dimotakis, N., & De Pater, I. E. (2010). Psychological and physiological reactions to high workloads: Implications for well-being. *Personnel Psychology, 63*(2), 407–436. doi: 10.1111/j.1744-6570.2010.01175.x

Johnson, W. (2009). So what or so everything? Bringing behavior genetics to entrepreneurship research. *Journal of Business Venturing, 24*(1), 23–26. doi: 10.1016/j.jbusvent.2007.11.002

Koellinger, P. D., van der Loos, M. J. H. M., Groenen, P. J. F., Thurik, A. R., Rivadeneira, F., van Rooij, F. J. A., . . . Hofman, A. (2010). Genome-wide association studies in economics and entrepreneurship research: Promises and limitations. *Small Business Economics, 35*(1), 1–18. doi: 10.1007/s11187-010-9286-3

Laureiro-Martínez, D., Brusoni, S., Canessa, N., & Zollo, M. (2015). Understanding the exploration–exploitation dilemma: An fMRI study of attention control and decision-making performance. *Strategic Management Journal, 36*(3), 319–338. doi: 10.1002/smj.2221

Lindquist, M. J., Sol, J., & Praag, M. V. (2015). Why do entrepreneurial parents have entrepreneurial children? *Journal of Labor Economics, 33*(2), 269–296. doi: 10.1086/678493

Logan, J. (2009). Dyslexic entrepreneurs: The incidence; their coping strategies and their business skills. *Dyslexia, 15*(4), 328–346. doi: 10.1002/dys.388

McCarthy, M. I., Abecasis, G. R., Cardon, L. R., Goldstein, D. B., Little, J., Ioannidis, J. P., & Hirschhorn, J. N. (2008). Genome-wide association studies for complex traits: consensus, uncertainty and challenges. *Nature Reviews Genetics, 9*(5), 356–369. doi: 10.1038/nrg2344

Narayanan, J., & Prasad, S. (2015). Neurobiological systems: Implications for organizational behavior. In S. M. Colarelli & R. D. Arvey (Eds.), *The biological foundations of organizational behavior:* Chicago, IL: University of Chicago Press.

Neave, N. (2007). *Hormones and behaviour: A psychological approach:* Cambridge, England: University Press.

Nicolaou, N., Patel, P., & Wolfe, M. (2017). Testosterone and the tendency to engage in self-employment. *Management Science.* doi: http://dx.doi.org/10.1287/mnsc.2016.2664

Nicolaou, N., & Shane, S. (2009). Can genetic factors influence the likelihood of engaging in entrepreneurial activity? *Journal of Business Venturing, 24*(1), 1–22. doi: 10.1016/j.jbusvent.2007.11.003

Nicolaou, N., & Shane, S. (2010). Entrepreneurship and occupational choice: Genetic and environmental influences. *Journal of Economic Behavior & Organization, 76*(1), 3–14. doi: 10.1016/j.jebo.2010.02.009

Nicolaou, N., & Shane, S. (2011). The genetics of entrepreneurship. In D. B. Audretsch, O. Falck, S. Heblich, & A. Lederer (Eds.), *Handbook of research on innovation and entrepreneurship.* Cheltenham, England: Elgar.

Nicolaou, N., & Shane, S. (2014). Biology, neuroscience, and entrepreneurship. *Journal of Management Inquiry, 23*(1), 98–100. doi: 10.1177/1056492613485914

Nicolaou, N., Shane, S., Adi, G., Mangino, M., & Harris, J. (2011). A polymorphism associated with entrepreneurship: Evidence from dopamine receptor candidate genes. *Small Business Economics, 36*(2), 151–155. doi: 10.1007/s11187-010-9308-1

Nicolaou, N., Shane, S., Cherkas, L., Hunkin, J., & Spector, T. D. (2008). Is the tendency to engage in entrepreneurship genetic? *Management Science, 54*(1), 167–179. doi: 10.1287/mnsc.1070.0761

Nicolaou, N., Shane, S., Cherkas, L., & Spector, T. D. (2008). The influence of sensation seeking in the heritability of entrepreneurship. *Strategic Entrepreneurship Journal, 2*(1), 7–21. doi: 10.1002/sej.37

Nicolaou, N., Shane, S., Cherkas, L., & Spector, T. D. (2009). Opportunity recognition and the tendency to be an entrepreneur: A bivariate genetics perspective. *Organizational Behavior and Human Decision Processes, 110*(2), 108–117. doi: 10.1016/j.obhdp.2009.08.005

Nicolaou, N., Ucbasaran, D., Lockett, A., Rees, G. (2017). *Exploring the potential and limits of a neuroscientific approach to entrepreneurship* (Working paper). Warwick Business School, England.

Niven, K., & Boorman, L. (2016). Assumptions beyond the science: Encouraging cautious conclusions about functional magnetic resonance imaging research on organizational behavior. *Journal of Organizational Behavior.* doi: 10.1002/job.2097

Parker, S. C., & van Praag, C. M. (2012). The entrepreneur's mode of entry: Business takeover or new venture start? *Journal of Business Venturing, 27*(1), 31–46. doi: 10.1016/j.jbusvent.2010.08.002

Plomin, R., DeFries, J. C., Knopik, V. S., & Neiderhiser, J. M. (2012). *Behavioral genetics:* New York, NY: Worth Publishers.

Plomin, R., DeFries, J. C., & Loehlin, J. C. (1977). Genotype-environment interaction and correlation in the analysis of human behavior. *Psychological Bulletin, 84*(2), 309–322. doi: 10.1037/0033-2909.84.2.309

Quaye, L., Nicolaou, N., Shane, S., & Harris, J. (2012). A study of gene-environment interactions in entrepreneurship. *Entrepreneurship Research Journal, 2*(2).

Quaye, L., Nicolaou, N., Shane, S., & Massimo, M. (2012). A discovery Genome-Wide Association Study of entrepreneurship. *International Journal of Developmental Science, 6*, 127–135.

Rietveld, C. A., van Kippersluis, H., & Thurik, A. R. (2014). Self-employment and health: Barriers or benefits? *Health Economics.* doi: 10.1002/hec.3087

Schermer, J. A., Johnson, A. M., Jang, K. L., & Vernon, P. A. (2015). Phenotypic, genetic, and environmental relationships between self-reported talents and measured intelligence. *Twin Research and Human Genetics, 18*(1), 36–42. doi: 10.1017/thg.2014.80

Shane, S. A. (2003). *A general theory of entrepreneurship: The individual-opportunity nexus:* Cheltenham, England: Edward Elgar.

Shane, S., & Nicolaou, N. (2013). The genetics of entrepreneurial performance. *International Small Business Journal, 31*(5), 473–495. doi: 10.1177/0266242613485767

Shane, S., & Nicolaou, N. (2015a). The Biological basis of entrepreneurship. In S. M. Colarelli & R. D. Arvey (Eds.), *The biological foundations of organizational behavior*: Chicago, IL: University of Chicago Press.

Shane, S., & Nicolaou, N. (2015b). Creative personality, opportunity recognition and the tendency to start businesses: A study of their genetic predispositions. *Journal of Business Venturing, 30*(3), 407–419. doi: 10.1016/j.jbusvent.2014.04.001

Shane, S., Nicolaou, N., Cherkas, L., & Spector, T. D. (2010a). Do openness to experience and recognizing opportunities have the same genetic source? *Human Resource Management, 49*(2), 291–303. doi: 10.1002/hrm.20343

Shane, S., Nicolaou, N., Cherkas, L., & Spector, T. D. (2010b). Genetics, the Big Five, and the tendency to be self-employed. *Journal of Applied Psychology, 95*(6), 1154–1162. doi: 10.1037/a0020294

Shane, S., & Venkataraman, S. (2000). The Promise of entrepreneurship as a field of research. *Academy of Management Review, 25*(1), 217–226.

Short, J. C., Ketchen, D. J., Shook, C. L., & Ireland, R. D. (2010). The concept of "opportunity" in entrepreneurship research: Past accomplishments and future challenges. *Journal of Management, 36*(1), 40–65. doi: 10.1177/0149206309342746

Simon, M., Houghton, S. M., & Aquino, K. (2000). Cognitive biases, risk perception, and venture formation: How individuals decide to start companies. *Journal of Business Venturing, 15*(2), 113–134. doi: 10.1016/S0883-9026(98)00003-2

Song, Z., Li, W., & Arvey, R. D. (2011). Associations between dopamine and serotonin genes and job satisfaction: Preliminary evidence from the Add Health Study. *Journal of Applied Psychology, 96*(6), 1223–1233. doi: 10.1037/a0024577

Song, Z., Li, W., & Wang, N. (2015). Progress in molecular genetics and its potential implications in organizational behavior research. In S. M. Colarelli & R. D. Arvey (Eds.), *The biological foundations of organizational behavior*. Chicago, IL: University of Chicago Press.

Tabor, H. K., Risch, N. J., & Myers, R. M. (2002). Candidate-gene approaches for studying complex genetic traits: Practical considerations. *Nature Reviews Genetics, 3*(5), 391–397. doi: 10.1038/nrg796

Thurik, R., Khedhaouria, A., Torrès, O., & Verheul, I. (2016). ADHD symptoms and entrepreneurial orientation of small firm owners. *Applied Psychology.* doi: 10.1111/apps.12062

Trahms, C. A., Coombs, J. E., & Barrick, M. (2010). Does biology matter? How prenatal testosterone, entrepreneur risk propensity, and entrepreneur risk perceptions influence venture performance. *Frontiers of entrepreneurship research 2010: Proceedings of the Thirtieth Annual Entrepreneurship Research Conference (pp. 217–229).* Wellesley, MA: Babson College.

Unger, J. M., Rauch, A., Weis, S. E., & Frese, M. (2015). Biology (prenatal testosterone), psychology (achievement need) and entrepreneurial impact. *Journal of Business Venturing Insights, 4,* 1–5. doi: 10.1016/j.jbvi.2015.05.001

van der Loos, M. J., Haring, R., Rietveld, C. A., Baumeister, S. E., Groenen, P. J. F., Hofman, A., . . . Thurik, A. R. (2013a). Serum testosterone levels in males are not associated with entrepreneurial behavior in two independent observational studies. *Physiology & Behavior, 119,* 110–114. doi: 10.1016/j.physbeh.2013.06.003

van der Loos, M. J., Rietveld, C. A., Eklund, N., Koellinger, P. D., Rivadeneira, F., Abecasis, G. R., . . . Thurik, A. R. (2013b). The molecular genetic architecture of self-employment. *PLoS One, 8*(4), e60542. doi: 10.1371/journal.pone.0060542

van der Loos, M. J. H. M., Koellinger, P. D., Groenen, P. J. F., Rietveld, C. A., Rivadeneira, F., van Rooij, F. J. A., . . . Thurik, A. R. (2011). Candidate gene studies and the quest for the entrepreneurial gene. *Small Business Economics, 37*(3), 269–275. doi: 10.1007/s11187-011-9339-2

Wernerfelt, N., Rand, D., Dreber, A., Montgomery, C., & Malhotra, D. (2012). *Arginine Vasopressin 1a Receptor (AVPR1a) RS3 repeat polymorphism associated with entrepreneurship.* Retrieved from http://ssrn.com/abstract=2141598

White, R. E., Thornhill, S., & Hampson, E. (2006). Entrepreneurs and evolutionary biology: The relationship between testosterone and new venture creation. *Organizational Behavior and Human Decision Processes, 100*(1), 21–34. doi: 10.1016/j.obhdp.2005.11.001

Wiklund, J., Patzelt, H., & Dimov, D. (2016). Entrepreneurship and psychological disorders: How ADHD can be productively harnessed. *Journal of Business Venturing Insights, 6,* 14–20. doi: 10.1016/j.jbvi.2016.07.001

Yeo, G. S. (2011). Where next for GWAS? *Briefings in Functional Genomics, 10*(2), 51. doi: 10.1093/bfgp/elr011

Zahra, S. A., Sapienza, H. J., & Davidsson, P. (2006). Entrepreneurship and dynamic capabilities: A review, model and research agenda. *Journal of Management Studies, 43*(4), 917–955. doi: 10.1111/j.1467-6486.2006.00616.x

Zhang, Z., & Ilies, R. (2010). *Moderating effects of earlier family environment on genetic influences on entrepreneurship.* Paper presented at the Symposium Presentation at the Annual Conference of the Academy of Management, Montreal, Canada.

Zhang, Z., Zyphur, M. J., Narayanan, J., Arvey, R. D., Chaturvedi, S., Avolio, B. J., . . . Larsson, G. (2009). The genetic basis of entrepreneurship: Effects of gender and personality. *Organizational Behavior and Human Decision Processes, 110*(2), 93–107. doi: 10.1016/j.obhdp.2009.07.002

13

"Born, Not Made" and Other Beliefs About Entrepreneurial Ability

Daniel P. Forbes[a]

[a] University of Minnesota

Introduction

The claim that "entrepreneurs are born, not made" is a colloquialism that captures the longstanding idea that entrepreneurial ability is a function of a person's inborn characteristics. This idea has been advanced for years in popular discussions of entrepreneurship as well as in scholarly circles (Gartner, 1989; Shook, Priem, & McGee, 2003), where it has motivated research on the entrepreneurial personality (e,g., Chell, 2008) and, more recently, on the genetic bases of entrepreneurial behavior (e.g., Shane, 2010). Despite longstanding scholarly interest in assessing the validity of this claim, *the belief* that entrepreneurial ability is inborn remains largely unexamined. This is unfortunate for several reasons.

First, people's beliefs have important implications for their behavior, regardless of whether those beliefs are true (Hong, Levy, & Chiu, 2001; Kruglanski, Dechesne, Orehek, & Pierro, 2009). Scholars have paid considerable attention to the beliefs people hold about their own entrepreneurial abilities—that is, their "entrepreneurial self-efficacy" (Hmieleski & Baron, 2008; Zhao, Seibert & Hills, 2005). But they have tended to ignore the more general beliefs people hold about the nature of entrepreneurial ability, even though general beliefs about ability have been shown to be highly consequential in other domains (Molden & Dweck, 2006). Second, notwithstanding the fact that people's behaviors are influenced by their personalities and genetic profiles, the simpler and more strongly deterministic claim that "entrepreneurs are born" is inconsistent with contemporary social science (Dar-Nimrod & Heine, 2011; Turkheimer, 2000). Nevertheless, there is evidence that many people—including, as I observe below, roughly half of the adults in several large, economically prominent countries—do in fact believe that "entrepreneurs are born" (Amway, 2014). This evidence is consistent with broader evidence showing that many people hold simplistic and erroneous beliefs about the genetic basis of human behavior (Lanie et al., 2004; Richards, 1996). At the same time, the increasing availability of genetic testing is making it more common for people to be interested in – and more liable to misinterpret – their own genetic profiles (Gollust, Hull, & Wilfond, 2002; Maron, 2015). Taken together, these factors make it important for

The Wiley Handbook of Entrepreneurship, First Edition.
Edited by Gorkan Ahmetoglu, Tomas Chamorro-Premuzic, Bailey Klinger, & Tessa Karcisky.
© 2017 John Wiley & Sons Ltd. Published 2017 by John Wiley & Sons Ltd.

scholars to consider more fully the implications of the frequently touted and widely held belief that "entrepreneurs are born."

In this chapter, I encourage entrepreneurship scholars to expand their focus beyond the longstanding question of whether (or to what degree) entrepreneurs are born and to consider newer, less-explored questions, such as when, why, and with what effects people actually believe this to be true. I begin by observing that significant numbers of people do in fact believe that entrepreneurs are born, and I show that some scholars have also endorsed this contention. I further explain, however, that the belief that entrepreneurs are "born, not made" is inconsistent with contemporary social science for a variety of reasons. I go on to review recent social psychological research on lay theory and, in particular, research on the concept of "essentialism," the idea that members of large social groups possess an underlying set of immutable characteristics. Extending those ideas, I apply them to the case of occupational groups and introduce a construct to capture the belief that entrepreneurs possess an underlying essence that is fixed and inborn. I proceed to discuss several ways in which this belief is likely to affect important choices people make about the creation and management of new ventures.

Taken together, these arguments advance research at the intersection of entrepreneurship and cognition by expanding scholarly conversations about entrepreneurial ability beyond matters of self-belief to include consideration of how and with what effects people think about ability in general (e.g., Molden & Dweck, 2006). This, in turn, helps to deepen our understanding of how people's beliefs shape their decisions about whether and how to exploit entrepreneurial opportunities (Ramoglou, 2011; Shepherd, McMullen, & Jennings, 2007).

"Born, Not Made": Beliefs and Evidence

The claim that entrepreneurs are born is commonly invoked in the popular press and even, to some extent, in academic literature. For example, in 2011 *Forbes* magazine ran a cover story in which it profiled a set of entrepreneurs whose children were also engaged in entrepreneurial pursuits (Adams, 2011). The story highlighted similarities that suggested the parents had passed on the "business gene" to their children. Other popular press articles have endorsed the claim even more explicitly (e.g., Gannett 2012; Maurya, 2015). Some scholars have also endorsed the claim, as Shane (2010) did in his book, *Born Entrepreneurs, Born Leaders* and as Fisher and Koch (2008) did in their book, *Born, not Made: The Entrepreneurial Personality*.[1]

Beyond these examples, there is evidence the born-not-made belief is prevalent within and across societies. For example, the Amway Global Entrepreneurship Report (2014) asked over 43,000 people in 38 countries around the world whether they believed entrepreneurs are born or, alternatively, whether entrepreneurial skills could be acquired. Thirty-seven percent of respondents worldwide indicated they believed entrepreneurs are born. The born-not-made belief was held by even larger percentages of the respondents in Great Britain (39%), Korea (42%), Brazil (46%), Slovakia (50%) and Japan (60%), among other countries.

---

[1] Shane carefully qualifies this claim in some parts of the text, but he is less qualified in other parts and, clearly, in the title. Fisher and Koch make the claim much more strongly.

Interest in the born-not-made claim is further reflected in some recent research studies which have documented evidence of a link between genetics and the entrepreneurial entry decision (Shane, 2010). For example, Nicolaou and colleagues (2008) analyzed the entrepreneurial entry behaviors of roughly 1,700 pairs of twins from the UK using commonly used measures of entrepreneurial entry. Through this study, they estimated the "heritability" of entrepreneurial behavior to be "high even after [adjusting] for potential confounders such as gender, age, income, education, marital status race and immigrant status" (p. 173).[2] Similarly, Zhang and colleagues (2009) studied the behaviors of roughly 2,000 pairs of twins, again using common measures of entrepreneurial entry. They concluded that entrepreneurial behavior was heritable among females but not among males.

To the extent that popular media outlets cover the findings of studies like these, they are liable to "hype" them and thereby convey the simplistic impression that scientists have validated the born-not-made thesis (Bubela & Caulfield, 2004). In fact, however, making sense of such studies requires us to position their findings in a larger theoretical and empirical context.

First, behavioral genetics has shown that nearly all complex human behaviors are at least partially heritable. Indeed, the effect of genes is generally stronger than the effect of being raised in a certain family (Turkheimer, 2000). Thus, we should not be surprised to find that genes exert some influence on entrepreneurial behavior as well. However, the causal chains through which genes influence human behavior are generally very long such that individual differences with regard to complex human behaviors (like entrepreneurship) are likely to be a function of a great many genetic variations, each of which accounts for only a small percentage of behavioral variability (Chabris, Lee, Cesarini, Benjamin, & Laibson, 2015). Moreover, a substantial portion of the remaining variation in human behavior is attributable to what behavioral geneticists call the "non-shared environment," or the set of environmental influences that are unique to a single organism, as opposed to those that are common to siblings within a family (Dick, 2005; Turkheimer, 2000). In fact, behavior is shaped significantly by a complex interaction of genes and environment that includes the "self-determinative ability of humans to chart a course for their own lives, constrained but not determined by the genes, family and culture, and in response to the vagaries of environmental experience with which they are presented" (Turkheimer, 2011; p. 826). Thus, there is no "gene for" entrepreneurship, and accepting the claim that entrepreneurs are born, not made would require us to embrace an oversimplified and exaggerated conception of how genes work.

Second, there is a meaningful difference between the characteristics that make someone more likely to become an entrepreneur and those that make someone more likely to perform well in that capacity. For example, consider Nicolaou and colleagues' (2008) proposition that people with a genetic predisposition for sensation-seeking are more likely to become entrepreneurs, owing to the capacity for entrepreneurial work to provide frequent exposure to novel and complex sensations. Even if we grant that this is true, it does not necessarily imply that people who are more predisposed to

---

[2] In genetic studies, claims of this kind are commonly based on heritability coefficients. However, Turkheimer (2011) has criticized the use of these coefficients as measures of "how determined" a trait is, given that heritability depends on the population in which it is measured, a point which underscores the need for care in interpreting genetics studies.

sensation-seeking are any more likely to succeed as entrepreneurs once they have made the entry decision. In fact, it is conceivable that, beyond a certain threshold level, higher levels of sensation-seeking might cause people to perform *less well* as entrepreneurs, given that high levels of sensation-seeking have been associated with substance abuse and other high-risk behaviors (Zuckerman, 2006). The claim that entrepreneurs are born glosses over such complexities by conflating the determinants of entrepreneurial entry with the determinants of success, a practice that is hard to reconcile with the high rates of failure new ventures generally experience.

Third, decades of social psychological research on entrepreneurs have shown that entrepreneurs as a group are highly heterogeneous and do not, in fact, share a set of fixed psychological characteristics (Gartner, 1989; Mitchell et al., 2002; Shook, Priem, & McGee, 2003). For example, Chell's (2008) exhaustive analysis of past scholarship in this vein yields an overall portrait of the "entrepreneurial personality" which, despite scattered elements of thematic consistency, remains highly diffuse and empirically inconclusive—a finding that prompted her to conclude that the concept of the entrepreneurial personality is best understood as a "social construction." To observe this is not to dispute that specific personality traits may influence specific behaviors relevant to entrepreneurship, as some scholars have concluded (e.g., Rauch & Frese, 2007; Zhao & Seibert, 2006), or that certain cognitive processes may facilitate the exploration or exploitation of opportunities. However, it is to say that there exists no scientifically grounded set of psychological characteristics that reliably distinguish born entrepreneurs from nonentrepreneurs.

Finally, research in entrepreneurship suggests that people who persist in entrepreneurial activities over time can develop knowledge that enhances their ability (e.g., Baron & Ensley, 2006; Parker, 2013; Sarasvathy, 2008). Research further indicates that entrepreneurial ability encompasses multiple components, including technical, social and cognitive skills (Markman, 2007; Mitchell et al., 2000), the significance of which may vary across environmental contexts (e.g., Aldrich & Martinez, 2001; Baron & Markman, 2003). Although the ability to acquire any given skill may vary across individuals, there exists a wide range of social settings within which innate talent has been shown to be less crucial than deliberate practice to task performance. Deliberate practice, meanwhile, has been shown to trigger improvements over time in memory, intuition, and other cognitive processes that further skill development and task performance (Baron & Henry, 2010). To the extent these findings indicate that the skills associated with entrepreneurial ability are diverse, learnable, and context-specific, they further contradict the idea that entrepreneurs are born.

In summary, notwithstanding the real influence that genes exert on entrepreneurial (or any other) behavior, the claim that entrepreneurs are born, not made is a significant exaggeration, and belief in the claim is inconsistent with contemporary social science. Nevertheless, as we have seen, the born-not-made thesis is often publicly advanced by influential people and sources, and it is widely held among members of the general population in a variety of cultural and institutional contexts. At a minimum, this state of affairs is noteworthy as an example of a disconnect between popular belief and research-based knowledge about entrepreneurship (Davidsson, 2002)—a disconnect that would seem to call for a knowledge transfer effort of the kind that scholars interested in evidence-based management have advocated (e.g., Rousseau & McCarthy, 2007). But this disconnect is all the more significant in light of recent scientific advances that have made it easier for people to access their own (and potentially others') genetic profiles (Maron, 2015). Given that such tests are already widely available and are increasingly marketed with reference to the information they can provide relevant to health, disease, and reproduction (Gollust et al., 2002), it is reasonable to expect such tests to be increasingly sought for work- and career-related purposes as well. For all of these reasons, there is a need for scholars to understand more fully the belief that entrepreneurs are born and to investigate its implications for entrepreneurial behavior. Tools appropriate to these tasks can be found in social psychological research on how people think about social groups.

Understanding How People Think About Entrepreneurs

Research relevant to understanding how people think about entrepreneurs as a social group can be found within certain streams of research on "lay theory." A lay theory is a knowledge structure possessed and used by lay people, as opposed to scientists (Furnham, 1988; Heath, 1999; Kruglanski et al., 2009). Among the earliest lay theories to be explored were "implicit" theories of personality and related psychological concepts (Furnham, 1988). More recently, the study of lay theory has examined the ideas people invoke in making sense of other aspects of the world, including physics and biology (e.g., Baron-Cohen, 1997; Jayaratne et al., 2009).

An important set of lay theories involves the beliefs people hold about the properties of social groups. In general, people tend to assign social groups to one of four main types: intimacy groups (e.g., groups of friends); social categories (e.g., gender categories such as men and women); task groups (e.g., project teams); and loose associations (e.g., people in an elevator) (Lickel, Hamilton, & Sherman, 2001). The type to which a specific group of people is assigned depends on that group's characteristics. Large groups of people that exist for long durations, for example, such as groups of people categorized with reference to their gender or occupation, are treated as social categories (Lickel et al., 2001). Clearly, however, social categories are highly heterogeneous, encompassing groups whose boundaries may be drawn with reference to a wide range of criteria. Most research attention has been devoted to how lay people make sense of large social categories, such as those defined with reference to race, ethnicity, religion, or gender (Levy, Chiu, & Hong, 2006). But by drawing on what we know about lay theorizing in connection with such groups, we can explore the way people think about occupational groups as well. In doing so, we can characterize more fully the belief that entrepreneurs are born and not made.

Essentialist Lay Beliefs

A key issue investigated in connection with lay theory is the extent to which people hold "essentialist" beliefs about social categories, or the extent to which they believe the people in these categories possess an underlying essence that is fixed (i.e., stable over time) and inductively potent, meaning it can serve as a strong basis for inferring other nonobvious properties (Rothbart & Taylor, 1992). For example, there is considerable evidence that lay beliefs about gender categories are highly essentialized (Haslam, Rothschild, & Ernst, 2000). In other words, many lay people believe the categories "men" and "women" each possess an underlying essence that is shared by the members of those categories. However, lay people vary with regard to the strength of their essentialist beliefs; in other words, some people hold these beliefs more strongly than do others. In addition, the prevalence and strength of essentialist lay beliefs varies significantly across social categories. For example, essentialist beliefs about gender categories are more widespread than are essentialist beliefs about ethnic groups, social classes, and personality types, although there is evidence that many lay people hold essentialist beliefs about all of these categories (Haslam & Whelan, 2008; Levy et al., 2006).

Essentialist beliefs are important, because research has shown that these beliefs affect how people make sense of their own behavior and that of others. For example, research has shown that when people hold essentialist beliefs about a social group, they are likely to endorse group stereotypes more readily, to exaggerate the homogeneity of the group, and to attribute people's behavior—their own and others'—to their "nature" as members of the group (Yzerbyt & Rocher, 2002; Demoulin, Leyens, & Yzerbyt, 2006). Thus, essentialist beliefs are related to stereotypes of social groups, but they differ from those beliefs in that essentialist beliefs do not entail any specific beliefs about the attributes or behaviors shared by members of a social group. Rather, they simply capture the belief that members of a group possess an underlying essence that is fixed and inductively potent.

The belief that members of a social group possess a fixed underlying essence is sometimes linked with lay beliefs about genes and human behavior (Nelkin & Lindee, 1995). Because lay theories of human biology are highly varied in their validity and sophistication, many lay people believe that genes play a much simpler and more direct role in shaping human behavior than they actually do (Lanie et al., 2004; Richards & Ponder, 1996). Researchers have gauged the prevalence and strength of such beliefs with instruments like the "belief in genetic determinism" scale, which asks people to register the extent to which they agree with statements such as, "The fate of each person lies in his or her genes" (Keller, 2005). Through this scale and similar ones, researchers have found that people who believe genes exert a simple and strong relationship on human behavior are also more likely to ascribe people's behavior to their membership in a particular social group, especially when they perceive that the group has a shared genetic foundation (Dar-Nimrod & Heine, 2011). Building on these findings, psychologists have introduced the idea of "genetic essentialism," a type of essentialism characterized by "the tendency to infer a person's characteristics and behaviors from his or her perceived genetic makeup" (Dar-Nimrod & Heine, 2011, p. 801).

Genetic Essentialist Lay Beliefs About Entrepreneurs

Past research on essentialist beliefs has tended to focus on how people think about large social categories, such as those defined with reference to race or ethnicity. However, people also hold beliefs about the members of occupational categories (e.g., Spencer-Rodgers, Hamilton, & Sherman, 2007). For example, research has shown that many people believe lawyers are generally dishonest and arrogant (Rhode, 1998), and a recent article in a major medical journal examined several common public perceptions of physicians (Jain & Cassell, 2010). Entrepreneurs are another occupational category about which people hold certain beliefs, and these beliefs sometimes represent a form of genetic essentialism.

Fisher and Koch (2008) provide a vivid illustration of these beliefs in their book, *Born, Not Made*. They write:

> The confident driven individuals who become entrepreneurs typically have different genetic endowments than those who are not entrepreneurial . . . Most are hardwired genetically to react differently than other individuals to external stimuli that portray risk, danger, excitement and change. (pp. 2–3)

This statement conveys key elements of genetic essentialism in that it defines entrepreneurs as a group of people whose occupational choice is attributable to an underlying psychological essence that is fixed and genetically based. I discuss these elements in turn.

The belief in a fixed entrepreneurial essence entails a belief that entrepreneurs as a group possess a set of underlying characteristics that are stable. This contrasts with the belief that a group's characteristics are dynamic, meaning they are malleable and can be changed over time (Wood & Bandura, 1989). People often disagree about whether particular characteristics are static or dynamic, and they may hold such beliefs with reference to a variety of characteristics (Dweck, 2000). Although lay beliefs about entrepreneurs often feature beliefs about an entrepreneurial essence, the characteristics to which that essence is attributable are not always clearly specified. Sometimes the characteristics are specified, as in the quotations above referencing confidence and risk-taking. But people can also believe that a social category has an essence without believing that they fully understand the essence. In these cases, essentialism functions as a kind of "placeholder" in that an unspecified essence stands in for belief in characteristics that are believed to exist but considered difficult to discern (Gelman, 2003). Whether the characteristics are specified or not, belief in a fixed entrepreneurial essence reflects the belief that the characteristics represented by the essence are ones that cannot be cultivated, learned, or otherwise acquired over time; rather, people possess those characteristics in certain quantities that remain stable over time (Dweck & Leggett, 1988).

The belief that a person's characteristics are rooted in his/her genes represents the second key element of genetic essentialism. Broadly speaking, alternative sources of people's characteristics include people's prior choices and their social environments as well as their genes (Jayaratne et al., 2009). People often disagree about which sources are responsible for particular human characteristics. But when people also believe that particular characteristics are stable, the set of plausible alternative sources is generally confined to sources exerting a distant or long-term effect on the person, such as genes or parenting, as opposed to sources based on recent personal choice (e.g., Phelan, 2002). Although much human behavior has some genetic basis, the belief I refer to here is belief in a relatively simple, direct process of translation, or a strong genetic explanation of the kind reflected in the above quotations, which quickly invoke DNA as a primary or even singular determinant of entrepreneurs' essential characteristics.

I summarize below the key elements of genetic essentialism as it applies to entrepreneurs.

Definition: People who hold genetic essentialist beliefs about entrepreneurs believe that entrepreneurs possess an underlying essence defined by one or more personal characteristics. They further believe that the extent to which any one person possesses the relevant characteristic(s) is: (a) fixed; and (b) strongly determined by his/her genes.

Born-Not-Made and General Beliefs About Entrepreneurial Ability

A corollary to the belief that entrepreneurs are born is the belief that entrepreneurial ability is itself a fixed attribute, as opposed to a malleable one. In social scientific theories, there is generally (but not always) a clear distinction drawn between a person's propensity to join an occupational category and the person's propensity to succeed in that category. However, people who subscribe to the born-not-made thesis are likely to conflate the set of fixed characteristics that they associate with entrepreneurial entry with a similar set of fixed characteristics that they believe to be associated with entrepreneurial performance.

Research on intergroup perception supports this expectation: For example, work by Levy and colleagues (2001) showed that people who subscribe to a "fixed" theory of human nature were more likely to exaggerate the homogeneity of social groups and more likely to exaggerate the differences between groups. Where occupational groups are concerned, this perspective is likely to have the effect of downplaying the very existence of performance differences among members of the group and of highlighting instead the shared attributes of occupational group members. To the extent that the shared attributes of entrepreneurs imply behaviors that may affect performance, it becomes easier for people to believe that those who are more entrepreneurial are also more likely to succeed as entrepreneurs. Consider, for example, the following remarks offered by the director of a regional business development program in the United States:

> Entrepreneurs have the vision to see what is possible. They have the creativity to develop new approaches to old problems and to muster the right resources in the right combination to bring their dreams to fruition. And, they have the self-assuredness to see the vision become reality, often in spite of seemingly insurmountable obstacles. (Paulsell, 2005)

This person is surely professionally acquainted with the reality that some entrepreneurs outperform others and that some fail outright. What is noteworthy about the quote, however, is the way it downplays that reality as well as its implication that those who manage to overcome the obstacles of entrepreneurship will be those who possess more of the essential characteristics of entrepreneurs. In light of this tendency to equate entrepreneurs' underlying essence with their performative capacity, people who subscribe to the born-not-made thesis are likely to conclude that entrepreneurial ability, like the essence itself, is a fixed attribute. Such a belief would be reflected in agreement with statements such as, "Each person has a certain amount of entrepreneurial ability, and he/she can't really do much to change it."

Proposition 1: People who hold genetic essentialist beliefs about entrepreneurs also believe that a person's entrepreneurial ability is a fixed attribute.

Implications of Belief in Born-Not-Made

In the sections that follow, I explore ways in which the beliefs described above may affect the behavior of two groups of people: (1) potential entrepreneurs, and (2) people tasked with evaluating others' entrepreneurial abilities.

Implications for the Judgments People Make About Their Own Entrepreneurial Abilities

An important implication of belief in the born-not-made thesis is its potential to discourage entrepreneurial activity among potential entrepreneurs. This is likely to occur to the extent that belief in born-not-made engenders in potential entrepreneurs a low sense of entrepreneurial self-efficacy (ESE).

The Global Entrepreneurship Monitor (GEM) defines potential entrepreneurs to be people who have identified an opportunity and believe they have the skills to exploit it (Kelley, Singer, & Herrington, 2011). Even under this relatively restrictive definition, GEM studies indicate that 30–55% of the adult population of many countries qualify as potential entrepreneurs. However, scholars have recognized that the supply of potential entrepreneurs in a society is not immutable but, rather, is subject to larger societal influences over time (e.g., Busenitz, Gomez, & Spencer, 2000). In a broader sense, therefore, the set of potential entrepreneurs may be understood to encompass more people, regardless of whether they already believe they have the skills to exploit a particular opportunity (Shook et al., 2003). Consistent with this view, I define potential entrepreneurs as people who have discovered an opportunity and are considering exploiting it. In McMullen and Shepherd's (2006) framework, this includes people who have identified a third-person opportunity but have not yet decided whether to pursue the opportunity themselves. This definition is broader than the GEM definition in that it includes people who possess a range of beliefs about their own entrepreneurial abilities—in other words people with varying levels of ESE.[3]

ESE is a construct that captures the degree to which people believe they have the ability to perform the tasks associated with launching a new business (Chen, Greene, & Crick, 1998; Hmieleski & Baron, 2008). Research has shown that people with higher levels of ESE are more likely to formulate entrepreneurial intentions (e.g., Wilson, Kickul, & Marlino, 2007; Zhao, Seibert, & Hills, 2005) and, ultimately, to act on them (e.g., Arenius & Minniti, 2005; Koellinger, Minniti, & Schade, 2007). More broadly, Levie and Autio (2008) argued that societies in which people possess higher levels of ESE will realize higher rates of new venture creation. Past research on the sources of ESE has focused on ways in which ESE is shaped by prior experiences, especially entrepreneurship-related educational experiences and prior entrepreneurial experiences (e.g., Ucbasaran, Alsos, Westhead, & Wright, 2008; Wilson et al., 2007; Zhao et al., 2005). But many potential entrepreneurs have not yet chosen to pursue either type of experience (Leibenstein, 1968). Moreover, beliefs are not entirely a function of experience; rather, they are likely to operate as part of a larger set of related beliefs (Bandura, 1993; Molden & Dweck, 2006). Born-not-made is an example of a general, topically relevant belief that is likely to exert an important influence on ESE.

One reason born-not-made is relevant to ESE is that controllability plays an important role in people's efficacy judgments (Bandura, 1997). In general, people possess lower levels of self-efficacy regarding tasks when they believe more strongly that the determinants of task performance are uncontrollable (Gist & Mitchell, 1992; Wood &

---

[3] Strictly speaking, the population of potential entrepreneurs may include people who have previously started other ventures. However, given that many potential entrepreneurs will also be novice entrepreneurs, I focus here on sources of ESE other than prior entrepreneurial experience.

Bandura, 1989). Consider, for example, that in many contemporary societies, it is relatively easy for people to encounter media accounts of highly successful entrepreneurs. Although it is possible for people to attribute such instances of success entirely to luck, people who believe in the born-not-made thesis will generally assign at least some portion of entrepreneurial performance to ability, and to the extent they do they are likely to infer that there exists a wide range of entrepreneurial abilities. However, their belief in the fixed nature of these abilities will also lead them to infer that ability-based determinants of entrepreneurial performance are uncontrollable, and this is likely to result in lower levels of ESE.

In addition, potential entrepreneurs' ESE assessments are likely to be shaped by social influences, including verbal persuasion (Bandura, 1997). Key sources of verbal persuasion that may affect a person's efficacy beliefs include appraisals of ability expressed by experienced others (Crundall & Foddy, 1981), which in the case of entrepreneurship may include experienced entrepreneurs or other businesspeople, investors or teachers. Potential entrepreneurs often experience feedback, including verbal feedback, from these and other sources about the opportunities they are considering (Gartner & Carter, 2003). Such feedback may include feedback on the strengths and weaknesses of a given opportunity, but it may also include explicit or implicit appraisals of a person's ability, and in both cases much of the feedback is negative (Brockner, Higgins & Low, 2004). This is important, because verbal persuasion is generally more powerful as a source of *discouragement* than as a means of producing enduringly high efficacy beliefs: Although people persuaded to adopt high efficacy beliefs will ultimately find those beliefs tested against other sources of information, people persuaded to adopt low beliefs can find that those beliefs "create their own behavioral validation" by "constricting choice of activities, undermining motivation and discouraging explorations" (Bandura, 1997, p. 104). Frese (2007) observed that negative feedback can provide entrepreneurs with motivation as well as information from which to learn. However, whether a potential entrepreneur processes negative feedback by drawing inferences that lead to persistence and learning or, alternatively, by drawing inferences that lead to discouragement is likely to be influenced by the more general beliefs he or she holds about the nature of entrepreneurial ability.

Potential entrepreneurs who believe entrepreneurs are born are likely to look to verbal feedback for clues that help reveal their own underlying entrepreneurial ability (Dweck, 2000). Accordingly, they are more likely to read negative feedback as a signal that they "don't have what it takes" to be an entrepreneur. This, in turn, is likely to amplify the negative effects of negative feedback on ESE. On the other hand, potential entrepreneurs who do not subscribe to the born-not-made thesis are likely to interpret verbal feedback more broadly—for example, as providing information about the opportunity itself or about specific alternative ways it might be exploited. To the extent they do encounter explicit, negative appraisals of their ability, they are more likely to conclude that the shortcomings can be remedied through additional effort or experience. This expectation is consistent with recent research in other settings, which has shown that belief in an incremental theory of ability (i.e., that abilities are malleable) mitigates the discouraging effects of negative information, including stereotypically negative portrayals of ability (Molden & Dweck, 2006; Pollack, Burnette, & Hoyt, 2012).

Proposition 2: Potential entrepreneurs who hold genetic essentialist beliefs about entrepreneurs will possess lower levels of ESE.

Implications for the Judgments People Make About Others' Entrepreneurial Abilities

Another way genetic essentialist beliefs may affect entrepreneurial behavior is by influencing how people make judgments about others' abilities to perform as entrepreneurs. I consider below two common contexts in which people make such judgments: (1) financing decisions and (2) the selection of entrepreneurial team members.

Entrepreneurial financing decisions are situations in which a person in control of financial resources (a "funder," to apply a generic label) is tasked with deciding which person(s) and/or firms represent the best investment opportunities among a set of available alternatives (DeClercq, Fried, Lehtonen, & Sapienza, 2007). The person in that role may be a venture capitalist or an angel investor deciding whether to invest in a start-up or a competition judge charged with awarding prize money. Because past research has shown that many funders consider the abilities of the entrepreneur(s) themselves to be of high importance (Huang & Pearce, 2015; Zott & Huy, 2007), financing decisions are likely to be significantly influenced by the beliefs funders hold about the nature of entrepreneurial ability.

When funders believe that entrepreneurs possess an underlying essence that is fixed and inborn, they are likely to direct their attention to information that they believe will help them determine the extent to which individual funding candidates possess that underlying essence. At the extreme, this could prompt funders to request detailed genetic information on specific individuals. But even if such behavior is inhibited by legal or ethical barriers, funders can try to discern a candidate's inborn essence on the basis of more readily available data, such as personality traits or the success of the candidate's prior entrepreneurial experiences. Such data often factor into funding decisions as a matter of course (Riquelme & Watson, 2002), but funders with genetic essentialist beliefs are likely to overweight those factors to the extent they interpret them as signals of an underlying inborn capacity. Relatedly, owing to the corollary belief that entrepreneurial ability is fixed, genetic essentialist beliefs are likely to prompt funders to assign diminished or negative values to career experiences that could represent significant episodes of learning and development, such as prior entrepreneurial failures.

Moreover, funders may look to even more simplistic cues as a basis for inferring whether an individual is a "born entrepreneur." For example, Brooks and colleagues (2014) found that investors were more likely to fund ventures when those ventures were pitched by males, as opposed to females, even when the content of the pitch was identical. That study did not determine why investors exhibited this preference; however, as Pollack and colleagues (2012) have observed, "[h]istorically, descriptions of entrepreneurs' activities and the success of new organizations have been unequivocally masculine" (p. 288). Accordingly, it is not difficult to imagine that investors who believe entrepreneurs are born could regard gender or other forms of visible difference to be suitable proxies for inferring whether individuals possess an entrepreneurial essence. Past research on essentialism and social judgment in other contexts is consistent with this expectation insofar as people with genetic essentialist beliefs have been shown to form faster judgments about others (Bastian & Haslam, 2007), to invoke group stereotypes more readily, and to subsequently pay less attention to data inconsistent with those stereotypes (Levy et al., 2001; Yzerbyt & Rocher, 2002).

Similar dynamics are likely to unfold when a person is tasked with deciding which person(s) represent the most compelling candidates for recruitment onto an entrepreneurial team. The person making this decision is often an entrepreneur seeking business partners, although an investor, board member, or other external advisor may also influence who is chosen (Klotz, Hmieleski, Bradley, & Busenitz, 2014). In both cases, the task calls for evaluation of a person's abilities, including those abilities relevant to the launch and management of a new venture. As with financing decisions, team member selection decisions may also be shaped by cognitive bias (Parker, 2009). Genetic essentialist beliefs are likely to trigger biased selection decisions, either by prompting selectors to consider candidates' genetic profiles directly or to misjudge the salience of other data, such as those described above, based on its perceived capacity to proxy for a person's inborn abilities. For example, data pertaining to candidates' subject-specific knowledge and skills or data pertaining to candidates' relationships with other people within or beyond the entrepreneurial team may be more likely to be underweighted or overlooked by selectors with genetic essentialist beliefs insofar as those data do not clearly correspond to a person's possession of an entrepreneurial essence—even though those data may in fact be highly relevant to a person's ability to perform well as an entrepreneurial team member (Beckman & Burton, 2008; Owens, Mannix, & Neale, 1998).

I have focused here on the initial selection decisions associated with financing and entrepreneurial team formation, but it is also possible for genetic essentialist beliefs to affect the ongoing evaluation of people in entrepreneurial roles. For example, people who join the board of a new venture after the initial funding and team formation decisions can find themselves monitoring and evaluating the performance of individuals they did not select. In such cases, as in many governance contexts, board members are tasked with disentangling the various internal and external drivers of firm performance and making appropriate attributions of responsibility (Mantere, Aula, Schildt, & Vaara, 2013; Walsh & Seward, 1990). Evaluators with genetic essentialist beliefs about entrepreneurs are likely to draw poorer inferences about the causes of performance insofar as they will be prompted to overweight internal determinants (positively or negatively) or to scrutinize performance data for evidence of whether specific individuals possess an inborn entrepreneurial essence.

In summary, genetic essentialist beliefs are likely to adversely affect the quality of the decision processes through which people select and evaluate others in connection with entrepreneurial roles. In particular, people who hold such beliefs are more likely to overweight their perceptions of individuals' personality traits, to underweight the value of past experience and training as sources of entrepreneurial ability, and to formulate interpretations of performance that are more skewed by attributional bias.

Proposition 3: When tasked with evaluating people's entrepreneurial abilities, people who hold genetic essentialist beliefs about entrepreneurs will render lower-quality evaluations relative to those who do not hold such beliefs.

Discussion

In this chapter I have called attention to a specific, widely held belief which, despite its familiarity, remains theoretically and empirically underexamined in the entrepreneurship literature: the belief that entrepreneurs are born and not made. Drawing on recent social psychological research on lay theory, I have introduced a construct that captures this belief and explained how the belief is likely to cause people to systematically overestimate or underestimate the entrepreneurial abilities that they and others possess.

Taken together, these arguments advance research at the intersection of entrepreneurship and cognition by expanding scholarly conversations about entrepreneurial ability beyond matters of self-belief (i.e., as reflected in the study of entrepreneurial self-efficacy, or ESE) to include consideration of how and with what effects people think about ability in general. This helps link entrepreneurship research with the large body of social psychology research that has underscored the significance of general ability-related beliefs as determinants of human behavior (e.g., Molden & Dweck, 2006; Wood & Bandura, 1989)—a body of work that entrepreneurship scholars have largely ignored to date. At the same time, it complements the recent efforts of other entrepreneurship scholars to deepen our understanding of how people's beliefs shape their decisions about whether and how to exploit entrepreneurial opportunities (e.g., Felin & Zenger, 2009; Ramoglou, 2011; Shepherd, McMullen, & Jennings, 2007). More broadly, by showing how entrepreneurial beliefs relate to larger systems of belief that operate within societies, this chapter responds to recent calls for research that clarifies how entrepreneurial cognition is shaped by the social systems and processes in which it is situated (Grégoire, Corbett, & McMullen, 2008; Mitchell, Smith, Seawright, & Morse, 2000).

Second, the arguments presented here help expand research on entrepreneurship and cognition beyond its traditional focus on existing entrepreneurs and toward the larger and less-understood population of potential entrepreneurs. In doing so, these arguments respond to Sarasvathy's (2004) call for scholars to pay more attention to the subset of people in a society "who want to become entrepreneurs but do not," owing to one or more barriers that may exist (p. 707) as well as to Shepherd and colleagues' (2007) call for research that helps clarify when and why individuals who identify a third-person opportunity refrain from exploiting it themselves. In particular, by showing how genetic essentialist beliefs may inhibit the exploitation of opportunities recognized by potential entrepreneurs, they help to show how such beliefs may exert a "drag" on the societies in which they are widely held.

These contributions carry several implications for future research and practice. First, there is a need for empirical research that tests these propositions and related ones, using data on the ability-related beliefs and perceptions of people who are not (yet) actively engaged in entrepreneurship. Such efforts could be linked to ongoing data collection efforts that gauge the general norms and beliefs people hold about entrepreneurship in countries around the world (e.g., the GEM). Relatedly, future studies could examine variations in the prevalence of the born-not-made thesis within and across societies (e.g., across cultures or education levels). Such studies could help elaborate some of the specific beliefs and inferences through which societal and institutional factors shape cross-national variations in entrepreneurial activity (Busenitz et al., 2000; Levie & Autio, 2008). It is common for entrepreneurship scholars to refer in broad terms to the existence and significance of these cognitive mechanisms, but there is a need for work that elaborates more fully what the relevant beliefs are and how they shape entrepreneurial activity (Busenitz et al., 2000; Grégoire et al., 2008). Finally, future research could shed light on linkages between the psychology of entrepreneurship and socioeconomic research on human capital in entrepreneurship (e.g., Aldrich & Yang, 2012; Lazear, 2004), for example by documenting differences in how people conceive of entrepreneurial ability and by assessing the validity of alternative conceptions of ability.

Methodologically, too, there is a need for scholars to adapt and refine the empirical research tools developed in psychological studies of essentialism and ability-related beliefs for application in entrepreneurship. Although most past research on lay beliefs has focused on large social categories, such as those defined with reference to gender and ethnicity, future scholars could build upon the survey instruments and experimental methods developed in the study of those categories to test predictions about what lay people believe about entrepreneurs and how those beliefs influence entrepreneurial behavior as well as business behavior more generally. Studies by Heath (1999) and Priem and Rosenstein (2000) provide examples of experimental studies that test lay beliefs related to management.

Finally, a practical implication of the ideas developed in this article is that they should prompt people who work closely with potential and existing entrepreneurs to surface and engage directly with the beliefs lay people hold about the sources of entrepreneurial ability. Clearly, individuals and societies stand to gain in many ways from the impending growth in scientific knowledge about how genetics shapes human behavior, as well as from the increasingly widespread availability of genetic tests. But such advances also increase the risk that people will formulate ability-related beliefs that are skewed by misinterpretations of genetic information. Thus, there exists both a need and an opportunity for teachers, consultants, and journalists, among others, to improve the accuracy of lay beliefs in this area and, in doing so, to improve the quality of the decisions people make about whether and how to engage in entrepreneurial activity.

References

Adams, S. (2011, May 23). Like father, like child. *Forbes 187*(9), 74–84.

Aldrich, H., & Martinez, M. A. (2001). Many are called but few are chosen. *Entrepreneurship Theory & Practice, 25*, 41–56.

Aldrich, H., & Yang, T. (2012). Lost in translation: Cultural codes are not blueprints. *Strategic Entrepreneurship Journal, 6*, 1–17.

Amway. (2014). *Global Entrepreneurship Report 2014*. Retrieved from http://www.amwayentrepreneurshipreport.com

Arenius, P., & Minniti, M. (2005). Perceptual variables and nascent entrepreneurship. *Small Business Economics, 24*, 233–247.

Bandura, A. (1993). Perceived self-efficacy in cognitive development and functioning. *Educational Psychologist, 28*, 117–148.

Bandura, A. (1997). *Self-efficacy: The exercise of control*. New York, NY: Freeman.

Baron, R., & Ensley, M. (2006). Opportunity recognition as the detection of meaningful patterns: Evidence from comparisons of novice and experienced entrepreneurs. *Management Science, 52*, 1331–1344.

Baron, R., & Henry, R. (2010). How entrepreneurs acquire the capacity to excel: Insights from research on expert performance. *Strategic Entrepreneurship Journal, 4*, 49–65.

Baron, R., & Markman, G. (2003). Beyond social capital: The role of entrepreneurs' social competence in their financial success. *Journal of Business Venturing, 18*, 41–60.

Baron-Cohen, S. (1997). Are children with autism superior at folk physics? In H. Wellman & K. Inagaki (Eds.), *The emergence of core domains of thought: Children's reasoning about physical, psychological and biological phenomena* (pp. 45–54). San Francisco, CA: Jossey-Bass.

Bastian, B., & Haslam, N. (2007). Psychological essentialism and attention allocation. *Journal of Social Psychology, 147*, 531–541.

Beckman, C., & Burton, D. (2008). Founding the future: Path dependence in the evolution of top management teams from founding to IPO. *Organization Science, 19,* 3–24.

Brockner, J., Higgins, E., & Low, M. (2004). Regulatory focus theory and the entrepreneurial process. *Journal of Business Venturing, 19,* 203–220.

Brooks, A.W., Huang, L., Kearney, S. W., & Murray, F. (2014). Investors prefer entrepreneurial ventures pitched by attractive men. *Proceedings of the National Academy of Sciences, 111,* 4427–4431.

Bubela, T., & Caulfield, T. (2004). Do the print media '"hype" genetics research? A comparison of newspaper stories and peer-reviewed research papers. *Canadian Medical Association Journal, 170,* 1399–1407.

Busenitz, L., Gomez, C., & Spencer, J. (2000). Country institutional profiles: Unlocking entrepreneurial phenomena. *Academy of Management Journal, 43,* 994–1003.

Chabris, C. F., Lee, J. J., Cesarini, D., Benjamin, D. J., & Laibson, D. I. (2015). The fourth law of behavior genetics. *Current Directions in Psychological Science, 24*(4), 304–312.

Chell, E. (2008). *The entrepreneurial personality: A social construction* (2nd ed.). London, England: Routledge.

Chen, C., Greene, P., & Crick, A. (1998). Does entrepreneurial self-efficacy distinguish entrepreneurs from managers? *Journal of Business Venturing, 13,* 295–316.

Crundall, I., & Foddy, M. (1981). Vicarious exposure to a task as a basis of evaluative competence. *Social Psychology Quarterly, 44,* 331–338.

Dar-Nimrod, I., & Heine, S. (2011). Genetic essentialism: On the deceptive determinism of DNA. *Psychological Bulletin, 137,* 800–818.

Davidsson, P. (2002). What entrepreneurship research can do for business policy practice. *International Journal of Entrepreneurship Education, 1,* 5–24.

DeClercq, D., Fried, V., Lehtonen, O., & Sapienza, H. (2007). An entrepreneur's guide to the venture capital galaxy. *Academy of Management Perspectives, 20,* 90–112.

Demoulin, S., Leyens, J., & Yzerbyt, V. (2006). Lay theories of essentialism. *Group Processes and Intergroup Relations, 9,* 25–42.

Dick, D. (2005). Shared environment. In B. Everitt & D. Howell (Eds.), *Encyclopedia of statistics in behavioral science* (Vol. 4, pp.1828–1830). Chichester, England: Wiley.

Dweck, C. (2000). *Self-theories: Their role in motivation, personality and development.* Philadelphia, PA: Taylor & Francis.

Dweck, C., & Leggett, E. (1988). A social cognitive approach to motivation and personality. *Psychological Review, 95,* 256–273.

Felin, T., & Zenger, T. (2009). Entrepreneurs as theorists: On the origins of collective beliefs and novel strategies. *Strategic Entrepreneurship Journal, 3,* 127–146.

Fisher, J., & Koch, J. (2008). *Born, not made: The entrepreneurial personality.* Westport, CT: Praeger.

Frese, M. (2007). The psychological actions and entrepreneurial success: An action theory approach. In J. R. Baum, M. Frese, & R. Baron (Eds.), *The psychology of entrepreneurship* (pp. 151–188). Mahwah, NJ: Erlbaum.

Furnham, A. (1988). *Lay theories: Everyday understanding of problems in the social sciences.* Elmsford, NY: Pergamon Press.

Gannett, A. (2012, March 10). Entrepreneurs are born. *Entrepreneur.* Retrieved from http://thenextweb.com/entrepreneur/2012/03/10/entrepreneurs-are-born

Gartner, W. (1989). "Who is an entrepreneur?" is the wrong question. *Entrepreneurship Theory and Practice,* 47–68.

Gartner, W., & Carter, N. (2003). Entrepreneurial behavior and firm organizing processes. In Z. Acs & D. Audretsch (Eds.), *Handbook of entrepreneurship research* (pp. 195–221). London, England: Kluwer.

Gelman, S. (2003). *The essential child: Origins of essentialism in everyday thought*. Oxford, England: Oxford University Press.

Gist, M., & Mitchell, T. (1992). Self-efficacy: A theoretical analysis of its determinants and malleability. *Academy of Management Review, 17*, 183–211.

Gollust, S., Hull, S. C., & Wilfond, B. (2002). Limitations of direct-to-consumer advertising for clinical genetic testing. *Journal of the American Medical Association, 288*(14), 1762–1767.

Grégoire, D., Corbett, A., & McMullen, J. (2008). The cognitive perspective in entrepreneurship research: An agenda for future research. *Journal of Management Studies, 48*, 1443–1477.

Haslam, N., Rothschild, L., & Ernst, D. (2000). Essentialist beliefs about social categories. *British Journal of Social Psychology, 39*, 113–127.

Haslam, N., & Whelan, J. (2008). Human natures: Psychological essentialism in thinking about differences between people. *Social and Personality Psychology Compass, 2*, 1297–1312.

Heath, C. (1999). On the social psychology of agency relationships: Lay theories of motivation overemphasize extrinsic incentives. *Organizational Behavior and Human Decision Processes, 78*, 25–62.

Hmieleski, K., & Baron, R. (2008). When does entrepreneurial self-efficacy enhance versus reduce firm performance? *Strategic Entrepreneurship Journal, 2*, 57–72.

Hong, Y., Levy, S., & Chiu, C. (2001). The contribution of the lay theories approach to the study of groups. *Personality and Social Psychology Review, 5*, 98–106.

Huang, L., & Pearce, J. (2015). Managing the unknowable: The effectiveness of early-stage investor gut feel in entrepreneurial investment decisions. *Administrative Science Quarterly, 60*, 634–670.

Jain, S., & Cassell, C. (2010). Societal perceptions of physicians: Knights, knaves or pawns? *Journal of the American Medical Association, 304*, 1009–1010.

Jayaratne, T. E., Gelman, S., Feldbaum, M., Sheldon, J., Petty, E., & Kardia, S.L.R. (2009). The perennial debate: Nature, nurture or choice? Black and White Americans' explanations for individual differences. *Review of General Psychology, 13*, 24–33.

Keller, J. (2005). In genes we trust: The biological component of psychological essentialism and its relationship to mechanisms of motivated social cognition. *Journal of Personality and Social Psychology, 88*, 686–702.

Kelley, D., Singer, S., & Herrington, M. (2011). *The Global Entrepreneurship Monitor: 2011 Global Report*. London, England: The Global Entrepreneurship Research Association.

Klotz, A., Hmieleski, K., Bradley, B., & Busenitz, L. (2014). New venture teams: A review of the literature and roadmap for future research. *Journal of Management, 40*, 226–255.

Koellinger, P., Minniti, M., & Schade, C. (2007). I think I can, I think I can: Overconfidence and entrepreneurial behavior. *Journal of Economic Psychology, 28*, 502–527.

Kruglanski, A., Dechesne, M., Orehek, E., & Pierro, A. (2009). Three decades of lay epistemics: The why, how and who of knowledge formation. *European Review of Social Psychology, 20*, 146–191.

Lanie, A., Jayaratne, T. E., Sheldon, J., Kardia, S. L. R., Anderson, E., Feldbaum, M., & Petty, E. (2004). Exploring the public understanding of basic genetic concepts. *Journal of Genetic Counseling, 13*, 305–320.

Lazear, E. (2004). Balanced skills and entrepreneurship. *American Economic Review, 94,* 208–211.

Leibenstein, H. (1968). Entrepreneurship and development. *American Economic Review, 58,* 72–83.

Levie, J., & Autio, E. (2008). A theoretical grounding and test of the GEM model. *Small Business Economics, 31,* 235–263.

Levy, S., Chiu, C., & Hong, Y. (2006). Lay theories and intergroup relations. *Group Processes and Intergroup Relations, 9,* 5–24.

Levy, S., Plaks, J., Hong, Y., Chiu, C., & Dweck, C. (2001). Static versus dynamic theories and the perception of groups: Different routes to different destinations. *Personality and Social Psychology Review, 5,* 156–168.

Lickel, B., Hamilton, D., & Sherman, S. (2001). Elements of a lay theory of groups: Types of groups, relational styles and the perception of group entitativity. *Personality and Social Psychology Review, 5,* 129–140.

Mantere, S., Aula, P., Schildt, H., & Vaara, E. (2013). Narrative attributions of entrepreneurial failure. *Journal of Business Venturing, 28,* 459–473.

Markman, G. (2007). Entrepreneurs' competencies. In J. Baum, M. Frese, & R. Baron (Eds.), *The psychology of entrepreneurship* (pp. 19–40). Mahwah, NJ: Erlbaum.

Maron, D. (2015, January 1). What rare disease is hiding in your DNA? *Scientific American, 312.* Retrieved from https://www.scientificamerican.com/article/what-rare-disorder-is-hiding-in-your-dna

Maurya, A. (2015, January 15). *Are entrepreneurs born or made?* Retrieved from https://blog.leanstack.com/are-entrepreneurs-born-or-made-fb4e6af89092#.5p9wjkad9

McMullen, J., & Shepherd, D. (2006). Entrepreneurial action and the role of uncertainty in the theory of the entrepreneur. *Academy of Management Review, 31,* 132–152.

Mitchell, R. K., Busenitz, L., Lant, T., McDougall, P., Morse, E., & Smith, J. B. (2002). Toward a theory of entrepreneurial cognition: Rethinking the people side of entrepreneurship research. *Entrepreneurship Theory and Practice, 27,* 93–104.

Mitchell, R. K., Smith, B., Seawright, K. W., & Morse, E. (2000). Cross-cultural cognitions and the venture creation decision. *Academy of Management Journal, 43,* 974–993.

Molden, D., & Dweck, C. (2006). Finding meaning in psychology: A lay theories approach to self-regulation, social perception and social development. *American Psychologist, 61,* 192–203.

Nelkin, D., & Lindee, M. (1995). *The DNA mystique: The gene as cultural icon.* Ann Arbor: University of Michigan Press.

Nicolaou, N., Shane, S., Cherkas, L., Hunkin, J., & Spector, T. (2008). Is the tendency to engage in entrepreneurship genetic? *Management Science, 54,* 167–179.

Owens, D., Mannix, E., & Neale, M. (1998). Strategic formation of groups: Issues in task performance and team member selection. In M. Neale, E. Mannix, & D. Gruenfeld (Eds.), *Research on managing groups and teams* (vol.1, pp. 149–165). Westport, CT: JAI Press.

Parker, S. (2009). Can cognitive biases explain venture team homophily? *Strategic Entrepreneurship Journal, 3,* 67–83.

Parker, S. (2013). Do serial entrepreneurs run successively better-performing businesses? *Journal of Business Venturing, 28,* 652–666.

Paulsell, S. (2005, December 28). What makes an entrepreneur? Retrieved from MissouriBusiness.net.

Phelan, J. (2002). Genetic bases of mental illness: A cure for stigma. *Trends in Neurosciences, 25,* 430–431.

Pollack, J., Burnette, J., & Hoyt, C. (2012). Self-efficacy in the face of threats to entrepreneurial success: Mind-sets matter. *Basic and Applied Social Psychology, 34,* 287–294.

Priem, R., & Rosenstein, J. (2000). Is organization theory obvious to practitioners? A test of one established theory. *Organization Science, 11,* 509–524.

Ramoglou, S. (2011). Who is a "non-entrepreneur?" Taking the "others" of entrepreneurship seriously. *International Small Business Journal, 31,* 432–453.

Rauch, A., & Frese, M. (2007). Born to be an entrepreneur? Revisiting the personality approach to entrepreneurship. In J. Baum, M. Frese, & R. Baron (Eds.), *The psychology of entrepreneurship* (pp. 41–66). Mahwah, NJ: Erlbaum.

Rhode, D. (1998). The professionalism problem. *William and Mary Law Review, 39,* 283–326.

Richards, M. (1996). Lay and professional knowledge of genetics and inheritance. *Public Understanding of Science, 5,* 217–230.

Richards, M., & Ponder, M. (1996). Lay understanding of genetics: A test of a hypothesis. *Journal of Medical Genetics, 33,* 1032–1036.

Riquelme, H., & Watson, J. (2002). Do venture capitalists' implicit theories on new business success/failure have empirical validity? *International Small Business Journal, 20,* 395–420.

Rothbart, M., & Taylor, M. (1992). Category labels and social reality: Do we view social categories as natural kinds. In G. Semin & K. Fiedler (Eds.), *Language, interaction and social cognition* (pp. 11–36). Thousand Oaks, CA: Sage.

Rousseau, D., & McCarthy, S. (2007). Educating managers from an evidence-based perspective. *Academy of Management Learning & Education, 6,* 84–101.

Sarasvathy, S. (2004). The questions we ask and the questions we care about: Reformulating some problems in entrepreneurship research. *Journal of Business Venturing, 19,* 707–717.

Sarasvathy, S. (2008). *Effectuation: Elements of entrepreneurial expertise.* Cheltenham, England: Elgar.

Shane, S. (2010). *Born entrepreneurs, born leaders: How genes affect your work life.* Oxford, England: Oxford University Press.

Shepherd, D., McMullen, J., & Jennings, P. D. (2007). The formation of opportunity beliefs: Overcoming ignorance and reducing doubt. *Strategic Entrepreneurship Journal, 1,* 75–95.

Shook, C., Priem, R., & McGee, J. (2003). Venture creation and the enterprising individual: A review and synthesis. *Journal of Management, 29,* 379–399.

Spencer-Rodgers, J., Hamilton, D., & Sherman, S. (2007). The central role of entitativity in stereotypes of social categories and task groups. *Journal of Personality and Social Psychology, 92,* 369–388.

Turkheimer, E. (2000). Three laws of behavior genetics and what they mean. *Current Directions in Psychological Science, 9,* 160–164.

Turkheimer, E. (2011). Genetics and human agency: Comment on Dar-Nimrod and Heine (2011). *Psychological Bulletin, 137,* 825–828.

Ucbasaran, D., Alsos, G. A., Westhead, P., & Wright, M. (2008). Habitual entrepreneurs. *Foundations and Trends in Entrepreneurship, 4,* 309–450.

Walsh, J., & Seward, J. (1990). On the efficiency of internal and external corporate control mechanisms. *Academy of Management Review, 15,* 421–458.

Wilson, F., Kickul, J., & Marlino, D. (2007). Gender, entrepreneurial self-efficacy and entrepreneurial career intentions: Implications for entrepreneurship education. *Entrepreneurship Theory and Practice, 31*, 387–406.

Wood, R., & Bandura, A. (1989). Social cognitive theory of organizational management. *Academy of Management Review, 14*, 361–384.

Yzerbyt, V., & Rocher, S. (2002). Subjective essentialism and the formation of stereotypes. In C. McGarty, V. Yzerbyt, & R. Spears (Eds.), *Stereotypes as explanations: The formation of meaningful beliefs about social groups* (pp. 38–66). Cambridge, England: Cambridge University Press.

Zhao, H., & Seibert, S. (2006). The Big Five personality dimensions and entrepreneurial status: A meta-analytical review. *Journal of Applied Psychology, 91*, 259–271.

Zhao, H., Seibert, S., & Hills, G. (2005). The mediating role of self-efficacy in the development of entrepreneurial intentions. *Journal of Applied Psychology, 90*, 1265–1272.

Zhang, Z., Zyphur, M., Narayanan, J., Arvey, R., Chaturvedi, S., Avolio, B., . . . Larsson, G. (2009). The genetic basis of entrepreneurship: The effects of gender and personality. *Organizational Behavior and Human Decision Processes, 100*, 93–107.

Zott, C., & Huy, Q. (2007). How entrepreneurs use symbolic management to acquire resources. *Administrative Science Quarterly, 52*, 70–105.

Zuckerman, M. (2006). *Sensation seeking and risky behavior*. Washington, DC: APA Press.

Acknowledgments

This chapter was stimulated by conversations held at the 2009 Carey-Darden Entrepreneurship Scholars' Retreat. I am grateful to Phil Phan for directing my attention to this topic and to Andrew Corbett, Dimo Dimov, Chuck Eesley, Vlad Griskevicius, Lisa Leslie, Annaleena Parhankangas, Phil Phan, Saras Sarasvathy, Vaish Subramani, Eric Turkheimer, and Hao Zhao, among others, for their feedback on these ideas. The chapter has also benefited from the insights of seminar participants at the University of Western Ontario, Drexel University, and the University of Minnesota. Finally, I am grateful to the University of Virginia's Batten Institute and the Richard M. Schulze Family Foundation for supporting the development of these ideas.

Section 3

The Organization: Corporate Entrepreneurship and Entrepreneurial Teams

3a: The Organization

14

Corporate Entrepreneurship & Innovation: Today's Leadership Challenge

Donald F. Kuratko[a]

[a] *Indiana University*

Introduction

The nature of business has been transformed in the 21st century. The dynamic that has driven this transformation is innovation/entrepreneurship, especially as it relates to existing companies. Seeking opportunities, taking risks beyond security, and having the tenacity to push an idea through to reality combine into a special perspective known as an entrepreneurial mindset which has become a challenge for most organizations to harness from their members (Kuratko, 2017). As this entrepreneurial mindset is about driving innovation, it has become a major strategic goal within organizations as they pursue significant competitive advantages (Morris, Kuratko, & Covin, 2011). Thus, the new leadership challenge is about promoting a new vision, fostering new possibilities, opening up new horizons, and inspiring others to unleash their entrepreneurial mindsets to create new venture concepts (Kuratko & Morris, 2013). It has been shown that the ability to trigger entrepreneurial action is a cornerstone of entrepreneurial leadership (McMullen & Shepherd, 2006). However, it may also be considered threatening because it is essentially disruptive, introducing change for individuals. The willingness to take on the risks associated with entrepreneurial action and encouraging others in the organization to address the obstacles to corporate entrepreneurship and innovation represent some of the keys to successful leadership in today's dynamic environment.

During the last decade large firms existing in mature industries realized that they need to restructure and reinvent themselves to become more entrepreneurial or they would simply not be able to sustain themselves for the future (Morris et al., 2011). A global entrepreneurial revolution has taken hold in an economic sense, and fostering individuals' entrepreneurial mindsets through corporate entrepreneurship/innovation is the dominant strategy. In trying to understand this strategy, it is important to first understand what exactly constitutes corporate entrepreneurship and innovation.

The Wiley Handbook of Entrepreneurship, First Edition.
Edited by Gorkan Ahmetoglu, Tomas Chamorro-Premuzic, Bailey Klinger, & Tessa Karcisky.
© 2017 John Wiley & Sons Ltd. Published 2017 by John Wiley & Sons Ltd.

What Constitutes the Domain of Corporate Entrepreneurship?

The concept of corporate entrepreneurship has evolved over the last five decades with various definitions and meanings. Kuratko and Nagelvoort (2015) provided a complete bibliography of corporate entrepreneurship, tracing its beginnings and developments over the years. They point out that "corporate entrepreneurship" describes entrepreneurial or innovative behavior inside established mid-sized and large organizations. The theoretical and empirical knowledge about the domain of corporate entrepreneurship/innovation has developed since the early 1970s and the entrepreneurial behavior on which it is based has improved with this academic research emphasis (Kuratko & Nagelvoort, 2015). Thus, many of the elements essential to constructing a theoretically grounded understanding of corporate entrepreneurship/innovation can now be readily identified from the previous literature.

For example, the early research in the 1970s focused on venture teams and how entrepreneurship inside existing organizations could be developed (Hanan, 1976; Hill & Hlavacek, 1972; Peterson & Berger, 1972). In the 1980s, researchers started to conceptualize corporate entrepreneurship as entrepreneurial behavior requiring organizational sanctions and resource commitments for the purpose of developing different types of value-creating innovations, viewing it as a process of organizational renewal (Alterowitz, 1988; Burgelman, 1983a, 1983b, 1984; Kanter, 1985; Pinchott, 1985; Sathe 1989; Schollhammer 1982; Sykes & Block, 1989).

By the 1990s researchers had adjusted their focus on corporate entrepreneurship to reenergizing and enhancing the firm's ability to develop the skills through which innovations could be created (Barringer & Bluedorn, 1999; Birkinshaw, 1997; Borch, Huse, & Senneseth, 1999; Jennings & Young, 1990; Merrifield, 1993; Zahra, 1991; Zahra, Kuratko, & Jennings, 1999). More comprehensive definitions began to take shape during the 1990s such as Guth and Ginsberg's (1990) approach that outlined two major types of phenomena: new venture creation within existing organizations and the transformation of ongoing organizations through strategic renewal. By the end of the decade Sharma and Chrisman (1999, p. 18) articulated that same approach by suggesting that corporate entrepreneurship "is the process where by an individual or a group of individuals, in association with an existing organization, create a new organization or instigate renewal or innovation within that organization."

The early 21st century found corporate entrepreneurship relatively well defined as a field of study due to the work of scholars in the late 20th century to reconcile past works into a holistic viewpoint. Measurement received increased focus in the 21st century's first decade and themes established in previous decades received further development. At the same time, the potential for corporate entrepreneurship to develop competencies continued to receive attention in this decade such as focusing on the role that corporate entrepreneurship plays in discovery (Ahuja & Lampert, 2001; Smith & Di Gregorio, 2002) and the learning interactions in corporate venturing (Schildt, Maula, & Kiel, 2005). It is also important to note that the early 2000s saw the introduction of the concept of strategic entrepreneurship (Hitt, Ireland, Camp, & Sexton, 2001).

With all these various aspects of corporate entrepreneurship taking shape in the 21st century, the concept evolved into a firm's efforts to establish sustainable competitive advantages as the foundation for profitable growth. All the previous research efforts suggested particular domains into which corporate entrepreneurial activities could be categorized. Because many of the elements essential to constructing a theoretically grounded understanding of the domains of corporate entrepreneurship can now be identified, three major research domains have emerged over the years that include: *corporate venturing, strategic entrepreneurship*, and *entrepreneurial orientation* (Kuratko & Nagelvoort, 2015).

Corporate venturing has generally been categorized as concerning two main activities. The first activity incorporates any innovation that is created *within* the firm, referred to as internal corporate ventures (ICVs). With internal corporate venturing, new businesses are created and owned by the corporation and typically reside within the current corporate structure. The second activity would be any innovation that is created *outside* of the firm, referred to as external corporate ventures (ECVs). External corporate venturing involves new businesses that are created by parties outside the corporation and subsequently invested in or acquired by the corporation. These external businesses are typically very young ventures or early growth-stage firms (Covin & Miles, 2007; Morris et al., 2011). Miles and Covin (2002) reported that firms pursue corporate venturing for three primary reasons: (1) to build an innovative capability as the basis for making the overall firm more entrepreneurial and accepting of change; (2) to appropriate greater value from current organizational competencies or to expand the firm's scope of operations and knowledge into areas of possible strategic importance; and (3) to generate quick financial returns.

Strategic entrepreneurship approaches refer to a broad array of significant entrepreneurial activities or innovations that are adopted in the firm's pursuit of competitive advantage which usually do not result in new businesses for the corporation. With reference to strategic entrepreneurship approaches, innovation can be found within any of five areas—the firm's strategy, product offerings, served markets, internal organization (i.e., structure, processes, and capabilities), or business model (Kuratko & Audretsch, 2013). These innovations can also represent a firm's fundamental differentiation from its industry rivals. Hence, there are two possible reference points that can be considered when a firm exhibits strategic entrepreneurship: (1) how much the firm is transforming itself relative to where it was before (e.g., transforming its products, markets, internal processes, etc.) and (2) how much the firm is transforming itself relative to industry conventions or standards (again, in terms of product offerings, market definitions, internal processes, and so forth). Strategic entrepreneurship can take one of five forms— *strategic renewal* (adoption of a new strategy), *sustained regeneration* (introduction of a new product into an existing category), *domain redefinition* (reconfiguration of existing product or market categories), *organizational rejuvenation* (internally focused innovation for strategy improvement), and *business model reconstruction* (redesign of existing business model) (Covin & Miles, 1999; Hitt et al., 2001; Ireland, Hitt & Sirmon, 2003; Ireland & Webb, 2007; Morris et al., 2011).

Entrepreneurial orientation (EO) was developed by Covin and Slevin (1989, 1991) who posited the existence of a continuum of a firm's strategic behavioral proclivities. The continuum ranged from more conservative to more entrepreneurial, with the entrepreneurial end of the spectrum evidenced by innovativeness (the introduction of new products, processes, and business models), proactiveness (actively entering new product/market spaces and seeking market leadership positions), and risk-taking (a willingness among strategic decision-makers to contribute resources to projects with uncertain outcomes). A focus on connecting EO to performance and measuring the dimensions of EO objectively arises in the late 1990s. Lumpkin and Dess (1996) and Rauch, Wiklund, Lumpkin, and Frese (2009) both focus on EO and business performance while Lumpkin and Dess (2001) and Lumpkin, Cogliser, and Schneider (2009) focus on measuring the various dimensions of EO. In the years following the Covin and Slevin (1991) specific conceptualization, scholars have offered alternative perspectives on the conceptual domain of a firm-level strategic orientation toward entrepreneurship (Anderson, Kreiser, Kuratko, Hornsby, & Eshima, 2015; Covin & Wales, 2012). As these perspectives show, the concept of EO is still an active emphasis within the corporate entrepreneurship/innovation area.

With any of the three main conceptual areas of corporate venturing, strategic entrepreneurship, or entrepreneurial orientation, the critical elements of the internal environment or company climate needed for corporate entrepreneurship to exist and prosper have been explored.

The Importance of a Climate Conducive for Innovative Activity

As Kuratko, Hornsby, and Covin (2014) state, "The willingness and ability to act upon one's innate entrepreneurial potential is based on a calculated assessment. Conditions in the internal work environment dictate the perceived costs and benefits associated with taking personal risks, challenging current practices, devoting time to unproven approaches, persevering in the face of organizational resistance, and enduring the ambiguity and stress that entrepreneurial behavior can create. Therefore, credible innovation is more likely in companies where all individuals' entrepreneurial potential is sought and nurtured and where organizational knowledge is widely shared. The managerial challenge becomes that of using workplace design elements to develop an "innovation friendly" internal environment." Employee perception of an innovative environment is critical for stressing the importance of the leadership's commitment to potential innovative projects (Hornsby, Kuratko, Shepherd, & Bott, 2009).

A firm's internal entrepreneurial climate should be assessed to evaluate in what manner it is supportive for entrepreneurial behavior to exist and how that is perceived by the leaders. As the foundation for successfully implementing corporate innovation, leaders need to create an inventory of the firm's current situation regarding its readiness for innovation; they need to identify (a) parts of the firm's structure, control systems, human resource management systems, and culture that inhibit entrepreneurial behavior, and (b) parts that facilitate entrepreneurial behavior (Ireland, Kuratko, & Morris, 2006a, 2006b).

In order to understand the most effective internal environment for corporate entrepreneurial activity, an examination of antecedents for individual entrepreneurial behavior is critical. Most of the research dealing with the impact of organizational antecedents on individual-level entrepreneurial behavior is based on the empirical work of Kuratko and his colleagues (Kuratko, Montagno, & Hornsby, 1990; Hornsby, Kuratko, & Montagno, 1999; Hornsby, Kuratko, & Zahra, 2002; Kuratko, Hornsby, & Goldsby, 2004; Kuratko, Ireland, Covin, & Hornsby, 2005; Hornsby et al., 2009). In the Kuratko et al. (1990) study, results from factor analysis showed that what had been theoretically argued to be five conceptually distinct factors that would elicit and support entrepreneurial behavior on the part of first- and middle-level managers (top management support, reward and resource availability, organizational structure and boundaries, risk-taking, and time availability) were actually only three in number. Based on how items loaded, they concluded that three factors—management support, organizational structure, and reward and resource availability—were important influences on the development of an organizational climate in which entrepreneurial behavior on the part of first- and middle-level managers could be expected.

In extending this early study, Hornsby et al. (1999) conducted empirical research to explore the effect of organizational culture on entrepreneurial behavior in a sample of Canadian and US firms. In particular, they sought to determine if organizational culture creates variance in entrepreneurial behavior on the part of managers. The results based on data collected from all levels of management showed no significant differences between Canadian and US managers' perceptions of the importance of five factors—management support, work discretion, rewards/reinforcement, time availability, and organizational boundaries—as antecedents to their entrepreneurial behavior. These findings partially validated those reported by Kuratko et al. (1990) and extended the importance of organizational antecedents of managers' entrepreneurial behavior into companies based in a second national culture.

Hornsby et al. (2002) then developed the Corporate Entrepreneurship Assessment Instrument (CEAI) to partially replicate the previous studies and provide a sound instrument for analyzing employee perceptions of the antecedents to an organizational climate conducive for entrepreneurial activity. The instrument featured 48 Likert-style questions that were used to assess antecedents of entrepreneurial behavior. Results from factor analyses supported the five stable antecedents of middle-level managers' entrepreneurial behavior. The five antecedents are: (1) *management support* (the willingness of top-level managers to facilitate and promote entrepreneurial behavior, including the championing of innovative ideas and providing the resources people require to behave entrepreneurially), (2) *work discretion/autonomy* (top-level managers' commitment to tolerate failure, provide decision-making latitude and freedom from excessive oversight and to delegate authority and responsibility to middle- and lower-level managers), (3) *rewards/reinforcement* (developing and using systems that reinforce entrepreneurial behavior, highlight significant achievements, and encourage pursuit of challenging work), (4) *time availability* (evaluating workloads to ensure that individuals and groups have the time needed to pursue innovations and that their jobs are structured in ways that support efforts to achieve short- and long-term organizational goals), and (5) *organizational boundaries* (precise explanations of outcomes expected from organizational work and development of mechanisms for evaluating, selecting and using innovations). This instrument measures the degree to which individuals within a firm perceive these five elements to be critical to an internal environment conducive for individual entrepreneurial activity (Kuratko, Hornsby, & Covin, 2014). Through the results of this instrument corporate entrepreneurial leaders are better able to assess, evaluate, and manage the firm's internal work environment in ways that support entrepreneurial behavior, which becomes the foundation for successfully implementing a corporate innovation strategy. Yet there are critical roles that must be fulfilled by the different levels of leadership.

Managerial Levels and Contributions to Entrepreneurial Efforts

Leaders at all organizational levels have critical strategic roles to fulfill for the organization to be successful (Ireland, Hitt, & Vaidyanath, 2002). According to Floyd and Lane (2000), senior-, middle-, and first-level managers (leaders) have distinct responsibilities which are then associated with particular managerial actions. Thus, each has specific contributions important to the entrepreneurial efforts of an organization.

In examining the role of senior-level managers, Burgelman (1984) contends that in successful corporate entrepreneurship senior-level management's principal involvement takes place within the strategic and structural context determination processes. In particular, senior-level managers are responsible for *retroactively rationalizing* certain new businesses into the firm's portfolio and concept of strategy based on their evaluations of those businesses' prospects as desirable, value-creating components of the firm. They are also responsible for *structuring* the organization in ways that accommodate and reinforce the business ventures embraced as part of the firm's strategic context. Overall, Burgelman (1984) sees such managers as having a *selecting* role in the corporate entrepreneurship.

Ling, Simsek, Lubatkin, and Veiga (2008) examined 152 firms in regard to how "transformational" CEOs impacted on corporate entrepreneurship. Their research demonstrated that CEOs had a significant role in directly shaping four salient characteristics of top management teams: behavioral integration, risk-taking propensity, decentralization of responsibilities, and long-term compensation. This study provided impetus to the importance of the *directing* role that top management must embrace. Thus, senior-level managers have critical roles in corporate entrepreneurial activity in the articulation of an entrepreneurial strategic vision and instigating the emergence of an organizational climate conducive to entrepreneurial activity. In addition, senior-level managers are also centrally involved in the defining processes of both the corporate venturing and strategic entrepreneurship domains, as they provide leadership to various entrepreneurial initiatives.

Evidence shows that middle-level managers are the hub through which most organizational knowledge flows (Floyd & Wooldridge, 1992; 1994; King, Fowler, & Zeithaml, 2001). To interact effectively with first-level managers, middle-level managers must possess the technical competence required to understand the firm's core competencies; simultaneously, interacting effectively with senior-level executives, middle-level managers must understand the firm's strategic intent and goals. Through interactions with senior- and first-level managers, those operating in the middle of an organization's leadership structure influence and shape their firms' corporate entrepreneurial strategies. Kuratko, Ireland, Covin, and Hornsby (2005) argue that middle-level managers' work as change agents and promoters of innovation is facilitated by their position in the organization hierarchy. They contend that middle-level managers *endorse, refine,* and *shepherd* entrepreneurial initiatives and *identify, acquire,* and *deploy* resources needed to pursue those initiatives.

The work of Kuratko, Ireland, et al. (2005), further described each of the roles for middle-level manager. In the *endorsement* role, middle-level managers often find themselves in evaluative positions with entrepreneurial initiatives emerging from lower organizational levels. Then middle-level managers must endorse those valued initiatives to the top level of the organization. They must also endorse the top-level initiatives and "sell" their value-creating potential to the primary implementers—first-level managers. In the *refinement* role, middle-level managers are molding the entrepreneurial opportunity into one that makes sense for the organization, given the organization's strategy, resources, and structure. Middle-level managers must convert potential entrepreneurial opportunities into initiatives that fit the organization. The *shepherding* role is where middle-level managers champion and guide the entrepreneurial initiative to assure that entrepreneurial initiatives originating at lower organizational levels are not abandoned once their continued development requires higher level support. With their *identification* role, middle-level managers must know which resources will be needed to convert the entrepreneurial initiative into a business reality as these initiatives tend to evolve in their scope, content, and focus as they develop (McGrath & MacMillan, 1995). Finally, the *acquisition and deployment* roles involve middle-level managers being responsible for redirecting resources away from existing operations and deploying them into entrepreneurial initiatives appearing to have greater strategic value for the firm (Burgelman, 1984). In short, it might be argued that the middle management level is where entrepreneurial opportunities are given the best chance to flourish based on the resources likely to be deployed in their pursuit.

According to Floyd and Lane (2000), first-level managers have *experimenting, adjusting,* and *conforming* roles. The *experimenting* role is expressed through the initiating of entrepreneurial projects. The *adjusting* role is expressed through, for example, first-level managers' responding to recognized and unplanned entrepreneurial challenges. Finally, the *conforming* role is expressed through first-level managers' adaptation of operating policies and procedures to the strategic initiatives endorsed at higher organizational levels.

In one empirical examination of managers' relation to employees in the corporate entrepreneurship process, Brundin, Patzelt, and Shepherd (2008) examined the entrepreneurial behavior of employees in entrepreneurially oriented firms and found a direct relation to manager's emotions and displays. The employees' willingness to act entrepreneurially increased when managers displayed confidence and satisfaction about an entrepreneurial project. It was also shown that the employees' willingness to act entrepreneurially decreased when managers displayed frustration, worry, or bewilderment about an entrepreneurial project.

In an effort to study entrepreneurial actions within the context of corporate entrepreneurship at different levels of management (leadership), Hornsby, Kuratko, Shepherd, and Bott (2009) conducted an empirical study of 458 managers at different levels in their firms. They found that the relationship between perceived internal antecedents (as measured by the CEAI mentioned earlier) and corporate entrepreneurial actions (measured by the number of new ideas implemented), differed depending on managerial level. Specifically, the positive relationship between managerial support and entrepreneurial action was more positive for senior- and middle-level managers than it was for first-level (lower level) managers, and the positive relationship between work discretion and entrepreneurial action was more positive for senior- and middle-level managers than it was for first-level managers. The few studies that have explored managerial level (primarily conceptual studies) have emphasized the role of first-level managers in a "bottom-up" process of corporate entrepreneurship (Burgelman, 1983a; 1983b; 1984). This study by Hornsby et al. (2009) offered a counterweight to this "bottom-up" process with arguments and empirical support for the notion that given a specific organizational environment more senior managers have greater structural ability to "make more of" the conditions and thus implement more entrepreneurial ideas than do first-level managers.

Even with the differences found with levels of management in the Hornsby et al. (2009) study, it reinforced the belief that working jointly, senior-, middle-, and first-level managers are responsible for developing the entrepreneurial behaviors that could be used to form the core competencies through which future competitive success can be pursued (Kuratko, Hornsby, & Bishop, 2005). Thus, organizations developing an environment conducive to entrepreneurial activity must recognize that there is an integrated set of roles at the senior, middle, and first levels of managerial leadership. Research continues to examine the impact of these differing levels. Even with all managerial responsibilities acknowledged, there are specific ingredients that should be considered for any corporate entrepreneurial strategy.

Ingredients for an Effective Corporate Entrepreneurial Strategy

A corporate entrepreneurial strategy is "a vision-directed, organization-wide reliance on entrepreneurial behavior that purposefully and continuously rejuvenates the organization and shapes the scope of its operations through the recognition and exploitation of entrepreneurial opportunity" (Ireland, Covin, & Kuratko, 2009, p. 21). As companies have found themselves continually redefining their markets, restructuring their operations, and modifying their business models, learning the skills to think and act entrepreneurially has become a major strategy for competitive advantage.

In order for corporate entrepreneurship to operate as a strategy, it must "run deep" within organizations. Top managers are increasingly recognizing the need to respond to the entrepreneurial imperatives created by their competitive landscapes. Minimal responses or superficial commitments to a corporate entrepreneurship strategy will lead to its failure. As discussed previously, the sustained and strong commitment from every level of management is needed for any entrepreneurial strategy to be successful. A corporate entrepreneurship strategy is hard to create and, perhaps, even harder to perpetuate in organizations. The presence of certain external environmental conditions may be sufficient to motivate an organization's leaders to explore the possibility of adopting a corporate entrepreneurship strategy. However, the commitment of individuals throughout the organization to making such a strategy work, and the realization of personal and organizational entrepreneurial outcomes that reinforce this commitment, will be necessary to assure that entrepreneurial behavior becomes a defining aspect of the organization. Moreover, alignments must be created in evaluation and reward systems such that congruence is achieved in the entrepreneurial behaviors induced at the individual and organizational levels. Although external conditions may be increasingly conducive to the adoption of corporate entrepreneurship strategies, managers should harbor no illusions that the effective implementation of these strategies will be easily accomplished (Kuratko, 2017).

Corporations that create an entrepreneurial strategy find that the ethos of the original enterprise often changes dramatically. Some members of the organization are unaccustomed to operating in this environment so they may choose to leave; while other members will be motivated by the new environment of creativity, ingenuity, risk-taking, teamwork, and informal networking, all designed to increase productivity and make the organization more viable.

It should be noted that entrepreneurial ability is a variable that each individual possesses and organizations exhibit at some level. The leadership challenge becomes one of determining the level of each particular entrepreneurial individual or action. This assessment may be done through identifying the *degree* and *frequency* of entrepreneurial actions (Morris et al., 2011). Using the three underlying dimensions of EO—innovativeness, risk-taking, and proactiveness (Covin & Slevin, 1991)—different combinations of these dimensions may help in identifying the degree of any entrepreneurial action. Morris et al. (2011) employed this distinction to suggest that each entrepreneurial action could be regarded as highly or only minimally innovative, risky, and proactive. Accordingly, the "degree" of entrepreneurial action refers to the extent to which events are innovative, risky, and proactive. The "frequency" of entrepreneurial actions refers to the number of actions pursued by an individual or organization over a given period of time. It may vary from those companies that produce a steady stream of new products, services, or processes, to other companies that rarely introduce something new.

The overall level of the degree and frequency of entrepreneurial actions demonstrated by an individual or organization is known as "entrepreneurial intensity." Morris et al. (2011) created a two-dimensional matrix ("entrepreneurial grid") with the frequency (number of entrepreneurial events) on the vertical axis, and the degree (extent of innovativeness, risk, and proactiveness) on the horizontal axis. As there are no absolute standards for degree or frequency of entrepreneurial actions, the results are relative, meaning that different points on the grid at different periods in time could be applied to the same organization or person depending on their activity. However, a firm's entrepreneurial intensity does provide some measure of an organization's entrepreneurial activity at any point in time that could then form the basis for the direction chosen for a corporate entrepreneurial strategy.

Initiating entrepreneurial actions through a corporate entrepreneurial strategy does not produce instant success. It requires considerable time and investment, and there must be continual reinforcement. By their nature, organizations impose constraints on entrepreneurial behavior. To be sustainable, the corporate entrepreneurial strategy must be integrated into the mission, goals, strategies, structure, processes, and values of the organization. Flexibility, speed, innovation, and entrepreneurial leadership are the cornerstones. The leadership mindset must become an opportunity-driven mindset, where actions are never constrained by resources currently controlled (Morris et al., 2011). This entrepreneurial mindset becomes the essence of corporate entrepreneurship.

Even with the proper ingredients considered, the actual implementation of corporate entrepreneurship has proven quite elusive for most senior leaders. While many organizations have initiated innovative efforts, there has been widespread disappointment with the implementation and outcomes of the strategies (Koetzier & Alon, 2013).

Challenges with Implementation of Corporate Entrepreneurship

The implementation of corporate entrepreneurship and innovation is usually a challenge for most organizations. While there are many reasons that can be offered for the continued frustration in implementing corporate entrepreneurship and innovation programs, recent research on corporate entrepreneurship/innovation (e.g., Kuratko, Hornsby, & Covin, 2014; Morris et al., 2011) demonstrates that there are some key implementation issues that most corporations are not recognizing or responding to effectively. Effective recognition and response to these issues may be the difference between those companies that are able to implement a successful corporate innovation strategy and those who do not. Three of the issues include: understanding what type of innovation is being sought, effective use of operating controls, and proper individual training and preparation. If these issues are understood and appropriately addressed by today's leaders they can create an effective innovative ecosystem within the organization (Kuratko, Covin, & Hornsby, 2014).

The first issue confronting leaders is what type of innovation the firm is seeking. There are numerous definitions of *innovation* so any discussion of corporate entrepreneurship must first address the matter of how we categorize innovation—specifically, by basic type or trajectory. The basic types of innovation include: *product innovation*—changes to physical products; *process innovation*—changes to the processes that produce products or services; and s*ervice innovation*—changes to services that customers use. The basic trajectory for innovation may be *radical*—the launching of inaugural breakthroughs; *incremental*—the systematic evolution of a product or service into newer or larger markets; and *disruptive*— transforms business practice to rewrite the rules of an industry. Disruptive innovation often occurs because new sciences and technology are introduced or applied to a new market that offers the potential to exceed the existing limits of technology (Kuratko, Goldsby, & Hornsby, 2012).

A second issue that permeates most organizations is how to effectively use operating controls with entrepreneurial strategy. Without proper operating control mechanisms, corporate entrepreneurial activity may "tend to generate an incoherent mass of interesting but unrelated opportunities that may have profit potential, but that don't move [those] firms toward a desirable future" (Getz & Tuttle, 2001, p. 277). As noted by Kuratko and Goldsby (2004), the encouragement of corporate entrepreneurship can and often does result in counterproductive, rogue behavior by organizational members. Thus, the deliberate design and development of organizational systems reflecting the organizational dimensions for an environment conducive to corporate innovation is critical. Therefore, successful corporate entrepreneurial activity is contingent upon a firm's ability to align operations control processes and mechanisms that select, guide, and possibly terminate innovative actions and initiatives (Morris, Allen, Schindehutte & Avila, 2006). The exhibition of certain controls is not antithetical to the interests of corporate entrepreneurship but rather inherent to those interests. As such, observations to the effect that control is the enemy of successful innovation are naive. Leaders have come to realize that a mixture of formality and discretion is a key to providing both high effectiveness and high efficiency (Naveh, 2007). Managers should understand that innovation is a process amenable to the application of structured, disciplined oversight. In a study of 177 firms operating in a wide variety of industries, Goodale,

Kuratko, Hornsby, and Covin (2011) investigated the effect on innovation performance of several recognized determinants of corporate innovation—namely, as discussed above, management support, work discretion/autonomy, rewards/reinforcements, time availability, and organizational boundaries (Kuratko, Hornsby, & Covin, 2014). Their results indicated that each of the five innovation determinants significantly interacted with one or both of the operations control variables, thereby, influencing innovation performance. This is a significant finding that supports the importance of effectively using control systems with innovation. In the Goodale et al. (2011) study, innovation performance was greatest when corporate entrepreneurship was combined with operating control.

A final issue that seems to be overlooked is the proper individual training and preparation of organizational members in understanding what exactly a corporate entrepreneurship strategy is and how they are to execute within that environment. It is clear that success with corporate entrepreneurship requires that those within the firm be educated and trained as to what constitutes the concept of corporate entrepreneurship within their organization (Kuratko, Ireland, & Hornsby, 2001). Leaders must create an understanding of the entrepreneurial process for their employees. Having assessed whether the firm's internal work environment supports innovative activity (Kuratko, Hornsby, & Covin, 2014), leaders should also determine if corporate innovation and entrepreneurial behavior are understood by the firms' employees. Experience demonstrates that executives need to develop a program with the purpose of helping all parties who will be affected by corporate innovation to understand the value of the entrepreneurial behavior the firm is requesting of them (Kuratko, Covin, & Hornsby, 2014). As a way for organizations to develop understanding of the need for innovation and entrepreneurial activity, corporate entrepreneurship and innovation training programs are often employed to include an overview of the corporate entrepreneurship experience, the process of thinking innovatively as individuals, the idea acceleration process, the barriers and facilitators to entrepreneurial activity, the recognition and handling of project failure (Shepherd & Kuratko, 2009), the concept of forming teams to focus on specific innovations (Kuratko et al., 2012), and the process of completing an action plan that includes setting goals, a step-by-step timetable for project completion, and project evaluation. While this is only one example of a training format, the outline at least depicts the type of education and preparation needed within an organization so a general understanding of corporate entrepreneurship can be accomplished.

If these major implementation issues are understood and appropriately addressed, the creation of an effective innovative ecosystem within the organization is certainly enhanced. In addressing these issues, executives are attempting to provide "entrepreneurial leadership" for their organization (Kuratko, 2007; Ling et al., 2008) yet they must also accept certain responsibilities in this leadership role.

Future Expectations

As highlighted in this chapter, corporate entrepreneurship provides the context within which innovation takes place in an established firm. However, there are certain future expectations that researchers, leaders, and decision-makers need to consider when designing a corporate entrepreneurial strategy for a firm. Based on the research reviewed in this chapter here are some critical questions that should be answered as well as issues to be considered in order to gauge the future expectations of the organization (Kuratko, 2012).

- Where does the firm want to be in terms of its level of entrepreneurial intensity (Morris et al., 2011)? Does the firm seek a condition of (1) high frequency and low degree, (2) high degree and low frequency, or (3) some other combination?
- To what extent are the firm's entrepreneurial efforts oriented toward growing new businesses and starting new ventures outside the current portfolio of businesses—corporate venturing (Covin & Miles, 2007)—versus transforming the existing businesses with the objective of developing new products and/or serving markets that are new to the firm—strategic entrepreneurship (Ireland, Hitt, & Sirmon, 2003)?
- In what areas of the firm are managers seeking higher versus lower levels of entrepreneurial behaviors? Which business units or product areas are expected to be the most innovative and to serve as a model for the remainder of the firm? How are team members prepared to understand and create entrepreneurial actions (Kuratko, Hornsby, et al., 2005)?
- What type of innovations is being sought? What is the relative importance over the next three or so years of product innovation - introducing new goods or services in the marketplace versus process innovation - developing more efficient and effective ways to produce the firm's goods and services (Kuratko et al., 2012)?
- To what extent are entrepreneurial stimuli expected to come from top-, middle-, or first-level managers? Are all managers clear about what the firm expects from them in terms of stimulating entrepreneurial behavior as the path to create product, process, and/or administrative innovations (Hornsby et al., 2009)?
- What will be accepted or not accepted as actions within the firm. In other words, what are the limiting conditions or control mechanisms that are in place within the organization. Once individuals understand and accept the parameters then far more entrepreneurial activity can be accomplished (Goodale et al., 2011).
- Are the entrepreneurial leaders prepared to understand the "grief" that may be associated with project failures (Shepherd, Covin, & Kuratko, 2009)? While failure can be an important source of information, learning is not automatic as emotions generated by failure such as grief can interfere with the learning process. Recognizing the grief process and providing assistance to manage it for individuals and organizations will be critical to the recovery process and lead to enhanced learning (Shepherd et al., 2009; Shepherd & Kuratko, 2009).

Once these questions and issues are considered, leaders can have their organizations better prepared to compete effectively in competitive markets. Today's executives agree that innovation is the most important pathway for companies to accelerate their pace of change in the global environment. Corporate entrepreneurship is envisioned as a process that can facilitate firms' efforts to innovate constantly and cope effectively with the competitive realities that companies encounter when competing in world markets.

However, today's leaders should understand that innovation is a process amenable to the application of structured, disciplined oversight. The successful pursuit of corporate entrepreneurship demands that managers approach the innovation challenge with the understanding that the means by which potentially desirable innovation outcomes might be generated can be well understood and deliberately constructed.

As shown in the research reviewed in this chapter, there are rules, methods, and general process knowledge that can be brought to bear as resources in facilitation of successful innovation efforts. As such, it's often not the absence of research and well-understood procedures that results in successful innovation, it's their presence.

Finally, keep in mind that every senior manager should seek to promote an innovation-friendly environment as a way of encouraging the best entrepreneurial behavior in individuals as well as designing the most effective procedures, decision processes, and actions necessary to pursue those newly discovered innovations. Firms with leaders focused on developing an "innovative mindset" in their employees are the ones where senior leadership is also continually assessing the degree to which their employees are prepared to engage in entrepreneurial behavior. Corporate entrepreneurship is a revitalization of innovation, creativity, and leadership. These may be the critical components needed for the future productivity of all organizations. If so, then corporate entrepreneurship is the real challenge of leadership in today's dynamic environment.

References

Ahuja, G., & Lampert, C. M. (2001). Entrepreneurship in the large corporation: A longitudinal study of how established firms create breakthrough inventions. *Strategic Management Journal, 22*(6–7), 521–543.

Alterowitz, R. (1988). *New corporate ventures.* New York, NY: Wiley.

Anderson, B. S., Kreiser, P. M., Kuratko, D. F., Hornsby, J. S., & Eshima, Y. (2015). Reconceptualizing entrepreneurial orientation, *Strategic Management Journal, 36*(10), 1579–1596.

Barringer, B. R., & Bluedorn, A. C. (1999). Corporate entrepreneurship and strategic management. *Strategic Management Journal, 20,* 421–444.

Birkinshaw, J. (1997). Entrepreneurship in multinational corporations: The characteristics of subsidiary initiatives. *Strategic Management Journal, 18,* 207–229.

Borch, O. J., Huse, M., & Senneseth, K. (1999). Resource configuration, competitive strategies, and corporate entrepreneurship: An empirical examination of small firms. *Entrepreneurship Theory & Practice, 24*(1), 49–70.

Brundin, E., Patzelt, H., & Shepherd, D. A. (2008). Managers' emotional displays and employees' willingness to act entrepreneurially. *Journal of Business Venturing, 23*(2), 221–243.

Burgelman, R. A. (1983a). A process model of internal corporate venturing in the major diversified firm. *Administrative Science Quarterly, 28*(2), 223–244.

Burgelman, R. A. (1983b). Corporate entrepreneurship and strategic management: Insights from a process study. *Management Science, 23,* 1349–1363.

Burgelman, R. A. (1984). Designs for corporate entrepreneurship in established firms. *California Management Review, 26*(3), 154–166.

Covin, J. G., & Miles, M. P. (1999). Corporate entrepreneurship and the pursuit of competitive advantage. *Entrepreneurship Theory & Practice, 23*(3), 47–64.

Covin, J. G., & Miles, M. P. (2007). Strategic use of corporate venturing. *Entrepreneurship Theory & Practice, 31*(2), 183–207.

Covin, J. G., & Slevin, D. P. (1989). Strategic management of small firms in hostile and benign environments. *Strategic Management Journal, 10,* 75–87.

Covin, J. G., & Slevin, D. P. (1991). A conceptual model of entrepreneurship as firm behavior. *Entrepreneurship Theory and Practice, 16*(1), 7–25.

Covin, J. G., & Wales, W. J. (2012). The measurement of entrepreneurial orientation. *Entrepreneurship Theory & Practice, 36*(4), 677–702.

Floyd, S. W., & Lane, P. J. (2000). Strategizing throughout the organization: Managing role conflict in strategic renewal. *Academy of Management Review, 25,* 154–177.

Floyd, S. W., & Wooldridge, B. (1992). Middle management involvement in strategy and its association with strategic type. *Strategic Management Journal, 13,* 53–168.

Floyd, S. W., & Wooldridge, B. (1994). Dinosaurs or dynamos? Recognizing middle management's strategic role. *Academy of Management Executive, 8*(4), 47–57.

Getz, G., & Tuttle, E. G. (2001). A comprehensive approach to corporate venturing. In *Handbook of business strategy.* New York, NY: Thompson Financial Media.

Goodale, J. C., Kuratko, D. F., Hornsby, J. S., & Covin, J. G. (2011). Operations management and corporate entrepreneurship: The moderating effect of operations control on the antecedents of corporate entrepreneurial activity in relation to innovation performance. *Journal of Operations Management, 29*(2), 116–127.

Guth, W. D., & Ginsberg A. (1990). Corporate entrepreneurship [Special issue]. *Strategic Management Journal, 11,* 5–15.

Hanan, M. (1976). Venturing corporations—Think small to stay strong. *Harvard Business Review, 54*(3), 139–148.

Hill, R. M., & Hlavacek, J. D. (1972). The venture team: A new concept in marketing organizations. *Journal of Marketing, 36,* 44–50.

Hitt, M. A., Ireland, R. D., Camp, S. M., & Sexton, D. L. (2001). Strategic entrepreneurship: Entrepreneurial strategies for wealth creation. *Strategic management journal, 22*(6–7), 479–491.

Hitt, M. A., Ireland, R. D., Sirmon, D. G., & Trahms, C. A. (2011). Strategic entrepreneurship: Creating value for individuals, organizations, and society. *Academy of Management Perspectives, 25*(2), 57–75.

Hornsby, J. S., Kuratko, D. F., & Montagno, R. V. (1999). Perception of internal factors for corporate entrepreneurship: A comparison of Canadian and U.S. managers. *Entrepreneurship Theory and Practice, 24*(2), 9–24.

Hornsby, J. S., Kuratko, D. F., Shepherd, D. A., & Bott, J. P. (2009). Managers' corporate entrepreneurial actions: Examining perception and position *Journal of Business Venturing, 24*(3), 236–247.

Hornsby, J. S., Kuratko, D. F., & Zahra, S. A. (2002). Middle managers' perception of the internal environment for corporate entrepreneurship: Assessing a measurement scale. *Journal of Business Venturing, 17,* 49–63.

Ireland, R. D., Covin, J. G., & Kuratko, D. F. (2009). Conceptualizing corporate entrepreneurship strategy, *Entrepreneurship Theory and Practice, 33*(1), 19–46.

Ireland, R. D., Hitt, M. A., & Sirmon, D. G. (2003). A model of strategic entrepreneurship: The construct and its dimensions. *Journal of Management, 29*(6), 963–989.

Ireland, R. D., Hitt, M. A., & Vaidyanath, D. (2002). Strategic alliances as a pathway to competitive success. *Journal of Management, 28,* 413–446.

Ireland, R. D., Kuratko, D. F., & Morris, M. H. (2006a). A health audit for corporate entrepreneurship: Innovation at all levels—Part I. *Journal of Business Strategy, 27*(1), 10–17.

Ireland, R. D., Kuratko, D. F., & Morris, M. H. (2006b). A health audit for corporate entrepreneurship: Innovation at all levels—Part 2. *Journal of Business Strategy*, 27(2), 21–30.

Ireland, R. D., & Webb, J. W. (2007). Strategic entrepreneurship: Creating competitive advantage through streams of innovation. *Business Horizons, 50,* 49–59.

Jennings, D. F., & Young, D. M. (1990). An empirical comparison between objective and subjective measures of the product innovation domain of corporate entrepreneurship. *Entrepreneurship Theory and Practice, 15*(1), 53–66.

Kanter, R. M. (1985). Supporting innovation and venture development in established companies. *Journal of Business Venturing, 1,* 47–60.

King, A. W., Fowler, S. W., & Zeithaml, C. P. (2001). Managing organizational competencies for competitive advantage: The middle-management edge. *Academy of Management Executive, 15*(2), 95–106.

Koetzier, W., & Alon, A. (2013). *Why "low risk" innovation is costly: Overcoming the perils of renovation and invention.* New York, NY: Accenture.

Kuratko, D. F. (2007, Summer). Entrepreneurial leadership for the 21st century. *Journal of Leadership & Organizational Studies, 14*(1).

Kuratko, D. F. (2012). A corporate innovation audit: Measuring readiness and results. In A. J. Sherman (Ed.), *Essays on governance.* Charleston, SC: Advantage Media.

Kuratko, D. F. (2017). *Entrepreneurship: Theory, process, practice* (10th ed.). Mason, OH: Cengage/Southwestern Publishing.

Kuratko, D. F., & Audretsch, D. B. (2013). Clarifying the domains of corporate entrepreneurship. *International Entrepreneurship & Management Journal, 9*(3), 323–335.

Kuratko, D. F., Covin, J. G., & Hornsby, J. S. (2014). Why implementing corporate innovation is so difficult. *Business Horizons, 57*(5), 647–655.

Kuratko, D. F., & Goldsby, M. G. (2004). Corporate entrepreneurs or rogue middle managers: A framework for ethical corporate entrepreneurship. *Journal of Business Ethics, 55*(1), 13–30.

Kuratko, D. F., Goldsby, M. G., & Hornsby, J. S. (2012). *Innovation acceleration: Transforming organizational thinking.* Upper Saddle River, NJ: Pearson/Prentice Hall.

Kuratko, D. F., Hornsby, J. S., & Bishop, J. W. (2005). Managers' corporate entrepreneurial actions and job satisfaction. *International Entrepreneurship and Management Journal, 1*(3), 275–291.

Kuratko, D. F., Hornsby, J. S., & Covin, J. G. (2014). Diagnosing a firm's internal environment for corporate entrepreneurship. *Business Horizons, 57*(1), 37–47.

Kuratko, D. F., Hornsby, J. S., & Goldsby, M. G. (2004). Sustaining corporate entrepreneurship: A proposed model of perceived implementation/outcome comparisons at the organizational and individual levels. *International Journal of Entrepreneurship and Innovation, 5*(2), 77–89.

Kuratko, D. F., Ireland, R. D., Covin, J. G., & Hornsby, J. S. (2005). A model of middle level managers' entrepreneurial behavior. *Entrepreneurship Theory & Practice, 29*(6), 699–716.

Kuratko, D. F., Ireland, R. D., & Hornsby, J. S. (2001). The power of entrepreneurial outcomes: Insights from Acordia, Inc. *Academy of Management Executive, 15*(4), 60–71.

Kuratko, D. F., Montagno, R. V., & Hornsby, J. S. (1990). Developing an entrepreneurial assessment instrument for an effective corporate entrepreneurial environment [Special issue]. *Strategic Management Journal, 11*, 49–58.

Kuratko, D. F., & Morris, M. H. (2013). *Entrepreneurship and leadership*. Cheltenham, England: Elgar.

Kuratko, D. F., & Nagelvoort, S. K. (2015). Corporate entrepreneurship. In R. W. Griffin. (Ed.), *Oxford bibliographies in management*. New York, NY: Oxford University Press.

Ling, Y., Simsek, Z., Lubatkin, M. H., & Veiga, J.F. (2008). Transformational leadership's role in promoting corporate entrepreneurship: Examining the CEO–TMT interface. *Academy of Management Journal, 51*(3), 557–576.

Lumpkin, G. T., Cogliser, C. C., & Schneider, D. R. (2009). Understanding and measuring autonomy: An entrepreneurial orientation perspective. *Entrepreneurship Theory & Practice, 33*(1), 47–69.

Lumpkin, G. T., & Dess, G. G. (1996). Clarifying the entrepreneurial orientation construct and linking it to performance. *Academy of Management Review, 21*(1), 135–172.

Lumpkin, G. T., & Dess, G. G. (2001). Linking two dimensions of entrepreneurial orientation to firm performance: The moderating role of environment and industry life cycle. *Journal of Business Venturing, 16*(5), 429–452.

McGrath, R. G., & MacMillan, I. C. (1995). Discovery-driven planning. *Harvard Business Review, 73*(4), 4–12.

McMullen, J. S., & Shepherd, D.A. (2006). Entrepreneurial action and the role of uncertainty in the theory of the entrepreneur. *Academy of Management Review, 31*(1), 132–152.

Merrifield, D. B. (1993). Intrapreneurial corporate renewal. *Journal of Business Venturing, 8*, 383–389.

Miles, M. P., & Covin, J. G. (2002). Exploring the practice of corporate venturing: Some common forms and their organizational implications. *Entrepreneurship Theory and Practice, 26*(3), 21–40.

Morris, M. H., Allen, J., Schindehutte, M., & Avila, R. (2006). Balanced management control systems as a mechanism for achieving corporate entrepreneurship. *Journal of Managerial Issues, 18*(4), 468–493.

Morris, M. H., Kuratko, D. F., & Covin, J. G. (2011). *Corporate entrepreneurship & innovation* (3rd ed.). Mason, OH: South-Western/Thomson Publishers.

Naveh, E. (2007). Formality and discretion in successful R&D projects. *Journal of Operations Management, 25*(1), 110–125.

Peterson, R., & Berger D. (1972). Entrepreneurship in organizations. *Administrative Science Quarterly, 16*, 97–106.

Pinchott, G. (1985). *Intrapreneurship*. New York, NY: Harper & Row.

Rauch, A., Wiklund, J., Lumpkin, G. T., & Frese, M. (2009). Entrepreneurial orientation and business performance: An assessment of past research and suggestions for the future. *Entrepreneurship Theory & Practice, 33*(3), 761–787.

Sathe, V. (1989). Fostering entrepreneurship in large diversified firm. *Organizational Dynamics, 18*(1), 20–32.

Schildt, H. A., Maula, M., & Keil, T. (2005). Explorative and exploitative learning from external corporate ventures. *Entrepreneurship Theory & Practice, 29*(4), 493–515.

Schollhammer, H. (1982). Internal corporate entrepreneurship. In C. Kent, D. Sexton, & K. Vesper (Eds.). *Encyclopedia of entrepreneurship*. Englewood Cliffs, NJ: Prentice-Hall.

Sharma, P., & Chrisman, J. J. (1999). Toward a reconciliation of the definitional issues in the field of corporate entrepreneurship. *Entrepreneurship Theory & Practice, 23*(3), 11–28.

Shepherd, D. A., Covin, J. G., & Kuratko, D. F. (2009). Project failure from corporate entrepreneurship: Managing the grief process, *Journal of Business Venturing, 24*(6), 588–600.

Shepherd, D. A., & Kuratko, D. F. (2009). The death of an innovative project: How grief recovery enhances learning, *Business Horizons, 52*(5), 451–458.

Smith, K. G., & Di Gregorio, D. (2002). Bisociation, discovery and the role of entrepreneurial action. In M. A. Hitt, R. D. Ireland, S. M. Camp, & D. L. Sexton (Eds.), *Strategic entrepreneurship: Creating a new mindset*. Oxford, England: Blackwell.

Sykes, H. B., & Block, Z. (1989). Corporate venturing obstacles: Sources and solutions. *Journal of Business Venturing, 4,* 159–167.

Zahra, S. A. (1991). Predictors and financial outcomes of corporate entrepreneurship: An exploratory study. *Journal of Business Venturing, 6,* 259–286.

Zahra, S. A., Kuratko, D. F., & Jennings, D. F. (1999). Entrepreneurship and the acquisition of dynamic organizational capabilities. *Entrepreneurship Theory & Practice, 23*(3), 5–10.

Section 3

The Organization: Corporate Entrepreneurship and Entrepreneurial Teams

3b: Entrepreneurial Teams

15

Unraveling the Black Box of New Venture Team Processes

Ekaterina S. Bjornali,[a,b] Mirjam Knockaert,[c] Nicolai Foss,[d] Daniel Leunbach[e] and Truls Erikson[e]

[a] *Norwegian University of Science and Technology, Norway*
[b] *Trondheim Business School, Norway*
[c] *Ghent University, Belgium*
[d] *Copenhagen Business School, Denmark*
[e] *University of Oslo, Norway*

Introduction

Traditionally, entrepreneurship research has been highly individual-centric (Foss & Lyngsie, 2014). However, over the last decade, academic interest has increasingly shifted toward recognizing and understanding the role of teams in starting up and managing new ventures (Harper, 2008; Vanaelst & Wright, 2009). This arguably reflects the increasing importance of entrepreneurial teams in the economy. For instance, the results of the Panel Study of Entrepreneurial Dynamics (PSED) demonstrate that around half of US founders share ownership and a substantial investment of time in their business start-ups (Ruef, 2010). The surge of team entrepreneurship is arguably caused by the need to pool complementary resources in order to recognize, create, evaluate, and exploit opportunities (Knockaert, Ucbasaran, Wright, & Clarysse, 2011). Uniting complementary skills may allow teams to realize distinct synergies in entrepreneurial activities. Further, team entrepreneurship allows for social processes that do not take place if a single individual, rather than a team of individuals, sets up a new venture.

In this chapter, we argue that new venture team (NVT) processes are relatively ill-understood in the entrepreneurship literature, and we describe various theoretical and empirical research avenues that may be pursued in order to improve our understanding of these processes. By "new venture teams" we mean "the group of individuals that is chiefly responsible for the strategic decision making and ongoing operations of a new venture" (Klotz, Hmieleski, Bradley, & Busenitz, 2014). NVTs are unique objects of inquiry as they are characterized by specific characteristics such as relatively unconstrained leadership processes, high managerial discretion, and weak social situations (Klotz et al., 2014). As such, the skills and strategies required to effectively handle the entrepreneurial challenges of a new venture may differ significantly from those required to manage the administrative challenges of established firms (Boeker & Wiltbank, 2005).

The Wiley Handbook of Entrepreneurship, First Edition.
Edited by Gorkan Ahmetoglu, Tomas Chamorro-Premuzic, Bailey Klinger, & Tessa Karcisky.
© 2017 John Wiley & Sons Ltd. Published 2017 by John Wiley & Sons Ltd.

So far, NVT researchers have to a large extent considered which (demographical) NVT characteristics are related to different types of firm outcomes (e.g., Amason, Shrader, & Tompson, 2006). However, this means that the processes occurring within the NVT are neglected, in the sense that NVT processes are not only empirically unobserved, but are also undertheorized. On the one hand, it is understandable that group processes are black boxed: by nature they are notoriously difficult to study. On the other hand, however, a number of recent contributions point to the need to open up the black box of NVT processes. Indeed, Austrian approaches point to the need to look at the dynamics of epistemics in NVT processes (Foss, Klein, Kor, & Mahoney, 2008). Along the same lines, the effectuation (Sarasvathy, 2001), bricolage (Baker & Nelson, 2005), creation (Alvarez & Barney, 2007), and imagination (Chiles, Bluedorn, & Gupta, 2007) perspectives articulate similar calls. Finally, Klotz et al. (2014), in their review of the NVT literature, also point to a gap with respect to theorizing and measuring intermediate processes.

Therefore, following recent calls in (team) entrepreneurship research, this chapter examines the NVT literature and particularly aims at responding to the following questions:

a) How can we *theoretically* further open up the black box of NVT processes?
b) What methods and tools may help dealing *empirically* with NVT processes?

By responding to these research questions we make the following contributions. First, we aim at contributing to the opening up of the black box of team processes (Klotz et al., 2014). We do so by integrating the theoretical foundations of entrepreneurial theorizing and entrepreneurial subjectivism and other theories that we believe have great potential to be instrumental in unraveling NVT processes. Second, by suggesting future research avenues for studying NVT processes within each of the selected theories, this chapter also indicates how research based on entrepreneurial theorizing and entrepreneurial subjectivism may be advanced. Third, methodologically, we contribute by outlining the major challenges associated with researching NVT processes, and how these can potentially be met in future research.

The chapter is structured as follows. First, we elaborate on what is unique about our object of inquiry, and suggest a framework for studying NVT processes. Second, we describe the selected theories within the theoretical foundations of entrepreneurial theorizing and subjectivism, and suggest future research opportunities for each of the selected theoretical perspectives. Third, we outline the methodological challenges and suggest selected methods that can address these challenges, before we provide a conclusion.

The New Venture Team as a Focal Object of Inquiry

In what follows, we elaborate on why we particularly focus on NVTs, which we relate to the nature of these teams (i.e. internal factors) and the specificity of the situation they are in (external factors).

Internal Factors

The nature of NVTs makes these teams particularly relevant objects of inquiry as they are typically composed of both principals and agents since NVT members often also (at least partially) own the new venture firm (Garg, 2013). Furthermore, NVTs typically display high levels of restricting homogeneity in terms of education and experience as they tend to select members from their own social networks (Ensley & Hmieleski, 2005; Williamson & Cable, 2003). Because of their nature, they often enjoy higher levels of managerial discretion compared to, for instance, corporate management teams (Klotz et al., 2014), but also suffer from a lack of clarity in the internal organization structure (Sine, Mitsushashi, & Kirsch, 2006; Stinchcombe, 1965). Finally, as NVT members often have a limited track record, they frequently lack clear norms, leading them to feel uncertain about their role and social standing in the team (Blatt, 2009; Klotz et al., 2014).

External Factors

Second, researchers have most commonly referred to liabilities of newness and smallness as main challenges that, coupled with the settings of novelty and uncertainty, confront NVTs with specific difficulties.

The liability of newness was argued by Freeman, Carroll, and Hannan (1983) as arising from the need to establish stable exchange relationships with clients, creditors, suppliers, and other organizations, which is suggested to be more challenging for new firms. In the entrepreneurship field, this liability is highly related to the "novelty" pertaining to the market, production, or management, as Shepherd, Douglas, and Shanley (2000) argue, or, to team-based, management-based, and market-based novelty, as indicated by Blatt (2009). As such, in the new venture context, novelty can be considered both a feature of the venture itself and, at the same time, a situational factor affecting it. As a consequence, new ventures are considered as varying along a continuum, ranging from imitative to highly innovative (Aldrich & Martinez, 2001; Amason et al., 2006; Jennings, Jennings, & Greenwood, 2009; Samuelsson & Davidsson, 2009). NVT decisions and actions then revolve around the creation of variety and the introduction of novelty of some kind into the economic sphere, for example new firms, new products, or new technologies (Becker, Knudsen, & March, 2006; Dew, Read, Sarasvathy, & Wiltbank, 2008; Felin, Kauffmann, Koppl, & Longo, 2014; Ruef, 2002; Schumpeter, 1934; Zahra, 2007). In such a setting of novelty and uncertainty, NVT members "may not know where to look for answers to their most pressing problems, or even what questions to ask in order to move their efforts forward" (Blatt, 2009). As such, they may experience feelings of disorientation, stress, anxiety and even excitement as they struggle to ascertain meaningful patterns and links between events (Blatt, 2009; Weick, 1979). NVT members do, however, have an advantage relative to single entrepreneurs because they can turn to other members in such situations.

The liability of smallness then originates from the limited resources and capabilities small firms have at their disposal, resulting in difficulties to buffer themselves from market contractions (Aldrich & Auster, 1986). Specifically, such liabilities originate from the fact that new organizations depend on new roles and tasks which are sometimes to be invented and learned at a cost (Bruderl & Schussler, 1990; Stinchcombe, 1965). As Stinchcombe (1965) further points out, both internal and external relationships result in the liability of smallness, with internal interactions resembling those between strangers, lacking common norms or information structures, whereas externally, links with partners, customers, and suppliers have to be established. The liability of newness and smallness are thus particularly related to each other, and as Kale and Arditi (1998) indicate, these contextual factors affect team functioning and make the company's survival problematic.

Hence, factors both internal and external to the NVT justify the particular focus of this chapter on NVTs. Indeed, such factors may explain why behavioral theories advanced to explain the functioning of well-established firms (e.g., upper echelon theory) do not always transfer well to the new venture context (Schjoedt, Monsen, Pearson, Barnett, & Chrisman, 2013). Specifically, the relation between antecedents/inputs and entrepreneurial outcomes is likely to be far from deterministic since NVTs may have few (or no) referent organizations (e.g., relevant competitors) to imitate and learn from. By consequence, NVTs leading highly novel ventures often have to rely on less-efficient, trial-by-trial (i.e., experiential) learning to acquire new knowledge, skills, and types of behavior (Aldrich & Martinez, 2001; Amason et al., 2006), making a process focus particularly warranted. In what follows, we explain why such a process focus is warranted, hereby building upon the widely established input-processes-outcome (IPO) framework.

Disentangling NVT "Processes" in the Input-Processes-Outcome Framework

Extant work on small groups and teams adopts an input-processes-outcome framework (or an antecedents-mediators-outcomes model; Klotz et al., 2014; Mathieu, Maynard, Rapp, & Gilson, 2008; Vykarnam & Handelberg, 2005). This framework has long been used within the field of organizational behavior (Mathieu et al., 2008) as it seeks to understand group performance and other group-level outcomes as the consequence of the inputs and processes that precede them. It is noteworthy that research has differentiated between extended and limited NVTs, in which the former includes the limited NVT as defined earlier, extended by outside board members, mentors, and consultants (Vanaelst et al., 2006; Zhang, Baden-Fuller, & Pool, 2011). For detailed literature reviews building upon the IPO framework, particularly providing an overview of inputs and outcomes studied in the new venture team literature, we refer to the excellent work by Mathieu et al. (2008) and Klotz et al. (2014).

In this chapter, we focus on selecting and discussing those theories we identify as instrumental in explaining the mediators, or the processes, that convert inputs into outputs in new venture teams. We deem a focus on these processes warranted as, in the antecedents-mediators-outcomes model, these mediators are typically unobserved mechanisms; the processes that mediate between "objective" antecedents and measured outcomes are inferred rather than observed and measured. Indeed, as Hambrick (2007, p. 335) more generally notes "the use of demographic indicators leaves us at a loss as to the real psychological and social processes that are driving executive behavior." At the same time, these unobserved mechanisms may be particularly critical in the case of NVTs given the challenges they are confronted with, and may explain why similarly composed NVTs produce different outcomes. In selecting and discussing our proposed theoretical perspectives, we particularly take these challenges into consideration.

Toward a Framework for Studying NVT Processes

In what follows, we present those theoretical foundations that we consider relevant in studying NVT processes. In doing so, we differentiate between the stage in which teams are formed (also referred to as the *prefounding phase*) and the stage thereafter, in which teams become operational and evolve (referred to as the *postfounding phase*). Specifically, for each of these stages, we build upon the theoretical foundations and related perspectives which guide us in our selection of theories which are likely to move our knowledge on NVT processes further.

Prefounding Phase

As to what the prefounding phase concerns, we build upon "Entrepreneurial Theorizing," developed by Felin and Zenger (2009). The process of *theorizing* explains the emergence of novel, entrepreneurial beliefs and strategies (Felin & Zenger, 2009). Entrepreneurial theorizing comprises three conceptual steps: (1) the triggering role of experiential and observational fragments, (2) the imagination of possibilities, and (3) the process of reasoning and justification. First, *experiences and observations* may trigger entrepreneurial belief formation. Though individuals may have similar experiences or make similar observations, teams of individuals with such similar experiences or observations may not necessarily share these beliefs or recognize similar opportunities as collective beliefs arise through social interaction (Felin & Zenger, 2009). More specifically, *faultlines* may emerge which affect team formation (Lim, Busenitz, & Chidambaram, 2013). Second, entrepreneurial imagination is a uniquely creative and generative act for supposing, conceiving, and considering various new possibilities for courses of entrepreneurial action (Felin & Zenger, 2009). *Creativity and imagination* (of possibilities) are likely important elements of entrepreneurial theorizing, as it, for instance, takes place during the brainstorming sessions within the new venture team at this stage. Third, imagined possibilities, triggered by fragmented observations, need to be reasoned and justified toward more full-fledged hypotheses, models, and theories (Chiles et al., 2007). *Organizational* and *team justice* (Folger & Cropanzano, 1998) are likely to be closely related to the processes of reasoning and justification of imagined possibilities. Entrepreneurs and other NVT members may need to sell their beliefs and ideas to others in an effort to ensure that a collective belief emerges. At this stage, the shift from a prefounding (idea) phase to a postfounding (nascent organization) phase may occur as the process of reasoning and justifying increases certainty of belief and intent about what the new venture is to do. NVT members with strong similar beliefs may stay in a team, while those who perceive unfairness due to disagreements about future ownership share or strategy in the venture, for instance, may leave the team.

As such, building upon the foundations of Entrepreneurial Theorizing, we will argue how and when specific theories such as faultline theory, creativity and imagination, and organizational and team justice may be instructive in studying NVT processes at the prefounding phase, and particularly the (self-)selection of individuals into (out of) the NVT through social interaction.

Postfounding phase

Regarding the postfounding phase, we build upon what may be called the "subjectivist approach" to team entrepreneurship in which a firm's productive range of possibilities is envisioned and enacted by an entrepreneurial management team (or NVT; Foss & Klein, 2012; Foss et al., 2008; Penrose, 1959). While the doctrine of subjectivism was originally implemented at the level of the individual, it may also serve as a key property of teams in the sense that each management team is unique in the productive opportunity set that it collectively envisions. Two essential elements of NVTs involve (1) heterogeneous managerial mindsets that are engaged in subjective processes of discovery, creativity, and learning; and (2) positive team dynamics that enable the team to capitalize on its knowledge assets (see Foss et al., 2008, for a rich discussion). First, following the heterogeneity suggested by subjectivism, *faultlines* may originate from diversity in terms of mental models and entrepreneurial beliefs, most likely in combination with other characteristics of the NVT, leading to changes in team composition and interaction. Second, *shared leadership, cognition, behavioral integration,* and *transactive memory systems (TMS)* are viewed as essential to achieve and maintain positive team dynamics in order "to make the best use of the team's diversity of talent, ideas, and perspectives," as well as to prevent negative consequences of diversity to occur (Foss et al., 2008, p. 84). Positive team dynamics may enable leveraging of the team's knowledge assets, thus enhancing the entrepreneurial firm's productivity. Third, as resource attributes are subjective and ultimately determined by NVT members' subjective values, knowledge, and beliefs, new ventures are inherently heterogeneous, even when possessing similar objective characteristics. In the *creativity and imagination* process, heterogeneous mental models interact, producing a superior collective output. As such, creative and imaginative NVTs may outperform other teams.

Building upon the foundations of Entrepreneurial Subjectivism, we will argue how and when specific theoretical lenses such as faultline theory, creativity and imagination, transactive memory systems, and organizational and team justice—like behavioral integration and shared cognition, and shared leadership—may be instructive in studying NVT processes at the postfounding phase, particularly the evolution in composition of and interactions within the NVT.

We present our theoretical foundations, selected theoretical perspectives, and implications for studying NVT processes in Figure 15.1 (prefounding phase) and Figure 15.2 (postfounding phase).

Table 15.1 subsequently systematically presents the selected theoretical perspectives, structured by the rubrics suggested by Low and MacMillan (1988). We elaborate on these theories in what follows.

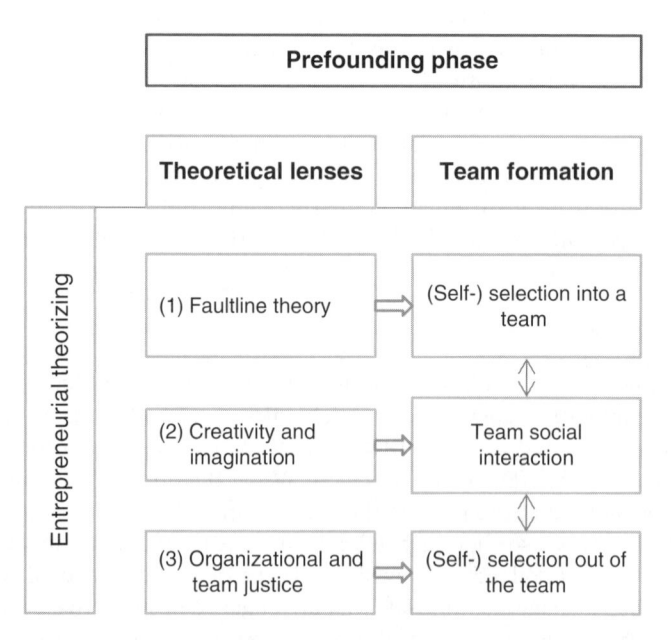

Figure 15.1 Team formation and prefounding phase through entrepreneurial theorizing and selected theories.

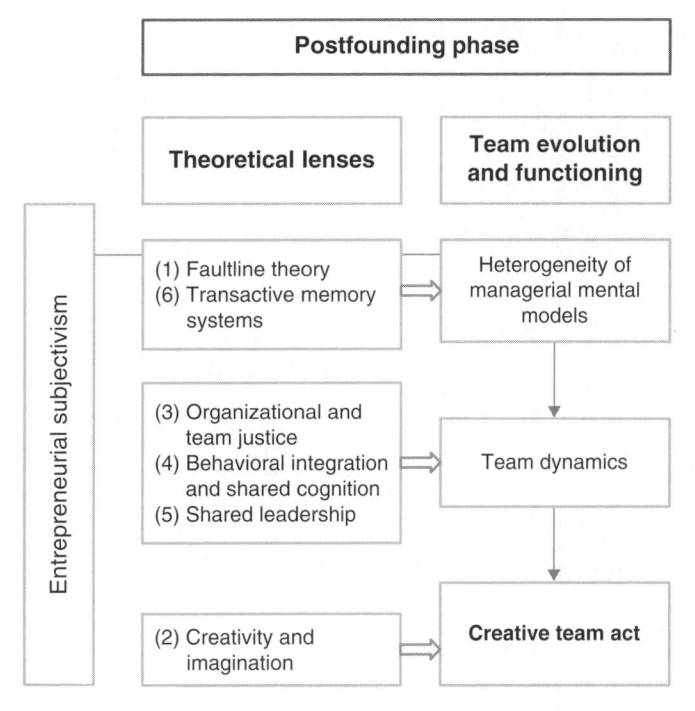

Figure 15.2 Team evolution and functioning and postfounding phase through entrepreneurial subjectivism and selected theories.

Selected Theories Within the Theoretical Foundations

Faultline Theory

Faultlines are defined as hypothetical dividing lines that split a group into relatively homogeneous subgroups based upon alignment of group members on social category demographic characteristics (Bezrukova, Jehn, Zanutto, & Thatcher, 2009). Faultlines originally draw from the similarity-attraction paradigm (Bryne, 1971) and the theory of self-categorization (Lim et al., 2013; Turner, 1987). Currently, faultline researchers draw from four additional theoretical streams to explain faultlines: (1) the categorization-elaboration model; (2) optimal distinctiveness theory; (3) social, psychological and cultural distance theories; and (4) the cross-categorization model (Thatcher & Patel, 2012). Most frequently, faultline research has considered age, gender, and ethnicity as characteristics leading to the origination of faultlines (Crucke & Knockaert, 2016), whereas job-related characteristics, for example functional background, tenure, and education (Bezrukova et al., 2009; Rico, Molleman, Sanchez-Manzanares, & Vegt, 2007), and personality traits (Thatcher & Patel, 2012) have received less attention. The construct of faultlines differs from diversity as the assumption is that it is not diversity per se which is problematic but rather the combination of diversity dimensions; it is this combination that may result in strong faultlines. Faultline strength is then determined by structural and cognitive dimensions (Lim et al., 2013) and faultlines may be dormant or active, depending on whether or not the members perceive the faultlines.

Table 15.1 Summarized presentation of the theories (and research streams) with potential for further insights in NVT processes.

Rubrics*	Rubric description	Faultline theory	Behavioral integration and shared cognition	Shared leadership
Purpose	What are the phenomena the theory aims to explain?	Faultlines are hypothetical dividing lines that split a group into subgroups. This division affects group and firm outcomes	To understand the influence of behaviorally integrated teams with high levels of shared cognition on team and firm outcomes	To understand leadership, which originally was referred to as the ability to influence a group toward the achievement of a vision or set of goals
Definition	Definition of the theoretical construct	See above	Behavioral integration (BI) includes quantity and quality of information exchange, collaborative behavior, and joint decision-making. Shared cognition refers to a group level thinking	Shared leadership refers to an emergent team property resulting from leadership functions being distributed across multiple team members
Theory	Main theories and key principals	Similarity-attraction paradigm, the theory of self-categorization, and a number of additional streams	Theory of BI belongs to the upper-echelon research stream. Research on entrepreneurial team collective cognition (ETTC) is empirical**	Theory of shared leadership stems from leadership and upper-echelon (TMT) research
Key references		Thatcher & Patel, 2011, 2012	Hambrick & Mason, 1984; Hambrick, 1994; West, 2007	Carson, Tesluk, & Marrone, 2007; Ensley, Pearson, & Pearce, 2003; Ensley, Hmieleski, & Pearce, 2006; Pearce & Sims, 2000
Focus	Which element of the IPO model does the theory focuses on?	Faultlines are determined by inputs, but may affect group and firm outcomes, e.g., conflict	Studies have linked BI/ETTC to outcomes, and examined antecedents of BI/ETTC	The positive relationship between shared leadership and team performance has been established
Levels	Units of analysis?	Intersubgroup and intrasubgroup	Team level and firm level	Team, firm levels
Methods	What are the dominant research design and typical statistical analyses used?	Vignette studies, lab setting experiment, surveys	Surveys, social grid analysis, cognitive mapping	Quantitative, surveys

Measurements	Typical measures	Faultline strength and distance	Scales		
Purpose	What are the phenomena the theory aims to explain?	Creativity and imagination refer to the production of ideas concerning products, services and practice that are novel and useful to the organization	To understand why people evaluate certain events as just or unjust, and the consequences that follow from such evaluations		To understand TMS referred to as a shared system that people in relationships develop for encoding, storing, and retrieving information about substantive different domains
Definition	Definition of the theoretical construct	Creativity and imagination is the process of engagement in creative acts	Justice is a shared perception of how team members judge the fairness with which they treat one another		TMS is the collection of knowledge possessed by each team member and a collective awareness of who knows what
Theory	Main theories and key principals	Great diversity in theories on the firm level (e.g., ten categories of creativity theory), but few on the team level	Fairness, equity theory, distributive justice primarily on a firm level		TMSs have two components: structure (store of knowledge) and processes (encoding, storage, retrieval)
Key references		Amabile, 1996, 1997; Chiles et al., 2007; Felin et al., 2014	Folger & Cropanzano, 1998		Wegner and colleagues, 1985; Wegner, 1987
Focus	Which element of the I-P-O model does the theory focus on?	Creativity and imagination is typically thought of as an outcome	The focus has been on the antecedents of justice and its consequences		There is a positive relationship between the presence of TMSs and both team performance and viability
Levels	Unit of analysis	Individual, group and organizational levels	Individual, group and firm levels		Group level
Methods	What are the dominant research design and typical statistical analyses used?	Field studies, lab experiments, survey, historiometric methods	Surveys and lab experiments		Lab experiments, field studies, surveys
Measurements	Typical measures	Scales	Perceptions of justice and fairness		Standard measures are developed to assess TMSs

*The theories were scrutinized using six key elements (or rubrics) as outlined by Low and MacMillan (1988, JM) and later used by e.g., Chiles et al. (2007, OS). Rubric "Time" applies to all theories, in the sense that time matters, is therefore left out.

**"Shared cognition" and "entrepreneurial team collective cognition" (ETCC) are used interchangeably in this study.

Faultline theory holds great promise for advancing our understanding of NVT processes. Specifically, while faultlines typically originate from combinations of input factors in the IPO model, they are likely to affect the processes the NVT goes through and to eventually affect team outcomes. Indeed, faultlines have been linked to different types of conflict (Thatcher & Patel, 2011), cohesion (Thatcher & Patel, 2012) and group and firm performance (Bezrukova et al., 2009; Crucke & Knockaert, 2016; Kaczmarek, Kimino, & Pye, 2012; Thatcher & Patel, 2012; van Knippenberg, Dawson, West, & Homan, 2011). At the same time, however, while faultlines have been widely applied in diverse literatures (including research in the domains of organizational behavior, corporate governance and family business), faultline theory has remained relatively under applied in entrepreneurial contexts. As we argue, the theory and its foundations hold great potential for disentangling how combinations of input factors (e.g., experience and tenure) affect the transformation of these inputs into (group or firm) outputs. Particularly, encouraging for the application of the theory is the fact that methodologies have been developed in other fields, which may guide research in the domain of entrepreneurship. We refer to Thatcher, Jehn, & Zanutto (2003) and Thatcher and Patel (2012) for an overview of methodologies and measures (including those for faultline strength and distance) which may guide further research in the entrepreneurship field in general, and NVT processes specifically.

Future Research Directions

Faultlines hold great potential for understanding NVT processes both in the prefounding and postfounding phases. Faultline theory may for instance help in understanding how team members select other members, why some team members leave and others join the NVT, how conflicts emerge and how and which social interactions take place. Focusing specifically on the postfounding phase, faultlines may additionally be instrumental in understanding how NVTs make decisions, how effective such decision-making is, and how it eventually leads to team and firm performance. In this context, research may focus on those social category characteristics that are likely to contribute to the formation of faultlines in an entrepreneurial context. In combination with "traditional" demographic characteristics such as age and gender, examples include: ownership distribution between NVT members, their (firm-specific and context-specific) social and human capital, their tenure within the firm, the stakeholder groups they represent (particularly relevant in the case of hybrid ventures such as social enterprises, and academic and corporate spin-offs), and the extent to which NVT members also belong to the board of directors. Furthermore, future entrepreneurship research could advance the entrepreneurship field and faultline literature by disentangling the circumstances under which the impact of faultlines is mitigated or strengthened by specific factors such as team-, firm-, or context-specific characteristics.

Behavioral Integration and Shared Cognition

Behavioral integration and shared cognition refer to emergent states within NVTs that unfold during team formation and evolution. As such, they are related to the postfounding phase. Behavioral integration is one of the most comprehensive behavioral characteristics representing an all-encompassing and multidimensional construct. Behavioral integration captures collaborative behavior, information exchange, and joint decision-making within a group, as originally suggested by Hambrick (1994). Behavioral integration within teams has been previously studied within the top management team (TMT) research stream that views TMT processes as critical antecedents of a firm's competitive behavior which may be associated with a firm's competitive advantage (Hambrick, 1994; Simsek, Veiga, Lubatkin, & Dino, 2005). Behaviorally integrated TMTs were found to make better decisions (Carmeli & Schaubroeck, 2006) and exhibit superior performance (Simsek et al., 2005). Research on behavioral integration in NVTs has so far, however, been limited (Bjornali & Ellingsen 2015).

Shared cognition, then, refers to group-level thinking (Ensley & Pearce, 2001) or what Weick and Roberts (1993) term the "collective mind," that is, the comprehension of unfolding events by teams of interacting individuals. While each entrepreneurial team member will have individual perspectives and cognitions about their new venture, "it is a collective perspective or a collective knowledge structure at the team level that guides the direction of the venture" (West, 2007). NVT researchers have tried to link various forms of shared cognition among team members—for example cognitive comprehensiveness, strategic consensus, collective mood, and polychronicity—to firm performance or other outcomes (Chowdhury, 2005; Perry-Smith & Coff, 2011; Souitaris & Maestro, 2010; Vissa & Chacar, 2009). The study by West (2007) stands out by positioning NVT shared (collective) cognition as a mediating mechanism between team inputs and outcomes, and supporting an inverted U-shaped relationship between shared cognition and new venture performance. Hence, shared cognition in NVTs remains an important domain in which to explore, for example, how and under which conditions it emerges and influences various outcomes.

Future Research Directions

Post-founding phase. The theories of behavioral integration and shared cognition are highly relevant for the postfounding phase, given that they are concerned with established teams. We suggest a number of future research avenues. First, future research aiming at more conceptual contributions could examine the fit of both constructs within the *entrepreneurial subjectivism* approach. Within this approach, heterogeneity of mental models within a NVT may stimulate fruitful debates, learning, and new ways of thinking among team members (Foss et al., 2008). Too much heterogeneity, nevertheless, may promote severe conflicts that can interrupt the processes of collective entrepreneurial behavior (Amason, 1996; Ensley, Pearson, & Amason, 2002; Kamm & Nurick, 1993; Miller, Burke, & Glick, 1998). Therefore, we propose that future research could explore how and to what extent behavioral integration and shared cognition may facilitate the emergence of a synergistic cognitive synthesis. How and to what extent will the shared team-specific cognition and behavioral integration contribute to the creation of a balance between a diversity of mental models and team dynamics that facilitates the group experimentation, cooperation, and learning necessary for activating a creative team act? For instance, similarly to shared cognition, the positive effect will most probably increase with more behavioral integration, but only up to a certain level, because too much behavioral integration may cause similarity in thinking and, as such, jeopardize the multiple viewpoints that are beneficial to innovation, team effectiveness, or other related outcomes (Jansen, Kostopoulos, Mihalache, & Papalexandris, 2016; Leunbach, Erikson, Ricciardi, Heggli, & Good, 2016).

Second, future research aiming at empirical contributions could investigate how and under which conditions both behavioral integration and shared cognition emerge and influence firm- and team-level outcomes. Behavioral integration and shared cognition are cognitive-based emergent states related to thinking and decision-making (Barsade & Knight, 2015). Given the contextual difficulties NVTs are faced with, these cognitive-based constructs are likely highly interlinked with the affective emergent states related to feelings and moods, for example team climate and affective tone (Klotz et al., 2014), and such relationships deserve further investigation. Future research may also explore how behavioral integration and shared cognition are related to "joint production motivation," that is, team members' capacity and motivation to actively engage in joint collaborative activities in the dynamic environments in which NVTs operate (Lindenberg & Foss, 2011).[1]

Third, methodologically, the above-suggested research questions call for longitudinal studies. So far, most studies have been cross-sectional. Ensley and Pearce (2001) used the shared cognition variable as a weak proxy for strategy content. The study by West (2007) addressed this limitation by thoroughly investigating the (true) entrepreneurial team collective (or shared) cognition (these terms are used interchangeably in this study) using sociocognitive grid analysis. Thus, it also overcame the limitations of other methods used for examining team cognitions in previous studies, for example by ensuring that the variables of interest reflect the full range of all members' underlying construct systems for thinking about strategy and strategic issues.[2] Hence, to explore further shared cognition represents a promising, albeit methodologically rather challenging, future research area. Whereas the behavioral integration measure (scale) has been established for upper-echelons (TMTs), it is yet to be tested in an NVT context.

Shared Leadership

Leadership is the ability to influence a group toward the achievement of a vision or set of goals (Robbins & Judge 2015). A number of thorough literature reviews on leadership in teams including a meta-analysis exist (e.g., Burke et al., 2006; Kozlowski & Bell, 2003; Kozlowski & Ilgen, 2006; Zaccaro, Rittman, & Marks, 2001) indicating that little is known about how leaders create and manage effective teams. Three aspects

---

[1] The construct "joint production motivation" captures the human capacity to actively engage in collaborative activities and is based on the insight that the motivation to engage in these collaborative activities is intricately related to cognitions about tasks, interdependencies, and common goals. Joint production refers to any productive activity that involves heterogeneous, but complementary, resources and a high degree of task and outcome interdependence. Joint production motivation is, therefore, by definition, optimally adapted to situations in which activities involve heterogeneous and complementary resources and in which the objective task and team structure are geared toward common goals (Lindenberg & Foss, 2011).

[2] A sociocognitive grid approach builds upon policy grid analysis and extends it in order to meet the research objectives in which strategic perspective is a key variable. Sociocognitive grid involves both method and analysis combining top managers and important strategy constructs. One of the limitations of other methods, including original policy grid approach, is that the selected dimensions do not reflect the full range of all managers' underlying construct systems for thinking about strategic issues. As such, the issue for researchers is to describe individual data in a format that is consistent across all individuals, while still allowing for the variation between individuals in construct use and importance to be represented within that format. Sociocognitive grid allows using factor scores as input, and thus, overcomes the above limitations by capturing both a complete set of strategic constructs explaining variance across all managers and individual managers' ratings of each construct indicating importance (West, 2007).

of leadership in teams that hold particular promise for future research efforts are external team-oriented leadership, team coaching, and shared leadership, as suggested by Mathieu et al. (2008).

External team-oriented leadership represents the traditional paradigm and focuses on the influence of a leader who is responsible for, and has authority over, the team. In this paradigm, leadership is viewed primarily as an input factor that influences team dynamics (e.g., creativity, and organizational and team perceptions of justice) and performance (Ahearn, Ferris, Hockwarter, Douglas, & Ammeter, 2006; Srivastava, Bartol, & Locke, 2006; Sy, Cote, & Saavedra, 2005). For instance, Kang, Solomon, and Choi (2015) find that both transformational and transactional leadership on the part of the CEO relate positively to managers' innovative behavior in (US) entrepreneurial companies.

Team coaching refers to "direct interaction with a team intended to help members make coordinated and task-appropriate use of their collective resources in accomplishing the team's work" (Hackman & Wageman, 2005). Examples of coaching behaviors include identifying team problems, process consultation, cueing and rewarding self-management, and problem-solving consultation (Wageman, 2001). With regard to the relationship between coaching and team performance, the results are ambiguous with some showing a positive influence (e.g., Edmondson, 1999) and others showing no influence (e.g., Wageman, 2001). Other research has suggested that the effects of coaching are contingent on other conditions, such as team design factors (e.g., Wageman, 2001) and the stability of the task environment (e.g., Morgeson, 2005).

Shared or distributed leadership refers to a type of leadership that emerges from within the team itself. Although research on shared leadership has recently gained attention, it has mainly been executed in the educational sector (Bolden, 2011; Thorpe, Gold & Lawler, 2011). Shared leadership refers to an emergent team property resulting from leadership functions being distributed across multiple team members rather than arising from a single, formal leader (Carson et al., 2007).

Despite shared leadership being a type of leadership that can be found in new ventures, relatively little research has been done in this area. Studies however demonstrate that shared leadership is positively associated with new venture growth rates and team performance (e.g., Sivasubramaniam, Murry, Avolio, & Jung, 2002; Carson et al., 2007; Ensley, Hmieleski, & Pearce, 2006; Hiller, Day, & Vance, 2006; Pearce & Sims 2000). For instance, Hmieleski and Ensley (2007) find that in dynamic industry environments, start-ups with heterogeneous TMTs perform best when led by directive leaders and those with homogeneous TMTs perform best when led by empowering leaders. In another study, Ensley et al. (2006) demonstrate that although both vertical and shared leadership are important predictors of new venture performance, the latter is an efficacious predictor that accounts for a significant amount of variance in new venture performance beyond the vertical leadership variables.

Future Research Directions

Postfounding phase. Theories of leadership most often address leadership in established new ventures, that is, the postfounding phase. Overall, NVT studies suggest that multileader teams (where multiple members participate in all leadership roles) help survive the novelty and complexity of entrepreneurial ventures (Dust & Ziegert, 2015; Ensley et al., 2003; Hmieleski, Cole, & Baron, 2012; Hoch, Pearce, & Welzel, 2010;

Patton & Higgs 2013; Pearce & Sims 2000). Shared leadership is highly relevant to NVTs and deserves more attention. Future research questions could for instance be: Under which conditions is shared leadership most beneficial to team and firm performance? How can lead entrepreneurs create a climate that encourages dialogue within the team (or positive team dynamics) and allows members to share their tacit knowledge, thus facilitating the creative team act?

The coaching aspect of leadership offers a promising avenue of research too (Mathieu et al., 2008). Indeed, new ventures are often coached through their development process, often in the postfounding phase, but also in the prefounding phase. Whereas in early stages, NVTs are coached by privileged witnesses (e.g., technology transfer officers; Vanaelst et al., 2006), in later stages they may be coached by external financiers (e.g., venture capital investors), often through their board involvement in both cases (Vohora, Wright, & Lockett, 2004). As such, future research could investigate to what degree coaching and the coaches participate in and influence the process of reasoning, justification, and testing of entrepreneurial beliefs and theories, which are final steps in *entrepreneurial theorizing*. Further, future research could explore how team coaches (as part of either team or board) may contribute to a fruitful mix of heterogeneity and dynamics and, thus, an emergence of a synergistic cognitive synthesis, which is the core condition for the creative team act taking place within the entrepreneurial subjectivism approach.

Further, within NVT studies the use of survey and leadership scales still dominates. Fitzsimons, James, and Denyer (2011) suggest alternative approaches for studying shared or distributed leadership. Depending on which approach is taken, various methods are applied ranging from variance methods (relational-entity approach) and social networks (relational-structural approach) to eclectic designs (relational-processual) and action research and ethnographic designs (relational-systemic approach). Additionally, while current research has primarily focused on the "positive" characteristics of leadership, the dark side of entrepreneurial leadership, for example hubris and particularly greed, has so far been much less explored (Haynes, Hitt, & Campbell, 2015).

Lastly, both shared leadership and NVT coaching can be studied to explore the interactions between NVTs and the board of directors since these management groups often work in tandem in new ventures (Bjørnåli, 2016; Garg, 2013; George, Erikson, & Parhankangas, 2014; Knockaert, Bjørnåli, & Erikson, 2014). For instance, Carson et al. (2007) found that important antecedents for shared (distributed) leadership are an overall supportive internal team environment (consisting of shared purpose, social support, and voice) and supportive coaching by an external leader (i.e., team manager). Methodologically, there are different proxies for shared leadership, and an accepted measure at the team level still needs to be developed (Anderson & Sun, 2015).

Creativity and Imagination

Psychologists have been studying creativity since the 1950s (Amabile & Pillemer, 2012). Creativity is an elusive concept and the field has struggled with definitional issues (Mumford, Hester & Robledo, 2012). Nevertheless, creativity (in an organizational context) is often defined as the production of ideas concerning products, practices, services, or procedures that are (1) novel or original and (2) potentially useful to the organization (Amabile, 1996; Shalley, Zhou, & Oldham, 2004). Although innovation and creativity are closely related concepts, creativity is typically considered conceptually distinct from innovation in that creativity focuses on idea production whereas innovation emphasizes implementation of creative ideas (Zhou, 2008).

There is great diversity in the theories employed. Kozbelt, Beghetto, and Runco (2010) offer a comprehensive summary of 10 different categories of creativity theory (e.g., evolutionary, systems, developmental, cognitive, etc.). In the entrepreneurship domain several studies, for example by Amabile (1997), Perry-Smith and Coff (2011), and Zhou (2008), draw explicitly on the creativity literature. Further, creativity is typically thought of as an outcome (i.e., dependent variable) and the literature has focused almost exclusively on understanding what factors can promote or inhibit creativity. A notable exception to the "creativity as outcome" perspective, is Drazin, Glynn, and Kazanjian (1999) who define creativity (across multiple levels) as "the process of engagement in creative acts, regardless of whether the resultant outcomes are novel, useful, or creative" (p. 287). Building on this notion of creativity as a process, Gilson and Shalley (2004) define the construct "team creative processes" as "members working together in such a manner that they link ideas from multiple sources, delve into unknown areas to find better or unique approaches to a problem, or seek out novel ways of performing a task." Paulus, Dzindolet, and Kohn (2011) provide a review of the factors that influence creative outcomes in teams.

Future Research Directions

Prefounding phase. Overall, there is limited empirical research on creativity at the group level. Although the attention has shifted to the group/team level of analysis more recently (Hennessey & Amabile, 2010), this research is still in its infancy compared to research examining creativity at the individual level (Reiter-Palmon, Wigert, & de Vreede, 2012). NVTs represent a fruitful context in which research can be developed at the group level, given the increasing focus on teams as "the locus of entrepreneurial creativity" (Foss et al., 2008; Perry-Smith & Coff, 2011, p. 248; Shalley & Perry-Smith, 2008). Creativity has so far been conceived mostly as an outcome (Shalley & Gilson, 2004). As George (2007) notes in her review of the literature on creativity in organizations, future theorizing and research might benefit from considering creativity not only as a dependent variable but also as an independent variable with multiple potential ramifications for organizations and their members.

Creativity and imagination might be important preconditions for entrepreneurial theorizing, especially in the phase where possibilities for future entrepreneurial actions are being imagined by potential entrepreneurs. Creative imagination has been considered by entrepreneurship scholars from the earliest days, with both Knight (1921) and Penrose's (1959) referring to "image." Further, Mahoney (1995) and Kor, Mahoney, and Michael (2007) refer to "heterogeneous mental models." Chiles et al. (2007) explore and elaborate the concept of creative imagination as developed by Lachmann (1956, 1976). Lachmann understood creative imagination as a forward-looking imagination, in which the forward-looking perspective was toward an "unknown but not unimaginable future" (Gloria-Palermo, 1999, p. 120). As such, creative imagination fills in the void created by Knight's (1921) longitudinal uncertainty. Hence, future research could explore how imagination and creativity facilitate imagination of new possibilities, including mental simulations and experimentation of thoughts about which new markets, new products, or new structures the new venture might pursue.

Postfounding phase. With regard to the effect of team diversity on the levels of creativity, two studies are noteworthy. First, Polzer, Milton, and Swann (2002) demonstrate that diversity (along many dimensions) tends to improve creative task performance in groups with high interpersonal congruence (i.e., the degree to which group members see others in the group as others see themselves) and undermine creative task performance of low interpersonal congruence groups. Second, Miron-Spektor, Gino, and Argote (2011) show that the adoption of paradoxical frames—mental templates that encourage individuals to recognize and embrace contradictions—increases creativity. This is very close to Koestler (1964)'s idea that any creative act is a bisociation (not mere association) of two (or more) apparently incompatible frames of thought. These studies' findings may imply that heterogeneous mental models from a team do not automatically lead to superior creative output (Foss et al., 2008). This indicates a need to study creativity and imagination as moderating and/or mediating factors in NVT processes. Future research may explore, for instance, how creativity and imagination may contribute to positive team dynamics, mitigating dysfunctional conflicts and stimulating creative NVT actions, which are necessary elements in entrepreneurial subjectivism.

Lab experiments, surveys, and historiometric and field studies are among methods applied in creativity studies (Amabile & Pillemer, 2012; Mumford et al., 2011). These methods can be inspiration sources when studying creativity in NVTs. Since team creativity develops and changes over time, time is an important parameter. Yet, time has not been taken into consideration properly by previous research on creativity. This calls for the incorporation of longitudinal and qualitative designs, which may serve as important approaches that complement existing methods in creativity studies.

Organizational and Team Justice

Organizational justice research seeks to understand why individuals evaluate certain events as just or injust (i.e., fair or unfair), and the consequences that follow from such evaluation (Cropanzano et al., 2007). The study of fairness in explaining organizational phenomena dates back to the 1960s (see Colquitt, Greenberg, & Zapata-Phelan, 2005, for a historical overview). The literature suggests that justice or fairness (these terms are used interchangeably) is an important means by which people make sense of their social worlds. As such, justice or fairness perceptions are thought to share much in common with stereotypes, schemas, heuristics, and attitudes (Folger & Cropanzano 1998). Contemporary justice research views organizational justice as a multidimensional construct consisting of four different components, that is, distributive, procedural, interpersonal, and informational justice. The latter two are sometimes treated as a single component referring to interactional justice. Justice perceptions in organizations have been tied to many individual level outcomes: for example job satisfaction, organizational commitment, organizational citizenship behaviors, job performance, withdrawal behaviors, counterproductive behaviors, and self-perceptions.

The organizational justice approach has traditionally been very much focused on individuals. However, the researchers' interest in the team level has increased recently (e.g., Cropanzano, Li, & Benson, 2011; Li & Cropanzano, 2009). There are few examples of studies in the entrepreneurship domain that explicitly draw on the organizational justice literature. A notable exception is the literature on the relationships between NVTs and venture capital investors (e.g., Busenitz, Moesel, Fiet, & Barney, 1997; Sapienza & Korsgaard, 1996; Zacharakis, Erikson, & George, 2010). Moreover, Breugst, Patzelt, and Rathgeber (2015) examined how perceptions of distributive justice concerning equity allocation influence NVT outcomes (i.e., performance and member exit).

Future Research Directions

Prefounding phase. Recent developments in the field in terms of conceptualizing justice as a team-level construct hold promise, implying the importing of organizational justice theory to the NVT context. Since there is a lack of research linking justice perceptions to organization level outcomes, the NVT context represents a promising future research avenue in this regard. Within entrepreneurial theorizing, future research could examine, for instance, how perceptions of justice within a group of future entrepreneurs lead to team member exit and whether such perceptions are related to the faith in different entrepreneurial beliefs about what the future course of entrepreneurial actions should be. As suggested by Felin and Zenger (2009), the reasoning and justification of the venture's idea (strategy, etc.) may occur when a would-be venture seeks funding. This is usually done by pitching to other vital external parties, for example venture capital investors. Such a setting will most likely surface many of the underlying cognitive processes, among them, perceptions of fairness in the relationships within the NVT and between NVT members and external parties.

Postfounding phase. Organizational and team justice appears to be relevant also for entrepreneurial subjectivism as it may influence team dynamics. As such, future research could investigate how and to what extent the NVT members' perceptions of justice may facilitate or inhibit positive team dynamics and thus the emergence of a synergistic cognitive synthesis. Alternative future research questions could assess how and to what extent perceptions of injustice lead to dysfunctional (detrimental) conflicts that hinder extracting benefits from task-related diversity in experience, skills, and so on within NVTs. Considering constructs used in the literature, an intraunit justice climate (Li & Cropanzano, 2009) or peer justice (Cropanzano et al., 2011) appear to be promising. Peer justice refers to "a shared perception regarding how individuals who work together within the same unit and who do not have formal authority over each other judge the fairness with which they treat one another" (Cropanzano et al., 2011).

Given the uncertain and unpredictable nature of NVT processes, another interesting future research avenue could be the use of fairness heuristics (uncertainty management theory; Lind, 2001; Lind & van den Bos, 2002; van den Bos, 2001) which argues that people use heuristics when evaluating and applying fairness information. Laboratory studies show that fairness is particularly salient for individuals who experience uncertainty. Hence, under such circumstances the founders may, for instance, use perceptions of procedural justice as a proxy for trust in judging individuals in positions of power (e.g., resource providers). For instance, Busenitz et al. (1997) examined the perceived quality of the relationships between NVT members and venture capital investors and found the NVT inputs, among them NVT members' industry experience and tenure, to negatively relate to perceptions of procedural justice. Future research could go beyond inputs and examine what cognitive processes and contingency factors affect the perceptions of procedural justice in such vital relationships as those between NVT members and external constituents.

Transactive Memory Systems

The concept of transactive memory systems (TMSs) was first introduced by Wegner, Giuliano, and Hertel (1985) and Wegner (1987). A TMS is now commonly defined as a shared system that people in relationships develop for encoding, storing, and retrieving information about substantive different domains (Hollingshead & Brandon, 2003; Ren, Carley & Argote, 2006). TMSs have two components: an organized store of knowledge (TMS structure) and a set of knowledge-relevant transactive processes (encoding, storage, and retrieval processes) that occur among members. TMSs are therefore more than just shared understandings of "who knows what?" (i.e., metaknowledge) because they involve these dynamic features (Lewis & Herndon, 2011). TMSs have been examined in a number of different empirical contexts including laboratory groups, air traffic control teams, top management teams, consulting teams, and software development teams (Lewis & Herndon, 2011). As such, they are thought to improve group performance by enabling both rapid and coordinated access to specialized expertise in the solving of collective tasks. TMS has been suggested as a potential "microfoundation of dynamic capabilities" (Argote & Ren, 2012).

Wegner (1987) first developed TMS when he examined why spouses perform certain jobs better than strangers. The concept has since been extended to groups/teams and even organizations (Ren & Argote, 2011). The predominant focus has been on the group or team level of analysis. A myriad of methods have been applied, including lab experiments, field studies and surveys and TMSs have been measured in various ways; however, more recently there has been some convergence towards standard assessment measures (e.g., Lewis, 2003; see also Ren & Argote, 2011, and Lewis & Herndon, 2011, for comprehensive overviews). TMS has also been employed as an explanatory device to account for relationships without it being measured directly. For instance, in a recent study Vera, Nemanich, Vélez-Castrillón, and Werner (2014) found that an R&D team's joint working experience (as a proxy for TMS) is positively related to its improvisation capability and that "minimal structures" (goal clarity combined with autonomy) further enhance this positive relationship (Kamoche, Pina, Cunha, & Da Cunha, 2003).

Future Research Directions

Postfounding phase. A number of review studies call for more research on TMSs in entrepreneurial settings. For instance, Lewis and Herndon (2011, p. 1262) note that "TMS provides an ideal—albeit underutilized—lens through which to consider the performance and development of groups engaged in complex, dynamic tasks." Similarly, Ren and Argote (2011) specifically call for research examining TMSs in the context of entrepreneurial ventures and suggest exploring the TMS as an explanation for why NVT members with prior shared experience are more innovative, which in turn may result in higher levels of new venture performance.

Indeed, TMS theory has been applied to a variety of contexts, but to a limited extent to new ventures. Examples of conceptual papers using TMSs in the entrepreneurship domain include Bryant (2014) and Aldrich and Yang (2014). Examples of empirical contributions to the TMS research applied to the NVT context are, to our knowledge, also few. First, Zheng (2012) found that the positive effect of prior shared experience within the NVT on new venture performance (growth) was partially mediated by TMS. Second, Zheng and Mai (2013) found that NVTs with strong TMSs are less inclined to acquire external knowledge, but more prone to improvise in response to unexpected events than NVTs with weak TMSs.

Hence, we argue that within the entrepreneurial subjectivism approach, TMS theory represents an interesting research opportunity where future investigators could examine the TMS as a potential mediator between heterogeneous mental models and creative team output (Foss et al., 2008). Future research could also explore in more detail the distinction between TMS structure and TMS processes between NVT members. If such a distinction exists in new ventures, this may have implications for recruitment and retention strategies, and may, consequently, represent a fruitful research avenue.

We also posit further that TMS theory can favorably augment Sarasvathy's effectuation model (2001), that is, make it more applicable to a team level by enabling transition from "Who am I? What do I know? Whom do I know? What can I do?" to "Who are we? What do we know? Whom do we know? What can we do?" For instance, a conceptual study by Harper (2008) examines the role of entrepreneurial teams (NVTs) in the processes of entrepreneurial discovery. Harper (2008, p. 614) advocates for "broadening our conception of entrepreneurial agency to include teams, not just enterprising individuals." The author further refers to emergent entrepreneurial teams that "can act jointly to make single discoveries of a particular opportunity" (Harper, 2008, p. 628). Emergent entrepreneurial team members view themselves as equal, and often understand each other without communicating, but must rely on improvised coordination and mutual responsiveness to function well under conditions of uncertainty. Future research could empirically test Harper's (2008) conceptualization of entrepreneurial teams, and, for instance, examine the role of TMSs in each team type.

Measuring New Venture Team Processes

In the previous sections, we have specified what the black box of NVTs is, how NVTs are unique as they face a number of liabilities and related challenges, and how NVT processes can be studied along the theoretical foundations of entrepreneurial theorizing and subjective judgement. Afterwards, we focused on a subset of theories that we believe hold potential value to theoretically advance the opening-up of the black box. Here, we briefly present the methods considerations that serve as potential road blocks for the empirical study of NVT processes.

Methodological Issues in NVT Studies

Alongside potential theoretical contributions, we identify three main methodological considerations that are associated with measuring antecedents (inputs), mediators (processes), and outcomes in new ventures: (1) collinearity; (2) dominant survey method; (3) the process challenge.

Collinearity

In their review of recent advancements in the research on team effectiveness Mathieu et al. (2008) note that empirical analyses demonstrate that various team mediators (both processes and emergent states) are *highly correlated*. The implications of such collinearity are as follows. First, the studies that investigate only one of the process/mediator variables are prone to the issues related to omitted variables. Second, if several mediators are highly correlated, one might question their discriminant validity. Some of these problems might be avoided if one measures the mediators in several points in time and from various sources. Moreover, "more elaborate research designs and measurement systems can better inform us about the empirical differentiation (or not) of various mediating mechanisms and their interrelationships" (Mathieu et al., 2008, p. 433).

Dominant Survey Method

Measuring at "more than one" level (at least both individual and team) is quite difficult and costly. This methodological consideration pertains to data collection, which becomes complicated in multilevel studies (of, e.g., dyadic incoming and outgoing relationships within a team) and is well illustrated in the review by Humphrey and Aime (2014). The authors show, with an example of 10-person teams and the number of items exceeding 1,000, how the survey would get tiresome quickly. Despite this, researchers have begun to acknowledge that shorter forms of scales (e.g., 3-item scales in contrast to 10-item scale) are psychometrically sound (Yarkoni, 2010), which make the consideration above possible to overcome.

Some constructs are inherently difficult to tap into, for example personality, intelligence, and general mental ability, as the data are usually not available. Similarly to TMT (upper-echelon) studies, NVT research has mostly used demographic variables as proxies for the underlying cognitive and behavioral traits. Despite the difficulty of obtaining psychometric data from teams (e.g., cognitive diversity, style, and personality), we echo the call by Shepherd and Rudd (2014, p. 348) for obtaining direct measures of constructs in order "to attain greater construct validity and to improve the explanatory ability of research."

Cross-Sectional Designs

There is a dominance of cross-sectional research design in team research (Humphrey & Aime (2014). This is echoed in NVT studies (Klotz et al., 2014). Such studies use variance theory and provide an outcome-driven explanation. A variance theory explanation is "built backwards" from a problematized outcome to "prior causally significant events" (Aldrich, 2001, p. 118). Hence, it is inherently difficult to capture processes with cross-sectional research designs (Weick, 1995). The need for multiperiod or longitudinal approaches to team research has been emphasized in previous research (Cronin, Weingart, & Todorova, 2011).

Longitudinal survey designs may capture some dimensions better than cross-sectional ones. As one of the board members of the *Organizational Research Methods* journal (ORM) indicated, entrepreneurship offers "a good opportunity to focus on longitudinal research" (Short, Ketchen, Combs & Ireland, 2010, p. 9). Yet, another ORM board member cautioned that "organization realities change with the times and *talking* about entrepreneurship from archival data 20 years ago doesn't really address what entrepreneurship is today" (Short et al., 2010, p. 10). Humphrey and Aime (2014) provide an overview of existing analytical techniques and commercial software for multilevel/multiperiod organizing approaches to teamwork, which are likely to be suitable for addressing research questions related to NVT processes.

Even then, many things are inherently difficult to measure by means of surveys. Even if traits can be measured, Austrian subjectivism indicates also that mental states matter a lot (Foss et al., 2008), and these are even more difficult to measure, raising further methodological challenges. For instance, longitudinal survey designs may still not correctly identify causality. Even though a process theory explanation (or event-driven explanation) is "built forwards" from "observed or recorded events to outcomes" (Aldrich, 2001, p. 119), there is still a successionist (linear) causality. In both variance and process theory explanations, "units of theory building are organized successively either in terms of causal antecedence in the case of variance theory or in terms of sequences of events in the case of process theory" (Fletcher & Selden, 2015, p. 108).

Meeting Methodological Challenges

In what follows, we provide guidance toward how the research on NVT processes can be advanced by focusing on a subset of methods (approaches, tools) that may help opening up the black box. A recent review on NVTs by Klotz et al. (2014) touches upon some methodological challenges and how future research may overcome these challenges. In the following, we offer a number of suggestions on how existing methodological approaches in the NVT research can be expanded (beyond the suggestions by Klotz et al., 2014) as an important next step to better understand NVT processes.

Improving Survey Instruments

Crook, Shook, Morris, and Madden (2009) made an assessment of the methodological state-of-the-art in the entrepreneurship domain. First, they conclude that, overall, the field's methodological rigor has made significant strides. In particular, improvements in major issues such as construct measurement and the use of more sophisticated modeling approaches (e.g., Hayes' (2013) process method simultaneously incorporating mediation and moderation). Second, while acknowledging the entrepreneurship field's inherent difficulties such as difficult data collection and sampling procedures resulting in smaller samples than those compared to the organization behavior and general management fields, important gaps were identified. Some of these involve common method bias, nonresponse bias, fit between design and method, reliability, and validity.

NVT research has traditionally borrowed and adapted the measurements from the TMT and small group research. Yet, in order to open the black box of NVT processes, new scales need to be developed that better capture NVT processes despite the fact that there may be difficulties when trying to publish papers with new scales. As Short et al. (2010) put it, "entrepreneurship scholars must . . . expect their work to be judged by discipline-wide empirical standards, which in some cases may be more demanding than those in the entrepreneurship field." Moderated mediation models (Hayes, 2013), for instance, take into account the conditions under which specific indirect effects occur, as such allowing the move from the study of causes to that of conditions (Hackman, 2012). Examining conditional indirect effect models of both the *how* and the *when* of the NVT processes is therefore a fruitful research avenue, even though the problems of successionist causality will still arise in such studies.

Simulation Exercises: Agent-Based Modeling

McMullen and Dimov (2013) outline bottom-up or agent-based computational modeling as one of the possibilities for studying entrepreneurship as a process ("journey") as opposed to entrepreneurship as an act. Unlike mathematical, top-down modeling, this approach enables closer correspondence with real-world agents of interest. Among other studies advocating for the use of agent-based modeling (ABM) are the studies by McKelvey (2004) and Yang and Chandra (2013) in relation to entrepreneurship, and by Davis, Eisenhardt, and Bingham (2007) in relation to management.

Yang and Chandra (2013) argue for the use of ABM as an alternative approach to advance research in entrepreneurship. They do so by discussing the shared conceptual foundations of ABM and entrepreneurship: autonomy, heterogeneity, and bounded rationality that gives rise to uncertainty, learning, and disequilibrium. An example of a general entrepreneurship research question suited to this research design could be "How do entrepreneurial phenomena emerge from the collective behaviors of agents?" Among methodological concerns indicated by the authors are the difficulties related to verification and validation of ABM models due to the possibility of the emergence of new patterns of macrobehavior, programming errors (bugs), and the fact that it may be hard to get accepted by empirical researchers. The authors provide an extensive list of further reading for those interested in advancing entrepreneurship research using the ABM.

As McMullen and Dimov (2013, p. 1506) point out, "given the challenges associated with obtaining data on the early stages of the entrepreneurial journey and its unfolding over long periods of time, ABM may be especially attractive to entrepreneurship researchers because it enables them to create their own datasets for theoretical exploration and insight." By systematically varying the contextual characteristics, agent characteristics, or rules of interaction, the suggested approach also allows for rigorous experimentation. Given difficulties in collecting data in the entrepreneurship field in general, and on the entrepreneurial team members particularly, ABM may serve as a favorable complementary research design. For instance, ABM could allow the simulation of certain situations and/or processes in the initial NVT prior to making data collection efforts in the field with samples of real entrepreneurial teams.

Neurostudies
Organizational cognitive neuroscience (OCN) is starting to gain speed in its theoretical development (Butler, O'Broin, Lee, & Senior, 2015). However, it is still in the exploratory phase of its emergence and diffusion since a relatively small number of empirical articles has been published between 2007 and the end of 2014. In their review, Butler et al. (2015) divide OCN into three clusters—economics, marketing, and organizational behavior—of which the latter is closest to entrepreneurship. Similarly to the economics and marketing clusters, the organizational behavior cluster encompasses research measuring the effect of testosterone levels on behavior (one article) and adopting neuroimaging methods (three articles). Contrary to other two clusters, the organizational behavior cluster includes experimental work using a greater variety of research methods—electroencephalography, facial morphology, and fluctuating physical asymmetry. Theoretically, the organizational behavior cluster investigates themes similar to those of the economics and marketing clusters. For instance, emotions and decision-making are explored through the memories of experiences with resonant and dissonant leaders (Boyatzis et al., 2012).

Boyatzis (2014, p. 302) reviews selected articles and their contributions to leadership and management development from neuroscience indicating that physiological and neuroscience studies are "creeping into print in AMJ, ASQ, JOM, and even Harvard Business Review." Both review studies by Boyatzis (2014) and Butler et al. (2015) encourage the application of neuroscience while also recommending cautiousness when integrating neuroscience and management. It is noteworthy that, of all reviewed articles in Butler et al. (2015) only one study examines team decision-making processes and the ways in which the brain system in different team members functions synchronously, yielding potential insight into how to compose effective teams (Woolley et al., 2007). Following these authors' advice, we would also recommend researchers to be cautious given the early stage of OCN. It is hard enough to make entrepreneurs respond to surveys, let alone placing them in MRI scanners; especially when all the entrepreneurial team members should ideally be taken into account.

We believe, however, that organizational cognitive neuroscience offers interesting research opportunities in the area of entrepreneurial team formation and early team functioning. Such studies could try to recruit business and entrepreneurship students who are often invited to a lab for experiments and simulations (e.g., Breugst & Patzelt, 2014; Johnson, van de Schoot, Delmar, & Crano, 2015). As such, the OCN research on entrepreneurial team formation and functioning has a great potential to uncover possible imprinting and path-dependent effects of socioemotional mechanisms (Baron, 2008) on decision-making in new ventures. Moreover, combined with grounded approach the OCN research design may be a valuable addition for studying the process of entrepreneurial theorizing, which consists of three conceptual steps—the triggering role of experience and perception, imagination of possibilities, reason and justification—and has, so far, remained a theoretical abstraction (Felin & Zenger, 2009).

Towards a Mixed Methods Approach
As mentioned, there have been recent calls for longitudinal approaches to team research (Cronin et al., 2011). Furthermore, Humphrey & Aime (2014) call for a microdynamics "organizing" approach which also emphasizes the multilevel and multitheoretical needs of the field and the interaction between them. As such, the authors offer a range of theories with potential value for the study of teams in organizational behavior research. A similar trend is found in the strategic decision-making process research where the need for multitheoretic models has been emphasized (Shepherd & Rudd, 2014). In the light of theoretical foundations eliminated above, we argue that such a trend is also valid for entrepreneurship implying that scholars interested in investigating NVT processes may benefit from incorporating longitudinal, multilevel and multi-theoretical approaches.

In this chapter, we have chosen to limit our discussion by focusing on a selection of quantitative methods that are instrumental in unraveling the black box of NVT processes. However, we suggest that these methods are complementary and should be reconciled with other methods when studying NVT processes. Undoubtedly, qualitative approaches (such as anthropological, ethnographic, narrative ones) must also be incorporated in studies of NVT processes (see Carsrud & Brännback, 2014; Martens, Jennings, & Jennings, 2007; McMullen & Dimov 2013; Neergaard & Ulhøi, 2007), independently or preferably as an essential element of a mixed methods approach. Qualitative methodologies may be particularly helpful in contextualizing the findings produced by quantitative studies of NVT processes and developing entirely new (or refining existing) theories.

Concluding Remarks

We started off with the observation that new venture team (NVT) processes remain a black box in entrepreneurship research. While research on input (demographic) characteristics influencing team and venture performance has received much attention

(Klotz et al., 2014), NVT processes have not been studied to the same extent. One reason for this is that the data on team demographic features is more readily available than the data on the processual characteristics, in addition to methodological challenges associated with measuring processes within the NVTs. Despite this, we argue that it is relevant and important for future research to address NVT processes.

In this chapter, we discussed why NVT processes are important and how we can theoretically further open up the black box of NVT processes. We also touched upon methodological challenges and suggested which methods and tools may help dealing with them. Particularly, we suggested that NVT processes may be approached by building upon two research foundations—entrepreneurial theorizing and entrepreneurial subjectivism—and by integrating a range of theoretical perspectives, namely: (1) faultlines, (2) creativity and imagination, (3) organizational and team justice, (4) behavioral integration and shared cognition, (5) shared leadership, (6) and transactive memory systems. Infusing these theories into entrepreneurial theorizing and entrepreneurial subjectivism, we offered future research directions on the processes associated with team formation in the prefounding phase as well as team evolution and functioning in the postfounding phase. We believe that our future research suggestions may not only advance the understanding of NVT processes, but also contribute to a further development of the streams of research on entrepreneurial theorizing and entrepreneurial subjectivism which have collective action as a common denominator.

We would like to emphasize that our selection of theories was not exhaustive and that future research could incorporate other theories as well. For instance, the theories on social interaction (e.g., Lechler, 2001), group affect (Barsade & Knight, 2015), sensemaking (Weick 1995; Weick, Sutcliffe, & Obstfeld, 2005) and signaling (Connelly, Certo, Ireland, & Reutzel, 2011) might be relevant and provide additional valuable insights surrounding team formation in the prefounding phase. Using theories of conflict, cohesion, emotions, resource orchestration, intrateam learning, team task design, boundary spanning, and so on (see e.g., reviews by Klotz et al., 2014, and Mathieu et al., 2008) could generate interesting insights into team evolution and formation in the postfounding phase. These theories were outside the scope of this chapter.

Our chapter has a number of implications. First, we aim at contributing to team research by developing increased awareness toward NVT processes and how these may be approached both theoretically and empirically. Second, these insights may prove useful not only to entrepreneurship researchers, but also to team researchers from other disciplines given recent calls for more in-depth examination of the role of team processes in explaining outcomes (e.g., Mathieu et al., 2008). Third, this chapter may also be relevant for practitioners who are entrepreneurs, team coaches (technology transfer officers, educators, and so on), or policymakers, who wish to better understand the processes within the teams in new ventures.

References

Ahearn, K., Ferris, G. R., Hockwarter, W. A., Douglas, C., & Ammeter, P. P. (2006). Leader political skill and team performance. *Journal of Management, 30,* 309–327.

Aldrich, H., & Auster, E. R. (1986). Even dwarfs started small: Liabilities of age and size and their strategic implications. In L. L. Cummings & B. M. Staw (Eds.), *Research in Organizational Behavior, 8,* 165–198. Greenwich, CT: JAI Press.

Aldrich, H. E. (2001). Who wants to be an evolutionary theorist: Remarks on the occasion of the Year 2000 OMT Distinguished Scholarly Career Award Presentation. *Journal of Management Inquiry, 10*, 115–127.

Aldrich, H. E., & Martinez, M. A. (2001). Many are called, but few are chosen: An evolutionary perspective for the study of entrepreneurship. *Entrepreneurship Theory and Practice, 25*, 41–56.

Aldrich, H. E., & Yang, T. (2014). How do entrepreneurs know what to do? Learning and organizing in new ventures. *Journal of Evolutionary Economics, 24*, 59–82.

Alvarez, S., & Barney, J. (2007). Discovery and creation: alternative theories of entrepreneurial action. *Strategic Entrepreneurship Journal, 1*, 11–26.

Amabile, T. M. (1996). *Creativity in context. Creativity in context: Update to the Social Psychology of Creativity*. Boulder, CO: Westview Press.

Amabile, T. M. (1997). Entrepreneurial creativity through motivational synergy. *The Journal of Creative Behavior, 31*, 18–26.

Amabile, T. M., & Pillemer, J. (2012). Perspectives on the social psychology of creativity. *Journal of Creative Behavior, 46*, 3–15.

Amason, A. (1996). Distinguishing the effects of functional and dysfunctional conflict on strategic decision making: Resolving a paradox for top management teams. *The Academy of Management Journal, 39*, 123–148.

Amason, A. C., Shrader, R. C., & Tompson, G. H. (2006). Newness and novelty: Relating top management team composition to new venture performance. *Journal of Business venturing, 21*, 125–148.

Anderson, M. H., & Sun, P. Y. T. (2015). Reviewing leadership styles: Overlaps and the need for a new "full-range" theory. *International Journal of Management Reviews*, 1–21.

Argote, L., & Ren, Y. (2012). Transactive memory systems: A microfoundation of dynamic capabilities. *Journal of Management Studies, 49*, 1375–1382.

Baker, T., & Nelson, R. (2005). Creating something from nothing: Resource construction through entrepreneurial bricolage. *Administrative Science Quarterly, 50*, 329–366.

Baron, R. A. (2008). The role of affect in the entrepreneurial process. *Academy of Management Review, 33*, 328–340.

Barsade, S. G., & Knight, A. P. (2015). Group affect. *Annual Review of Organizational Psychology and Organizational Behavior, 2*, 14.1–14.26.

Becker, M. C., Knudsen, T., & March, J. G. (2006). Schumpeter, Winter, and the sources of novelty. *Industrial and Corporate Change, 15*, 353–371.

Bezrukova, K., Jehn, K. A., Zanutto, E. L., & Thatcher, S. M. B. (2009). Do workgroup faultlines help or hurt? A moderated model of faultlines, team identification, and group performance. *Organization Science, 20*, 35–50.

Bjørnåli, E. S. (2016). Research on boards of directors in high-tech start-ups: An assessment and suggestions for future research. In J. Gabrielsson (Ed.), *Handbook of corporate governance and entrepreneurship*. Cheltenham, England: Elgar.

Bjørnåli, E. S., & Ellingsen, A. (2015). Exploring antecedents and impact of board effectiveness in clean-tech enterprises. In L. Gnan, A. Hinna, & F. Monteduro (Eds.), *Contingency, behavioural and evolutionary perspectives on public and non-profit governance*. Bingley, England: Emerald.

Blatt, R. (2009). Tough love: How communal schemas and contracting practices build relational capital in entrepreneurial teams. *Academy of Management Review, 34*, 533–551.

Boeker, W., & Wiltbank, R. (2005). New venture evolution and managerial capabilities. *Organization Science, 16*, 123–133.

Bolden, R. (2011). Distributed leadership in organizations: A review of theory and research. *International Journal of Management Reviews, 13*, 251–269.

Boyatzis, R. E. (2014). Possible contributions to leadership and management development from neuroscience. *Academy of Management Learning & Education, 13*, 300–303.

Boyatzis, R. E., Passarelli, A. M., Koenig, K., Lowe, M., Mathew, B., Stoller, J. K., & Philips, M. (2012). Examination of the neural substrates activated in memories of experiences with resonant and dissonant leaders. *Leadership Quarterly, 23*, 259–272.

Breugst, N., & Patzelt, H. (2014).Thinking about team decisions in entrepreneurial tasks. *Academy of Management Proceedings, 2014*(1).

Breugst, N., Patzelt, H., & Rathgeber, P. (2015). How should we divide the pie? Equity distribution and its impact on entrepreneurial teams. *Journal of Business Venturing, 30*, 66–94.

Bruderl, J., & Schussler, R. (1990). Organizational mortality: the liabilities of newness and adolescence. *Administrative Science Quarterly, 35*, 530–547.

Bryant, P. T. (2014). Imprinting by design: The microfoundations of entrepreneurial adaptation. *Entrepreneurship Theory and Practice, 38*, 1081–1102.

Bryne, D. E. (1971). *The attraction paradigm.* New York, NY: Academic Press.

Burke, C. S., Stagl, K. C., Klein, C., Goodwin, G. F., Salas, E., & Halpin, S. M. (2006).What type of leadership behaviors are functional in teams? A meta-analysis. *Leadership Quarterly, 17*, 288–307.

Busenitz, L. W., Moesel, D. D., Fiet, J. O., & Barney, J. B. (1997). The framing of perceptions of fairness in the relationship between venture capitalists and new venture teams. *Entrepreneurship Theory and Practice, 21*, 5–21.

Butler, M. J. R., O'Broin, H. L. R., Lee, N., & Senior, C. (2015). How organizational cognitive neuroscience can deepen understanding of managerial decision-making: A review of the recent literature and future directions. *International Journal of Management Reviews, 18*(4), 542–559.

Carmeli, A., & Schaubroeck, J. (2006). Top management team behavioural integration, decision quality, and organizational decline. *Leadership Quarterly, 17*, 441–453.

Carson, J. B., Tesluk, P. E., & Marrone, J. A. (2007). Shared leadership in teams: An investigation of antecedent conditions and performance. *Academy of Management Journal, 50*, 1217–1234.

Carsrud, A., & Brännback, M. (Ed.). (2014). *Handbook of research methods and applications in entrepreneurship and small business.* Cheltenham, England: Elgar.

Chiles, T. H., Bluedorn, A. C., & Gupta, V. K. (2007). Beyond creative destruction and entrepreneurial discovery: A radical Austrian approach to entrepreneurship. *Organization Studies, 28*, 467–493.

Chowdhury, S. (2005). Demographic diversity for building an effective entrepreneurial team: Is it important? *Journal of Business Venturing, 20*, 727–746.

Colquitt, J. A., Greenberg, J., & Zapata-Phelan, C. P. (2005). What Is organizational justice? A historical overview. In J. Greenberg & J. A. Colquitt (Eds.), *Handbook of organizational justice* (pp. 3–58). Mahwah, NJ: Erlbaum.

Connelly, B. L., Certo, S. T., Ireland, R. D., & Reutzel, C. R. (2011). Signaling theory: A review and assessment. *Journal of Management, 37*, 39–67.

Cronin, M. A., Weingart, L. R., & Todorova, G. (2011). Dynamics in groups: Are we there yet? *Academy of Management Annals, 5*, 571-612.

Crook, T. R., Shook, C. L., Morris, M. L., & Madden, T. M. (2009). Are we there yet? An assessment of research design and construct measurement practices in entrepreneurship research. *Organizational Research Methods, 13*, 192–206.

Cropanzano, R., Bowen, D. E., & Gilliland, S. W. (2007). The management of organizational justice. *Academy of Management Perspectives, 21*, 34–48.

Cropanzano, R., Li, A., & Benson, L. (2011). Peer justice and teamwork process. *Group & Organization Management, 36*, 567–596.

Crucke, S., & Knockaert M. (2016). When stakeholder representation leads to faultlines. A study of board service performance in social enterprises. *Journal of Management Studies, 53*(5), 768–793.

Davis, J. P., Eisenhardt, K. M., & Bingham, C .B. (2007). Developing theory through simulation methods. *Academy of Management Review, 32*, 480–499.

Dew, N., Read, S., Sarasvathy, S. D., & Wiltbank, R. (2008). Outlines of a behavioral theory of the entrepreneurial firm. *Journal of Economic Behavior & Organization, 66*, 37–59.

Drazin, R., Glynn, M. A., & Kazanjian, R. K. (1999). Multilevel theorizing about creativity in organizations: A sensemaking perspective. *Academy of Management Review, 24*, 286–307.

Dust, S. B., & Ziegert, J. C. (2015). Multi-leader teams in review: A contingent-configuration perspective of effectiveness. *International Journal of Management Reviews, 18*(4), 518–541.

Edmondson, A. (1999). Psychological safety and learning behavior in work teams. *Administrative Science Quarterly, 44*, 350–383.

Ensley, M., & Hmieleski, K. (2005). A comparative study of new venture top management team composition, dynamics and performance between university-based and independent start-ups. *Research Policy, 34*, 1091–1105.

Ensley, M. D., Hmieleski, K. M., & Pearce, C. L. (2006). The importance of vertical and shared leadership within new venture top management teams: implications for the performance of start ups. *Leadership Quarterly, 17*, 217–231.

Ensley, M. D., & Pearce, C. L. (2001). Shared cognition in top management teams: Implications for new venture performance. *Journal of Organizational Behavior, 22*, 145–160.

Ensley, M. D., Pearson, A. W., & Amason, A. C. (2002). Understanding the dynamics of new venture top management teams: Cohesion, conflict, and new venture performance. *Journal of Business Venturing, 17*, 365–386.

Ensley, M. D., Pearson, A., & Pearce, C. L. (2003). Top management team process, shared leadership, and new venture performance: A theoretical model and research agenda. *Human Resource Management Review, 13*, 329–346.

Felin, T., Kauffman, S., Koppl, R., & Longo, G. (2014). Economic opportunity and evolution: Beyond landscapes and bounded rationality. *Strategic Entrepreneurship Journal, 8*, 269–282,

Felin, T., & Zenger, T. (2009). Entrepreneurs as theorists: On the origins of collective beliefs and novel strategies. *Strategic Entrepreneurship Journal, 3*, 127–146.

Fitzsimons, D., James, K. T., & Denyer, D. (2011). Alternative approaches for studying shared and distributed leadership. *International Journal of Management Reviews, 13*, 313–328.

Fletcher, D., & Selden, P. (2015). Navigating the growing field of entrepreneurship inquiry: successionist and relational modes of theory development. In A. Fayolle & P. Riot (Eds.), *Rethinking entrepreneurship: Debating research orientations*. New York, NY: Routledge.

Folger, R., & Cropanzano, R. (1998). *Organizational justice and human resource management* Thousand Oaks, CA: Sage.

Foss, N. J., & Klein, P. G. (2012). *Entrepreneurial judgment and the theory of the firm.* Cambridge, England: Cambridge University Press.

Foss, N. J, & Lyngsie, J. (2014).The strategic organization of the entrepreneurial established firm. *Strategic Organization, 12*(3), 208–215.

Foss, N. J., Klein, P. G., Kor, Y. Y., & Mahoney, J. T. (2008). Entrepreneurship, subjectivism, and the resource-based view: Toward a new synthesis. *Strategic Entrepreneurship Journal, 2*, 73–94.

Freeman, J., Carroll, G. R., & Hannan, M. T. (1983). the liability of newness: age dependence in organizational death rates. *American Sociological Review, 48*, 692–710.

Garg, S. (2013). Venture boards: Distinctive monitoring and implications for firm performance. *Academy of Management Review, 38*, 90–108.

George, B. A., Erikson, T., Parhankangas, A. (2014). Preventing dysfunctional conflict: Examining the relationship between different types of managerial conflict in VC-backed firms. *Frontiers of Entrepreneurship Research, 33*, 11–15.

George, J. M. (2007). Creativity in organizations. *The Academy of Management Annals, 1*, 439–477.

Gilson, L. L., & Shalley, C. E. (2004). A little creativity goes a long way: An examination of teams' engagement in creative processes. *Journal of Management, 30*, 453–470.

Gloria-Palermo, S. (1999). *The evolution of Austrian economics. From Menger to Lachmann.* New York, NY: Routledge.

Hackman, J. R. (2012). From cause to conditions in group research. *Journal of Organizational Behavior, 33*, 428–444.

Hackman, J. R., & Wageman, R. (2005). A theory of team coaching. *Academy of Management Review, 30*, 269–287.

Hambrick, D. C. (1994). Top management groups: A conceptual integration and reconsideration of the team label. In B. M. Staw & L. L. Cummings (Eds.), *Research in Organizational Behavior* (Vol. 16, pp. 171–214). Greenwich, CT: JAI Press.

Hambrick, D. C. (2007). Upper echelons theory: An update. *Academy of Management Review, 32*, 334–343.

Hambrick, D. C., & Mason, P. A. (1984). Upper echelons: The organization as a reflection of its top managers. *Academy of Management Review, 9*, 193–207.

Harper, D. A. (2008). Towards a theory of entrepreneurial teams. *Journal of Business Venturing, 23*, 613–626.

Hayes, A. F. (2013). *Introduction to mediation, moderation, and conditional process analysis: A regression-based approach.* New York, NY: Guilford.

Haynes, K. T., Hitt, M. A., Campbell, J. T. (2015). The dark side of leadership: Towards a mid-range theory of hubris and greed in entrepreneurial contexts. *Journal of Management Studies, 52*, 1467–6486.

Hennessey, B. A., & Amabile, T. M. (2010). Creativity. *Annual Review of Psychology, 61*, 569–598.

Hiller, N. J., Day, D. V., & Vance, R. J. (2006). Collective enactment of leadership roles and team effectiveness: A field study. *The Leadership Quarterly, 17*, 387–397.

Hmieleski, K. M., Cole, M. S., & Baron, R. A. (2012). Shared authentic leadership and new venture performance. *Journal of Management, 38*, 1476–1499.

Hmieleski, K. M., & M. D. Ensley (2007). A contextual examination of new venture performance: Entrepreneur leadership behavior, top management team heterogeneity, and environmental dynamism. *Journal of Organizational Behavior, 28*, 865–889.

Hoch, J. E., Pearce, C. L., & Welzel, L. (2010). Is the most effective team leadership shared? *Journal of Personnel Psychology, 9*, 105–116.

Hollingshead, A. B., & Brandon, D. P. (2003). Potential benefits of communication in transactive memory systems. *Human Communication Research, 29*, 607–615.

Humphrey, S. E., & Aime, F. (2014). Team microdynamics: Toward an organizing approach to teamwork. *The Academy of Management Annals, 8*, 443–503.

Jansen J. P., Kostopoulos, K. C., Mihalache, O. R., & Papalexandris A. (2016). A sociopsychological perspective on team ambidexterity: The contingency role of supportive leadership behaviours. *Journal of Management Studies*. Version of Record online: Feb 5 2016. doi: 10.1111/joms.12183

Jennings, J. E., Jennings, P. D., & Greenwood, R. (2009). Novelty and new firm performance: The case of employment systems in knowledge-intensive service organizations. *Journal of Business Venturing, 24*, 338–359.

Johnson, A. R., van de Schoot, R., Delmar F., & Crano, W. D. (2015). Social influence interpretation of interpersonal processes and team performance over time using Bayesian model selection. *Journal of Management, 41*, 574–606.

Kaczmarek, S., Kimino, S., & Pye, A. (2012) Board task-related faultlines and firm performance: A decade of evidence. *Corporate Governance: An International Review, 20*(4), 337–351.

Kale, S., & Arditi, D. (1998). Business failures: Liabilities of newness, adolescence, and smallness. *Journal of Construction and Engineering Management, 124*, 458–464.

Kamm, J., & Nurick, A. (1993). The stage of team venture formation: A decision-making model. *Entrepreneurship Theory and Practice, 17*, 17–27.

Kamoche, K., Pina E., Cunha, M., & Da Cunha, J. V. (2003). Towards a theory of organizational improvisation: Looking beyond the jazz metaphor. *Journal of Management Studies, 40*, 2023–2051.

Kang, J. H., Solomon, G. T., & Choi, D. Y. (2015). CEOs' leadership styles and managers' innovative behaviour: Investigation of intervening effects in an entrepreneurial context. *Journal of Management Studies, 52*, 531–554.

Klotz, A. C., Hmieleski, K. M., Bradley, B. H., & Busenitz, L. W. (2014). New venture teams: A review of the literature and roadmap for future research. *Journal of Management, 40*, 226–255.

Knight, F. H. (1921). *Risk, uncertainty, and profit*. Boston, MA: Hart, Schaffner & Marx/ Houghton Mifflin.

Knockaert, M., Ucbasaran, D., Wright, M., & Clarysse, B. (2011). The relationship between knowledge transfer, top management team composition and performance: The case of science based entrepreneurial firms. *Entrepreneurship Theory and Practice, 35*, 777–803.

Knockaert, M., Bjørnåli, E. S., & Erikson, T. (2014). Joining forces: Top management team and board chair characteristics as antecedents of board service involvement. *Journal of Business Venturing, 30*, 420–435.

Koestler, A. (1964). *The act of creation*. Oxford, England: Macmillan.

Kor, Y. Y., Mahoney J. T., Michael, S. C. (2007). Resources, capabilities, and entrepreneurial perceptions. *Journal of Management Studies, 44*, 1185–1210.

Kozbelt, A., Beghetto, R. A., & Runco, M. A. (2010). Theories of creativity. In J. C. Kaufman & R. J. Sternberg (Eds.), *The Cambridge handbook of creativity* (pp. 20–48). New York, NY: Cambridge University Press.

Kozlowski, S. W. J., & Bell, B. S. (2003). Work groups and teams in organizations. In W. C. Borman, D. R. Ilgen, & R. J. Klimoski (Eds.). *Handbook of psychology: Industrial and organizational psychology* (Vol. 12, pp. 333–375) London, England: Wiley.

Kozlowski, S. W. J., & Ilgen, D. R. (2006). Enhancing the effectiveness of work groups and teams. *Psychological Science in the Public Interest, 7*, 77–124.

Lachmann, L. M. (1956/1978). *Capital and its structure*. Kansas City, MO: Sheed Andrews and McMeel.

Lachmann, L. M. (1976). From Mises to Shackle: An essay on Austrian economics and the kaleidic society. *Journal of Economic Literature, 14*, 54–61.

Lechler, T. (2001). Social interaction: A determinant of entrepreneurial team venture success. *Small Business Economics, 16*, 263–278.

Leunbach, D., Erikson, T., Ricciardi, L., Heggli, K., & Good, M. (2016, June 8–11). Muddling through Akerlofian and Knightean uncertainties: The role of team positive affective tone and polychronicity. Paper presented at the 2016 Babson College Entrepreneurship Research Conference (BCERC), Bodo, Norway.

Lewis, K. (2003). Measuring transactive memory systems in the field: Scale development and validation. *Journal of Applied Psychology, 88*, 587–604.

Lewis, K., & Herndon, B. (2011). Transactive memory systems: Current issues and future research directions. *Organization Science, 22*, 1254–1265.

Li, A., & Cropanzano, R. (2009). Fairness at the group level: Justice climate and intraunit justice climate. *Journal of Management, 35*, 564–599.

Lim, J. Y. K., Busenitz, L. W., & Chidambaram, L. (2013). New venture teams and the quality of business opportunities identified: Faultlines between subgroups of founders and investors. *Entrepreneurship Theory and Practice, 37*, 47–67.

Lind, E. A. (2001). Fairness heuristic theory: Justice judgments as pivotal cognitions in organizational relations. In J. Greenberg & R. Cropanzano (Eds.), *Advances in organization justice* (pp. 56–88). Stanford, CA: Stanford University Press.

Lind, E. A., & van den Bos, K. (2002). When fairness works: Toward a general theory of uncertainty management. *Research in Organizational Behavior, 24*, 181–223.

Lindenberg, S., & Foss, N. J. (2011). Managing joint production motivation: The role of goal framing and governance mechanisms. *Academy of Management Review, 36*, 500–525.

Low, M. B., & MacMillan, I. C. (1988). Entrepreneurship: Past research and future challenges. *Journal of Management, 14*, 139–161.

Mahoney, J. T. (1995). The management of resources and the resource of management. *Journal of Business Research, 33*, 91–101.

Martens, M. L., Jennings, J. E., & Jennings, P. D. (2007). Do the stories they tell get them the money they need? The role of entrepreneurial narratives in resource acquisition. *Academy of Management Journal, 50*, 1107–1132.

Mathieu, J. E., Maynard, M. T., Rapp, T., & Gilson, L. (2008). Team effectiveness 1997–2007: A review of recent advancements and a glimpse into the future. *Journal of Management, 34*, 410–476.

McKelvey, B. (2004). Toward a complexity science of entrepreneurship. *Journal of Business Venturing, 19*, 313–341.

McMullen, J. S., & Dimov, D. (2013). Time and the entrepreneurial journey: The problems and promise of studying entrepreneurship as a process. *Journal of Management Studies, 50*, 1481–1512.

Miller, C., Burke, L., & Glick, W. (1998). Cognitive diversity among upper-echelon executives: Implications for strategic decision processes. *Strategic Management Journal, 19*, 39–58.

Miron-Spektor, E., Gino, F., & Argote, L. (2011). Paradoxical frames and creative sparks: Enhancing individual creativity through conflict and integration. *Organizational Behavior and Human Decision Processes, 116*, 229–240.

Morgeson, F. P. (2005). The external leadership of self-managing teams: Intervening in the context of novel and disruptive events. *Journal of Applied Psychology, 90*, 497–508.

Mumford, M. D., Hester, K. S., & Robledo, I. C. (2011). Creativity in organizations: Importance and approaches. In M. D. Mumford (Ed.), *Handbook of organizational creativity* (pp. 3–16). London, England: Elsevier.

Neergaard, H., Ulhøi, J. P. (Eds.). (2007). *Handbook of qualitative research methods in entrepreneurship*. Cheltenham, England: Elgar.

Patton, D., & Higgs, M. (2013). The role of shared leadership in the strategic decision making processes of new technology based firms. *International Journal of Innovation Management, 17*, pp. 1–24.

Paulus, P. B., Dzindolet, M., & Kohn, N. W. (2011). Collaborative creativity-group creativity and team innovation. In M. D. Mumford (Ed.), *Handbook of organizational creativity* (pp. 327–357). London, England: Elsevier.

Pearce, C. L., & Sims, H. P. (2000). Shared leadership: Toward a multi-level theory of leadership. In M. M. Beyerlein, D. A. Johnson, & S. T. Beyerlein (Eds.), *Advances in interdisciplinary studies of work teams: Team development* (Vol. 7, pp.115–139). Greenwich, CT: JAI Press.

Penrose E. T. (1959). *The theory of the growth of the firm*. Cambridge, England: Wiley.

Perry-Smith, J. E., & Coff, R. W. (2011). In the mood for entrepreneurial creativity? How optimal group affect differs for generating and selecting ideas for new ventures. *Strategic Entrepreneurship Journal, 5*, 247–268.

Polzer, J. T., Milton, L. P., & Swann, W. B. J. (2002). Capitalizing on diversity: Interpersonal congruence in small work groups. *Academy of Management Proceedings & Membership Directory, 47*, 296–324.

Reiter-Palmon, R., Wigert, B., & de Vreede, T. (2012). Team creativity and innovation: The effect of group composition, social processes, and cognition. In L. C. Kaufman, J. C. & R. J. Sternberg (Eds.). *Handbook of organizational creativity* (pp. 295–326). New York, NY: Cambridge University Press.

Ren, Y., & Argote, L. (2011). Transactive Memory Systems 1985 – 2010: An Integrative Framework of Key Dimensions, Antecedents and Consequences. *The Academy of Management Annals, 5*, 37–41.

Ren, Y., Carley, K. M., & Argote, L. (2006) The contingent effects of transactive memory: When is it more beneficial to know what others know? *Management Science, 52*(5), 671–682.

Rico, R., Molleman, E., Sanchez-Manzanares, M., & Vegt, G. S. V. d. (2007). The Effects of Diversity Faultlines and Team Task Autonomy on Decision Quality and Social Integration. *Journal of Management, 33*, 111–132.

Robbins, S. P., & Judge, T. A. (2015). *Organizational behaviour* (16th ed.). Pearson Education Ltd., Essex.

Ruef, M. (2002). Strong ties, weak ties and islands: Structural and cultural predictors of organizational innovation. *Industrial and Corporate Change, 11*, 427–449.

Ruef, M. (2010). *Entrepreneurial Group: Social Identities, Relations, and Collective Action*. Princeton University Press, Princeton.

Samuelsson, M., & Davidsson, P. (2009). Does venture opportunity variation matter? Investigating systematic process differences between innovative and imitative new ventures. *Small Business Economics, 33*, 229–255.

Sapienza, H. J., & Korsgaard, M. A. (1996). Procedural justice in entrepreneur-investor relations. *Academy of Management Journal, 39*, 544–574.

Sarasvathy, S. D. (2001). Causation and effectuation: Toward a theoretical shift from economic inevitability to entrepreneurial contingency. *Academy of Management Review, 26*, 243-263.

Schjoedt, L., Monsen, E., Pearson, A., Barnett, T., & Chrisman, J. J. (2013). New venture and family business teams: Understanding team formation, composition, behaviors, and performance. *Entrepreneurship Theory and Practice, 37*, 1–15.

Schumpeter, J. A. (1934). *The theory of economic development*. Cambridge, MA: Harvard University Press.

Shalley, C. E., & Gilson, L. L. (2004). What leaders need to know: A review of social and contextual factors that can foster or hinder creativity. *Leadership Quarterly, 15*, 33–53.

Shalley C. E., & Perry-Smith J. E. (2008). The emergence of team creative cognition: The role of diverse outside ties, sociocognitive network centrality, and team evolution. *Strategic Entrepreneurship Journal, 2*, 23–41.

Shalley, C. E., Zhou, J., & Oldham, G. R. (2004). The effects of personal and contextual characteristics on creativity: Where should we go from here? *Journal of Management, 30*, 933–958.

Shepherd, D. A., Douglas, E. J., & Shanley, M. (2000). New venture survival: Ignorance, external shocks, and risk reduction strategies. *Journal of Business Venturing, 15*, 393–410.

Shepherd, N. G., & Rudd, J. M. (2014). The influence of context on the strategic decision-making process: A review of the literature. *International Journal of Management Reviews, 16*, 340–364.

Short, J. C., Ketchen, D. J., Jr., Combs, J. G., & Ireland, R. D. (2010). Research methods in entrepreneurship: Opportunities and challenges. *Organizational Research Methods, 13*, 6–15.

Simsek, Z., Veiga, J., Lubatkin, M. H., & Dino, R. N. (2005). Modeling the multilevel determinants of top management team behavioral integration. *Academy of Management Journal, 48*, 69–84.

Sine, W. D., Mitsuhashi, H., & Kirsch, D. A. (2006). Revisiting Burns and Stalker: Formal structure and new venture performance in emerging economic sectors. *Academy of Management Journal, 49*, 121–132.

Sivasubramaniam, N., Murry, W. D., Avolio, B. J., & Jung, D. I. (2002). A longitudinal model of the effects of team leadership and group potency on group performance. *Group and Organization Management, 27*, 66–96.

Souitaris, V., & Maestro, B. M. M. (2010). Polychronicity in top management teams: The impact on strategic decision processes and performance of new technology ventures. *Strategic Management Journal, 31*, 652–678.

Srivastava, A., Bartol, K. M., & Locke, E. A. (2006). Empowering leadership in management teams: Effects on knowledge sharing, efficacy, and performance. *Academy of Management Journal, 49*, 1239–1251.

Stinchcombe, A. L. (1965). Social structure and organizations. In J. G. March (Ed.), *Handbook of organizations* (pp. 142–193). Chicago, IL: Rand McNally.

Sy, T., Cote, S., & Saavedra, R. (2005). The contagious leader: Impact of the leader's mood on the mood of group members, group affective tone, and group processes. *Journal of Applied Psychology, 90*, 295–305.

Thatcher, S. M. B., Jehn, K. A., & Zanutto, E. (2003). Cracks in diversity research: The effects of diversity faultlines on conflict and performance. *Group Decision and Negotiation, 12*, 217–241.

Thatcher, S. M. B., & Patel, P. C. (2011). Demographic faultlines: A meta-analysis of the literature. *Journal of Applied Psychology, 96*, 1119–1139.

Thatcher, S. M. B., & Patel, P. C. (2012). Group faultlines: A review, integration, and guide to future research. *Journal of Management, 38*, 969–1009.

Thorpe, R., Gold, J., & Lawler, J. (2011). Locating distributed leadership. *International Journal of Management Reviews, 13*, 239–250.

Turner, J. (1987). *Rediscovering the social group: A social categorization theory*. Oxford, England: Blackwell.

van den Bos, K. (2001). Uncertainty management: The influence of uncertainty salience on reactions to perceived procedural fairness. *Journal of personality and social psychology, 80*, 931–941.

van Knippenberg, D., Dawson, J. F., West, M. A., & Homan, A. C. (2011). Diversity faultlines, shared objectives, and top management team performance. *Human Relations, 64*, 307–336.

Vanaelst, I., & Wright, M. (2009). *Entrepreneurial teams and new business creation*. Cheltenham, England: Elgar.

Vanaelst, I., Clarysse, B., Wright, M., Lockett, A., Moray, N., & S'Jegers, R. (2006). Entrepreneurial team development in academic spinouts: An examination of team heterogeneity. *Entrepreneurship Theory and Practice, 30*, 249–271.

Vera, D., Nemanich, L., Vélez-Castrillón, S., & Werner., S. (2014). Knowledge-based and contextual factors associated with R&D teams' improvisation capability. *Journal of Management, 42*(7), 1874–1903.

Vissa, B., & Chacar, A. S. (2009). Leveraging ties: The contingent value of entrepreneurial teams' external advice networks on Indian software venture performance. *Strategic Management Journal, 30*, 1179–1191.

Vohora, A., Wright, M., & Lockett, A. (2004). Critical junctures in the development of university high-tech spinout companies, *Research Policy, 33*, 147–175.

Vykarnam, S., & Handelberg, J. (2005). Four themes of the impact of management teams on organizational performance: Implications for future research of entrepreneurial teams. *International Small Business Journal, 23*, 236–256.

Wageman, R. (2001). How leaders foster self-managing team effectiveness: Design choices versus hands-on coaching. *Organization Science, 12*, 559–577.

Wegner, D. M. (1987). Transactive memory: A contemporary analysis of the group mind. In B. Mullen & G. R. Goethals (Eds.), *Theories of group behavior* (pp. 185–208). New York, NY: Springer.

Wegner, D. M., Giuliano, T., & Hertel, P. T. (1985). Cognitive interdependence in close relationships. In W. J. Ickes (Ed.), *Compatible and incompatible relationships* (pp. 253–276). New York, NY: Springer.

Weick, K. E. (1979). *The social psychology of organizing*. New York, NY: McGraw-Hill.

Weick, K. E. (1995). *Sensemaking in organizations*. Thousand Oaks, CA: Sage.

Weick, K. E., & Roberts, K. H. (1993). Collective mind in organizations: Heedful interrelating on flight decks. *Administrative Science Quarterly, 38*, 357–381.

Weick, K. E., Sutcliffe, K. M., & Obstfeld, D. (2005). Organizing and the process of sensemaking. *Organization Science, 16*, 409–421.

West, G. P. (2007). Collective cognition: When entrepreneurial teams, not individuals, make decisions. *Entrepreneurship Theory and Practice, 31*, 77–102.

Williamson, I. O., & Cable, D. M. (2003). Organizational hiring patterns, interfirm network ties, and interorganizational imitation. *Academy of Management Journal, 46*, 349–358.

Woolley, A. W., Hackman, J. R., Jerde, T. E., Chabris, C. F., Bennett, S. L., & Kosslyn, S. M. (2007). Using brain-based measures to compose teams: How individual capabilities and team collaboration strategies jointly shape performance. *Social Neuroscience, 2*, 96–105.

Yang, S.-J. S., & Chandra, Y. (2013). Growing artificial entrepreneurs: Advancing entrepreneurship research using agent-based simulation approach. *International Journal of Entrepreneurial Behaviour & Research, 19*, 210–237.

Yarkoni, T. (2010). The abbreviation of personality, or how to measure 200 personality scales with 200 items. *Journal of Research in Personality, 44*, 180–198.

Zaccaro, S. J., Rittman, A. L., & Marks, M. A. (2001). Team leadership. *Leadership Quarterly, 12*, 451–483.

Zacharakis, A. Erikson, T., & George, B. A. (2010). Conflict between the VC and entrepreneur: The entrepreneur's perspective. *Venture Capital: An International Journal of Entrepreneurial Finance, 12*, 109–126.

Zahra, S. A. (2007). Contextualizing theory building in entrepreneurship research. *Journal of Business Venturing, 22*, 443–452.

Zhang, H. J., Baden-Fuller, C., & Pool, J. K. (2011). Resolving the tensions between monitoring, resourcing and strategizing: Structures and processes in high technology venture boards. *Long Range Planning, 44*, 95–117.

Zheng, Y., & Mai, Y. (2013). A contextualized transactive memory system view on how founding teams respond to surprises: Evidence from China. *Strategic Entrepreneurship Journal, 7*, 197–213.

Zheng, Y. (2012). Unlocking founding team prior shared experience: A transactive memory system perspective. *Journal of Business Venturing, 27*, 577–591.

Zhou, J. (2008). New look at creativity in the entrepreneurial process. *Strategic Entrepreneurship Journal, 2*, 1–5.

Section 4

National and International Entrepreneurship

4a. National Entrepreneurship

16

The Knowledge Spillover Theory of Entrepreneurship and the Strategic Management of Places

David B. Audretsch[a] and Erik E. Lehmann[b,c]

[a] Indiana University
[b] University of Augsburg, Germany
[c] CISAlpino Institute for Comparative Studies in Europe, Germany

Introduction

In addressing perhaps the two most central questions in the scholarly field of economics—how to achieve economic growth and wealth and how to distribute them among society—much economic research has focused on "the wealth of nations" and has tried to understand why countries differ according their business cycles, why some countries grow faster than others, and why income varies across countries. Yet, the within-country differences in productivity, income, and wealth accumulation or innovation capacity are also striking, leading Krugman (1991) to criticize the theoretical predictions of neoclassical growth theory, where we should expect that not only countries, but also places within countries, converge. In this chapter we try to give some answers on how and why regions differ within and across countries. We introduce the knowledge spillover theory of entrepreneurship (KSTE) as a refinement combining growth theory with the theory of entrepreneurship in the spatial context of places.

It has long been observed that certain places become the locus of creative activity at specific times when individuals are in close contact, exchanging ideas, and creating economic and social values; examples include the medieval cities in Italy, Augsburg in Bavaria, Birmingham and Manchester in the UK, and Alexandria and Athens among others (Lehmann, 2015). What has changed in recent times is the variation in regional competitiveness: within a short period, regions or places may improve their competitiveness and then lose it, this loss then followed either by a sharp increase in income and productivity or by a sharp decline (Audretsch, 2015). Countless examples of the latter abound, ranging from the devastation wreaked by the closure of steel mills in places like Gary, Indiana, Youngstown, Ohio, and Dortmund, the Rhine-Ruhr Valley in Germany, to the reduction of employment due to outsourcing and offshoring in the automotive industry in places like Detroit, US and Birmingham, UK (Audretsch, 2015, pp. 22–24; Audretsch & Lehmann, 2016a).

It is not that places were spared a negative economic performance in the past. As learned from economic history, the business cycle is an economic reality that, to this

The Wiley Handbook of Entrepreneurship, First Edition.
Edited by Gorkan Ahmetoglu, Tomas Chamorro-Premuzic, Bailey Klinger, & Tessa Karcisky.
© 2017 John Wiley & Sons Ltd. Published 2017 by John Wiley & Sons Ltd.

day, has not been solved or mitigated. Economic downturns and recessions are an inevitable part of economic reality. Nor are individual places immune to the economic cycle. When an economic downturn comes along, unemployment rises, local economies stagnate or fall, and places seem to suffer from diminished prospects. Thus, the economic performance of a place seems invariably tied to the business cycle, at least to some degree. When the overall conditions are stagnant, many, if not most, places suffer. When the overall economy is thriving, most places benefit—but not all and not all in the same way. It turns out that business cycles are at least a national or supranational phenomenon, as reflected by the Asian crises (1997–1998), the Euro crises (2010 until the time of writing), and the Latin-American crises (1980–1990) (Audretsch & Lehmann, 2016b). However, while the business cycle is at least as old as capitalism itself, the idea that a place needs to be strategically managed is considerably newer and would no doubt startle many people. What has changed in the last decades is the skill-biased technological change and globalization that has rendered strategic opportunities from countries to places and from sectors to specialized industries, and from the strategic management of countries toward a strategic management of places.

Even in the Solow (1956) model of economic growth, knowledge, or what was termed as constituting "technical change," was a driving force of economic performance. However, knowledge is viewed as being outside the model and reflected in the residual, and thus is beyond the reach of policy influence. As Solow famously pointed out, such knowledge "falls like manna from heaven," which would seemingly put it out of the reach of entrepreneurship or any other particular organizational form or behavior. By contrast, in the endogenous growth models introduced by Romer (1990) and Lucas (1993), knowledge is not only included within the models' parameters, but has a particularly potent impact on growth, because of its strong propensity, as Arrow (1962) made clear, to spill over from the firm or organization creating it to other third-party firms accessing it for a cost less than its value. While the Romer (1990) model assumes that knowledge spills over automatically, Acs, Audretsch, Braunerhjelm, and Carlsson (2004), Audretsch, Keilbach, and Lehmann (2006), Braunerhjelm, Acs, Audretsch, and Carlsson (2010), and Acs, Audretsch, Braunerhjelm, and Carlsson (2012) suggest that instead, the automatic spillover of knowledge from its source is impeded by what they term "the knowledge filter." The knowledge filter prevents or at least impedes knowledge from automatically spilling over for innovation and commercialization. Regulations and legal restrictions may account for some of the knowledge filter. However, the broadest and most prevalent source contributing to the knowledge filter is the conditions inherent in knowledge—uncertainty, asymmetries, and high costs of transaction. Knowledge spillover entrepreneurship is important and significant because it provides a conduit that penetrates the knowledge filter and serves as a catalyst for the commercialization of knowledge and ideas that are created in one organizational context but generate innovative activity in the context of a new firm, which ultimately contributes to economic growth, employment creation, and global competitiveness (Acs, Audretsch, Lehmann, & Licht, 2016a, 2016b).

The next section of this chapter explains the causes of the inequality of places and why places should be the objects of interest. The subsequent section introduces the concept of the knowledge spillover of entrepreneurship, and why knowledge spillover of entrepreneurship matters for the competitiveness of places. This is followed by a section identifying what has been gained from the literature about the knowledge spillover theory of entrepreneurship and introducing a framework for the strategic management of places. The final section of the chapter provides a summary and conclusions.

The Challenge of Inequality of Places

Globalization and Regionalization

Globalization has been widely associated with the end of geography, famously captured in Friedman's phrase "The world is flat" (2005). For nearly all activities—whether economic, social, or political, and whether public or private—distance between people, physical or not, will no longer serve as a barrier. Everything can be done at any time at any place in the world and at decreasing costs. However, with the world flattening, why have we observed that it is bumpy? The number of megacities is increasing drastically, and some regions and places have gained from agglomerating people and activities, while others have lost. Globalization is about regionalization, as Rugman (2005) and Rugman and Oh (2008) point out. Despite the increasing number of multinational firms worldwide and the individual use of personal computers, smartphones and the Internet, production, and personnel relationships are bounded geographically, using and absorbing the positive effects of agglomeration. Friedman (2005) concentrates on the skill-biased technological change that leads to an increase in outsourcing activities toward the lowest labor costs, and has important effects for regions. This skill-biased technological change leads to sunrise sectors in regions with a competitive advantage in labor costs, such as Eastern Europe and Asia. There, the agglomeration of industries has led to an increase in employment and positive spillover effects, for example technological and knowledge spillovers. The roots of many multinational companies from Asia, in particular India and China, lie in the workbench of Western companies. On the other hand, this effect of globalization has rendered formerly rich places like Detroit, Gary, Indiana, the Ruhr-Valley in Germany, and Birmingham in the UK to become sunset regions. Another aspect is that globalization and technological change were unambiguously skill-biased as long as the advances in IT, telecommunications, and logistics could be used to lower the costs of existing tasks (Snower, Brown, & Merkl, 2009). This requires increasing investment in technology, human capital, knowledge, and skills—which is in turn dependent on positive spillover effects, and thus agglomeration. High-tech companies, whether they are established organizations like Google, Facebook, Microsoft, and Amazon or are new start-ups, still depend on clustering effects. And these clustering effects lead to anything other than a flat world. While Friedman's focus is on the centrifugal force of globalization, the skill biased technological change spreading out economic activities, he misses the centripetal force, the clustering and agglomeration effects (Florida & Mellander, 2015, p. 41). Or, to use a more technical statement: There is no action without reaction. This paradigm shift has also shifted the focus of interest in economics, business, and politics from nations toward regions and places (Audretsch & Lehmann, 2016b).

The Mediating Role of Entrepreneurship in Transforming Places

The centrifugal forces of globalization lead to a specialization and a geographic decomposition of value chains and a disaggregation of competition at a lower, regional level, rendering places into the focus of agents. Thus, location still matters—in the location of outsourcing activities but also for the activities pushing the centripetal forces. The specialization and new organization patterns of production and work on the one hand and the innovation of new technologies on the other gave rise to new winners and losers from globalization, mirrored in new patterns of inequality and agglomeration, sunset and sunrise places, and regions. At the same time an emerging and moderating role of entrepreneurship has come about. Entrepreneurs have become a key force by devoting time, knowledge, effort, and money to making new machines, processes, and tools to do the old jobs or to innovate and create new jobs for new tasks. The pivotal point in preventing places from declining into sunset places is entrepreneurship. In a place with low labor costs, entrepreneurs create new companies to do the old jobs using a low-skilled labor force. In places with a high-skilled labor force, high-tech and knowledge-based entrepreneurs create new ideas and technologies for new jobs and tasks.

As far back as history will allow us to look, individuals have acted as opportunity seekers in order to improve their own wealth status and general well-being. Changes and developments in the environment have led to new challenges and thus new opportunities, which have consequently led to a new type of actor entering society in the last decades: the entrepreneur as an economic agent. While the individual incentives to start up a firm may be quite constant over time, technological, political, and social factors endogenously changed over time. The industrial revolution, starting in the UK and spilling over to the US and Europe, generated a new generation of agents, namely the entrepreneurs founding and establishing new companies. These inventors, who recognized an opportunity and made the risky decision to invest in a new venture and to commercialize their ideas, made the majority of their inventions in the previous century. Most of the organizations continue to exist and continue to be named after their initial founder and entrepreneur, for example Daimler, Siemens, Johnson & Johnson, and Eli Lilly, among others, and have had a sustainable impact on their location and place that still continues. While many of them still exist, a myriad of new ventures created at the same time have gone and are going under, and have disappeared beyond our memory. What they all have in common is that they dramatically changed the place where they founded their company. Places changed from being agricultural, becoming industrial districts with new challenges for society and politics, and creating new winners and losers.

While this industrial revolution has changed the economic and societal landscape in Western countries dramatically, it has bypassed the former Communist countries of the 20th century (see Lehmann & Seitz, 2016). What Shleifer described as the "Age of Milton Friedman" (Shleifer, 2009) in Western countries started decades later, in 1979, in the former Communistic countries. Ten years before the Berlin Wall fell, Deng Xiao Ping started market reforms in China, spilling over to other countries. Strongly protected by the government, a new type of economic agent appeared in those countries—entrepreneurs. Innovation policy in those countries was primarily dedicated to fostering and promoting entrepreneurs offering possibilities for doing the same jobs as those in companies in Western countries. New firms were founded as manufacturing workbenches for the old jobs, benefiting from providing outsourcing activities to Western companies. New ventures in the regions in Eastern Europe and Asia have thus led to the well-known erosion of previously existing sunrise industries and sectors in the West. Many of these start-ups founded in the recent past are now multinational companies, having totally shaped and changed their places and regions into hot-spots and megacities.[1]

At the same time, sunrise sectors and regions in Western countries have loosened their competitive advantages within a few years; the skill-biased technological change

---

[1] Haier (founded in 1984 as a joint venture with Liebherr, a German hidden champion) and Lenovo (founded in 1984 by young Chinese researchers) are prominent examples.

has entered a new stage, a stage in which entrepreneurs have begun to discover new opportunities for creating new jobs and tasks for new ideas, products, and services. These entrepreneurs devote their effort and time not primarily to do the old jobs for existing solutions and in a better way, but to create new jobs for new challenges and new desires. These entrepreneurs have again changed and shaped regions and places.

Entrepreneurship thus plays an important and necessary role in mediating places. As the "single most important player in a modern economy" (Lazear, 2002, p. 1), they are the engine of economic growth (Audretsch et al., 2006, p. 3). They are the answer to the question of who determines which consumer needs have to be fulfilled, in which ways and, in particular, where. They set themselves in places that they think are the best in which to create new ventures, or they create places, leading other market participants to follow them. Entrepreneurship transforms regions into places.

Transforming Regions to Places

It has long been observed that certain places become the locus of creative, inventive activity when individuals are in close contact, and exchange and share ideas, knowledge, and resources in order to create economic and social welfare. Much economic research has thus focused on providing answers to the question of why certain places prosper and achieve a higher standard of living compared to others. Krugman (1991) observed that rather than converging as predicted by neoclassical economics, national economies were becoming more divergent over time. Since then, economic research has shifted the lens towards geography as a platform for organizing economic activities, away from the national or country perspective (Audretsch, 2015; Audretsch & Lehmann, 2016b). Glasear and Gottlieb (2009, p. 984), point out that instead of macroeconomics, urban economics now tries to find answers in order to understand why there are such great differences in gross domestic product (GDP), manufacturing, productivity, creativity, and living standards across space within countries. Several objectives for investigation have been defined and suggested for capturing the disaggregated levels of space within countries: regions, metropolitan areas, regional clusters, cities, or at least municipal districts. What makes these concepts investigation objectives is the underlying concept of measuring the boundaries. In the same way that a national borderline separates two countries, measures are used to separate one geographical location or area from another, and just as the boundaries of organizations are hard to define and measure, so too are geographic areas. Regions often encompass several clusters, metropolitan areas, and cities, and inequality within regions often exceeds inequality across countries. Clusters are sometimes widespread, swapping over from region to others. While the conceptual frameworks of clusters, regions, or cities stem from the recent past, the conceptual framework of places dates at least back to von Thünen (1783–1850), a Prussian geographer, social reformer, and agronomist. Von Thünen termed the expression *Standortpolitik*, which means "management of places." The framework of places, as defined by Audretsch (2015, pp. 9–10), is on the one hand vague and undefined, and just considers a particular geographical area, a town, a city, a region, a state or even a country. But this vague and undefined concept, analogous to the concept of an organization and its boundaries, makes it a flexible and elastic object of investigation as defined by the interested party. A place is thus a location of specific interest, encompassing all relevant dimensions which confirm the boundary of this specific location for a specific interest. Or, as Florida and Mellander (2015, p. 43), point out, a place is characterized by at least three dimensions: what's there, who's there, and what's going on.

Places thus differ from regions and other geographical units in these aspects, which may culminate in at least one point: The concept of places, in the historical roots of *Standortpolitik*, indicates an active reference. The active reference, like the one of a policymaker, defines a place as a geographical sphere of influence. For policymakers in the European Union, the *Standort*, or place, is the sphere of influence—the member countries. From the viewpoint of a national government, it is the country, and from that of a single decision-maker it is the place of her or his interest. A place thus differs from concepts of geographical or climate boundaries, such as regions, and from economic areas, such as clusters, or social and political areas, such as countries, states, cities, or metropolitan areas. Finally, a place is a more dynamic and less static concept.

Because entrepreneurs are active agents, searching for opportunities, places are considered as dynamic. A region without entrepreneurship is not a place. Entrepreneurship transforms regions to places of interest, because of either their abundance or their scarcity.

This leads two to aspects discussed in the next sections of this chapter—the importance of places as the most relevant aspects of investigation and, as Krugman (1991) points out, revisions of the neoclassical theory are needed to better predict why places differ across countries more than countries differ from each other. The next section introduces the knowledge spillover theory of entrepreneurship as a refinement of the existing neoclassical theory, followed by a framework for the strategic management of places.

The Knowledge Spillover Theory of Entrepreneurship

Defining the Knowledge Spillover Theory of Entrepreneurship[2]

Like any theory of entrepreneurship, the knowledge spillover theory of entrepreneurship explains why some people take action, while others opt for inaction, when an entrepreneurial opportunity presents itself. The theory is based on the proposition that entrepreneurial behavior is a response to profitable or utility enhancing opportunities from knowledge spillovers. The reason people start entrepreneurial firms is because they have access to knowledge spillovers. In particular, the potential for taking advantage of a knowledge spillover creates the entrepreneurial opportunity, which then drives knowledge spillover entrepreneurship. Thus, theory focuses on entrepreneurial behavior within the context of knowledge spillovers, and by doing so, links traditional entrepreneurship theory to the theory and literature on knowledge spillovers (see Ghio, Guerini, Lehmann, & Rossi-Lamastra, 2015).

The traditional theoretical approach that has become well established throughout the scholarly literature on entrepreneurship has been focused on the role of opportunities, both recognizing or creating opportunities, as well as acting upon or exploiting those opportunities. (See Arenius & De Clercq, 2005; Arentz, Sautet, & Storr, 2012; Braunerhjelm, 2008; Buenstorf, 2007); Casson, 2005; Casson & Wadeson, 2007a, 2007b; Gaglio & Katz, 2001; McMullen, Plummer, & Acs, 2007; Robson, Akuetteh, Westhead,

---

[2] This chapter follows and is an updated version of "The Knowledge Spillover Theory of Entrepreneurship" (Acs, Audretsch, & Lehmann, 2013).

& Wright, 2012; Shane, 2003; Ucbasaran, Westhead, & Wright, 2008). As Sarasvathy, Dew, Velamuri, and Venkataraman (2003, p. 142) point out, "An entrepreneurial opportunity consists of a set of ideas, beliefs and actions that enable the creation of future goods and services in the absence of current markets for them." They decompose entrepreneurial opportunities into three types—opportunity recognition, opportunity discovery, and opportunity creation. According to Krueger (2003, p. 105), "The heart of entrepreneurship is an orientation toward seeing opportunities," which frames the research questions: What is the nature of entrepreneurial thinking and what cognitive phenomena are associated with seeing and acting on opportunities?

Thus, the traditional theories of entrepreneurship consider the context external to the individual as given or constant and then focus instead on the cognitive decision made by the individual in deciding whether or not to enter into, or remain in, entrepreneurship. By contrast, the knowledge spillover theory of entrepreneurship has an alternative starting point. Rather than focusing on the heterogeneity of individuals, the starting point is instead the heterogeneity of contexts with which individuals find themselves. The salient characteristic of the context involves the creation of new knowledge and ideas. As Arrow (1962) emphasized, decisions involving economic knowledge have three characteristics that distinguish them from decisions with normal economic goods (see Audretsch & Lehmann, 2017). The first is the high degree of uncertainty. As Alvarez, Barney, and Young (2010) argue, neither the outcomes nor any of the associated likelihood of distributions can be associated with decisions involving uncertainty. While decision-making under risky conditions has known outcomes, which are likely to occur with known probabilities, the outcomes based on knowledge involve inherent uncertainty where there are no certain outcomes. The second condition distinguishing the uncertainty inherent in knowledge from risky decision-making involving information is the asymmetric nature of knowledge and ideas. The valuation of any uncertain idea or knowledge will vary across individuals due to moral differences between those individuals. The third condition is that the cost of transacting those differences leading to heterogeneous valuations in knowledge and ideas is nontrivial.

Taken together, these three conditions contribute to disparities in the valuation of new ideas across individuals in general, and in particular, within decision-making hierarchies. Such disparities in the value of a new idea create commensurate disparities about whether to act upon such an idea, that is, to develop that idea and commercialize it in the form of an innovative activity. The asymmetries in knowledge across individuals also create asymmetries in opportunities across individuals. In the case where an individual places a higher valuation on a new idea, as opposed to a decision-making hierarchy within an incumbent firm or organization, this individual is confronted by an entrepreneurial opportunity because they perceive an opportunity while the incumbent organization does not. The entrepreneurial opportunity is derived from the creation of knowledge that has not been fully appropriated within the incumbent organization from which that knowledge originated. Thus, what distinguishes this theory from other theories of entrepreneurship is that the source of the entrepreneurial opportunity involves knowledge spillovers.

Examples of knowledge spillover entrepreneurship are illustrated by companies like Microsoft, Google, Amazon, and Facebook. The knowledge spillover theory of entrepreneurship explains the entrepreneurial act—why certain people become entrepreneurs while others abstain from entrepreneurship—as a response to knowledge spillovers, and these spillovers are geographically bounded.

The Emergence of the Knowledge Spillover Theory of Entrepreneurship

Although several theoretical streams and thoughts from a variety of disciplines in the social sciences shape the theory, its primary roots can be traced back to early thoughts on how to create value and wealth, and how to distribute it within society. Long before Adam Smith, philosophers, policymakers, and practitioners were concerned about seeking answers to these questions and to the present day the body of knowledge is continuing to expand. The KSTE is perhaps the most recent theoretical structure in providing answers to the aforementioned questions. The answer, according to KSTE, is the individual entrepreneurs.

One of the earliest concepts explaining economic growth dates back to the 16th century with the expansion and growth of trade companies—mercantilism, named later after the Latin noun *mercator* and the French adverb *mercantile*. The 16th century was characterized by absolutistic policy regimes such as those found in France, England, Spain, and Portugal, their expansions across the New World, and the growth of trade companies. Economic value was generated by export activities under a strong protection (subsidies, monetary policy, and import restrictions) of the absolutistic monarchies. Economic value was thus distributed among the actors—the monarchy and the trade companies. Regarding the societal and political environment, mercantilism could be treated as an efficient way to produce wealth and distribute said wealth among members of a society. Changes in the technological and political environment increased the costs of governmental protectionism and increased the advantages of division of labor and specialization, leading to a complete rethinking and reformulating of economic strategy.

In the middle of the 20th century, economists began to formulate models directed towards explaining economic growth and distribution. Growth and wealth in a society could be simply expressed by something such as gross domestic production, and the main questions were concerned with how to increase GDP and which factors were the most relevant. Harrod (1939) and Domar (1946) showed that GDP growth depends primarily on the stock of capital, the investment made, and the savings ratio. Economic growth thus increases, ceteris paribus, with the investments made, and investments strongly increase with the saving rate. However, production growth and income are also shaped by the costs of production, the amount of capital needed to produce a single unit of GDP. Accordingly, wealth is generated by the production of goods and therefore by the actors who make the investments and hence the people who save money (instead of consuming) and thus are rewarded by interest rates. Regarding the industrial landscape at this time—large firms producing mainly standardized products in tailored-style mass production (automobile, steel, railways, weapons, food, energy)—the main drivers of GDP on the supply side were investments in plants and transportation, and the only scarcity was access to financial resources and therefore the money saved and spent on banks or equity invested in the stock market. Observed variations on the demand side, a decrease in consumption, should be removed by the forces of the free market (which is the neoclassical point of view) or policy inventions (Keynesianism). The production process from inputs to outputs was approximately best described by production functions, based on capital and labor as the main inputs, and only varying in the elasticity in the final production function (Cobb–Douglas type). Economic wealth was distributed in society by the interest rates (compensation for not consuming and thus saving money) and the wage for providing labor force.

After World War II, new inventions led to product differentiation, new products and production processes. The input factors began to vary from standardized inputs like unskilled to skilled labor workforce, different types of services, and other inputs. Product differentiation, endogenously driven by investments not only in plants or transportation but also in new production processes and products and exogenously driven by inventions, like the first computer, led to a rethinking of the existing models explaining growth and the production process. One of the first scholars taking this development into account was Robert Solow, reformulating the existing model of growth by explicitly implementing technological progress. In steady-state equilibrium, investments in capital equal its depreciation rate (or growth of population). Additional growth rates could only be achieved through technological progress. Solow himself provided empirical evidence for his revised growth model by testing a revised version of the Cobb–Douglas production function. Considerable research was subsequently published based on Solow's theoretical article, linking physical capital and (unskilled) labor to growth rates (see Nelson, 1981).

However, knowledge is not only exogenously given but also the result of investments in education and R&D (Mansfield, John, Anthony, Edmond et al., 1977; Mansfield, John, Anthony, Samuel, & George, 1977). Knowledge spills over, like a reinforcing process, and thus is attributed to the unexpected residual in explaining growth rates increases over time. In addition, the political landscape evolved, leading to openness between countries with increases in trade and foreign investments. The Solow model, based on exogenously given technology within a closed economy and mass production, leaves a great amount of variation of growth rates unexplained and leads to the question of where these unexplained growth rates come from, if not falling from heaven.

This was the starting point for economists like Romer (1986, 1990), Lucas (1988), Aghion and Howitt (1992), among others. Romer effectively remodeled the industrial sector from how it had been formulated by Solow, by explicitly including the research and development sector, the role of patents and trademarks, the sector for intermediate inputs, and the consumer sector, thus using endogenous technology as the main driver of economic performance. Thus, technological change became the central factor in explaining economic growth, and the rate of per capita GDP growth equals the rate of technological change on the steady-state growth path: "And the efficiency of technology and knowledge production is enhanced by the—historically developed—stock of scientific-technology knowledge" (Acs, Audretsch, Braunerhjelm, & Carlsson, 2009, p. 16). Fundamental to the Romer model are the assumptions that, first, all knowledge is economic knowledge and, second, that knowledge spills over. Arrow (1962) emphasized knowledge as being inherently different from traditional factors of production, resulting in a gap between new knowledge and what he termed "economic knowledge." While new knowledge leads to opportunities that can be exploited commercially, economic knowledge holds commercial opportunities. Economically useful scientific-technological knowledge consists of non-rival, partially excludable elements of knowledge such as codified knowledge published in books, papers, or patent documentations, and rival, excludable knowledge. The latter contains elements of tacit knowledge of individuals, like experience, insights, and individual learning. Knowledge spillovers are the result of intertemporal spillovers, which yield the endogenous growth. In other words, investment in R&D in the present period automatically generates returns in future periods.

Endogenous growth theory stimulated the emergence of fruitful promising new fields in academia, not only in economics and management but also in geography, sociology, and finance. In particular, endogenous growth theory refocuses the light away from capital and labor as the main drivers of wealth and growth toward technology, education, and various forms of financial resources, social developments, and different forms of public policy. Stimulating growth could thus not only be done in a Keynesian way but also by fostering firm R&D, education policy or by increasing the market forces to stimulate agents to invest in knowledge and technology. The introduction of knowledge into macroeconomic growth models leads to the formulation of a knowledge production function (KPF). As before, physical capital and labor were econometrically linked to growth, but now in a revised form by considering knowledge and knowledge spillovers. One of the most prevalent models found in the literature of technological change is the Griliches (1979) model of the KPF. Firms exist exogenously and engage in the pursuit of new economic knowledge as an input into the process of generating innovative activity and thus economic growth. The most decisive input into the KPF is new economic knowledge. Subsequent to Griliches' article, a plethora of studies empirically tested the KPF. Though the economic concept of innovative activity does not automatically lend itself to exact measurements (Griliches, 1990), a number of measurements are developed such as patent inventions, new product introductions, market growth of new products, growth in productivity, or export performance of new products as proxies for innovative output. The ensuing literature that empirically tested the KPF model generated a series of econometrically robust results substantiating Griliches' view. Several refinements were subsequently made. Jaffe (1989), extending the findings from Mansfield, John, Anthony, Edmond et al. (1977) and Mansfield, John, Anthony, Samuel et al. (1977) considered that R&D spillovers constitute unambiguous positive externalities. Cohen and Levinthal (1990) introduced the capacity to adapt new knowledge and ideas in other firms and to absorb external knowledge. This key insight implied that by investing in R&D, firms could develop the absorptive capacity to appropriate at least some of the returns accruing to investments in new technology made external to the firm.[3]

While considerable empirical evidence supports the KPF model, linking knowledge inputs to innovative output, this relationship apparently becomes stronger as the unit of observation becomes increasingly aggregated, particularly at the country level of analysis (Acs & Audretsch, 1990; Audretsch, 1995, Acs et al., 2016a, 2016b). This raises several questions, in particular, whether knowledge is only firm specific, automatically spills over, or is only embedded in large and established firms (incumbents), and why the relationship between knowledge inputs and innovative outputs in empirical studies is strongest on the country level. Providing answers to these questions are in the core of the knowledge spillover theory.

Knowledge Spillover Theory and Places

Globalization combined with skill-biased technological change, in particular the information and communication technology breakthroughs, have rendered obsolete the

---

[3] Worthwhile to notice recent research results from Harvard Center for International development (CID) on knowledge diffusion, both across countries and within countries and industries (Neffke & Henning, 2013; Neffke, Henning, & Boschma, 2011; Neffke, Otto, & Weyh, 2016).

comparative advantage in low technology and even traditional moderate-technology industries. This revolution has also brought developments that were largely unanticipated, like the evolvement of economic geography and the organizational context of the sources of knowledge production and absorption. The fact that countries differ considerably according to the economic growth of their regions is a well-known phenomenon. Differences in climate, natural resources, and culture, among other reasons have played a major role in explaining different levels of growth and path dependencies. The question regarding external sources of knowledge spillovers turned academic attention to one of the largest inventions of mankind—the university. Since their first appearance in the 13th century, universities have played a crucial role in developing regions by the spillovers of the knowledge produced within their boundaries (Lehmann, 2015). Thus, place and geographic proximity have (re)emerged as important spatial units of economic activity. While knowledge generated and produced within large and incumbent firms was a focal point of analysis, that knowledge generated by large incumbent firms may spill over to other firms (Mansfield, John, Anthony, Edmond et al., 1977; Mansfield, John, Anthony, Samuel et al., 1977, for the chemical industry), the role of universities and research industries as sources of knowledge was rather neglected. With the observation that some regions, in particular Silicon Valley in the United States, as well as Route 128, and places such as San Antonio, Raleigh, and Durham among others, are not only the center of commercial innovation showing above average growth rates, but they are also located around research intensive and prestigious universities. Due to this phenomenon, new streams of literature began analyzing the geographic proximity to universities and the role of knowledge spillovers. Jaffe (1986, p. 957) states that it is "certainly plausible that the pool of talented graduates, the ideas generated by faculty, and the high quality libraries and other facilities of research universities facilitate the process of commercial innovation in their neighborhood." For example, as Carlsson and Fridh (2002) find, only half of the invention disclosures in US universities result in patent applications, from which only about half result in actual patents. Only one third of these patents are licensed, and only 10–20% of licenses yield a significant income. Thus, Braunerhjelm et al. (2010, p. 107) state, "only 1% or 2% of inventions are successful in reaching the market." However, we ask, what about the other 98% of uncommercialized ideas? Only about 25% of the inventions resulted in patents as codified knowledge—the overwhelming amount rests in tacit knowledge. The higher the level of R&D activities, the more knowledge is produced, the greater the level of absorptive capacity as well as the pool of tacit knowledge which remains unexplored and could potentially be exploited and transformed into economic knowledge. The ability to transform knowledge into economic knowledge involves not only a set of skills and insights, but also local proximity to the source of the knowledge. The matching mechanism between inventors and economic agents who commercialize the inventions works best when both parties have access to R&D and entrepreneurial skills (Michelacci, 2003).

As one of the first who systematically and empirically analyzed this phenomenon, Jaffe (1986) finds compelling evidence to support the theory of geographic proximity and knowledge spillovers of universities (Acs, Audretsch, & Feldman, 1994; Audretsch & Feldman, 1996; Audretsch & Lehmann, 2005a, 2005b; Audretsch & Stephan 1996, 1999). The underlying trigger or the mechanism between geographical proximity and knowledge spillovers is tacit knowledge. While codified knowledge as patents, academic articles, and books among others, could easily be transmitted over long distances at quite low cost, tacit knowledge is bound to the individual as the source of knowledge (Kogut & Zander, 1992). The transport mechanism, according to Jaffe (1986, p. 957), is informal conversation and thus geographic proximity to the spillover source may be not only helpful but also even necessary in capturing the spillover benefits. University research as a source of spillovers has been measured in various studies by quantity and quality. Quantity is often measured by the amount of money spent on R&D, the number of articles published in scientific and academic journals, the number of employees engaged in research, or the number of patents (Hall, Link, & Scott, 2003; Henderson, Jaffe, & Trajtenberg, 1998; McWilliams & Siegel 2000; Varga 2000), while quality effects are expressed by the number of citations of patents and articles, the specific human capital of researchers, or the position in national and international research rankings. While earlier research was more concerned about quantity effects, more recent work highlights the importance of quality and the nature of spillovers, and differentiates between the social sciences and the natural sciences, between tacit and codified knowledge (Audretsch, Lehmann, & Warning, 2004, 2005) and the mobility of human capital (Neffke, Henning, & Boschma, 2011; Neffke, Otto, & Weyh, 2016).

The emergence of innovative clusters around universities and the explosion of new firms within these clusters questioned the dominant role of large and established firms as the main and sole source of knowledge and innovation (see Audretsch, Lehmann, & Menter, 2016). Most of the budget spent in R&D was invested to increase production efficiency via investments in automatization and therefore the replacement of human labor by machines, logistics, and firm infrastructure. The amount of capital spent in R&D today leads to an increase in profits tomorrow and thus economic growth. These intertime knowledge spillovers are captured in the Solow model, where large-scale firms have been observed as the backbone of industry, welfare and growth, and mass-production, which serves as the primary guarantee for employment (see Chandler, 1977).

Academic researchers increasingly criticize this perspective, instead arguing that innovation output is linked to firm size, and they promote compelling evidence for the importance of small and medium sized firms within the innovation process (Acs & Audretsch 1988, 1990; Audretsch, 1995). This also leads to a renaissance of Schumpeter's work on the role played by entrepreneurial firms in society. Instead of living in a neoclassical world without entrepreneurial firms in the steady-state equilibrium, entrepreneurial firms are not real and existing; they also play an increasing role expressed by employment rates, growth rates, and innovation (Audretsch, 1995). Entrepreneurial activity has long been observed to vary not only across industries but also across geographic space (Audretsch & Fritsch, 2002; Reynolds, Storey, & Westhead, 1994).

This moves the interest of research toward the relationship between knowledge spillovers from scientific institutes and entrepreneurial activities. Audretsch and Stephan (1996, 1999) use joint articles written together by scientists working in the industry and university context. They show that the spillover of knowledge to a new start-up firm facilitates the appropriation of knowledge for the individual scientist but not necessarily for the organization that was the originator of that new knowledge. Linking universities and start-ups in the biotech sector, Zucker, Darby, and Armstrong (1998) find evidence suggesting that it is not spillovers per se but rather the intellectual capital of prominent scientists that plays a major role in shaping both location and timing of the new firm entry into the market. Shane (2001a, 2001b) finds compelling evidence that universities create technological spillovers that are exploited by new firms. Audretsch et al.

(2004, 2005) show that the kind of knowledge matters for entrepreneurial activities. They differentiate between knowledge in the natural science and in the social science and show that geographic proximity plays a greater role in accessing and absorbing university spillovers when knowledge is tacit.

Although the relationship between research output on the one hand and entrepreneurial activities on the other could be confirmed empirically, the empirical link is strongest the less aggregated the unit of observations becomes, which is why we observe the strongest relationship in studies characterized with individual cases. This creates an interesting dilemma since the production of knowledge as measured by patents, patent inventions, or academic and scientific research articles has increased drastically since the 1990s (see Kortum & Lerner, 1997, p. 1).[4] Thus, a large part of the new ideas and inventions are not turned into knowledge that necessarily constitutes a commercial opportunity. As suggested by Arrow (1962), not all of the knowledge produced is economically useful. Since the production of knowledge is far from being costless, the production of knowledge that could not be converted into economic knowledge is a sunk-cost of capital and other resources. Bahar, Hausman, and Hidalgo (2014) point out that knowledge decays strongly with distance. They show that the probability that a product is added to a country's export basket is, on average, 65% larger if a neighboring country is a successful exporter of that same product and that a growth of exports in a country is 1.5% higher per annum if it has a neighbor with comparative advantage in these products. This may lead to competitive disadvantages, particularly for the new emerging countries like China, Russia, and India.

Therefore, the question arises about which factors prevent or constrain spillovers that limit the efficient conversion of new knowledge into economic knowledge. The answer to this is provided by the concept of the knowledge filter leading to the knowledge spillover theory of entrepreneurship.

The Knowledge Filter and the Strategic Management of Place

In their early framework, Acs et al. (2004) develop the concept of a knowledge filter. They conceptualized the combination of factors that function as barriers limiting the total conversion of innovative knowledge into economic knowledge to be utilized in the market via new products, processes, and organizations. They argue that the knowledge filter "must be penetrated for knowledge to be appropriated, packaged, modified, and enhanced for it to ultimately contribute to economic growth" (Acs & Plummer, 2005, p. 442). Those willing and able to penetrate the filter, in order to enable and absorb knowledge spillovers, are either incumbent firms or new ventures. While incumbent firms are endowed with the capacity to recognize, evaluate, and absorb knowledge from external resources, they also account for about 25%–50% of the patents produced that are not used in an economic sense. This sheds some light on the importance of new ventures as a means to penetrate the knowledge filter. The initial contribution of Acs et al. (2004) influenced several studies testing the importance of new ventures

---

[4] A large part of this observed patent inflation among universities and research laboratories is driven by changes in incentive structures by universities and inventors. The Bayle–Dhole Act in the US and the Employment Invention Act 2002 in Germany increased the incentives for the organization to increase the number of patent applications and patent licensing (Hülsbeck, Lehmann, & Starnecker, 2013).

and entrepreneurship in penetrating the knowledge filter (Acs & Plummer, 2005; Mueller, 2006). They all confirm that the stock of knowledge is mainly transformed to economic knowledge by new ventures. It is the entrepreneur who acts as the opportunity seeker because the arbitrage of knowledge resources is a particular specialty of alert and motivated entrepreneurs (Foss, 2016; Kirzner, 1979, 1997).

These agents actively penetrate the knowledge filter, incurring the costs of doing so with the expectation that they will reap the returns. New ideas and knowledge are characterized by uncertainty, and the inertia inherent in decision-making under uncertainty within incumbent organizations reflects the knowledge filter (Acs et al., 2004; Audretsch et al., 2006).

Holding the individual attributes constant, as well as varying the knowledge context, gives rise to the KSTE. However, the consideration of entrepreneurship as an endogenous response to the incomplete commercialization of new knowledge resulting in entrepreneurial activity provides the missing link in recently developed economic growth models. By serving as a conduit of knowledge spillovers, entrepreneurship serves as an important source of economic growth that otherwise will remain missing (Audretsch, 1995). Therefore, entrepreneurship is the mechanism by which society more fully appropriates its investments into the development of new knowledge, such as research and education. The knowledge spillover theory of entrepreneurship posits one source of entrepreneurial opportunities: new knowledge and ideas (Acs & Armington, 2004, 2006; Acs et al., 2004; Audretsch & Keilbach, 2004, 2007; Audretsch et al., 2006). As shown in the previous sections, ideas and knowledge created within one organizational context such as an incumbent firm or university (see Bonaccorsi, Colombo, Guerrini, & Rossi-Lamastra, 2013), but left uncommercialized as a result of the uncertainty inherent in knowledge, serve as a source of knowledge generating entrepreneurial opportunity (Audretsch & Keilbach, 2007).

Three core conjectures derive from the KSTE. First, the knowledge hypothesis states that, "ceteris paribus, entrepreneurial activity will tend to be greater in [spatial] contexts where investments in new knowledge are relatively high, since the new firm will be started from knowledge that has spilled over from the source producing that new knowledge" (Audretsch et al., 2006, p. 44). Second, the commercialization efficiency hypothesis predicts the "the more efficiently incumbents exploit knowledge flows, the smaller the effect of new knowledge on entrepreneurship" (Acs et al., 2009, p. 17). Finally, since acquiring knowledge requires spatial proximity, the localization hypothesis predicts that "knowledge spillover entrepreneurship will tend to be spatially located within close geographic proximity to the source of knowledge actually producing that knowledge" (Audretsch et al., 2006, p. 29).

While the commercialization efficiency hypothesis has yet to be tested directly, the evidence that does exist is inconclusive. Even if commercialization efficiency can be properly measured and analyzed, the focus on such efficiency as a constraint on the entrepreneurial opportunities available for *discovery* causes the KSTE to overlook and obscure the factors that reduce an entrepreneur's incentive to *exploit* the opportunity she does discover.

First, building on a regional knowledge production framework, Plummer and Acs (2012) start from the premise that within a region all the knowledge created by private industry and universities (as well as other public entities such as federal labs) is subject to potential discovery by alert entrepreneurs. Second, whether an opportunity is exploited depends on the degree of competition for opportunity in the region.

Integrating this second premise into the KSTE involves nothing more than expanding Jane Jacobs' view of "localized competition" already naturally embedded into the KSTE (Audretsch, 2015; Audretsch, Hülsbeck, & Lehmann, 2012; Audretsch & Keilbach, 2004; Audretsch et al. 2006).

To extend and generalize the KSTE, Plummer and Acs (2012) start by establishing the KPF by which new knowledge is created in a region. The most common conceptual framework for analyzing the geographic spillover of new knowledge is a regional KPF whereby the knowledge output in a given region is the product of the research and development performed by private industry and the research performed by universities given local economic conditions (Jaffe, 1986, 1989). A key premise of the knowledge production framework is that university research creates both new ideas for industry research to adopt and develop and supplies industry R&D labs with key human capital in the form of scientific and technical expertise (Feldman, 1999). Thus, both the prevailing theory and empirical evidence suggest that local university research and industry research spatially interact in a way that boosts the knowledge output of the region (Acs & Varga, 2005; Anselin, Varga, & Acs, 1997; Klarl, 2013). Moreover, a key assumption of the knowledge production framework is that knowledge spillovers are more prevalent in regions with greater knowledge investments (Audretsch & Feldman, 1996).

Plummer and Acs (2012) extend the theory by positing that, given broad institutional constraints, knowledge-driven entrepreneurship reflects the attempt by individual entrepreneurs to profit by exploiting new knowledge produced in the region conditional on the intensity of the local competition for opportunity. The knowledge-based opportunities available for entrepreneurial exploitation are the product of both industry research and university research given local economic conditions. Consistent with established theory, an individual chooses to become an entrepreneur and start a new venture when the expected profit of the opportunity exceeds the sum costs of needed resources and the anticipated wage earned by working for an incumbent enterprise.

In this theory, local competition for opportunity is related to the number of agents pursuing the same opportunity as the entrepreneur. If other potential agents move to exploit the same opportunity, such competition would reduce the entrepreneur's entrepreneurial profit to the point at which she no longer has an incentive to act (Fiet, 2002). Moreover, as Casson (2005) points out, the concurrent discovery of the opportunity by other agents has no bearing on the focal entrepreneur's recognition of the opportunity; instead, it is the concurrent exploitation of the opportunity by other agents that reduces the incentive for the focal entrepreneur to act. Indeed, the focal entrepreneur becomes aware of the competition for opportunity only when she seeks to exploit the opportunity and finds it difficult to obtain the necessary resources at a favorable price (Casson, 2005). This point may seem trivial, but this logic suggests that the "agents" that reduce the incentive for the focal entrepreneur to act are not other *individual* entrepreneurs who have merely discovered the same opportunity, but rather the *organizations* that have marshaled the resources needed to exploit the opportunity. Therefore, this suggests that the competition for opportunity represents the number of existing firms in a place.

If localized competition for knowledge threatens an incumbent's viability and thus drives it to be more innovative, then such localized competition must also be a major influence on entrepreneurs' decisions to exploit opportunities manifest in new knowledge. Given this, the effect localized competition has on regional entrepreneurial activity is twofold. First, as Feldman and Audretsch (1999) find in their analysis, greater localized competition will put pressure on incumbents to be more innovative, which in turn will tend to expand the pool of opportunities for entrepreneurs to discover. Second, because localized competition by definition means the ruthless adoption and imitation of a firm's innovations by other neighboring firms, it also follows that greater localized competition will tend to reduce the likelihood that knowledge-based opportunities will be exploited by entrepreneurs. As discussed, the reason is that localized competition makes it less likely that, in the entrepreneur's judgment, the rewards for pursuing the given opportunity will outweigh the costs of doing so (Casson, 2005). Thus, in sum, it follows that localized competition will accelerate the rate of innovation in the region, which in turn begets more entrepreneurial activity; however, it also follows that with greater localized competition less new knowledge is commercialized by new ventures.

Extant versions of the KSTE contend that the creation of new knowledge will result in entrepreneurial activity conditional on how efficiently incumbent firms exploit or commercialize new knowledge (Acs et al., 2009). Plummer and Acs' findings are broadly consistent with Jacobs' (1969) concept of localized competition. First, using simultaneous equations they find that greater localized competition leads to more knowledge and to higher rates of knowledge-driven entrepreneurship. Second, they find that the positive relationship between new knowledge and high-tech firm birth rates is negatively moderated by greater localized competition. This evidence supports the premise that localized competition has a twofold effect on knowledge-driven entrepreneurship by increasing the pool of opportunities for entrepreneurs for discovery, but also reducing the share of these opportunities exploited by entrepreneurs.

Moreover, the finding concerning the effect of population density fits the conjecture central to agglomeration theory that dense concentrations of firms, households, and people blunts the forces of competition that would otherwise erode a firm's competitive advantage and performance (see McCann & Folta, 2008). In particular, the effect of density operates by reversing the effect localized competition has on negatively moderating the relationship between new knowledge and high-tech firm births. Density neither has a direct effect on entrepreneurial activity nor moderates the respective relationships between localized competition, new knowledge, and the rate of high-tech firm births. This suggests that regions with prodigious capacities for new knowledge creation and a large number of incumbent firms tightly packed in a relatively small geographic area are particularly conducive to knowledge spillover entrepreneurship because the negative effects of localized competition cannot take hold. More to the point, this finding buttresses the view that localized competition is an important driver of knowledge spillover entrepreneurship.

Absorptive Capacity of Place

Qian and Acs (2013) extend the KSTE by introducing absorptive capacity. First, the term "entrepreneurial absorptive capacity" is introduced, based on which an absorptive capacity theory of knowledge spillover entrepreneurship is developed. Second, deviating from exogenously assumed knowledge, the new model posits that new knowledge is endogenously created. Reflecting this assumption in the theory, the KPF is integrated into the knowledge spillover theory of entrepreneurship. These efforts enable a better understanding of the relationships between knowledge, new knowledge, and entrepreneurship, thus further unveiling the mechanism of knowledge spillover entrepreneurship.

The focus is then shifted to advancing the KSTE. The absorptive capacity theory of knowledge spillover entrepreneurship argues that, the level of knowledge spillover entrepreneurship depends not only on the speed of knowledge creation, or on the level of new knowledge, but also on entrepreneurial absorptive capacity. Entrepreneurial absorptive capacity is defined as "the ability of an entrepreneur to understand new knowledge, recognize its value, and subsequently commercialize it by creating a firm."

Entrepreneurial absorptive capacity varies among people who are potential entrepreneurs. It basically has two dimensions. On the one hand, it involves *scientific knowledge* the individual should have in order to understand what a new invention really is and, further, to recognize its market value. On the other hand, it relies on *market or business knowledge* with which the individual can successfully create and further operate a new firm. Both types of knowledge are indispensable for knowledge spillover entrepreneurship. In the typical case of the knowledge spillover theory of entrepreneurship, as discussed by Acs et al. (2009) and Audretsch (1995), the inventor who develops a new technology already has the scientific knowledge, and thus her/his success in commercializing the new technology to a great extent depends on the market knowledge she/he bears to start up and operate a business (Audretsch, Lehmann, & Plummer, 2009).

Introducing entrepreneurial absorptive capacity makes two major contributions to the KSTE. First, it connects new knowledge and the entrepreneurial action of starting a new firm. The act of entrepreneurship involves not only where the opportunity is but also the process of discovering and exploiting the opportunity. The theory, while clarifying new knowledge as one source of entrepreneurial opportunities, has not well explained whether entrepreneurs can discover and exploit entrepreneurial opportunities. The single conduit of knowledge spillover suggested by the theory is the previously discussed inventors' career choice model. In this case, entrepreneurial discovery is less important since the inventor simply needs to estimate the potential market value of the invention and does not need to learn what the invention exactly is (because she/he already knows). The inventors' career choice model may suggest whether to exploit a new invention, but sheds little light on whether the inventor is capable of doing it. Entrepreneurial absorptive capacity addresses such capability especially in terms of market knowledge to undertake entrepreneurial discovery and exploitation.

Second, noninventors' entrepreneurial actions to appropriate the market value of new knowledge developed in large firms and universities can be integrated into the knowledge spillover theory of entrepreneurship through entrepreneurial absorptive capacity. With strong absorptive capacity, an entrepreneur will have sufficient scientific and market knowledge to understand a new invention developed by others, recognize its market value, and apply it at the commercial end by creating a new firm (Lehmann & Schwerdtfeger, 2016). For noninventor entrepreneurs who are generally businessmen and already have certain market knowledge and resources, scientific knowledge must be obtained at the start so as to perceive an entrepreneurial opportunity embedded in a new invention. Entrepreneurial absorptive capacity is important for both inventors' and noninventors' entrepreneurial activity. In the former case, the inventors' capacity to commercialize new knowledge (i.e., market knowledge) is the more necessary condition. In the latter case, by contrast, what is more desired is the entrepreneurs' capacity to identify and understand new knowledge (i.e., scientific knowledge).

The second effort to extend the KSTE by Qian and Acs (2013) is consistent with Agarwal, Audretsch, and Sarkar (2007), to endogenize the knowledge production process, which contributes to a better clarification of the mechanism by which knowledge influences entrepreneurship. In this specific context, endogenizing knowledge production is also desired because knowledge is closely associated with entrepreneurial absorptive capacity that has been introduced. To do that, the KPF developed by Romer (1990) is adopted, but is simplified as a human capital model:

$$d(A) = f(H)$$

where new knowledge is simply a function of human capital. There are two reasons why this simplification works. First, human capital refers to knowledge and skills embodied in people, thus capturing not only the knowledge stock but also R&D workers, both of which are input factors in Romer's KPF. Second, even for Romer's KPF, new knowledge is ultimately reliant on human capital, since the knowledge stock is the inter-temporal accumulation of new knowledge.

Qian and Acs (2013) identify two conduits through which human capital or knowledge embodied in people influences entrepreneurship. The first one is via the creation of new knowledge that contains entrepreneurial opportunities, and the second one is via the building of entrepreneurial absorptive capacity, which allows the entrepreneur to successfully commercialize new knowledge by starting a new firm. This dual-conduit mechanism can better explain the role of knowledge in entrepreneurial activity, or in other words, provide better insights on knowledge-based entrepreneurship than can the knowledge spillover theory of entrepreneurship.

Emergence of a Strategic Management Approach of Place[5]

The knowledge spillover theory of entrepreneurship integrates the context in which decision-making is undertaken in order to explain how value and wealth are generated in societies and how they should be distributed across the society. The theory contributes to the existing body of knowledge by explaining how and why knowledge spills over, and in what manner entrepreneurship acts as the mechanism by which knowledge is transformed into economic knowledge within a strategic framework. Technological change and progress have been considered drivers of economic growth since the first industrial revolution and are still in the emerging countries. The most influential factors in the last few decades can be characterized by a shift in the costs and benefits of the contextual factors, which have led to innovations and new venture creation far beyond exogenous factors (Lehmann & Menter, 2015). Not only innovations, but new ventures and entrepreneurial firms also often fall like manna from heaven. However, the place where they drop down from heaven is not necessarily exogenously given.

Thus, what is still missing is a framework for how to create and manage places in a strategic sense. Having a coherent and well-formulated strategy is fundamental to generating a strong performance for a place. Places in the past had not developed the discipline and practice of systematically and explicitly articulating their strategy—the physical capital

---

[5] This section follows the second chapter in Audretsch, 2015.

strategy—because, since there was only one strategy available, there was no point in analyzing and reflecting on it; to do so would be squandering precious time and resources.

However, as it became increasingly clear that the strategy was failing, the intellectual void that existed presented a challenge to those mandated with ensuring a strong economic performance for their place. Where could policymakers and place-advocates look for guidance and for a framework to help structure a strategy designed to improve their place? Where could city and regional leadership find insights as to why some cities and regions prosper while others stagnate or deteriorate? Typically, policymakers responded to the failure of their existing strategy with a stunned immobility, reminiscent of a deer staring into headlights.

In fact, there were many contributions from a broad spectrum of scholarly fields and academic disciplines that filled the ensuing intellectual void, suggesting new approaches and strategies to deliver a strong economic performance. City and regional economic performance is not a new topic. In particular, the field of urban economics has many studies focusing on why some places do better and others struggle. As Glaeser and Gottlieb (2009, p. 985) point out, "Just as macroeconomics explores both differences in growth rates and differences in GDP levels across countries, urban economists wonder why some cities are rich, some cities are growing, and others are doing neither."

Contributions did not just come from urban economics. Understanding the problem and proposed strategies originated from sociology, innovation, and technological change, labor economics, entrepreneurship, growth economics, sociology, psychology, regional studies, economic geography, and management—to name a few. In addition, economic development professionals, ranging from experts on cities, states, and national-based agencies, to nonprofit organizations, foundations, and consulting firms have all contributed their thoughts and wisdom (Audretsch et al., 2016).

Out of all this research, thought, and practical experience is a diverse set of insights, which taken together, provide the basis for identifying and articulating the underlying forces shaping and influencing the performance of a place, along with what a place in turn can do to influence those underlying forces. This framework, based on the insights offered by scholarly research and insights from practitioners is depicted in Figure 16.1 and provides the basis for the strategic management of places. It is organized into four main elements: the three elements of (1) factors of production, (2) spatial and organizational dimension, and (3) the human dimension inform the fourth element, public policy.

Factors of production and resources. This first element expands on the set of factors influencing the performance of a place. This includes not just the traditional factors of natural resources, as well as physical capital and infrastructure, but also human capital, skilled labor, creative workers, finance, and knowledge capital (Lehmann, Seitz, & Wirsching, 2017). Just as the resource-based view of the firm has become a cornerstone for the field of strategic management of organizations, the role of resources and factors also plays a central role for the strategic management of a place. The role of sources of knowledge, such as universities and their commercialization activities embodied in science parks, incubators, and offices of technology transfer, are included as factors enhancing the knowledge capabilities of a place. The main point is that having a strong endowment of productive factors, including both the traditional ones such as natural resources, physical capital and infrastructure, and the less traditional ones, such as universities, creative and high human capital workers, research institutes, and venture capital institutions, will contribute positively to the economic performance of a place.

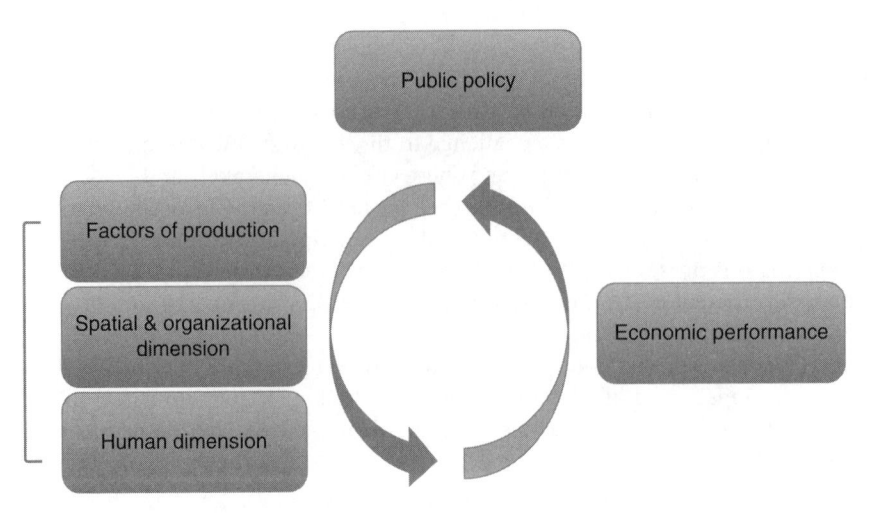

Figure 16.1 Framework for the strategic management of places. *Source:* Audretsch, 2015, p.24.

Spatial and organizational dimension. This second element explains why even having an abundance of key resources and factors at a place may not be enough to generate a strong economic performance. Rather, what is done with those resources and, in particular, how they are organized and structured into coherent and fluid meaningful economic units within a specific spatial dimension makes a difference between places. It is the configuration—the structure and organization of those factors—that influences the performance of places. Organizational and structural dimensions, such as the degree of specialization, the extent of diversification, monopolization, and decentralization all seem to influence a place's economic performance. Certainly the strategy that has readily captured the attention of the policymaking community focuses on clusters and their positive impact on economic performance. Although headlines are grabbed by Silicon Valley in California and Research Triangle Park in North Carolina, such spatial clusters exist in many places. They also involve less well-known but no less impressive technology clusters, such as life sciences in Madison, Wisconsin, or software engineering in Austin, Texas. Outside the United States there are software engineering clusters in Ottawa, Canada, and Bangalore, India; information technology is in Stockholm; and biotechnology in Cambridge, UK, and Jena, Germany. A very different but important dimension of the structure of assets and resources at a place involves whether they are organized in large, mature firms or in entrepreneurial start-ups and small business. The extent to which the organization of economic activity is characterized by entrepreneurship also influences the economic performance of that place. Entrepreneurship, in the form of a new-firm start-up, is considered to have a positive impact on city economic growth by serving as a conduit for the spillover of knowledge from an organization—whether a firm or university—where that knowledge is created, to a new firm, where that knowledge is commercialized. Examples of such knowledge-spillover entrepreneurship include Google, which was founded from knowledge created at Stanford University. Similarly, Intel is an example of knowledge spillover entrepreneurship, as it was founded from knowledge created in Fairchild. A European example is SAP Software and Solutions, which was founded from knowledge created at IBM. In each of these cases the founder(s) left an established organization where they obtained the crucial knowledge and ideas, and then started a new firm where those ideas were commercialized first. These entrepreneurial firms, in many cases, drove economic growth. Many of these ideas were ignored and thrown away in the organization where they originated. It took an entrepreneurial act to get these ideas out into society and, in the process, generate innovations and growth.

Human dimension. The focus on resources and factors, as well as how they are deployed and structured by differently structured organizations overlooks a key element that is the focus of the third element – the human dimension, or the fact that people and individuals make a key difference in how well a place performs. In particular, the literature developed in sociology has identified an important role for individuals who engage in social networks. Places where people like to engage with others, in a plethora of venues, are considered to possess a high degree of social capital (Audretsch & Keilbach, 2007). Similarly, just as leadership has been identified as providing a crucial contribution to the strategic management of organizations, it is also important for the strategic management of places. Thus, while factors refer to the extent that productive inputs exist in a region, and structure refers to their organization and configuration within the region, this strand of literature identifies that certain processes involving the main economic actors and institutions are needed for harnessing the potential performance from the first two sources. For example, inspired leadership plus the existence of vital, dynamic, networks and linkages both contribute to the economic performance of a place.

These three underlying elements—factors and resources, spatial and organizational structure, and the human dimension—provide the cornerstones highlighting the varied underlying forces shaping the performance of a place. However, while it is one thing to identify the cornerstones shaping the economic performance of a place, it is a very different thing to advocate policy intervention and institutional change in order to change or influence those underlying forces in such a way as to improve or enhance economic performance. In fact, as it became clear that relying on physical capital was no longer working, experimentation with a myriad of policy approaches and attempts blossomed, resulting in a broad range of results and outcomes. This helps us explicitly identify the role of policy in formulating and implementing the strategic management of places. In particular, the focus is on what places can and should do to positively influence their economic performance.

Conclusions

How places have strived to attain a strong economic performance has changed dramatically within a generation. The tried and true formula from the post-World War II era of attracting and retaining physical capital—plants and factories—was rendered ineffective by globalization. This simple, singular mantra of local economic development was replaced, at first, by shock; it no longer worked. As time has passed, however, it has gradually and painstakingly given way to a mandate for the strategic management of individual places.

As US President Henry S. Truman observed, when signing the Employment Act of 1946, which mandated a nationally coherent and cohesive strategy to be formulated and implemented, "The Employment Act of 1946 is not the end of the road, but rather the beginning. It is a commitment by the Government to the people—a commitment to take any and all of the measures necessary for a healthy economy, one that provides opportunities for those able, willing, and seeking to work. We shall all try to honor that commitment." What neither Truman nor the Congressional leadership anticipated is that the relevant locus for developing and implementing this strategy may be more important at the local than at the federal level.

The pragmatism of policymakers, in combination with academics from varied scholarly fields and disciplines, has made considerable progress in filling in this void, resulting in what has emerged as the mandate for the strategic management of places. This strategy revolves around a framework consisting of four main pillars—resources and factors, spatial organization and structure, the human dimension, and public policy.

References

Acs, Z. J., & Armington, C. (2004). Employment growth and entrepreneurial activities in cities. *Regional Studies, 38*, 911–927.

Acs, Z. J., & Armington, C. (2006). *Entrepreneurship, geography, and American economic growth*. New York, NY: Cambridge University Press.

Acs, Z. J., & Audretsch, D. B. (1988). Innovation in large and small firms: An empirical analysis. *The American Economic Review, 78*(4), 678–690.

Acs, Z. J., & Audretsch, D. B. (1990). Innovation and Small Firms, MIT Press.

Acs, Z. J., Audretsch, D. B., Braunerhjelm, P., & Carlsson, B. (2004). *The missing link: The knowledge filter and endogenous growth* (Discussion paper). Center for Business and Policy Studies, Stockholm, Sweden.

Acs, Z. J., Audretsch, D. B., Braunerhjelm, P., & Carlsson B. (2009). The knowledge spillover theory of entrepreneurship. *Small Business Economics, 32*(1), 15-30.

Acs, Z. J., Audretsch, D. B., Braunerhjelm, P., & Carlsson, B. (2012). Growth and entrepreneurship. *Small Business Economics, 39*(2), 213–245.

Acs, Z. J, Audretsch, D. B., & Feldman, M. (1994). R&D spillovers and recipient firm size. *Review of Economics and Statistics, 76*, 336–340.

Acs, Z. J., Audretsch, D. B., & Lehmann, E. E. (2013), The knowledge spillover theory of entrepreneurship. *Small Business Economics, 41*(4), 757–774.

Acs, Z. J., Audretsch, D. B., Lehmann, E. E., & Licht, G. (2016a). National systems of entrepreneurship. *Small Business Economics, 46*(4), 527–535.

Acs, Z. J., Audretsch, D. B., Lehmann, E. E., & Licht, G. (2016b), National systems of innovation. *Journal of Technology Transfer*. doi:10.1007/s10961-016-9481-8

Acs, Z. J., & Plummer, L. (2005). Penetrating the "knowledge filter" in regional economies. *The Annals of Regional Science, 39*(3), 439–456.

Acs, Z. J., & Varga, A. (2005). Entrepreneurship, agglomeration and technological change. *Small Business Economics, 24*(3), 323–334.

Agarwal, R., Audretsch, D. B., & Sarkar. M. B. (2007). The process of creative construction: Knowledge spillovers, entrepreneurship and economic growth. *Strategic Entrepreneurship Journal, 1*, 263–286.

Aghion, P., & Howitt, P. (1992). A model of growth and creative destruction. *Econometrica, 60*, 323–351.

Alvarez, S., Barney, J., & Young, S. (2010). Debates in entrepreneurship: Opportunity formation and implications for the field of entrepreneurship. In Z. J. Acs & D. B. Audretsch (Eds.), *Handbook of entrepreneurship* (pp. 23–46). New York, NY: Springer.

Anselin, L., Varga, A., Acs, Z. J. (1997). Local geographic spillovers between university research and high technology innovations. *Journal of Urban Economics, 42*(3), 422–448.

Arenius, P., & De Clercq, D. (2005). A network-based approach on opportunity recognition. *Small Business Economics, 24,* 249–265.

Arentz, J., Sautet, F., & Storr, V. (2012). Prior-knowledge and opportunity identification. *Small Business Economics, 41,* 461–478.

Arrow, K. (1962). Economic Welfare and the allocation of resources for invention. In R. R. Nelson (Ed.), *The rate and direction of inventive activity* (pp. 609–626). Princeton, NJ: Princeton University Press.

Audretsch, D. (1995). *Innovation and industry evolution*, Cambridge, MA: MIT Press.

Audretsch, D. B. (2015). *Everything in its place. Entrepreneurship and the strategic management of cities, regions, and states.* New York, NY: Oxford University Press.

Audretsch, D. B., & Feldman, M. (1996). R&D spillovers and the geography of innovation and production. *American Economic Review, 86,* 630–640.

Audretsch, D. B., & Fritsch, M. (2002). Growth regimes over time and space. *Regional Studies, 36,* 113–124.

Audretsch, D. B., Hülsbeck, M., & Lehmann, E. E. (2012). Regional competitiveness, university spillovers, and entrepreneurial activity. *Small Business Economics, 39*(3), 587–601.

Audretsch, D. B., & Keilbach, M. (2004). Entrepreneurship capital and economic performance. *Regional Studies, 38*(8), 949–959.

Audretsch, D. B., & Keilbach, M. (2007). The theory of knowledge spillover entrepreneurship. *Journal of Management Studies, 44,* 1242–1254.

Audretsch, D. B., Keilbach, M., & Lehmann, E. E. (2006). Entrepreneurship and economic growth. Oxford, England: Oxford University Press.

Audretsch, D. B., & Lehmann, E. E. (2005a). Does the knowledge spillover theory of entrepreneurship hold for regions? *Research Policy, 34,* 1191–1202.

Audretsch, D. B., & Lehmann, E. E. (2005b). Mansfield's missing link: The impact of knowledge spillovers on firm growth. *Journal of Technology Transfer, 30* (1/2), 207–210.

Audretsch, D. B., & Lehmann, E. E. (2016a). *The seven secrets of Germany. Economic resilience in an area of global turbulence.* New York, NY: Oxford University Press.

Audretsch, D. B., & Lehmann, E. E. (2016b). Industrial policy in Italy and Germany: Yet another look. *Journal of Industrial and Business Economics.* doi: 10.1007/s40812-016-0046-5

Audretsch, D. B., & Lehmann, E. E. (Eds.). (2017). *The Routledge companion to the makers of modern entrepreneurship.* Oxford, England: Taylor & Francis.

Audretsch, D. B., Lehmann, E. E., & Menter, M. (2016). Public cluster policy and new venture creation. *Journal of Industrial and Business Economics.* doi: 10.1007/s40812-016-0050-9

Audretsch, D. B., Lehmann, E. E., & L. A. Plummer (2009). Agency and governance in strategic entrepreneurship. *Entrepreneurship Theory and Practice, 33*(1), 149–166.

Audretsch, D. B., Lehmann, E. E., & Warning, S. (2005). University spillovers and new firm location. *Research Policy, 34*(7), 1113–1122.

Audretsch, D. B., Lehmann, E. E., & Warning, S. (2004). University spillovers: Does the kind of science matter? *Industry and Innovation*, *11*(3), 193–205.

Audretsch, D. B., & Stephan, P. (1996). Company-scientist locational links: The case of biotechnology. *The American Economic Review*, *86*(3), 641–652.

Audretsch, D. B., & Stephan, P. (1999). How and why does knowledge spill over in biotechnology? In D. B. Audretsch & R. Thurik (Eds.), *Innovation, industry evolution, and employment* (pp. 216–229). Cambridge, England: Cambridge University Press.

Bahar, D., Hausmann, R., & Hidalgo, C. A. (2014). Neighbors and the evolution of the comparative advantage of nations: Evidence of international knowledge diffusion? *Journal of International Economics*, *92*, 111–123.

Bonaccorsi, A., Colombo, M. G., Guerrini, M., & Rossi-Lamastra, C. (2013). University specialization and new firm creation across industries. *Small Business Economics*, *41*(4), 837–863.

Braunerhjelm, P. (2008). Entrepreneurship, knowledge, and growth. *Foundations and Trends in Entrepreneurship*, *4*, 451–533.

Braunerhjelm, P., Acs, Z. J., Audretsch, D. B., & Carlsson, B. (2010). The missing link: Knowledge diffusion and entrepreneurship in endogenous growth. *Small Business Economics*, *34*(2), 105–125.

Buenstorf, G. (2007). *Opportunity spin-offs and necessity spin-offs* (Papers on Economics and Evolution, No. 0718). Evolutionary Economics Group, Max Planck Institute of Economics, Jena, Germany.

Carlsson, B., & Fridh, A.-C. (2002). Technology transfer in United States universities. *Journal of Evolutionary Economics*, *12*(1–2), 199–232.

Casson, M. (2005). The individual–opportunity nexus. *Small Business Economics*, *24*(5), 423–430.

Casson, M., & Wadeson, N. (2007a). The discovery of opportunities: Extending the economic theory of the entrepreneur. *Small Business Economics*, *28*(4), 285–300.

Casson, M., & Wadeson, N. (2007b). Entrepreneurship and macroeconomic performance. *Strategic Entrepreneurship Journal*, *1*(3–4), 239–262.

Chandler, A. (1977). *The visible hand: The managerial revolution in American business*. Cambridge, MA: Belknap Press.

Cohen, W., & Levinthal, D. (1990). Absorptive capacity: A new perspective on learning and innovation. *Administrative Science Quarterly*, *35*, 128–152.

Domar, E. (1946). Capital expansion, rate of growth, and employment. *Econometrica*, *14*(2), 137–147.

Feldman, M. P. (1999). The new economics of innovation, spillovers and agglomeration: A review of empirical studies. *Economics of Innovation and New Technology*, *8*(1): 5–25.

Feldman, M. P., & Audretsch, D. B. (1999). Innovation in cities: Science-based diversity, specialization and localized competition. *European Economic Review*, *43*, 409–429.

Fiet, J. O. (2002). *The systematic search for entrepreneurial discoveries*. Santa Barbara, CA: Greenwood Publishers.

Florida, R., & Mellander, C. (2015). Talent, cities, and competitiveness. In D. B. Audretsch, A. N. Link, & M. Lindenstein Walshok (Eds.), *The Oxford handbook of local competitiveness* (p. 34–53). New York, NY: Oxford University Press.

Foss, N. (2016). Judgement, the theory of the firm, and the economics of institutions: My contributions to the entrepreneurship field. In D. B. Audretsch & E. E. Lehmann (Eds.),

The Routledge companion to the makers of modern entrepreneurship (p. 101–111). London, England: Routledge.

Friedman, T. L. (2005). *The world is flat: A brief history of the twenty-first century.* New York, NY: Picador.

Gaglio, C., & Katz, J. (2001). The psychological basis of opportunity identification: Entrepreneurial alertness. *Small Business Economics, 16,* 95–111.

Ghio, N., Guerini, M., Lehmann, E. E., & Rossi-Lamastra C. (2015). The emergence of the knowledge spillover theory of entrepreneurship. *Small Business Economics, 44*(1), 1–18.

Glasear, E. L., & Gottlieb, J. (2009). The wealth of cities: Agglomeration economies and spatial equilibrium in the Untited States. *Journal of Economic Literature, 47*(4), 983–1028.

Griliches, Z. (1979). Issues in assessing the contribution of research and development to productivity growth. *Bell Journal of Economics, 10,* 92–116.

Griliches, Z. (1990). Patent statistics as economic indicators: A survey. *Journal of Economic Literature, 28,* 1661–1707.

Hall, B., Link, A., & Scott, J. (2003). Universities as research partners. *Review of Economics and Statistics, 85,* 485–491.

Harrod, R. (1939). An essay in dynamic theory. *The Economic Journal, 49*(193), 14–33.

Henderson, R., Jaffe, A., & Trajtenberg, M. (1998). Universities as a source of commercial technology: A detailed analysis of university patenting 1965–1988. *Review of Economics and Statistics, 65,* 119–127.

Hülsbeck, M., Lehmann, E. E., & Starnecker, A. (2013). Performance of technology transfer offices in Germany. *Journal of Technology Transfer, 38,* 199–215.

Jacobs, J. (1969). *The economy of cities.* New York, NY: Random House.

Jaffe, A. B. (1986). Technological opportunity and spillovers of R&D: Evidence from firms' patents, profits, and market value. *American Economic Review, 76*(5), 984–1001.

Jaffe, A. B. (1989). The real effects of academic research. *American Economic Review, 79,* 957–970.

Kirzner, I. M. (1979). *Perception, opportunity, and profit.* Chicago, IL: University of Chicago Press.

Kirzner, I. M. (1997). Entrepreneurial discovery and the competitive market process: An Austrian approach. *Journal of Economic Literature, 35*(1), 60–85.

Klarl, T. (2013). Comment on Acs and Varga: Entrepreneurship, agglomeration and technological change. *Small Business Economics, 41,* 215–218.

Kogut, B., & Zander, U. (1992). Knowledge of the firm, combinative capabilities, and replication of technology. *Organizational Science, 3,* 383–397.

Kortum, J., & Lerner, S. (1997). *Stronger protection or technological revolution: What is behind the recent surge in patenting?* (NBER Working Paper 6204). Cambridge, MA: National Bureau of Economic Research.

Krueger, N. (2003). The cognitive psychology of entrepreneurship. In Z. J. Acs & D. B. Audretsch (Eds.), *Handbook of entrepreneurship research* (pp. 105–140). Dordrecht, Netherlands: Kluwer.

Krugman, P. (1991). *Geography and trade.* Cambridge, MA: MIT Press.

Lazear, E. (2002). *Entrepreneurship.* (NBER Working Paper 9109). Cambridge, MA: National Bureau of Economic Research.

Lehmann, E. E. (2015). The role of universities in local and regional competitiveness. In D. B., Audretsch, A. N. Link, & M. Lindenstein Walshok (Eds.), *The Oxford handbook of local competitiveness* (pp. 211–236). New York, NY: Oxford University Press.

Lehmann, E. E., & Menter, M. (2015). University–industry collaboration and regional wealth, *Journal of Technology Transfer, 41,* 1284 doi: 10.1007/s10961-015-9445-4

Lehmann, E. E., & Schwerdtfeger, M. (2016). Evaluation of IPO-firm takeovers: An event study. *Small Business Economics, 47*(4), 921938. doi: 10.1007/s11187-016-9740-y

Lehmann, E. E., & Seitz, N. (2016). Freedom and innovation: A country and state level analysis, *Journal of Technology Transfer.* doi: 10.1007/s10961-016-9478-3

Lehmann, E. E., Seitz, N., & Wirsching, K. (2017). Smart finance for smart places to foster new venture creation, *Journal of Industrial and Business Economics, 44*(1), 51–75. doi: 10.1007/s40812-016-0052-7

Lucas, R. (1988). On the mechanics of economic development, *Journal of Monetary Economics, 22,* 3–39.

Lucas, R. (1993). Making a miracle. *Econometrica, 61,* 251–272.

Mansfield, E., John, R., Anthony, R., Edmond, V., Samuel, W., & Frank, H. (1977). *The production and application of new industrial technology.* New York, NY: Norton.

Mansfield, E., John, R., Anthony, R., Samuel, W., & George, B. (1977). Social and private rates of return from industrial innovations. *Quarterly Journal of Economics, 91*(2), 221–240.

McCann, B. T., & Folta, T. B. (2008). Location matters: Where we have been and where we might go in agglomeration research. *Journal of Management, 34,* 532–565.

McMullen, J. S., Plummer, L., & Acs, Z. (2007). What is an entrepreneurial opportunity? *Small Business Economics, 28*(4), 273–283.

McWilliams, A., & Siegel, D. (2000). Corporate social responsibility and financial performance: Correlation or misspecification? *Strategic Management Journal, 21,* 603–609.

Michelacci, C. (2003). Low returns in R&D due to the lack of entrepreneurial skills. *The Economic Journal, 113,* 207–225.

Mueller, P. (2006). Exploring the knowledge filter: How entrepreneurship and university–Industry relationships drive economic growth. *Research Policy, 35*(10), 1499–1508.

Neffke, F. M. H., & Henning, M. (2013). Skill-relatedness and firm diversification. *Strategic Management Journal, 34*(3), 297–316.

Neffke, F. M. H., Henning, M., & Boschma, R. A. (2011). How do regions diversify over time? Industry relatedness and the development of new growth paths in regions. *Economic Geography, 87*(3), 237–265.

Neffke, F., Otto, A., & Weyh, A. (2016). *Inter-industry labor flows* (CID Research Fellow and Graduate Student Working Paper No. 72), Harvard University, MA.

Nelson, R. (1981). Research on productivity growth and differences: Dead ends and new departures. *Journal of Economic Literature, 19,* 1029–1064.

Plummer, L. A., & Acs, Z. J. (2012). Localized competition in the knowledge spillover theory of entrepreneurship. *Journal of Business Venturing, 29*(1), 121–136.

Qian, H., & Acs, Z. J. (2013). An absorptive capacity of knowledge spillover entrepreneurship. *Small Business Economics, 40*(2), 185–199.

Reynolds, P. D., Storey, D. J., & Westhead, P. (1994). Cross-national comparisons of the variation in new firm formation rates. *Regional Studies, 28*(4), 443–456.

Robson, P., Akuetteh, C., Westhead, P., & Wright, M. (2012). Innovative opportunity pursuit, human capital and business ownership experience in an emerging region: Evidence from Ghana. *Small Business Economics, 39*(3), 603–625.

Romer, P. (1986). Increasing returns and long-run growth. *Journal of Political Economy, 94*(5), 1002–1037.

Romer, P. (1990). Endogenous technological change. *Journal of Political Economy, 98*, 71–102.

Rugman, A. M. (2005). *The regional multinationals*. Cambridge, England: Cambridge University Press.

Rugman, A. M., & Oh, C. H. (2008). Friedman's follies: Insights on the globalization/regionalization debate. *Business and Politics, 10*(2), 1–14.

Sarasvathy, S., Dew, N., Velamuri, R., & Venkataraman, S. (2003). Three views of entrepreneurial opportunity. In Z. J. Acs & D. B. Audretsch (Eds.), *Handbook of entrepreneurship* (pp. 141–160). Dordrecht, Netherlands: Kluwer.

Shane, S. (2001a). Technological opportunities and new firm creation. *Management Science, 47*, 205–220.

Shane, S. (2001b). Technology regimes and new firm formation. *Management Science, 47*, 1173–1190.

Shane, S. (2003). *A general theory of entrepreneurship: The individual opportunity nexus*. Northampton, MA: Elgar.

Shleifer, A. (2009). The age of Milton Friedman. *Journal of Economic Literature, 47*(19), 123–135.

Snower, D., Brown, A. J. G., & Merkl, C. (2009). Globalization and the welfare state: A review of Hans-Werner Sinn's *Can Germany be Survived*. *Journal of Economic Literature, 47*(1), 136–158.

Solow, R. (1956). A contribution to the theory of economic growth. *Quarterly Journal of Economics, 70*, 65–94.

Ucbasaran, D., Westhead, P., & Wright, M. (2008). Opportunity identification and pursuit: Does an entrepreneur's human capital matter? *Small Business Economics, 30*, 153–73.

Varga, A. (2000). Local Academic knowledge transfers and the concentration of economic activity. *Journal of Regional Science, 40*, 289–309.

Zucker, L., Darby, M., & Armstrong, J. (1998). Intellectual human capital and the birth of U.S. biotechnology enterprises. *American Economic Review, 88*, 290–306.

17

The Effect of New Business Formation on Regional Development

Michael Fritsch[a]

[a] *Friedrich Schiller University Jena, Germany*

Introduction

It is a widespread belief that new business formation is a source of economic growth. This belief has been a strong motivation for a great deal of research in entrepreneurship. It has also motivated politicians in many countries to devise strategies aimed at stimulating the formation of new firms. For a long time, however, the theoretical as well as the empirical foundations for this belief were remarkably weak. Empirical research on the issue started late and only recently have researchers begun to assess the effects of new businesses on economic development in more detail. There can hardly be any doubt that a proper understanding of the effect of new business formation on regional development may provide valuable inputs for policies aimed at stimulating growth.

This chapter gives an overview of the current state of knowledge about the effects that new businesses have on regional development. The focus is on regions for three reasons. First, geographical units of observation are much better suited to such an analysis than are industries.[1] The results may not only apply to regions in terms of sub-national geographic entities but could also hold for whole nations. Second, empirical research has shown that the level of new business formation, the type of new businesses, as well as the magnitude of the effects of new business formation on growth differ considerably across regions (and nations) pointing to the importance of geographic-specific factors (for an extensive review see Fritsch, 2013). Third, regions (and nations) are an important arena for policy.

---

[1] The reasoning behind this statement is that if industries follow a lifecycle (Klepper, 1997), then the number of entries and the start-up rate will be relatively high in the early stages of the lifecycle when the industry is growing, and comparatively low in later stages when the industry is in decline. In such a setting, the positive correlation between the start-up rate and the development of the industry in subsequent periods can hardly be regarded as evidence for a positive causal effect of entry on growth, but it may be appropriate to view entry as a symptom of industry development. Accordingly, the results of empirical analyses at the regional level can be considerably different from those found in an analysis at the industry level.

The Wiley Handbook of Entrepreneurship, First Edition.
Edited by Gorkan Ahmetoglu, Tomas Chamorro-Premuzic, Bailey Klinger, & Tessa Karcisky.
© 2017 John Wiley & Sons Ltd. Published 2017 by John Wiley & Sons Ltd.

In what follows I will first deal with the main effects that new businesses may have on the performance of the economy and then identify a number of factors that shape these effects. The chapter then summarizes the main results of research on the magnitude of direct and indirect effects of new business formation, and on differences of these effects across regions. In the following section I discuss possible reasons and implications for the pronounced persistence of regional levels of entrepreneurship that can be found in reality. This is followed by a section that draws a number of policy implications, and a further section that suggests main avenues for further research. There is then a final concluding section.

The Basic Relationships

The formation of a new business is a market entry that results in intensified competition and is, therefore, a challenge to the incumbent firms. Hence, *the basic mechanism that transforms new business formation into growth is the competition between entries and incumbent firms*. The overall effect of new business formation on development results from this competitive process. It includes not only the development of the start-ups—the *direct effect*—but also the development of the incumbent firms caused by entry of the newcomers—the *indirect effect* (Figure 17.1). These indirect effects are influenced by diverse factors that can be specific to the respective firms, markets, or regions.

One important indirect effect of new business formation is the displacement of incumbents by new competitors. Given that competition and market selection are based on survival of the fittest, firms with relatively high productivity will remain in the market, whereas those with low productivity will either have to reduce their output or exit. Since this type of market selection leads to an overall productivity increase, fewer resources are needed to produce a given amount of goods and services. Hence, if regional output remains constant, the increased productivity due to new business formation should cause a decline in employment instead of the creation of additional jobs. Thus, the effect of new business formation on the number of jobs will not necessarily be positive but could just as well be negative.

However, a well-functioning market process is not a zero-sum game in which the gains of one actor are necessarily at the expense of the other actors. There are several ways in which competition by entry of new businesses can stimulate competitiveness on the supply side of the economy. Such supply-side improvements can then attract

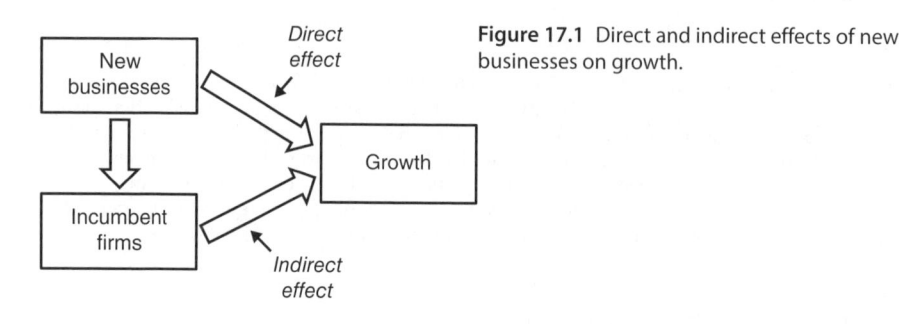

Figure 17.1 Direct and indirect effects of new businesses on growth.

additional demand that leads to growth of output and employment. Main supply-side effects of entry could include:

- *Securing efficiency and stimulating incumbent's productivity by contesting established market positions* (Aghion, 2017; Fritsch & Changoluisa, 2017). The pressure of competition is not limited to actual entry but also the very possibility of entry can force incumbents to perform more efficiently (Baumol, Panzar, & Willig, 1988).
- *Acceleration of structural change.* Frequently, structural change is accomplished by a turnover of economic units, that is, by the entry of new firms and the simultaneous exit of established incumbents. In this case, the incumbents do not make the necessary internal changes, but are substituted by newcomers. This type of process is emphasized in J. A. Schumpeter's (1911/1934, 1942) concept of creative destruction and by Alfred Marshall's (1920) analogy of a forest in which the old trees must fall to make way for new ones.
- *Amplified innovation,* particularly the creation of new markets. There are many examples of radical innovations introduced by new firms (Baumol, 2004).
- *Knowledge spillovers.* Generally, a start-up can be regarded an experiment (Kerr, Nanda, & Rhodes-Kropf, 2014). It generates knowledge about the economic viability of a certain business concept in a certain location and in a certain period of time. Such spillovers could be particularly expected if a new business introduces new products or new ways of production that can be imitated by the incumbent firms (Greenstone, Hornbeck, & Moretti, 2010).
- *Better quality and greater variety of products and problem solutions.* If the products and services of a newcomer are of higher quality than those of the incumbents, or if an entrant introduces significant process innovation, firms in downstream markets may benefit from these innovations by realizing a productivity increase. Generally, a greater variety of available goods and problem-solving methods may create new opportunities for an intensified division of labor, as well as follow-up innovation and, therefore, may stimulate economic development (Saviotti, & Pyka, 2004). Greater variety can particularly mean a diversification of the regional industry structure and the respective knowledge base that may make regions more resilient to external shocks (Boschma & Frenken, 2011).

Like the displacement effects, the supply-side effects are indirect in nature. They are not necessarily limited to the industry to which a start-up belongs, but may occur in completely different industries, such as those that use the improved supply as an input. Neither are these effects restricted to the region in which entry occurs; they can manifest in other regions, for example, regions where competitors are located. The indirect supply-side effects are the drivers of competitiveness in the respective industries and regions, which may induce employment growth and improve welfare by attracting additional demand. They are the main reason why one may expect positive employment effects of new business formation, thus turning "creative destruction" into "creative construction" (Audretsch, Keilbach, & Lehmann, 2006). Figure 17.2 gives an overview of the different effects.

It is important to note that the occurrence of supply-side effects of new business formation does not necessarily require the newcomers to be economically successful and survive. As long as entry induces improvements by incumbents, it will lead to enhanced competitiveness in the respective region or industry even if most of the new businesses

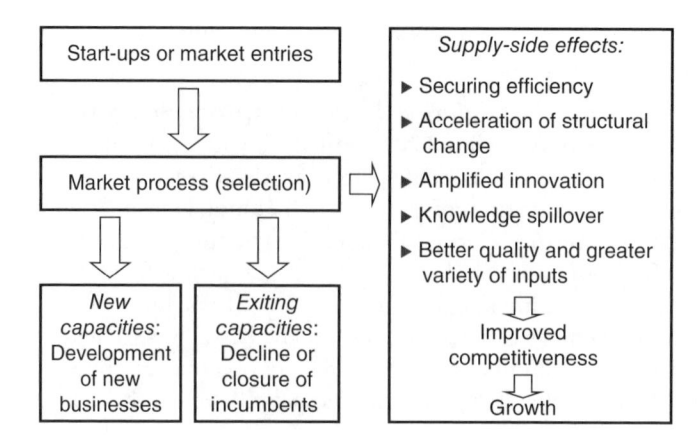

Figure 17.2 New firm formation and the market process.

```
Start-ups or market entries          Supply-side effects:
            ↓                        ▶ Securing efficiency
                                     ▶ Acceleration of structural
  Market process (selection)  ⇨        change
            ↓         ↓              ▶ Amplified innovation
                                     ▶ Knowledge spillover
     New        Exiting              ▶ Better quality and greater
  capacities:  capacities:             variety of inputs
  Development  Decline or                    ⇩
   of new     closure of              Improved
  businesses  incumbents            competitiveness
                                            ⇩
                                         Growth
```

fail and exit the market soon after entry. If new or incumbent firms fail, their knowledge is not necessarily lost; instead, it can be further diffused by the persons who were engaged in the failed firm (Hoetker & Agarwal, 2007; Stam, Audretsch, & Meijaard, 2008). Hence, even failed start-ups can make a significant contribution to growth.

The above review of the different impacts of new business formation on market processes makes very clear that the evolution of start-ups is only a portion of their total effect on development. Many important influences that start-ups have on growth and employment are of an indirect nature and occur on the supply side of the market. If market selection is indeed based on survival of the fittest, the direct employment effects, that is, the growth of new businesses, as well as the displacement of incumbents, should lead to increased productivity that actually results in a decline in employment. Hence, under a properly functioning market regime, growth from new business formation can only be expected from improvements on the supply side. If, however, the process of market selection is not working properly and allows relatively unproductive competitors to survive, the economy's competitiveness will decline and, thus, cause the supply-side effects to become negative.

The recognition that the effects of new business formation emerge from competition between newcomers and incumbent firms[2] means that the magnitude of the effects will depend on:

- **The quality of the newcomers** in terms of the competitive pressure they exert on incumbents. A strongly challenging entry such as a radical innovation introduced by a Schumpeterian entrepreneur may revolutionize the market and create a completely new industry; the effect of imitative new businesses ("ma and pa businesses") will be much smaller or even negligible.
- **The way the incumbent firms react to the challenge of new competition,** for example, by product innovation, process innovation, outsourcing to low-wage regions, and the like.

---

[2] One indication for the importance of the competition between the newcomers and incumbent firms is that the long-run effect of new business formation on the development of the incumbents as a whole is found to be significantly positive (Fritsch & Noseleit, 2013).

- **The characteristics of the competitive process,** which may be considerably dependent on factors such as the number of competitors, demand conditions, and technological developments, as well as on barriers to entry and exit. Literature on industry evolution strongly suggests that the stage of an industry in its lifecycle will play an important role here (Audretsch, 1995; Klepper, 1997). According to the lifecycle perspective, the domain of challenging entry is in the early stages of market development that are characterized by an "entrepreneurial regime" while competition by newcomers plays only a minor role in the latter stages where a "routinized regime" prevails.

A further type of indirect effect could be the influence of entrepreneurial role models on a region's "culture" of entrepreneurship (see below for a more detailed treatment of this issue). Moreover, there may be "second-round" indirect effects that result from the impetus given to regional development from new business formation, such as increasing agglomeration economies and diseconomies, growth-induced start-ups, and the like (see Greenstone, Hornbeck, & Moretti, 2010). Such second-round effects, however, are not discussed here.

The Magnitude of Direct and Indirect Effects

Research has for a long time focused on the direct effects of new businesses—the development of the newly founded firms—and has largely neglected their indirect effects, such as the displaced jobs. As a result, statements about the contribution of new business formation to growth have been in many cases restricted to the number of jobs that have been created by start-ups (direct effects) but have remained largely silent about how many jobs have been lost in incumbent firms due to the new competition.

Empirical analyses of start-up cohorts clearly show that many of the new businesses fail and have to exit the market after only a rather short period of time. As a rule of thumb, about 40–50% of start-ups exit the market within the first five years.[3] Most of the surviving new businesses stay very small, often without any employees. Some exceptional start-ups, the so-called gazelles, may show high growth. However, the possibility of high growth is not at all limited to newcomers but can also be found in incumbent firms (Henrekson & Johansson, 2010). In Germany, for example, the typical start-up cohort shows some employment increase in the first one or two years followed by continuing decline (Figure 17.3). The reason for this employment decline is that the job losses due to exits are not fully compensated by growth of surviving firms. After about eight years, employment falls below the initial level and after 20 years the overall number of employees in a cohort is slightly less than 80% of what it was in the year the new businesses were set up. After 29 years (the maximum length of the currently available time series), the overall number of employees is about 50% of the initial number of employees.

---

[3] See, for example, Horrell & Litan (2010), Schindele & Weyh (2011), Spletzer (2000), and Stangler & Kedrosky (2010) for the United States; and Bartelsman, Haltiwanger, & Scarpetta (2009) for a cross-country comparison.

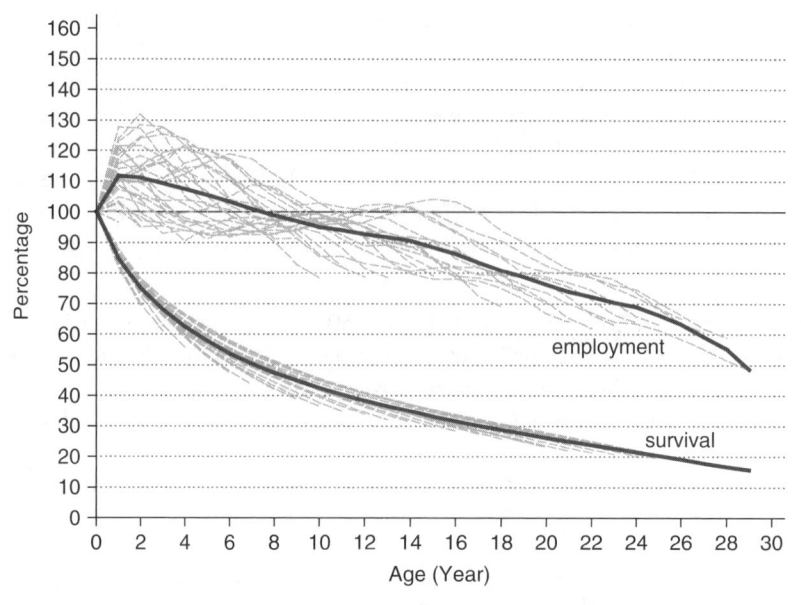

Figure 17.3 Evolution of employment and survival rates in entry cohorts in West Germany, 1976–2004. *Source:* Schindele & Weyh, 2011.

Notes: Thin dotted lines represent individual cohorts; dark thick lines represent average values over all cohorts for which information in the respective year is available.

Empirical studies for a number of countries found an S-shaped lag structure that suggests a certain sequence of the different effects of new business formation on employment (for details, see Fritsch, 2013). According to these results, the positive direct effect of new business formation prevails in the first and maybe also the second year after start-up, followed by a period where the overall effect is only weakly positive or even negative, suggesting dominance of the displacement effect. About five years after the new businesses have been set up the indirect supply-side effects—increased competitiveness of the regional suppliers resulting from competition and market selection—lead to a positive overall effect that remains statistically significant until about year 10 after entry. This pattern implies that new business formation is not a short-run solution to problems of lack of growth but rather its effects will unfold over a longer period of time.

In an analysis for West Germany, Fritsch and Noseleit (2013) quantify the magnitude of the direct and indirect effects. They find that in the year in which the start-ups enter the market, they account for an employment increase of about 1.5–1.8%. In the first year after entry, this effect is also positive but much smaller. Because the start-up cohorts tend to experience an employment decline in later years, their direct contribution to employment change becomes slightly negative. Hence, the largest direct contribution of start-ups to employment change occurs in the year they are set up. According to the analysis of Fritsch and Noseleit (2013) for West Germany, the start-ups of a certain vintage have on average led to a 3.8% increase in regional employment over a period of 11 years. About 40% of this increase is attributable to employment in new businesses;

the other 60% is due to the "first round" indirect effects described above. Hence, nearly two-thirds of the employment change generated by new business formation arises from the interaction between newcomers and incumbents in the region. The authors conclude that employment in the start-ups—the direct effect of new business formation on regional employment—is clearly the smaller part of the overall effect. Hence, disregarding indirect effects on incumbents is not a forgivable oversight, but a mistake so big that it may render the analysis meaningless.

The recognition that the effect of entry on growth is the outcome of a competitive process between newcomers and incumbents implies that the share of the direct and indirect effect in the contribution to growth depends on the relative competitive strength of both parties. If the start-ups pose only a rather weak challenge to the incumbents, then the overall effect may be quite small. High quality and competitiveness of the newcomers combined with low abilities of the incumbents to react to the competitive challenge in a productive way may lead to a pronounced direct effect, but the indirect effect is likely to be rather small. The better the incumbents are able to cope with the challenge of the new competitors, the larger will be the overall impact on growth as well as the share of the indirect effect.

Differences in the Contribution of New Business Formation to Economic Growth Across Industries and Regions

The number and the quality of entries as well as the ability of the incumbents to react productively are significantly shaped by industry-specific conditions as well as by the regional environment. For these reasons, the effect of new business formation on growth varies considerably across regions. Figure 17.4 shows a number of factors that may be responsible for such regional differences in the effect of new businesses on regional development.

An important factor that may shape the level of entry as well as its effect on growth is the *market structure and the intensity of competition*. Although economic theory is, as yet, ambiguous about the relationship between market structure and the intensity of competition, it seems reasonable to assume that easy entry and a high number of competitors lead to rather strong competition that results in relatively large effects of new business formation. To what extent certain barriers to entry, such as minimum efficient size and capital requirements, influence the effects of new business formation is a priori unclear. On the one hand, entry rates will be relatively low in industries with a high minimum efficient size (Fritsch & Falck, 2007), which should lead to lower intensity of competition and a less pronounced role of new businesses in industry development. On the other hand, a high minimum efficient size can induce larger-size entries, which will tend to have a more pronounced effect than smaller start-ups (Acs & Mueller, 2008). A large minimum efficient size may also constitute higher sunk costs of exit, which can motivate incumbents to seek a productive response to the challenge of entry instead of simply quitting the market. Hence, start-ups in the manufacturing sector, which is characterized by a relatively large minimum efficient size, are more likely to have a strong effect on growth than new businesses in small-scale industries with low barriers to entry and exit, such as many types of consumer-oriented services.

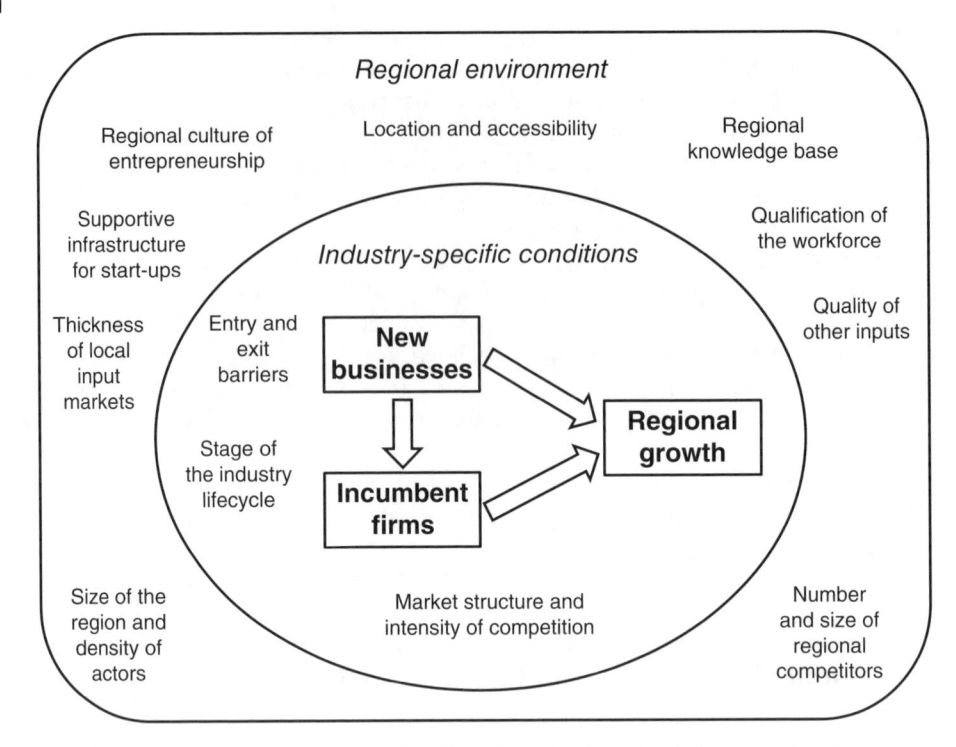

Figure 17.4 Factors that may determine the effect of new business formation on regional development.

A factor that significantly shapes the level of entry as well as the type of competition is the stage of an industry in its lifecycle (Klepper, 1997). For example, the empirical correlation between the level of new business formation and employment may be relatively pronounced in industries that are at the early stage of their industry lifecycle because these industries benefit from growing demand for their products or services. Such an early stage of industry development is characterized by relatively conducive conditions for start-ups (entrepreneurial technological regime) with small and young firms performing a considerable share of the R&D and competition being more to do with quality than price. In mature industries characterized by a routinized technological regime, the incumbents typically enjoy a strong competitive position, so an entrant's prospects for survival and growth are modest. As a consequence, the level of entry in such mature industries tends to be rather low and their effects on growth can be expected to be relatively small.

There are several reasons why factors at the national and the regional level play a pronounced role in the emergence of new businesses and their effect on economic development. Generally, entrepreneurship is a regional event (Feldman, 2001; Sternberg, 2009) in that new businesses emerge from the regional context and are shaped by regional conditions. Hence, governing formal and informal institutions, the stage of economic development, the quality of the regional workforce, the size and the characteristics of the knowledge base, the presence of supportive infrastructure for start-ups, the intensity of local competition, as well as agglomeration economies, such as availability of necessary resources, may be important influences on the number and quality of new businesses.

The *regional knowledge base*, which is partly embodied in the regional workforce as well as in regional organizations for research and education (e.g., universities), plays a significant role not only in the formation of new businesses, but also in the competitive response of incumbent firms. On the one hand, the regional knowledge base can be regarded as a main source of opportunities for innovative entrepreneurship, possibly stimulating a large number of high-quality start-ups posing a strong challenge to incumbent firms (Acs, Braunerhjelm, Audretsch, & Carlsson, 2009; Fritsch & Aamoucke, 2013). On the other hand, the regional knowledge base may also enable local incumbents to productively react to the challenges posed by new businesses. Thus, a well-developed regional knowledge base may be conducive to productive competition between newcomers and incumbent firms, leading to pronounced supply-side effects. In particular, the type of regional knowledge base can have a strong influence on the type and diversity of industry that will be founded in the region (Boschma & Frenken, 2011; Helfat & Lieberman, 2002).

Another region-specific characteristic that may be important for the effect of start-ups on development is the intensity of local competition for the goods and services supplied by the newcomers, that is, the presence of direct competitors. Spatial proximity to direct competitors constitutes localization economies and diseconomies. The number of regional competitors in the same industry or market should be one of the main factors determining the magnitude of those intraregional indirect effects of new business formation—displacement and supply side—that stem from competition on the output market. Hence, these effects are likely to be much more pronounced for entries that emerge in regional clusters, that is, in regions with many competitors supplying the same market, as compared to new businesses that have very little spatially proximate competition.

A number of studies deal specifically with the relationship between regional *clustering* and the level of new business formation. This work finds that regional clusters are formed chiefly as a result of the tendency of spin-offs from public research organizations and from private firms to locate themselves near to their parents (Boschma & Frenken, 2011; Buenstorf & Klepper, 2009; Klepper, 2010). Given the important role of entrepreneurship for the emergence of spatial clusters, it is not surprising that a number of studies find that the level of new business formation tends to be higher in such clusters than in regions where firms of the same industry are absent or relatively scarce (for an overview, see Frenken, Cefis, & Stam, 2015). The available empirical evidence provides, however, only weak support for the hypothesis that new firms set up in clusters of the same industry have higher survival rates and grow faster than new businesses outside such clusters (Frenken, Cefis & Stam, 2015; Wennberg & Lindqvist, 2010). Although spatial proximity between firms of the same industry may be conducive to the transfer of knowledge, clustered firms are not found to be generally more innovative than firms located outside of clusters (Martin & Sunley, 2003).

Relatively wide *availability of resources* in thick regional input markets in cities can have two main advantages for new businesses (Helsley & Strange, 2011). First, wide availability of inputs can lead to faster project completion that may increase the success of new ventures. Second, thick input markets may enable firms to successfully manage quite complex projects such as innovations that would be infeasible in regions with relatively thin markets. Generally, a richly diverse supply of inputs can compensate for skill deficits in that it allows entrepreneurs with a limited variety or balance of skills (Lazear, 2004, 2005) to hire local personnel with the appropriate qualifications, thereby substituting market thickness for own skill imbalance. Due to such agglomeration advantages, one may expect that larger cities have a comparatively high share of entries that pose a significant challenge to incumbent firms. However, large cities are also characterized by fairly intensive competition on input markets that—in contrast to competition on output markets—is not necessarily limited to the same industry. Since many input markets are much more local in character than output markets, the competition effects in input markets will more often occur in the same region where a new business is located as compared to the competition on output markets.

Empirical analyses have shown remarkable variation in the effect of new businesses on employment across regions. In some regions, the effect has even been found to be negative. A main finding of these analyses is that the effect of new business formation on employment tends to be much more pronounced in high-density areas as compared to rural regions (Fritsch & Schroeter, 2011). There are several factors that may be responsible for this pattern. One of these factors is that larger cities tend to have a greater knowledge base due to their sheer size, the presence of public research facilities (e.g., universities), and the relatively high share of well-educated persons in the workforce, and because of their relatively high ability to attract private and public R&D. Generally, the greater knowledge base and the higher share of creative activity found in larger cities (Bosma & Sternberg, 2014; Florida, 2004) can be a source of innovative entrepreneurship.

Another factor that might explain the stronger effects of new business formation on growth in high-density areas is that agglomerations have relatively thick input markets that provide a rich variety of complementary skills and resources, thereby enabling entrepreneurs to complete their projects more quickly and to successfully engage in more complex projects than would be feasible in smaller cities (Helsley & Strange, 2011). Moreover, knowledge exchange between actors in large cities can be more intense as a result of relatively rich opportunities for communication and large, differentiated labor markets. A higher density of actors may lead to a correspondingly high level of competition between newcomers and incumbents for inputs, which stimulates market selection. For example, intense competition for inputs could explain why survival rates of new businesses are lower in regions with high population density (Fritsch, Brixy, & Falck, 2006; Renski, 2009). As a result of the lower survival rates in agglomerations, the direct effects of entry in such regional environments may be relatively small. Competition between newcomers and incumbent firms in agglomerations may also be relatively intense on the output side, depending on the number and the quality of competitors located in the same region.

A further factor that may play a significant role in the effects of entry on growth could be the presence of a regional culture of entrepreneurship that is characterized by high levels of new business formation as well as a relatively pronounced effect of the new firms on growth. The nature and the role of such a regional culture of entrepreneurship are explained in the following section.

The Persistence of Regional Entrepreneurship

A number of recent studies have found a significant effect of historical self-employment levels on regional entrepreneurship many decades later on (Andersson & Koster, 2011; Fotopoulos, 2014; Fritsch & Wyrwich, 2014; Glaeser, Pekkala Kerr, & Kerr, 2015). This persistence of regional entrepreneurship is one type of the second-round indirect effects of new business formation mentioned earlier.

There are at least three types of reasons for persistence of the level of regional entrepreneurship. One of these explanations could be that the region's determinants of entrepreneurial activity, such as the regional knowledge stock and the availability of resources, also remain largely unchanged. Fotopoulos (2014) and Fritsch and Kublina (2016) demonstrate that such durable and spatially "sticky" regional characteristics may explain a large part of the persistence of regional new business formation activity that can be observed. A second reason may be the presence of a regional entrepreneurship culture that affects the level of new business formation. A regional entrepreneurial culture is described as a "positive collective programming of the mind" (Beugelsdijk, 2007, p. 190) or an "aggregate psychological trait" (Freytag & Thurik, 2007, p. 123) of the local population. A well-developed entrepreneurial culture may be characterized by a high level of social acceptance or legitimacy of entrepreneurship (Kibler, Kautonen, & Fink, 2014) among the population that manifests itself in the acceptance of values such as individualism, independence, and achievement (e.g., Hofstede & McCrae, 2008; McClelland, 1961). Regions with a pronounced entrepreneurial culture are likely to have a high share of persons with pronounced entrepreneurial personality traits such as extraversion, openness to experience, and conscientiousness, as well as a high ability to bear risk (Obschonka, Schmitt-Rodermund, Gosling, & Silbereisen, 2013; Rauch & Frese, 2007; Zhao & Seibert, 2006). Generally, an entrepreneurship culture can be regarded as an informal institution that comprises norms, values, and codes of conduct (Baumol, 1990; North, 1994). Historical research provides many examples for informal institutions, such as a culture changing only very slowly, much slower than the formal institutions or governance structures (e.g., North, 1994; Nunn, 2012; Williamson, 2000).

Analyzing the development of entrepreneurship in the regions of Germany from 1925 to 2005, Fritsch and Wyrwich (2014) show that a regional entrepreneurship culture can persist through even drastic changes in the socioeconomic environment, such as a devastating war or long decades of a socialist regime that undertakes severe efforts to extinguish private sector economic initiative. Hence, a regional culture of entrepreneurship may also be regarded as a spatially sticky characteristic. In contrast to the determinants of new business formation, however, a culture of entrepreneurship will particularly shape the responsiveness of a region to these determinants.

One of the transmission mechanisms of an entrepreneurial culture could be the well-documented transfer of positive entrepreneurial attitudes in the regional population across generations (Laspita, Breugst, Heblich, & Patzelt, 2012). Moreover, a large number of self-employed persons in a region may reinforce a regional culture of entrepreneurship through demonstration and peer effects. Such role models provide a nonpecuniary externality that reduces ambiguity and influences the decision to pursue an entrepreneurial career (Minniti, 2005). Furthermore, observing active entrepreneurs, especially successful ones, may increase social acceptance of entrepreneurship and self-confidence of people in regard to their ability to successfully set up their own business

(Bosma, Hessels, Schutjens, van Praag, & Verheul, 2012; Kibler, Kautonen, & Fink, 2014; Stuart & Sorenson, 2003).

A third type of explanation for the persistence of high levels of regional entrepreneurship that may contribute to the persistence of a regional entrepreneurship culture is path dependency, in the sense that current entrepreneurial activities can be regarded as a response to similar activities in a region's history (Martin & Sunley, 2006). One type of such a path dependency could be that high levels of new business formation create additional entrepreneurial opportunities that induce further start-ups. Another type of path dependency may result from the observation that most new businesses remain rather small and that small firms are a fertile seedbed for future entrepreneurs (Elfenbein, Hamilton, & Zenger, 2010; Parker, 2009).

An important result of recent research (see Fritsch & Wyrwich 2016; Glaeser, Pekkala Kerr, & Kerr, 2015) is that regions with relatively high levels of historical entrepreneurship tend to exhibit relatively high growth rates several decades later. In particular, regions with high levels of historical entrepreneurship tend to be economically more resilient in that they are better able to deal with drastic changes in economic conditions. This may be regarded as an indication that a well-developed culture of entrepreneurship in a region can have long-lasting positive effects on regional growth.

Our knowledge about the emergence of high levels of regional entrepreneurship is currently rather limited, leaving much room for speculation. In many regions, the sources of an entrepreneurship culture may be deeply rooted in economic history. Maybe the type of agriculture that prevailed in a region—for example large-scale farming with many employees versus small family-run farms—plays a role. Differences in the structure of agriculture may be based in sociopolitical reasons, but they may also have to do with the quality of the soil or with particular social practices, such as the mode of inheritance. Where, for example, it has been common practice in a region to divide the land among the beneficiaries in real terms (*Realteilung*), the resulting small lots have created an incentive to shift economic activity toward some type of craft business, maybe initially as a secondary occupation but which would later became the main source of income.[4] This type of economic shift would not have been so likely to occur, however, if land was cohesively transferred to one beneficiary only (*Anerberecht*). Such examples suggest that attempts to explain the emergence of a regional entrepreneurship culture will need to reach far back into the economic history of regions. Another example of the role of historical developments is the presence of mining and heavy industries (Chinitz, 1961; Glaeser et al., 2015; Stuetzer et al., 2016). Due to the usually large scale of the respective firms, the share of entrepreneurship and the level of entrepreneurial peer effects in such regions was relatively low so that an entrepreneurial spirit was not widespread.

The long-term persistence of regional levels of entrepreneurship and its effects raises the question, How can the emergence of such a culture be created? Generally, what can policy do in order to raise the level of new business formation in those regions that have relatively low start-up rates?

---

[4] This is an often-heard explanation for the emergence of an economic structure characterized by the relatively large number of small firms in some regions in the south of Germany.

Policy Implications

Recent empirical analyses of the effects of new businesses on economic development have made it very clear that start-ups need to be understood as an integral part of the market process. According to this view, new businesses are a challenge to incumbents and may induce improvement of overall economic performance, given that market selection is operating on a survival of the fittest basis. Although our understanding of the effects of new business formation on regional development is still incomplete, the current state of knowledge suggests a number of important implications for an entrepreneurship policy aimed at stimulating regional growth.

One of these policy implications pertains to the quality of start-ups. The research clearly suggests that it is not so much the sheer number of start-ups, but their ability to compete successfully with incumbents and to survive, that is important for their effect on regional development. Hence, to be truly effective, the policy must concern itself with the quality of the start-ups it encourages. Just increasing the overall number of start-ups may not be an appropriate strategy for stimulating growth; rather, policy should focus on improving the quality of start-ups and on increasing the number of high-quality new businesses. This implies that start-up rates or business ownership rates that include all types of businesses are of only limited relevance for assessing the level of growth-relevant entrepreneurship in a region.

Policy intended to stimulate high-quality start-ups should be firmly based on the preconditions necessary for successful entrepreneurship, such as general as well as entrepreneurship education, and provide qualified advice to potential founders. Entrepreneurship education, in particular, could be very useful in helping people make a more realistic assessment of their ability to run a business and, where necessary, convince those ill-suited to such a venture not to embark on it (von Graevenitz, Harhoff, & Weber, 2010). The empirical results particularly indicate that a highly educated regional workforce and good availability of labor are generally conducive to the employment contribution of new businesses. Moreover, policy should be especially designed to include measures aimed at the regional knowledge base, which is an important source of spatially bounded knowledge externalities that may enhance the recognition of promising entrepreneurial opportunities and the emergence of high-quality start-ups. For innovative start-ups, this includes building a high-quality university system that provides cutting-edge scientific knowledge and technology, facilitates access to higher education by talented people, and effective technology transfer. There is considerable indication that trying to increase the number of high-quality start-ups means actively creating an entrepreneurial culture (Astebro & Bazzazian, 2011).

Further, the results of recent research clearly show that region-specific factors play an important role in the development of new businesses and their contribution to employment. Growth conditions for new businesses and their impact on regional development will vary according to the regional environment, and thus different regions may have quite different types of growth regimes (Audretsch & Fritsch, 2002; Fritsch, 2004; Fritsch & Kublina, 2015). This suggests that policy measures aimed at creating an environment for successful entrepreneurship should be region-specific and take into consideration both the advantages and disadvantages of a region's economic structure.

There is considerable evidence that new business formation may produce a number of important indirect effects that have a strong impact on regional competitiveness and growth. These competitiveness-enhancing supply-side effects of new business formation are dependent on markets operating according to a survival of the fittest basis. If the market does not operate according to these principles, which when functioning properly force less productive firms to exit, entry may not stimulate growth. Therefore, a growth-oriented entrepreneurship policy needs to be accompanied by an appropriate competition policy ensuring that the market truly is determined by survival of the fittest. Such a competition policy should be particularly alert to the possibility of "unfair" attempts at entry deterrence by incumbents. In a sufficiently well-operating market, policymakers should avoid any action that will disturb market selection. Hence, direct support of new businesses by means of special subsidies that are not available to incumbents must be regarded as of questionable utility.

All these issues point to the important role of institutions in new business formation and its impact on economic development. Institutions, both formal and informal, not only shape the incentives for different types of entrepreneurship but particularly govern the interaction between newcomers and incumbent firms, which, as mentioned at the beginning of this chapter, is the main mechanism by which new business formation transforms into growth. However, our knowledge about the appropriate framework of formal institutions for productive entrepreneurship is still incomplete (Boettke & Coyne, 2009).

The pronounced persistence of the regional level of entrepreneurial activity that has been found in recent research clearly suggests that an important part of the regional conditions for entrepreneurship may have a long-lasting (second round) effect. In particular, there is compelling evidence that a regional culture of entrepreneurship may exist that stimulates not only new business formation but also the effects of these new businesses on growth and generally makes the respective region more resilient with regard to external shocks.

As far as changes in the level of regional start-up activity do occur, they emerge over a long time period, and they are in most cases rather small. This high degree of persistence suggests that there are only weak prospects for rapid change with regard to regional new business formation activity. Therefore, a policy aimed at stimulating the regional level of entrepreneurship and building up a regional entrepreneurship culture needs patience and a long-term orientation.

Avenues for Further Research

Although recent research has substantially improved our understanding of the factors that influence the effect of new business formation on economic development, there is considerable room for further investigation. In what follows, I sketch some particularly important avenues for further research in the field.

Quality of entry. Although the theoretical considerations (see earlier) clearly suggest the key importance of the quality of entry for its effect on growth, our knowledge about those characteristics of new businesses that make them particularly challenging to incumbents is somewhat incomplete. The quality of a new business may be indicated by factors such as the innovativeness of the supplied goods and services, the entrepreneur's qualifications, her or his motivations (e.g., opportunity versus necessity start-ups) and growth ambitions, the marketing strategy pursued, the amount and quality of resources mobilized for the new business, its productivity, survival over a certain period of time, and the like. Only a few studies analyze the factors that are conducive to the emergence of high-quality entry such as innovative start-ups or new businesses with high growth expectations. To derive policy recommendations for increasing the number of high-quality start-ups, much more needs to be known about the determinants of this type of entry. What circumstances are conducive for the emergence of these firms? How can the emergence of these firms be stimulated?

Indicators for growth-relevant new businesses. Nearly all currently available studies on how new business formation affects regional development are based on start-up rates for the entire regional economy or for broad economic sectors. If it is true that only a small portion of new businesses has a significant effect on regional development, then start-up rates that include all new businesses produce a too-diffuse picture and are not well suited to assessing the level of growth-relevant entrepreneurship in a region. Hence, more informative indicators for this type of entrepreneurship should be developed.

Universities and other research institutions as incubators. Although our knowledge about the characteristics of those new businesses that are of particular importance for regional growth processes is not well developed, there is good evidence that the regional knowledge base, particularly universities and other research institutions, plays an important role in this respect. Hence the role of these knowledge sources as incubators of new businesses should be further investigated (for a review of this field, see Astebro & Bazzazian, 2011). A more comprehensive understanding of the role played by these institutions could be particularly helpful in designing effective policy.

The role of noninnovative entry. Although there is strong reason to believe that innovative entry is of key importance for economic development, noninnovative new businesses may also play a role at least by providing role models of self-employment that are conducive to the emergence of new businesses and by generating peer effects (Bosma et al. 2012; Minniti & Lévesque, 2010). Hence, the effects, particularly the indirect effects of noninnovative new businesses, should be further explored.

Gazelles. Fast-growing new businesses (gazelles) are a special case of high-quality start-ups. Although these firms have attracted a fair amount of attention and research in recent years (Acs, 2011; Henrekson & Johansson, 2010), not much is known about them. This is particularly true with regard to their effect on the respective industry and region. What regional conditions are conducive to the emergence of gazelles? What impact do these fast-growing new businesses have on overall regional development? Does the emergence of gazelles lead to a particularly pronounced response by incumbents?

Effects of entry on competition in input markets and output markets. The available evidence about the competitive processes induced by newcomers is incomplete and somewhat speculative. For example, it is still a largely open question as to why we can observe such pronounced supply-side effects of new business formation in many regions when output markets are interregional or even global. Accordingly, a study by Fritsch and Changoluisa (2017) does not find the effect of output market competition between start-ups and incumbents to be limited to the region. They speculate that a regional concentration of the effects of entry may be explained by competition for local inputs such as floor space and labor. The relative importance of competition on output markets compared to input market competition remains, however, still unclear.

Characteristics of output markets. Entry conditions and the competitive process vary considerably with the characteristics of the industry, such as the stage of the industry lifecycle (Audretsch, 1995; Klepper, 1997). Such characteristics of output markets should have consequences for the performance of newcomers as well as for their effect on their competitors and on economic overall development. They may also have some influence on the quality of entry. Empirical evidence about the impact of start-ups in different industries on overall economic performance, however, is less than clear and is contradictory. And nothing is known about the influence that the intensity of competition and the importance of particular parameters in the competitive process of a particular market, such as price and quality, have on the direct and the indirect effects of entry.

Institutional environment. Generally, the role the institutional environment plays in entrepreneurship is a research "blind spot." This is particularly true for the effects of new business formation on development. Formal as well as informal institutions may be important at all stages of the entrepreneurial process and can affect the number and quality of start-ups as well as their impact on input and output markets (for a more detailed treatment of this topic, see Boettke & Coyne, 2009; Henrekson, 2007; Henrekson & Johansson, 2011).

Regional characteristics. A number of studies clearly show that regional characteristics can play a considerable role in the employment effects of new business formation. For example, population density seems to have a particularly dominant effect. These regional differences are not yet well understood and should be further investigated.

The role of the level of new business formation. Several studies show that the effect of start-ups is higher in regions with a relatively low level of new business formation and considerably less pronounced in high start-up regions (Bosma, Stam, & Schutjens, 2011; Fritsch & Schroeter, 2011; Fritsch & Noseleit, 2013). According to these studies, the marginal effect of new business formation declines with a growing number of regional start-ups, suggesting that there is an optimum level of new business formation at which the effect of start-ups on development attains a maximum. The reasons behind this phenomenon are largely unknown and should be further investigated.

The role of the economic development level. Most of the empirical research on the effect of new business formation on regional development involves the well-developed countries of Western Europe or the United States. Empirical evidence for other countries, particularly for less-developed countries, is more or less entirely based on Global Entrepreneurship Monitor data and does not include sufficiently long time lags. The available empirical evidence suggests that developing countries are indeed a special case in that high levels of entrepreneurship and new business formation are not positively linked to economic growth (Acs & Virgill, 2010; Naudé, 2011; Vivarelli, 2013). One possible explanation for the rather weak or nonexistent link between new business formation and economic growth in developing countries could be deficiencies in the institutional framework and a less than optimum level of division of labor (Sautet, 2013). More needs to be learned about such peculiarities of new business formation and its effects in developing countries.

Entry as a cause or as a symptom of growth? Research in this important field is particularly hampered by the lack of appropriate data. Time series are often too short for adequately investigating this important issue. Although the few available studies clearly indicate that start-ups can have an effect on subsequent growth that is independent from long-term development trajectories (Fritsch & Wyrwich, 2017; Glaeser, Pekkala Kerr, & Kerr, 2015), more such studies for countries of different wealth levels would be desirable. It would be particularly interesting to know whether it is possible to identify types of new businesses that are mainly induced by increasing domestic demand and have no significant effect on future development (start-ups as a symptom of growth). Accordingly, it would be desirable to know what types of new ventures are growth initiators and to what extent their emergence is a result of development processes.

Longer-run effects of new business formation on regional development. Research on regional growth regimes and regional entrepreneurship culture has produced evidence of rather long-run positive effects of new business formation for development. For example, research shows that high regional levels of new business formation and self-employment can be persistent and survive dramatic changes in the framework conditions. This evidence raises at least three questions. First, how does a regional entrepreneurship culture emerge? Second, what are the factors that make such a regional entrepreneurship culture so persistent? Third, to what extent is a regional culture of entrepreneurship conducive to coping with necessary structural change? That is, are regions with a well-developed culture of entrepreneurship more resilient than other regions? There are some indications that entrepreneurship culture does indeed have such effects (see earlier) but much more needs to be learned about this issue.

Entrepreneurship policy. Finally, all the research directions proposed above should lead to the design of an appropriate growth-oriented entrepreneurship policy. A great deal of the entrepreneurship policy currently in place in many countries and regions is motivated by stimulating regional growth. However, these policy instruments have been designed more or less ad hoc, without a sufficient understanding of the underlying processes. The effects of the current strategies should be analyzed and considerable effort should be devoted to translating research results into appropriate and effective policy strategies.

This catalog of open questions makes very clear that much more needs to be learned about how different types of new businesses impact economic development in different regional environments.

Final Remarks

The relationship between new business formation and regional development is still a largely underresearched field. This is remarkable given the importance of the issue, particularly since regional development is often the stated justification for policy measures intended to promote the emergence of new ventures. Recent research shows that new business formation can indeed benefit regional development, but it would be naïve to expect that all, or even most, of these new businesses create a substantial number of jobs. Many and probably the most important effects of new business formation on growth are indirect in nature and much depends on factors such as the quality of the start-ups and the regional environment. Our knowledge about these influences has increased considerably in recent years, but still a great deal of research is necessary before we will arrive at an appropriate understanding of the effects.

The empirical evidence clearly shows that the main effect of new business formation on economic development comes from spurring the competitive process. Much of this process's outcome in terms of the economic performance of regions, nations, or industries is indirect in nature. This implies that the strong focus often put on the performance of the newly founded firms—their direct effect—is misguided because it neglects the often more important indirect effects. The results of empirical research suggest that successful new businesses that pose a strong challenge to incumbent firms are likely to also induce strong indirect effects, but that such indirect effects can also occur even if many of the newcomers fail and exit the market after a short time.

Against the background of current theory and empirical evidence, it is obvious that highly challenging new businesses have a relatively strong stimulating effect on economic growth. They can be assumed to be much more important for economic development than, for example, purely imitative start-ups that represent routine entrepreneurship and serve only small local markets. This result has some important implications for policy as well as for empirical descriptions and analyses of new business formation. The main implication for policy intended to stimulate economic development is that such policy should particularly focus on challenging entrepreneurship, for example by trying to improve the entrepreneurial qualifications of founders and stimulating the emergence of innovative start-ups (for a discussion of possible policy measures, see Brown, Mason, & Mawson, 2014, and Stam, Hartog, van Stel, & Thurik, 2011). An important implication for the description and analysis of new business formation processes is that measures for the numbers of challenging or high-quality new businesses are needed. This is particularly relevant because the shares of highly innovative start-ups (Fritsch, 2011), of fast growing "gazelles" (Henrekson & Johansson, 2010), or of "ambitious" start-ups (Stam et al., 2011) in all new businesses tend to be small so that measures for the overall level of new business formation in a country or region may be an only vague and imprecise representation of those start-ups that have a particular impact on growth.

References

Acs, Z. J. (2011). High-impact firms: Gazelles revisited. In M. Fritsch (Ed.), *Handbook of research on entrepreneurship and regional development* (pp. 133–174). Cheltenham, England: Elgar.

Acs, Z. J., Braunerhjelm, P., Audretsch, D. B., & Carlsson, B. (2009). The knowledge spillover theory of entrepreneurship. *Small Business Economics, 32*, 15–30.

Acs, Z. J., & Mueller, P. (2008). Employment effects of business dynamics: Mice, gazelles and elephants. *Small Business Economics, 30*, 85–100.

Acs, Z. J., & Virgill, N. (2010). Entrepreneurship in developing countries. *Foundations and Trends in Entrepreneurship, 6*, 1–68.

Aghion, P. (2017). Entrepreneurship and growth: Lessons from an intellectual journey. *Small Business Economics, 49*, 9-24.

Andersson, M., & Koster, S. (2011). Sources of persistence in regional start-up rates—Evidence from Sweden. *Journal of Economic Geography, 11*, 179–201.

Astebro, T., & Bazzazian, N. (2011). Universities, entrepreneurship and local economic development. In M. Fritsch (Ed.), *Handbook of research on entrepreneurship and regional development* (pp. 252–333). Cheltenham, England: Elgar.

Audretsch, D. B. (1995). *Innovation and industry evolution*. Cambridge, MA: MIT Press.

Audretsch, D. B., & Fritsch, M. (2002). Growth regimes over time and space. *Regional Studies, 36*, 113–124.

Audretsch, D. B., Keilbach, M., & Lehmann, E. (2006). *Entrepreneurship and economic growth*. Oxford, England: Oxford University Press.

Bartelsman, E., Haltiwanger, J., & Scarpetta, S. (2009). Measuring and analyzing cross-country differences in firm dynamics. In T. Dunne, J. Bradford Jensen, & and M. J. Roberts (Eds.), *Producer dynamics—New evidence from micro data* (pp. 15–76). Chicago, IL: University of Chicago Press.

Baumol, W. J. (1990). Entrepreneurship: Productive, unproductive, and destructive. *Journal of Political Economy, 98*, 893–921.

Baumol, W. J. (2004). Entrepreneurial Enterprises, Large Established Firms and Other Components of the Free-Market Growth-Machine. *Small Business Economics, 23*, 9–21.

Baumol, W. J., Panzar, J. C., & Willig, R. D. (1988). *Contestable markets and the theory of industry structure* (rev. ed.). San Diego, CA: Harcourt Brace Jovanovich.

Beugelsdijk, S. (2007). Entrepreneurial culture, regional innovativeness and economic growth. *Journal of Evolutionary Economics, 17*, 187–210.

Boettke, P. J., & Coyne, C. J. (2009). Context matters: Institutions and entrepreneurship. *Foundations and Trends in Entrepreneurship, 5*, 135–209.

Boschma, R., & Frenken, K. (2011). The emerging empirics of evolutionary economic geography. *Journal of Economic Geography, 11*, 295–307.

Bosma, N., Stam, E., & Schutjens, V. (2011). Creative destruction and regional productivity growth: Evidence from the Dutch manufacturing and services industries. *Small Business Economics, 36*, 401–418.

Bosma, N., Hessels, J., Schutjens, V., van Praag, M., & Verheul, I. (2012). Entrepreneurship and role models. *Journal of Economic Psychology, 33*, 410–424.

Bosma, N., & Sternberg, R. (2014). Entrepreneurship as an urban event? Empirical evidence from European cities. *Regional Studies, 48*, 1016–1033.

Brown, R., Mason, C., & Mawson, S. (2014). *Increasing "The vital 6 percent": Designing effective public policy to support high growth firms* (Working Paper). London, England: Nesta.

Buenstorf, G., & Klepper, S. (2009). Heritage and agglomeration: The Akron tyre cluster revisited. *Economic Journal, 119*, 705–733.

Chinitz, B. (1961). Contrasts in agglomeration: New York and Pittsburgh (Papers and Proceedings). *American Economic Review, 51*, 279–289.

Elfenbein, D. W., Hamilton, B. H., &. Zenger, T. R. (2010). The small firm effect and the entrepreneurial spawning of scientists and engineers. *Management Science, 56*, 659–681.

Feldman, M. P. (2001). The entrepreneurial event revisited: Firm formation in a regional context. *Industrial and Corporate Change, 10*, 861–891.

Florida, R. (2004). *The rise of the creative class* (revised paperback ed.). New York, NY: Basic Books.

Fotopoulos, G. (2014). On the spatial stickiness of UK New firm formation rates. *Journal of Economic Geography, 14*, 651–679.

Frenken, K., Cefis, E., & Stam, E. (2015). Industrial dynamics and clusters: A survey. *Regional Studies, 49*, 10–27.

Freytag, A., & Thurik, R. (2007). Entrepreneurship and its determinants in a cross-country setting. *Journal of Evolutionary Economics, 17*, 117–131.

Fritsch, M. (2004). Entrepreneurship, entry and performance of new businesses compared in two growth regimes: East and West Germany. *Journal of Evolutionary Economics, 14*, 525–542.

Fritsch, M. (2011). Start-ups in innovative industries—Causes and effects. In D. B. Audretsch, O. Falck, S. Heblich, & A. Lederer (Eds.), *Handbook of innovation and entrepreneurship* (pp. 365–381). Cheltenham, England: Elgar.

Fritsch, M. (2013). New business formation and regional development: A survey and assessment of the evidence. *Foundations and Trends in Entrepreneurship, 9*, 249–364.

Fritsch, M., & Aamoucke, R. (2013). Regional public research, higher education, and innovative start-ups—an empirical investigation. *Small Business Economics, 41*, 865–885.

Fritsch, M., Brixy, U., & Falck, O. (2006). The effect of industry, region and time on new business survival—A multi-dimensional analysis. *Review of Industrial Organization, 28*, 285–306.

Fritsch, M., & Changoluisa, J. (2017). New business formation and the productivity of manufacturing incumbents: Effects and mechanisms. *Journal of Business Venturing, 32*, 237–259.

Fritsch, M., & Falck, O. (2007). New business formation by industry over space and time: A multi-dimensional analysis. *Regional Studies, 41*, 157–172.

Fritsch, M., & Kublina, S. (2015). Entrepreneurship, growth, regional growth regimes (Jena Economic Research Papers No. 2015-002), Friedrich Schiller University Jena, Germany.

Fritsch, M., & Kublina, S. (2016). Persistence and change of regional new business formation in the national league table (Jena Economic Research Papers No. 2016-001, Friedrich Schiller University Jena, Germany.

Fritsch, M., & Noseleit, F. (2013). Investigating the anatomy of the employment effects of new business formation. *Cambridge Journal of Economics, 37*, 349–377.

Fritsch, M., & Schroeter, A. (2011). Why does the effect of new business formation differ across regions? *Small Business Economics, 36*, 383–400.

Fritsch, M., & Wyrwich, M. (2014). The long persistence of regional entrepreneurship culture: Germany 1925–2005. *Regional Studies, 48*, 955–973.

Fritsch, M., & Wyrwich, M. (2016). The effect of entrepreneurship on economic development—an empirical analysis using regional entrepreneurship culture. *Journal of Economic Geography, 1* (1), 157–189. doi: 10.1093/jeg/lbv049

Fritsch, M., & Wyrwich, M. (2017). Persistence of Regional Entrepreneurship: Causes, Effects, and Directions for Future Research. *Jena Economic Research Papers*, No. 2017-003. Retrieved from https://ideas.repec.org/p/jrp/jrpwrp/2017-003.html

Glaeser, E. L., Pekkala Kerr, S., & Kerr, W. R. (2015). Entrepreneurship and urban growth: An empirical assessment with historical mines. *Review of Economics and Statistics, 97*, 498–520.

Graevenitz, G. von, Harhoff, D., & Weber, R. (2010). The effects of entrepreneurship education. *Journal of Economic Behavior & Organization, 76*, 90–112.

Greenstone, M., Hornbeck, R., & Moretti, E. (2010). Identifying agglomeration spillovers: Evidence from winners and losers of large plant openings. *Journal of Political Economy, 118*, 536–598.

Helfat, C. E., & Lieberman, M. B. (2002). The birth of capabilities: Market entry and the importance of pre-history. *Industrial and Corporate Change, 11*, 725–760.

Helsley, R. W., & Strange, W. C. (2011). Entrepreneurs and cities: Complexity, thickness and balance. *Regional Science and Urban Economics, 41*, 550–559.

Henrekson, M. (2007). Entrepreneurship and institutions. *Comparative Labor Law & Policy Journal, 28*, 717–742.

Henrekson, M., & Johansson, D. (2010). Gazelles as job creators: A survey and interpretation of the evidence. *Small Business Economics, 35*, 227–244.

Henrekson, M., & Johansson, D. (2011). Firm growth, institutions, and structural transformation. In M. Fritsch (Ed.), *Handbook of research on entrepreneurship and regional development* (pp. 175–215).Cheltenham, England: Elgar.

Hoetker, G., & Agarwal, R. (2007). Death hurts, but it isn't fatal: The postexit diffusion of knowledge created by innovative companies. *Academy of Management Journal, 50*, 446–467.

Hofstede, G., & McCrae, R. R. (2008). Personality and culture revisited, linking traits and dimensions of culture. *Cross-Cultural Research, 38*, 52–87.

Horrell, M., & Litan, R. (2010). *After inception: How enduring is job creation by startups?* Kansan City, MO: Kauffman Foundation.

Kerr, W. R., Nanda, R., & Rhodes-Kropf, M. (2014). Entrepreneurship as Experimentation. *Journal of Economic Perspectives, 28(3)*, 25–48.

Kibler, E., Kautonen, T., & Fink, M. (2014). Regional social legitimacy of entrepreneurship: Implications for entrepreneurial intention and start-up behaviour. *Regional Studies, 48*, 995–1015.

Klepper, S. (1997). Industry life cycles. *Industrial and Corporate Change, 6*, 145–181.

Klepper, S. (2010). The origin and growth of industry clusters: The making of Silicon Valley and Detroit. *Journal of Urban Economics, 67*, 15–32.

Laspita, S., Breugst, N., Heblich, S., & Patzelt, H. (2012). Intergenerational transmission of entrepreneurial intentions. *Journal of Business Venturing, 27*, 414–435.

Lazear, E. P. (2004). Balanced skills and entrepreneurship. *American Economic Review, 94*, 208–211.

Lazear, E. P. (2005). Entrepreneurship. *Journal of Labor Economics, 23*, 649–680.

Marshall, A. (1920). *Principles of economics* (8th ed.). London, England: MacMillan.

Martin, R., & Sunley, P. (2003). Deconstructing clusters: Chaotic concept or policy panacea? *Journal of Economic Geography, 3*, 5–35.

Martin, R., & Sunley, P. (2006). Path dependence and regional economic evolution. *Journal of Economic Geography, 6*, 395–437.

McClelland, D. C. (1961). *The achieving society*. Princeton, NJ: Van Nostrand Reinhold.

Minniti, M. (2005). Entrepreneurship and network externalities. *Journal of Economic Behavior and Organization, 57*, 1–27.

Minniti, M., & Lévesque. M. (2010). Entrepreneurial types and economic growth. *Journal of Business Venturing, 25*, 305–314.

Naudé, W. (Ed.). (2011). *Entrepreneurship and economic development*. Houndmills, England: Palgrave MacMillan.

North, D. C. (1994). Economic performance through time. *American Economic Review, 84*, 359–368.

Nunn, N. (2012). Culture and the historical process. *Economic History of Developing Regions, 27,* S108–S126.

Obschonka, M., Schmitt-Rodermund, E., Gosling, S. D., &. Silbereisen, R. K. (2013). The regional distribution and correlates of an entrepreneurship-prone personality profile in the United States, Germany, and the United Kingdom: A socioecological perspective. *Journal of Personality and Social Psychology, 105,* 104–122.

Parker, S. (2009). Why do small firms produce the entrepreneurs? *Journal of Socio-Economics, 38,* 484–494.

Rauch, A., & Frese, M. (2007). Let's put the person back into entrepreneurship research. *European Journal of Work and Organizational Psychology, 16,* 353–385.

Renski, H. (2009). New firm entry, survival, and growth in the United States: A comparison of urban, suburban, and rural areas. *Journal of the American Planning Association, 75,* 60–77.

Sautet, F. (2013). Local and systemic entrepreneurship: Solving the puzzle of entrepreneurship and economic development. *Entrepreneurship in Theory and Practice, 37,* 387–402.

Saviotti, P. P., & Pyka, A. (2004). Economic development, variety and employment. *Revue Économique, 55,* 1023–1049.

Schindele, Y., & Weyh, A. (2011). The direct employment effects of new businesses in Germany revisited: An empirical investigation for 1976–2004. *Small Business Economics, 36,* 353–363.

Schumpeter, J. A. (1911/1934). *Theorie der wirtschaftlichen Entwicklung,* Leipzig 1911: Duncker & Humblot; revised English edition: *The Theory of Economic Development.* Cambridge, MA: Cambridge University Press.

Schumpeter, J. A. (1942). *Capitalism, socialism and democracy.* New York, NY: Harper & Row.

Spletzer, J. R. (2000). The contribution of establishment births and deaths to employment growth. *Journal of Business and Economic Statistics, 18,* 113–126.

Stam, E., Audretsch, D. B., & Meijaard, J. (2008). Renascent entrepreneurship. *Journal of Evolutionary Economics, 18,* 493–507.

Stam, E., Hartog, C., van Stel, A., & Thurik, R. (2011). Ambitious entrepreneurship, high-growth firms and macroeconomic growth. In M. Minniti (Ed.), *The dynamics of entrepreneurship: Evidence from the Global Entrepreneurship Monitor Data* (pp. 231–249). Oxford, England: Oxford University Press.

Stangler, D., & Kedrosky, P. (2010). Neutralism and entrepreneurship: The structural dynamics of startups, young firms, and job creation. Kansas City, MO: Kauffman Foundation.

Sternberg, R. (2009). Regional dimensions of entrepreneurship. *Foundations and Trends in Entrepreneurship, 5,* 211–340.

Stuart, T. E., & Sorensen, O. (2003). The geography of opportunity: Spatial heterogeneity in founding rates and the performance of biotechnology firms. *Research Policy, 32,* 229–253.

Stuetzer, M., Obschonka, M., Audretsch, D. B., Wyrwich, M., Rentfrow, P. J., Coombes, M., ... Satchell, M. (2016). Industry structure, entrepreneurship, and culture: An empirical analysis using historical coalfields. *European Economic Review, 86,* 52–72.

Vivarelli, M. (2013). Is entrepreneurship necessarily good? Microeconomic evidence from developed and developing countries. *Industrial and Corporate Change, 22,* 1453–1495.

Wennberg, K., & Lindqvist, G. (2010). The effect of clusters on the survival and performance of new firms. *Small Business Economics, 34,* 221–241.

Williamson, O. (2000). The new institutional economics: Taking stock, looking ahead. *Journal of Economic Literature, 38,* 595–613.

Zhao, H., & Seibert, S. E. (2006). The Big-Five personality dimensions and entrepreneurial status: A meta-analytical review. *Journal of Applied Psychology, 91,* 259–271.

18

National Culture and Entrepreneurship

Gabriella Cacciotti[a] and James C. Hayton[b]

[a] *Aalto University, Finland*
[b] *Rutgers University*

Introduction

In the last decades, national culture has emerged as an important concept within the entrepreneurship literature to help explain differences in entrepreneurial outcomes at national and individual levels of analysis (Hayton & Cacciotti, 2013; Hayton, George, & Zahra, 2002). Despite the extensive research on the topic, questions remain regarding the existence of an entrepreneurial culture as well as consistent theories about how national culture influences the entrepreneurial process.

We offer this review of the current literature to shed light on the main challenges and issues associated with the research on the relationship between national culture and entrepreneurship. We note that scholars have used two different approaches to defining national culture: culture as values, and culture as norms and practices. While this theoretical pluralism may suggest researchers' enthusiasm for the topic, it also creates a challenge, as scholars try to make sense of the diverse theoretical frameworks used to explain the role of national culture in entrepreneurship. In this review, we analyze the literature that is related to each approach. We also highlight its limitations and use it as a starting point for proposing a more coherent approach to defining and measuring national culture in entrepreneurship research. We conclude the chapter by proposing fear of failure as one of the cognitive variables able to capture the mechanisms through which national culture influences entrepreneurial behavior.

Method

We took as a starting point the reviews by Hayton et al. (2002) and Hayton and Cacciotti (2013). We complemented them by conducting a systematic review of the empirical studies published between January 2013 and September 2016 (Denyer & Tranfield, 2008; Tranfield, Denyer, & Smart, 2003). To identify articles for inclusion, we traced the conceptual boundaries of the relationship between culture and entrepreneurship. We focused on national culture with no reference to a specific conceptualization. We assumed that

The Wiley Handbook of Entrepreneurship, First Edition.
Edited by Gorkan Ahmetoglu, Tomas Chamorro-Premuzic, Bailey Klinger, & Tessa Karcisky.
© 2017 John Wiley & Sons Ltd. Published 2017 by John Wiley & Sons Ltd.

national culture can influence a variety of entrepreneurial outcomes at a different level of analysis. Therefore we did not constrain our search to specific phases of the entrepreneurial process, but rather we adopted a comprehensive approach to include entrepreneurial intention and action reported at an individual or national level of analysis.

We then searched leading electronic databases relevant to this topic, such as the *Journal of Business Venturing, Entrepreneurship Theory and Practice, Entrepreneurship and Regional Development, Journal of International Business Studies, Academy of Management Journal*, and *Strategic Entrepreneurship Journal*. We used the search terms "national culture" AND "entrepreneur*." We included only single or multicountry studies that address the significance of national culture, however defined or operationalized, for entrepreneurship. Consistent with Hayton et al. (2002), and Hayton and Cacciotti (2013), we excluded articles that focused on immigrant entrepreneurship and corporate entrepreneurship. This process resulted in 10 additional studies on national culture and entrepreneurship that were not covered by the prior reviews.

Conceptualization of National Culture in Entrepreneurship Research

Our review of the relevant literature reveals two prominent conceptualizations of national culture used by entrepreneurship scholars: as values, and as norms and/or practices (e.g., Autio, Pathak, & Wennberg, 2013; Liñán & Fernandez-Serrano, 2014; Shane, 1993; Urban, 2006; Wennberg, Pathak, & Autio, 2013). A summary of each framework's dominant focus and selected studies that make use of it is given in Table 18.1.

Table 18.1 Approaches to national culture in entrepreneurship.

Definition	Measure(s)	Sample studies
National culture as values	Hofstede's model (Hofstede 1980, 2006)	Liñán & Fernandez-Serrano, 2014
		Moriano et al., 2012
	Schwartz's Value Survey (SVS) (Schwartz 1994, 2004, 2006, 2008)	Mueller & Thomas, 2000
		Nguyen et al., 2009
		Pinillos & Reyes, 2011
		Pruett et al., 2009
		Rarick & Thuang, 2015
		Shane, 1993
		Shneor et al., 2013
		Urban, 2006
National culture as norms and practices	GLOBE index (House et al., 2004)	Autio et al., 2013
	GLOBE framework (House et al. 2004)	Harms & Groen, 2016
		Rauch et al., 2013
	Gelfand et al.'s study (2011)	Wennberg et al., 2013

To facilitate a better understanding of the different conceptualizations, we discuss each in turn focusing on the core definition of national culture, the measures, the outcomes, and the limitations associated with each particular conceptualization.

National Culture as Values

Definition

The concept of national culture as values is probably the most well-known among entrepreneurship scholars. Building from Hofstede's (1980) classic study, national culture is defined as the values, beliefs, and expected behaviors that are common to a group of people living (or coming from) the same region or nation (Herbig 1994; Hofstede, 1980). Values are described as desires that direct behavior and "imbue it with meaning, defining what is good to attain and the ideal manner in which one should attain it" (Longest, Hitlin, & Vaisey, 2013, p. 1500). Therefore, individuals do not act in a social vacuum but within a given set of values and cultural standards that influence needs, motives, beliefs, cognition, and behavior (Fink, Neyer, & Kölling, 2007; Hayton et al., 2002). As such, cultural values provide a good framework for understanding how different societies deal with entrepreneurship and associated outcomes (Krueger, Liñán, & Nabi, 2013).

Measures

A long-standing tradition in entrepreneurship studies measures cultural values by the use of Hofstede's cultural dimensions (e.g., Rinne, Steel, & Fairweather, 2012; Shane, 1992; 1993; Williams & McGuire, 2010). Hofstede's model originally comprised four dimensions: power distance, individualism versus collectivism, masculinity versus femininity, and uncertainty avoidance. Power distance refers to the extent to which members of society are more or less likely to accept differences in power and wealth (Hofstede & Bond, 1988). High power distance nations include India, France, and Mexico. Low power distance nations include the United States, Australia, and Israel. Individualistic societies have loose ties among their members and place more value on personal interest than communal interest. On the contrary, collectivistic societies emphasize the importance of strong ties between group members and their communal interest. Examples of individualistic societies include United States, Canada, and Australia. Examples of collectivistic societies include Colombia, China, and Japan.

The third cultural value dimension identified by Hofstede is that of masculine versus feminine values. Masculine societies place value on performance, money, and personal ambition, whereas feminine societies are less oriented toward oneself and appreciate more helping others, the quality of life, and preservation of the environment. Examples of more masculine cultures include Italy, Mexico, and Japan. More feminine cultures include Denmark, Thailand, and the Netherlands. Finally, uncertainty avoidance refers to the extent to which societies tolerate uncertainty and security. Countries high on uncertainty avoidance include France, Belgium, and Greece. Countries low on this dimension include Singapore, the United States, and Canada. A fifth dimension was later added to Hofstede's model: long-term versus short-term orientation. A society with a long-term orientation is focused on the future and values persistence and perseverance. Conversely, a society with a short-term orientation is focused on the present and values tradition and the fulfillment of social obligations. Scores of this dimension are not available for every country.

The use of the Hofstede model varies within the entrepreneurship literature. Several entrepreneurship studies have focused on the influence of the single dimensions on entrepreneurial outcomes (e.g., Rinne et al., 2012; Shane, 1992, 1993; Wennekers, Thurik, van Stel, & Noorderhaven, 2007). Others consider culture as an umbrella construct: "Culture is a construct composed of factors that are interdependent and should be considered together" (Williams & McGuire, 2010, p. 398). As a result, cultural dimensions are sometimes aggregated into a single measure of national culture (e.g., Williams & McGuire, 2010). This operationalization of culture might be problematic because it implies substitutability of the underlying dimensions in an unknown way. Further, it does not allow for possible complementarity among different poles of each subdimension (e.g., masculinity and individualism; Hayton & Cacciotti, 2013). Nor does it allow for different cultural configurations—combinations of distinct patterns of cultural dimensions— to be considered. As a result, we suggest caution with respect to the practice of reducing cultural dimensions to a single score or index.

Another measurement tool of cultural values used in entrepreneurship research is Schwartz's Value Survey (SVS) (1994; 2004; 2006; 2008). Currently, data are available for more than 60 countries. Schwartz identified seven values that guide human behavior and that can be grouped into three bipolar dimensions: embeddedness versus autonomy, hierarchy versus egalitarianism, and mastery versus harmony. The first bipolar dimension refers to the degree of inclusiveness of a person within a community versus the degree a person see herself as an autonomous body that finds meaning in her own differences. The second bipolar dimension refers to the degree to which the unequal distribution of power, roles, and resources is seen as legitimate versus the degree to which people are considered equal human beings who cooperate for the pursuit of a common good. Finally, mastery versus harmony refers to the degree to which people search for personal gain through the exploitation and domination of nature versus individuals' search of a harmonious fit with nature.

An example of the use of the SVS within entrepreneurship literature is provided by Liñán and Fernandez-Serrano (2014). They considered data from the period 1985–2005 and calculated the average for each country in relation to the seven dimensions. The national-level scores of the seven cultural values were then grouped into the three bipolar cultural dimensions. These three variables were then used for the empirical analysis.

Outcomes

By definition, cultural values influence needs, motives, beliefs, cognition, and behavior (Fink et al., 2007). Accordingly, entrepreneurship scholars have focused on cultural variations in needs, motives and beliefs, cognition, and behaviors of entrepreneurs at the individual and national level of analysis. We thus divide studies using the Hofstede model upon the dependent variable that is supposed to be influenced by national culture.

Cultural values and the decision to start. Early studies examine the association between national culture and needs, motives, and beliefs, which, in turn, influence the decision to start a business (e.g., Aoyama, 2009; Pruett et al., 2009; Rarick & Thaung, 2015; Scheinberg & MacMillan, 1988; Shane, Kolvereid, & Westhead, 1991). Motive dispositions associated with entrepreneurship (e.g., need for achievement, risk-taking, locus of control, innovativeness) have been found to vary across countries (e.g., Garcia-Cabrera & Garcia-Soto, 2008;

Kristiansen & Indarti, 2004; Lee-Ross & Mitchell, 2007; Mueller & Thomas, 2000; Stewart, Carland, Carland, Watson, & Sweo, 2003; Thomas & Mueller, 2000). For example, Stewart et al. (2003) reported significantly higher levels of need for achievement in US entrepreneurs relative to their Russian counterparts. This is suggested to be the result of the individualistic, masculine nature of US culture as opposed to the more feminine and collectivistic culture that characterizes Russia (Hofstede, 1980). Achievement motivation theory had already discussed the dispositional nature of need for achievement and its relevance for entrepreneurship (McClelland, Atkinson, Clark, & Lowell, 1953). While Stewart et al.'s (2003) study confirms that learned dispositions can be influenced by cultural values, their findings that Russian entrepreneurs have lower levels of need for achievement somewhat undermine arguments for the universal importance of this motive for entrepreneurship (Hayton & Cacciotti, 2013).

Particular emphasis has been given to the influence of cultural dimensions on locus of control. Thomas and Mueller (2000) showed that locus of control differs systematically with cultural distance from the United States. Further studies have supported the idea that locus of control is dominant in cultures high in individualism and uncertainty avoidance (e.g., Garcia-Cabrera & Garcia-Soto, 2008; Mueller & Thomas, 2000). These findings support the argument that cultures high in individualism and uncertainty avoidance encourage entrepreneurship. However, this conclusion has to be treated with caution for two reasons. First, these studies have looked at students and have not linked locus of control to any entrepreneurial outcome. In addition, a replication study also considering students in different countries (Indonesia and Norway) has not found strong differences in locus of control among the participants (Kristiansen & Indarti, 2004). Second, high rates of entrepreneurial activity have also been found in collectivist and uncertainty avoiding cultures (e.g., Pinillos & Reyes, 2011), in direct contradiction to earlier studies, suggesting that focusing only on individualism, uncertainty avoidance, and locus of control is not enough to understand what is needed to build an entrepreneurial culture.

Drawing on the idea that there is a common entrepreneurial culture that is shared by entrepreneurs across national boundaries, many studies have compared entrepreneurs and managers in different countries (e.g., Baum et al., 1993; McGrath & MacMillan, 1992; McGrath, MacMillan, & Scheinberg, 1992). While some scholars examine whether entrepreneurs and nonentrepreneurs differ in terms of motives (e.g., Baum et al., 1993; Tan, 2002), others focus on differences in terms of Hofstede's dimensions of culture (e.g., McGrath, et al., 1992). Findings from these studies show once again that there is weak evidence for an entrepreneurial "type" across cultures. However, when McGrath et al. (1992) have compared entrepreneurs with nonentrepreneurs in 13 countries, they have found that entrepreneurs are higher in power distance, individualism, and masculinity and lower in uncertainty avoidance than nonentrepreneurs. This finding suggests the possibility of an entrepreneurial culture that differentiates entrepreneurs from the rest of the population.

Cultural values and cognition. Entrepreneurship scholars have also focused on the influence of cultural dimensions on entrepreneurs' cognition (e.g., Goktan & Gunay, 2011; Mitchell, Smith, Morse et al., 2002; Mitchell, Smith, Seawright, & Morse, 2000; Tan, 2002). For example, Mitchell et al. (2000) examined whether cognitive scripts that vary according to individualism and power distance can be associated with venture creation. They found that a script describing knowledge of appropriable ideas is negatively related with individualism and positively related with power distance. Conversely, a script describing access to resources is positively associated with individualism and negatively associated with power distance. While cognitive scripts are found to be associated with cultural variation, this study contradicts the idea that there is a single entrepreneurial culture that universally stimulates or supports the cognition hypothesized to support entrepreneurial behavior (Hayton & Cacciotti, 2013).

Interestingly, Tan (2002) has raised the question whether entrepreneurs' cognition is influenced by the national context rather than the cultural context. To address the issue, he has compared the perceptions and orientations of mainland Chinese, Chinese American, and Caucasian American entrepreneurs. Tan has found significant differences between mainland Chinese entrepreneurs and both Chinese American and Caucasian entrepreneurs. However, no significant differences have been found between the latter two groups. He suggests that differences that we tend to attribute to national culture might actually stem from differences in the national institutional environment. This conclusion emphasizes the idea that we cannot ignore the role of the institutional environment when investigating the relationship between national culture and the entrepreneurship phenomenon. This is a point to which we will return.

Cultural values and entrepreneurial behaviors. A consistent number of articles have focused on the relationship between national culture and (intended or actual) entrepreneurial behavior at an individual, regional, or national level of analysis (e.g., Iakovleva, Kolvereid, Gorgievski, & Sørhaug, 2014; Liñán & Chen, 2009; Moriano, Gorgievski, Laguna, Stephan, & Zarafshani, 2012; Mueller, Zapkau, & Schwens, 2014; Shinnar, Giacomin, & Janssen, 2012; Shneor, Camgöz, & Karapinar, 2013; Urban, 2006). At the individual level of analysis, scholars have been particularly interested in how national culture influences the intention to engage in entrepreneurship. Most of this research draws upon the *theory of planned behavior* (TPB; Ajzen, 1991), where cultural values are assumed to interact with the three motivational antecedents (personal attitudes, subjective norms, and perceived behavioral control) and determine the strength of their relationship with entrepreneurial intentions (e.g., Liñán & Chen, 2009; Shinnar et al., 2012; Shneor et al., 2013; Urban, 2006). Using this theoretical lens, Liñán and Chen (2009) have shown that cultural and social differences can influence the perceptions of those antecedents of intentional behavior. However, empirical findings within this stream of research have been inconsistent (e.g., Moriano et al., 2012; Shneor et al., 2013; Urban, 2006). For example, Urban (2006) did not find support for the positive influence of moderate individualism/collectivism, low uncertainty avoidance, high masculinity, low power distance, and high long-term orientation on entrepreneurial intention within a multicultural society such as South Africa. Similarly, Moriano et al. (2012) report that the influence of subjective norms does not vary according to levels of individualism/collectivism across multiple countries (Germany, India, Iran, Poland, Spain, and the Netherlands). They have reached the same conclusion: entrepreneurial intentions do not covary significantly with cultural dimensions.

Notwithstanding the lack of strong and clear relationship between cultural dimensions and entrepreneurial intentions (Hayton & Cacciotti, 2013), these studies emphasize two important points. First, culture cannot be considered in isolation (Busenitz, Gomez, & Spencer, 2000). Cross-national differences in entrepreneurship might be best explained by a broader set of institutions in addition to culture (e.g., Iakovleva et al., 2014; Nguyen et al., 2009; Urban, 2006). This is evident in Nguyen et al.'s (2009) study, where they considered variations in entrepreneurial intentions among Vietnam, Taiwan, and the United States. Contrary to their expectations, Vietnamese respondents scored higher on intention to create a business than those from the two other countries. Nguyen and colleagues have argued that this is the result of both institutional and cultural factors. In Vietnam, renovation policies brought institutional development that encouraged new venture formation. At the same time, these policies increase the levels of uncertainty, which are perceived as opportunities by Confucian entrepreneurs. In addition to national differences, we have to consider regulatory and institutional structures that may influence or stimulate business start-up (Iakovleva et al., 2014). Second, inconsistent findings can be attributed to the operational definition of culture through country level data collection (House, Hanges, Mansour, Dorfman, & Gupta, 2004); a problem that could be addressed by the use of direct measures of this construct (Moriano et al., 2012).

Cultural values and national rates of entrepreneurship. It is important to recognize that efforts to explain the influence of cultural dimensions on entrepreneurship go beyond the focus on individual level outcomes. Several studies have examined the relationship between culture and aggregate rates of innovation (e.g., Rinne et al., 2012; Shane 1992, 1993; Sun, 2009; Williams & McGuire, 2010) and country-level of entrepreneurial activity (e.g., Davidsson & Wiklund, 1997; Liñán & Fernandez-Serrano, 2014; Pinillos & Reyes, 2011; Wennekers et al., 2007). There is strong evidence for the association of individualism, power distance and uncertainty avoidance (both as single dimensions and aggregate construct) with national rates of innovation (e.g., Rinne et al., 2012; Shane, 1992, 1993; Williams & McGuire, 2010). However, a deeper examination reveals that the relationship is not stable over time (Shane, 1993), different sources of innovation rates have been considered (Porter & Stern, 2001), and potential confounding factors such as gross domestic product (GDP) or stage of development are often ignored (Rinne et al., 2012). This decreases the confidence in assuming that variation in rates of innovations can be explained by differences in cultural dimensions.

Within this stream of research, levels of entrepreneurial activity are operationalized as new firm formation or firm ownership rates. Individualism and uncertainty avoidance seem to be associated with variations in the regional and country-level entrepreneurial activity (e.g., Davidsson & Wiklund, 1997; Pinillos & Reyes, 2011; Wennekers et al., 2007). However, similarly to the previous stream of research, these relationships are not stable over time (Wennekers et al., 2007), and factors such as GDP and general level of economic development can increase the complexity of these relationship (from liner to curvilinear; see Wennekers et al., 2007) or even change their direction (see Pinillos & Reyes, 2011). These observations suggest that two more factors should be included in the theoretical model that relates national culture to entrepreneurship: time and stage of economic development.

Limitations. Although Hofstede's model has contributed to the acceleration of the study of the role of national culture in entrepreneurship (Hayton & Cacciotti, 2013), it has been criticized for several reasons. First, Hofstede's definition of culture depicts it as a relatively static concept (Signorini, Wiesemes, & Murphy, 2009). He believes that cultural change is slow, especially in terms of values and assumes a-one-way relationship between cultural values and the social structure (Hofstede, 2006). Contrary to these assumptions, other scholars have emphasized the mutable nature of culture (e.g., Signorini, Wiesemes, & Murphy, 2009; Spencer-Oatey, 2005), which has been also confirmed in entrepreneurship research (e.g., Shane, 1993; Wennekers et al., 2007). Furthermore, it has been suggested that there is a bidirectional relationship between values and other components of culture (e.g., other individual/group activities; Spencer-Oatey, 2005). For example, it has been demonstrated that radical political, social, and educational reforms, and/or globalization and technological revolutions are able to transform nations and influence the relevance of certain values (Signorini et al., 2009). This is evident in Vietnam, for example, where renovation policies have encouraged entrepreneurship regardless the absence of an alleged entrepreneurial culture (Nguyen et al., 2009). Because of its static nature, Hofstede's model seems to be unable to capture the complexity of national culture (McSweeney, 2002).

Second, by defining culture as "the collective programming of the mind," Hofstede (1991, p. 5) emphasizes the social nature of national culture and focuses mainly on the role of values in influencing motives, thoughts, and behavior. Building on the previous point on the interaction between values and other cultural elements as well as evidence from entrepreneurship studies (e.g., Busenitz et al., 2000; Iakovleva et al., 2014; Pinillos & Reyes, 2011; Wennekers et al., 2007), culture cannot be considered in isolation. There must be a systematic consideration of culture along with dimensions of the institutional and economic environment (Hayton et al., 2002).

Third, in terms of measurement, Hofstede's model assumes that a country's culture is typically represented by the mean aggregated individual scores of personal preferences (or values) of that country's respondents (Hofstede, 2001). However, it is suggested that values might be only loosely related to behavior since individuals do not necessarily act in line with their expressed personal preferences (see Stephan & Uhlaner, 2010). This also applies to the values measured through the SVS. Accordingly, a more direct measure of national culture is needed to capture something that exerts a more normative influence on entrepreneurial behavior within a certain culture (Fisher, 2006). This influence can be captured by descriptive norms. This is an approach to national culture that we describe next.

National Culture as Norms and Practices

Definition
Within the entrepreneurship literature, national culture is also defined in terms of descriptive norms and practices (House et al., 2004). Descriptive norms are conceptualized as perceived patterns of typical behavior approved in certain contexts, generally accompanied by the expectation that people will behave according to the pattern (Stephan & Uhlaner, 2010). Cultural practices represent the individual's perception of how cultural norms are actually enacted in societal behaviors (Segall, Lonner, & Berry, 1998). While cultural values represent an individual's views of how society should behave (Hofstede, 2001), norms and practices are the "actual ways in which members

of a culture go about dealing with their collective challenges" (Javidan, House, Dorfman, Hanges, & De Luque, 2006, p. 899).

Building on this approach, national culture influences behavior by imposing a legitimacy judgment on individuals' actions (Kibler, Kautonen, & Fink, 2015). In terms of entrepreneurial behavior, a supportive cultural environment makes potential entrepreneurs more likely to see their behavior as socially legitimate and increase their likelihood to acting entrepreneurially (Krueger & Brazeal, 1994). Thus, at individual level, that social legitimacy enhances the link between an individual's entrepreneurial attitudes and their intention to act (Kibler, Fink, Lang, & Munoz, 2014). Accordingly, at the national level, a nation that regards entrepreneurship as legitimate is expected to exhibit a higher level of national entrepreneurial activity (Harms & Groen, 2016; van Gelderen, Kautonen, & Fink, 2015).

Measures

One of the most developed measures of descriptive norms is provided by the Global Leadership Organizational Behavior Effectiveness (GLOBE) study (House et al., 2004). This project involved the study of 17,300 middle managers from 951 organizations in 62 societies. House and colleagues identified nine cultural dimensions that make it possible to capture the similarities and/or differences in norms and practices among societies. They were: power distance, uncertainty avoidance, institutional collectivism, in-group collectivism, gender egalitarianism, future orientation, performance orientation, assertiveness, and human orientation.

Some of these dimensions are very similar to those which Hofstede proposed (e.g., power distance, uncertainty avoidance, and future orientation). However, House et al. (2004) distinguish two types of collectivisms: institutional, and in-group collectivism. The former refers to the degree to which societal institutional practices encourage and reward collective distribution of resources and collective action. The latter refers to the degree to which individuals express pride, loyalty, and cohesiveness in their organizations or families. While Hofstede talks about masculine versus feminine societies, House focuses on the concept of gender egalitarianism that is the degree to which a collective minimizes gender inequalities. Performance orientation refers to the degree to which a collective encourages and rewards group members for performance improvement and excellence. Assertiveness is the degree to which individuals are assertive, confrontational, and aggressive in relating to others. Finally, human orientation is the degree to which a collective encourages and rewards individuals for being fair and kind to others.

The use of these dimensions varies within the entrepreneurship literature. For example Autio et al. (2013), Rauch et al. (2013), and Wennberg et al. (2013) have each focused on only a single dimensions that they see as being relevant to entrepreneurship such as institutional collectivism, uncertainty avoidance, assertiveness, and performance orientation. However, these authors felt the need to emphasize the necessity to conceptualize different levels of culture. They used the GLOBE index as well as more direct measures of national culture such as individuals' cultural orientations, captured through a questionnaire based on the GLOBE framework (König, Steinmetz, Frese, Rauch, & Wang, 2007; Rauch et al., 2013). This technique appears to achieve more consistent results in cross-cultural entrepreneurship research. It also overcomes ecological or individualistic fallacies due to the mix of a fundamentally collective phenomenon (i.e., culture) with a fundamentally individual-level behavior (i.e., entrepreneurship) (Autio et al., 2013; Wennberg et al., 2013).

Stephan & Uhlaner (2010) focused only on the GLOBE index and considered seven of the original nine dimensions and created two second-order factors, which they label performance-based culture and socially-supportive culture. The performance-based culture factor is representative of cultures with high positive loadings of future orientation, uncertainty avoidance, and performance orientation and high negative loadings of in-group collectivism and power distance. Examples of societies scoring high on performance orientation are Germanic, North European, and Anglo countries. Eastern European and Latin American countries scored very low on performance orientation, whereas Confucian and Southern Asian countries exhibited scores in the middle.

The socially supportive culture factor is representative of cultures with high positive loadings of human orientation and high negative loadings of assertiveness. Stephan and Uhlaner (2010) see this factor as a direct measure of social capital as it is representative of countries characterized by norms that support cooperation and fellowship (Fukuyama, 2001; Woolcock & Narayan, 2000). Societies scoring high on social supportiveness are Southern and Confucian Asian countries and some Anglo and North European countries. Latin American societies score in the middle and societies from Germanic, Eastern, and Latin Europe exhibited very low scores.

Another approach to the measurement of the effect of norms and practices has been proposed by Harms and Groen (2016). They have considered the role of "tightness" which has been shown to be a significant cultural characteristic in modern societies (Gelfand et al., 2011). Tightness refers to "the degree to which social norms are pervasive, clearly defined and reliably imposed within nations" (Gelfand et al., 2011, p. 2). Harms and Groen have observed that some cultures emphasize cultural standards very firmly and consistently (e.g., Malaysia, India, and Pakistan), while others grant more leeway (e.g., the Netherlands, Estonia, and Hungary). Tightness reflects at institutional and individual levels. At the institutional level, tighter countries tend to have more autocratic and sociopolitical institutions. At the individual level, individuals in tight countries show corresponding levels of psychological adaptation, such as being more concerned with avoiding mistakes, adhering more strictly to internalized norms, and having a higher need for structure (Gelfand, Erez, & Aycan, 2007, 2011).

Outcomes

As with cultural values, the effects of cultural norms and practices on entrepreneurial behavior have been studied at multiple level of analysis. Although very few studies have used this approach (Autio et al., 2013; Harms and Groen, 2016; Rauch et al., 2013; Wennberg et al. 2013), their findings are extremely relevant in advancing our understanding of the relationship between national culture and entrepreneurship.

Cultural norms and individual behavior. At the individual level, some studies challenge the idea that individualist cultures are supportive of entrepreneurship (Autio et al., 2013; Wennberg et al., 2013). Using multilevel techniques, Autio et al. (2013) have highlighted the differential effects of cultural practices (societal institutional collectivism, uncertainty avoidance, and performance orientation) on entrepreneurial entry and growth aspirations. Specifically, they have found that societal institutional collectivism practices are negatively associated with entrepreneurial entry, but positively associated with entrepreneurial growth aspirations. Uncertainty avoidance practices are negatively associated with entry but not with growth aspirations, and performance orientation practices are positively associated with entry. The most interesting result here is the positive effect of collectivism on entrepreneurial entry which contrasts with the accepted theorizing and empirical findings that highlight only the detrimental effect of this dimension on entrepreneurial entry (Autio et al., 2013).

In fact, most of the research on national culture and entrepreneurship has emphasized the relevance of individualism versus collectivism in facilitating entrepreneurship (Mueller & Thomas 2000). The rational for this assumption is that, in individualistic cultures, entrepreneurial behavior is more consistent with the dominant cultural values of individual accomplishments and thus recognized as more legitimate and appropriate within that society (Morris, Avila, & Alien, 1993; Pinillos & Reyes, 2001). However, the positive effects of institutional collectivism on entrepreneurship are also confirmed by Wennberg et al. (2013). Using data from the GLOBE study and from the Global Entrepreneurship Monitor (GEM), they have found that institutional collectivism enhances the positive effect of self-efficacy on entrepreneurial entry. Contrary to their expectations, they have also found that cultural landscape favoring institutional collectivism does not exacerbate the negative effects of individuals' fear of failure on entry. They explain these findings through the distinction between variance-generating and resource-mobilizing aspects of entrepreneurship (Thessen, 1997). This distinction suggests that entrepreneurs need both a societal setting that allows for deviance and playfulness (Hjorth, 2004) and a social fabric that facilities resource mobilization (Sørensen & Sorenson, 2003). This would explain the positive relationship between institutional collectivism and entrepreneurship.

Also at firm level, it is possible to observe that the innovation–growth relationship is stronger in more collectivistic countries. Rauch et al. (2013) have considered a sample of 857 business owners from five different countries: China, Germany, the Netherlands, Peru, and Russia. They have found that high collectivism and high power distance are very functional for effective innovation implementation. This challenges once again the assumption that "entrepreneurship is facilitated by cultures that are high in individualism, low in power distance, and low in uncertainty avoidance" (Hayton et al., 2002, p. 34)

Interestingly, the beneficial effect of collectivism on entrepreneurship is also confirmed at the national level of analysis. Stephan and Uhlaner (2010) have found that a socially supportive culture is related to several different measures of entrepreneurial activity. This is even more interesting when considering that they have not found any significant relationship between performance-based culture and entrepreneurship. Although Stephan and Uhlaner (2010) are not able to provide evidence for how and why social supportiveness influences entrepreneurship, their findings stimulate discussion on the role of cooperative and supportive cultures. It is plausible that higher social capital enhances weak ties among individuals of a population, increasing the number of opportunities discovered (Granovetter, 1973), or that it reduces transaction costs (Hayton & Cacciotti, 2013).

Harms and Groen (2016) have also reported surprising results at the national level of analysis. Contrary to their expectations, the cultural dimension of tightness has neither a direct nor a moderating effect on entrepreneurship. They also consider the cultural values of individualism and uncertainty avoidance, which do not show any significant impact on high-growth entrepreneurship or social entrepreneurship. These results emphasize the role of institutions in driving entrepreneurship behavior. Even if national culture is not supportive, policymakers can always use formal institutions to foster high-growth entrepreneurship and social entrepreneurship. This is in line with the idea that national culture does not have a predominant effect; it mainly works as moderator of the influence of institutional and economic context variables on entrepreneurial outcomes (Hayton et al., 2002).

Limitations. Although informative, this second stream of research on national culture and entrepreneurship is not without limitations. First, there are a limited number of investigations approaching national culture in terms of norms and practices. This becomes especially significant in light of the counterintuitive results emerging from these few studies: the relevance of institutional collectivism in entrepreneurship. The use of a different measure of national culture is suggesting a different and more coherent picture than the one emerging from the literature that measure national culture as values. However, we need more studies using this approach to claim that the operationalization of national culture as norms and practices is able to provide a more consistent understanding of what can be defined as entrepreneurial culture.

Second, some of these studies only focus on culture-specific effects (e.g., Harms & Groen, 2016; Rauch et al., 2013). As already highlighted, national culture and entrepreneurship studies require additional investigations because the countries considered within a single study often differ not only in culture but in other ways as well. We know that institutional environment (e.g., Nguyen et al., 2009), and/or economic development (e.g., Pinillos & Reyes, 2011; Wennekers et al., 2007) may impact reported relationships and there might be temporal effects as well (e.g., Shane, 1993). These influences cannot be ruled out. On the contrary, they have to be part of a more comprehensive theoretical framework through which we observe the relationship between national culture and entrepreneurship (Hayton et al., 2002; Hayton & Cacciotti, 2013). This should be a clear starting point for future research as we explain next.

Summary

Our review of the existing literature on national culture and entrepreneurship reveals that it is characterized by two definitions of national culture: culture as values and culture as norms and practices. Following the values approach, national culture is an aggregate of what individuals claim as their desired goals in life. The sum of individual values constitutes a national culture. This approach is also known as the "aggregate traits approach" because these individual values may be rooted in individual traits (Hofstede et al., 2004). For this reason, several researchers proposed a direct link between cultural dimensions and the relative frequency with which corresponding individual traits (e.g., locus of control, innovativeness, risk-taking, and proactiveness) appear in a population (e.g., Mueller & Thomas, 2000; Stewart et al., 2003; Thomas & Mueller, 2000). Hayton et al. (2002) have already criticized this approach. They suggested that if culture is assumed to be "an aggregation of individual values and beliefs, it is not surprising that measures of cultural values are correlated with measures of individual values" (Hayton et al., 2002; p. 47). The same argument applies to traits. The result is a tautology: when differences in the national level are derived from the aggregation of individual differences, it is hardly surprising that conceptually related individual differences are predicted based on nationality (Hayton & Cacciotti, 2013).

Research that focuses on the influence of cultural values on cognition partially overcomes this problem. By examining how culture as an exogenous factor influences perceptions and cognitions, it is possible to develop plausible, testable and nontautological models of a culture's influence (e.g., Gotkan & Gunay, 2011; Mitchell et al., 2000; Tan, 2002). This may be direct or indirect. Hayton and Cacciotti (2013) note that very limited research has been conducted on the influence of culture on cognition. That which has been conducted suggests systematic differences, although so far no coherent framework has been worked out and successfully tested.

A similar concern arises when considering the studies on the influence of cultural values on entrepreneurial intentions. The theory of planned behavior represents a dominant approach to explaining individuals' intention to act entrepreneurially. In principle, we would expect that the beliefs concerning the social desirability and personal desirability of entrepreneurship are plausibly influenced by the cultural and institutional environment. Despite this conceptual plausibility, due to methodological shortcomings, the studies in this area have yet to test a more comprehensive framework to fulfill the promise of explaining the process through which culture and institutions influence intentions to behave entrepreneurially (e.g., Hayton & Cacciotti, 2013; Nguyen et al., 2009; Urban 2006).

At the national level of analysis, studies reveal that consideration of only cultural values is not enough to explain variation of entrepreneurship rates, start-up rates, and firm formation (e.g., Davidsson, 1995; Davidsson & Wicklund, 1997). For example, Pinillos and Reyes (2011) have shown that the association between individualism and entrepreneurial activity varies with the stage of economic development. This suggests that cultural values interact with economic development in ways that allow for dynamism in the influence of culture, without necessarily suggesting instability in cultural values themselves (Hayton & Cacciotti, 2013). Accordingly, an absolute concept of "entrepreneurial culture" cannot exist as the influence of certain values (e.g., individualism, uncertainty tolerance, and lower power distance) is subject to levels of economic development (Wennekers et al., 2007).

Following the descriptive norms approach, national culture is described in terms of typical behavior accepted within a society (Stephan & Uhlaner, 2010). A supportive cultural environment makes potential entrepreneurs more likely to evaluate entrepreneurial behavior as socially legitimate and be more motivated to act. Because cultural norms seem to be a strong determinant of behavior, some scholars believe that this approach provides higher fidelity with the action theory of entrepreneurship (Autio et al., 2013; McMullen & Shepherd, 2006). This means that societal cultural norms and practices condition the degree to which observed third-person opportunities (i.e., opportunities for someone) are evaluated to represent feasible and desirable first-person opportunities (i.e., opportunities for oneself). Since entrepreneurship can be regulated by how important others react to this behavior, observable cultural norms and practices are likely to be salient predictors of entrepreneurial behaviors. This has resulted in the examination of a direct relationship between these norms and practices and individuals' decision to start a business (e.g., Autio et al., 2013).

Nevertheless, this direct approach ignores the fact that national norms and practices are a collective level phenomenon and as such operate at a higher level of analysis than the individual (Hofstede, 2001). For this reason, Wennberg et al. (2013) have preferred to examine the contingent role of national culture on the relationship between individual level constructs: self-efficacy and fear of failure, and individuals' entrepreneurial entry. However, much has yet to be discovered about the process of this interaction between individual differences and national norms, and the cognitive processes through which these elements interact, and indeed the outcomes of these cognitive processes. For example, if being an entrepreneur involves extreme deviation from national cultural norms, what is the impact of such deviation for individuals, or the achievement of entrepreneurial objectives? More research is needed within this stream of research. We provide some direction for future investigations in the next section.

Directions for Future Research

As suggested by Hayton & Caccioti (2013), research on national culture and entrepreneurship requires the development of a more rigorous theoretical framework. However, given the presence of two different conceptualizations of national culture, the path forward should begin by establishing the relevance of one over the other. We agree with Javidan et al.'s assertion, mentioned earlier, that culture can be theoretically defined as "both values and actual ways in which members of a culture go about dealing with their collective challenges" (Javidan et al., 2006, p. 899). However, the need to commit to one or the other definition becomes relevant in terms of measurement. The two predominant approaches to the measurement of national culture as values and national culture as norms and practices are respectively the Hofstede study (1980; 2001) and the GLOBE project (House et al., 2004). Javidan et al. (2006) offers an accurate comparison between the two. Although our aim is not to make a judgment of superiority, we follow Wennberg et al. (2013) and suggest that the appropriateness of each model depends on the context of investigation. Building on intention-based theories of entrepreneurial entry (e.g., Krueger & Carsrud, 1993), they stated that people consider not only their own ability to achieve success and the risk of failure, but also how entrepreneurial action is "consistent with prevailing cultural norms and practices"(p.758). Cultural practices refers to the actual manifestation of a culture in individuals' daily lives (House et al. 2004) and is useful for theorizing about the culture–entrepreneurship link since distinctively from more abstract "values," "practices" are more proximate concepts dealing with the decisions important in entrepreneurship (Javidan et al., 2006). We agree with Wennberg et al. (2013) and suggest that cultural norms and practices are a more concrete tool for assessing the influence of national culture on entrepreneurship.

Although scholars can use the GLOBE index (House et al., 2004) to classify and compare national cultures, relying only on this database can have some limitations. First, like the Hofstede's study, the GLOBE index is not available for every country in the world. Second, these studies create country-level proxies, ignoring intracultural variation. Minkov and Hofstede (2012) have shown that 299 in-country regions from 28 countries do not intermix much when they are clustered on the basis of cultural values. However, we cannot exclude that historical, geographical, political, ethnic, linguistic, religious, and economic elements can generate regional cultural variations that can manifest over time (e.g., Liñán & Fernandez-Serrano, 2014; Shane, 1993).

These limitations can be partially overcome by applying multilevel research designs to study the culture–entrepreneurship link (e.g., Autio et al., 2013; Rauch et al., 2013;

Wennberg et al., 2013). For example, Rauch et al. (2013) suggest investigating both individuals' cultural orientations and national culture. Studying culture only at a single level of analysis can be problematic because scholars can generate an ecological fallacy when generalizing from relationships at the country level to relationships at the individual level (Brett, Trinsley, Janssens, Berness, & Lytle, 1997). The same problem emerges when scholars use only individuals' perceptions of culture to study their entrepreneurial behavior. They assume that collective attributes can be directly reflected in the behaviors and values of individuals, confusing individuals' perceptions and motivations with those of the national culture (Hofmann, Griffi, & Gavin, 2000; Wennberg et al., 2013). Accordingly, multilevel models allow researchers to better understand the complex mechanisms between culture and entrepreneurship.

Now that we have clarified how national culture can be operationalized, it is important to provide a more coherent framing of the connection between national culture, individual traits, motives, beliefs, cognition, and behavior. Future research must be concerned with how individual difference variables or individual cognitions are influenced by both national culture and institutions, as well as how these factors might interact. Hayton and Cacciotti (2013) proposed the Busenitz and Lau model (1996) as the logical foundation for this integration. Building on the assumption that individual preferences for entrepreneurship are influenced by contextual contingencies (Shane & Venkataraman, 2000), we can place cognitive processes as a mediating variable between (a) stable individual differences, cultural, and institutional factors, and (b) entrepreneurship behavior. However, what remains to be decided is what and how specific cognitions (e.g., perceptions or preferences) arise in contexts characterized by certain cultural and institutional environments.

With the purpose of facilitating future research in this field, we propose fear of failure as one of the cognitive mechanisms through which we can capture the connection between national culture and entrepreneurial behavior. The cultural norm and practice approach to culture assumes that people are motivated to start a business if this activity is congruent with a society's legitimate behavior. The decision to pursue entrepreneurial activity "involves significant legitimacy trade-offs that may be regulated by cultural practices, prompting careful weighting of social legitimacy costs arising from the interpretation of the symbolic value of alternative behaviors, resource investment, and the preclusion of alternative pursuits" (Autio et al, 2013, p. 358). However, this legitimacy judgment is often elaborated around the extent to which culture punishes or stigmatizes the failure of this activity (e.g., Tezuka, 1997). It is suggested that some cultural norms can render losing to be a shameful experience and expose entrepreneurs to the stigma of negative social judgments (Cacciotti & Hayton, 2015; Goffman, 1963; Tezuka, 1997). Accordingly, the fear of failure can capture this variation.

A recent conceptualization of fear of failure in entrepreneurship shows that experiencing fear of failure in this context depends on how strongly individuals believe or anticipate that aversive consequences will occur (Cacciotti, Hayton, Mitchell, & Giazitzoglu, 2016). The relevant appraisals include threats to entrepreneurs' financial security, to their personal ability, and to their ability to obtain financing for the venture, the venture's ability to execute (distinct from that of the individual entrepreneur), the potential of the idea, social esteem, and the fears arising from perceived lost opportunities to spend time or resources elsewhere. Taken together, these aspects relate to the expectancy (feasibility) and instrumentality (desirability) of actions and are consistent with extant theories such as expectancy theory and the theory of planned behavior.

Drawing on the multidimensionality of fear of failure, we can assume the following mechanisms. For instance, cultural and social norms associated with failure stigmatization can be expected to promote fear of failure resulting from the perceived threat to social esteem. Importantly, the same social norms can be hypothesized to moderate the *effect* of fear of failure on entrepreneurial entry. Similarly, government policies—for example, bankruptcy regulation—can be expected to influence the extent to which particular threat cues are experienced, and also to moderate the effects of threat appraisals on entrepreneurial entry. The multidimensionality of fear of failure ensures that the cognitive processes associated with it arise not only in responses to social norms that stigmatize fear of failure (e.g., threat to social esteem) but also to institutional conditions that can hamper or facilitate entrepreneurship as career option (e.g., threat to financial security, ability to fund the venture, and opportunity costs).

However, the relationship between fear of failure and entrepreneurial entry is not straightforward. Research has demonstrated that fear does not always and only prevent people from following an entrepreneurial career (Cacciotti et al., 2016). Fear of failure can also motivate entrepreneurial action (e.g., Mitchell & Shepherd, 2011; Morgan & Sisak, 2016). Although this seems to result in a more complicated theoretical framework, it offers the possibility of considering once again the context contingencies as moderators that can decide the direction of the relationship between fear of failure and the decision to start a business. We invite future research to think about specific moderators and to test to what extent fear of failure mediates the relationship between ecosystem characteristics (social norms and institutional factors) and entrepreneurial inhibition/entry. Finally, since fear of failure can also be experienced at any stage of the entrepreneurial process (see Cacciotti et al., 2016), scholars can consider its mediating effect when assessing the influence of national culture on entrepreneurial actions beyond the decision to start a business (e.g., growth intentions).

Conclusion

Culture is a complex phenomenon. Our review of the literature has emphasized the presence of two different approaches to defining national culture in entrepreneurship. This has resulted in contrasting findings and the inability to confirm the presence of a clear entrepreneurial culture. We have tried to give some suggestions to move the research in this field forward. Fear of failure is proposed as one of the cognitive variables placed in the middle to explain the mechanisms through which national culture influences entrepreneurship. Although this is only a suggestion, we hope that it can be considered as a starting point for finally resolving the inconsistencies that currently characterize the literature on national culture and entrepreneurship.

References

Ajzen, I. (1991). The theory of planned behavior. *Organizational Behavior and Human Decision Processes, 50*, 179–211.

Aoyama, Y. (2009). Entrepreneurship and regional culture: The case of Hamamatsu and Kyoto, Japan. *Regional Studies, 43*(3), 495–512.

Autio, E., Pathak, S., & Wennberg, K. (2013). Consequences of Cultural Practices for Entrepreneurial Behaviors. *Journal of International Business Studies, 44*: 334–362.

Baum, J. R., Olian, J. D., Erez, M., Schnell, E. R., Smith, K. G., Sims, H. P., . . . Smith K. A. (1993). Nationality and work role interactions: A cultural contrast of Israeli and U.S. entrepreneurs' versus managers' needs. *Journal of Business Venturing, 8*, 449–512.

Brett, J. M., Trinsley, C. H., Janssens, M., Berness, Z. I., & Lytle, A. L. (1997). New approaches to the study of culture in industrial/organizational psychology. In P. C. Earley & M. Erez (Eds.), *New perspectives in international industrial/organizational psychology* (pp. 75–129). San Francisco, CA: New Lexington Press.

Busenitz, L. W., Gomez, C., & Spencer, J. W. (2000). Country institutional profiles: Unlocking entrepreneurial phenomena. *Academy of Management Journal, 43*, 994–1003.

Busenitz, L. W., & Lau, C. M. (1996). A cross-cultural cognitive model of new venture creation. *Entrepreneurship Theory and Practice, 20*, 25–39.

Cacciotti, G., & Hayton, J. C. (2015). Fear and entrepreneurship: A review and research agenda. *International Journal of Management Review, 17*, 165–190. doi: 10.1111/ijmr.12052

Cacciotti, G., Hayton J. C., Mitchell J. R., & Giazitzoglu A. (2016). A reconceptualization of fear of failure in entrepreneurship. *Journal of Business Venturing, 31*(3), 302–325.

Davidsson, P. (1995). Culture, structure and regional levels of entrepreneurship. *Entrepreneurship and Regional Development, 7*, 41–62.

Davidsson, P., & Wiklund, J. (1997). Values, beliefs and regional variations in new firm formation rates. *Journal of Economic Psychology, 18*, 179–199.

Denyer, D., & Tranfield, D. (2008). Producing a systematic review. In D. Buchanan (Ed.), *The Sage handbook of organizational research methods* (pp. 671–689). London, England: Sage.

Fink, G., Neyer, A.K., & Kölling, M. (2007). Understanding cross-cultural management interaction: Research into cultural standards to complement cultural value dimensions and personality traits. *International Studies of Management & Organization, 36*(4), 38–60.

Fischer, R. (2006). Congruence and functions of personal and cultural values: Do my values reflect my culture's values? *Personality and Social Psychology Bulletin, 32*(11), 1419–1431.

Fukuyama, F. (2001). Social capital, civil society and development. *Third World Quarterly, 22*(1): 7–20.

Garcia-Cabrera, A. M., & Garcia-Soto, M. G. (2008). Cultural differences and entrepreneurial behavior: An intra-country cross-cultural analysis in Cape Verde. *Entrepreneurship & Regional Development: An International Journal, 20*(5): 451–483.

Gelfand, M. J., Erez, M., & Aycan, Z. (2007). Cross-cultural organizational behavior. *Annual Review of Psychology, 58*, 479–514.

Gelfand, M. J., Raver, J. L., Nishii, L., Leslie, L. M., Lun, J., Lim, B. C., . . . Yamaguchi, S. (2011). Differences between tight and loose cultures: A 33-nation study. *Science, 332*, 1100–1104.

Goffman, E. (1963). *Stigma: Notes on Management of Spoiled Identity*. Englewood Cliffs, NJ: Prentice Hall.

Goktan, A. B., & Gunay, G. (2011). Is entrepreneurial cognition culturally bound? A comparative study conducted in Turkey and United States. *Journal of Small Business and Entrepreneurship, 24*(4): 445–470.

Granovetter, M. S. (1973). The strength of weak ties. *American Journal of Sociology, 78*(6): 1360–1380.

Harms, R., & Groen, A. (2016). Loosen up? Cultural tightness and national entrepreneurial activity. *Technological Forecasting & Social Change*, 1–9.

Hayton, J. C., & Cacciotti, G. (2013). Is there an entrepreneurial culture? A review of empirical research. *Entrepreneurship & Regional Development, 25*(9–10): 708–731. doi: 10.1080/08985626.2013.862962

Hayton, J. C., George, G., & Zahra, S. A. (2002). National culture and entrepreneurship: A review of behavioral research. *Entrepreneurship: Theory & Practice, 26*(4): 33–52.

Herbig, P. (1994). *The innovation matrix: Culture and structure prerequisites to innovation*. Westport, CT: Quorum.

Hjorth, D. (2004). Creating space for play/invention-concepts of space and organizational entrepreneurship. *Entrepreneurship and Regional Development, 16*, 413–432.

Hofmann, D., Griffi, M., & Gavin, M. (2000). The application of hierarchical linear modeling to organizational research. In K. J. Klein & S. W. J. Kozlowski (Eds.), *Multilevel theory, research, and methods in organizations: Foundations, extensions, and new directions* (pp. 467–511). San Francisco, CA: Jossey-Bass.

Hofstede, G. (1980). *Culture's consequences: International differences in work related values*. Beverly Hills, CA: Sage.

Hofstede, G. (1991). *Cultures and organizations: Software of the mind*. Newbury, England: McGraw-Hill.

Hofstede, G. (2001).*Culture's consequences: Comparing values, behaviors, institutions and organizations across nations* (2nd ed.). Thousands Oaks, CA: Sage.

Hofstede, G. (2006). What did GLOBE really measure? Researcher's minds versus respondents' minds, *Journal of International Business Studies, 37*(6), 882–896.

Hofstede, G., & Bond, M. H. (1988). The Confucian connection: From cultural roots to economic growth. *Organizational Dynamics, 16*(1), 4–21.

House, R. J., Hanges, P. W., Mansour, J., Dorfman, P. W., & Gupta, V. (2004). *Culture, leadership and organization: The GLOBE study of 62 societies*. Thousand Oaks, CA: Sage.

Iakovleva, T., Kolvereid, L., Gorgievski, M. J., & Sørhaug, O. (2014). Comparison of perceived barriers to entrepreneurship in Eastern and Western European countries. *International Journal of Entrepreneurship & Innovation Management, 18*(2/3), 115-133. doi: 10.1504/IJEIM.2014.062874

Javidan, M., House, R., Dorfman, P., Hanges, P., & De Luque, M. (2006). Conceptualizing and measuring cultures and their consequences: A comparative review of GLOBE's and Hofstede's approaches. *Journal of International Business Studies, 37*, 897–914.

Kibler, E., Fink, M., Lang, R., & Munoz, P. (2014). Place attachment and social legitimacy: Revisiting the sustainable entrepreneurship journey. *Journal of Business Venturing. Insights, 3*, 24–29.

Kibler, E., Kautonen, T., & Fink, M. (2015). Regional social legitimacy of entrepreneurship: Implications for entrepreneurial intention and start-up behaviour. *Regional Studies, 48*, 995–1015.

König, C., Steinmetz, H., Frese, M., Rauch, A., & Wang, Z. (2007). Scenario-based scales measuring cultural orientations of business owners. *Journal of Evolutionary Economics, 17*, 211–239.

Kristiansen, S., & Indarti, N. (2004). Entrepreneurial intention among Indonesian and Norwegian students. *Journal of Enterprising Culture, 12*(1), 55–78.

Krueger, N. F., & Brazeal, D. V. (1994). Entrepreneurial potential and potential entrepreneurs. *Enterpreneurship Theory Practice, 18,* 91–104.

Krueger, N. F., & Carsrud, A. L. (1993). Entrepreneurial intentions: Applying the theory of planned behavior. *Entrepreneurship and Regional Development, 5,* 315–330.

Krueger, N., Liñán, F., & Nabi, G. (2013). Cultural values and entrepreneurship. *Entrepreneurship & Regional Development, 25*(9–10), 703–707. doi: 10.1080/08985626.2013.862961

Lee-Ross, D., & Mitchell, B. (2007). Doing business in the Torres Straits: A study of the relationship between culture and the nature of indigenous entrepreneurship. *Journal of Developmental Entrepreneurship, 12*(2), 199–216.

Liñán, F., & Chen, Y.-W. (2009). Development and cross-cultural application of specific instrument to measure entrepreneurial intentions. *Entrepreneurship Theory and Practice, 33*(3): 593–617.

Liñán, F., & Fernandez-Serrano, J. (2014). National culture, entrepreneurship and economic development: Different patterns across the European Union. *Small Business Economics,. 42*(4), 685–701. 17. doi: 10.1007/s11187-013-9520-x

Longest, K. C., Hitlin, S., & Vaisey, S. (2013). Position and disposition: The contextual development of human values. *Social Forces, 91,* 1499–1528.

McClelland, D. C., Atkinson, J. W., Clark, R. A., & Lowell, E. L. (1953). The achievement motive. New York, NY: Appleton-Century-Crofts.

McGrath, R. G., & MacMillan, I. C. (1992). More like each other than anyone else? A cross-cultural study of entrepreneurial perceptions. *Journal of Business Venturing, 7,* 419–429.

McGrath, R. G., MacMillan, I. C., & Scheinberg, S. (1992). Elitists, risk-takers, and rugged individualists? An exploratory analysis of cultural differences between entrepreneurs and non-entrepreneurs. *Journal of Business Venturing, 7,* 115–135.

McMullen, J. S., & Shepherd, D. A. (2006). Entrepreneurial action and the role of uncertainty in the theory of the entrepreneur. *Academy of Management Review, 31*(1), 132–152.

McSweeney, B. (2002). Hofstede's model of national cultural differences and their consequences: A triumph of faith—a failure of analysis. *Human Relation, 55,* 89–118.

Minkov, M., & Hofstede, G. (2012). Is national culture a meaningful concept? Cultural values delineate homogeneous national clusters of in-country regions. *Cross-Cultural Research, 46*(2), 133–159. doi:10.1177/1069397111427262

Mitchell, R. K., Smith, J. B., Morse, E. A., Seawright, K. W., Peredo, A. M., & McKenzie, B. (2002). Are entrepreneurial cognitions universal? Assessing entrepreneurial cognitions across cultures. *Entrepreneurship Theory and Practice, 26*(4), 9–32.

Mitchell, R. K., Smith, B., Seawright, K. W., & Morse, E. A. (2000). Cross-cultural cognitions and the venture creation decision. *Academy of Management Journal, 43,* 974–993.

Mitchell, J. R., & Shepherd, D. A. (2011). Afraid of opportunity: The effects of fear of failure on entrepreneurial decisions. *Frontiers of Entrepreneurship Research, 31*(6), Article 1.

Morgan, J., & Sisak, D. (2016). Aspiring to succeed: A model of entrepreneurship and fear of failure. *Journal of Business Venturing, 31,* 1–21.

Moriano, J. A., Gorgievski, M., Laguna, M., Stephan, U., & Zarafshani, K. (2012). A cross cultural approach to understanding entrepreneurial intention. *Journal of Career Development, 39*(2), 162–185.

Morris, M. H., Avila, R. A., & Alien, J. (1993). Individualism and the modern corporation: Implications for innovation and entrepreneurship. *Journal of Management, 19,* 595–612.

Mueller, J., Zapkau, F. B., & Schwens, C. (2014). Impact of prior entrepreneurial exposure on entrepreneurial intention—cross-cultural evidence. *Journal of Enterprising Culture, 22*(3), 251-282. doi: 10.1142/S0218495814500113

Mueller, S. L., & Thomas, A. S. (2000). Culture and entrepreneurial potential: A nine country study of locus of control and innovativeness. *Journal of Business Venturing, 16*, 51–75.

Nguyen, T. V., Bryant, S. E., Rose, J., Tseng, C.-H., & Kapasuwan, S. (2009). Cultural values, market, institutions, and entrepreneurship potential: A comparative study of the Unites States, Taiwan, and Vietnam. *Journal of Developmental Entrepreneurship, 14*(1), 21–37.

Pinillos, M. J., & Reyes, L. (2011). Relationship between individualist–collectivist culture and entrepreneurial activity: Evidence from global entrepreneurship monitor data. *Small Business Economics, 37*, 23–37.

Porter, M. E., & Stern, S. (2001, Summer). Innovation: Location matters. *MIT Sloan Management Review, 42*(4), 28–36.

Pruett, M., Shinnar, R., Toney, B., Llopis, F., & Fox, J. (2009). Explaining entrepreneurial intentions of university students: Across-cultural study. *International Journal of Entrepreneurial Behaviour & Research, 15*(6), 571–594.

Rarick, C., & Thaung H. (2015). The role of culture in shaping an entrepreneurial mindset. *International Journal of Entrepreneurship, 19*, 119–125.

Rauch, A., Frese, M., Wang, Z., Unger, J., Lozada, M., Kupcha, V., & Spirina, T. (2013). National culture and cultural orientations of owners affecting the innovation–growth relationship in five countries. *Entrepreneurship & Regional Development, 25*(9–10), 732–755. doi: 10.1080/08985626.2013.862972

Rinne, T., Steel, G. D., & Fairweather, J. (2012). Hofstede and Shane revisited: The role of power distance and individualism in national-level innovation success. *Cross-Cultural Research, 46*(2), 91–108.

Scheinberg, S., & MacMillan, I. C. (1988). An 11 country study of motivations to start a business. In B. A Kirchoff, W. A. Long, W. E. McMullan, K. H. Vesper, & W. E. Wetzel (Eds.), *Frontiers of Entrepreneurship Research* (pp. 669–687). Wellesley, MA: Babson College.

Schwartz, S. H. (1994). Beyond individualism/collectivism: New cultural dimensions of values. In U. Kim, H. C. Triandis, C. Kagitçibasi, S. C. Choi, & G. Yoon (Eds.), *Individualism and collectivism. Theory, method, and applications* (pp. 85–119). Thousand Oaks, CA: Sage.

Schwartz, S. H. (2004). Mapping and interpreting cultural differences around the world. In H. Vinken, J. Soeters, & P. Ester (Eds.), *Comparing cultures, dimensions of culture in a comparative perspective*. Leiden, Netherlands: Brill.

Schwartz, S. H. (2006). A theory of cultural value orientations: Explication and applications. *Comparative Sociology, 5*(2–3), 137–182. doi: 10.1163/156913306778667357

Schwartz, S. H. (2008). *Cultural value orientations: Nature and implications of national differences*. Moscow: SU HSE.

Segall, M. H., Lonner, W. J., & Berry, J. W. (1998). Cross-cultural psychology as a scholarly discipline: On the flowering of culture in behavioral research. *American Psychologist, 53*, 1101–1110.

Shane, S. (1992). Why do some societies invent more than others? *Journal of Business Venturing, 7*, 29–46.

Shane, S. (1993). Cultural influences on national rates of innovation. *Journal of Business Venturing, 8*, 59–73.

Shane, S., Kolvereid, L., & Westhead, P. (1991). An exploratory examination of the reasons leading to new firm formation across country and gender. *Journal of Business Venturing, 6*, 431–446.

Shane, S., & Venkataraman, S.. (2000). The promise of entrepreneurship as a field of research. *Academy of Management Review, 25*, 217–266.

Shinnar, R. S., Giacomin, O., & Janssen, F. (2012). Entrepreneurial perceptions and intentions: The role of gender and culture. *Entrepreneurship Theory and Practice, 36*, 465–493.

Shneor, R., Camgöz, S. M., & Karapinar, P. B. (2013). The interaction between culture and sex in the formation of entrepreneurial intentions. *Entrepreneurship & Regional Development, 25*(9–10), 781–803. doi: 10.1080/08985626.2013.862973

Signorini, P., Wiesemes, R., & Murphy, R. (2009). Developing alternative frameworks for exploring intercultural learning: A critique of Hofstede's cultural difference model. *Teaching in Higher Education, 14*(3), 253–264.

Sørensen, J. B., & Sorenson, O. (2003). From conception to birth: Opportunity perception and resource mobilization in entrepreneurship. *Advances in Strategic Management, 20*, 89–117.

Spenser-Oatey, H. (2005). (Im)politeness, face and perceptions of rapport: Unpackaging their bases and interrelationships. *Journal of Politeness Research, 1*, 95–119.

Stephan, U., & Uhlaner, L. M. (2010). Performance-based vs. socially supportive culture: A cross-national study of descriptive norms and entrepreneurship. *Journal of International Business Studies, 41*, 1347–1364.

Stewart, W. H., Jr., Carland, J. C. Carland, J. W., Watson, W. E., & Sweo, R. (2003). Entrepreneurial dispositions and goal orientation: A comparative exploration of United States and Russian entrepreneurs. *Journal of Small Business Management, 41*(1), 27–46.

Sun, H. (2009). A meta-analysis on the influence of national culture on innovation capability. *International Journal of Entrepreneurship and Innovation Management, 10*(3/4), 353–360.

Tan, J. (2002). Culture, nation, and entrepreneurial strategic orientations: Implications for an emerging economy. *Entrepreneurship Theory and Practice, 26*(4), 95–111.

Tezuka, H. (1997). Success as the source of failure? Competition and cooperation in the Japanese economy. *Sloan Management Review, 38*, 83–89.

Thessen, J. H. (1997). Individualism, collectivism, and entrepreneurship: A framework for international comparative research. *Journal of Business Venturing, 12*, 367–384.

Thomas, A. S., & Mueller, S. L. (2000). A case for comparative entrepreneurship: assessing the relevance of culture. *Journal of International Business Studies, 31*, 287–301.

Tranfield, D., Denyer, D., & Smart, P. (2003). Towards a methodology for developing evidence-informed management knowledge by means of systematic review. *British Journal of Management, 14*, 207–222.

Urban, B. (2006). Entrepreneurship in the Rainbow Nation: Effect of cultural values and ESE on intentions. *Journal of Developmental Entrepreneurship, 11*(3), 171–186.

van Gelderen, M., Kautonen, T., & Fink, M. (2015). From entrepreneurial intentions to actions: Self- control and action-related doubt, fear, and aversion. *Journal of Business Venturing, 30*, 655–673.

Wennberg, K., Pathak, S., & Autio, E. (2013). How culture moulds the effects of self-efficacy and fear of failure on entrepreneurship. *Entrepreneurship & Regional Development*, *25*(9–10), 756–780. doi: /10.1080/08985626.2013.862975

Wennekers, S., Thurik, R., van Stel, A., & Noorderhaven, N. (2007). Uncertainty avoidance and the rate of business ownership across 21 OECD countries, 1976–2004. *Journal of Evolutionary Economics*, *17*, 133–160.

Williams, L. K., & McGuire, S. J. (2010). Economic creativity and innovation implementation: The entrepreneurial drivers of growth? Evidence from 63 countries. *Small Business Economics*, *34*, 391–412.

Woolcock, M., & Narayan, D. (2000) Social capital: Implications for development theory, research, and policy. *World Bank Research Observer, 15*(2), 225–250.

19

Management of Entrepreneurial Ecosystems

Erkko Autio[a] and Jonathan Levie[b]

[a] *Imperial College Business School, UK*
[b] *University of Strathclyde, UK*

Introduction

The notion of entrepreneurial ecosystems has become increasingly prevalent in the entrepreneurship policy literature (Acs, Autio, & Szerb, 2014; Auerswald, 2014; Drexler et al., 2014; Spigel, 2017; Stam, 2014). However, there is little evidence that entrepreneurship policy itself has become more systemic in nature. Like many socioeconomic policy areas, entrepreneurship policy has traditionally employed top-down, siloed approaches designed to address specific, well-defined market and structural failures by, for example, providing subsidized funding for new businesses or enhancing SME access to R&D facilities (Audretsch, 2011; Lundström, & Stevenson, 2005). However, siloed approaches may not be effective in redressing complex, systemic challenges that span across policy domains (Blackburn, & Schaper, 2012; Stam, 2015). In this chapter, we explore alternative approaches to managing entrepreneurial ecosystems.

Acs et al. (2014, p. 479) defined entrepreneurial ecosystems as: "dynamic, institutionally embedded interaction between entrepreneurial attitudes, ability, and aspirations, by individuals, which drives the allocation of resources through the creation and operation of new ventures." Entrepreneurial ecosystems are complex socioeconomic structures that are brought to life by individual-level action (Spigel, 2017). This action is embedded in complex interactions between multiple individual and organizational stakeholders that make up the ecosystem, and it is expressed through the creation and operation of new ventures. The ultimate outcome of this trial-and-error dynamic is the allocation of resources toward productive uses, as entrepreneurs are more likely to abandon the pursuit of poor-quality opportunities than they are to abandon high-quality opportunities—that is, those which enable them to gain high returns on their resource allocation.

In the ecological literature, the benefits generated by natural ecosystems are commonly referred to as "ecosystem services," and the practice of managing and enhancing such benefits is referred to as "ecosystem management" (Anderies, Janssen, & Ostrom, 2004; Grumbine, 1994; Seppelt, Dormann, Eppink, Lautenbach, & Schmidt, 2011). The dual service created by entrepreneurial ecosystems is resource allocation towards productive uses and the innovative, high-growth ventures that drive this process. Because

The Wiley Handbook of Entrepreneurship, First Edition.
Edited by Gorkan Ahmetoglu, Tomas Chamorro-Premuzic, Bailey Klinger, & Tessa Karcisky.
© 2017 John Wiley & Sons Ltd. Published 2017 by John Wiley & Sons Ltd.

entrepreneurial ecosystem services are created through myriad localized interactions between ecosystem stakeholders, it is not easy to trace gaps in ecosystem performance back to specific, well-defined market and structural failures that could be addressed in a top-down mode. This undermines the effectiveness of "market failure" and "system failure" approaches to policy-making in entrepreneurial ecosystems (Bergek, Jacobsson, Carlsson, Lindmark, & Rickne, 2008; Woolthuis, Lankhuizen, & Gilsing, 2005). Yet, there has been little theoretical work exploring alternative policy approaches in entrepreneurial ecosystems.

We address this gap by drawing on literature that discusses policy approaches in socioeconomic and socioecological systems that are comparable to entrepreneurial ecosystems in their complexity (e.g., socioecological ecosystems, multistakeholder communities). We find that policy approaches to address such systems share several common features, such as deep stakeholder engagement, reinforcement of generalized reciprocity and prosocial behaviors, multipolar coordination, and collective action (Bowles & Gintis, 2002; Kofinas, 2009; Vollan & Ostrom, 2010). Such approaches are yet to be discussed in the context of entrepreneurial ecosystems. In this chapter, we contribute to entrepreneurial ecosystem theory and practice by applying socioecological and community governance theories to develop a model for collective management of entrepreneurial ecosystems. We show how policymakers and other stakeholders can assume a leadership role in system renewal by acting as stewards of the entrepreneurial ecosystem and engaging a balanced set of relevant stakeholders to find ways to mutually coordinate their actions (Feld, 2012; Ostrom, 1990).

We summarize our insights in three propositions for successful entrepreneurial ecosystem management: one highlighting an approach to data and analysis, another highlighting an approach to design of activities, and a third highlighting an approach to implementation that set entrepreneurial ecosystem policymaking apart from traditional approaches to entrepreneurship policy. We then reflect these propositions against a live case of regional entrepreneurial ecosystem policymaking in practice in Scotland to check their face validity. Finally, we draw conclusions regarding the role of policymakers in entrepreneurial ecosystems and present normative suggestions.

We advance four contributions to the entrepreneurial ecosystem literature with this design. First, this is the first study to identify analysis and management challenges to policymaking, as posed by the systemic characteristics of entrepreneurial ecosystems. Second, this is the first study to translate policy insights accumulated in other socioeconomic and socioecological ecosystem domains to the context of entrepreneurial ecosystems. Third, we link deep stakeholder engagement, a feature of policy approaches in socioecological ecosystems, to stakeholder theory to generate insights on stakeholder selection and engagement. Finally, through our empirical case, we confirm the face validity of the propositions using a recent policymaking experience of entrepreneurial ecosystem management and draw lessons for entrepreneurial ecosystem management in national and regional contexts.

In the next section, we discuss characteristics of entrepreneurial ecosystems and associated challenges for policymaking. In the subsequent section, we review policy research that focuses on policy analysis and management in complex socioeconomic and socioecological systems. From this review we derive three general propositions for effective entrepreneurial ecosystem management. We follow this with a section in which we reflect these propositions against a case study of an ongoing process of Scottish entrepreneurial ecosystem facilitation, noting examples of good practice and instances where following the propositions could have generated superior outcomes. We then discuss the results and finish with a concluding section that outlines the implications of our contribution to entrepreneurial ecosystem policy.

Entrepreneurial Ecosystems: Definitions and Policy Challenges

It is increasingly appreciated that entrepreneurial action by individuals and entrepreneurial teams is subject to contextual influences (Autio, Kenney, Mustar, Siegal, & Wright, 2014). Yet, the systems approach to entrepreneurship remains nascent and theoretical and conceptual work conspicuously scarce (Autio, Kenney, Mustar, Siegel, & Wright, 2014; Auerswald, 2014; Spigel, 2017). The early works in this area have been mostly practitioner-oriented and eschewed conceptual discussion of their object (Feld, 2012; Isenberg, 2010). Such works tend to focus on regional agglomerations and specialized resources and also cover tacit aspects such as culture and institutions, but formal definitions are seldom offered. This problem even extends to more formal attempts to measure and assess entrepreneurial ecosystems (Spigel, 2017; Stangler & Bell-Masterson, 2015).

The lack of coherent theoretical underpinnings is reflected in definitional diversity. Stam (2014) suggested that an entrepreneurial ecosystem is an interdependent set of actors that is governed in such a way that it enables entrepreneurial action. However, entrepreneurial action is defined as the "pursuit of opportunities for innovation" (and not opportunities for generating entrepreneurial profit), and the definition does not specify welfare outcomes of the process.[1] Mason and Brown (2014, p. 5) suggested a rather more comprehensive definition as:

> a set of interconnected entrepreneurial actors (both potential and existing), organizations (e.g. firms, venture capitalists, business angels and banks), institutions (universities, public sector agencies and financial bodies), and processes (business birth rate, rate of [high-growth firms], number of serial entrepreneurs and blockbuster entrepreneurs, and levels of entrepreneurial ambition and sell-out mentality in the society).

This definition lists structural, dynamic, and institutional elements attributed to entrepreneurial ecosystems in the literature but does not specify ecosystem outcomes. Another (unpublished) definition in the OECD LEED (Local Economic and Employment Development) initiative was proposed by Voegel (2013, p. 6):

> an interactive community within a geographic region, composed of varied and interdependent actors (e.g. entrepreneurs, institutions and organizations) and factors (e.g. markets, regulatory framework, support setting, entrepreneurial culture), which evolves over time and whose actors and factors coexist and interact to promote new venture creation.

---

[1] Stam also presents a graphical illustration which includes "framework conditions," "systemic conditions," outputs (entrepreneurial businesses), and outcomes including productivity, employment, and well-being. These are not included in the formal definition, however.

This definition is the most specific of the three in terms of its explicit focus on new venture creation—but consequent system-level benefits are not elaborated.

The only peer-reviewed definition of entrepreneurial ecosystems, or as they called it, systems of entrepreneurship, is the one proposed by Acs et al. (2014) and adopted in this paper (quoted in the introduction).[2] The distinctive aspect of this definition is its emphasis on system-level resource allocation, rather than new venture creation, as the outcome of the entrepreneurial ecosystem dynamic. In this definition, the creation of new ventures is the mechanism that drives the resource allocation dynamic. This trial-and-error dynamic is driven by individuals who mobilize resources to pursue opportunities they perceive. This dynamic should drive productivity, as if the perceived opportunity turns out not to be real, the entrepreneurs will abandon the opportunity pursuit, and the resources will be reallocated towards alternative uses that yield a higher return. If, however, entrepreneurs persist in opportunity pursuit, this implies that that no alternative use of the mobilized resources can be found that offers a higher return. This, then, means that successful opportunity pursuits will allocate economic resources to their most productive use, implying welfare-increasing allocation for the resources. While Acs et al.'s (2014) definition does not elaborate specific components of the ecosystem, their discussion and proposed measurement approach resonates with received works by highlighting elements such as attitudes, culture, institutions, finance, technology transfer, and infrastructure.

As a context for policy action, entrepreneurial ecosystems differ from contexts usually addressed by entrepreneurship policy: those of "markets" (industries) and "systems of innovation" (Dodgson, Hughes, Foster, & Metcalfe, 2011). Markets and industries consist of sets of mostly independent actors who may link to form value chains. A typical policy challenge in such a context would arise when the market fails to perform a given activity (say, R&D) or supply the necessary resources for entrepreneurial firms (say, funding). A market failure mode of policy would address such gaps in a top-down mode by providing economic incentives (usually through subsidies) to encourage specific activities; or plug resource gaps through public intervention (Arrow, 1962; Audretsch, 2011). In contrast, a system failure policy would address structural, institutional, and other failures in the structure, activities, and functions of a given innovation system (Bergek et al., 2008; Carlsson & Jacobsson, 1997; Wooldhuis et al., 2005). While in this approach the structures and mechanisms governing the production of innovations are more complex and often multilayered, the focus of this approach remains on plugging gaps in different aspects of the system structure by means of top-down policy analysis and design; system-level outcomes are seen as produced by abstract "activities" and "functions" rather than by individual agents (Markard & Truffer, 2008). As Acs et al. (2014) noted, the systems of innovation approach, while recognizing the role of "entrepreneurial experimentation," still fails to see the individuals and teams behind the function they perform.

Entrepreneurial ecosystems differ from markets and systems of innovation by positioning the entrepreneurial individual or team at the center of the system dynamic (see also Stam, 2015). The ecosystem influences both individual-level decision-making and aspirations (i.e., who decides to pursue opportunities through a new venture and with

---

[2] Spigel (2017) does not advance a formal definition.

which aspirations), as well as the ability of the new venture to reach its full potential (regulated through, e.g., resource availability and governance systems). This focus on entrepreneurial action and the realization of the welfare-generating potential set up by that action constitutes perhaps the most important differentiator of the entrepreneurial ecosystem concept relative to market failure and system failure approaches. In the market failure thinking, action is assumed to follow automatically once the appropriate economic incentives and price signals are in place. In the system failure thinking, action (in the form of functions performed by the system) is assumed to follow automatically once the proper structures and institutions are in place. The entrepreneurial ecosystems approach recognizes that cause–effect relationships in an ecosystem are complex; economic incentives alone do not fully explain individual-level motivations to act, and the welfare resulting from an action may depend on whether the ecosystem as a whole supports the realization of the full potential of that action.

We suggest that the complexity of entrepreneurial ecosystems challenges traditional approaches to policy-making, for four reasons. First, knowledge of the inner workings of the ecosystem is distributed across multiple stakeholders, whose localized, often one-to-one, interactions collectively coproduce ecosystem-level outcomes. Second, actions taken by stakeholders can have direct and indirect cascading effects within complex causal chains, some of which may be mutually reinforcing. Third, the stakeholders may be imperfectly aligned, both in goals and activities. Fourth, their interlocking relationships, combined with imperfectly distributed information, can produce a high level of inertia. We explore these four features below.

As noted above, the services rendered by entrepreneurial ecosystems are diffuse: the allocation of resources towards productive uses through the creation and operation of innovative, high-growth new ventures. This trial-and-error activity is carried out in myriad microlevel interactions, which are embedded in an idiosyncratic ecosystem structure. Because opportunity pursuit decisions are influenced not only by opportunity size but also by local factors such as personal opportunity costs and local social norms, much of the knowledge relevant for understanding the ecosystem dynamic is embedded in the ecosystem structure itself, and therefore, not easily extracted and codified (Hayek, 1945; Kirzner, 1997). This embeddedness means that no single individual or organization is likely to have a full and complete insight into how the ecosystem works, nor is it trivial to create comprehensive enough statistics to support such insight. Codified data on the ecosystem inputs and outputs alone does not yet inform us how inputs are converted into outputs.

The second challenge, that of fully understanding how exactly entrepreneurial ecosystems work, goes beyond mapping ecosystem structure (a reasonably straightforward exercise), because ecosystem outcomes are often produced in cascading effect chains. For example, if a given ecosystem does not facilitate sufficient numbers of high-growth ventures, is the problem caused by funding gaps, lack of high-growth expertise, or failure of high-potential individuals to start new businesses? Tracking real causes of ecosystem bottlenecks often requires a fine-grained understanding of a range of interrelated causal chains. If the cascading effects that coproduce system-level outcomes are not fully known, policies designed to facilitate a given favored outcome may end up producing unintended consequences (Merton, 1936). The possibility of unintended consequences grows higher as the cascading effect chains grow more complex.

The third feature of the challenge is stakeholder misalignment. Although collaboration and rational alignment of stakeholders is often assumed, there is a strong possibility of stakeholder misalignment arising from diverging and competing stakeholder interests and imperfect information flows between stakeholders, resulting in suboptimal local equilibria. If left unattended, this may undermine collective commitment to implementing policy actions, sustain inefficient generalism among competing stakeholders, and inhibit productive interactions in entrepreneurial ecosystems.

The fourth feature of the challenge is system inertia. Due to their complexity, socioeconomic systems tend to exhibit strong inertial properties and high path dependency (Gustafsson & Autio, 2011). Because of complex interactions between system elements, top-down policy effort may simply dissipate into the system without leaving much visible impact on the system dynamic.

Although these four features of entrepreneurial ecosystems—also common to natural ecosystems—undermine the feasibility of market and system failure policies, the entrepreneurial ecosystems literature has not discussed their implications for entrepreneurial ecosystem management. However, these challenges have been explored in socioecological ecosystem and collective governance literature. We next review insights and approaches from this literature to develop theoretical propositions applicable in the context of entrepreneurial ecosystems.

Management of Complex Socioecological Ecosystems

Socioecological and collective governance literatures have explored policy approaches that address head on the challenges of distributed knowledge, cascading cause–effect chains, stakeholder misalignment, and system inertia (e.g., Bowles & Gintis, 1998, 2002; Stringer et al., 2006; Vollan & Ostrom, 2010). These literatures have explored policy-making approaches that entail multipolar coordination and generation of collective commitment among hierarchically independent, yet mutually dependent, cospecialized agents to manage shared resources for common good and resolve ecosystem bottlenecks to enhance the overall functioning of the ecosystem. Examples of collective governance challenges explored in these literatures include the management of fish stocks to prevent overexploitation (Gutiérrez, Hilborn, & Defeo, 2011; McClanahan, Castilla, White, & Defeo, 2009) and the collective management of forests to prevent exhaustion of firewood stocks (Vatn, 2007).

Entrepreneurial ecosystems resemble socioecological ecosystems in that stakeholders need to undertake essentially voluntary action to generate common-good benefits that materialize in the future. The collective governance literature suggests that voluntary action to enhance ecosystem functioning cannot be motivated by economic self-interest alone, as short-term financial incentives for participation in the common project may distort and even crowd out common-good motivations (Vollan, 2008). Therefore, collaborative governance literature emphasizes deep forms of stakeholder engagement, which harness intrinsic motivations, foster a stewardship attitude towards the ecosystem, and encourage voluntary contribution (Bowles & Gintis, 1998; Das & Teng, 2002; Ekeh, 1974; Kofinas, 2009). Although the emphasis is on the generation of common-good benefits, this is not purely altruistic behavior, as common-good outcomes through collective action benefit all ecosystem stakeholders. Applied in the context of entrepreneurial ecosystems, ecosystem management needs to rely on voluntary participation motivated by "enlightened entrepreneurial self-interest" that recognizes that the pursuit of private and common good benefits can be more effective when aligned (Van de Ven, Sapienza, & Villanueva, 2007).

Stakeholder engagement is central for multipolar policy-making and implementation. The depth of engagement with ecosystem stakeholders can range from shallow top-down communication to bottom-up consultation, and to the deepest form, participation, where information flows both ways in an iterative fashion (Stringer et al., 2006). Deep stakeholder engagement can tap knowledge within the ecosystem and uncover hidden interactions and cause–effect chains. It can also facilitate multipolar coordination and collective governance (Seppelt et al., 2011). By facilitating mutual coalignment and specialization among ecosystem stakeholders, deep stakeholder engagement can preempt potential conflicts due to lack of trust and mutual awareness (Lichtenstein, 2014). Even when hard facts are available, they may not be accepted by key stakeholders if these have not been constructively engaged in the ecosystem analysis and management processes (McClanahan et al., 2009; van den Belt, 2004, p. 7). In summary, deep stakeholder engagement can overcome system inertia by allowing stakeholders to become active participants in ecosystem analysis and management, thus facilitating joint action to resolve ecosystem constraints (Pahl-Wostl, 2002; Smit & Wandel, 2006).

Several approaches have been developed to promote deep stakeholder engagement and discourage free-riding in socioecological and socioeconomic systems. These include adaptive governance (Ostrom, 1990), polycentric governance (Pahl-Wostl, 2002), adaptive management (Stringer et al., 2006), community governance (Bowles & Gintis, 2002), generative leadership (Lichtenstein, 2014), and transition management (Nill & Kemp, 2009). These approaches harness the knowledge, attitudes, and actions of individual stakeholders to produce a broader and deeper understanding of the ecosystem dynamic, promote collective commitment to resolving problems, and incorporate learning into policy analysis and management through feedback loops that engage these actors (Bowles & Gintis, 2002; Vollan & Ostrom, 2010; Wilson & Howarth, 2002). We next review stakeholder consultation and participation approaches and elaborate implications for entrepreneurial ecosystem management.

Stakeholder Consultation

Stakeholder consultation facilitates bottom-up flow of information from ecosystem stakeholders to policy-makers (Stringer et al., 2006). With consultation, ecosystem stakeholders are identified and consulted in order to help policymakers understand the ecosystem, sometimes with the help of approaches such as Integrated Assessment (IA) methodologies (Rotmans, 1998) or systems dynamics modeling (van den Belt, 2004). The breadth and depth of information gleaned in basic stakeholder consultation may vary with the method of engagement. These range from semistructured individual or group interviews (Kaplowitz & Hoehn, 2001) to participant observation and focus groups (Kahan, 2001; Markova, Linell, Grossen, & Salazar Orvig, 2007; Smit & Wandel, 2006) to surveys (BenDor, Shoemaker, Thill, Dorning, & Meentemeyer, 2014).

Whereas stakeholder interviews and surveys are typically broad-based, focus groups are designed to produce insight into more narrowly defined aspects of the ecosystem (Kahan, 2001; Kaplowitz & Hoehn, 2001). Interviews and surveys solicit broad understandings of the ecosystem as a whole, drawing on inputs from a range of different stakeholders. In contrast, focus groups facilitate deep insight on specific issues. This has implications for how focus groups are organized. As the purpose is digging deep into a specific issue, coherence in participant backgrounds takes precedence over diversity. Focus group participants need to be well aware of the domain area, and their participants need to be able to communicate effectively with one another. Also, focus group discussions tend to be more narrowly focused on sets of closely related issues, in lieu of exploring and uncovering previously unexplored issues. Finally, consensus-building and commitment-building play less of a role in focus groups, whose purpose is more on the production of well-defined outputs such as specific calls to action. This tends to imply less free-flowing and more intense sessions that tend to be shorter in duration than stakeholder discussion groups (Kahan, 2001).

Stakeholder Participation

Stakeholder participation assigns a more active role than stakeholder consultation to ecosystem stakeholders, engaging stakeholders not just in ecosystem analysis but also in ecosystem management (Stringer et al., 2006). Several methods have been reported in the socioecological and collective governance literatures. For example, adaptive management uses both "hard" facts (i.e., codified data) and insight derived through deep stakeholder engagement to encourage social learning and develop simulation models to better manage socioecological systems (Holling, 1978; Stringer et al., 2006). Feedback mechanisms are built into this approach to enhance adaptation. Collective action draws on the theory of adaptive governance (Ostrom, 1990) as an alternative to top-down governance (Meinzen-Dick, & Di Gregorio, 2004). This approach is increasingly deployed in large-scale renewal of neighbourhoods and even cities, under the term "collective impact" (Hanleybrown, Kania, & Kramer, 2012). It also has parallels in the transition approach to sustainable innovation policy in the Netherlands (Nill & Kemp, 2009).

Collective action requires careful and sensitive management. The ecosystem needs to be at a scale that is big enough to be self-sustaining but small enough so that the major stakeholders know each other. Some key principles to avoid unintended consequences, misalignment, and inertia include reciprocity, recognition, validation, and differentiation (Meilasari-Sugiana, 2012). These help bind people collectively to the mission, whether it is to facilitate a sustainable yield of biomass or of high-quality entrepreneurs.

The approach known as collective impact follows similar principles: common agenda, shared measurement systems, mutually reinforcing activities, continuous communication, and the presence of a backbone organization (Hanleybrown et al., 2012). Transition management exhibits the following features: long-term thinking (at least 25 years) as a framework for short-term action; thinking in terms of multiple domains; and a focus on learning, including learning-by-doing, doing-by-learning, and learning about a variety of options (Nill & Kemp, 2009).

In stakeholder participation, stakeholders engage with each other, repeatedly, with a view to their coordinated, collective action to pursue a shared vision. Policymakers can facilitate this by creating relational space for stakeholders, that is, opportunities for "reflective learning across organizational boundaries, which is enabled by, and in turn gives rise to, collaborative projects" (Bradbury-Huang, Lichtenstein, Carroll, & Senge, 2010, p. 109).

Finally, Lichtenstein (2014) provides a set of techniques for managing emergence or renewal of human systems based on complexity science that map onto a generalized five-stage model of ecosystem emergence and renewal. They include disrupting existing patterns, encouraging experiments, surfacing conflict, supporting rich interaction, catalysing collective action, correlating the system, recombining resources, leaders accepting tags as role models, and leveraging local resources. Many of these techniques can also be seen in descriptions of the collective management of other complex socioeconomic systems (e.g., Meilasari-Sugiana, 2012; Meinzen-Dick & Di Gregorio, 2004; Nill & Kemp, 2009). By linking them to phases of emergence, Lichtenstein offers a manual on managing system change to managers of complex systems.

Summarizing, the ecosystem management approaches reviewed above share numerous commonalities, deep stakeholder engagement being the defining one. This is employed to uncover hard-to-access information on ecosystem interactions, to enhance multipolar coordination, and to motivate and commit stakeholders to ecosystem improvement. These characteristics respond to ecosystem management challenges created by distributed knowledge, cascading cause–effect chains, stakeholder misalignment, and resulting system inertia. The arguments suggest three theoretical propositions that we explore next in our case study of the Scottish innovation-based entrepreneurial ecosystem:

Propostion 1: In entrepreneurial ecosystems, deep stakeholder engagement will produce richer and more actionable insight into ecosystem workings than will information and data derived from external observation alone.

Propostion 2: An understanding of cascading effects will help generate more productive insight (from a policy perspective) than will the study of market and structural failures in entrepreneurial ecosystems.

Propostion 3: A careful consideration of entrepreneurial ecosystem stakeholders, their motivations, and power relations will enable more efficient policy action than one that considers all stakeholders as homogenous.

By drawing on the entrepreneurial ecosystem facilitation case in Scotland, we can see how deep and participative stakeholder engagement approaches can be harnessed to enhance the functioning of entrepreneurial ecosystems.

Scottish Innovation-Based Entrepreneurial Ecosystem

Method

Because of the novelty of the ecosystems approach to entrepreneurship policy, there have been relatively few policy initiatives that qualify as entrepreneurial ecosystem analysis and management initiatives, and there is no database storing data on entrepreneurial ecosystem policy effectiveness. A quantitative method of testing hypotheses drawn from our propositions is therefore not feasible. We therefore adopt systematic process analysis as our research method (Hall, 2006). Systematic process analysis uses rich longitudinal data and reflects on findings against what the researchers would expect to see. It enables the investigation of the face validity of propositions. Specifically, we chose a qualitative approach called "pattern matching" (Geels & Penna, 2015; Yin, 1994), in which the pattern of events predicted by theory is compared with the pattern of events exhibited in the case. To avoid confirmation bias, we actively sought chains of events that did not fit our theory, and compared theorized patterns against competing propositions.

Because the still ongoing initiative has progressed in stages, we are able to compare insights produced by codified secondary data alone to insights produced through stakeholder engagement, allowing us to compare the effectiveness of alternative approaches to ecosystem facilitation. Because one of the authors has participated in the initiative as a participant-observer, we had rich data available to gauge levels of stakeholder alignment, commitment, and inertia during the initiative, enabling us to compare the effectiveness of participative approaches against more traditional approaches to entrepreneurship policy. We next describe our empirical context.

REAP Scotland

The Scottish entrepreneurial ecosystem policy initiative was triggered by participation of a Scottish team in a series of workshops organized by Massachusetts Institute of Technology (MIT) from 2012 to 2014. This programme, known as REAP (Regional Entrepreneurship Acceleration Program) sought to facilitate policy targeting high-potential innovation-based entrepreneurship (IBE). The Scottish team comprised two senior enterprise agency managers, a university representative (the second author), and three entrepreneurs. The team met regularly (usually once a month) from December 2011 to March 2015, and there were also four intensive three-day sessions with participating teams from other countries between 2012 and 2014.

The Scottish exercise used secondary data and interviews to assess regional innovation capacity and entrepreneurship capacity under six themes: people, funding, infrastructure, policy, rewards and norms, and demand. Potential growth clusters were then identified. Early work in the Scottish exercise found that while good quality secondary data was often available at the regional level for innovation capacity and clusters, measures of entrepreneurial capacity were unsatisfactory. There was also a need for rigorous benchmarking of elements of the regional ecosystem against each other and against equivalent elements in other regions or equivalent sized nations.

The Scottish team decided to ground their analysis of the Scottish entrepreneurial ecosystem on data provided by the Global Entrepreneurship and Development Index (GEDI) method (Acs et al., 2014). The GEDI methodology builds on the systems of entrepreneurship theory and portrays the quality (instead of quantity) of the entrepreneurially driven resource allocation dynamic in entrepreneurial ecosystems. It does so by combining individual-level data on entrepreneurial attitudes, ability, and aspirations with data describing the context within which these processes are expressed or repressed. The outcome of this methodology is an index composed of a set of interactions between national-level measures of rates of individual attitudes, ability, and aspirations and institutional-level variables that moderate the impact of individual-level variables on productivity growth. Unlike measures quantifying rates of self-employment, which tend to decline with increasing rates of economic development at a decreasing rate (Carree & Thurik, 2008), the GEDI is positively associated with gross domestic product (GDP) per capita for most of its range (Acs et al., 2014).

The distinctive characteristics of the GEDI methodology reflect well the complexity of entrepreneurial ecosystems, and therefore, the policy challenges described earlier.

First, the GEDI methodology contextualizes individual-level data by weighting it with data describing a country's framework conditions for entrepreneurship, thereby seeking to capture embedded complexity in entrepreneurial ecosystems. Complexity is further reflected in GEDI's use of 14 context-weighted measures to portray entrepreneurial attitudes, ability and aspirations in the ecosystem. The GEDI methodology also allows different index pillars to interact and, thus, coproduce ecosystem performance. This last feature also captures the notion that national entrepreneurial performance may be held back by "bottleneck factors"—that is, poorly performing pillars that may constrain system performance (see Acs et al., 2014 for a description of the Penalty for Bottleneck methodology).

The distinctive aspects of the GEDI approach fitted well with the aim of the Scottish team to describe, diagnose, and enhance the Scottish entrepreneurial ecosystem. For example, the GEDI features a holistic approach in which a deficiency in one factor can have knock-on effects on other parts of the ecosystem, simulating the notion of cascading effects. The index also appeared to provide comprehensive coverage of all elements of an entrepreneurial ecosystem outlined above with the exception of policy measures, though it did cover current institutions which could reflect past and current policy. It also contained a combination of multiple input and output measures, which is necessary in any assessment of an ecosystem.[3] What GEDI did not do was engage in any form of sectoral cluster analysis. Fortunately, a great deal of work on clusters had already been done and designated growth sectors formed part of the Scottish Government's Economic Strategy (Scottish Government, 2011). At no time did the Scottish team consider that additional analysis was required in this area.

The Scottish team adapted the GEDI methodology to a regional level of analysis and used this to identify possible gaps between the areas of current policy focus and bottlenecks in the entrepreneurial ecosystem suggested by the GEDI analysis. It was recognized, first, that the GEDI analysis was only as good as the quality and choice of data, and second, that it could stimulate wider debate on the health of an innovative entrepreneurial ecosystem, but should not be used as a computerized "policy-creating machine."

Policymakers want to know how they can achieve most leverage in enhancing an entrepreneurial ecosystem. Understanding the strength of the links between pillars that appear to be linked might help reveal critical leverage points. Unfortunately, the GEDI analysis did not reveal the strength of links between pillars. Because all ecosystems are unique, the GEDI methodology assumes that all links have the same strength and that all pillars cost the same to change. Furthermore, it could not reveal whether the bottlenecks were causal or merely symptoms of underlying, deep-seated weaknesses in an innovation-based entrepreneurial ecosystem. Therefore, the Scottish team decided it had to be supplemented by expert stakeholder judgment.

The method of entrepreneurial ecosystem analysis and management developed by the Scottish team is outlined in Figure 19.1. The process begins with data collection of each variable in the GEDI framework for the focal region and appropriate benchmark regions or nations. Once bottlenecks have been identified using sensitivity analysis, the next step is to test the convergent validity of the bottlenecks themselves by

---

[3] A table of these measures is available from the authors on request.

```
Locate regional measures of GEDI variables
                    ↓
Establish national or regional benchmarks for the region
                    ↓
Relative and absolute comparison with benchmarks
                    ↓
Sensitivity analysis to elicit a bottleneck configuration
                    ↓
Validity test of bottleneck pillars
                    ↓
Group bottlenecks under themes
                    ↓
Engage with 10–15 stakeholders per theme to assess face
validity of bottlenecks/ uncover underlying causes
                    ↓
Smaller short-term task groups of stakeholders focused
on solutions to bottlenecks/underlying causes
                    ↓
Set of actions agreed and monitoring of actors in place
                    ↓
Monitoring of outcomes and impact
```

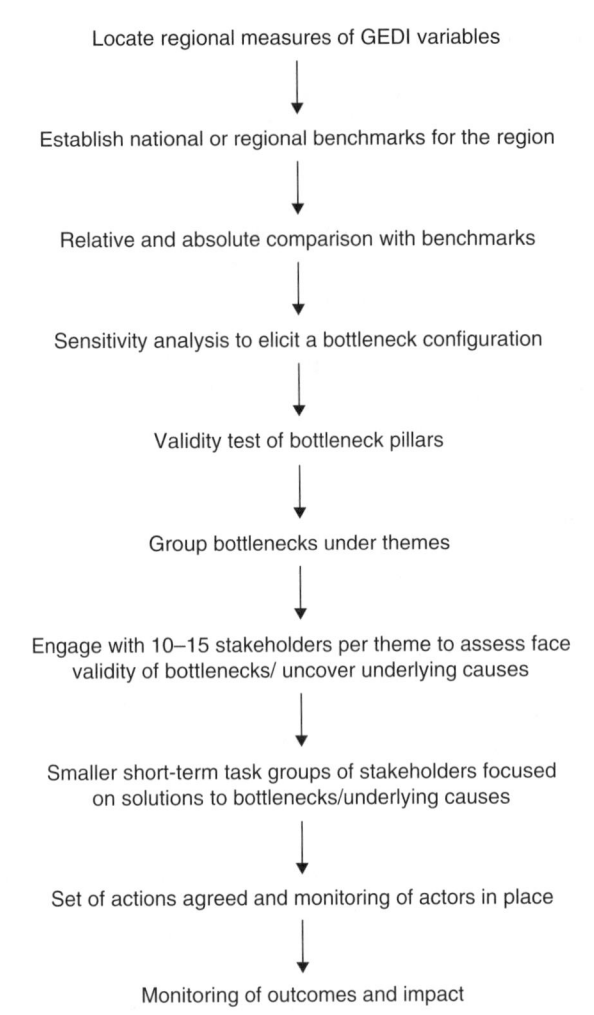

Figure 19.1 Process model of the Scottish entrepreneurial ecosystem exercise.

employing alternative measures of institutional variables. If the bottleneck measures are robust to alternative specifications, the next step is to group them under themes and then test them on groups of expert stakeholders. Assuming the GEDI assessment passes this test, one could explore possible links between bottleneck pillars, underlying causes, and priorities for action with the experts. If there are a limited number of underlying causes, this should be apparent in the degree of agreement across the different stakeholder groups, providing both convergent validity and face validity to the assessment.

Assuming this consultative phase delivers a consensus on a limited number of linked causes and priorities for action, the next stage is to appoint short-term task groups of lead stakeholders to actively participate in the process by developing solutions and taking action. This, in turn, could lead to a monitoring and learning phase in which momentum is maintained and the effect of different actions is compared.

Field Trial in Scotland

The Scottish core team drew up a project specification which, first, requested a GEDI-type assessment of Scotland's entrepreneurial performance against benchmark nations within and outside the UK on the set of six priority themes and, second, requested a sensitivity analysis of the results to identify likely bottlenecks to the acceleration of innovative entrepreneurship in Scotland.

The first stage was to regionalize the individual and institutional variables that the GEDI research team had found to best represent the quality and size of the entrepreneurial ecosystem at the national level. The actual individual and framework variables employed are described in Levie et al. (2013), and the pillars are described in Autio et al. (2012). This list was debated by the Scottish team both before and after the list was populated with data, resulting in several changes to the data specification, including a change from two-year to four-year moving averages because of the low frequency of entrepreneurs in the population, and a change in the institutional measure used for risk capital, which was subsequently adopted more generally by GEDI. This corresponds to the first step of the method.

Six of the 14 measures were taken from perceptual measures generated for the Global Competitiveness Index (a complex index of national competitiveness devised for the World Economic Forum) by senior corporate managers in different countries, and it was not possible to find equivalent regional measures. These measures were of business risk, technology absorption capability, staff training, market dominance, technology transfer, and business strategy. Another three measures—business freedom, globalization, and venture capital—all drawn from different global indices with national-level indicators, were assumed to differ little at the home nation level of the UK. Truly regional estimates were found from published sources for seven of the 14 institutional measures.

The Scottish team requested four benchmarking assessments: Scotland versus all 78 economies for which data was available; Scotland versus 27 innovation-driven economies according to the 2011 World Economic Forum's *Global Competitiveness Report 2011*; Scotland versus "Arc of Prosperity" countries, a Scottish Government term for small modern nations located around Scotland (Ireland, Iceland, Norway, Denmark, and Finland); and Scotland versus other home nations within the UK (England, Wales, and Northern Ireland).

A second work package consisted of a sensitivity analysis of the results, which used the Penalty for Bottleneck methodology to simulate how weaknesses in one component might affect the entrepreneurial ecosystem as a whole. In this analysis, weak pillars were artificially boosted to gauge the effect of additional policy effort to improve them. Due to simplifying assumptions, the purpose of this sensitivity analysis was not to be prescriptive, but rather, to serve as a basis for discussion by stakeholders in the next phase of assessment.

Figure 19.2 is an example of benchmarking using a spider diagram, in this case against Arc of Prosperity countries. It plots Scotland's scores and shows visually where Scotland fits relative to the other countries. Denmark appears strong in pillars where Scotland is relatively weak, such as process innovation and networking, and where it is absolutely weak, such as Opportunity Perception. Ireland follows a similar pattern to Scotland, and is worse in some pillars, such as Opportunity Perception and Opportunity Start-up. Iceland fares worse than Scotland in Competition but better in some pillars where

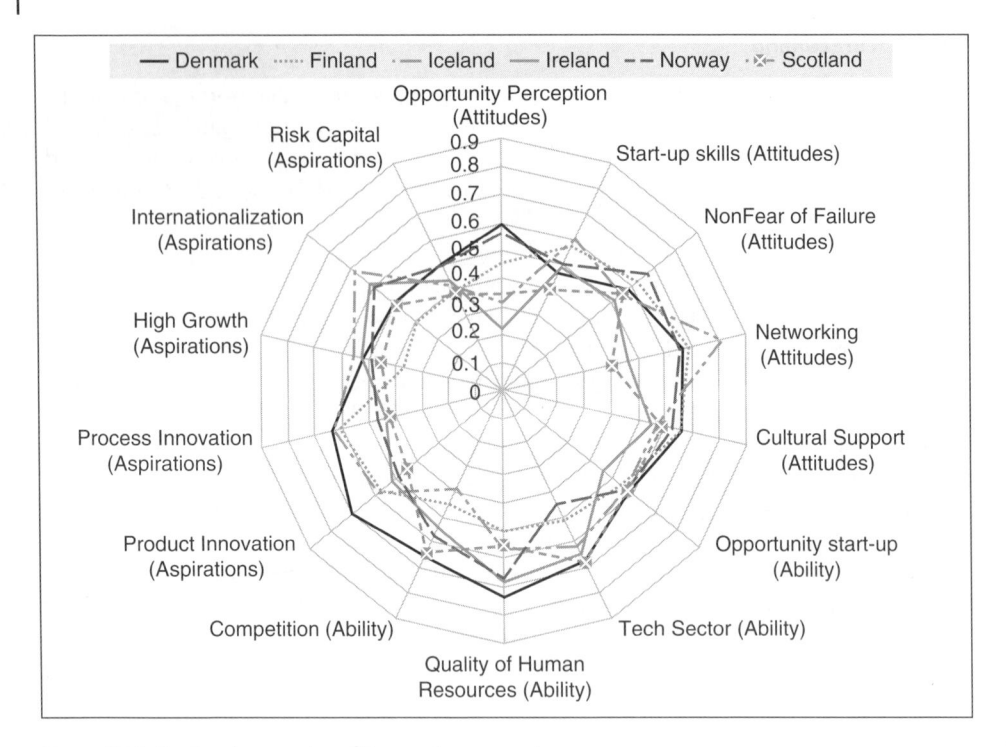

Figure 19.2 Scotland versus Arc of Prosperity economies.

Scotland is weak, such as Process Innovation and Networking. Finland does better than Scotland in most Attitudes measures and the innovation-related Aspiration measures.

Against the UK's other home nations—England, Wales, and Northern Ireland—Scotland appeared as performing less well than England in Opportunity Perception and Start-up Skills, and better than Wales and Northern Ireland in some ability measures and Opportunity Perception. (A full set of benchmark figures and tables is included in Levie et al., 2013.)

In relation to 27 innovation-driven countries, three weak institutional variables were apparent: the current level of participation in postsecondary education among young adults (aged 18–22), the level of internet usage, and Gross Expenditure in R&D (GERD). These had knock-on effects on their respective pillars: Start-up skills, Networking, and Process Innovation. Most individual aspiration variables were also relatively weak. Scotland was in the fourth quartile of innovation-driven nations in Process Innovation, Product Innovation and Risk Capital. The benchmarking also revealed areas where Scotland compared well with other countries. Scotland ranked second out of 78 countries in the Tech Sector, third in the Competition pillar, and fourth in the Opportunity Start-up pillar.

A sensitivity analysis estimated "optimum" additional allocation of policy effort for a 20% improvement in Scotland's GEDI score, based on simplifying assumptions. This improvement would bring Scotland from 16th place to around 4th place in the rank of 78 countries in the GEDI database, behind the United States, Denmark, and Sweden and just ahead of Australia. The analysis suggested that almost 50% of additional allocation should be focused on Aspiration pillars, with another 35% on three Attitudes pillars. This sensitivity analysis assumed that the cost of improving each pillar is the same, which of course is unrealistic. It nevertheless provided a basis for stakeholders to debate alternative scenarios, a useful guide to possible areas for further investigation, and facilitated debate as to where the goals should be set. The team reached a consensus that an absolute score of less than 0.5 or a ranking of 19 or higher justified further investigation of a given pillar. Three Attitude pillars (Opportunity Perception, Start-up Skills, Networking) and all five Aspiration pillars met this criterion.

Having identified eight pillars to focus on, the next stage was to validate the bottleneck pillars with four stakeholder consultation meetings in February 2013, to which a mix of prominent and representative members of Scotland's entrepreneurial ecosystem were invited to debate between one and three of the eight pillars. (In October 2012, these individuals had all been invited to a dinner in Edinburgh. The Scottish core team felt that this would help to give a sense of purpose and legitimacy to subsequent stakeholder engagement.) Four different sets of about a dozen stakeholders attended one of four consultation meetings, which were chaired by members of the core team and recorded verbatim by a professional court recorder. These consultation meetings suggested a set of perceived weaknesses in Scotland's entrepreneurial ecosystem that cross-linked the bottlenecks. A 23-page summary report was written based on a content analysis of the stakeholder consultation meetings. Identified concerns included: networking and networks (67 mentions); business, management and commercial skills (28 mentions) and in particular sales and selling skills (21 mentions); global outlook (10 mentions) and the need to connect with other cultures (11 mentions); the contribution of Scottish universities (12 mentions); mentors (12 mentions); role models (eight mentions); access to markets (four mentions) and finance (12 mentions) including those outside Scotland; and exits (four mentions). Several participants noted how individuals who had had the opportunity to experience entrepreneurial environments such as Boston returned to Scotland fired with enthusiasm.

In a 24-hour retreat in May 2013, the core team whittled down the identified issues (and underlying causes) into five priority themes: financing for growth (including exits for investors in angel-backed companies, increasing access to institutional and international funds, etc.); effective connections (this included networks but was more fundamental than mere networking); skills for growth for leadership teams within IBE ventures; role of the universities in the IBE ecosystem; and role models and positive messages. Chairs and members of the stakeholder community were identified for high-level task groups who would be charged with developing and implementing solutions to each of the five themes. (This corresponds to "stakeholder participation": the deepest level of stakeholder engagement identified in the literature review above.) At least one member of the Scottish core team was appointed to each task group to facilitate information flows between task groups. In developing the briefs for the task groups, the team agreed to adopt the collective impact approach of Hanleybrown et al. (2012) that seeks to get wide stakeholder buy-in and consensus on the direction of travel rather than a top-down directive approach. As a reminder, the five key aspects of this approach are a common agenda, shared measurement systems, mutually reinforcing activities, continuous communication, and the presence of a backbone organization.

Between May 2013 and August 2015, the task groups evolved in different ways. The Financing for Growth task group was already formed as a separate committee of the Royal Society of Edinburgh, charged with coming up with proposals for the Scottish

Government on the financing of early-stage growth companies. It published an advice paper in June 2014. An online questionnaire to assess the demand for growth finance was piloted. The effective connections group developed a guide to networking within Scotland for entrepreneurs, which was updated annually, and the group organized an event to bring networking organizations together in November 2014. The universities group developed a set of actions and planned a series of five workshops for relevant university staff on each action point in 2015–2016 plus a manual on enhancing university entrepreneurial ecosystems, sponsored by an enterprise agency. The Scottish team also consulted with experienced entrepreneurs to draw up a list of critical skills for CEOs of growth companies under the "skills for growth" bottleneck. The enterprise agencies took this forward to create SCALE, a skills for growth program for early-stage entrepreneurs, launched in August 2015 with 70 entrepreneurs and input from MIT and Harvard Business School; and the University of Strathclyde with Santander Bank launched the Growth Advantage Programme (GAP) for established entrepreneurs in May 2015, with 20 CEOs in the first cohort. Under the role models theme, an enterprise agency ran a series of events and initiatives to encourage women to become entrepreneurs and to encourage women entrepreneurs to serve as role models to other women. It also greatly expanded its online suite of videos of Scottish entrepreneurs of growing businesses.

In June 2014, a 48-page report was released by the Scottish team to all stakeholders who had been consulted or had participated in the Scottish exercise (Chisholm et al., 2014). The team deliberately chose a soft launch with minimal publicity, as it wished to ensure that the process did not end with a report that might, like so many before it, be shelved and forgotten. The report listed the calls for action under each of the five themes, and also called for a backbone organization independent of government agencies to take on the management of the process. At the time of the report, the team thought that a new organization might need to be formed to do this. However, coinciding with the release of the report, the merger of two prominent independent stakeholder organizations in the Scottish entrepreneurial ecosystem, the Entrepreneurial Exchange and the Saltire Foundation, was announced. Subsequently, the incoming chief executive of this new organization, Entrepreneurial Scotland, was invited to join the core team and, at the time of writing, a proposal that Entrepreneurial Scotland serve as the backbone organization was under active consideration.

Case Reflection

We now consider the applicability of alternative policy approaches against the chain of events presented in the previous section. A traditional approach to correcting system failures would rely on secondary data describing the structures and processes of the system to be improved. Based on our literature review above, we suggest that codified (i.e., externally observable) data alone is not likely to be sufficient to fully understand the complexities of emergent systemic processes and uncover cascading effect chains. If the traditional approach holds (i.e., that of relying on externally observable data alone and not engaging the multiple stakeholders), then a policymaker that engages stakeholders for entrepreneurial ecosystem analysis should find discrepancies between the understanding supported by codified data and the understanding emerging from stakeholder consultations. We illustrate this logical implication with examples of stakeholders questioning and finding weaknesses in the secondary data, finding gaps in the secondary data, and generating actions in priority areas that were not highlighted by the secondary data. Together, these examples suggest that a participative stakeholder engagement approach is likely to produce better results than external observation alone.

First, the core team driving the process of entrepreneurial ecosystem management in Scotland actively questioned the results in several of the items included in the secondary data analysis conducted for it by a third party. For example, the UK scored relatively poorly on the institutional measure of risk capital used by GEDI (a measure of corporate managers' perceptions of the availability of venture capital to early-stage ventures, published by the Global Competitiveness Index), but measured relatively well on other international measures of venture capital availability. The Scottish REAP team included several experts in young venture finance, and their knowledge of the UK risk capital market conflicted with this measure. On reflection, the GEDI team realized that the perceptions of middle managers in corporations might not accurately reflect financial flows on the ground and this measure was replaced with a measure of the Depth of the Capital Market for Venture Capital published by the the University of Navarre's Business School (IESE) and Ernst & Young Venture in the Capital and Private Equity Country Attractiveness Index. This did not rely on perceptions of managers with little exposure to venture capital, but instead was composed of measures of capital flows relevant to venture exits. This measure correlated highly with actual venture capital flows at the national level, and also reflected the expectations of the experts in the Scottish team. It was subsequently adopted by GEDI as the default measure of institutional risk capital.

In another example, secondary data indicated that Scotland has a relatively low proportion of individuals who invest in other individuals' new businesses, leading the secondary analysis to identify risk capital as a bottleneck. But stakeholders pointed out in consultation meetings that Scotland has a relatively well-developed business angel infrastructure, with some 22 angel syndicates and a transparent angel market, and the UK has exceptionally attractive incentives for wealthy individuals to invest in new ventures. Also this discrepancy triggered debate leading to the identification of funding flows (rather than business angels) as the real constraint of the Scottish ecosystem.

Further reflection on the pillars in which Scotland did well raised some doubts within the core team as to what was being measured within these pillars. For example, in the Competition pillar, the individual-level measure was the percentage of early-stage entrepreneurs who operate in markets where not many businesses offer the same product. The GEDI authors intended it to be a relative measure of product-market uniqueness, but it could also be interpreted as lack of competition due to low overall levels of entrepreneurship. Thus, Scotland appeared to do well on this measure, but it could actually be a sign of weakness rather than strength, because of the way the original survey item was worded. The institutional measure for this pillar was for the UK rather than Scotland, and might therefore not reflect the dominance of firms in a regional market like Scotland. Again, this could have flattered Scotland's ranking.

Because Scotland had relatively few necessity-driven entrepreneurs, it scored highly on a secondary measure of nascent and new early-stage entrepreneurs who initiated their business because of opportunity start-up motive. This measure intended to penalize countries with high proportions of necessity-driven, and by implication low-quality, start-ups. But, in Scotland, which had a relatively advanced social welfare system and a strong class-based society, it may simply have reflected the lack of perceived economic need or self-efficacy on the part of those without employment.

A second implication of our first theoretical conjecture was that by combining codified (secondary) data and stakeholder insights, a policymaker will produce a more complete understanding of the ecosystem. There is evidence to support this from the Scottish case. The four stakeholder consultation meetings conducted by the Scottish team identified links between the bottlenecks in the entrepreneurial ecosystem suggested by the secondary data. This is something the hard data itself did not do. Following a content analysis of the stakeholder consultation meetings and a full day of discussion by the core team, combining the GEDI and stakeholder analyses, the Scottish team was able to identify five linked issues that, if tackled comprehensively, could lift a range of pillars. These five themes only partially overlapped with the bottlenecks thrown up by the hard data analysis. For example, one issue raised repeatedly by entrepreneurs in the stakeholder group sessions was the relatively low perceived contribution by universities to the Scottish entrepreneurial ecosystem. This was not identified as an issue by the GEDI analysis. If indeed the university sector was a bottleneck, proceeding with policy based on the hard data alone would have omitted a bottleneck in the ecosystem. If it was not, a false attribution of a bottleneck in the system would have been identified. In the end, while the empirical evidence did not fully support the view of the stakeholders (and this evidence was published in the June 2014 report), the high-level task group on universities identified that the contribution of universities was uneven across Scotland and that there was much that Scottish universities could learn from each other.

The university theme is interesting because it was raised repeatedly as a bottleneck by entrepreneurs. Yet many of their claims were based on misunderstandings and not borne out by hard evidence subsequently collected by the Scottish team and incorporated into its June 2014 report. Examples included the belief that entrepreneurs taught all entrepreneurship classes in US universities, that universities were detached from industry, that it was extremely difficult to get technology out of a university, and that academics and researchers were unwilling to network. In fact, Scotland had one of the highest rates of R&D expenditure in Higher Education (HERD) and one of the lowest rates of R&D expenditure in the business sector (BERD) in the OECD, and Scottish universities had relatively high rates of knowledge exchange compared with the rest of the UK (Chisholm et al., 2014, p. 19). One of the tasks of the university task group, composed of "entrepreneurial professors" rather than professors of entrepreneurship, became not just how to enhance the connectivity of Scottish universities but also to educate entrepreneurs on how Scottish universities do engage in the ecosystem. On the other hand, it demonstrated that the degree of engagement varied greatly across the university sector and that universities had much to learn from each other: pockets of best practice were scattered through the university sector and not visible. This led the university task group to the idea of the sharing of best practice within the sector.

Our second proposition stated that deep stakeholder engagement produces causative insights that identify areas where concerted action can bring about productive change within an entrepreneurial ecosystem, lower the risk of unintended consequences in entrepreneurial ecosystem management, improve stakeholder alignment, and reduce the risk of ecosystem inertia dissipating the effect of policy action. If this proposition holds, then we should see instances where deep stakeholder engagement produced causative insights that identified areas where concerted action could bring about productive change within the Scottish entrepreneurial ecosystem. These could include recommendations for action that were identified as a result of the stakeholder participation but for which secondary data did not suggest a gap, thus demonstrating what the Scottish team might have missed by relying on the secondary data alone. Crucially, in order for this proposition to be supported, these actions would not be ones that provided incentives to address perceived market failure.

Of the five priority themes identified by the core team, the role of universities was not suggested by secondary data, while the priority action within the financing for growth theme, enabling an exit mechanism for investors, was not immediately obvious from the secondary data. Similarly, it was not obvious from the low networking score in the secondary data that, although Scotland had many networking organizations for entrepreneurs, many entrepreneurs did not know this and the networking organizations were not themselves well networked to each other. This prevented the Scottish team from needlessly developing new networking organizations but instead led it to create a guide to networking and an event that brought networking organizations together to inform each other on their activities. These actions improved alignment, lowered the risk of unintended consequences, and prevented inertia, which would have been the likely result of action that created a new networking organization. Significantly, the Scottish entrepreneurial ecosystem support landscape began to shift significantly in 2014 with the merger of the two major support organizations, the Entrepreneurial Exchange and the Saltire Foundation.

In another example, in addition to agreeing on the sharing of best practice, the entrepreneurial professors group agreed a set of stretch goals for the sector, including "enterprise for all." This combination of sharing of best practice to produce quick wins and long-term ambitious goals helped promote alignment and avoid inertia. Where one might have expected competitive stances between universities, instead a positive spirit of cooperation developed. This initiative developed independently of the existing range of financial incentives for universities to engage in knowledge exchange activity.

Under the skills for growth theme, there is evidence of actions that could be interpreted as market failure interventions and actions that were independent of market failure approaches. Both were initiated by stakeholders active in Scotland. For example, the Scottish enterprise agencies launched SCALE and the University of Strathclyde with Santander Bank launched GAP, as detailed above.

Our third proposition stated that in selecting and engaging stakeholders in an entrepreneurial ecosystem, policymakers need to understand and balance the power, legitimacy and urgency of different stakeholders. The Scottish core team looked for a balance between entrepreneurs, entrepreneurial financiers, government, corporates, and universities among participating stakeholders. A prime example of the wisdom of this approach is the issue of finance, where the two finance experts on the panel queried the measure of risk finance used by GEDI. Another example is where the stakeholder consultations raised the issues of exit for investors and the universities as bottlenecks, areas not covered by the GEDI framework. Because of the wide differences in background within the core team and the stakeholders they engaged with through consultation and participation, many differences of perspective on the problem were raised and as learning developed, core team members and task team members changed the way they perceived how they and their organizations could address the goal.

The makeup of the Scottish team was a difficult issue for the enterprise agencies who funded the Scottish exercise and invited stakeholders to join it. While civil servants responsible for entrepreneurship policy in Scotland were kept informed of the team's progress, they were not invited to become core team members. On the one hand, the Scottish team was concerned that in the heated political atmosphere leading up to the Scottish independence referendum in September 2014, part-formulated policy solutions might be prematurely adopted and announced rather than analyzed fully and managed bottom-up. In other words, a civil servant as a core team member might have too much power and urgency, upsetting the stakeholder balance. But on the other hand, absence of the central policymaker's perspective may have led to some blind spots on the part of the core team, and a chance was missed for social learning by civil servants.

Another constituency that was missing from the core team was corporate Scotland. While a representative group of senior corporate executives did participate at a separate stakeholder workshop, the presence of a corporate representative on the core team might have changed the dynamics of the team. The three sectors represented—enterprise agencies, universities and entrepreneurs—all had their disagreements at times and sometimes felt they had to defend their sectors. A corporate representative might have been seen as an honest broker, more objective, and more results-focused—and was, in fact, recommended by MIT.

Balance within the high-level task groups was also important. The core team opted to invite senior entrepreneurial professors in the main Scottish research universities to form the high-level task group for universities rather than professors of entrepreneurship or officials in technology transfer or enterprise centers. Entrepreneurial professors possessed relatively high levels of power, legitimacy and urgency within their institutions. They bought into the vision relatively quickly and recognized the value that could be gained from sharing best practice across the sector. They also attracted similar individuals from other universities, expanding the group to cover almost all higher education institutes in Scotland.

Experience with the high-level task groups to date suggests that regular monitoring and "holding of feet to the fire" is necessary to maintain momentum and prevent inertia. The core team regularly reviewed activity under each action plan and it became clear that "what gets measured gets done." At the same time, however, the high-level task groups represent a form of relational space that enables stakeholders, who might normally act as competitors, to collaborate and devise new actions or spread existing successful ones in ways that policymakers might not have imagined (Bradbury-Huang et al., 2010, p. 109). The actions produced by the effective connections and university groups were examples of this.

In summary, our empirical analysis provides consistent support for the propositions we derived from our theoretical analysis of entrepreneurial ecosystems, demonstrating the importance of deep stakeholder engagement in entrepreneurial ecosystem policy interventions.

Discussion

This chapter was inspired by the observation that while the concepts of entrepreneurial ecosystems and start-up ecosystems have rapidly gained currency in policy practitioner circles, both the concepts themselves and their implications for policy analysis and management of policy implementation have remained undertheorized. To address this gap, we have drawn on policy research in ecological economics to infer distinctive challenges faced by entrepreneurial ecosystem policy analysis and management, and, also, elaborated on the implications they pose for policy practice. Our core observation was that in complex, multipolar entrepreneurial ecosystems, where system performance is coproduced in localized, embedded interactions among ecosystem stakeholders, performance gaps are not easily reducible to well-defined market failures that can be addressed by top-down approaches in which stakeholder engagement is reduced to communication, such as those described by Arshed, Carter, and Mason (2014). Instead, stakeholder consultation and participation are required to enhance the understanding of how the system works, identify coherent policy actions that are more likely to yield a desired impact, realign stakeholders, and build stakeholder commitment to overcome systems inertia. Moreover, the choice of stakeholder should be determined by their current and potential influence on the ecosystem. We used the context provided by a Scottish entrepreneurial ecosystem facilitation initiative to explore the face validity of these propositions.

As such, participative approaches to policy design and implementation are not new—even to the increasing number of ecosystem management exercises currently under way in the area of entrepreneurship. Nevertheless, conceptual and theoretical underpinnings have lagged behind burgeoning policy practice. In this chapter, we have provided a theoretical treatment of the concept of entrepreneurial ecosystems, highlighting how they differ from other concepts that have guided policy theory and thinking—notably, those of markets and innovation systems. In our theoretical review, we highlighted four distinct challenges that characterize entrepreneurial ecosystems—and potentially undermine the applicability of market and structural failure approaches: (1) the creation of the ecosystem service through localized interactions among hierarchically independent, yet mutually codependent, cospecialized system stakeholders; (2) the potential for emergent cascading effects created by cross-dyad influences; (3) the resulting potential for ecosystem inertia; and (4) the need for commitment, action, and multipolar coordination by ecosystem stakeholders. Our major conceptual contribution has been to highlight and explicate such challenges and elaborate why received approaches to entrepreneurial ecosystem policy are not well equipped to deal with them.

Our main contribution to policy practice was to review policy approaches discussed in socioecological ecosystem and collective governance literatures and apply these insights in the context of entrepreneurial ecosystem management. Specifically, we highlighted the importance of soliciting deep stakeholder engagement in entrepreneurial ecosystem management and reviewed policy approaches for achieving this goal. We have illustrated why it is important to go beyond secondary, quantified data in entrepreneurial ecosystem analysis and why exactly deep stakeholder engagement matters in practice. While these approaches may seem like common sense to many a policy practitioner, examples of success in entrepreneurial ecosystem management nevertheless remain frustratingly few. As highlighted by Arshed et al. (2014), top-down policy declarations arguably remain the norm in entrepreneurship and policy initiatives vulnerable to capture by politicians. Similarly, most policy initiatives remain siloed, consistent with the market and structural failure approaches, and comprehensive, ecosystem-wide actions are few. This perhaps helps explain why the majority of attempts to replicate successful entrepreneurial hot-spots such as Silicon Valley have failed. By explicating and theoretically justifying principles of good management of entrepreneurial ecosystems, and by illustrating the application of these principles with rich case evidence from Scotland, we hope to contribute toward a wider and more meaningful adoption of an ecosystem management approach to entrepreneurship policy. We contend that, from a policy perspective, entrepreneurship should be viewed as a complex, dynamic ecosystem, and the effective management of such ecosystems is only possible when their distinctive management challenges are clearly understood.

Although we have illustrated advantages of an ecosystem approach to entrepreneurship policy, we are not implying that traditional policy approaches have no role to play in entrepreneurial ecosystem management. In the Scottish case, while our explorations supported the validity of Propositions 1, 2 and 3, there was also evidence that participative approaches alone—in the absence of codified data—may, in themselves, provide an insufficient picture of entrepreneurial ecosystem dynamics for policy analysis and management. In the Scottish case, evidence of the importance of codified data included stakeholders being informed and even surprised by the hard data. For example, Scottish team members were surprised that in relation to other innovation-driven countries, the current gross enrolment ratio in tertiary education in Scotland (proportion of 18- to 22-year-olds undergoing third level education) was relatively low. A second surprise was that Scotland fared best in the Ability pillars. The quantity of entrepreneurship in Scotland has long been perceived as relatively low. This demonstrated the advantage of the GEDI choice of Ability variables that reflect innovative entrepreneurship, not all entrepreneurship. Examples like this illustrate how successful ecosystem practices should be employed to complement and enhance insights achieved through market and structural failure practices, not blindly replace them.

Interestingly, throughout the whole Scottish exercise, no suggestions were made to add dimensions to the GEDI framework, only to improve certain measures of constructs. The hard data provided a foil, or basis for discussion rather than being accepted as the last word on the state of the ecosystem. It also enabled statements made by stakeholders to be compared with the hard data. In some cases, these statements were found to be untrue. In other cases, knowledge held by stakeholders revealed that the measures used for the hard data were unsuitable.

In an example where the systematic analysis of the hard data countered subjective bias, the sensitivity analysis highlighted the need to focus on areas of absolute weakness, rather than relative weakness. Scotland ranks in the fourth quartile of innovation-driven countries for three Aspiration pillars but no Attitude pillars. Yet the worse score of any pillar was Opportunity Perception, and this was identified as the bottleneck deserving the greatest allocation of additional effort. Because the GEDI methodology is based on the premise that the weakest pillars, not the relatively weak pillars, hold the entire entrepreneurial ecosystem in check, the sensitivity analysis spotlighted Opportunity Perception more than the relatively weak Aspiration pillars. This example again suggests that "soft" insights complement, but do not replace, "hard" facts.

While it is too early to conclusively assess the full impact of the ecosystem management approach in Scotland, it is striking that not one of the actions proposed in the Scottish report summarizing its findings required government to introduce new policies or change old ones. The actions focused on other stakeholders in the system, challenging them to commit to specific actions; through the high-level task groups, critical stakeholders had already been co-opted, helped to shape, and were committed to these actions. This stands in stark contrast to contemporary practices in the

UK of superficial conference-style communication with stakeholders and ministerial "surprise" announcements of policy decisions (Arshed et al., 2014; Bridge, 2010). This ecosystem analysis and management approach seems more humble, more cautious, more engaged, and more long term-oriented; the analysis took around two years, and the action phase has only just begun and is intended to last for the foreseeable future.

A limitation of this study is that we have focused on a single, albeit rich, case example, that of Scotland. In addition to allowing deep longitudinal immersion into rich data, this choice nevertheless carries obvious limitations, particularly where it comes to possible bias induced by idiosyncratic institutional conditions. For example, one reason for the absence of a clear role for central government in the actions may be that the general regulatory background for entrepreneurship in Scotland is relatively favorable. In 2014, the UK ranked eighth in the World Bank Ease of Doing Business ranking (World Bank, 2014). This may be why regulatory issues were not identified as bottlenecks. This raises the possibility that our propositions may be contingent on the relative maturity of the regulatory regime for entrepreneurship in a country. In countries where regulation is burdensome or rule of law is weak, there may indeed be a need for government as the central policy actor, at least in relation to the regulatory regime (Autio & Fu, 2015; Levie & Autio, 2011). Given that entrepreneurial ecosystem management engages stakeholder communities, there is little doubt that local and regional cultural and social norms will influence the effectiveness of alternative approaches to such engagement, for example. Future research should compare the effectiveness of attempts at analysis and management in different entrepreneurial ecosystems, using systematic process analysis to compare across cases (Hall, 2006).

Another limitation is that we have focused more on country-level rather than regional-level analysis. Although part of the UK, Scotland has its own parliament and considerable independence in economic and fiscal policy. The focus of the Scottish exercise was on the Scottish national ecosystem framework, within which a number of regional clusters can be found (e.g., Scotland's "Silicon Glen"). It is quite well recognized (although not sufficiently theorized) that country-level and regional entrepreneurial ecosystems are different and may exhibit different dynamics (Sobel & Hall, 2008; Szerb, Acs, Autio, Ortega-Argiles, & Komlosi, 2013). It is left for future research to tease out nuances of entrepreneurial ecosystem management in national and regional contexts.

Conclusion

In conclusion, this chapter has explored the various challenges an ecosystems approach to entrepreneurship policy presents for policy analysis and management. After 30 or so years of a market failure approach to entrepreneurship policy, an ecosystems management approach offers the potential of new insights and, if correctly implemented, higher effectiveness. This chapter has provided conceptual grounding to understand entrepreneurial ecosystems, elaborated resulting challenges for entrepreneurship policy, derived principles of successful management of entrepreneurial ecosystems, and highlighted these using rich case data from Scotland. We hope that our study will inspire further explorations of this important, yet underresearched domain.

References

Acs, Z. J., Autio, E., & Szerb, L. (2014). National systems of entrepreneurship: Measurement issues and policy implications. *Research Policy, 43*, 476–494.

Anderies, J. M., Janssen, M. A., & Ostrom, E. (2004). A framework to analyze the robustness of social-ecological systems from an institutional perspective. *Ecology and Society, 9*, 18–35.

Arrow, K. (1962). Economic welfare and the allocation of resources for invention. In R. Nelson (Ed.), *The rate and direction of inventive activity* (pp. 609–625). Princeton, NJ: Princeton University Press.

Arshed, N., Carter, S., & Mason, C. (2014). The ineffectiveness of entrepreneurship policy: Is policy formulation to blame? *Small Business Economics, 43*, 639–659.

Audretsch, D. (2011). Entrepreneurship policy. In L. P. Dana (Ed.), *World encyclopedia of entrepreneurship* (pp. 111–121). Cheltenham, England: Elgar.

Auerswald, P. E. (2014). Enabling entrepreneurial ecosystems. In D. Audretsch, A. Link, & M. Walshok (Eds.), *The Oxford handbook of local competitiveness*. Oxford, England: Oxford University Press.

Autio, E., & Fu, K. (2015). Economic and political institutions and entry into formal and informal entrepreneurship. *Asia Pacific Journal of Management, 32*, 67–94.

Autio, E., Kenney, M., Mustar, P., Siegel, D. S., & Wright, M. (2014). Entrepreneurial innovation: The importance of context. *Research Policy, 43*, 1097–1108.

BenDor, T., Shoemaker, D. A., Thill, J.-C., Dorning, M. A., & Meentemeyer, R. K. (2014). A mixed-methods analysis of social-ecological feedbacks between urbanization and forest persistence. *Ecology and Society, 19*, 1–22.

Bergek, A., Jacobsson, S., Carlsson, B., Lindmark, S., & Rickne, A. (2008). Analyzing the functional dynamics of technological innovation systems: A scheme of analysis. *Research Policy, 37*, 407–429.

Blackburn, R. A., & Schaper, M. T. (2012). Government, SMEs and entrepreneurship development: Policy, practice and challenges., Farnham, England. Gower.

Bowles, S., & Gintis, H. (1998). The moral economy of communities: Structured populations and the evolution of pro-social norms. *Evolution and Human Behavior, 19*, 3–25.

Bowles, S., & Gintis, H. (2002). Social capital and community governance. *The Economic Journal, 112*, 419–436.

Bradbury-Huang, H., Lichtenstein, B. L., Carroll, J. S., & Senge, P. M. (2010). Relational space and learning experiments: The heart of sustainability collaborations. *Research in Organizational Change and Development, 18*, 109–148.

Bridge, S. (2010). *Rethinking enterprise policy: Can failure trigger new understanding?* Basingstoke, England: Palgrave Macmillan.

Carlsson, B., & Jacobsson, S. (1997). In search of useful public policies: Key lessons and issues for policy makers. In B. Carlsson (Ed.), *Technological systems and industrial dynamics*. Alphen aan den Rijn, Netherlands: Kluwer.

Carree, M. A., & Thurik, A. R. (2008). The lag structure of the impact of business ownership on economic growth in OECD countries. *Small Business Economics, 30*, 101–110.

Chisholm, D., Grey, S., Harris, J., Levie, J., Reeves, C., & Ritchie, I. (2014). *Increasing innovation-driven entrepreneurship in Scotland through collective impact*. Inverness, Scotland: Highlands and Islands Enterprise/Scottish Enterprise.

Das, T. K., & Teng, B.-S. (2002). Alliance constellations: A social exchange perspective. *Academy of Management Review, 27*, 445–456.

Dodgson, M., Hughes, A., Foster, J., & Metcalfe, S. (2011). Systems thinking, market failure, and the development of innovation policy: The case of Australia. *Research Policy, 40*, 1145–1156.

Drexler, M., Eltogby, M., Foster, G., Shimizu, C., Ciesinski, S., Davila, A., . . . McLenithan, M. (2014). *Entrepreneurial ecosystems around the globe and early-stage company growth dynamics*. Geneva, Switzerland: World Economic Forum.

Ekeh, P. P. (1974). *Social exchange theory: Two traditions*. Princeton, NJ: Princeton University Press.

Feld, B. (2012). *Start-up communities: Building an entrepreneurial ecosystem in your city*. Hoboken, NJ: Wiley.

Geels, F. W., & Penna, C. C. R. (2015). Societal problems and industry reorientation: Elaborating the Dialectic Issue Life Cycle (DILC) model and a case study of car safety in the USA (1900–1995). *Research Policy, 44*, 67–82.

Grumbine, R. E. (1994). What is ecosystem management? *Conservation Biology, 8*(1), 27–38.

Gustafsson, R., & Autio, E. (2011). A failure trichotomy in knowledge exploration and exploitation. *Research Policy, 40*, 819–831.

Gutiérrez, N. L., Hilborn, R., & Defeo, O. (2011). Leadership, social capital and incentives promote successful fisheries. *Nature, 470*, 386–389.

Hall, P. A. (2006). Systematic process analysis: When and how to use it. *European Management Review, 3*, 24–31.

Hanleybrown, F., Kania, J., & Kramer, M. (2012, January). Channeling change: Making collective impact work. *Stanford Social Innovation Review*, 1–8.

Hayek, F. A. (1945). The use of knowledge in society. *American Economic Review, 35*(4), 519–530.

Holling, C. S. (Ed.). (1978). *Adaptive environmental assessment and management*. Chichester, England: Wiley.

Isenberg, D. J. (2010). How to start an entrepreneurial revolution. *Harvard Business Review, 88*, 41–49.

Kahan, J. P. (2001). Focus groups as a tool for policy analysis. *Analyses of Social Issues and Public Policy*, 129–146.

Kaplowitz, M. D., & Hoehn, J. P. (2001). Do focus groups and individual interviews reveal the same information for natural resource valuation? *Ecological Economics, 36*, 23–47.

Kirzner, I. (1997). Entrepreneurial discovery and the competitive market process: An Austrian approach. *Journal of Economic Literature, 35*, 60–85.

Kofinas, G. P. (2009). Adaptive co-management in social-ecological governance. In C. Folke, G.P. Kofinas, & Chapin F. S. (Eds.), *Principles of ecosystem stewardship* (pp. 77–101). New York, NY: Springer.

Levie, J., & Autio, E. (2011). Regulatory burden, rule of law, and entry of strategic entrepreneurs: An international panel study. *Journal of Management Studies, 48*, 1392–1419.

Levie, J., Autio, E., Reeves, C., Chisholm, D., Harris, J., Grey, S., . . . Cleevely, M. (2013, June). *Assessing regional innovative entrepreneurship ecosystems with the global entrepreneurship and development index: The case of Scotland. Global Entrepreneurship Monitor Research Conference*, Barcelona, Spain.

Lichtenstein, B. (2014). *Generative emergence: A new discipline of organizational, entrepreneurial, and social innovation.* Oxford, England: Oxford University Press.

Lundström, A., & Stevenson, L. A. (2005). *Entrepreneurship policy: Theory and practice.* Boston, MA: Springer.

Markard, J., & Truffer, B. (2008). Technological innovation systems and the multi-level perspective: Towards an integrated framework. *Research Policy, 37*, 596–615.

Markova, I., Linell, P., Grossen, M., & Salazar Orvig, A. (2007). *Dialogue in focus groups: Exploring socially shared knowledge.* London, England: Equinox.

Mason, C., & Brown, R. (2014). *Entrepreneurial ecosystems and growth oriented entrepreneurship.* Paris, France: OECD LEED Programme.

McClanahan, T. R., Castilla, J. C., White, A. T., & Defeo, O. (2009). Healing small-scale fisheries by facilitating complex socio-ecological systems. *Reviews in Fish Biology and Fisheries, 19*, 33–47.

Meilasari-Sugiana, A. (2012). Collective action and ecological sensibility for sustainable mangrove governance in Indonesia: Challenges and opportunities. *Journal of Political Ecology, 19*, 184–201.

Meinzen-Dick, R. S., & Di Gregorio, M. (2004, February). *Collective action and property rights for sustainable development* (Focus 11, Brief 1). Washington, DC: International Food Policy Research Institute.,

Merton, R. K. (1936). The unanticipated consequences of purposive social action. *American Sociological Review, 1*, 894–904.

Nill, J., & Kemp, R. (2009). Evolutionary approaches for sustainable innovation policies: From niche to paradigm? *Research Policy, 38*, 668–680.

Ostrom, E. (1990). *Governing the commons: The evolution of institutions for collective action.* Cambridge, England: Cambridge University Press.

Pahl-Wostl, C. (2002). Participative and stakeholder-based policy design, evaluation and modeling processes. *Integrated Assessment, 3*, 3–14.

Rotmans, J. (1998). Methods for integrated assessment: The challenges and opportunities ahead. *Environmental Modelling and Assessment, 3*, 155–180.

Scottish Government (2011). *The Government Economic Strategy.* The Scottish Government, Edinburgh.

Seppelt, R., Dormann, C. F., Eppink, F. V., Lautenbach, S., & Schmidt, S. (2011). A quantitative review of ecosystem service studies: Approaches, shortcomings and the road ahead. *Journal of Applied Ecology, 48*, 630–636.

Smit, B., & Wandel, J. (2006). Adaptation, adaptive capacity and vulnerability. *Global Environmental Change, 16*, 282–292.

Sobel, R. S., & Hall, J. C. (2008). Institutions, entrepreneurship, and regional differences in economic growth. *American Journal of Entrepreneurship*, 69–96.

Spigel, B. (2017). The relational organization of entrepreneurial ecosystems. *Entrepreneurship Theory and Practice, 41*, 49–72. doi:10.1111/etap.12167

Stam, E. (2014). *The Dutch entrepreneurial ecosystem.* Utrecht, Netherlands: Birch Research.

Stam, E. (2015). Entrepreneurial ecosystems and regional policy: A sympathetic critique. *European Planning Studies, 23*, 1759–1769.

Stangler, D., & Bell-Masterson, J. (2015). *Measuring an entrepreneurial ecosystem, Kauffman Foundation Research Series on City, Metro, and Regional Entrepreneurship.* Kansas City, MO: Ewing Marion Kauffman Foundation.

Stringer, L. C., Dougill, A. J., Fraser, E., Hubacek, K., Prell, C., & Reed, M. S. (2006). Unpacking "participation" in the adaptive management of social–ecological systems: A critical review. *Ecology and Society, 11*, 1–22.

Szerb, L., Acs, Z., Autio, E., Ortega-Argiles, R., & Komlosi, E. (2013). *REDI: the Regional Entrepreneurship and Development Index*. Brussels, Belgium: Directorate-General for Regional and Urban Policy, European Commission.

Van de Ven, A. H., Sapienza, H. J., & Villanueva, J. (2007). Entrepreneurial pursuits of self- and collective interests. *Strategic Entrepreneurship Journal, 1*, 353–370.

van den Belt M. (2004). *Mediated modeling: A system dynamics approach to environmental consensus building*. Washington, DC: Island Press.

Vatn, A. (2007). Resource regimes and cooperation. *Land Use Policy, 24*, 624–632.

Voegel, P. (2013). *The employment outlook for youth: Building entrepreneurial ecosystems as a way forward*. Paper presented at the G20 Youth Forum, St Petersburg, Russia.

Vollan, B. (2008). Socio-ecological explanations for crowding-out effects from economic field experiments in southern Africa. *Ecological Economics, 67*, 560–573.

Vollan, B., & Ostrom, E. (2010). Cooperation and the commons. *Science 330*, 923–924.

Wilson, M. A., & Howarth, R. B. (2002). Discourse-based valuation of ecosystem services: Establishing fair outcomes through group deliberation. *Ecological Economics, 41*, 431–443.

Woolthuis, R. K., Lankhuizen, M., & Gilsing, V. (2005). A system failure framework for innovation policy design. *Technovation, 25*, 609–619.

World Bank (2014). *Doing business 2015: Going beyond efficiency*. Washington, DC: World Bank.

Yin, R. K. (1994). *Case study research: Design and methods*. Thousand Oaks, CA: Sage.

Section 4

National and International Entrepreneurship

4b: International Entrepreneurship

20

International Entrepreneurship and Networks

Salman Ahmad[a] and Pavlos Dimitratos[b]

[a,b] University of Glasgow, UK

Introduction

During the 1980s and 1990s, the international business environment was significantly changed due to rapid globalization of the world economy. This global change was coupled with worldwide measures to gradually remove obstacles from international trade and to enforce harmonization of international law. This whole process became more efficient with dramatic developments in information and communication technologies, and falling political borders, which facilitated the cross border interactions and transformed our world into a global village (Mathews & Zander, 2007). Moreover, the growing cross-border interactions also helped to remove psychological and practical barriers in doing business abroad and firms were no longer bound to follow any process model for internationalization. On the basis of this progress new opportunities emerged for unconventional business models and many small firms internationalized more innovatively, faster, and more deliberately than ever before (McDougall, 1989). Therefore, many researchers started studying this changing behavior and new models were introduced based on the assumption that these firms were innately entrepreneurial (Bell, Crick, & Young, 2004; Oviatt & McDougall 1994; Zahra, 2005), which gave rise to the concept of international entrepreneurship.

Over the last two decades, international entrepreneurship has attracted many scholars and is now being recognized as a distinguished field of study (Autio, George, & Alexy, 2011; Dimitratos, Voudouris, Plakoyiannaki, E., & Nakos, 2012; Gabrielsson & Gabrielsson, 2013) with great potential for future research in international business, entrepreneurship, and strategic management domains (see Hitt & Ireland, 2000; Wright & Ricks, 1994; Zahra, Jennings, & Kuratko, 1999). Despite its dramatic growth in the last two decades, the domain of international entrepreneurship is still in its infancy with multiplicity of approaches requiring separation of its key theoretical aspects and delineation of its boundaries (Young, Dimitratos, & Dana, 2003). Moreover, there is a deficiency of solid theoretical frameworks that may cause fragmentation and lack of focus in this domain (Jones, Coviello, & Tang, 2011; McDougall & Oviatt, 2000; Nummela & Welch, 2006). McDougall, Shane, and Oviatt (1994) have also argued that the behavior

---

The Wiley Handbook of Entrepreneurship, First Edition.
Edited by Gorkan Ahmetoglu, Tomas Chamorro-Premuzic, Bailey Klinger, & Tessa Karcisky.
© 2017 John Wiley & Sons Ltd. Published 2017 by John Wiley & Sons Ltd.

of international new ventures (or "born globals") cannot be explained in the light of existing concepts or models of international business including traditional internationalization theories, oligopolistic reaction, product life cycle and monopolistic advantage. Thus, many scholars have used different theories, models, and perspectives to elucidate the firm's international entrepreneurial behavior and activities. In this regard, network and social capital theory is extensively used to explain how international entrepreneurial firms access necessary resources and develop capabilities to successfully operate beyond their national boundaries. Both aspects of this theory have contributed toward better understanding the phenomenon: whereas network aspects helped to explore the antecedents of internationalization from the perspective of the firm, the social capital has enlightened the study domain by including all interpersonal ties of entrepreneurs (Ellis, 2011).

Based on a systematic literature review of the network perspective in international entrepreneurship research, this chapter (a) discusses different definitions of international entrepreneurship (IE), (b) identifies different themes in which network perspective is used in IE research, and (c) highlights the theories used to comprehend the interaction between networks and international entrepreneurship.

International Entrepreneurship: Definition

Until the 1990s, international entrepreneurship had not emerged as a proper distinguished field of study but rather both entrepreneurship and international business were being studied separately as two distinct areas of research that rarely intersected (McDougall & Oviatt, 2000). While entrepreneurship researchers focused on studying the creation and management of new small ventures, researchers in international business emphasized on business activities of large multinational enterprises (MNEs). Rapid globalization, however, changed the whole research setting and international entrepreneurship has become an important research topic with the intersection of entrepreneurship and international business due to the emergence of born globals (McDougall & Oviatt, 2000).

According to Zahra and George (2002), Morrow (1988) first introduced international entrepreneurship in 1988 as a fresh opportunity for established as well as new ventures. Further, McDougall's study on international new ventures significantly supported the international entrepreneurship research domain with initial empirical evidence to present structural and strategic differences between domestic new ventures and international new ventures (McDougall, 1989). This study made a pioneering contribution to the field of international business as McDougall (1989 p. 388) focused on "the development of international new ventures or startups that, from inception, engage in international business." According to McDougall (1989), international new ventures engage in cross-border business activities from their very inception stage and draw their operational domain significantly as international.

Since then, the definitional paradigm of international entrepreneurship has significantly evolved as different researchers have tried to integrate entrepreneurship, international business, and even strategic management perspectives into their definitions. Wright and Ricks (1994) regarded international entrepreneurship as an activity at the firm level that extends beyond national boundaries and focused on the relationship between the firm and its international environment. Further, McDougall and Oviatt (2000), defined international entrepreneurship as the study of "innovative, proactive and risk seeking behaviors across borders" (p. 903), and Zahra and George (2002) defined it as the "process of creatively discovering and exploiting (entrepreneurial) opportunities that lie outside a firm's domestic market" (p. 261). These definitions centered on the process of international entrepreneurship, whereas many important issues were largely neglected such as why some firms successfully identify and exploit cross-border opportunities while others in a similar position fail to act on them. According to Zahra, Korri, and Yu (2005) the dilemma of how entrepreneurs spot international business opportunities and exploit them can be understood by applying cognitive perspectives. Another unaddressed but important issue is whether it is essential for international entrepreneurs to have a business in their domestic markets or are able to start their firms from any international market, assuming they do not see the same opportunity in their home country.

According to Fletcher (2004), born global are the sole firms that truly qualify as internationally entrepreneurial firms. Although this definition is based on the ideas of innovation and novelty, it may potentially exclude many firms from the domain of international entrepreneurship, even though they go international just because of their prolonged presence in their domestic markets. Brush (1995) suggested that the firm's age is important in predicting internationalization. In the same way, Zahra, Neubaum, and Huse (1997) also found that a firm's age has an impact on the intensity of internationalization but the firm's size does not have an impact. However, Zahra, Matherne, and Carleton (2003) later questioned the impact of both firm's size and firm's age including past performance on the degree and speed of internationalization of sales, that is, international intensity. Moreover, Schwens and Kabst (2009) concluded that the prior experience of primary decision-makers has positive impacts on the internationalization efforts of the firm. Further, Acedo and Florin (2006) revealed that risk perception and cognition of CEOs, which also depend upon prior experiences, can affect their decision-making about internationalization.

However, Oviatt and McDougall (2005) stressed that any definition of international entrepreneurship will be regarded as imperfect if it does not consider the effects of networks, knowledge, competition, technology, and culture in its domain. Moreover, it is important to acknowledge that the international entrepreneurial culture certainly has an important role to play among forces affecting international entrepreneurship. According to Dimitratos and Plakoyiannaki (2003), organizational culture plays a very central role in facilitating and accommodating entrepreneurial activities in the process of internationalizing the firm. Moreover, institutions that hinder or facilitate internationalization are very important and cannot be excluded from its scope (Dimitratos & Jones, 2005). In the past, it was very challenging for small firms to internationalize their operations since they had to face many disadvantages in their decisions (Lamb & Liesch, 2002). However, more and more firms are going international, irrespective of their size. Besides that, new small firms of the contemporary world do not need to carry the burden of a status-quo-seeking culture that hinders their international expansion.

The focus of initial international entrepreneurship research was mainly on born global firms, as international new ventures were also examined in the pioneering study of McDougall (1989). However, Zahra (1993) suggested that the scope of international entrepreneurship should incorporate both new as well as existing firms since entrepreneurship is an ongoing process that unfolds gradually and applies to all firms. The task force of the Academy of Management—an international professional association for management and organization scholars—also agreed with this opinion and recommended that the international entrepreneurship domain should be seen in a broader perspective (Giamartino, McDougall, & Bird, 1993). Moreover, this intent to include big companies in the study of international entrepreneurship was confirmed by the emergence of "corporate entrepreneurship" as an important area of interest within the domain of international entrepreneurship.

Previous definitions of international entrepreneurship provided by Miller (1983) and Wright and Ricks (1994) defined this phenomenon through a firm level approach. However, according to Oviatt and McDougall (2005) the actors who identify, exploit, assess, or take advantage of international opportunities to create solutions in the form of services and goods can be individual, groups, or organizations. Oviatt and McDougall (2005) provided another, even more comprehensive definition of international entrepreneurship as "the discovery, enactment, evaluation, and exploitation of opportunities—across national borders—to create future goods and services" (p. 540). In this definition, the entrepreneurial dimension is stressed by introducing the concept of "opportunity"; however, the international perspective of opportunity is also emphasized through their cross-border nature (Mainela, Puhakka, & Servais, 2014). Oviatt and McDougall (2005) further described actors (individuals, groups, or organizations) who engage in the process of identification and exploitation of opportunities to develop services and goods, and cross their national boundaries, as internationally entrepreneurial actors. Oviatt and McDougall (2005) also summarized past research on international entrepreneurship as falling into two broad areas: the first stresses cross-national behavior of entrepreneurial actors, and the second highlights cross-national comparisons of entrepreneurs, their behavior, and the overall environment in which they operate.

According to Mainela et al. (2014) the notion of international opportunity has also gained fundamental importance because research in the field of firms' internationalization has moved away from the study of internal experience and gradual learning about international markets (Bilkey & Tesar, 1977; Cavusgil, 1980; Johanson & Vahlne, 1977) toward the study of internal opportunity development in relationship networks (Johanson & Vahlne, 2006, 2009). Over the last decade, opportunity identification and exploitation are investigated as central functions of entrepreneurship (Eckhardt & Shane, 2003; Shane & Venkataraman, 2000; Short, Ketchen, Shook, & Ireland, 2010). According to Murphy (2011), it is largely believed that entrepreneurship as a research field can best be explained through the concept of opportunity. Moreover, identification of opportunities and entrepreneurial innovation are also considered central to MNEs (Casson, Dark, & Gulamhussen, 2009; Casson, & Godley, 2007).

Network Perspective

Originally the network perspective (e.g., Hammarkvist, Håkansson, & Lars-Gunnar, 1982) was introduced in the marketing field as an alternate mechanism of the dominant marketing management perspective (e.g., Kotler, 1997). Initially, the focus of network perspective was narrowly defined by the buyer–seller relationship, but it has been developed over time and currently it also considers larger networks with more than two actors. Many researchers have built their studies on the network perspective but there is still a lack of consensus about definitions, especially in social sciences. In those, different phenomena such as interlocks, dyadic relations, and whole networks are simultaneously referred to by the same term "networks." According to Axelsson and Easton (1992, p. 365), "sets of two or more connected exchange relationships" are called a network. In another definition, Laumann, Galaskiewicz, and Marsden (1978) explained networks as "a set of nodes (e.g. persons, organizations) linked by a set of social relationships (e.g. friendships, transfer of funds, overlapping membership) of a specified type" (p. 458). Given this, markets can also be seen as systems of social and industrial relationships among suppliers, customers, competitors, friends, family, etc. Håkansson and Johanson (1992) divided networks into three concepts—actors, resources, and activities—and also argued that all of them create their own networks but at the same time are dependent on each other. Moreover, it is important to understand the relationship between different actors to understand the network as a whole because these relationships are characterized by specificity, multiplicity, and continuity. Alliance relationships between firms are also referred to as an important type of network, which is defined as an "inter-firm collaboration over a given economic space and time for the attainment of mutually defined goals" (Buckley, 1992, p. 91).

Thus, in a network, actors can be linked to each other through economic, legal, cognitive, social, technical, and other different types of ties, whereas mutual trust and knowledge create a framework over time to facilitate the future business among these actors (Hammarkvist et al., 1982). Further, relationships established among different actors in the network also facilitate the exchange of resources and influence their strategic decisions (Sharma, 1993), and networks help to minimize and control opportunistic behaviors because their members give more importance to their relationships than discrete transactions.

In the past few decades, the extensive research on networks has assisted in extending the stock of knowledge (Borgatti & Foster, 2003; Brass, Galaskiewicz, Greve, & Tsai, 2004; Parkhe, Wasserman, & Ralston, 2006) in a vast and diverse range of fields (such as strategy, organization theory, political science, and organizational sociology) at different levels of analysis (such as the country, industry, firm, group, and interpersonal or individual) (Zaheer, Gözübüyük, & Milanov, 2010).

Networks and International Entrepreneurship

Even though marketing researchers have identified the value of networks (Anderson, Hakansson, & Johanson, 1994; Hammarkvist et al., 1982; Sharma & Johanson, 1987), the network perspective is considered equally important among scholars of both entrepreneurship (e.g., Aldrich & Zimmer, 1986; Larson & Starr, 1993) and international business (e.g., Axelsson & Easton, 1992; Bartlett & Ghoshal, 1991; Forsgren, 1989; Johanson & Mattsson, 1988). The network perspective has also received considerable attention among scholars of international entrepreneurship as they recognized the importance of network theory in the search for an explanation of international entrepreneurial activities. In particular, many scholars have put forth calls to extend knowledge in international entrepreneurship based on network theory (Bell, 1995; Coviello & Munro, 1995, 1997; Oviatt & McDougall, 1994).

Relevant works include Oviatt and McDougall's (1995) study in which they found that strong international business networks played a very central role in the success of global start-ups. Oviatt and McDougall (1994) presented networks as an important alternative seeking essential resources for firm internationalization in their work on new venture internationalization theory. In another comparative study, Bell (1995) identified the important role of networks in export behavior of entrepreneurial software firms. Moreover, in their revised model, Johanson and Vahlne (2003) also advised entrepreneurship scholars to incorporate the network perspective into traditional theories of firm internationalization.

Overall, the network perspective goes beyond the traditional stages theory, which posits that firms pursue their international strategies in incremental ways as it argues that the firm's international strategy emerges as a pattern of behavior influenced by a range of network relationships. As stated by Benito and Welch (1994) "the sometimes erratic character of internationalization for individual firms appears to be related to the seeming randomness with which opportunities and threats relevant to international activity arise in a company's external environment." (p. 14).

Internationalization requires strong resource commitment from the firm's management, whereas insufficient resources create major obstacles to expansion, especially for small firms and new ventures. In this regard, networks help firms overcome their constraints and internationalize by accessing necessary resources through network exchange structures without the need for huge investments, and also enable them to maximize their adaptability to the environment (Larson 1992). For example, studies have revealed that networks played a central role in the process of internationalization of firms from the US (Oviatt & McDougall, 1994), UK (Crick & Spence, 2005), New Zealand (Coviello & Munro 1995), Scandinavian countries (Bell, 1995), Germany (Al-Laham & Souitaris, 2008). and China (Zhou, Wu, & Luo, 2007). Considering this extensive research on the role of networks in international entrepreneurship, this chapter elaborates on how networks influence international entrepreneurial activities, an influence summarized in Figure 20.1.

Important Themes: Intersection of International Entrepreneurship and Networks Research

Since 1980, when the seminal work of McDougall on international new ventures was published, many scholars have started studying the firms that internationalize at their very early age to understand their behavior and omission of stages that were believed to be very important in traditional internationalization theories. In this quest for an explanation, the network perspective played very important role as many studies revealed that internationalization of these firms was strongly influenced by their network structures (Bell, 1995; Coviello, & Munro, 1995; Oviatt, & McDougall, 1994). This large number of studies, conducted in the past few decades, can be categorized into five different thematic areas to comprehend how networks affect international entrepreneurial activities: (1) the influence of network creation/development, (2) network types, (3) the network structure on international entrepreneurship, (4) the network evolution with the firm's age and growth, and (5) network benefits for international entrepreneurial activities (see Figure 20.1).

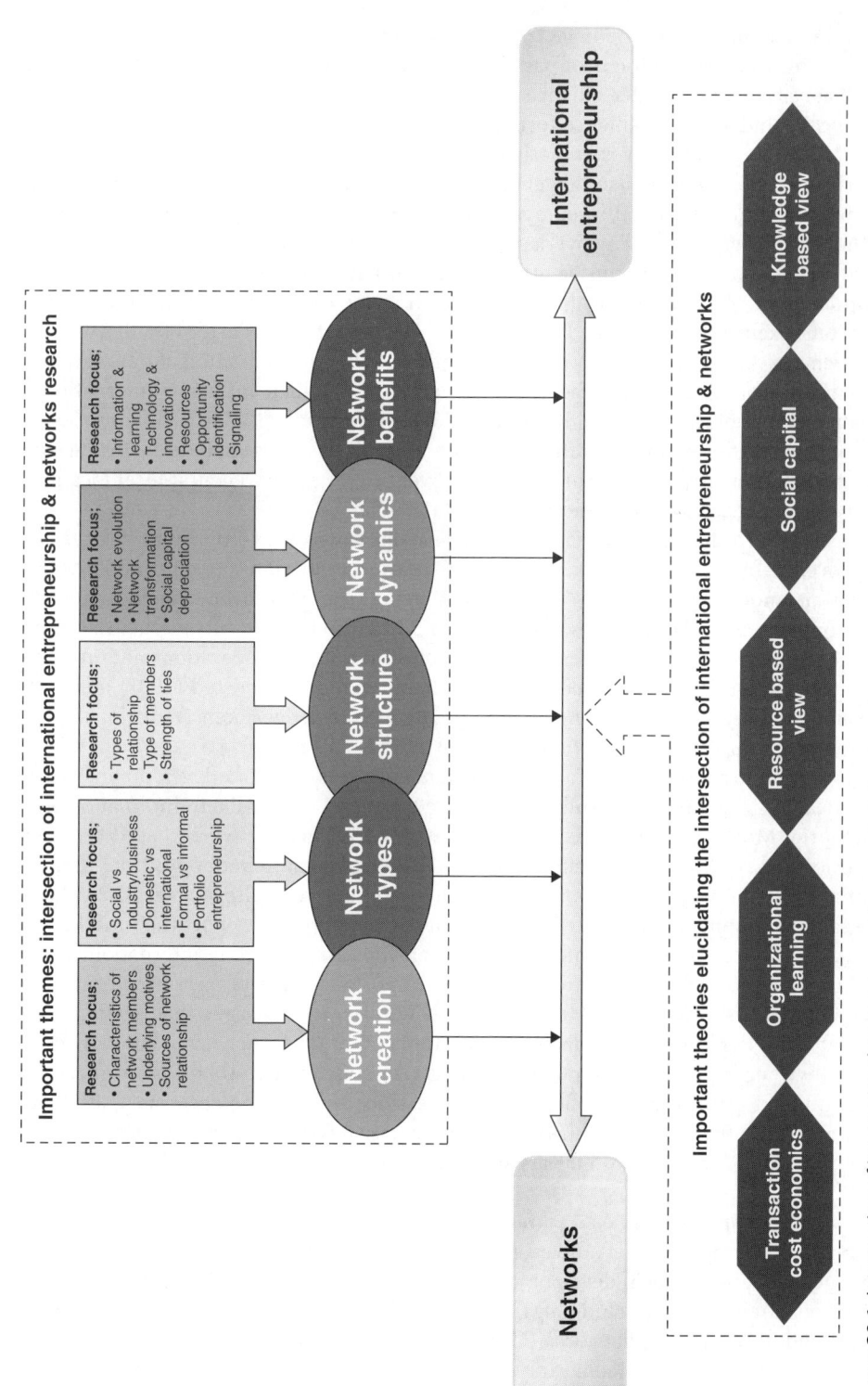

Figure 20.1 Intersection of international entrepreneurship and networks research.

Network Creation and International Entrepreneurship

Within this domain the focus of past studies was on the motives behind the creation of alliances. In the broader alliance literature, many authors have discussed various reasons behind strategic alliance formation. Mariti and Smiley (1983) discussed some primary strategic objectives underlying the formation of strategic alliances, while Harrigan (1985) identified some general motives of alliance creation and categorized them into strategic benefits, competitive benefits and internal benefits. Different authors have suggested many overlapping motives. Glaister and Buckley (1996) developed an list of mutually exclusive motives, such as risk-sharing (Porter & Fuller, 1986), economies of scale (Mariti & Smiley, 1983), transfer of complementary technology or patent exchange (Harrigan, 1985), shaping of competition (Porter & Fuller, 1986), adherence to host government policies (Beamish, 1988) and facilitation of international expansion (Young, Hamill, Wheeler, & Davies, 1989), which influence international alliance formation. Glaister and Buckley (1996) also concluded that with different levels of importance, these motives influence the firm's internationalization decisions such as partner's nationality, industry of the alliance, venture's primary geographical location, relative partner size, and contractual form of the alliance.

Tolstoy (2010) has argued that network development is very important in order to improve the firm's capabilities of knowledge creation in foreign markets and in developing an understanding of regional market structures. Moreover, ongoing network development in foreign markets is also very important in helping entrepreneurial firms to access important business resources for their international operations and innovation (Greve & Salaff, 2003). According to Johannisson and Monsted (1997), network development is more crucial when firms operate in knowledge-intensive regional markets, where future prediction of market behavior is a hard task.

In addition to successful operations in regional markets, network development is also significant in enabling small and medium-sized enterprises (SMEs) to internationalize (Gregorio, Musteen, & Thomas, 2009). SMEs develop their networks based on their experience in offshore outsourcing which helps them to create a better positions in their home markets as well as internationalizing into other markets (Gregorio et al., 2009). In the same way, some firms create international partnerships to support their marketing and sales services, and sometimes these relationships assist them in internationalizing and provide access to other networks that are important in the process of internationalization (Harris & Wheeler, 2005). Harris and Wheeler (2005) argue that relationships do not always originate from distributors, suppliers, or customer firms but can come from anywhere in social or work settings. It is also quite evident that firms with excellent networking skills can establish close partnerships with foreign customers, distributors, and other firms, and are likely to achieve better internationalization performance (Aaby & Slater, 1989; Leonidou, Katsikeas, & Samiee, 2002; Zou & Stan, 1998).

Network Types and International Entrepreneurship

Networks have become very diverse phenomena as various types of networks have emerged along with global developments, such as social networks (Crick, Chaudhry, & Batstone, 2001; Freeman, Hutchings, Lazaris, & Zyngier, 2010; Marshall, 2011; Pruthi, 2014), industry/business networks (Crick et al., 2001), clusters (Al-Laham & Souitaris, 2008; Iriyama, Li, & Madhavan, 2010), home country networks (Prashantham & Birkinshaw, 2015; Yiu, Lau, & Bruton, 2007), international joint ventures

(Li & Shenkar, 2003) and intraorganizational networks (McGaughey, 2007). Research examining the impact of different types of networks on international entrepreneurship started mainly in the first decade of the 21st century.

Social Networks Social networks are interpersonal ties of entrepreneurs and managers (e.g., family, friends, colleagues, ethnic groups) in any firm. The significant value of social networks in the process of entrepreneurship is well recognized in the social capital (Adler & Kwon, 2002) and entrepreneurship (Aldrich, & Zimmer, 1986; Greve & Salaff, 2003) literature streams. Social capital theory posits that professional and personal ties of entrepreneurs help create social capital (Davidsson & Honig, 2003), and therefore impact on the perceived possibility of new venture development (Bandura, 2001), provide resources, and trigger opportunities (Aldrich & Zimmer, 1986; Sullivan & Ford, 2014). In the same way, the impact of social networks on international entrepreneurship is also confirmed in past literature. According to Coviello (2006), social networks assist international new ventures in minimizing their risks of new market entry by providing them business connections, local market information, and access to sale and distribution channels at local levels. Riddle and Gillespie (2003) conducted research on internationalization of the Turkish textile industry and revealed that social networks involving, for example, family and friends were the main sources of information among owners of new ventures, especially regarding suppliers and technological developments. Loane, Bell, and McNaughton (2007) revealed a positive relationship between top management team networks and internationalization speed. They also concluded that firms address their deficiencies by adding new members into their management teams. In more recent literature, scholars have also evaluated the role of ethnic networks in a firm's entry into the home market of entrepreneurs and found significant positive impacts (Chung & Tung, 2013) because ethnic networks reduce the perceived distance between home and host countries (Saxenian, 2002, 2005). Social networks or social capital do not always have positive effects on the process of knowledge acquisition and internationalization; Presuttia, Boaria, & Fratocchi (2007) have argued that social capital is a diverse and multifaceted concept and different characteristics of social capital could have dissimilar effects. Overall, the importance of social networks in international entrepreneurship is well established, but the literature does also suggest that not all types of social networks influence positively, as some also have negative effects on firm internationalization (Prashantham & Birkinshaw, 2015).

Industry/Business Networks Industry/business networks are another type of network that is frequently studied in the literature whereby the relationship exists between two or more organizations (Crick et al., 2001). This type of network also includes industry clusters (Al-Laham & Souitaris, 2008; Iriyama et al., 2010), business associations (Riddle & Gillespie, 2003) and corporate alliances (Baucus, Baucus, & Human, 1996; Contractor & Kundu, 1998; Li, 2008). Business networks can be an important source of information in enabling firms to internationalize, such as when they outsource their business operations, and also help them learn from their partners as well as internationalize their sales (Gregorio et al., 2009). Similarly, Harris and Wheeler (2005) support the idea that many firms create business partners to get support for their marketing and sales functions and these partnerships also help them in knowledge accumulation and access of resources for internationalization. In addition, Glaister and Buckley (1996) have argued that many firms create international alliances for business expansion across national boundaries and their motives also influence partner selection and location of alliance region. International alliances also help firms to learn and accumulate knowledge from their foreign partners and then use that knowledge to further internationalize and make decisions about the speed with which to do this.

Small firm partnerships with MNEs also influence their internationalization process and sometimes those MNEs become their initial foreign clients (Prashantham & Birkinshaw, 2015). Just like interfirm relationships with buyers, customers, or distributors, firms also use their links with business associations to get information and resources for internationalization. According to Riddle and Gillespie (2003), business associations played a very important role in the internationalization of textile manufacturers by providing them information about export processes, foreign markets, and legal matters and helping them connect with foreign buyers through trade shows and export promotion services. In their same study, it was also found that it was easy for textile manufacturer associations to support firms in internationalization because of the industrial clustering in Istanbul. Istanbul is the hub of Turkish textile industry and this geographical concentration of the industry helped business associations focus their support services. Clusters are established on two primary bases, namely sector and location, and Andersson, Evers, and Griot (2013) have argued that both types of industrial clusters have an influence on internationalization of firms. Moreover, a firm's embeddedness in regional industrial and research clusters also accommodates knowledge accumulation and resources, which facilitates its internationalization and partnerships with foreign firms because the cluster's international experience and partnerships create knowledge spillover for other firms in that region (Al-Laham & Souitaris, 2008).

Other Types of Network Besides social and industrial networks, several other types of networks are discussed in the literature from the perspective of international entrepreneurship. While studying local and international networks, Andersson et al. (2013) have revealed that both international and local ties influence firms' internationalization in four different ways. First, the extent of network influence on internationalization of the firm is determined by cluster location, industry dynamics, and the enterprise's life cycle. Second, there are two types of international entrepreneurial firms, one born global with global market orientation from the start and led by proactive entrepreneurs, and the other born again global with rapid internationalization due to some critical incident such as foreign acquisition or new management. Third, firms' networking in local industrial clusters helps born globals in their initial internationalization while, in contrast, international networks influence born again globals in their relaunching in international markets. Fourth, the firm's connections and networking with local research institutions assist both born globals and born again globals in their internationalization based on innovation. Yiu et al. (2007) have argued that network ties with domestic financial institutions, banks, and regulatory and administrative agencies help firms access critical resources for international venturing such as financial backup, information about foreign markets, and outward foreign direct investment (FDI) opportunities. Moreover, networks with domestic institutions also provide firms from emerging economies additional ownership advantages for internationalization.

Sigfusson and Harris (2013) have studied domestic and international networks for software firms and found that strong domestic ties do not support their internationalization because the window of opportunity in this high tech industry is very short and domestic ties are not very helpful in enabling quick international distribution. Similarly, Prashantham and Birkinshaw (2015) have also studied the impact of domestic and international networks on a firm's internationalization, looking at software companies from India. Their study found low international intensity in firms that had strong ties with MNEs' subsidiaries and with SMEs in the home market, but higher intensity for strong networks based on clusters or industry groups. Home country networks are bounded by domestic markets and are therefore unlikely to help firms in internationalization and relationship development beyond these networks (Prashantham & Birkinshaw, 2015).

In a study to evaluate the formal (alliance partners) and informal (geographically proximate firms) network relationships, Fernhaber and Li (2013) have found that both types of network facilitate internationalization of new ventures but their effects vary according to the venture's age. Relatively older firms get more benefits from formal networks and newer firms get more international exposure from informal networks. McGaughey (2007) has discussed networks established in portfolio entrepreneurship. This refers to the case when an entrepreneur establishes, owns, controls, and manages more than one venture simultaneously and all new ventures differ from each other and existing ventures (Scott & Rosa, 1996; Westhead & Wright, 1998). McGaughey (2007) has revealed that a network established on the basis of portfolio entrepreneurship, in which one venture in the portfolio is connected with the others, facilitates internationalization in three ways. First, it provides access to critical resources such as physical, knowledge, and organizational resources through their transfer between ventures. Second, this type of network also provides legitimacy through positive spillover, which is typically difficult for international new ventures to get in a short time. Third, the diversity of markets, products, and business lines within the network enhances the stock of knowledge, experimentation, and learning across ventures being managed under the portfolio.

Network Structures and International Entrepreneurship
The network structure is also discussed in the literature from different angles that include the type of relationships among network members, type of members, strength of relationships, and nature of alliance (Milanov & Fernhaber, 2014; Osborn & Baughn, 1990; Styles & Genua, 2008; Yeung, 2002). Osborn and Baughn (1990) have evaluated contractual agreements (e.g., licensing and supply agreements) and joint ventures in the context of international business and found that firms operating in technologically intense sectors prefer contractual agreements as they allow them to control and limit the flow of proprietary information across boundaries, whereas firms intending to form joint R&D alliances prefer joint ventures because they help them align the interests of the partners, build day-to-day coordination, reduce opportunism, and facilitate information flows. Contractual agreements can be a very useful substitute for alliances based on equity ownership when firms have less fear of opportunism from counterparts due to the strong control that international partners have over strategic business resources (Contractor & Kundu, 1998).

Another factor influencing the selection of alliance type is the religious background of the partner organization. According to Li (2008), if both firms belong to countries that are religious (Christian) countries, they are *less* likely to choose joint ventures when entering the partner's country and are *more* likely to choose joint ventures if one or both of the partner firms belongs to an atheist country.

Riddle and Gillespie (2003) have studied the role of two different types of networks provided by business associations in the internationalization of the firm, namely a government-operated mandatory association and a privately led voluntary association. Their research revealed that the public sector association was more successful in facilitating the internationalization of firms than the privately led voluntary association. Apart from the ownership and control of the network, the types of members in the network also influence internationalization of firms. Nakos, Brouthers, and Dimitratos (2014) have studied alliances with competitors and noncompetitors and concluded that alliances with competitors have a negative impact on the firm's international performance, and alliances with noncompetitors improve the firm's international performance. In another study, Dimitratos, Amorós, Etchebarne, and Felzensztein (2014) have established the predictive validity of networking perspective and international entrepreneurship, which means if firms engage in networking with international as well as domestic firms their likelihood of becoming microMNEs increases. However, Milanov and Fernhaber (2014) have argued that domestic ties, when partners have no experience abroad, decrease the new venture's international intensity, but have a positive impact if domestic partners have prior international experience, especially when the firm's top management also has international exposure. In a similar study, Prashantham and Dhanaraj (2015) found that local ties with MNEs have positive effects on the firm's internationalization capabilities but there are negative effects if the ties are with local small firms.

Network Dynamics and International Entrepreneurship

Network dynamics means how networks evolve alongside the growth of the firm. Coviello and Munro (1995, 1997) studied the impact of business and social ties on the internationalization of new ventures and concluded that both networks of international new ventures (INVs) and resultant growth change over time. According to Coviello (2006), a network changes as the firm evolves from idea stage to internationalization and growth. Further, this research suggests that the network's density is reduced and its range increased with the firm's growth. In turn, this helps improve network effectiveness and INVs social capital. Likewise, it is also argued that network ties are process based and dynamic (Hite & Hesterly, 2001; Hoang & Antoncic, 2003; Larson & Starr, 1993). Johanson and Vahlne (2003) have also revised their classic process theory (1977, 1990) to integrate a network model of internationalization, but their focus is still on the process of expansion in international markets rather than networks. Larson and Starr (1993) presented a classic model of network evolution and argued that networks change over time from one dimensional simple dyadic exchanges to multilayered and multidimensional intense relationships. Hite and Hesterly (2001) provided a conceptualization of network development arguing that in initial stages firms' networks are likely to be more cohesive and based on social ties, but as the firm grows the network changes to weak ties that are well managed to facilitate growth. Moreover, Prashantham and Dhanaraj (2010) have argued that social capital also depreciates over time and have identified three main forces involved in this change. First, is tie decay, which is referred to the weakening and fading of some relationships over time (Burt, 2002). Second, is tie obsolescence, which means some relationships become obsolete over time because the utility of ties is context specific. Third is utility life cycle, which means some networks lose their ability to yield new business opportunities over time. All three forces exert negative pressure on social capital over time, and therefore, it is important for firms to continuously replenish their stock of social capital (Prashantham & Dhanaraj, 2010). Network relationships play a crucial role in both early internationalization of the firm and its scope of international expansion (Cannone & Ughetto, 2014). The importance of networks is also evidenced in reinternationalization of firms where past networks help firms in reentry and take-off (Welch & Welch, 2009). Baum, Schwens, and Kabst (2015) have also found a strong positive relationship between intense networks and the patterns of born again globals.

Network's Benefits and International Entrepreneurship

Past studies have identified many ways in which networks facilitate international entrepreneurial activities, such as by helping new ventures access resources (Crick & Spence, 2005; Gabrielsson & Kirpalani, 2004; Riddle & Gillespie, 2003), technologies (Lee & Williams, 2007; McArthur & Schill, 1995; Witt, 1998; Young, Huang, & McDermott, 1996;), information (Sharma & Blomstermo, 2003), knowledge (Al-Laham & Souitaris, 2008; Mahnke & Venzin, 2003; Pak & Park, 2004), learning (Chandra & Coviello, 2010; Coviello, 2006; Prashantham & Floyd, 2012; Witt, 1998), finance (Harrison & Mason, 1992; Moen, Sørheim, & Erikson, 2008) and opportunities (Ciravegna, Majano, & Zhan, 2014; Crick & Spence, 2005; Kontinen & Ojala, 2011). In this section some key benefits of networking for international entrepreneurship are discussed.

Information and Learning The network literature emphasizes the value of interpersonal and interfirm relationships in accumulating and utilizing new knowledge (Al-Laham & Souitaris, 2008; Mahnke &Venzin, 2003; Pak & Park, 2004) and learning (Chandra & Coviello, 2010; Coviello, 2006; Prashantham & Floyd, 2012; Witt, 1998) for the firm's internationalization process. Leibeskind (1996) has defined knowledge as "information whose validity has been established through tests of proof.... what we can use without further experimentation" (p. 94). As to international entrepreneurship activities, the knowledge about how firms can apply their skills, beliefs, and information to their foreign operations is crucial for new ventures in their internationalization (Fernhaber, Mcdougall-Covin, & Shepherd, 2009). Further, how firms learn and accumulate new knowledge and develop core capabilities is a fundamental issue in international entrepreneurship (Freeman et al., 2010; Freeman, Hutchings, & Chetty, 2012; Zhou Barnes, & Lu, 2010). Many researchers have highlighted the role of network ties in helping firms internationalize through learning and knowledge accumulation (Majkgård & Sharma, 1998; Sharma & Johanson, 1987). According to Johanson and Vahlne (1977), the internationalization process of firms is driven by their knowledge base. Networks are crucial because, just like social actions and outcomes, economic actions and their outcomes are also influenced by dyadic ties between actors and their overall network structure (Granovetter, 1992). Networks ties cannot be imitated easily and provide firms channels that they can use to share knowledge with each other (Sharma & Blomstermo, 2003). Ties have impacts along three dimensions, namely (1) available information, (2) referrals, and (3) timing (Burt, 1992). Pak and Park (2004) have argued that firms create international alliances to learn and accumulate new knowledge and/ or skills in order to internationalize. Even though tacit knowledge is difficult to transfer, equity ownership in international alliances helps firms control mechanisms (Makhija & Ganesh, 1997) and take up a central position within the network (Tsai, 2001). In turn, it enables them to accumulate more tacit knowledge from their foreign partners than any other type of ties (Mowery, Oxley, & Silverman, 1996). Knowledge transfer within international cooperative alliances is significantly influenced by the knowledge and relation-specific factors, such as the nature of knowledge and absorption capacity of the organization (Pak & Park, 2004). Internationalization of born globals depends highly on learning through their networks (Sharma & Blomstermo, 2003) and similarly SMEs also rely on networks for experiential knowledge to select and expand into foreign markets, which they cannot get otherwise (Lindqvist, 1997).

Technology and Innovation   R&D, innovation, and new technologies have critical value in enabling born globals to achieve success in their international markets (Knight & Cavusgil, 2004). The role of networks in helping the firms access technological resources is frequently observed in past studies (Lee & Williams, 2007; McArthur & Schill, 1995; Witt, 1998; Young et al., 1996). According to Witt (1998), firms use information networks to acquire new technologies and internationalize their business. Roman (1991) has argued that firms use their alliances with international firms to learn and develop new technologies that enable them to internationalize their own operations. Even though firms can use their networks to acquire and create new technologies, how they use these technologies to build their competitive advantage is an entirely different thing and mere acquisition of new technologies does not help firms achieve any advantage (Dodgson, 1991; Schill & McArthur, 1991). Thus, firms should use their networks strategically to access technologies. McArthur and Schill (1995) have suggested that the process of technology acquisition through networks should be based on a twofold rationale. First, a strategic rationale should be applied to all stages of this process, including selection of technology, its acquisition and its final exploitation with formal technology strategy, because this will help in the management of new technology. Second, firms depend on other firms for new technologies, hence cooperative arrangements can assist the firm achieve a competitive advantage.

In a study to explore entrepreneurship and innovation in big companies, Lee and Williams (2007) revealed that entrepreneurial communities within big multinationals are also a very important source of new technology developments and entrepreneurship. These communities thrive on the knowledge and unique resources of their host company and significantly contribute to its innovation process. Moreover, internationalization is no longer a choice but has become an inevitable need, especially for high technology sectors (Spence, 2003) because quick diffusion of new technologies around the world is very important. According to Zhang and Dodgson (2007), networks also help firms in quick diffusion of their innovation and new technologies because technological developments and the level of acceptability also differ from one country to another. The network economy has enabled firms to increase their technical compatibility standards and as a result new technology diffusion across borders has become quicker and smoother than ever before (Zhang & Dodgson, 2007).

Resources   Internationalization can be a risky choice because it involves additional costs related to management of cross-border business activities; it is therefore important for firms to possess a significant competitive advantage that will help them overcome the costs of operating in foreign markets (Dunning, 2000; Rugman, 1981). Firms build their competitive advantage on the basis of their unique set of tangible and intangible resources and networking is a very effective way through which firms can overcome their scarcity of resources and learn from each other simultaneously (Gabrielsson & Kirpalani, 2004). In addition, internationalization requires a strong commitment of resources, but new ventures and small firms lack these resources that are necessary for them to succeed in international markets and must therefore use different channels such as networks, MNEs as distributors, and the internet, either in combination or separately (Gabrielsson & Kirpalani, 2004). Moreover, international new ventures can build their sustainable competitive advantage based on their access to different unique resources and capability to control them, especially "knowledge" (Oviatt & McDougall, 1994). According to Oviatt and McDougall (1994) new ventures can use alternative governance structures, such as network partners and close relationships, to acquire critical resources for internationalization. Past literature has discussed several types of resources that firms acquire through their networks such as entrepreneurial capability (Zhang et al., 2009), firm capabilities and intangible resources (Rialp & Rialp, 2007), institutional capital (Lu, Zhou, Bruton, & Li, 2010), network resources (Coviello & Cox, 2006; Loane & Bell 2006), market knowledge (Lamb & Liesch 2002), and firm-level knowledge (Knight & Kim 2009). According to Peng (2001), new ventures cannot compete on tangible resources with bigger counterparts such as state-owned enterprises and MNEs, but only on stronger effectiveness of minimum available resources.

Other Benefits Networking is a diverse phenomenon and all firms use their networks in different ways to get different advantages. Besides information, technology, and resources, many other benefits of networking for firms have been discussed in past studies. Harrison and Mason (1992) have argued that informal investors use their social networks to identify investment opportunities and this is a likely channel used by new ventures to acquire early finance. In another study, Moen et al. (2008) have also found that born globals access their early investments through personal and professional network ties established by entrepreneurs, whereas ties with formal investors help firms grow in later stages. According to Peng (2001), international network ties having strong social capital cannot be replicated by competitors, thus they help firms develop competitive advantage and achieve higher international performance. Moreover, small firms can achieve higher performance by participating in research and marketing alliances that are aligned with their internal capabilities (Brouthers, Nakos, & Dimitratos, 2014). Ciravegna et al. (2014) argued that networks increase entrepreneurs' proactive behavior in searching for new opportunities for international expansion. According to Nowinski and Rialp (2016), network ties help firms form international opportunity perceptions, as the weak ties increase desirability of nascent entrepreneurs for international opportunities and strong ties influence experienced entrepreneurs to perceive the high feasibility of international opportunities. Moreover, formal networks can be more useful in identification of international opportunities than informal or family networks (Kontinen & Ojala, 2011), and this may be because of the presence of weak ties in formal networks and strong ties in informal networks. In addition, transnational entrepreneurs with good networks are more likely to find international opportunities and exploit them because their networks provide them social and institutional embeddedness in their foreign markets (Yeung, 2002). Signaling is another important benefit that transnational entrepreneurs get from their international ties. According to Reuer and Ragozzino (2014), affiliations with strong financial institutions enable firms to create a signal for their international stakeholders about their strength and also assist them in creating international collaborative agreements. Moreover, membership of prominent networks also helps firms create signals about their product quality and resources (Reuer & Ragozzino, 2014). Oviatt and McDougall (2005) have also found that entrepreneurs use networks to identify international opportunities, achieve legitimacy, and build strategic partnerships, and altogether help them achieve higher internationalization speed. In another study, Presuttia et al. (2007) concluded that the combined networks of top management help firms internalize rapidly. Social networks also enable firms attain higher speed of international expansion (Casillas & Acedo, 2013).

Theoretical Basis: Intersection of International Entrepreneurship Networks Research

According to Etemad (2004), most internationalization theories are focused on big multinationals, and subsequently, fail to provide any comprehensive explanation for small firm internationalization. Moreover, they use firms as the unit of analysis and thus cannot provide satisfactory information about international entrepreneurship, which is inclined towards an individual (entrepreneur) as a unit of analysis. Apart from this, one of the basic rationalizations of international entrepreneurship is based on the criticisms of traditional concepts and models of international business (Young et al., 2003). In particular, the incremental proposition of the stages theory is criticized among scholars of international entrepreneurship mostly because it posits that firms should allocate their resources for international business in small steps based on accumulated knowledge (Bilkey, & Tesar, 1977; Johanson & Vahlne, 1977). In the early1990s, many cases were witnessed of many firms from knowledge-intensive sectors going for internationalization by following an opposite path (Bloodgood, Sapienza, & Almeida, 1996; McDougall et al., 1994). Further, firms in these studies showed more assertive behaviors towards their international markets from their inception, while disregarding their domestic markets. Since then, a quest for an acceptable theoretical explanation of the international new venture's behavior appeared among scholars of international entrepreneurship. In this regard, network perspective was extensively used to search for answers for why and how new ventures internationalize by overcoming their deficiencies in comparison to their big counterparts such as MNEs, established ventures, and state owned enterprises. The network perspective was highlighted by Oviatt and McDougall (1994) as an important alternative to seeking essential resources for internationalization and Johanson and Vahlne (2003) advised researchers of international business to incorporate a network perspective into traditional theories of firm internationalization. Different theoretical grounds used in past studies to explain international new ventures' behavior alongside the network perspective are the following.

Transaction Cost Economics (TCE)

A prominent theory used in network and international entrepreneurship research is transaction cost economics (Chandra & Coviello, 2010; Coase, 1937; Glaister & Buckley, 1996; Mazzanti, Montresor, & Pini, 2011; Osborn & Baughn, 1990; Williamson, 1985;). It suggests that any decision related to international expansion should be evaluated based on its costs and benefits. The core argument of TCE depends on the interplay of three primary assumptions, namely opportunism, bounded rationality, and asset specificity (Contractor & Kundu, 1998; Li, 2008). Opportunism assumption suggests that people try to use situations in their own interest, especially in the absence of market constraints such as contracts. Also, bounded rationality means individual decisions are limited due to several factors such as available information, cognitive ability of decision-makers, and resources. Asset specificity is another important assumption and it refers to the degree of reuse of an asset as an alternative without diminishing its productive value. Asset specificity increases bilateral dependency and creates contracting hazards between parties (Williamson, 1975, 1985, 1991).

According to Williamson (1975), the costs linked with different aspects of dealing with other firms, such as the costs of finding, building, and managing the ties and costs associated with specifying, monitoring, and enforcing the conditions of the relationship, are regarded as transaction costs. TCE suggests that any relationship and governance structure that minimizes transaction costs should be preferred (Williamson, 1975, 1985). TCE helps to explain a firm's decision in establishing networks and alliances and also specifying the features of the relationship because the network's structure and management incur costs and should not exceed their benefits (Li, 2008; Osborn & Baughn, 1990). TCE is also concerned with how to defend the firm's existing tangible and intangible resources from opportunism of other members in the network (Li & Shenkar, 2003). Besides these challenges, networks also help firms to reduce costs related to internationalization by providing network-specific benefits and resources, which are otherwise difficult for new ventures to collect because of large capital costs (Crick & Spence, 2005; Moen et al.. 2008). Further, international networks enable firms to minimize their costs related to liabilities of foreignness (Zhou et al., 2010).

Organizational Learning

Vera and Crossan (2003) have defined organizational learning as a process that facilitates "the continually evolving knowledge stored in individuals, groups and the organization, and constitutes the fundamental infrastructure that supports a firm's strategy formulation and implementation systems" (p. 123). Organizational learning is frequently used in international entrepreneurship to explain how networks facilitate learning process in new ventures (Glaister & Buckley, 1996; Milanov & Fernhaber, 2014; Voudouris, Dimitratos, & Salavou, 2010; Wang & Nicholas, 2005).

Johanson and Vahlne (1977) used the learning approach to treat internationalization as a sequential and evolutionary process of increase in international commitments over time. According to Costello (1996) learning is accumulated over time and therefore it is path-dependent by nature. The engagement of the firm in networks improves its learning process and the different types and structures of networks have different impacts on organizational learning (Fletcher, 2001; Glaister & Buckley, 1996; Wang & Nicholas, 2005). Voudouris et al. (2010) argue that entrepreneurial learning scope starts at the individual level through experiential learning, and gradually involves higher levels of intraorganizational and interorganizational networks, whereby interaction and ties in the network assist the learning process.

Resource-Based View

The resource-based view, also called resource-based theory (Barney, Ketchen, & Wright, 2011), is one dominant and widely used theoretical explanation for understanding networks and international entrepreneurship (Baum et al., 2015; Gerschewski, Rose, & Lindsay, 2015; Peng, 2001; Sigfusson & Chetty, 2013). According to the resource-based theory, firms accumulate a unique bundle of tangible and intangible resources, such as knowledge, routines, processes, capabilities, and assets (Roth, 1995), which help them build their competitive advantage (Peng, 2001). According to McDougall et al. (1994), the resource-based view can potentially be used as a valid framework to explain the international entrepreneurial activities.

Moreover, international new ventures can build their sustainable competitive advantage based on their access to different unique resources and ability to control (Oviatt & McDougall, 1994). The resource-based view suggests that firms use their networks to access several resources that are necessary for their internationalization, such as knowledge, capital, technologies, and finances, and then use these resources to build their competitive advantage. However, access to resources and knowledge about how to use them effectively are two different crucial things. Hence, the knowledge about how to use the resources is as important as access itself and networks help firms to accumulate both (Riddle & Gillespie, 2003).

Social Capital

Social capital is another prominent theoretical framework that helps understand new venture internationalization on the basis of their networks. It is defined as the "the sum of the actual and potential resources embedded within, available through, and derived from network relationships possessed by an individual or social unit" (Nahapiet & Ghoshal, 1998, p. 243). According to Lin, Cook, and Burt (2001), a social network is the value of all resources accumulated by a firm or individuals through all their network ties. Moreover, the importance of social capital depends on the resources and their usefulness to the firm. Social capital is further divided into three dimensions that include relational embeddedness, cognitive embeddedness, and structural embeddedness (Nahapiet & Ghoshal, 1998). Relational aspects of networking, such as interpersonal trust and emotional closeness, are termed as relational embeddedness; the extent to which network members share similar systems of meaning including shared narratives, codes, and language is called "cognitive embeddedness"; and, overall configuration and architecture of networks are regarded as "structural embeddedness." According to Musteen, Francis, and Datta (2010), each dimension of social capital influences firms' access to resources in different ways. For example, Inkpen and Tsang (2005) have argued that relational embeddedness enables network members to share knowledge by increasing the trust level and minimizing the chances of opportunistic behavior. On the other hand, a shared system of meanings in cognitive embeddedness facilitates knowledge sharing among international network members through mutual understanding and advanced communication (Edelmanet, Bresnen, Newell, Scarbrough, & Swan, 2004). Lastly, structural embeddedness determines the amount and quality of resources that members can access through their network (Burt, 1992); for instance, if network members are geographically dispersed in international markets, they can share information and resources about international opportunities.

Knowledge-Based View

The knowledge-based perspective, which has emerged as an extension of the resource-based view, separates knowledge as the most important strategic resource that any firm can possess (Grant, 1996). It is also evident from past studies that knowledge helps firms in the development of competitive advantage (McEvily & Chakravarthy, 2002; Wiklund & Shepherd, 2003). Moreover, the nature of knowledge can range from explicit to tacit, where explicit knowledge is the one that we can easily record and transfer (Nonaka, 1994) but tacit knowledge is nonprogrammable, experiential, and cannot be transferred easily (Nelson & Winter, 1982; Penrose, 1959; Polanyi, 1966).

Over the last few decades, a significant amount of research has been done on experiential knowledge (Johanson & Vahlne, 1977). According to Autio, Sapienza, and Almeida (2000), the knowledge-based view in international entrepreneurship is connected to knowledge intensity, which refers to the dependence of the firm on its existing knowledge base. Fernhaber et al. (2009) found that firms' alliances are an important source of new knowledge. In another study, Gassmann and Keupp (2007) tried to integrate the knowledge-based view with social capital theory to understand the foundations of competitive advantage of born global firms. According to Pak and Park (2004), cooperative alliances facilitate cross-border transfer of knowledge between member firms. Freeman et al. (2010) have also used knowledge-based perspectives and found that networks help build relational trust that facilitates the transfer of knowledge between network members.

Other Theories

Several other theories have also been used in past studies to understand the network's role in explaining the international entrepreneurial activity. For example, Glaister and Buckley (1996) have used resource dependence theory to understand the motives behind network creation among small businesses. Yeung (2002) has applied institutional theory to suggest that transnational entrepreneurs who have network ties with institutional actors can have better access to international opportunities. By applying the economies of scale theory, Glaister and Buckley (1996) revealed that firms also engage in networks and international expansion to achieve economies of scale. Al-Laham and Souitaris (2008) used the embeddedness theory to highlight that firms' embeddedness in their regional clusters significantly supports their international expansion. The tie strengths approach is also used to evaluate how the strength of different network ties facilitates firms in their internationalization process (Nowinski & Rialp, 2016; Pruthi, 2014). The effectuation theory is an emerging theme among researchers of networks and international entrepreneurship as it explains entrepreneurial logic, which is how entrepreneurs take existing resources available internally and through their networks to create international value from them (Galkina & Chetty, 2015). Similarly, the signaling and reference group theories help to understand how firms use their network ties and alliances as a signaling mechanism of quality and business strength (Prashantham & Birkinshaw, 2015; Reuer & Ragozzino, 2014). The liability of foreignness is another important framework used to describe how embeddedness in international networks helps new ventures internationalize by overcoming their liabilities of foreignness (Brouthers et al., 2014).

Practical Implications

This chapter has substantial implications for managers. By having a better understanding of networks and their influence on international expansion, firms can apply better management practices to align their network resources with their strategic objectives. The success in recognizing the benefits of networking can create the leverage to achieve higher international performance and competitive advantage in foreign markets. Hence, proactive and strategically aligned networking can enable firms to augment their chances of international success by minimizing their costs related to risks and uncertainty abroad.

This chapter is also important for policy initiatives as it highlights the critical role of networks in international trade and business. It informs policymakers about different implications of networks for facilitating the internationalization of firms. Hence, they should take policy measures that develop networking capabilities among local firms and provide them opportunities to network in local as well as in international markets.

Future Research

The use of multiple theoretical frameworks in past studies suggests that the use of a network perspective to explain international entrepreneurship is still in its infancy and that there is a lack of strong, equally accepted theoretical frameworks. Furthermore, network management is a largely understudied domain and there is a significant need to elucidate network management from both network as well as members' perspectives. It is important to study different approaches used by firms to manage their network relationships and their effects on internationalization. Similarly, future research that studies the network as a whole distinct unit and how it is managed will definitely improve our understanding about differently managed networks and their effects on firms' internationalization.

Conclusion

Research on international entrepreneurship is growing, but there is still a deficit of solid theoretical frameworks. The application of the network perspective has added a considerable value to fill this gap, but the use of networks to understand the international behavior of new ventures is largely fragmented. This chapter has summarized the existing debate concerning different aspects of networks and their influence on international entrepreneurial activities. In earlier literature, the network perspective was connected with international entrepreneurship research under five different thematic areas. First, how network creation influences international entrepreneurial activities and what the impact of motives and the process behind network creation is on international entrepreneurship. Second, the impact of different types of networks on international entrepreneurship is another important theme and social and business networks emerged as the most frequently researched types of networks. In the third important theme, network structures and their influence on international entrepreneurship, the key areas are seen as network centrality, strength of ties, tie characteristics, and geographical origin of network members. Fourth, network evolution and international entrepreneurship examines how networks change along with the firm's growth and age. Fifth, the network's benefits for international entrepreneurship are highlighted and how firms access the resource, information, learning, technology, and innovation-related benefits are observed as primary advantages of networks. This chapter also highlighted important theoretical frameworks that are used to explore how networks influence new ventures' international expansion. The TCE, organizational learning, resource-based view, social capital, and knowledge-based view emerge as important theoretical frameworks frequently used in past research to explain international entrepreneurial activities from a network perspective.

References

Aaby, N., & Slater, S. F. (1989). Management influences on export performance: A review of the empirical literature 1978–1988. *International Marketing Review, 6*(4), 7–23.

Acedo, F., & Florin, J. (2006). An entrepreneurial cognition perspective on the internationalization of SMEs. *Journal of International Entrepreneurship, 4*(1), 49–67.

Al-Laham, A., & Souitaris, V. (2008). Network embeddedness and new-venture internationalization: Analyzing international linkages in the German biotech industry. *Journal of Business Venturing, 23*, 67–586.

Adler, P. S., & Kwon, S. W. (2002). Social capital: Prospects for a new concept. *Academy of Management Review, 27*(1), 17–40.

Aldrich, H. E., & Zimmer, C. (1986). *Entrepreneurship through social networks*. In D. Sexton & R. Smilor (Eds.), *The art and science of entrepreneurship*. New York, NY: Ballinger.

Anderson, J., Hakansson, H., & Johanson, J. (1994, October). Dyadic Business relationships within a business network context. *Journal of Marketing, 58*, 1–15.

Andersson, S., Evers, N., & Griot, C. (2013). Local and international networks in small firm internationalization: cases from the Rhône-Alpes medical technology regional cluster. *Entrepreneurship & Regional Development, 25*(9–10), 867–888.

Autio, E., George, G., & Alexy, O. (2011). International entrepreneurship and capability development—qualitative evidence and future research directions. *Entrepreneurship Theory and Practice, 35*, 11–37.

Autio, E., Sapienza, H., & Almeida, J. (2000). Effects of age at entry, knowledge intensity, and imitability on international growth. *Academy of Management Journal, 43*(5), 909–924.

Axelsson, B., & Easton, G. (Eds.). (1992). *Industrial networks: A new view of reality*. London, England: Routledge.

Bandura, A. (2001). Social cognitive theory: An agentic perspective. *Annual Review of Psychology, 52*, 1–26.

Barney J. B., Ketchen, D. J., & Wright, M. (2011). The future of resource-based theory: revitalization or decline? *Journal of Management, 37*(5), 1299–1315.

Bartlett, C. A., & Ghoshal, S. (1991). Global strategic management: Impact on the new frontiers of strategy research. *Strategic Management Journal, 12*, 5–16.

Baucus, D. A., Baucus, M. S., & Human, S. E. (1996). Consensus In franchise organizations: A cooperative arrangement among entrepreneurs. *Journal of Business Venturing, 11*, 359–378.

Baum, M., Schwens, C., & Kabst, R. (2015). A latent class analysis of small firms' internationalization patterns. *Journal of World Business, 50*, 754–768.

Beamish, P. W. (1988). *Multinational joint ventures in developing countries*. London, England: Routledge.

Bell, J. (1995). The internationalization of small computer software firms—a further challenge to "stage theories." *European Journal of Marketing, 28*(8), 60–75.

Bell, J., Crick, D., & Young, S. (2004). Small firm internationalization and business strategy: An exploratory study of knowledge-intensive and traditional manufacturing firms in the UK. *International Small Business Journal, 22*(1), 23–56.

Benito, G. R. G., & Welch, L. S. (1994). Foreign market servicing: Beyond choice of entry mode. *Journal of International Marketing, 2*(2), 7–27.

Bilkey, W., & Tesar, G. (1977). The export behavior of smaller-sized Wisconsin manufacturing firms. *Journal of International Business Studies, 8*, 93–98.

Bloodgood, J., Sapienza, H. J., & Almeida, J. G. (1996). The internationalization of new high potential US ventures: Antecedents and outcomes. *Entrepreneurship Theory and Practice, 20*(4), 61–76.

Borgatti, S. P., & Foster, P. C. (2003). The network paradigm in organizational research: A review and typology. *Journal of Management, 29*(6), 991–1013.

Brass, D. J., Galaskiewicz, J., Greve, H. R., & Tsai, W. (2004). Taking stock of networks and organizations: A multilevel perspective. *Academy of Management Journal, 47*(6), 795–817.

Brouthers, K. D., Nakos, G., & Dimitratos, P. (2014). SME entrepreneurial orientation, international performance, and the moderating role of strategic alliances. *Entrepreneurship Theory and Practice*, 1161–1187.

Brush, C. G. (1995). *International entrepreneurship: The effect of firm age on motives for internationalization*. New York, NY: Garland.

Buckley, P. J. (1992). Alliances, technology and markets: a cautionary tale. In P. J. Buckley (Ed.), *Studies in international business*. London, England: Macmillan.

Burt, R. S. (1992). The social structure of competition. In N. Nohria & R. G. Eccles (Eds.), *Networks and organizations*. Boston, MA: Harvard Business School Press.

Burt, R. (2002). Bridge decay. *Social Networks, 24*, 333–63.

Cannone, G., & Ughetto, E. (2014). Born globals: A cross-country survey on high-tech start-ups. *International Business Review, 23*, 272–283.

Casillas, J. C., & Acedo, F. J. (2013). Speed in the internationalization process of the firm. *International Journal of Management Reviews, 15*, 15–29.

Casson, M., Dark, K., & Gulamhussen, M. A. (2009). Extending internalisaton theory: From the multinational enterprise to the knowledge-based empire. *International Business Review, 18*, 236–256.

Casson, M., & Godley, A. (2007). Revisiting the emergence of the modern business enterprise: Entrepreneurship and the Singer global distribution system. *Journal of Management Studies, 44*, 1064–1077.

Cavusgil, S. T. (1980). On the internationalization process of firms. *European Research, 8*, 273–281.

Chandra, Y., & Coviello, N. (2010). Broadening the concept of international entrepreneurship: "Consumers as international entrepreneurs." *Journal of World Business, 45*, 228–236.

Chung, H., & Tung, R. L. (2013). Immigrant social networks and foreign entry: Australia and New Zealand firms in the European Union and Greater China. *International Business Review, 22*(1), 18–31.

Ciravegna, L., Majano, S. B., & Zhan, G. (2014). The inception of internationalization of small and medium enterprises: The role of activeness and networks. *Journal of Business Research, 67*, 1081–1089.

Coase, R. H. (1937). The nature of the firm. *Economica, 4*(16): 386–405.

Contractor, F. J., & Kundu, S. K. (1998). Modal choice in a world of alliances: Analyzing organizational forms in the international hotel sector. *Journal of International Business Studies, 29*(2), 325–357.

Costello, N. (1996). Learning and routines in high-tech SMEs: Analyzing rich case study material. *Journal of Economic Issues, 30*(2), 591.

Coviello, N. E. (2006). The Network dynamics of international new ventures. *Journal of International Business Studies, 37*(5), 713–731.

Coviello, N. E., & Cox, M. P. (2006). The resource dynamics of international new venture networks. *Journal of International Entrepreneurship, 4*(2), 113–132.

Coviello, N. E., & Munro, H. J. (1995). Growing the entrepreneurial firm: Networking for international market development. *European Journal of Marketing, 29*(7), 49–61.

Coviello, N., & Munro, H. (1997). Network relationships and the internationalization process of small software firms. *International Business Review, 6*(4), 361–386.

Crick, D., Chaudhry, S., & Batstone, S. (2001). An investigation into the overseas expansion of small Asian-owned U.K. firms. *Small Business Economics, 16*(2), 75–94.

Crick, D., & Spence, M. (2005). The internationalisation of "high performing" UK high-tech SMEs: A study of planned and unplanned strategies. *International Business Review, 14*, 167–185.

Davidsson, P., & Honig, B. (2003). The role of social and human capital among nascent entrepreneurs. *Journal of Business Venturing, 18*, 301–331.

Dimitratos, P., Amorós, J. E., Etchebarne, M. S., & Felzensztein, C. (2014). Micro-multinational or not? International entrepreneurship, networking and learning effects. *Journal of Business Research, 67*, 908–915.

Dimitratos P., & Jones, M. V. (2005). Future directions for international entrepreneurship research. *International Business Review, 14*(2), 119–128.

Dimitratos, P., & Plakoyiannaki, E. (2003). Theoretical foundations of an international entrepreneurial culture. *Journal of International Entrepreneurship, 1*(2), 187–215.

Dimitratos, P., Voudouris, I., Plakoyiannaki, E., & Nakos, G. (2012). International entrepreneurial culture—toward a comprehensive opportunity-based operationalization of international entrepreneurship. *International Business Review, 21*(4), 708–721.

Dodgson, M. (1992). The management of technological collaboration. *Engineering Management Journal, 1*(4), 187–191.

Dunning, J. H. (2000). The eclectic paradigm as an envelope for economic and business theories of MNE activity. *International Business Review, 9*, 163–190.

Eckhardt, J., & Shane, S. (2003). Opportunities and entrepreneurship. *Journal of Management, 29,* 333–349.

Edelman, L. F., Bresnen, M., Newell, S., Scarbrough, H., & Swan, J. (2004). The benefits and pitfalls of social capital: Empirical evidence from two organizations in the United Kingdom. *British Journal of Management, 15,* 59–69.

Ellis, P. D. (2011). Social ties and international entrepreneurship: Opportunities and constraints affecting firm internationalization. *Journal of International Business Studies, 42*(1), 99–127.

Etemad, H. (2004). International entrepreneurship as a dynamic adaptive system: Towards a grounded theory. *Journal of International Entrepreneurship, 2,* 5–59.

Fernhaber, S. A., & Li, D. (2013). International exposure through network relationships: Implications for new venture internationalization. *Journal of Business Venturing, 28,* 316–334.

Fernhaber, S. A., Mcdougall-Covin, P. P., & Shepherd, D. A. (2009). International entrepreneurship: Leveraging internal and external knowledge sources. *Strategic Entrepreneurship Journal, 3,* 297–320.

Fletcher, D. (2004). International entrepreneurship and the small business. *Entrepreneurship & Regional Development, 16*(4), 289–305.

Fletcher, R. (2001). A holistic approach to internationalisation. *International Business Review, 10,* 25–49.

Forsgren, M. (1989). *Managing the internationalisation process: The Swedish case.* London, England: Routledge.

Freeman, S., Hutchings, K., Lazaris, M., & Zyngier, S. (2010). A model of rapid knowledge development: The smaller born-global firm. *International Business Review, 19,* 70–84.

Freeman, S., Hutchings, K., & Chetty, S. (2012). Born-globals and culturally proximate markets. *Management International Review, 52*(3), 425–460.

Gabrielsson, M., & Kirpalani, V. M. (2004). Born globals: How to reach new business space rapidly. *International Business Review, 13,* 555–571.

Gabrielsson, P., & Gabrielsson, M. (2013). A dynamic model of growth phases and survival in international business-to-business new ventures: The moderating effect of decision-making logic. *Industrial Marketing Management, 42*(8), 1357–1373.

Galkina, T., & Chetty, S. (2015). Effectuation and networking of internationalizing SMEs. *Management International Review, 55,* 647–676.

Gassmann, O., & Keupp, M. M. (2007). The competitive advantage of early and rapidly internationalizing in the biotechnology industry: A knowledge-based view. *Journal of World Business, 42,* 350–366.

Gerschewski, S., Rose, E. L., & Lindsay, V. J. (2015). Understanding the drivers of international performance for born global firms: An integrated perspective. *Journal of World Business, 50,* 558–575.

Giamartino, G. A., McDougall, P. P., & Bird, B. J. (1993). International entrepreneurship: The state of the field. *Entrepreneurship Theory and Practice, 18,* 37–42.

Glaister, K. W., & Buckley, P. J. (1996). Strategic motives for international alliance formation. *Journal of Management Studies, 33*(3), 301–332.

Granovetter, M. (1992). Economic institutions as social constructions: A framework for analysis. *Acta Sociologica, 35*(1), 3–32.

Grant, R. M. (1996). Prospering in dynamically-competitive environments: Organisational capability as knowledge integration. *Organisation Science, 7*(4), 375–87.

Gregorio, D. D., Musteen, M., & Thomas, D. E. (2009). Offshore outsourcing as a source of international competitiveness for SMEs. *Journal of International Business Studies, 40*(6), 969–988.

Greve, A., & Salaff, J. W. (2003). Social networks and entrepreneurship. *Entrepreneurship Theory and Practice, 28*(1), 1–22.

Håkansson, H., & Johanson, J. (1992). A model of industrial networks. In B. Axelsson & G. Easton (Eds.), *Industrial networks. A New view of reality* (pp. 28–34). London: England: Routledge.

Hammarkvist, K.-O., Håkansson, H., & Lars-Gunnar, M. (1982). *Marknadsföring för konkurrenskraftt*. Malmo, Sweden: Liber.

Harris, S., & Wheeler, C. (2005). Entrepreneurs' relationships for internationalization: Functions, origins and strategies. *International Business Review, 14*, 187–207.

Harrigan, K. R. (1985). *Strategies for joint ventures*. Lexington, MA: Lexington Books.

Harrison, R. T., & Mason, C. M. (1992). International perspectives on the supply of informal venture capital. *Journal of Business Venturing, 7*, 459–475.

Hite, J. M., & Hesterly, W. S. (2001). The evolution of firm networks: From emergence to early growth of the firm. *Strategic Management Journal, 22*(3), 275–286.

Hitt, M., & Ireland, R. D. (2000). The intersection of entrepreneurship and strategic management research. In D. L. Sexton & H. Landstrom (Eds.), *Handbook of entrepreneurship* (pp. 45–63). Oxford, England: Blackwell.

Hoang, H., & Antoncic, B. (2003). Network-based research in entrepreneurship: A critical review. *Journal of Business Venturing, 18*(2), 165–187.

Inkpen, A. C., & Tsang, E. W. K. (2005). Social capital, networks, and knowledge transfer. *Academy of Management Review, 30*, 146–165.

Iriyama, A., Li, Y., & Madhavan, R. (2010). Spiky globalization of venture capital investments: The influence of prior human networks. *Strategic Entrepreneurship Journal, 4*, 128–145.

Johannisson, B., & M. Monsted. (1997). Contextualizing entrepreneurial networking. *International Studies of Management & Organization, 27*(3), 109–36.

Johanson, J., & Mattsson, L.-G. (1988). Internationalization in industrial systems—a network approach. In N. Hood & J.-E. Vahlne (Eds.), *Strategies in global competition* (pp. 303–321). New York, NY: Croom Helm.

Johanson, J., & Vahlne, J. (1977). The internationalization process of the firm—A model of knowledge development and increasing foreign market commitments. *Journal of International Business Studies, 8*(1), 23–32.

Johanson, J., & Vahlne, J.-E. (1990). The mechanism of internationalization. *International Marketing Review, 7*(4), 11–24.

Johanson, J., & Vahlne, J.-E. (2003). Business relationship learning and commitment in the internationalization process. *Journal of International Entrepreneurship, 1*(1), 83–101.

Johanson, J., & Vahlne, J.-E. (2006). Commitment and opportunity development in the internationalization process: A note on the Uppsala internationalization process model. *Management International Review, 46*, 165–178.

Johanson J., & Vahlne J.-E. (2009). The Uppsala internationalization process model revisited: From liability of foreignness to liability of outsidership. *Journal of International Business Studies, 40*(9), 1411–1431.

Jones, M. V., Coviello, N., & Tang, Y. K. (2011). International entrepreneurship research (1989– 2009): A domain ontology and thematic analysis. *Journal of Business Venturing, 26*(6), 632–659.

Knight, G. A., & Cavusgil, S. T. (2004). Innovation, organizational capabilities, and the born-global firm. *Journal of International Business Studies, 35*(2), 124–141.

Knight, G. A., & Kim, D. (2009). International business competence and the contemporary firm. *Journal of International Business Studies, 40,* 255–273.

Kontinen, T., & Ojala, A. (2011). International opportunity recognition among small and medium-sized family firms. *Journal of Small Business Management, 49*(3), 490–514.

Kotler, P. (1997). *Marketing management* (9th ed.). Englewood Cliffs, NJ: Prentice-Hall.

Lamb, P., & Liesch, P. W. (2002). Re-framing the relationships between market commitment, knowledge and involvement. *Management International Review, 42*(1), 7–26.

Larson, A. (1992). Network dyads in entrepreneurial settings: A study of the governance of exchange relationships. *Administrative Science Quarterly, 37*(1), 76–104.

Larson, A., & Starr, J. A. (1993). A network model of organization formation. *Entrepreneurship: Theory and Practice, 17*(2), 5–15.

Laumann, E. O., Galaskiewicz, J., & Marsden, P. V. (1978). Community structure as interorganizational linkages. *Annual Review of Sociology, 4,* 455–84.

Lee, S. H., & Williams, C. (2007). Dispersed entrepreneurship within multinational corporations: A community perspective. *Journal of World Business, 42,* 505–519.

Leibeskind, J. P. (1996). Knowledge, strategy and the theory of the firm. *Strategic Management Journal, 17,* 93–107.

Leonidou, L. C., Katsikeas, C. S., & Samiee, S. (2002). Marketing strategy determinants of export performance: A meta-analysis. *Journal of Business Research, 55*(1), 51–67.

Li, N. (2008). Religion, opportunism, and international market entry via non-equity alliances or joint ventures. *Journal of Business Ethics, 80*(4), 771–789.

Li, J., & Shenkar, O. (2003). Knowledge search and governance choice: International joint ventures in the People's Republic of China. *Management International Review, 43*(3), 91–109.

Lin, N., Cook, K. S., & Burt, R. S. (Eds.). (2001). *Social capital.* Chicago, IL: Aldine de Gruyter.

Lindqvist, M. (1997). Infant multinationals: Internationalisation of small technology-based firms. In D. Jones, & M. Klofsten (Eds.), *Technology, innovation and enterprise: The European experience* (pp. 303–24). Basingstoke, England: Macmillan.

Loane, S., & Bell, J. (2006). Rapid internationalization among entrepreneurial firms in Australia, Canada, Ireland and New Zealand: An extension to the network approach. *International Marketing Review, 23*(5), 467–485.

Loane, S., Bell, J., & McNaughton, R. (2007). A cross-national study on the impact of management teams on the rapid internationalization of small firms. *Journal of World Business, 42,* 489–504.

Lu, Y., Zhou, L., Bruton, G., & Li, W. (2010). Capabilities as a mediator linking resources and the international performance of entrepreneurial firms in an emerging economy. *Journal of International Business Studies, 41,* 419–436.

Mahnke, V., & Venzin, M. (2003). The internationalization process of digital information good providers. *Management International Review, 43*(1), 115–142.

Mainela, T., Puhakka, V., & Servais, P. (2014). The concept of international opportunity in international entrepreneurship: A review and a research agenda. *International Journal of Management Reviews, 16,* 105–129.

Majkgård, A., & Sharma, D. D. (1998). Client-following and market-seeking strategies in the internationalization of service firms. *Journal of Business-to-Business Marketing, 4*(3), 1–41.

Makhija, M. V., & Ganesh, U. (1997). The relationship between control and partner learning in learning-related joint ventures. *Organization Science, 8*(5), 508–527.

Mariti, P., & Smiley, R. H. (1983). Co-operative agreements and the organisation of industry. *The Journal of Industrial Economics, 31*(4), 437–451.

Marshall, R. S. (2011). Conceptualizing the international for-profit social entrepreneur. *Journal of Business Ethics, 98*(2), 183–198.

Mathews, J. A., & Zander, I. (2007). The international entrepreneurial dynamics of accelerated internationalisation. *Journal of International Business Studies, 38*(3), 387–403.

Mazzanti, M., Montresor, S., & Pini, P. (2011). Outsourcing, delocalization and firm organization: Transaction costs versus industrial relations in a local production system of Emilia Romagna. *Entrepreneurship & Regional Development, 23*(7–8), 419–447.

McArthur, D. N., & Schill, R. L. (1995). International cooperative technology arrangements: Improving their role in competitive strategy. *Journal of Business Research, 32*, 67–79.

McDougall, P. P. (1989). International versus domestic entrepreneurship: New venture strategic behavior and industry structure. *Journal of Business Venturing, 4*(6), 387–400.

McDougall, P. P., & Oviatt, B. M. (2000). International entrepreneurship: The intersection of two research paths. *Academy of Management Journal, 43*, 902–908.

McDougall, P. P., Shane, S., & Oviatt, B. M. (1994). Explaining the formation of international new ventures: The limits of theories from international business research. *Journal of Business Venturing, 9*, 469–487.

McEvily S. K., & Chakravarthy, B. (2002). The persistence of knowledge-based advantage: An empirical test for product performance and technological knowledge. *Strategic Management Journal, 23*(4), 285–305.

McGaughey, S. L. (2007). Hidden ties in international new venturing: The case of portfolio entrepreneurship. *Journal of World Business, 42*, 307–321.

Milanov, H., & Fernhaber, S. A. (2014). When do domestic alliances help ventures abroad? Direct and moderating effects from a learning perspective. *Journal of Business Venturing, 29*, 377–391.

Miller, D. (1983). The correlates of entrepreneurship in three types of firms. *Management Science, 29*, 770–791.

Moen, Ø., Sørheim, R., & Erikson, T. (2008). Born global firms and informal investors: Examining investor characteristics. *Journal of Small Business Management, 46*(4), 536–549.

Morrow, J. F. (1988). International entrepreneurship: A new growth opportunity. *New Management, 5*(3), 59–60.

Mowery, D. V., Oxley, J., & Silverman, B. (1996, Winter). Strategic alliances and interfirm knowledge transfer. *Strategic Management Journal, 17*, 77–91. (Special issue).

Murphy, P. J. (2011). A 2 + 2 conceptual foundation for entrepreneurial discovery theory. *Entrepreneurship Theory and Practice, 35*, 359–374.

Musteen, M., Francis, J., & Datta, D. K. (2010). The influence of international networks on internationalization speed and performance: A study of Czech SMEs. *Journal of World Business, 45*, 197–205.

Nahapiet, J., & Ghoshal, S. (1998). Social capital, intellectual capital, and the organizational advantage. *Academy of Management Review, 23*, 242–266.

Nakos, G., Brouthers, K. D., & Dimitratos, P. (2014). International alliances with competitors and non-competitors: The disparate impact on sme international performance. *Strategic Entrepreneurship Journal, 8*, 167–182.

Nelson, R., & Winter, S. (1982). *An evolutionary theory of economic change*. Cambridge, MA: Balkan.

Nonaka, I. (1994). A dynamic theory of organizational knowledge creation. *Organization Science, 5*, 14–37.

Nowinski, W., & Rialp, A. (2016). The impact of social networks on perceptions of international opportunities. *Journal of Small Business Management, 54*(2), 445–461.

Nummela, N., & Welch, C. (2006). Qualitative research methods in international entrepreneurship: Introduction to the Special Issue. *Journal of International Entrepreneurship, 4*(4), 133–136.

Osborn, R. N., & Baughn, C. C. (1990). Forms of interorganizational governance for multinational alliances. *The Academy of Management Journal, 33*(3), 503–519.

Oviatt, B. M., & McDougall P. P. (1994). Toward a theory of international new ventures. *Journal of International Business Studies, 25*(1), 45–64.

Oviatt, B. M., & McDougall, P. P. (1995). Global start-ups: Entrepreneurs on a worldwide stage. *Academy of Management Executive, 9*(2), 30–43.

Oviatt, B. M., & McDougall, P. P. (2005). Defining international entrepreneurship and modelling the speed of internationalization. *Entrepreneurship Theory and Practice, 29*(5), 537–553.

Pak, Y. S., & Park, Y.-R. (2004). A framework of knowledge transfer in cross-border joint ventures: An empirical test of the Korean context. *Management International Review, 44*(4), 417–434.

Parkhe, A., Wasserman, S., & Ralston, D. A. (2006). New frontiers in network theory development. *Academy of Management Review, 31*(3), 560–568.

Peng, M. W. (2001). The resource-based view and International Business. *Journal of Management, 27*, 803–829.

Penrose, E. (1959). *Theory of the growth of the firm*. Oxford, England: Blackwell.

Polanyi, M. (1966). *The tacit dimension*. Garden City, NY: Doubleday.

Porter, M. E., & Fuller, M. B. (1986), Coalitions and global strategy. In M. E. Porter (Ed.), *Competition in global industries*. Boston, MA: Harvard Business School.

Prashantham, S., & Birkinshaw, J. (2015). Choose your friends carefully: Home-country ties and new venture internationalisation. *Management International Review, 55*, 207–234.

Prashantham, S., & Dhanaraj, C. (2010). The dynamic influence of social capital on the international growth of new ventures. *Journal of Management Studies, 47*, 967–994.

Prashantham, S., & Dhanaraj, C. (2015). MNE ties and new venture internationalization: Exploratory insights from India. *Asia Pacific Journal of Management, 32*, 901–924.

Prashantham, S., & Floyd, S. W. (2012). Routine micro processes and capability learning in international new ventures. *Journal of International Business Studies, 43*(6), 544–562.

Presuttia, M., Boaria, C., & Fratocchi, L. (2007). Knowledge acquisition and the foreign development of high-tech start-ups: A social capital approach. *International Business Review, 16*, 23–46.

Pruthi, S. (2014). Social ties and venture creation by returnee entrepreneurs. *International Business Review, 23*, 1139–1152.

Reuer, J. J., & Ragozzino, R. (2014). Signals and international alliance formation: The roles of affiliations and international activities. *Journal of International Business Studies, 45*, 321–337.

Rialp, A., & Rialp, J. (2007). Faster and more successful exporters: An exploratory study of born global firms from the resource based view. *Journal of Euromarketing, 16*(1/2), 73–86.

Riddle, L. A., & Gillespie, K. (2003). Information Sources for new ventures in the Turkish clothing export industry. *Small Business Economics, 20*(1), 105–120.

Roman, Z. (1991). Entrepreneurship and small business: The Hungarian trajectory. *Journal of Business Venturing, 6*, 474–465.

Roth, K. (1995). Managing international interdependence: CEO characteristics in resource-based framework. *Academy of Management Journal, 38*(1), 200–231

Rugman, A. M. (1981). *Inside the multinationals: The economics of internal markets*. New York, NY: Columbia University Press.

Saxenian, A. (2002). Transnational communities and the evolution of global production networks: Taiwan, China and India. *Industry and Innovation, 9*(3), 183–202.

Saxenian, A. I., (2005). From brain drain to brain circulation: Transnational communities and regional upgrading in India and China. *Studies in Comparative International Development , 40*(2), 35–61.

Schill, R. L., & McArthur, D. (1991). *Technology strategy: What is it and how can it be used?* Paper presented at the Portland International Conference on Technology Management, Portland, OR.

Schwens, C., & Kabst, R. (2009). How early opposed to late internationalizers learn: Experience of others and paradigms of interpretation. *International Business Review, 18*, 509–522.

Scott, M., & Rosa, P. (1996). Opinion: Has firm level analysis reached its limits? Time for a rethink. *International Small Business Journal, 14*(4), 81–89.

Shane, S., & Venkataraman, S. (2000). The promise of entrepreneurship as a field of research. *Academy of Management Review, 25*(1), 217–226.

Sharma, D. (1993). Introduction: Industrial networks in marketing. In T. Cavusgil & D. Sharma (Eds.), *Advances in international marketing* (Vol. 5, pp. 1–9). Greenwich, CT: JAI Press.

Sharma, D. D., & Blomstermo, A. (2003). The internationalization process of born globals: A network view. *International Business Review, 12*, 739–753.

Sharma, D. D., & Johanson, J. (1987, Winter). Technical consultancy in internationalisation. *International Marketing Review, 4*, 20–29.

Short, J., Ketchen, D., Shook, C., & Ireland, R. D. (2010). The concept of "opportunity" in entrepreneurship research: Past accomplishments and future challenges. *Journal of Management, 36*, 40–65.

Sigfusson, T., & Chetty, S. (2013). Building international entrepreneurial virtual networks in cyberspace. *Journal of World Business, 48*, 260–270.

Sigfusson, T., & Harris, S. (2013). Domestic market context and international entrepreneurs' relationship portfolios. *International Business Review, 22*, 243–258.

Spence, M. (2003). International strategy formation in small Canadian high-technology companies—a case study approach. *Journal of International Entrepreneurship, 1*(3), 277–296.

Styles, C., & Genua, T. (2008). The rapid internationalization of high technology firms created through the commercialization of academic research. *Journal of World Business, 43*, 146–157.

Sullivan, D. M., & Ford, C. M. (2014). How entrepreneurs use networks to address changing resource requirements during early venture development. *Entrepreneurship Theory and Practice, 38*(3), 551–574.

Tolstoy, D. (2010). Network development and knowledge creation within the foreign market: A study of international entrepreneurial firms. *Entrepreneurship & Regional Development, 22*(5), 379–402.

Tsai, W. (2001). Knowledge transfer in intraorganizational networks: Effects of network position and absorptive capacity on business unit innovation and performance. *Academy of Management Journal, 44*(5), 996–1004.

Vera D., & Crossan, M. (2003). Organizational learning and knowledge management: Toward an integrative framework. In M. Easterby-Smith & M. A. Lyles (Eds.), *Handbook of organizational learning and knowledge management* (pp. 122–141). Oxford, England: Blackwell.

Voudouris, I., Dimitratos, P., & Salavou, H. (2010). Entrepreneurial learning in the international new high-technology venture. *International Small Business Journal, 29*(3), 238–258.

Wang, Y., & Nicholas, S. (2005). Knowledge transfer, knowledge replication, and learning in non-equity alliances: Operating contractual joint ventures in China. *Management International Review, 45*, 99–118.

Welch, C. L., & Welch, L. S. (2009). Re-internationalisation: Exploration and conceptualisation. *International Business Review, 18*, 567–577.

Westhead, P., & Wright, M. (1998). Novice, portfolio and serial founders: Are they different? *Journal of Business Venturing, 13*, 173–204.

Wiklund J., & Shepherd, D. (2003). Knowledge-based resources, entrepreneurial orientation, and the performance of small- and medium-sized businesses. *Strategic Management Journal, 24*(13), 1307–1314.

Williamson, O. E. (1975). *Markets and hierarchies: Analysis and antitrust implications*. New York: NY: The Free Press.

Williamson, O. E. (1985). *The economic institutions of capitalism*. New York, NY: The Free Press.

Williamson, O. E. (1991). Comparative economic organization: The analysis of discrete structural alternatives. *Administrative Science Quarterly, 36*(2), 269–296.

Witt, P. (1998). Strategies of technical innovation in Eastern European firms. *Management International Review, 38*(2), 161–174.

Wright, R. W., & Ricks, D. A. (1994). Trends in international business research: Twenty-five years later. *Journal of International Business Studies, 25*, 687–701.

Yeung, H. W.-C. (2002). Entrepreneurship in international business: An institutional perspective. *Asia Pacific Journal of Management, 19*, 29–61.

Yiu, D. W., Lau, C. M., & Bruton, G. D. (2007). International venturing by emerging economy firms: The effects of firm capabilities, home country networks, and corporate entrepreneurship. *Journal of International Business Studies, 38*(4), 519–540.

Young S, Dimitratos, P., & Dana, L. (2003). International entrepreneurship research: What scope for international business theories? *Journal of International Entrepreneurship, 1*(1), 31–42.

Young, S., Hamill, J., Wheeler, C., & Davies, J. R. (1989). *International market entry and development: Stages and management*. Hemel Hempstead, England: Harvester Wheatsheaf.

Young, S., Huang, C.-H., & McDermott, M. (1996). Internationalization and competitive catch-up processes: Case study evidence on Chinese multinational enterprises. *Management International Review, 36*(4), 295–314.

Zaheer, A., Gözübüyük, R., & Milanov, H. (2010). It's the connections: The network perspective in interorganizational research. *Academy of Management Perspectives, 24*(1), 62–77.

Zahra, S. A. (1993). Conceptual model of entrepreneurship as firm behaviour: A critique and extension. *Entrepreneurship Theory and Practice, 14*(4), 5–21.

Zahra, S. (2005). A theory of international new ventures: A decade of research. *Journal of International Business Studies, 36*(1), 20–28.

Zahra, S. A., & George, G. (2002). International entrepreneurship: The current status of the field and future research agenda. In M. Hitt, R. Ireland, S. Camp, & D. Sexton (Eds.), *Strategic entrepreneurship: Creating a new mindset* (pp. 255–288). Malden, MA: Blackwell.

Zahra, S. A., Jennings, D.F., & Kuratko, D. F. (1999). The antecedents and consequences of firm level entrepreneurship: The state of the field. *Entrepreneurship Theory and Practice, 24*(2), 45–63.

Zahra, S. A., Korri, J. S., & Yu, J. (2005). Cognition and international entrepreneurship: Implications for research on international opportunity recognition and exploitation (Management Department Faculty Publications, Paper 113). Retrieved from http://digitalcommons.unl.edu/managementfacpub/113

Zahra, S. A., Matherne, B. P., & Carleton, J. M. (2003). Technological resource leveraging and the internationalization of new ventures. *Journal of International Entrepreneurship, 1*(2), 163–186.

Zahra, S. A., Neubaum, D. O., & Huse, M. (1997). The effect of the environment on the export performance among telecommunications new ventures. *Entrepreneurship Theory & Practice, 22*(1), 25–46.

Zhang, M. Y., & Dodgson, M. (2007). "A roasted duck can still fly away": A case study of technology, nationality, culture and the rapid and early internationalization of the firm. *Journal of World Business, 42*, 336–349.

Zhang, Z., Zyphur, M. J., Narayanan, J., Arvey, R. D., Chaturvedi, S., Avolio, B. J., . . . Larsson, G. (2009). The genetic basis of entrepreneurship: Effects of gender and personality. *Organizational Behavior and Human Decision Processes, 110*, 93–107.

Zhou, L., Barnes, B. R., & Lu, Y. (2010). Entrepreneurial proclivity, capability upgrading and performance advantage of newness among international new ventures. *Journal of International Business Studies, 41*(5), 882–905.

Zhou, L., Wu, W.-p., & Luo, X. (2007). Internationalization and the performance of born-global SMEs: The mediating role of social networks. *Journal of International Business Studies, 38*(4), 673–690.

Zou, S., & Stan, S. (1998). The determinants of export performance: A review of the empirical literature between 1987 and 1997. *International Marketing Review, 15*(5), 333–356.

Index

Page numbers in **bold** refer to Tables; page numbers in *italics* refer to Figures

a

ability, 250, 273–286, 298, 303, 469–470
   entrepreneurial ecosystems, 423, 432–433, *436*, 436, 444
   entrepreneurial teams, **322**, 326, 333
   KSTE and place, 366, 367
   national culture, 414, 415, 416
   new business and regional development, 385, 389–390
absorptive capacity, 366–368
abstraction, 9–12
academic entrepreneurship, **41**
Academy of Management, 456
achievement motivation theory, 98–99, 100, 405
achievement need, 174–177, 237, 404–405
   social entrepreneurship, **209**, 212–213, 217
adaptive entrepreneurship, 61–62, 64–65
adolescent entrepreneurial competence, 176
adoption studies, 260
adversity, 131–133
affect, **124**, 231–232, 236, 238, 240
Africa, 195
age, 25, 29–31, 40, **41**, 42, 275
   faultline theory, 321, 324
   psychology, 107, 108–109
agent-based modeling (ABM), 335–336
agents of change, 38, 46, 300
agglomeration, 353, 366, 383, 387–388, 425

agreeableness, 101–102, 126, 176, **209**, 216, 263
alertness, 47–48, 77, **134**, 241, 364
Algeria, 193, **201**
alliance creation, 460, 462–464, 466
Amazon, 353, 357
ambidexterity theory, 140, 147–149
ambitious entrepreneurship, 38, 40, **41**, 42–45, **50**, 52–53, 61–65
ambitious innovators, 44–45, **50**, 57–58, *58*, 61
ambitious replicators, 58–59, *59*, 61
angel finance, 64, 131, 283, 425, 437, 439
Angola, 195, **201**
Apple, 52
Arc of Prosperity, 435, *436*
Argentina, **201**
artistic personality, 176
Asia, 352, 353, 354, 410
attention deficit hyperactivity disorder (ADHD), 32, 98, 261, 264, 266–267
attraction, selection, attrition (ASA) theory, 125, 132, 206, 239
attribution process, 104
automobile industry, 52, 53, 131, 351, 358
autonomy, 100, 121, 336, 404
   corporate entrepreneurship, 299, 305
   personality, 174, 176, 177
   self-employment, 43–44, 53–54, 56, *60*
   social entrepreneurship, **209**, **210**, 212, 218

The Wiley Handbook of Entrepreneurship, First Edition.
Edited by Gorkan Ahmetoglu, Tomas Chamorro-Premuzic, Bailey Klinger, & Tessa Karcisky.
© 2017 John Wiley & Sons Ltd. Published 2017 by John Wiley & Sons Ltd.

types of entrepreneurship, **51**, 51, **55**, *61*, 62
Australia, **201**, 219, 403, 436
Austria, 26, 45, 47, **201**, 316, 335

b

Bangladesh, **201**
Barbados, **201**
Baron, Robert A., 32, 130–132, 146–147, 161
 entrepreneurial phases, 28–29, 140, 143, 146–147, 149, 151–152, 161
Baumol, William, 134
Bavaria, 351
behavioral combination, 79, 81–82, 84, 87–88
behavioral integration and shared cognition, 320, *321*, **322**, 324–326, 338
behavioral repertoire, 79, 89–81, 83–88
behavioral selection, 79, 81–88
behavioral sequence, 79, 81, 82, 84, 87
behavioral stage, 27–28
behavioral variation, 80, 81–85, 88
behavior execution, 79, 79, 82–83, 85, 88
behavior-specific outcomes, 79, 79, 81–88
Belgium, **201**, 403
benchmarking, 63, 189, 191, 433–434, *434*, 435–436
bias, 7, 13, 17, 75, 109, 444–445
 belief in inborn characteristics, 284
 cognitive traps, **124**, 124–125
 confirmation, **124**, 124, **134**, 432
 entrepreneurial teams, 335
 entrepreneurial tendencies, 241, 244
 female entrepreneurship and IQ, 187
 hormone tests, 265
 optimistic, **124**
 self-serving, **124**, 124–125, **134**
 skills, 352, 353, 354, 360
 social entrepreneurship, 220
Big Five personality traits (OCEAN), 101–103, 107, 110, 126–127, 175–176
 entrepreneurial tendencies, 235–236, 241, 248–250
 genetics, 263

social entrepreneurship, 207, **209**, 216
Big Six personality traits (HEXACO), 102, 103, 110
biology, 259–268
blame, 104, 133
Bolivia, **201**
bonding social capital, 130
born globals, 454–455, 462, 466–467
Bosnia, **201**
Botswana, 195, **202**
bottlenecks, 427–428, 433, *434*, 434–435, 437–440, 445
boundary conditions, 157–159, 160
Brazil, **202**, 274
bricolage, 73, 76, 316
broad sets of personality dimensions, 100–102, 111
business freedom, 435
business plans, 28, 120, 152, 156, 248
 cognitive traps, **124**, 135
 entrepreneurial behavior, 72, 82, 84, 87–88
business-to-business (B2B), 43, 49, 53
business-to-consumer (B2C), 43

c

California Psychological Inventory (CPI), 100–101
Canada, 299, 370, 403
candidate-genes, 263–264
career reasons, 103–104
Carlson, Chester, 119, 123
characteristics needed, 125, 126–127, 128, 133
Chile, **202**
China, 32, **202**, 214, 458
 KSTE and place, 353, 354, 363
 national culture, 403, 406, 411
Choice Dilemmas, Questionnaire, 99
Churchill, Winston, 133
clusters and clustering, 47, 109, 207, 336, 387
 entrepreneurial ecosystems, 432, 433
 international entrepreneurship, 460–463, 471
 management of place, 353, 355–356, 362, 370
 personality traits, 176, 181, 207

Cobb-Douglas function, 358, 359
cognition, 231–232, 236, 238, 240, 455
    national culture, 405–406, 413–416
    stages, 27–28
    tools needed, 120, 121–123, **124**, 124–125
    traps and errors, 123, **124**, **134**
collectivism, 403, 405–407, 409–412, 414
    entrepreneurial ecosystems, 424, 427–431, 443
collinearity, 333, 334
Colombia, **202**, 403
commercialization efficiency hypothesis, 364
community governance, 424, 429
competition and competitiveness, 5, 40, 46–48, 51–55, 57–62, 387
    corporate entrepreneurship, 295–297, 302, 306
    creativity, 150–152
    entrepreneurial behavior, 75, 83, 88
    entrepreneurial ecosystems, 435, *436*, 436
    entrepreneurial personality, 176
    KSTE and place, 351–354, 363–366
    new business and regional development, 380–388, 392–394, 396
    NVT processes, 318, 325
    roles, effects and contributions, **51**, **55**, *58*, *59*, *60*, *61*
    social entrepreneurship, 218, 219
    tools needed, 119, 123, **124**, 126, 135
complex socioecological ecosystems, 428–431
conceptual clarity, 9–12
confirmation bias, **124**, 124, **134**, 432
conscientiousness, 101–102, 126, 175–176, 389
    entrepreneurial tendencies, 236, 248
    social entrepreneurship, 216
context recognition, 13–14
conventional personality, 176
convergent thinking, 139, 143–145, 147, *148*, 148–162
corporate entrepreneurship, 37–38, 40–45, 63, 65, 402
    dimensions, **41**
    domain, *40*, 296–298
    innovation, 295–307
    international, 456
    managerial levels, 300–302
Corporate Entrepreneurship Assessment Instrument (CEAI), 299, 301
corporate venturing, 296, 297–298, 300
correlation matrix, 193, **193**
cortisol, 265
Costa Rica, **202**
countries and country differences, 30–31, 32, 40, 42, 403–406
    belief in inborn characteristics, 274, 281, 285
    entrepreneurial ecosystems, 435–436, *436*, 439, 444–445
    female entrepreneurship and IQ, 188–193, 195–198, **201–203**
    international entrepreneurship and networks, 463–464
    KSTE and place, 351, 353–356, 361, 368
    new business and regional development, 394–395
    psychology, 109
craftsman entrepreneurship, **41**
creation theory, 77
Creative Achievement Questionnaire, 246
creativity, 121–122, **134**, 134, 139–162, 328–330
    belief in inborn characteristics, 280
    characteristics and skills, 125–128
    corporate entrepreneurship, 303, 307
    cumulative process model, 140, 143–148, *148*, 149–157, 161–162
    effect on entrepreneurship, **141**, 141–143
    entrepreneurial personality, **141**, 142, 149, 176
    entrepreneurial tendencies, 233, 244, 246
    genetics, 261
    international entrepreneurship, 455
    KSTE and place, 355, 369
    NVT processes, 319–320, *320*, *321*, **323**, 328–330, 338
    opportunity recognition, 122–125
    social entrepreneurship, 207, **210**, 214, 216
Croatia, **202**
cross-sectional designs, 334–335
crowdfunding, 6, 79

culture, 6–7, 9, 12, 15, 39, 361, 389–390
　belief in inborn characteristics, 275–276, 285
　conceptualization, **402**, 402–412
　corporate entrepreneurship, 299
　entrepreneurial behavior, 76, 404, 406–413, 415–416
　entrepreneurial ecosystems, 425–426, *436*, 437
　entrepreneurial tendencies, 239, 244, 248, 250
　female entrepreneurship and IQ, 187, 197
　national, 401–416
　regional, 383, *386*, 388–392, 395
　social entrepreneurship, 211, 219
cumulative process model, 140, 143–148, *148*, 149–157, 161–162
Czech Republic, 31, **202**

d

Daimler, 354
data and data sources, 3, 6–7, 9, 12–13
　female entrepreneurship, 191–193
decision feedback loop, 79, 83–84, 88
delineation of entrepreneurial research, 3–6
Denmark, **202**, 403, 435–436, *436*
dependent variable (DV), 4, 11–12
destructive entrepreneurship, 39–40, 134
detachment, 16
disability, **41**, 49, 54
Disney, Walt, 131, 133
disruptive innovation, 304
divergent thinking, 139, 143–145, 147, *148*, 148–162
diversity, 107–111, 320, 329–330
　faultline theory, 321
　information, 157–159, 160
dominance, 176, 179, 181
dominant survey method, 333, 334
dopamine, 263–264, 265
dynamic exploitation, 49, **50**, **51**, 51–53, 62
　ambitious innovators, 57, *58*
　ambitious replicators, 58–59, *59*
dyslexia, 262, 264, 266

e

Eastern Europe, 353, 354, 410
economic cycle, 351–352

Economic Freedom of the World Index (EFWI), 192–193, **193**, **194**, 195
　data sources, 204
economic growth, 38, 44, 48, 54–63, 76
　ambitious innovators, 57–58, *58*
　ambitious replicators, 58–59, *59*
　entrepreneurial tendencies, 231, 233
　female entrepreneurship and IQ, 187, 190–191, 198
　final contribution, 54, **55**, 55, 57–58, *58*, 59, *59*
　intermediary effects, 50, 51–54, **55**, 57–58, *58*, *59*, 59
　KSTE and place, 351–352, 355, 358–364, 368, 370–371
　managerial employers, *61*
　new business and regional development, 379, *380*, 385, *386*, 386–388, 395–306
　solo self-employed, *60*
Ecuador, **202**
Edison, Thomas, 127
educational attainment, 29–31, 40, **41**, 42, 317, 321
　data sources, 204
　entrepreneurial behavior, 275, 281, 285
　entrepreneurial ecosystems, 436
　female entrepreneurship and IQ, 188, 190, 196, **196**, 197–198
　genetics, 262, 264
　human capital, 10–11
　new business and regional development, 388, 391
　self-employment, 49, 54
　social entrepreneurship, 221, 223
effectuation, 73, 76, 78
egalitarianism, 404, 409
Egypt, **202**, 351
Einstein, Albert, 122, 128
electroencephalography, 266, 267, 336
Eli Lilly, 354
El Salvador, **202**
empathy, **210**, 214, 217, 220, 223
empirical fact-finding, 8, 15
employees, 28, 73, 99, 129, 131, 179
　corporate entrepreneurship, 298, 301, 305
　creativity, 140, 146, 152, 154

entrepreneurial tendencies, 249–250
productive entrepreneurship, *40*, 42, 44, 47–49, 53, 56, 60, 64
social entrepreneurship, **209–211**, 211, 214–215, 219, 221
employer entrepreneurship, 40, **41**, 42–44
emotionality, 102
emotional stability, 126, 175–176, 178, **209**, 248
enablers and enabling, 10, 49, 53–54, *60*, 61, 62
intermediary effects, **51**, 51
role of entrepreneurs, 43–44, 49, **50**, 53–54
engagement levels, 25–33
England, 358, 435, 436
entrepreneurial alertness, 47–48, 77, **134**, 241, 364
entrepreneurial behavior, 37, 40, *40*, 242–247, 324–326, 356, 406–407
belief in inborn characteristics, 273, 275–286
corporate, 296, 298–307
definition, 74–76, 87
differences and tendencies, 231–236, 238–240, 242–247, 250–251
engagement level, 26–27, 32
integration, 320, *321*, **322**, 324–326
international, 454
model, *79*
national culture, 404, 406–413, 415–416
NVT processes, 317–318, **322**, 324, 327, 330, 334–337
personality, 174, 176–177
physiology, 266
psychology, 98, 104, 111
tools needed, 120
toward a theory, 71–88
entrepreneurial ecosystems, 423–445
definition, 423, 425–428
Scottish innovation-based, 431–434, *434*, 435, *436*, 436–442
entrepreneurial exchange, 438, 441
entrepreneurial exiting, 27, 46
entrepreneurial grid, 303
entrepreneurial intensity, 303, 306
Entrepreneurial Intensity Measure, 246
entrepreneurial intentions, 11, 262–263, 281

biology, 259, 262–263, 265
engagement levels, 26–27, 32–33
national culture, 402, 406–407
personality, 175–177, 178, 179
entrepreneurial judgment, 46
entrepreneurial ladder, 27, 28, 31–32
entrepreneurial orientation (EO), 241, 243, 297–298, 301, 303
ADHD, 261
Entrepreneurial Orientation Scale, 241, 243
Entrepreneurial Scotland, 438
entrepreneurial self-efficacy (ESE), 281, 282, 285
entrepreneurial subjectivism, 316, 319–320, *321*, 325, 328–330, 333 335, 338
entrepreneurial success, 177–179
personality, 173, 175, 177–179, 181–184
entrepreneurial survival *see* survival
entrepreneurial team collective cognition (ETCC), **322**
entrepreneurial teams *see* teams
entrepreneurial tendencies, 231–251, 259, 260–261
genetics, 260–264
hormones, 265
physiology, 266
redefining, 237–238
entrepreneurial theorizing, 316, 319, *320*, 328–39, 331, 333, 337–338
entrepreneurship dichotomies, 40, **41**, 41
environmental concerns, 259, 262, 268
belief in inborn characteristics, 275, 276
genetics, 260–262, 264
social entrepreneurship, 205–206, **209**, 212
essentialism, 274, 277–285
established business ownership, 27, 29, 33
Estonia, **202**, 410
Ethiopia, 192, 195, **202**
ethnicity *see* race and ethnicity
Euro crisis, 352
Europe, 32, 44, 53, 354, 356, 394, 410
creativity, 142
self-employment, 49, 54, 56
exaptation, 81
expectancy theory, 104, 105, 109, 120, 415
experimentation, 7, 46, 48, 72

exploitation of opportunities, 27, 45, 47–48, *48*, 53
  ambitious innovators, *58*
  ambitious replicators, 58, *59*
  belief in inborn characteristics, 274, 276, 281, 295
  corporate entrepreneurship, 302
  creativity, 140, 146–147, 152–153, 155–156
  dynamic, 49, **50, 51**, 51–53, 57–58, *58*, *59*
  entrepreneurial behavior, 77
  entrepreneurial tendencies, 231, 233, 235, 238, 240, 248–251
  final contribution, 55
  intermediary effects, **51**, 51–53
  international entrepreneurship and networking, 456, 467–468
  KSTE and place, 359, 364, 365, 367
  NVT processes, 315
  social entrepreneurship, 212
  static, 49, **50, 51**, 51, 53
  see also opportunity recognition
exploration and creation, 46, 48, *48*, **50**, 62, 140, 155–156
  ambitious innovations, 57, *58*
  ambitious replicators, 58, *59*
  final contribution, 55
  intermediary effects, **51**, 51–53
external corporate ventures (ECVs), 297
extraversion, 101–102, 126, 176, 178, 389
  entrepreneurial tendencies, 232, 234, 236, 248
  genetics, 261, 263
  social entrepreneurship, **209**, 216

f

Facebook, 353, 357
factors of production, 369, *370*, 371
failure, 4, 9, 16, 46, 119, 131–133
  cognitive traps, 125
  corporate entrepreneurship, 299, 302, 306
  entrepreneurial behavior, 75, 88
  entrepreneurial ecosystems, 423–424, 426–428, 431, *436*, 438, 441, 443, 445
  entrepreneurial personality, 175, 179, 180–181
  entrepreneurial tendencies, 235, 239, 249
  financial cost, 133
  national culture, 401, 411, 414, 415–416
  new business and regional development, 382, 383
  psychology, 98–99, 104
  social costs, 133
  social entrepreneurship, **210**, 216
Faith, Paloma, 136
families, 4, 38, **41**, 41, 262, 263
  belief in inborn characteristics, 274, 275
  entrepreneurial behavior, 86
  entrepreneurial personality, 180, 182
  female entrepreneurship and IQ, 197
  national culture, 409
  new business and regional development, 387, 390
  NVT processes, 332
  social entrepreneurship, 214, 222, 223
  social networks, 129, 461, 467
fast-thinking effect, **124**
faultline theory, 321, 324
  NVT processes, 319–320, *320*, *321*, 321, **322–323**, 324, 338
feedback, 105, 128, 282, 429
  creativity, 140, 153
  entrepreneurial behavior, 78, *79*, 83–84, 88
female entrepreneurship and IQ, 187–198, **201–203**, 204
Female Entrepreneurship Index (FEI), 188–193, **193, 194**, 195–197
  data sources, 204
  country scores, **201–203**
femininity, 403, 405, 406, 409
final contributions, 50–51, 54–57, *60*, *61*, 62
  ambitious innovators, 57, *58*
  ambitious replicators, *59*
Financing for Growth, 437–438
Finland, **202**, 435, *436*
firm and venture growth, 38, *60*, 60, *61*, 64, 177
  ambitious innovators, *58*
  ambitious replicators, *59*, 59
  creativity, **141**, 154–155
  final contribution, **51**, 55, 55
  intermediate effects, 51, **51**, 52–54, **55**

Flash Eurobarometer, 32
flexibility, 149, 151, 153, 156–157, 160
Ford, Henry, 131, 133
foreign direct investment (FDI), 462
founders and founding, 7, 10, 25, 31, 315, 354
  entrepreneurial roles, 46, 48
  entrepreneurial tendencies, 238–239, 245, 246, 248
  psychology, 97, 103–104, 109
  regional development, 391, 396
  social entrepreneurship, 218, 221
  tools needed, 119, 128
founding teams *see* teams
France, 44, **202**, 358, 403
franchise entrepreneurship, **41**
freelancers, 38
functional magnetic resonance imaging (fMRI), 266, 267

g
Gates, Bill, 119
gazelles, 6, 383, 393, 396
gender, 25, 29–32, 40, **41**, 42, 108, 277–278
  belief in inborn characteristics, 275, 277–278, 283, 286
  country scores, **201–203**
  data sources, 204
  entrepreneurial behavior, 275
  entrepreneurship ecosystems, 438
  faultline theory, 321, 324
  female entrepreneurship and IQ, 187–198
  hormones, 261, 265
  national culture, 409
  psychology, 103, 104, 108, 109
  self-employment, 49, 54
  sex ratios, 196, **196**, 204
  social entrepreneurship, 221
genetics, 32, 259, 260–264, 267–268
  belief in inborn characteristics, 273–286
  essentialism, 278–280, 282–285
genome-wide association studies (GWAS), 264
Germany, **202**, 410, 411, 458
  KSTE and place, 351, 353–354, 363, 370

new business and regional development, 383–384, 389–390
Ghana, 195, **202**
Global Competitiveness Index, 435, 439
Global Entrepreneurship Development Index (GEDI), 189–190, 192, 197
  entrepreneurial ecosystem, 432–433, *434*, 434–436, 439–441, 444
Global Entrepreneurship Monitor (GEM), 6, 7, 33, 44, 62, 109
  belief in inborn characteristics, 281, 285
  female entrepreneurship and IQ, 188–189, 191–192
  national culture, 411
  new business and regional development, 394
globalization, 352, 353, 360, 408, 435
  international entrepreneurship, 453–454
GLOBE, **402**, 409, 411 414
goals, 16, 43, 63, 120–121
  entrepreneurial behavior, 75, 78, 87
  psychology, 100, 106
  self-employment, 54
  tools needed, 119–121, 135–136
Google, 208, 353, 357, 370
Great Britain, 274
Greece, 31, **202**, 351, 403, 406
green economy, 62–63
green entrepreneurship, 5, **41**, 63
Griliches' model, 360
gross domestic product (GDP), 355, 358–359, 369, 407
  entrepreneurial ecosystems, 432
  female entrepreneurship and IQ, 191–193
  see also real GDP per capita (RGDPCAP)
group differences approach, 234–235, 239, 250
Growth Advantage Programme (GAP), 438, 441
growth orientation, 4, 213, 392, 395
Guatemala, **202**

h
Haier, 354
happiness, **55**, 56–57, *60*, *61*
harmony, 404
heredity, 260–262, 273–286

heuristics, **124**, 127, 330, 331
HEXACO personality traits (Big Six), 102, 103, 110
hierarchy, 404, 409
Hofstede's model, **402**, 403–405, 407–409, 414
Holland, John, 176, 177, 212
honesty, 102
hope, 132
hormones, 32, 259, 261, 263, 265–266
hubris, 174, 178, 181, 183, 328
hubristic pride, 124–125
human capital (HC), 10–11, 13, 72, 109, 285, 324
   female entrepreneurship and IQ, 198
   KSTE and place, 353, 365, 368, 369
   social entrepreneurship, 223
Human Development Index (HDI), 192–193, **193**, **194**, 195
   data source, 204
human dimension, 369, *370*, 371
humility, 102
Hungary, **202**, 410

i

Iceland, **202**, 435–436, *436*
identity, 207–207, **210**, 217–218, 222–223
ill-health, 205, 206
illusion of control, 178
imitative entrepreneurship, 40, **41**, 42–45, 47–48, **50**
immigration status, 25, **41**, 49, 53, 188, 275, 402
improvisation, 126–127, **134**
incentives, 354, 363–365
inclusive economy, **55**, 56–57
income inequality (GINI), 196, **196**, 204
incremental innovation, 42, 47–48, **50**, 57–58, 62, 155, 304
incumbent entrepreneurship, 40, **41**, 42–44, 61
incumbent firms, 357, 360–361, 363–366
   entrepreneurial tendencies, 239, 246, 249
   new business, 380–381, *382*, 382–383, 385, *386*, 386–388, 391–392
independent entrepreneurship, 37, 40, *40*, **41**, 42–45, 63
India, **202**, 353, 363, 370
national culture, 403, 406, 410
individual differences, 231–251
   pillars, 232–233
individualism, 403, 405–407, 409–411, 413
Indonesia, 405
industry/business networks, 460, 461–462
innovation and innovative entrepreneurship, 4, 46–47, 155, 431–433, 435, 437
   challenges with implementation, 304–305
   corporate entrepreneurship, 295–307
   creativity, 140, **141**, 142, 144, 146–147, *148*, 149–151, 155–156
   disruptive, 304
   entrepreneurial behavior, 72, 76, 78
   entrepreneurial ecosystems, 423, 425–427, 430–433, 435–436, *436*, 443–444
   entrepreneurial personality, 176, 177, 179
   entrepreneurial tendencies, 231, 233, 235, 237–240, 243–246, 248–249
   exploitative, 155, 156–157
   exploratory, 155, 156–157
   incremental, 42, 47–48, **50**, 57–58, 62, 155
   intermediary effects, 51–52
   international entrepreneurship, 453, 455, 460
   KSTE and place, 352–354, 360–363, 368–369
   national culture, 404, 407, 411, 412
   new business and regional development, 381–382, *382*, 387–388, 393, 396
   NVT processes, 317, 327, 328–329, 332
   social entrepreneurship, 207, 212, 215, 217, 222
   types and roles, 40–41, **41**, 42–48, *48*, **50**, 61–62, 64–65
   see also radical innovation
input-process-output (IPO) framework, 318, **322–323**, 324
instrumentality, 105, 415
insulin, 265
Integrated Assessment (IA), 429
Intel, 52, 370

Index | 493

intellectual property rights, 28, 152
    patents, 28, 149, 361–362, 363
intelligence quotient (IQ), 187–198
    correlations, **193**
    country scores, **201–203**
    data sources, 204
    regression results, **194**
    summary statistics, **193**
intermediary effects, 50–51, **51**, 51–54, 62
    ambitious innovators, 57, *58*
    ambitious replicators, *59*
    managerial employers, *61*
    solo self-employed, *60*
internal corporate ventures (ICVs), 297
international entrepreneurship (IE), **41**, 453–473
    networks, 457–458, *459*, 460–469
international new ventures (INVs), 464
International Personality Item Pool (IPIP), 101
internships, 135
intrapreneurs, 38
intuition, 9, 73, 155, 276
investigative personality, 176
Iran, **202**, 406
Ireland, **202**, 435, *436*
Israel, **202**
Italy, **202**, 351, 403

j

Jackson Personality Inventory (JPI), 100–101
Jamaica, 190, **202**
Japan, 190, **202**, 274, 403
job creation, 42, 44, 50, 54–56
    ambitious innovators, 57, *58*
    ambitious replicators, *59*
    entrepreneurial tendencies, 231
    final contributions, 54–55, **55**, 56
    managerial employers, *61*
    new business and regional development, 380, 383, *384*, 384–385, 388, 396
    solo self-employed, *60*
    types of entrepreneurship, 42, 44, 50, 54–63
Jobs, Steve, 174
job satisfaction, 43, 44, 50, **55**, 56–57
    genetics, 264
    social entrepreneurship, 215
    solo self-employed, *60*
Johnson & Johnson, 354
Jordan, Michael, 127

k

Kirzner, I., 47–48, 76–77
knowledge-based view, 471, 473
    regional, 381, *386*, 386–388, 391, 393
knowledge filter, 352, 363–366
Knowledge Production Function (KPF), 366, 368
knowledge spillover theory of entrepreneurship (KSTE), 356–368
    definition, 356–357
    inequality of places, 353–356
    management of places, 351–369, *370*, 371–372
    new business and regional development, 381, *382*
Korea, 190, **202**, 274
Kullback-Leibler Divergence (KLD), 182

l

last is best effect, **124**
latent behaviors, 81
latent dimensions, 101–102
latent entrepreneurship, 26, 29, 30
Latin America, 352, 410
Latvia, **202**
launch phase, 28, 151–154
    creativity, 140, **141**, 142–143, 146–147, *148*, 151–157, 161
    entrepreneurial personality, 176
    entrepreneurial tendencies, 248
lay theories, 277–279
leadership, 218–220, 295–307, 326–328, 371
    creativity, 154
    entrepreneurial behavior, 72
    neuroscience, 267
    NVT processes, 315, 320, *321*, **322**, 326–328, 338
    shared, 320, *321*, **322**, 326–328, 338
    social entrepreneurship, 207–208, **211**, 218–220, 222
learning feedback loop, *79*, 83–84, 88
Lenovo, 354

level of mastery, 83, 404
  entrepreneurial behavior, *79*, 79–85, 88
life course, 108–109
life expectancy, 196, **196**, 197, 204
Lithuania, **202**
Local Economic and Employment
    Development (LEED), 425
locus of control, 86, 177, 237
  national culture, 404, 405, 412
  psychology, 98, 100, 109, 110
  social entrepreneurship, **210**, 216, 220
long-term/short-term orientation, 403
long-term unemployment, 49, 54
Lynn-Vanhanen (LV), IQ data, 190–191, 195, 197

m

Macedonia, **202**
Machiavellianism 98, 176, 179, 181
macroeconomic growth, 38, 355, 360, 369
macroeconomic productivity, 51, 52, 62
magnetic resonance imaging (MRI), 337
Malawi, 193, 195, **202**
Malaysia, **203**, 410
managerial employers, 43, 44, **50**, 56, 60–61, *61*
marital status, 25, 107, 109, 275
marketing, 146, 152–153
Marshall, Alfred, 381
masculinity, 403, 405, 406, 409
Massachusetts Institute of Technology
    (MIT), 432, 438, 442
mastery, 83, *79*, 79–85, 88, 404
mercantilism, 358
metacognition, 127
Mexico, 190, **203**, 403
Microsoft, 52, 119, 353, 357
Miller, Danny, 174–176, 178–182
mindset, 6, 16, 319
  corporate entrepreneurship, 295, 303, 307
minimum efficient size, 385
Minnesota Multiphase Personality
    Inventory (MMPI), 100
mixed methods approach, 337
modest majority, 4–5

molecular genetics, 263–264
Montenegro, **203**
moral obligation, **210**, 217, 220
motivation, 105, 109, 120–121, 177, 208, **209**, 211–216
  achievement, 98–99, 100, 405
  belief in inborn characteristics, 282
  corporate entrepreneurship, 302–303
  entrepreneurial behavior, 77–78
  entrepreneurial ecosystems, 428, 431, 439
  entrepreneurial tendencies, 237
  international entrepreneurship, 460, 462, 471, 473
  national culture, 404, 405, 415–416
  new business and regional development, 385, 393, 395
  NVT processes, 326
  social entrepreneurship, 205–208, **209**, 211–218, 220, 222–223
  tools needed, 119, 120–121, 126, 133, **134**, 135
multinational enterprises (MNEs), 353–354, 454, 456, 462–464, 467–468
multiple dimensions, 110
multipolar coordination, 424, 428, 429, 431, 443
Musk, Elon, 181

n

narcissism, 98, 174, 176, 179, 181
nascent entrepreneurship, 75, 246, 439, 467
  engagement level, 26–27, 30, 32–33
  psychology, 103–105, 108
necessity entrepreneurship, **41**, 44, 50
neoclassical theory, 351, 355–356, 358
Netherlands, **203**, 403, 406, 410, 411
networks and networking, 233, 457–458, *459*, 460–468
  corporate entrepreneurship, 303
  entrepreneurial behavior, 72, 78, 88
  entrepreneurial ecosystems, 435, *436*, 436–438, 440–441
  entrepreneurial teams, 106
  entrepreneurial tendencies, 244, 245
  gender, 108

international entrepreneurship, 457–458, *459*, 460–469
  intersection of research, 468–472
  perspective, 456–457
  race and ethnicity, 108, 461
  ties, 454, 457, *459*, 461–473
  see also social networks
neuroscience, 259, 266–267, 268, 336–337
neuroticism, 101–102, 126, 176, 178, 216, 236, 261
new business formation *see* start-ups
new markets, 38, 46–47, 49, 53, 57
  entrepreneurial behavior, 75–76, 78
new technology-based firms, 10, 38, 48, 63, 466
  entrepreneurial teams, 317
  KSTE and place, 353, 360, 367
new venture team (NVT) processes, 315–320, *320*, *321*, 321, **322–323**, 324–338
  external factors, 317–318
  internal factors, 316–317
New Zealand, 458
Nigeria, 195, **203**
nonambitious entrepreneurship, 41, 42–43, 61, 65
norms and practices, 408–412
  national culture, **402**, 402, 408–415
Northern Ireland, 435, 436
Norway, 188, 193, **203**, 405, 435, *436*
null hypothesis, 13

o

occupational entrepreneurship, 37, 40, 45
OCEAN *see* Big Five personality traits (OCEAN)
online shopping, 52
openness to change, **209**, 211–212
openness to experience, 101–102, 126, 216, 236, 389
  entrepreneurial personality, 175, 176, 177–178
  genetics, 261, 263
operationalization, 9–12, 14
opportunity entrepreneurship, 9–10, 37, 40, **41**, 47–48
  processes, 27, 30–31
opportunity identification, 76–78, 189, 435–436, *436*, 456
  creativity, 139–141, **141**, 142–144, 147, *148*, 149–157, 160–162
opportunity recognition, 122–125, **134**, 135, 259
  corporate entrepreneurship, 302
  entrepreneurial tendencies, 237–238, 240, 248–251
  genetics, 260, 262
  KSTE and place, 354, 356–357, 365
  NVT processes, 315, 319
  see also exploitation of opportunities
optimism, 132, **210**, 216
  entrepreneurial personality, 175, 178, 181, 183
optimistic bias, **124**
Organisation for Economic Cooperation and Development (OECD), 44, 55, 425, 440
organizational cognitive neuroscience (OCN), 336–337
organizational learning, 469–470, 473
organization and team justice, 330–332
  NVT processes, 319–320, *320*, *321*, 330–332, 338
outsiders, 43–44, **50**, 54, 61, 64
  self-employed, 49–51, **51**, 54, *60*
oxytocin, 265

p

Pakistan, 192, **203**, 410
Panama, **203**
Panel Study of Entrepreneurial Dynamics (PSED), 6, 28, 32, 315
  psychology, 103–104, 105, 106, 110
  social entrepreneurship, 215
parental status, 25, 107, 109, 187, 198
passion, 128, **134**, 135
path dependency, 337, 361, 390
pattern matching, 431–432
pattern recognition, 123
PercentMan, 191, 192, **193**, **194**, 195
  data sources, 204

persistence, **210**, 216, 276, 282, 389–390
　new business and regional development, 380, 389–390, 392, 395
personal computer market, 52
personality, 98–102, 111, 173–184, 207, 389
　belief in inborn characteristics, 273, 276–278, 284
　creativity, **141**, 142, 149, 176
　dark side, 173–184, **221**, 223
　entrepreneurial intentions, 175–177, 178, 179
　entrepreneurial success, 173, 175, 177–179, 181–184
　entrepreneurial tendencies, 233–234, 235–236, 250
　future research, 174–175, 180–183, 220, **221**, 221–223
　genetics, 263
　NVT processes, 321, 334
　reviewed studies, 207–208
　review findings, 208, **209–211**, 211–220
　social entrepreneurship, 205–223
　tools needed, 125–128, 133, 135
　see also traits
Peru, 190, **203**, 411
phenotypes, 259–261, 263–267
physical appearance, 261, 266
physiology, 259, 266, 268
　genetic influences, 261, 263
Picasso, Pablo, 122
pitching, 80, 83, 88, 331
　gender, 283
places *see* strategic management of places
Poland, **203**, 406
Portugal, **203**, 358
positive affect, 126–127, 128, **134**, 175
PostComm, 192, **193**, **194**, 195
postfounding phase, 319–320, *321*, 330–333
　NVT processes, 319–320, *321*, 324–325, 327–328, 330–333, 338
postlaunch phase, 28, 154–157, 248
　creativity, 140, **141**, 142–143, 146–147, *148*, 154–157, 161
power distance, 403, 405–407, 409–411, 413
practical relevance, 3, 9, 12–13, 14–17
predictions, 13, 14, 286, 351, 460

entrepreneurial tendencies, 233, 235, 242–244, 246
　psychology, 105, 109
prefounding phase, 319, *320*, 329, 331
　NVT processes, 318–319, *320*, 324, 328–329, 331, 338
prelaunch phase, 28, 149–151, 248
　creativity, 140, **141**, 142–143, 146–147, *148*, 149–151, 153, 155–157, 161
proactivity, 297, 303, 412, 455
　social entrepreneurship, 207, 217, 220
productive entrepreneurship, 5, 37–65
productivity and competitiveness, **51**, 52, **55**, 55
　ambitious innovators, *58*
　ambitious replicators, *59*, 59
　managerial employers, 60, *61*
　solo self-employed, 59–60, *60*
profit-oriented entrepreneurship, 40, **41**
progesterone, 265
Program for International Student Assessment (PISA), 190
prosocial values, 206, **209**, 211–215, 220, 223
psychological capital, 132–133, 176, 181
psychology, 97–111, 233–234
　cost of failure, 133
　critical evaluation, 234–236
　entrepreneurial tendencies, 232–236, 240–241, 247
　personality approach, 98–102
　social cognition approach, 102–106
　teams, 97, 104, 106–107, 110–111
psychometric testing, 237, 241
psychopathy, 98, 176–177, 178–179, 181

q

quality of entry, 391, 392–393, 394, 396
quantitative electroencephalogram (qEEG), 266, 267
quantitative genetics, 260–263

r

race and ethnicity, 108, 109, 321, 461
　belief in inborn characteristics, 277, 278, 286

self-employment, 49, 54
radical innovation, **141**, 142, 155, 304, 382
   types of entrepreneurship, 42, 46–48, **50**, 57–58, 62, 65
real GDP per capita (RGDPCAP), 191–193, **193**, **194**, 195
   data sources, 204
realistic personality, 176
regional development, 379–396
   differences in contributions of new businesses, 385, *386*, 386–387
   direct and indirect effects, 383, *384*, 384–385
   basic relationships, *380*
   policy implications, 391–392
   relationship to business, *380*, 380–381, *382*, 382–383
Regional Entrepreneurship Acceleration Program (REAP), 432–434, *434*, 439
regionalization, 353
regions, 6, 9, 14, 52, 55, 353, 355–356
   belief in inborn characteristics, 280
   creativity, **141**, 142
   entrepreneurship process, 28
   entrepreneurship tendencies, 246, 248, 251
   female entrepreneurs and IQ, 192, **194**
   KSTE and place, 351, 353–356, 361–366, 369, 371
   social entrepreneurship, 223
   see also regional development
regression models, 191–194, **194**, 195–196
Relationship Closeness Inventory, 107
religion, 277, 463–464
replication, 11, 14, 110, 11
replicative entrepreneurship, 40, **41**, 42–45, 47–48, **50**
   adaptive, 61–62, 64–65
research and development (R&D), 332, 386, 388, 463, 466
   entrepreneurial ecosystems, 423, 426, 436, 440
   KSTE and place, 359–362, 365, 368
   types, 46, 48, 63, 64
resilience, 131, 132
resource-based view, 470, 473
restaurants, 53

risk-taking, 29, 31, 40, *40*, 61, 99
   corporate entrepreneurship, 295, 297–300, 303
   creativity, 152
   entrepreneurial personality, 177, 178
   entrepreneurial roles, 45, 49, 54
   entrepreneurial tendencies, 233
   hormones, 265
   international entrepreneurship, 455
   KSTE and place, 354, 357
   national culture, 404, 412
   psychology, 98–100
   regional entrepreneurship, 389
   self-employment, 56
   social entrepreneurship, **210**, 216, 217, 220
   tools needed, 127
Rockefeller, John D., 174
Rokeach value theory, 211
Romania, **203**
Russia, **203**, 363, 405, 411
ruthlessness, 174, 179

S

Saltire Foundation, 438, 441
samples and sampling, 4, 6–7, 9, 26, 142
   corporate entrepreneurship, 299
   entrepreneurial behavior, 73, 81
   entrepreneurial personality, 178, 181
   entrepreneurial teams, 106, 108, 335, 336
   entrepreneurial tendencies, 246, 250
   female entrepreneurship and IQ, 190, 192–193, **193**, 195, **201–203**
   genetics, 260, 262, 263, 265, 266
   national culture, **402**, 411
   size, 9, 12–13, **193**, 213, 217, 335
   social entrepreneurship, 208, 211–214, 216–217, 219–221
   twin studies, 260, 262
Sanders, Colonel Harlan, 131, 133
Saudi Arabia, 190, **203**
SCALE, 438, 441
Scandinavia, 111, 458
Schumpeter, Joseph A., 45, 46–47, 49, 76, 237, 362
   new business and regional development, 381–382

Schwartz's Value Survey (SVS), 211, 215, **402**, 404, 408
Scotland, 424, 431–434, *434*, 435, *436*, 436–442, 443–445
  field trial, 435–438
  REAP, 432–434, *434*, 439
self-assurance, 174, 178, 181
self-control, 127, **134**, 135
self-determination theory, 56, 104, 109, 214–215
self-efficacy, 86, 126–127, 414, 439
  belief in inborn characteristics, 273, 281–282, 285
  entrepreneurial personality, 174–175, 177–178, 181
  psychology, 98, 100, 106, 109, 132
  social entrepreneurship, 207, **210**, 216, 220
  tools needed, 121, 126–127, 128, 132
self-employment, 4, 54, 206, 260, 432
  entrepreneurial tendencies, 234, 239
  female entrepreneurship and IQ, 188, 192
  new business and regional development, 389, 393, 395
  outsiders, 49–51, **51**, 54, *60*
  process stages, 25, 27, 29
  see also solo self-employment
self-esteem, 56, 175
self-regulation, 127–128, **134**
self-serving bias, **124**, 124–125, **134**
self-transcendence values, **209**, 211
sensation-seeking, 99, 261, 275–276
sensitivity analysis, 433, *434*, 434–437
separation, 4, 16, 249, 453
serial entrepreneurship, 38, **41**, 181–182, 264, 266, 425
serotonin, 263, 265
Shakespeare, William, 122, 134
Shkreli, Martin, 99
Siemens, 354
Silicon Glen, 445
Silicon Valley, 361, 370, 443
simulation exercises, 7, 335–336
Singapore, 193, **203**, 403
single firm entrepreneurship, **41**
single traits, 98–99, 110, 111
skills, 9, 10–11, 16, 80, 125–129, 218–220

belief in inborn characteristics, 276, 281, 284
corporate entrepreneurship, 296, 302
entrepreneurial behavior, 80, 83, 84–85
entrepreneurial ecosystems, 435–436, *436*, 437–438
entrepreneurial process, 30
genetics, 261
KSTE and place, 352–354, 360, 369
leadership and management, 218–220
new business and regional development, 388
NVT processes, 315, 318
social entrepreneurship, 206–208, **210–211**, 218–220, 222–223
tools needed, 119, 125–128, 130–131, 133, **134**, 135
types of entrepreneurship, 44, 57
Slovakia, **203**, 274
Slovenia, **203**
small and medium-sized enterprises (SMEs), 460, 463
small businesses, 3–4, 8
social capital, 13, 129–131, 132–133, 217, 470–471
  international entrepreneurship, 4544, 461, 464–465, 467, 470–471
social class, 278
social cognition, 102–106, 111
social costs of failure, 133
social entrepreneurship, 38, **41**, 206–207, 412
  future research, 220, **221**, 221–223
  personality, 205–223
  review findings, 208, **209–211**, 211–220
social esteem, 415–416
social exclusion, 205, 206
social networks, 32, 129–131, 220, 371, 460–462, 467–468
  creativity, 158–159
  NVT processes, 317
  teams, 107, 317, 328
  tools needed, 129–131, 133, **134**
social personality, 176
societal problems, 174, 175, 179–180
sociocognitive grid, 325
socioecological systems, 424, 428–431

solo self-employed, 38, 56, 59–60, *60*, 61–62, 64–65
   dimensions, **41**
   domain, *40*
   types of entrepreneurship, 40, 42–45, **50**
Solow, Robert, 352, 359, 362
South Africa, 195, **203**, 406
Spain, **203**, 211, 215, 358, 406
spatial and organizational dimension, 369, *370*, 370–371
stakeholders, 424, 427–442
   consultation, 429–430, 440–441
   participation, 430–431, 437, 441
   Scotland, 431–433, *434*, 434–445
start-ups, 6, 8, 11–13, 16, 61, 63, 379–396
   belief in inborn characteristics, 283
   enabling, 54
   entrepreneurial behavior, 75, 81–82, 84–85, 87
   entrepreneurial ecosystems, 425–427, 435–436, *436*, 439
   entrepreneurial roles, 45, 49
   entrepreneurial tendencies, 239, 244, 246, 249
   evolution of employment and survival, *384*
   exploration and creation, 52
   female entrepreneurship and IQ, 190
   final contributions, 56
   international entrepreneurship, 454, 458
   KSTE and place, 353–354, 362, 367, 370
   national culture, 407, 413
   physiology, 266
   process, 25, 26, 28
   psychology, 106, 109
   regional development, 379–380, *380*, 381, *382*, 382–385, *384*, 386–396
   social entrepreneurship, 215, 222, 223
   teams, 106, 315, 327
   types of entrepreneurship, 40, **41**, 41–44
static exploitation, 49, **50**, 51, **51**, 53, *61*, 62
statistical significance, 9, 12–13
stereotypes, 278, 282, 283, 330
strategic entrepreneurship, 296, 297–298, 300, 302–303, 306
strategic management of places, 363–366
   KSTE and place, 351–372
   challenge of inequality, 353–356
   emergence of approach, 368–369, *370*, 370–371
stress, 132–133, **134**, 177
substance misuse, 276
sunk costs, **124**, 125, 385
survey instruments improvement, 335
survival of ventures, 27, 54, 101, 215
   creativity, 140, 147, 154–155
   final contributions, **55**, 56
   intermediary effects, **51**, 51, **55**
   managerial employers, 60, *61*
   regional development, 381–383, *384*, 386, 388, 391–392, 396
   solo self-employment, *60*
   tools needed, 126, 128
Sweden, **203**, 370, 436
Switzerland, **203**
systematic process analysis, 431

t

Taiwan, 190, **203**, 407
teams, **41**, 106–107, 110–111, 315–338
   belief in inborn characteristics, 283–284
   corporate entrepreneurship, 296, 306
   divergent and convergent thinking, 161–162
   entrepreneurial behavior, 78–81, 84–85, 87
   entrepreneurial personality, 181
   new venture processes, 315–320, *320*, *321*, 321, **322–323**, 324–338
   psychology, 97, 104, 106–107, 110–111
   tools needed, 129, **134**
testosterone, 261, 265–266, 336
Thailand, **203**, 403
Thematic Apperception Test (TAT), 98, 237
theoretical precision, 3, 7–8, *8*, 9–14, 109
theory of planned behavior (TPB), 104, 105–106, 109, 406
Third International Mathematics and Science Study (TIMSS), 190
tightness, 410, 411
tools needed, 119–136, 316
   cognitive, 121–123, **124**, 124–125
   successful kit, 133–134, **134**
training, 10, 123, 181, 197, 284

corporate entrepreneurship, 304, 305
creativity, **141**, 142, 144, 159–160
entrepreneurial behavior, 75, 80
traits, **208–209**, 216–217, 276
   activation theory, 239, 244, 247, 248
   entrepreneurial tendencies, 232–236, 239, 243–244, 247–250
   inventories, 100–101
   latent dimensions, 101–102
   national culture, 412, 415
   NVT processes, 321, 334
   psychology, 98–99, 100–102, 107, 110–111
   single, 98–99, 110, 111
   social entrepreneurship, 205–208, **208–209**, 212, 216–217, 222–223
   see also personality
transaction cost economics (TCE), 469, 473
transactive memory systems (TMS), 332–333
   NVT processes, 320, *321*, **323**, 332–333, 338
transition ratio, 27, 28
Trinidad, **203**
Truman, President Harry S., 371–372
Tunisia, **203**
Turkey, 190, **203**, 461, 462
twin studies, 260, 262, 275

u

Uganda, 193, 195, **203**
uncertainty avoidance, 403, 405–407, 409–411, 413
unemployment, 49, 54, 56–57
unicorns, 6
United Arab Emirates (UAE), 192, **203**
United Kingdom (UK), 15, 44, **203**, 458
   entrepreneurial ecosystems, 435–346, 439–440, 445
   KSTE and place, 351, 353, 354, 370
United States of America (USA), 15, 32–33, 280, 458

corporate entrepreneurship, 299
creativity, 142
entrepreneurial ecosystems, 436, 440
entrepreneurial processes, 26–27, 31–32
entrepreneurial teams, 106
female entrepreneurship and IQ, 192, **203**
KSTE and place, 351, 353–354, 358, 361, 363, 370–372
national culture, 403, 405–407
new business and regional development, 383, 394
NVT processes, 315, 327
psychology, 110
social entrepreneurship, 215, 219
universities, 361–365, 367, 369, 393
   new business and regional development, 387–388, 391, 393
   Scotland, 437–438, 440–442
unproductive entrepreneurship, 39–40
urbanization, 196, **196**, 204
Uruguay, **203**
user entrepreneurs, 75, 76, 78

v

valence, 105
values, 403–408
   national culture, **402**, 402–408, 412–415
Vanderbilt, Cornelius, 174
Venezuela, 193, **203**
venture capital, 15, 64, 106, 108, 283, 369
   creativity, 152
   entrepreneurial ecosystems, 425, 435, 439
   NVT processes, 328, 331
   tools needed, 120, 122
venture growth *see* firm and venture growth
venture outcomes, 79, 82–85, 87–88
Vietnam, 407, 408

w

Wales, 435, 436
Walton, Sam, 119

wealth redistribution, 5
West, Mae, 127
World Bank Ease of Doing Business ranking, 445
world-changing tools, 119, 134–136
World Economic Forum, 435

y

Yerkes-Dodson Law, 175, 178
young business ownership, 27, 29, 31, 33

z

Zambia, 195, **203**